Integrating Social Media Tools Into Hotel Operations and Marketing

Ankit Shukla
https://orcid.org/0000-0002-7646-3517
Rajamangala University of Technology, Thanyaburi, Thailand

Nagendra Yadav
https://orcid.org/0009-0008-9743-9250
Welcomgroup Graduate School of Hotel Administration, Manipal Academy of Higher Education, Manipal, India

Karan Berry
https://orcid.org/0000-0002-8641-5228
Symbiosis International University, Pune, India

Siddharatha Sharma
https://orcid.org/0000-0003-4902-5199
Government of Punjab, India

Ghamaliel M. Villalobos
https://orcid.org/0009-0001-1169-2917
Rajamangala University of Technology, Thanyaburi, Thailand

IGI Global
Scientific Publishing
Publishing Tomorrow's Research Today

Vice President of Editorial Melissa Wagner
Director of Acquisitions Mikaela Felty
Director of Book Development Jocelynn Hessler
Production Manager Mike Brehm
Cover Design Jose Rosado

Published in the United States of America by
IGI Global Scientific Publishing
701 East Chocolate Avenue
Hershey, PA, 17033, USA
Tel: 717-533-8845 | Fax: 717-533-7115
Website: https://www.igi-global.com E-mail: cust@igi-global.com

Library of Congress Cataloging-in-Publication Data

LCCN: 2025042343 (CIP Data Pending)
ISBN13: 9798337367415
Isbn13Softcover: 9798337367422
EISBN13: 9798337367439

British Cataloguing in Publication Data
A Cataloguing in Publication record for this book is available from the British Library.

Table of Contents

Detailed Table of Contents

among others. Also, blockchain loyalty programs, immersive online experiences, and the use of the Internet of Things (IoT) will boost transparency, trust, and consumer interaction. The study determines the paths that the future marketing technologies in the hospitality industry could follow to bring about change in brand positioning, customer experiences, and competitive advantage. It emphasizes that it is necessary that companies constantly innovate to keep up with the changing and technological world.

The digital technologies revolution in the global hospitality industry, where it is particularly concerned with the introduction of the latest technologies applications examines how these technologies are revolutionizing the manner in which hotels operate, market themselves, and undertake sustainability initiatives to ensure individualized guest experiences, real-time decision-making, and operational effectiveness. Among the opportunities presented by digital transformation, and addressed the increased customer interaction, brand loyalty and competitive advantage, the challenges of technological integration and providing a service that is human-centred. It also talks about the future trend in hospitality marketing, which involves AI-powered content, social commerce, and immersive technologies. Lastly, it can take advantage of the effectiveness of technology and the traditional service standards to become successful in a more consumer-oriented hospitality industry

This chapter explores the transformative impact of emerging technologies on hospitality marketing, tracing the sectors evolution from traditional, localised promotion to a dynamic, data driven and immersive ecosystem. It examines how innovations such as artificial intelligence, augmented l reality, blockchain and social media storytelling are reshaping guest engagement, brand reputation and operational efficiency. The discussion highlights the shift from mass messaging to personalised, predictive and adaptive marketing, emphasizing the importance of real time analytics, sentiment tracking and dynamic pricing. Through global case studies including Marriot's use of VR and AL, Accor's blockchain based loyalty programmes, among others, the chapter illustrates how technology adoption is tailored to local contexts while reflecting global trends. The chapter concludes by proposing s strategic framework for responsible technology adoption, stressing the need for digital maturity, staff training, cross functional integration, and alignment with brand identity and guest expectations.

AI is rapidly transforming the service sector, opening new research opportunities in hospitality and tourism. It has gradually changed the service sector, leading to significant innovations. This review aims to evaluate the application of AI in the hospitality industry in service delivery to improve the visitor experience. The primary focus of this paper is to discuss the optimum use of artificial intelligence tools by implementing AI technology in the travel and hospitality industry. The study adopts SPAR-4-SLR to review the articles systematically. The literature and data sources have been obtained from Scopus and Web of Science. This review covers research papers published from 2013 to 2025. Using the TCM-ADO framework, this article holistically analyzes the relationship between the varied use of AI tools in the hospitality industry. This review paper adds to the body of knowledge on the application of AI in the hospitality industry.

The present study examines the fusion of social media constructs to obtain a model of the Unified Theory of Acceptance and Use of Technology (UTAUT2) for predicting the behavioural intentions of hotel guests in Tricity of India. Acknowledging the increasing impact of digital social connectedness on hospitality consumption, e.g., in the form of electronic word of mouth (e-WOM), perceived trust and information quality are integrated in addition to original UTAUT2 determinants like performance expectancy, social influence and hedonic motivation. Applying hierarchical regression and structural equation modelling on meta-analytic secondary data, our findings

association has been established between irritation and attitude toward Instagram advertisements. Looking at the interrelationship, advertising value does mediate the relationship between the predictor variable attitude towards Instagram advertising except irritation. Furthermore, the present study also supports that the hierarchy of effect (HOE) does exist, and there is a strong positive relationship between attitude towards Instagram advertising and purchase intention.

The hospitality industry has experienced significant changes in the age of social media, where online interactions increasingly influence customer opinions and booking choices. One of the most effective approaches in transforming hotel marketing and operations is influencer marketing, along with strategic collaborations between brands. This chapter investigates how hotels can benefit from the trustworthiness, creativity, and extensive online presence of influencers to forge genuine connections with their target audiences. Also, it looks into the advantages of partnership with lifestyle, travel, and luxury brands to enhance guest experiences, distinguish offerings, and reinforce brand identity. This chapter illustrates, through industry-leading practices and cutting-edge research, how campaigns and partnerships driven by influencers can enhance hotel visibility. The focus is particularly on the integration of operations—highlighting how hotel managers can align influencer initiatives with service execution, guest interaction, and revenue strategies to guarantee a cohesive brand.

This paper discusses the distinction between micro and mega-influencers in consumer persuasion and authenticity cues. It examines the existence of the effect of follower scale on consumer trust, purchase intention, and brand engagement. Data, with a quantitative research design that used 390 respondents, were analyzed using factor Analysis and mediation analysis. Consequences of chapter designate that micro-influencers can create more visions of authenticity and consumer trust, which translates to increased persuasion and purchase intention than mega-influencers whose endorsements are perceived to be more commercial. The research points to

Preface

ABOUT THIS BOOK

The rapid evolution of digital technologies has fundamentally transformed the global hospitality industry, with social media emerging as one of the most influential forces reshaping hotel operations and marketing practices. Once regarded merely as promotional platforms, social media tools have now become integral to nearly every aspect of hotel management—from customer engagement, brand positioning, and revenue generation to service innovation, reputation management, and operational decision-making. *Integrating Social Media Tools Into Hotel Operations and Marketing* is conceived in response to this paradigm shift, addressing the growing need for a comprehensive, research-informed, and practice-oriented exploration of social media integration within contemporary hotel environments.

In an era characterized by user-generated content, real-time communication, and digitally empowered travelers, hotels can no longer rely solely on traditional marketing channels or standardized service delivery models. Guests increasingly evaluate hotels based on online reviews, influencer endorsements, interactive brand narratives, and personalized digital interactions before, during, and after their stay. Social media platforms such as Instagram, Facebook, TikTok, X (formerly Twitter), LinkedIn, and emerging community-based applications have become critical touchpoints in the guest journey, shaping perceptions, expectations, and loyalty. This book recognizes social media not as an auxiliary function, but as a strategic and operational asset that directly influences hotel performance and competitiveness.

The primary objective of this book is to examine how social media tools can be effectively integrated into hotel operations and marketing strategies to enhance guest experience, operational efficiency, and brand equity. It brings together theoretical perspectives, empirical research, and real-world case studies to offer a holistic understanding of social media's role in hospitality management. Special attention is given to data-driven decision-making, customer relationship management, electronic word-of-mouth (e-WOM), online reputation management, influencer marketing, and the alignment of social media strategies with broader organizational goals.

Integrating Social Media Tools Into Hotel Operations and Marketing is designed for a diverse audience, including academics, researchers, postgraduate students, hotel managers, marketing professionals, and policymakers in tourism and hospitality. For scholars, it provides conceptual frameworks and research directions that contribute to the growing body of literature on digital hospitality. For practitioners, it offers actionable strategies and evidence-based insights that can be adapted across different hotel categories, from budget and boutique properties to luxury and multinational chains.

Ultimately, this book seeks to bridge the gap between theory and practice by demonstrating how strategically integrated social media tools can create value for both hotels and guests. As the hospitality industry continues to evolve in response to technological innovation and changing consumer behavior, this volume aspires to serve as a timely and authoritative reference for understanding and leveraging the transformative power of social media in hotel operations and marketing.

Acknowledgement

The completion of this book, *Integrating Social Media Tools Into Hotel Operations and Marketing*, would not have been possible without the support, encouragement, and contributions of many individuals to whom I owe my sincere gratitude.

First and foremost, I express my deepest appreciation and heartfelt thanks to my wife, *Dipika Sharma*, whose unwavering support, patience, and understanding have been a constant source of strength throughout this academic journey. Her encouragement during long hours of research, writing, and editing made this work possible. I am equally grateful to my son, *Anvit Shukla*, whose presence, love, and innocence provided motivation, balance, and renewed energy during the most demanding phases of this project. This book is as much theirs as it is mine.

I extend my sincere thanks to all the *editors and contributors* who shared their expertise, insights, and scholarly efforts in shaping this volume. Their intellectual rigor, commitment to quality, and collaborative spirit significantly enhanced the academic value and practical relevance of this book. Each chapter reflects their dedication to advancing knowledge in hospitality, tourism, and digital marketing.

I am also grateful to the *reviewers and academic peers* whose constructive feedback and suggestions helped strengthen the conceptual clarity, structure, and scholarly depth of this work. My appreciation further extends to the *publisher and editorial team* for their professional guidance, support, and patience throughout the publication process.

Special thanks are due to colleagues, mentors, researchers, and industry professionals whose discussions, ideas, and experiences indirectly contributed to the development of this book. Their perspectives enriched the content and ensured its relevance to both academia and industry practice.

Finally, I acknowledge all students, researchers, and hospitality professionals who continue to inspire meaningful research and innovation in the field. It is my hope that this book serves as a valuable resource for learning, research, and practical application in the evolving landscape of hotel operations and marketing.

Chapter 1
Innovations in Hospitality Marketing:
Past, Present, and Future

Dilip Kumar
http://orcid.org/0000-0002-2503-1394
Great Lakes Institute of Management, Gurgaon, India

Abhinav Kumar Shandilya
http://orcid.org/0000-0001-5186-9433
Birla Institute of Technology Mesra, Patna, India

Sushil Kumar
http://orcid.org/0009-0007-1087-9150
Birla Institute of Technology Mesra, Patna, India

ABSTRACT

Innovation is the key to survival for individuals, businesses, and societies alike. In today's fast-paced and evolving environment, adopting a problem-solving and value-creation approach is essential to meet the growing demands of consumers and guests. This review seeks to examine the competitive landscape of the hospitality industry by analysing literature published in the Scopus database since its inception. From an initial query yielding 258 articles, 91 documents were finalized after applying the inclusion and exclusion criteria explained through the PRISMA framework. To address the research questions both performance analysis and science mapping approaches were employed. The findings reveal that this area of research has witnessed rapid growth over the years, with contributions from a diverse range of countries and authors. Building on these insights, this review proposes future research directions that can serve as a valuable guide for budding researchers, business practitioners, and policymakers engaged in the hospitality domain.

DOI: 10.4018/979-8-3373-6741-5.ch001

1. INTRODUCTION

Innovation and development of new products or services are crucial for sustainable growth in any industry. It becomes more critical where market demand is driven by the standards of the services offered, such as in the hospitality and tourism industry. As per Lee et al. (2025), "innovation is developing a product, service, business model, or strategy that is both novel and useful." Hisrich et al. (2016) defined innovation as a new product, characterised by the degree of newness based on how much new learning is required by the customer to use the product or avail of the service. These definitions reiterate that innovation in the hospitality and tourism industry can be acceptable to customers only when services are customised according to their requirements. In other words, customising products and services in the hospitality and tourism industry is one of the most essential ways to innovate.

Innovation in the hospitality sector has emerged as a central focus of discussion among researchers, particularly in the face of intense competition within the industry. Innovations are essential not only for survival but also for sustainability and profitability (Aggarwal et al., 2024). Therefore, successful hospitality organisations need to implement realistic and attractive marketing strategies through successful innovations (de Oliveira et al., 2024). The hospitality and tourism industry encompasses various dimensions, including service quality, quality of tangible products, perception, employee training, organisational culture, competition, profitability, and sustainability. These dimensions being too numerous pose a challenge to the service provider, while at the same time providing opportunities to innovate. To develop a competitive hospitality organisation, marketing of hospitality services is essential, and the activities of the marketing department extend beyond marketing strategies. The domain of marketing strategies has expanded beyond product or service innovation. Ahmad & Rasheed (2025) argued that innovation in the hospitality sector can be achieved through innovation in accommodation and human resource management. Badraoui & Smith (2025) highlighted that hotels can be competitive through marketing innovation and effective use of information technology. Liasidou & Pipyros (2025) explored the importance of sustainable hotel engineering and organisation of facilities in the hospitality business, along with combined innovation in economic and marketing areas.

In the recent past, innovation has been driven by technology adoption. Use of technology has accelerated the achievement of efficiency in the hospitality industry. Demirović Bajrami et al. (2025) argued that the development of technologies introduced numerous changes in the hospitality sector that affected both the service offerings and demand. Increase in demand for hospitality services, enhancing efficiency, and improving customer satisfaction has forced the hospitality sector to adopt technology (Law et al., 2014; Mu et al., 2025). Technology-driven practices have benefited street vendors by introducing innovation in digital marketing, online payment systems, and linkage with suppliers (Sigala et al., 2025). Recently introduced blockchain technology has been useful for both operational and strategic purposes in the hospitality industry. It has helped the hospitality managers in managing operations of the service creation and offerings (Fraga et al., 2025; Tsou et al., 2025; Willie, 2019). Artificial intelligence has redesigned the internal processes, supported in the customisation of products and services, remodelled the distribution models, and contributed to co-creation practices, transforming the interaction between customers and service providers in the hospitality and tourism industry (Borges-Tiago & Avelar, 2025; Sackey et al., 2025).

Although a considerable amount of work has been done in the area of innovation in hospitality marketing, it has been observed that there is a lack of systematic literature reviews encompassing all the works undertaken in the area of innovation in the hospitality sector. Through this research work, the authors attempted to summarise the existing research in the field of innovation in the hospitality industry. As suggested by (Ridley, 2012), good research is based on a well-formulated research question (RQ), the following RQs are formulated, and further analysis is presented in the results section.

> RQ1: *What are the current publication trends in Innovation in Hospitality Marketing (IHM) in terms of publication volume, time evolution, and citation impact?*

Purpose: To identify how research activity has evolved over time (e.g., publication growth, citation patterns) and to understand the maturity and momentum of the field.

> RQ2: *Who are the leading contributors (authors and countries) in the field, and which regions or entities are underrepresented?*

Purpose: To map the global research landscape - identifying major hubs of innovation and gaps in scholarly participation or collaboration.

> RQ3: *How are the most highly cited publications contributing to the conceptual and methodological development of research in IHM?*

Purpose: To examine the intellectual foundations and influential works that have shaped the direction of research.

> RQ4: *How does the bibliographic coupling of documents reveal the underlying research clusters and emerging trends in IHM?*

Purpose: To use bibliographic coupling to detect thematic relationships, clusters, and future research frontiers based on shared references among papers.

2. RESEARCH METHODOLOGY

A literature review helps in strengthening the knowledge by integrating previous studies and provides a comprehensive overview of the literature (Paul & Criado, 2020). Simultaneously, it significantly contributes to the development of thematic, conceptual and methodological domains (Hulland & Houston, 2020). A systematic literature review (SLR) is classified into four categories: domain-based, method-based, theory-based, and meta-analysis, which explore quantitative effects (Hulland & Houston, 2020). Domain-based review covers Structured review, Framework-based review, Bibliometric review, Hybrid-Narrative with a future research agenda, and Model/Framework development. A large number of domain-based reviews are available in both technical (engineering, medical, pharmaceuticals, etc.) and non-technical fields (tourism, hospitality, marketing, entrepreneurship, etc.), and have been published in well-established journals.

In the present study, Bibliometric analysis (BA) is chosen over other domain-based reviews due to its scalable, reproducible nature, which helps to map the intellectual structure of relevant research published in the same domain. Quantitative indicators, such as citation counts, co-occurrence, and bibliographic coupling, reveal macro-level patterns (performance analysis and science mapping) that are difficult to obtain via conventional methods (Öztürk et al., 2024). The use of visualisation tools and reproducible workflows helps in creating thematic clusters, collaboration networks, and identifying emerging topics, which can provide a foundation for future research directions (Montazeri et al., 2023). A recent study in hospitality and marketing suggested that identifying research gaps and developing a guiding theory supports the appropriateness of uncovering trends and high-impact works in the innovation sub-domain (Giraldo et al., 2024).

A systematic bibliometric review was conducted using the Scopus database. A comprehensive search using a search string - ((TITLE-ABS-KEY(Innovation) AND TITLE-ABS-KEY(hospitality marketing)) AND (LIMIT-TO (DOCTYPE, "ar")) AND (LIMIT-TO (LANGUAGE, "English"))) was carried out on 25th August 2025. The initial search returned 258 records. After deduplication and screening in accordance with PRISMA guidelines, 91 documents were retained for analysis. Preferred Reporting Items for Systematic Reviews and Meta-Analysis (PRISMA) is followed for selection (inclusion and exclusion) of articles, as suggested by Page et al. (2021) is shown in *Figure 1*. Metadata were exported and analysed using the bibliometrix R-package (Biblioshiny) 4.4.1. Finally, authors performed a performance analysis (annual trends, productive authors & countries, and highly cited articles) and science mapping (bibliographic coupling) to gain insight into the context of the RQs.

Figure 1. PRISMA Flowchart

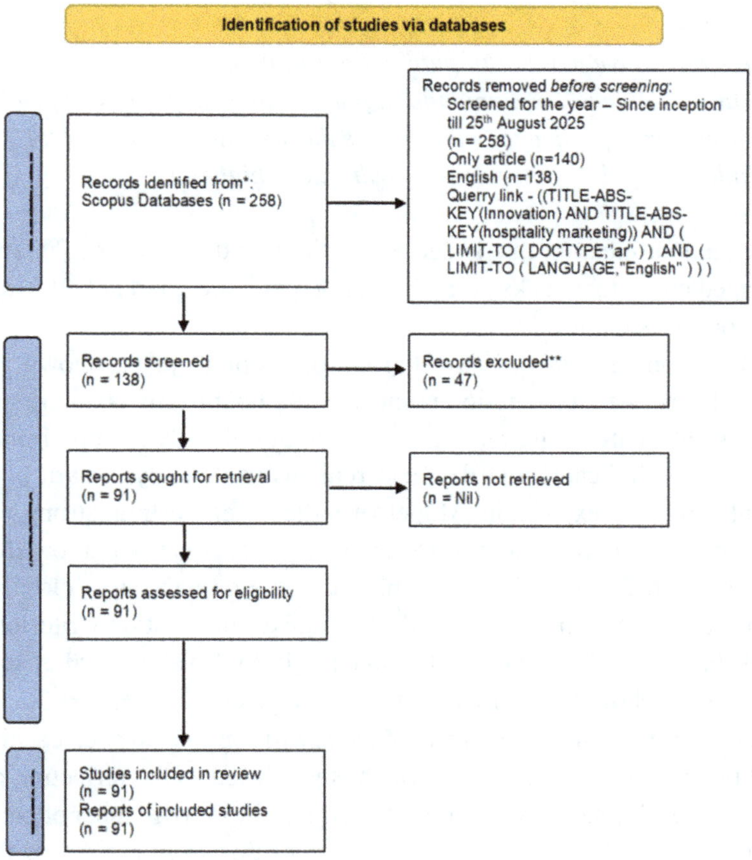

3. RESULTS AND DISCUSSION

3.1. Overview

The temporal dynamics of the research topic are analysed by implementing a logistic growth model through the Life Cycle of Scientific Production module (LCSPM). This approach evolved from the theory of "*scientific paradigms* and *in-*

novation diffusion", which allows researchers to identify the current developmental stage, predict future trends and estimate the maturity or saturation stage.

Formula:

$P(t) = K / (1 + exp(-b(t - t_0)))$

Where:

- *P(t): Cumulative number of publications at time t*
- *K: Saturation level (maximum total publications the topic will produce)*
- *b: Growth rate parameter (determines the steepness of the curve)*
- *t_0: Inflection point (time when growth rate is highest)*

The annual publication rate is derived as the first derivative of P(t), producing a bell-shaped curve that peaks at the inflection point and gradually declines as the topic approaches saturation.

The IHM domain, which is a subgroup of hospitality, has shown promising statistics. The estimated saturation point (K = 910 publications) suggests that the domain has substantial long-term potential, with only 10% of this limit reached as of 2025. This indicates that the field remains in its early growth phase, with significant scope for expansion. Model fit indices demonstrate strong reliability, evidenced by an R^2 (Coefficient of Determination) of 0.818 and a low Root Mean Square Error (RMSE) of 1.73, confirming that the growth curve closely reflects the historical publication pattern. Both the Akaike Information Criterion (AIC is 30.0) and Bayesian Information Criterion (BIC is 33.3) values further support the suitability of the chosen model without overfitting, shown in *Figure 2*.

The model predicts that annual publications will continue to rise, reaching a peak of 39 publications per year in 2038, which is identified as the inflection point (T) of the topic's development. At this midpoint, the cumulative number of publications is projected to reach 50% of K, marking the transition from rapid growth to early maturity. Milestone analysis reveals that the field will cross 90% saturation by 2051 and 99% saturation by 2065, indicating a long maturation period extending over the next four decades. These trends align with the typical evolution of emerging research domains in the social sciences and management disciplines, where adoption and interest gradually peak, as shown in *Figure 3*.

Forecasting results further reinforce the upward trajectory: cumulative publications are expected to reach 178 by 2030 and 332 by 2035, corresponding to annual outputs of 25 and 36 publications, respectively. These values highlight continuous research momentum and growing scholarly engagement. Overall, the results confirm that the topic is currently positioned within the rapid growth stage (10–50% of K), as shown in *Figure 4*. This phase is characterised by increasing academic attention, expanding theoretical development, and rising publication rates. Researchers entering this field are therefore likely to encounter fertile opportunities for high-impact contributions before the topic approaches maturity in the coming decades. The logistic growth model provides meaningful insights into the developmental stage and future trajectory of the research field.

Figure 2. Model overview; Software – Biblioshiny

Figure 3. Publication life cycle; Software - Biblioshiny

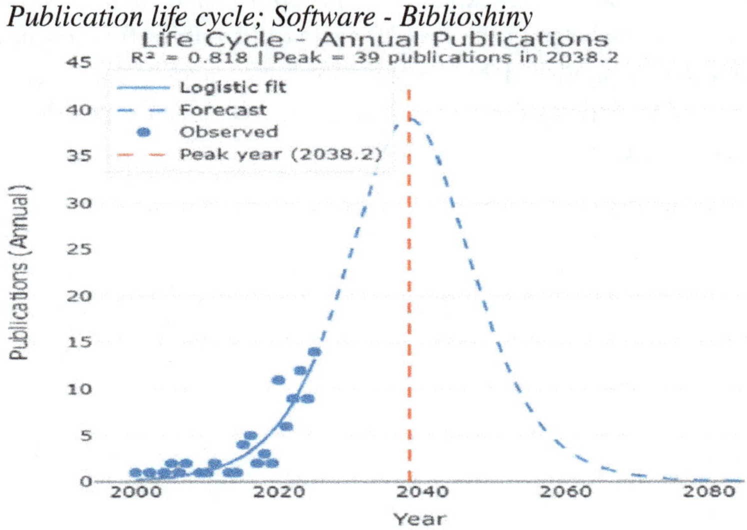

Figure 4. Cumulative Publication growth curve; Software - Biblioshiny

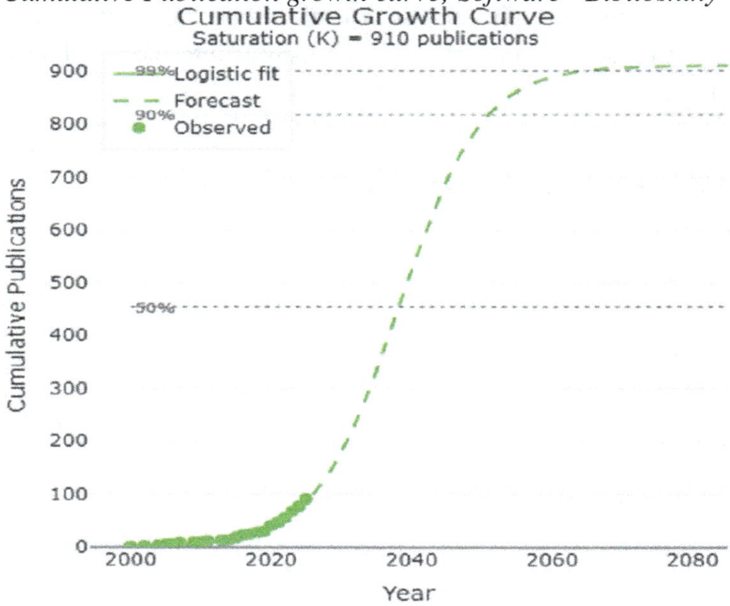

3.2. RQ1: Publication and citation trends

Identifying research activity in the IHM field, which evolved over time (e.g., publication growth, citation patterns), is done with the data extracted from the Scopus database from inception to 25th August 2025. Initially, 258 articles (metadata) were extracted, and after screening (explained in *Figure 1*), a metadata of 91 articles was used for the final analysis. In the first 20 years of its publication journey, only 30 (33%) articles were published, but received 61% of total citations; however, in the next six years, 61 (67%) articles were published. It shows a drastic upward trend and the maturity and momentum of the field, as shown in *Figure 5*.

Figure 5. Publication and Citation Trends; Software – MS Excel (NP – Number of Publications, TC-Total Citations)

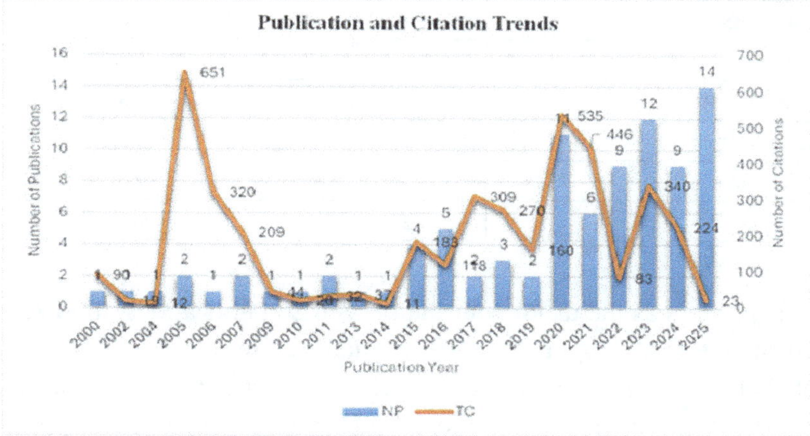

3.3. RQ2: Leading contributors (authors and countries) in the field

The IHM area has attracted researchers in the last six years (since 2020). 55.51% of total published articles were published in the last six years, which shows steep upward growth. Buhalis, Dimitrios and O'Connor, Peter appeared as the highest contributors of 3 articles with the same articles' fractionalised value of 1.08. Pappas, Nikolaos V., contributed only two articles but has the highest articles' fractionalised value of 2.00 (sole author). The article's fractionalised value refers to "the total credit for a single article is split equally among all listed authors or affiliated institutions. The core idea is to reflect the actual contribution to the work more accurately, rather than giving each author full credit for the entire paper." The top 10 productive authors in the IHM domain over the period of time are presented in *Table 1.*

Table 1. Top 10 Productive Authors

Author	Articles	Articles Fractionalised
Buhalis, Dimitrios	3	1.08
O'Connor, Peter	3	1.08
Floričić, Tamara	2	1.33
Hallak, Rob	2	0.58

continued on following page

Table 1. Continued

Author	Articles	Articles Fractionalised
Hassanien, Ahmed	2	1.00
Lee, Craig	2	0.58
Lee, Minwoo	2	0.67
Ottenbacher, Michael C.	2	1.50
Pappas, Nikolaos V.	2	2.00
Abdullah, Taufik	1	0.25

China appeared as the major contributor with 26 publications, followed by the UK (20) and the USA (19). The top 10 contributors are shown in *Table 2*. Several key global innovation and marketing research hubs, such as Germany, France, Switzerland, the UAE, Singapore, South Korea and Japan, are either underrepresented or completely missing from the list. Countries like Germany, France, Neatherlands and Singapore publish their work in general marketing and services marketing. Many European countries focus on tourism development, sustainable tourism and destination branding, not exactly innovation within hospitality marketing only. Exclusion of articles other than English and only the Scopus database used for data extraction can also be a reason behind the underrepresented or missing contributor list.

Table 2. Top 10 Productive Countries

Country	China	UK	USA	Brazil	Spain	India	Malaysia	Greece	Canada	Portugal
Frequency	26	20	19	9	9	8	8	7	6	6

3.4. RQ3: Highly Cited Publications in IHM

The top 10 highly cited articles are presented in *Table 3*. Buhalis & O'connor (2005) received the maximum citations of 337, where the role of information and communication technologies (ICTs) was highlighted to support customer-centric and personalised marketing through digitalisation to empower consumers and create new marketing models to reshape value chains. Williams (2006) received the second highest citation of 320, where experiential marketing has been highlighted as the key to differentiation and hospitality environments act as "cathedrals of consumption." M. C. Ottenbacher (2007) and M. Ottenbacher & Gnoth (2005) highlighted the requirement of systematic organisational support, cross-functional collaboration and experimentation for innovation. Strategic alignment can play a pivotal role between marketing and technology. Kuo et al. (2017 and Tuomi et al. (2021) identified the utilitarian and hedonic dimensions of service enhancements through robot-employee collaboration. Factors such as trust, perceived usefulness, and culture play a pivotal role in the acceptance of robot-employee collaboration. Jung et al. (2018) highlighted the role of intuitive, culturally adapted design, behavioural adoption shaped by cultural and demographic differences. Augmented reality (AR) plays a crucial role in increasing tourist engagement and learning.

Buhalis et al. (2023) highlighted the integration of ecosystem collaboration with ICTs, as the future of smart hospitality lies in it through personalisation, co-creation and optimised operations. Bulchand-Gidumal et al. (2024) highlighted the role of AI in reshaping hotel marketing across various processes and networks. Mass personalisation and recommendation systems, predictive and smart customer service, augmented workers and strategic integration across organisations and platforms are some of the key Artificial Intelligence (AI) driven transformations which can be very helpful for hospitality and tourism marketing. Filimonau & Naumova (2020) suggested the application of blockchain in supply chain management (removal of intermediaries), authenticating online reviews, customer loyalty programmes, cashless payment and sustainable. Secure data exchange between hotels and suppliers, and traceable food supply chains.

Table 3. Top 10 highly cited articles published in IHM domain

Authors	Title	PY	Source	TC	TCpY	NTC
(Buhalis & O'connor, 2005)	Information Communication Technology Revolutionizing Tourism	2005	Tourism Recreation Research	337	16.05	1.04
(Williams, 2006)	Tourism and Hospitality Marketing: Fantasy, Feeling and Fun	2006	International Journal of Contemporary Hospitality Management	320	16.00	1.00
(M. Ottenbacher & Gnoth, 2005)	How to Develop Successful Hospitality Innovation	2005	Cornell Hotel and Restaurant Administration Quarterly	314	14.95	0.96
(Kuo et al., 2017)	Investigating an Innovative Service with Hospitality Robots	2017	International Journal of Contemporary Hospitality Management	283	31.44	1.83
(Tuomi et al., 2021)	Applications and Implications of Service Robots in Hospitality	2021	Cornell Hospitality Quarterly	272	54.40	3.66

continued on following page

Table 3. Continued

Authors	Title	PY	Source	TC	TCpY	NTC
(Jung et al., 2018)	Cross-Cultural Differences in Adopting Mobile Augmented Reality at Cultural Heritage Tourism Sites	2018	International Journal of Contemporary Hospitality Management	225	28.13	2.50
(M. C. Ottenbacher, 2007)	Innovation Management in the Hospitality Industry: Different Strategies for Achieving Success	2007	Journal of Hospitality and Tourism Research	200	10.53	1.91
(Buhalis et al., 2023)	Smart Hospitality: From Smart Cities and Smart Tourism towards Agile Business Ecosystems in Networked Destinations	2023	International Journal of Contemporary Hospitality Management	196	65.33	6.92
(Bulchand-Gidumal et al., 2024)	Artificial Intelligence's Impact on Hospitality and Tourism Marketing: Exploring Key Themes and Addressing Challenges	2024	Current Issues in Tourism	166	83.00	6.67
(Filimonau & Naumova, 2020)	The Blockchain Technology and the Scope of its Application in Hospitality Operations	2020	International Journal of Hospitality Management	155	25.83	3.19

(PY-Publications year, TC-Total Citation, TCpY-Total Citation per year, NTC-Normalised total citation)

Top 10 highly cited articles published in the IHM domain highlight a transition of innovation from products/services to digitalisation and an ecosystem-driven model. Technology and experience are two pillars of hospitality marketing decision-making, and to design an emotionally rich experience amongst customers/guests, their integration is highly important. Blockchain and AI are innovation catalysts which can be used to enhance trust and personalisation, which can be helpful in transforming marketing and guest experience, enabling smarter and sustainable operations and supporting data-driven revenue and loyalty systems.

3.5. RQ4: The clusters identified by bibliographic coupling of documents

Cluster -1 Innovation through functional areas of hospitality

Innovation within an organisation cannot be achieved without involving all functional areas of the organisation. Lee et al. (2025) provided the insights of organisation-level innovation by examining the role of innovation in improving the performance of functions of the hospitality organisation (product, process, organisational, and marketing). Demirović Bajrami et al. (2025) found that competitiveness in the hospitality sector can be achieved through innovation in accommodation, human resource management and marketing. Ahmad & Rasheed (2025) proposed a framework to examine the influence of service innovation on customer satisfaction. They highlighted the importance of innovative service delivery in enhancing customer behavioural intentions. On similar lines, Wilkesmann & Bassyiouny (2025) focused on innovation in the tourism and hospitality industry through service innovation, especially in the post-crisis scenario. They initiated a discussion on the role of service innovation in reducing the impact of COVID-19 pandemic on the tourism and hospitality industry. Liasidou & Pipyros (2025) examined and evaluated the hotels' marketing strategies during the recession using a nationwide survey of hospitality managers in Greece. The result revealed that hotels can overcome crises through marketing innovation and effective use of information technology.

Aggarwal et al. (2024) emphasised creating a competitive advantage for innovative entrepreneurs in the tourism and hospital industry, especially those involved with accommodation and food, and travel agencies. With reference to the Canadian tourism and hospitality industry, Mu et al. (2025) argued that innovative economic policies, such as reinvesting a portion of tax from international visitors, can boost tourism marketing in Canada. Badraoui & Smith (2025) adopted an interdisciplinary approach to explore the importance of sustainable hotel engineering and organisation of facilities in the hospitality business, along with combined innovation in economic and marketing areas.

Cluster-2 Innovation and Service Quality

Quality of the service in the hospitality sector is an important factor that can help the service provider gain a competitive advantage in the industry. Borges-Tiago & Avelar (2025) explored the effect of technological innovation on the scope of outreach of hospitality services to customers. They found that service providers, using innovative technology for improving service quality, can benefit in reaching out to target customers effectively. Fraga et al. (2025) investigated the moderating role of operational innovation on the relationship between service quality and marketing performance among hotels. A survey was conducted by collecting data from general managers of hotels in Jordan. The results presented a positive relationship between quality of service and marketing performance, moderated by operational innovation. In the recent past, Sigala et al. (2025) developed a scale to measure restaurant innovativeness across three different restaurant formats: casual dining, fast food, and coffee shops. The respondents were Generation Z individuals availing services across all three formats. On similar lines, Tsou et al. (2025) established a model representing the relationship between restaurant innovativeness and customer loyalty with the mediating role of perceived service quality.

Cluster-3 Customer-employee participation for service innovation

Customer and employee participation is crucial for creating services, as it leads to greater value to customers through service customisation. Innovativeness in involving service providers and service receivers may lead to greater competitive advantage. One of the pioneering studies examined differences in value co-creation appraisal between employees and customers of a destination resort (Zhang et al., 2025). The results showed that employees appraised significantly higher of co-created value. Positive satisfaction and competitive advantage were appraised as higher by both employees and customers. Sackey et al. (2025) revealed how the involvement of customers in the hospitality industry drives the employees of the sector by surveying employees and managers working in hotels in Vietnam. Meng et al. (2025) analysed the interrelationship among three key forces of service innovation in the hospitality sector. They studied how internal marketing processes influence employee involvement, training and empowerment of the employee, and service advantage. Chung (2025) explored the mediation of service innovation and customer relationship management in the relationship between market orientation and competitive advantage. Kaban & Augustinus (2025) assessed the influence of knowledge resources on marketing innovation and evaluated how the learning capacity of employees mediates this relationship.

Cluster-4 Innovation behaviour in city hotels

This cluster is a summary of works related to innovativeness and innovation behaviour in city hotels. Magoutas et al. (2024) assessed innovation in Swedish hotels to investigate organisational and structural factors of hotels that affect the creation of product or service, process, and marketing innovation. They asserted that managers can influence the innovation strategy in the hotel sector by engaging in non-traditional R&D activities. Lim et al. (2024) unravelled the impacts of soft innovation in the city hotels. They also figured out if vitality on the components of soft innovation varies among the 4-star, 5-star, and boutique hotels in Izmir, Turkey. The results revealed that all soft innovation applications are crucial regardless of their categories. Duarte Alonso et al. (2024) argued that hotels must seek innovation, and must exhibit innovative service behaviours of hotel employees to attract customers. Based on the survey of hotel employees working at the front office and the F&B department, the study found that internal service quality and climate positively affect employee job satisfaction. Ausejo Sánchez et al. (2024) explored the dimensions and determinants of innovation that are hotel-specific. Results from Portuguese hotels showed that information & communication technology, and marketing were the leading innovation areas. Size of the hotel, hotel's star ratings, hotel chain, and employee training are significantly related to hotel innovation behaviour, which in turn positively affects the hotel performance. With the purpose of exploring the distribution channels and identifying the important elements of the online distribution system leading to the success of the hotel, Zeng et al. (2024), through research findings, presented the benefits of online travel agents, tour operators, and social networks in improved performance of the hotels. Sánchez Jiménez et al. (2024) examined the customers' perceptions of the technology, innovation, and marketing communications within the hotel. The Hotel guests of 4-star and 5-star hotels located in two Mediterranean countries – Croatia and Italy were surveyed to find that customers' perceptions of technology are moderate, and perception of communication consistency is high.

Cluster-5 Technology and Innovation in the Hospitality Industry

In this cluster, new technologies being used by the hospitality industry are discussed. The use of a recently developed concept of blockchain technology in the hospitality industry has been studied by Panda et al. (2024). This study is an attempt to explore the scope of blockchain technology applications in the context of operations management in the hospitality sector. Based on the grounded theory approach, Han et al. (2024) used in-depth interviews, focus groups, and a questionnaire-based survey to explore the effect of artificial intelligence on the marketing function of hotels. The results pointed out that artificial intelligence redesigns the internal process, helps in the customisation of products and services, transforming distribution models, and integrating organisations in the hospitality and tourism industry. On similar lines, Ramachandran et al. (2024) explored the benefits of co-creation using artificial intelligence in the hospitality industry. They found that co-creation practices driven by technology transformed the way customers and service providers interact.

It further demonstrated how co-creation drives innovation, encourages customer engagement, and manages challenges.

Technology-driven services have even penetrated micro-enterprises in the hospitality industry, like street food vendors. These vendors contribute to the success of tourism and hospitality as they cater to both local residents and tourists, acting as ambassadors of local culture and culinary traditions. Prevolšek et al. (2024) emphasised that the performance of street vendors is influenced by technology-driven innovative practices such as digital marketing, online payment systems, and strong links with local suppliers. Bilgihan & Ricci (2024) examined the impact of communities of practice on the development of innovations in the hospitality sector. Using the snowball method, data were collected from renowned chefs through in-depth interviews. The findings revealed that by using communities of practice, chefs obtained the knowledge to innovate their menus.

4. CONCLUSION

Effective and impactful marketing is essential for every business, and in today's competitive environment, innovation plays a crucial role in ensuring long-term survival. The hospitality sector is no exception-innovation in hospitality marketing is just as important as in any other industry, helping businesses stay ahead of competitors and meet evolving guest expectations.

The present study reveals that research output in the IHM domain is still limited, with only 91 published articles to date. However, the trend indicates significant growth ahead. While the highest number of publications so far appeared in 2025 (14 articles), projections suggest this number may rise to 39 by the year 2038. This upward trajectory highlights a promising opportunity for researchers to further develop the theoretical foundations and practical contributions of the field. The growth curve analysis provides compelling evidence that the topic is on a steep upward trajectory, with substantial room for scholarly expansion. The strong predictive performance of the model reinforces the credibility of the projected publication patterns. The long maturation horizon further highlights the field's potential to remain academically vibrant and impactful for several decades.

Summarising and analysing the research work undertaken in past in the domain of innovation in hospitality marketing using Bibliographic Coupling Analysis (BCA), five clusters have been generated. Underlining the importance of integrating various sections or departments of an organisation, Cluster-1 focuses on introducing innovation in the hospitality industry through integrating functional areas of a hospitality organisation. Cluster-2 highlights the contribution of innovation in bringing out the better quality of the hospitality services for efficient operations and enhanced marketing performance. Cluster-3 emphasises the importance of customer and employee participation for creating innovative services through a greater degree of service customisation. Cluster-4 brings forward the innovativeness and innovation practices in the city hotels by engaging in non-traditional R&D activities that have helped front office management, food & beverages department, and housekeeping department for a comfortable stay for guests. Lastly, cluster-5 showcases how the innovation has been initiated through the application of technologies in the hospitality industry, ranging from using digital marketing tools, online payment systems, to using artificial intelligence and blockchain technology. Together, these five clusters substantiate the significance and necessity of innovation in hospitality marketing through integrating operations, customer-employee participation, and technological applications for improved service quality, enhanced marketing performance, and gaining a competitive advantage.

5. CONCEPTUAL INTEGRATION OF FINDINGS:

Conceptually, the findings converge on a unified framework in which innovation in hospitality marketing functions as a *systemic capability* rather than a set of discrete practices. The five clusters collectively demonstrate that IHM emerges from the dynamic alignment of three interdependent domains: organisational integration, relational co-creation, and technological enablement. At the organisational level (Clusters 1 and 2), innovation is embedded across functional boundaries, transforming marketing into an enterprise-wide logic that aligns operations, service design, and performance outcomes. At the relational level (Cluster 3), value is no longer produced unilaterally by firms but co-created through continuous interaction among employees and guests, where customisation and experiential differentiation become central marketing mechanisms. At the contextual and operational level (Cluster 4), innovation materialises within everyday service encounters, particularly in city hotels, where non-traditional R&D practices convert frontline departments into strategic innovation nodes. Finally, at the infrastructural level (Cluster 5), digital and intelligent technologies act as integrative enablers, connecting organisational processes with customer experiences through data-driven personalisation, seamless transactions, and trust-enhancing systems.

Together, these dimensions form an integrated conceptual architecture in which innovation in hospitality marketing operates as a recursive cycle: organisational integration enables service innovation; service innovation fosters relational co-creation; co-creation generates experiential differentiation; and technology amplifies and scales these processes. This cycle continuously feeds back into organisational learning and strategic renewal. Hence, IHM can be conceptualised as a *multi-layered adaptive system* that synchronises internal capabilities, human interactions, and digital infrastructures to produce sustained competitive advantage. This integrative perspective advances the field beyond fragmented tool-centric or department-specific approaches, positioning innovation as the central mechanism through which hospitality firms orchestrate value creation, experience design, and market performance in an evolving service ecosystem.

6. MANAGERIAL IMPLICATIONS:

From a managerial perspective, the findings suggest that hospitality leaders must reconceptualise marketing as an enterprise-wide innovation function. Managers should foster cross-departmental collaboration, ensuring that marketing objectives are embedded in service design, employee training, and operational workflows. Empowering frontline employees and engaging guests as co-creators can generate differentiated experiences that are difficult for competitors to imitate. Moreover, investments in digital infrastructure should not be limited to promotional activities; rather, technologies such as AI-driven personalisation, seamless payment systems, and data-integrated platforms should be aligned with service strategy to enhance responsiveness and trust. Innovation, therefore, should be managed as a portfolio of organisational, relational, and technological initiatives rather than as isolated projects.

Policy implications are equally significant. Tourism authorities and hospitality regulators can play a catalytic role by encouraging innovation ecosystems that connect academia, industry, and technology providers. Targeted funding for digital transformation, innovation labs for small and medium hospitality enterprises, and skill-development programmes focused on data literacy and service design can accelerate sector-wide capability building. Furthermore, policy frameworks that promote ethical data use, cybersecurity, and technological transparency will strengthen consumer trust and support sustainable digital adoption.

In sum, this study establishes innovation in hospitality marketing as a rapidly emerging and strategically consequential field. By integrating organisational processes, human participation, and technological advancement, the five identified clusters offer a comprehensive roadmap for both scholarly inquiry and managerial action. As the field matures, future research can build on this foundation to develop integrative theories, longitudinal models, and cross-cultural insights that further elevate the academic and practical relevance of IHM.

REFERENCES

Aggarwal, A., Baker, H. K., & Joshi, N. A. (2024). Organizational Innovation as Business Strategy: A Review and Bibliometric Analysis. *Journal of the Knowledge Economy*, *16*(2), 6550–6576. DOI: 10.1007/s13132-024-01830-2

Ahmad, N., & Rasheed, H. M. W. (2025). Tourism and hospitality SMEs and digital marketing: What factors influence their attitude and intention to use from the perspective of BRT, TAM and IRT. *Journal of Hospitality and Tourism Insights*, *8*(4), 1546–1563. DOI: 10.1108/JHTI-05-2024-0508

Ausejo Sánchez, J. L., Soto, F. G. C., La Rosa, P. E. R., Palma, D. F. M., Campos, G. A. C., & Cadillo, A. J. R. (2024). Big data research in the business, management and accounting field: Revealing the thematic structure based on co-word analysis. *Iberoamerican Journal of Science Measurement and Communication*, *4*(1), 1–8. DOI: 10.47909/ijsmc.116

Badraoui, B., & Smith, S. J. (2025). Innovative interiors: An evaluation of guest perceptions and booking responses to robotic furniture in hotel rooms. *Journal of Hospitality and Tourism Insights*, *8*(4), 1355–1373. DOI: 10.1108/JHTI-05-2024-0479

Bilgihan, A., & Ricci, P. (2024). The new era of hotel marketing: Integrating cutting-edge technologies with core marketing principles. *Journal of Hospitality and Tourism Technology*, *15*(1), 123–137. DOI: 10.1108/JHTT-04-2023-0095

Borges-Tiago, M. T., & Avelar, S. (2025). Co-creation dynamics in tourism and hospitality: A horizon 2050 paper. *Tourism Review*, *80*(1), 194–208. DOI: 10.1108/TR-06-2024-0500

Buhalis, D., O'Connor, P., & Leung, R. (2023). Smart hospitality: From smart cities and smart tourism towards agile business ecosystems in networked destinations. *International Journal of Contemporary Hospitality Management*, *35*(1), 369–393. DOI: 10.1108/IJCHM-04-2022-0497

Bulchand-Gidumal, J., William Secin, E., O'Connor, P., & Buhalis, D. (2024). Artificial intelligence's impact on hospitality and tourism marketing: Exploring key themes and addressing challenges. *Current Issues in Tourism*, *27*(14), 2345–2362. DOI: 10.1080/13683500.2023.2229480

Chung, K.-C. (2025). The evolution of creativity: How generative AI is reshaping the hospitality landscape. *Enterprise Information Systems*, *19*(3–4). Advance online publication. DOI: 10.1080/17517575.2024.2427024 de Oliveira, P. S. G., da Silva, L. F., de Oliveira, S. I., da Silva, R. C., & de Mesquita Spinola, M. (2024). Chefs' Communities of Practice for Managing Innovations in the Tourism and Hospitality Sectors. *Journal of the Knowledge Economy*, *16*(2), 8660–8686. DOI: 10.1007/s13132-023-01616-y

Demirović Bajrami, D., Cimbaljević, M., Petrović, M. D., Radovanović, M. M., & Gajić, T. (2025). Internal marketing and employees' personality traits toward green innovative hospitality. *Tourism Review*, *80*(3), 710–724. DOI: 10.1108/TR-05-2023-0307

Duarte Alonso, A., Vu, O. T. K., Tran, T. D., Nguyen, T. T., Dang, Q. T., & Maheshwari, G. (2024). Perceived advantages and disadvantages of information communication technology adoption among restaurants in an emerging economy: A diffusion of innovations view. *International Journal of Hospitality Management*, *122*, 103837. DOI: 10.1016/j.ijhm.2024.103837

Filimonau, V., & Naumova, E. (2020). The blockchain technology and the scope of its application in hospitality operations. *International Journal of Hospitality Management*, *87*. Advance online publication. DOI: 10.1016/j.ijhm.2019.102383

Fraga, C., Cardoso, L., de Stefano, E., Lima Santos, L., & Motta, N. (2025). Mapping Gamification for Sustainable Urban Development: Generating New Insights for Tourism Education. *Tourism and Hospitality*, *6*(1), 17. DOI: 10.3390/tourhosp6010017

Giraldo, L. F. G., Pineda, V. G., Arias, J. V., Palacios-Moya, L., & López Goycochea, J. (2024). Exploring the evolution of marketing strategies in hospitality and tourism: A bibliometric study. *Progress in Industrial Ecology*, *17*(3), 240–251. DOI: 10.1504/PIE.2024.143784

Han, H., Ayalew, Z. A., & Kim, S. (Sam), Quan, W., Lho, L. H., Jung, I., & Al-Ansi, A. (2024). Drivers of digital currency adoption and their configurational impact assessment in tourism and hospitality: Loss aversion under prospect theory. *Current Issues in Tourism*, •••, 1–18. DOI: 10.1080/13683500.2024.2413665

Hisrich, R. D., Peters, M. P., & Shepherd, D. A. (2016). *Entrepreneurship* (10th ed.). McGraw Hill.

Hulland, J., & Houston, M. B. (2020). Why systematic review papers and meta-analyses matter: An introduction to the special issue on generalizations in marketing. *Journal of the Academy of Marketing Science*, *48*(3), 351–359. DOI: 10.1007/s11747-020-00721-7

Jung, T. H., Lee, H., Chung, N., & tom Dieck, M. C. (2018). Cross-cultural differences in adopting mobile augmented reality at cultural heritage tourism sites. *International Journal of Contemporary Hospitality Management, 30*(3), 1621–1645. DOI: 10.1108/IJCHM-02-2017-0084

Kaban, L. M., & Augustinus, D. C. (2025). Understanding brand recommendation and loyalty strategy across local and international chain hotels. *Corporate and Business Strategy Review, 6*(2), 52. DOI: 10.22495/cbsrv6i2art5

Kuo, C. M., Chen, L. C., & Tseng, C. Y. (2017). Investigating an innovative service with hospitality robots. *International Journal of Contemporary Hospitality Management, 29*(5), 1305–1321. DOI: 10.1108/IJCHM-08-2015-0414

Law, R., Buhalis, D., & Cobanoglu, C. (2014). Progress on information and communication technologies in hospitality and tourism. *International Journal of Contemporary Hospitality Management, 26*(5), 727–750. DOI: 10.1108/IJCHM-08-2013-0367

Lee, C., Abdullah, T., Hallak, R., & Kallmuenzer, A. (2025). Hospitality on the streets: A mixed-method study of Indonesian street food micro-enterprises. *International Journal of Hospitality Management, 130*, 104236. DOI: 10.1016/j.ijhm.2025.104236

Liasidou, S., & Pipyros, K. (2025). Conclusion: What is the transformative relationship between tourism and technology? *Worldwide Hospitality and Tourism Themes, 17*(1), 144–148. DOI: 10.1108/WHATT-12-2024-0314

Lim, S. (Edward), Ok, C. M., & Yang, Y. (2024). A meta-analytic investigation of innovation predictors in tourism and hospitality organizations. *Tourism Management, 105*, 104965. DOI: 10.1016/j.tourman.2024.104965

Magoutas, A. I., Manolopoulos, D., Manouka, M., & Dimitropoulou, M. (2024). Digitalization of the Alternative Tourism Marketspace: Evidence from an EU Peripheral Economy. *Tourism and Hospitality, 5*(4), 1151–1166. DOI: 10.3390/tourhosp5040064

Meng, J., Begum, M., Na, M., & Shah Alam, S. (2025). The Impact of Innovative Culture on Adaptive Marketing and Service Innovation in Hospitality: A Strategic Perspective. *Journal of Quality Assurance in Hospitality & Tourism*, •••, 1–38. DOI: 10.1080/1528008X.2025.2509230

Montazeri, A., Mohammadi, S. M., Hesari, P., Ghaemi, M., Riazi, H., & Sheikhi-Mobarakeh, Z. (2023). Preliminary guideline for reporting bibliometric reviews of the biomedical literature (BIBLIO): A minimum requirements. *Systematic Reviews, 12*(1), 239. PMID: 38102710

Mu, L., Guo, Q., & Yang, L. (2025). Revolutionizing Hospitality: Unraveling the Transformative Potential of Big Data in Tourism and Hotel Management. *HighTech and Innovation Journal*, *6*(1), 201–215. DOI: 10.28991/HIJ-2025-06-01-014

Ottenbacher, M., & Gnoth, J. (2005). How to develop successful hospitality innovation. *The Cornell Hotel and Restaurant Administration Quarterly*, *46*(2), 205–222. DOI: 10.1177/0010880404271097

Ottenbacher, M. C. (2007). Innovation Management in the Hospitality Industry: Different Strategies for Achieving Success. *Journal of Hospitality & Tourism Research (Washington, D.C.)*, *31*(4), 431–454. DOI: 10.1177/1096348007302352

Öztürk, O., Kocaman, R., & Kanbach, D. K. (2024). How to design bibliometric research: An overview and a framework proposal. *Review of Managerial Science*, *18*(11), 3333–3361.

Page, M. J., McKenzie, J. E., Bossuyt, P. M., Boutron, I., Hoffmann, T. C., Mulrow, C. D., Shamseer, L., Tetzlaff, J. M., Akl, E. A., Brennan, S. E., Chou, R., Glanville, J., Grimshaw, J. M., Hróbjartsson, A., Lalu, M. M., Li, T., Loder, E. W., Mayo-Wilson, E., McDonald, S., . . . Moher, D. (2021). The PRISMA 2020 statement: An updated guideline for reporting systematic reviews. In *The BMJ* (Vol. 372). BMJ Publishing Group. https://doi.org/DOI: 10.1136/bmj.n71

Panda, G. C., Rout, P. K., Nayak, M., Mohanty, B. R., & Sana, S. S. (2024). *Social media as a catalyst for hotel business growth: a pls-sem approach in odisha's smart cities*. OPSEARCH., DOI: 10.1007/s12597-024-00859-w

Paul, J., & Criado, A. R. (2020). The art of writing literature review: What do we know and what do we need to know? *International Business Review*, *29*(4), 101717. DOI: 10.1016/j.ibusrev.2020.101717

Prevolšek, D., Kukurin, Ž., & Golja, T. (2024). Collaborative Synergies for Elevated Destination Experiences: A Model of Cooperation between Hotel Companies, DMOs, and Local Stakeholders. *Organizacija*, *57*(1), 20–38. DOI: 10.2478/orga-2024-0002

Ramachandran, S., Ugokwe, C. K., Latiff, K., & Ibrahim, M. R. (2024). Continued innovation beyond COVID-19 crisis: toward mitigating the challenges in the tourism and hospitality industry. *Journal of Tourism Futures*. https://doi.org/DOI: 10.1108/JTF-10-2023-0221

Ridley, D. (2012). *The literature review: A step-by-step guide for students*.

Sackey, B. B., Yang, J., Quansah, P. E., Ekumah, C. A., Arboh, F., & Boadu, B. (2025). Internal marketing orientation and employee innovative behaviour: The mediating role of workforce agility and moderating role of psychological empowerment. *Journal of Hospitality and Tourism Insights*, *8*(2), 674–693. DOI: 10.1108/JHTI-01-2024-0063

Sánchez Jiménez, M. Á., Gómez Carmona, D., & Moral Moral, M. (2024). Evolution of the impact of social media in hospitality: A bibliometric analysis. *Journal of Destination Marketing & Management*, *31*, 100868. DOI: 10.1016/j.jdmm.2024.100868

Sigala, M., Goh, E., Leung, X., Rasoolimanesh, S. M., Su, C.-H. (Joan), & Tham, A. (2025). 30 Years of contribution and future directions in tourism, hospitality, and events research: A Quo Vadis perspective from the Journal of Hospitality and Tourism Management. *Journal of Hospitality and Tourism Management, 62*, 258–265. https://doi.org/DOI: 10.1016/j.jhtm.2025.02.001

Tsou, H.-T., Chen, J.-S., Mai, T. O., & Jade, N. B. N. (2025). Soft HRM Practices Fostering Service Innovations and Performance in Hospitality Firms. *Sustainability*, *17*(3), 895. DOI: 10.3390/su17030895

Tuomi, A., Tussyadiah, I. P., & Stienmetz, J. (2021). Applications and Implications of Service Robots in Hospitality. *Cornell Hospitality Quarterly*, *62*(2), 232–247. DOI: 10.1177/1938965520923961

Wilkesmann, M., & Bassyiouny, M. (2025). From leisure to labor: How workations are reshaping hospitality and destination marketing in the era of New Work. *Journal of Destination Marketing & Management*, *36*, 100991. DOI: 10.1016/j.jdmm.2025.100991

Williams, A. (2006). Tourism and hospitality marketing: Fantasy, feeling and fun. *International Journal of Contemporary Hospitality Management*, *18*(6), 482–495. DOI: 10.1108/09596110610681520

Willie, P. (2019). Can all sectors of the hospitality and tourism industry be influenced by the innovation of Blockchain technology? *Worldwide Hospitality and Tourism Themes*, *11*(2), 112–120. DOI: 10.1108/WHATT-11-2018-0077

Zeng, Z., Shen, C., Wang, H., & Lin, I. Y. (2024). Luckin Coffee in China: An Innovative Coffee Brand Dominating the Chinese Market amid the Covid-19 Pandemic. *Journal of Hospitality & Tourism Cases*, *12*(1), 3–10. DOI: 10.1177/21649987241241913

Zhang, M., & Li, J. (Justin), & Li, X. (2025). Can esports help with hospitality marketing for Generation Z? The interaction of esports, novelty seeking, and subjective knowledge. *International Journal of Hospitality Management*, *124*, 103963. DOI: 10.1016/j.ijhm.2024.103963

Chapter 2
Technology-Driven Transformation in Hospitality Marketing

Mohammad Badruddoza Talukder
http://orcid.org/0009-0008-1662-9221
International University of Business Agriculture and Technology, Bangladesh

Sanjeev Kumar
http://orcid.org/0000-0002-7375-7341
Lovely Professional University, India

Farhana Lina
http://orcid.org/0009-0006-8308-5549
Daffodil International University, Bangladesh

ABSTRACT

The hospitality world is undergoing a huge paradigm shift and technology is fueling a lot of it. Even more captivating user experiences and data-driven decisions are expected to be offered by new enhancements that are expected to revolutionize the process of serving the clients of hotels, restaurants, and tourism companies. The human relations with the brands will be characterized by new technologies such as AI and machine learning, AR and VR, chatbots, predictive analytics and big data, among others. Also, blockchain loyalty programs, immersive online experiences, and the use of the Internet of Things (IoT) will boost transparency, trust, and consumer interaction. The study determines the paths that the future marketing technologies in the hospitality industry could follow to bring about change in brand positioning,

DOI: 10.4018/979-8-3373-6741-5.ch002

customer experiences, and competitive advantage. It emphasizes that it is necessary that companies constantly innovate to keep up with the changing and technological world.

INTRODUCTION

The hospitality sector has reached a stage of inflexion, with technology currently bringing together the customary marketing frameworks and customer interaction approaches. With the growing tendency of consumer behavior in fast-paced digital development, the implementation of the newest marketing technologies has become a necessity as well as a source of competition for hospitality companies. Besides restaurants, lodgings, and hotels are also employing increasingly sophisticated tools such as artificial intelligence (AI), big data analytics, augmented reality (AR), virtual reality (VR), chatbots, blockchain systems, and the Internet-of-Things (IoT) to create communication convenience, accessibility, generation, personification, and distribution of customized services provided (Gursoy 2018). Not only do they create interactive, immersive, and value-driven experiences, but they also allow companies to more effectively capture, comprehend, and apply consumer data in more informative forms than ever before. Using artificial intelligence (AI) as an example, recommendation systems and predictive analytics may assist marketers to predict consumer preference levels, creating tailored marketing plans and maximizing price optimization models in order to increase brand loyalty and engagement (Lee et al., 2021). Similarly, AR and VR have presented new interactive marketing opportunities that bridge the gap between the real and virtual world, with potential travelers being able to virtually walk into a destination, into a hotel room, or into a dining establishment online before booking. In the meantime, blockchain technology is shaking the loyalty programs with a transparent, fraud-resistant, and secure decentralized apparatus to monitor the reward drivers. Collectively, these innovations imply that the marketing ecosystem is becoming more intelligent, customer-focused in terms of experience market - a shift that will not only improve the level of competitiveness but also increase operational efficiency, cost-efficiency, and sustainability (Talukder et al., 2024; Hoque et al., 2025).

In the meantime, the new technologies in hospitality marketing are not about the need to adopt new digital technologies only, but also about redefining how the new technologies can be applied to mirror the efforts of the changing consumer behavior, global problem-solving, and industry sustainability efforts better. The viewpoint and principles that direct the path towards a digitalization of the hospitality marketing are designed into the voyage of presenting the brand storytelling, experience design, and ethical innovation (Muller, 2010). Due to the increased importance of convenience, authenticity, and individuality among consumers than ever before, the emergence of marketing innovations should feel natural at all the Points of contact within the customer journey, including the inspiration and research phases, booking and check-out, as well as post-travel interactions. As IoT-enabled smart devices become the new reality, marketers can now access real-time data about the behavior of their guests that drives ultra-personalized campaigns that can change on the fly to satisfy the wants of their guests. Meanwhile, the AI-based analytics that drive social media are altering the ways in which brand reputation and consumer trust are established based on pinpointed and participatory mediations. The digital eco-badge or green blockchain certificates are also part of the sustainability-oriented marketing technology that will become a prominent area of distinction when trying to appeal to the environmentally conscious travelers. In terms of the future, the future of hospitality marketing will be more integrated into bigger and global tendencies, including the experience economy, smart cities, and sustainable tourism (Bilgihan and Ricci, 2024). A progressive mindset that prioritizes flexibility, digital literacy, and innovation as an ongoing operation will be required of hospitality companies in order to succeed in this changing environment. Therefore, it is not only the future of hotel marketing technology but the path of development that is going to turn it into genuine, enduring, sustainable, and robust business-to-consumer relationships (Singh et al., 2024).

Although the literature outlines the potential of emerging technologies to revolutionize hospitality marketing, certain gaps remain. To begin with, most studies are conceptual or exploratory and provide minimal data on the quantifiable effects of AI, AR/VR, blockchain, and IoT on the adoption of marketing strategies. Secondly, the ethical and privacy concerns related to data collection and use are not given enough consideration, particularly when there is a severe implementation of AI and IoT. Thirdly, the amount of cross-cultural and comparative research is insufficient to help gain a clearer insight into the disparities in consumer behavior towards marketing novelties in different regions and consumer profiles. Moreover, there is a necessity for longitudinal research on the sustainability and financial impact of the implementation of the technologies in the long term, and more informed research is needed to determine the direction of future research. Also, students suggest the idea of following an interdisciplinary direction, which combines marketing, technology, and sustainability visions to create an integrated strategy in the future marketing of hospitality.

THEORETICAL OVERVIEW

An examination of the probable effects on technology marketing within the hospitality sector may be based on a theoretical basis, taking into account the effect of using technology on the organizational strategy, customer interaction, and market success. A part of the foundations is the Technology Acceptance Model (TAM), where it is assumed that the perceived ease of use and the perceived usefulness of new technologies are mostly important in their adoption by the hospitality business and consumers (Tlili et al., 2021). When applied to the hospitality marketing industry, TAM implies that AI-based recommendation engines, AR applications, or blockchain-based reward programs have a higher chance of being accepted when employees and consumers view them as helpful solutions that allow them to make decisions and improve the experience overall. Expanding the range of this model is the Unified Theory of Acceptance and Use of Technology (UTAUT) that introduces the concepts of performance expectancy, effort expectancy, social influence, and facilitating conditions to be able to consider the applicability of this model to explore how hospitality businesses can integrate emergent marketing technologies into their work and promotion methods (Talukder et al., 2025).

The other applicable framework is the Service-Dominant Logic (SDL) of Marketing that puts the focus not on the physical goods but on value co-creation between the company and the consumer. This logic of co-creation between the firm and the customer is also applicable to the new hospitality marketing trends. Customers are transforming into more active participants in the creation of their own experiences and value creation in hotels with the help of IoT-based personalization or chatbots powered by AI. Additionally, the Innovation Diffusion Theory (IDT) provides an understanding of the reasons behind new marketing technologies being diffused across the hospitality industry and how it changes. Three groupings of the concepts have been identified, namely innovators, early adopters, and laggards, that affect the rate and the extent of adoption. Besides that, the Relationship Marketing Theory also focuses on the value of long-term loyalty and trust in customer relationships that platform players can improve with the help of such tools as blockchain transparency, immersive VR marketing experience, or personalized digital campaigns (Martin-Rios and Ciobanu, 2019). Finally, the Triple Bottom Line (TBL) framework can also be utilized to analyze sustainability-based innovations by evaluating the marketing strategies on the basis of the financial performance in addition to societal responsibility and environmental impact (Oh et al., 2004).

Combined, these theoretical frameworks provide a complex perspective of the possible effects of future marketing technologies on the hospitality industry. They highlight the relationship between user acceptance, value co-creation, and innovation diffusion and relational engagement with dynamic companies that must transform traditional marketing approaches into a sustainable digital one, which offers a general framework to explore the opportunities and challenges of digital transformation in hospitality marketing.

LITERATURE REVIEW

The pace of digital development of the hospitality industry has been coupled with the slowly growing literature on innovative marketing technologies. Scholars emphasize that the transformation of marketing approaches is based on artificial intelligence (AI) to personalize marketing with data, adjust prices dynamically, and use predictive analytics. AI-enabled systems are also used to operate Chabots, such as customer service in real-time and gathering an abundant source of information on consumer behavior (Dewangan and Kumar, 2024). Equally, in the literature, the use of machine learning models in demand forecasting and targeted campaigning, followed by customer satisfaction and loyalty, is also highlighted. AR and VR are becoming a formidable type of experiential marketing, which enables one to tour hotel rooms, conference halls, or tourist spots and then buy them (Valenca et al., 2020). Such immersive experiences are already being identified to be used in enabling physical and online experiences, especially prior to travel decisions.

The second component of the literature explores the use of blockchain in tourism marketing. Studies show that blockchain can bring a new dawn to the loyalty program since it provides the potential of transparency, decentralization, and fraud deterrence, which enhance confidence between companies and their customers (Salazar, 2018). Another developing topic that is growing rapidly in the field of marketing is the use of the Internet of Things (IoT), specifically in customized services and time-sensitive promotions. The IoT-related devices can be used to gather the preferences of the guests, allowing the marketers to customize their offers in real-time, and also to help reduce the expenses and enhance sustainability. Moreover, social media marketing and engagement of influencers are identified as the main points in the existing literature, where Instagram, TikTok, and Facebook are the main platforms that make brands more visible and help to formulate the thoughts of consumers (Shin et al., 2023). The scholars state that AI-driven analytics, when utilized in social marketing campaigns, may reinforce customer-brand relationships and build brand loyalty.

Although such developments have been made, there are some gaps in the literature. To start with, despite the high number of literature that praises the merits of such technology, there is not much concrete data regarding the impact of these applications on trust, loyalty, and financial performance in the long term. Second, the ethical aspect of collecting and using data in marketing, namely in AI- and IoT-based marketing, should be investigated further. Thirdly, there is a scarcity of information regarding how sustainability-related marketing technologies (e.g., digital eco-certifications, green blockchain practices) affect consumer intentions and behaviors regarding eco-friendly travel. Finally, comparative cross-country and cross-market research is done in very few studies, which restricts a comprehensive perception of country-specific differences in technological adoption used in marketing a hotel (Talukder et al., 2025). These gaps imply that the study of hospitality marketing innovation needs to be conceptualized in a more inclusive way to a certain degree, including an interdisciplinary perspective that integrates marketing, technology, and sustainability perspectives to form a comprehensive conceptualization of the phenomenon.

Data-Driven Marketing and Artificial Intelligence

Scholars have paid attention to AI as a tool in marketing in hospitality, as it can process massive volumes of data that come in about customers and draw insights. Chatbots, recommendation systems, and sentiment analysis platforms are artificial intelligence (AI)-based solutions that are becoming more and more popular to increase customer engagement and optimize promotional activities. It was also pointed out that AI interventions can allow the hotel and restaurant sectors to provide personalized, up-to-date services and become more satisfied and loyal to the company (Abakouy et al., 2019). Moreover, AIs can be used in predictive consumer demand analysis, which enables firms to dynamically adjust pricing regimes and thereby get the highest rents (A et al., 2025). When there is an addition of ML models, customer behavior can even be predicted. Marketers may use this knowledge to do micro-segmentation and a targeted advertising campaign. Notwithstanding such advantages, scientists caution that the implementation of AI creates problems in the context of data security and ethical use, and it needs precise instructions to the consumer and confidence (Talukder et al., 2025).

Experiential Marketing of AR and VR

AR and VR as Game-Changing is Experiential Hospitality Augmented Reality (AR) and Virtual Reality (VR) become progressively regarded as the game-changing components of experiential hospitality marketing. The platforms provide an interactive experience, allowing potential visitors to interact with products, such as accommodations and attractions, and make a purchasing choice. According to Trivedi et al. (2025), virtual hotel tour applications and VR destination previews influence consumer intention greatly as they decrease the uncertainty and enhance the perceived value. AR has also been applied in mobile apps, which overlay digital content on real spaces, e.g., an interactive restaurant menu or a promotion based on location.

The literature (4) adds that AR and VR fill the gap between the physical and digital spectrum, which also provides a try-before-you-buy experience, generating a sense of consumer confidence. However, the problem of affordability, accessibility, and the necessity of consumers to utilize these technologies do not go down the drain (Talukder et al., 2025). Academicians expect that in the marketing of the hospitality industry, consistent innovation and improved cost-effectiveness will be one of the drivers of AR/VR proliferation.

Loyalty Programs and Blockchain

The use of blockchain as a possible new tool that could enhance the transparency, safety, and trust in marketing the hospitality industry has also been explored. According to Sharma et al. (2023), blockchain is capable of disrupting loyalty programs by decentralizing point-of-sale rewards systems and rewards based on promotion, which will reduce fraud and offer a high degree of transferability across platforms. This becomes one more way in which we reinvent ourselves, and we assist customers in managing their rewards in a better way. Bob Mack, an executive vice president and Strategy of Texas Capital Bank. Also, the blockchain supports secure transactions via booking systems, reducing the risk of being exposed to issues that are associated with data breaches and identity theft. The recent research has emphasized its potential in sustainability, including the idea of using blockchain-based digital certifications to authorize eco-friendly methods and convey them to green consumers (Sarkar et al., 2025). Nevertheless, regulatory limitations, the complexity of technology, and the lack of consumer awareness are factors that limit the use of blockchain in the hospitality marketing field.

Personalization in Marketing and IoT

In its turn, the Internet of Things (IoT) has become a popular topic in the marketing literature of the hospitality industry because of the possibility of obtaining and processing real-time information using networked devices. To illustrate this point, the hotel rooms with IoT can learn about the preferences of guests (in relation to lighting, temperature, or entertainment) and utilize this information to implement highly personalized marketing campaigns. As emphasized by Mariani and Chakrabarti et al. (2024), the IoT not only offers service personalization but also contributes to enhancing operating efficiency through energy reduction, which would lead to sustainability. Researchers note that the marketing opportunity of the IoT is in the marketing of the smart device, including sending push notifications and personalized offers to guests during their stay, which will help to increase cross-selling or upselling. Nonetheless, the introduction of the IoT has also created certain cybersecurity and privacy concerns that have proven to be a major concern to consumers and businesses alike (R. Sharma & Kumar, 2025).

Influence Marketing, Social Media, and AI Analytics

You Can Not Escape Social Media in 2018: How to maximize your Hotel Socio-Online Resume / Author: Sanjay Nijhawan Convention. On the basis of another quotation - Subtitle Goes Here Summary: This dissertation will discuss. In recent years, it has become even more challenging not to come across marketing strategies oriented towards the hospitality and travel industries. R. Khan & Shalini (2024) emphasize that social media interaction is a trust-building factor and enhances the consumer-brand relationship. The visual platforms, including Instagram, TikTok, and YouTube, have become a pillar of the experiential marketing campaign, as the consumer decision-making process can be shaped with the help of high-quality content. Influencer marketing may also have a more comprehensive purpose, as literature implies the use of the top social media celebrities to promote a brand and make it more authentic (Aziz et al., 2024). Moreover, AI-based analytics may be combined with social media, which allows hotel companies to monitor the sentiment of the consumers, brand reputation, and the performance of the campaigns in real-time. However, taking into consideration misinformation, authenticity, and overpopulating influencer content makes the situation more complicated, and a considerate approach to future social media marketing activities is required.

Marketing Innovations in Sustainability

An increasing body of literature on the topic highlights the relevance of marketing technologies based on sustainability as a way of dealing with the high rate of sustainable tourism. Consumers are also demanding green and socially responsible hospitality brands, and the companies are implementing green marketing strategies with the assistance of technology. New technological tools, specifically digital environmental certification, ecolabeling based on blockchain, and AI-driven systems to manage energy, are called the reinforcement of an eco-friendly brand image (Gil-Saura et al., 2024). According to researchers, these outreach programs not only create corporate image/s but also alter consumer attitudes through the appeal to the values of being green. Nevertheless, the authors of this paper also mention that, despite the discussion of sustainability-oriented innovations, empirical evidence is still required to prove that a sustainable innovation approach can affect long-term consumer loyalty and business performance.

Predictive Personalization and Artificial Intelligence

Most of the research that is being conducted by hospitality marketing specialists is currently centered on artificial intelligence. In addition to Chatbots and suggestions, AI has been used more and more to handle unstructured data, including customer reviews, social media posts, and verbal communication. Sentiment analysis applications that run on natural language processing (NLP) allow businesses to gauge customer satisfaction instantly and act immediately in an emergency (Verma & Diwan, 2025). In the case of hotels, AI is being used to monitor TripAdvisor and Google Reviews so that the hotel can be notified of negative comments early enough to make timely amends. The researchers also note the importance of AI in predictive personalization, where MLC forecasts anticipate the demand of guests even prior to their requests, like suggesting guests spa offers when they easily book wellness services (Krishnan and Mariappan, 2024). Nevertheless, AI is not without the ethical issues that are inherent to data-driven technologies, including consumer privacy, algorithmic bias, and surveillance, the most prominent of which.

Destination Marketing: AR and VR in Destination content in the Tourism e-kit

AR and VR have been widely studied in the marketing of destinations and organizations (DMOs) in the hotel marketing context. (S. Kumar et al., 2025) revealed that VR destination experiences positively affected emotional thought, and the emotional impact had a positive impact on travel intentions. Similarly, regarding the aspect of AR application in City Tourism, it has resulted in the improvement of the storytelling and visitor engagement elements (Altinay Ozdemir, 2021), including interactive maps and tours to heritage sites. The literature further adds that these AR/VR technologies can be applicable in presale and pre-experience marketing, but there are technological barriers, which are costly equipment and consumer perceptions. According to some researchers, the greater ease of use of mobile AR applications will be used to encourage usage in business, including hospitality, via the impact of improved visualization, which reduces uncertainty and creates consumer confidence.

Blockchain as a Trust and Transparency

Another area of research has been the use of blockchain to address long-term challenges of trust and transparency in hospitality marketing. Indicatively, Centobelli et al. (2022) assert that blockchain provides transparent customer transaction records, which reduces fraudulent activities in online booking. Recent research has indicated that tokenized loyalty points, which are implemented on blockchain, can be exchanged between brands and, as a result, will result in higher levels of customer engagement due to greater mobility (Kumar et al., 2021). Moreover, blockchain has the ability to demonstrate sustainable practices, including the responsible sourcing of seafood in a hotel restaurant, which will enable support for marketing claims with evidence. However, it is not widely adopted because of technical knowledge, cost of infrastructure, and lack of clarity on the legal framework (Scott et al., 2023).

Radical technologies - hyper-personalization and IoT

The IoT literature emphasizes that the IoT bridges the gap between the physical and virtual worlds. Smart devices that provide real-time information include connected thermostats, in-room entertainment, and voice assistants, and marketers can use this information to create hyper-personalized marketing campaigns for guests. Moreover, (Gupta et al., 2022) also add that the IoT can provide marketers with a chance to target guests in a timely manner and provide them with incentives (e.g., a discount at the restaurant at times when customers are few). Moreover, using IoT, it is possible to provide a sustainable marketing message to the guests, showing them energy-efficient and smart waste management solutions as an eco-traveler. However, the prospect of the IoT is counterbalanced by security issues and the lack of willingness of people to exchange personal data among the devices connected to each other.

Influencer-Driven Campaigns and Social Media

The use of social media as a marketing tool within the hospitality industry has always been popular in literature. The use of Instagram and TikTok has a strong impact on the perception of destinations and accommodation by the consumer, especially due to the content displayed in their images (Jamir et al., 2025). Nevertheless, the authenticity will be increased by collaborations between influencers when the followers view the appropriate influencer as someone they can relate to (Mohammadian and Valilai, 2024). Nevertheless, other researchers cautiously note that the surface-level popularity of the so-called fake influencers and fake content overall has already started to undermine trust, so AI-based tools to calculate the authenticity of engagements will become essential in the future. The research also examines the user-generated content (UGC), which possibly implies that customer-created photos and reviews are more persuasive than advertisement messages, which can offer authenticity and peer approval (Fotis, 2018).

Customer Relationship and Customer Experience Marketing

More and more, the hospitality innovations are discussed within the framework of relationship marketing theory, where the emphasis is made on long-term, as opposed to one-time, transactions (see Choi et al.). Such solutions as the CRM systems with AI and IoT can be used to strengthen the loyalty programs, achieve the ability to track the preferences of the guests, and provide them with the ability to interact with the guests personally (Suharto and Hoti, 2023).

Research has shown that loyalty in the digital age is not just about the transactions, but also about the construction through the creation of immersive experiences, frictionless service, and constant digital contact. Chatbots, applications, and loyalty systems are important in the development of these enduring relations.

The Voice of the Consumer and Big Data Analytics

There is an increasing body of literature on the topic of big data analytics in hospitality marketing. STP can be presented with enormous prospects when it comes to big data, which involves mammoth volumes of data that are generated by booking engines, loyalty programs, and online reviews (Manoharan et al., 2024). Researchers have suggested that predictive analytics may facilitate the prediction of demand patterns during the seasons, the creation of efficient pricing frameworks, and the promotion timing. Customer journey mapping is also enhanced by big data that enables the marketer to observe and impact touchpoints between inspiration and after travel review. Nevertheless, there are certain recurrent issues, including the fear of information overload and inadequate analytical skills in hospitality companies, that are recurrent in the literature.

Ethical Marketing Innovations and Sustainability

Sustainability is one of the key strings in the sphere of hospitality research, and marketing technologies have become more and more oriented as the means of communication with environmental and social responsibility. According to Dossa & Kaeufer (2014), green blockchain checking, digital eco-certifications, and AI-assisted energy monitoring enable hotels to make their sustainability initiatives credible. As most studies have demonstrated that environmentally friendly travelers also appreciate the importance of decreased plastic consumption, the shift towards renewable energy, and carbon offsetting, a number of marketing campaigns should be considered. Greenwashing refers to a situation where firms exaggerate their sustainability efforts without presenting any objective data.

Worldview and International Adoption

Although a Western-dominated market has been most researched in the literature, a limited number of works have also been done on consumer adoption of IM across countries. As an example, the Asian consumer is more enthusiastic about mobile-based innovation than the European market, and Europeans 1 are more concerned with privacy issues than Asians (Talukder et al., 2024). This means that the international hospitality firms will need to localize their marketing innovations to suit the regional contingencies. Nevertheless, there is a need to carry out more cross-cultural comparative studies to determine the dissemination of technology marketing innovation within different cultures.

Loyalty, trust, and sustainability blockchains

Blockchain research in the context of hospitality marketing does not solely concern the loyalty programmes, but also the sustainability validation. Eco-certificates based on blockchains would certify sustainability algorithms, including power generation or fair trade ones, and allow brands to trade on credibility proxying.

Express credibility to more and more environment-conscious tourists (Mastilak et al., 2023). Studies highlight the fact that LP can be decentralized with the help of blockchain technology that may allow the customers to redeem the points in other hotel/serviced apartments chains/airlines/f&b outlets, etc (Afif and Susanto, 2025). This promotes network effect, which subsequently enhances consumer interest. Nevertheless, analysts cite factors like unpredictable laws, consumer ignorance, and the cost of infrastructure that are depressing the large-scale deployment. Additional comparisons should also be conducted to understand whether blockchain loyalty programs prove to be more efficient than traditional centralized loyalty programs in the area of customer retention.

Smart Internet of Things (IoT) and Smart Hospitality Marketing

Operational efficiency is one thing, but capitalizing on the connected consumer is a big leap. Smart technology at the property level, including in-wall smart thermostats, televisions, and voice-activated assistants, creates a continuous flow of consumer data, which the marketer can use to direct their campaigns. As an illustration, hotels can sell their spa to customers with usage behaviors that show their interest in wellness packages. All you should know about IoT. Also, the Internet of Things opens the prospects of real-time contextual marketing; for example, the location data will show that a guest is approaching a hotel restaurant. However, the literature raises the problem of cyber vulnerabilities and consumer rejection of surveillance as important issues. It is suggested that future research should integrate IoT and blockchain to increase trust and security of the data in hospitality marketing.

Social Media, Influencers, and User-Generated Content

The use of social media marketing in hospitality is a major concern in the hospitality literature. Special attention should be paid to such apps as Instagram and TikTok, which influence the perception of destinations and hotel brands by using visual storytelling (Smith et al., 2023). According to researchers, influencer marketing is worthwhile because it is authentic; nevertheless, Smith and Hilton (2022) maintain that the over-commercialization of influencer marketing can undermine consumer confidence. The user-generated content (UGC) (customer photos and customer reviews) is more convincing than the conventional advertisement, as it promotes peer-to-peer trust. This implies that when AI is integrated with social platforms, the firms will be able to monitor sentiment in real-time and optimize campaigns on the fly. Nevertheless, debates still persist about the misinformation, influencer content burnout, and the psychological effects of constant online interaction.

Neuromarketing and Big Data Analytics

Big data analytics have gained much interest in the past years in consumer segmentation, demand forecasting, and pricing optimization. However, researchers are also exploring the field of neuromarketing, with biometrics, including eye-tracking, facial recognition, and brain wave monitoring, being the most commonly used techniques to monitor consumer reactions to advertisements and promotion campaigns (Azman et al., 2023). These technologies provide a means through which marketers can follow subconscious emotional response, which is beyond self-reported liking. The hospitality industry has now grown to be mature in neuromarketing to determine the success of digital advertisements, VR campaigns, and web design. This may be an attractive option, but it brings about ethical issues about consumer freedom and informed consent.

Customer Service Robotics and AI

Most of the literature on hospitality robotics is operational, but in recent times, there have been attempts at 360-degree coverage- the marketing potential of the robots. Hotel robots in the lobbies and restaurants are utilized as service staff and brand ambassadors that attract media coverage and make the properties shine in the overcrowded markets (Webster and Ivanov, 2020). The humanoid robots will be capable of attracting guests by having personalized conversations, providing promotions and destination information, and also acting as an interactive marketing ambassador, which is AI-driven. Nevertheless, the level of acceptance among consumers is quite diverse; some people consider robots to be cool and entertaining, while others find them frightening and intimidating. Thus, it can be estimated that the marketing of robotics should be rather a complement, and not a replacement, of human contact.

Experience economy and customer relationship marketing

Experience marketing of hospitality is a paradigm that is increasingly becoming visible, whereby the value addition is done by experiences that generate long-term memories, rather than merely providing services. The new technologies, including AI, IoT, and VR, contribute to the emergence of hyper-personalized experiences, which is why they correspond to the relationship marketing theory, aimed at establishing long-term emotional connections with consumers (Pine and Gilmore, 2013). Loyalty programs are also shifting out of the transactional and into an experience-based model of engagement, where a customer can enjoy an offer or event that is more valuable to the brand, building value of the customer relationship, be it in the form of VIP experiences, digital communities, or simply going to the premises of a brand. It is reported in literature that the next stage in evolution will be the combination of emotional intelligence and digital personalization to maintain the originality of relationships.

Ethical Marketing Innovations and Sustainability

The issue of sustainability is still a point of discussion in hospitality marketing. According to Kumar (2015), digital certificates and clear demonstrations of green behaviors are valued by environmentally informed travelers. Supply chain verification by blockchain, AI by energy optimization, and IoT by waste management are all plausible technologies that can add more marketing stories. However, researchers warn of the dangers of greenwashing, where unproven sustainability claims may work in both directions. The studies also indicate that the demand for ethical innovation among consumers is increasing, and hospitality brands are obligated not only to utilize AI in a responsible manner but also to treat employees fairly and interact with communities in multiple aspects, such as environmental sustainability.

Adoption across Cultural Divides and International Understandings

Even though the literature is based on the Western perspective of the world, it highlights major regional discrepancies. They also established that Asian users are more receptive to the innovation of mobile technology than their European counterparts, who have greater privacy issues (Shoib & Nandhakumar, 2003). The level of digital knowledge, regulations, and culture also plays an important part in the process of adoption. There is a lack of comparative studies; thus, multinational research on consumer acceptance of AI, blockchain, and AR/VR in hospitality marketing is justified. The study would help give the contextualization of innovation by these MNEs in hospitality operations.

Rise of a New Frontier: Metaverse, Generative AI, and Beyond

The new literature offers a few frontiers that may make the marketing of the hospitality industry revolutionary. Hotels and destinations are envisioned to create a digital twin of their real estate to invite guests to the Metaverse, a virtual world that is an alternative to the real world. Even now, you can make custom promotional content, whether custom-made travel plans or generative AI-generated images and videos, in a few seconds with the help of generative AI. Academics also identify V-commerce, which is a trend where guests make bookings and buy through voice-activated assistants. The introduction of 5G connectivity into this equation is merely going to expedite these features, which will allow seamless and real-time experiences. However, there are ethical, economic, and technical issues that involve these frontiers and that academic research should take into consideration.

Marketing Artificial Intelligence and Big Data

One of the most controversial questions is the influence of AI and big data analytics on hospitality marketing. According to experts, AI-driven devices allow extremely targeted marketing. Real-time campaigns through researching what consumers like, do, and purchase. Hospitality businesses are able to forecast consumer demand correctly and make good use of pricing strategies with predictive analytics and allocate resources more efficiently (Webster and Ivanov, 2020). Recommendation engines are becoming increasingly popular in OTAs and hotel booking sites, although they have also been applied by OTAs to cross-sell related services, such as spa programs, F&B offerings, or local tours (Mariani et al., 2021). More to the point, in case we are able to increase the amount of satisfaction people experience with the personalization services provided by applying and utilizing AI, it is also a competitive edge. However, the concerns of data privacy and algorithmic transparency remain at the center of the discussion in AI in marketing, and scholars insist on the creation of ethical models that will guarantee the safe usage of AI in marketing.

AR and VR Experiences

Experiential marketing is one of the areas of influence, as noted by the literature on AR and VR. AR applications can allow potential guests to see what the hotel has to offer in and out and explore the destination experiences through the use of smartphones or headsets, which will also reduce uncertainty and boost purchase confidence (Tussyadiah et al., 2018). VR, in its turn, provides highly immersive pre-travel experiences, including virtual tours of hotels or tours of destinations, which, undoubtedly, contribute to the formation of a booking intention. The introduction of immersive VR storytelling is in line with the increasing trend of consumers in terms of experiencing economy, where people not only want products but also unforgettable and emotional experiences with their brands (Storchevoyi throwback nostalgia). However, adoption remains diverse due to the high cost of creating immersive content, and many consumers do not have access to VR hardware, which creates a problem of scalability to mainstream hospitality marketing.

Loyalty Programs and Blockchain

Another similar key theme in the literature is the disruptive attribute of blockchain technology in hospitality marketing. It is possible to increase the trust of customers in online transactions and loyalty programs with the help of transparency, security, and decentralization of blockchain (Onder and Treiblmaier, 2018). As an example, such loyalty tokens utilizing blockchain could be used in other platforms, allowing them to be redeemed by consumers anywhere, resolving the problem of lost points lying idle. Scholars have indicated that these breakthroughs could redefine the nature of customer-brand relationships and establish a marketing world that is founded on trust and value. Nonetheless, the adoption is still in its initial phases, and even though not all studies provide empirical analysis, research has shown that hospitality managers lack sufficient skills and awareness (Mariani and Borghi, 2021).

Hyper-Personalization and Internet of Things (IoT)

The Internet of Things is one of the most frequently discussed topics in the hospitality marketing literature because of its potential to provide the opportunity to gather data in real-time. Voice-controlled gadgets and voice-controlled thermostats in Smart Hotel Guest rooms provide personalized experiences that track the behavior of the guests, and the marketers can use the information to customize the offers (Neuhofer et al., 2015). As an example, a guest with an eco-friendly or wellness interest can lead to nature-friendly or wellness-oriented offers in accordance with the trends of sustainability and wellness. The IoT also supports the provision of context-based advertising that is premised on the location and activity of a customer. Nevertheless, scholars warn that relying excessively on this type of IoT data would cause ethical concerns about consent, surveillance, and access to such data, particularly with the strict data protection regulations such as the GDPR in the EU.

Influencers, Social Media, and Digital Stories

The literature is pervasive with respect to the place of social media marketing. Instagram, TikTok, and Facebook are the platforms on which brands in the hospitality industry can narrate their story using powerful images and leverage influencer relationships to improve their visibility (Leung et al., 2019). Exposure to such content has been observed to increase brand authenticity and engagement, especially in younger consumers who consume peer-generated content more than corporate messages in the case of influencer marketing (Mariani and Filieri, 2021). The constantly increasing role of AI-driven social media analytics that allow marketers to monitor sentiment, predict trends, and evaluate the performance of campaigns in real-time has also become the focus of researchers. Despite these advancements, some challenges remain to be overcome in the process of measuring the return on investment (ROI) and authenticating the influencer, especially in the era of increasing cynicism about sponsored content.

Sustainability and Ethical Marketing Technologies

In more recent times, there has been a section of literature that has arisen that focuses on the intersection of sustainability and marketing innovations. With consumers becoming more conscious of climate change and environmental degradation, the use of eco-marketing is becoming very common, particularly in the hotel industry. It includes ecolabels on online platforms, the verification of sustainable practices through blockchain or gamified applications, and rewarding guests who do eco-friendly things (Jones et al., 2021). The long-term competition in the market has been proposed by academics to be a core, and not a side-show, component of market strategies in the long term. Nevertheless, empirical studies show that although the attitude of consumers towards sustainable supply chains could be relatively high, their behavior is mostly the manifestation of the attitude-behavior gap, suggesting that technology-based sustainability campaigns should be accompanied by effective nudges to support pro-social actions.

FINDINGS FROM LITERATURE

Review of literature. The overall position of the literature reviewed can be described as indicating that AI and big data analytics are transforming a new era in marketing hotels. According to research, AI-based technologies provide a hyper-personalized customer experience through the use of predictive analytics, recommendation systems, and automated service delivery. These technologies strive to enhance the satisfaction of the guests and create long-term loyalty because they predict consumer trends more accurately than ever before, and they are more effective than traditional marketing. Nonetheless, scientists also warn that there are still some unresolved attendant ethical concerns, such as data privacy and algorithmic transparency, which point to the significance of a solid regulatory framework to promote the responsible use of AI.

Another significant conclusion is the ubiquitous nature of immersive technologies, such as AR and VR. According to the literature, these tools are potent types of experiential marketing, which allow prospective guests to sample the hotel products, destination, and services before they commit to a booking. This vicarious narration is in line with the principles of the experience economy, and it has been demonstrated to positively influence booking intentions. Despite these advantages, the problem of scalability remains in connection to the expenditure of development and the rates of consumer access demarcation, which impact mostly smaller segments of the hospitality industry.

Another innovation that has high potential of being used in reorganizing loyalty programs and trust systems in hospitality marketing is blockchain technology. These loyalty points inefficiencies and fraud dilemmas can be resolved through the provision of a decentralized, visible, and unchangeable service blockchain. Lessons. The findings indicate that blockchain might bring more transparent and trustworthy marketing conditions, but with a condition, researchers have found that the adoption rate is low because hospitality managers are not aware of it or have no technical expertise.

Similarly, the Internet of Things (IoT) is highly promoted as a driving force of hyper-personalization and real-time marketing. Smart gadgets gather behavioral information as well as situational data that can be leveraged by marketers in order to make pertinent offers or facilitate operational efficiencies. It is noteworthy that in the literature, a number of works discuss how the implementation of IoT can be used to facilitate context-sensitive marketing, including location-based services, to enable a company to gain a better customer engagement. Nevertheless, scholars warn that marketing with the IoT creates ethical issues of surveillance and consent, and a further spread of the discussion of data ownership in the aesthetic world of hospitality.

Findings also indicate that social media and influencer marketing remain at the top of the list in consumer perception of hospitality brands. The study indicates that platforms such as Instagram, TikTok, and Facebook make it possible to tell visual stories, socialize with peers, and send direct messages. Partnerships with influencers, specifically, may be a perfect solution to achieve credibility and trust among younger audiences. At the same time, the literature also points to the difficulties with the calculation of return on investment (ROI) and the reduction of risk related to influencer credibility, and consumer distrust toward sponsored content.

The combination of sustainability and digital marketing innovations is an emerging phenomenon, but few studies in the literature cover it. Other studies indicate that some technologies related to eco-marketing (blockchain-based sustainability tracking, digital certification, and gamified green behavior application) are attracting the attention of environmentally conscious consumers. These tools assist in positioning hospitality marketing in line with the global sustainability objectives and provide new dimensions of differentiation for a brand. Nonetheless, even research evidence indicates that the fact that the attitude-behavior gap persists shows that it is not sufficient that consumers declare their preference for sustainable products and services.

Overall, according to the literature, despite all the opportunities provided by future marketing technology in enhancing personalization, engagement, and trust in the hospitality service encounter, the literature indicates that there are barriers. These are high implementation costs, uneven distribution of developed and developing markets, ethical issues connected to the problem of data privacy, and fragmented strategies that comprise the integration of a wide range of technologies into complete systems. The findings suggest that future studies and practice must not just focus on technological adoption in marketing innovation in the hospitality industry, but also come up with holistic, ethical, and sustainable mechanisms that will add value in the long-term of marketing innovations.

DISCUSSIONS

The literature has indicated that big data analytics and artificial intelligence are changing the nature of hospitality marketing by hyper-personalizing customer experiences and making decisions that are future-oriented. Conversational AI can anticipate the needs of guests, which makes it proactive in serving guests and automating communication throughout the visitor journey, moving towards one-to-one, data-driven, participatory marketing instead of mass-marketing-type messaging strategies. This reorganization, of course, follows the concept of the experience economy: the value is co-created with the customer. Nevertheless, the discussion also reveals that ethics and privacy issues are the reasons behind the use of AI.

Hospitality companies need to embrace open data governance frameworks that can facilitate technological innovations and consumer trust with a single slip, and damage control will ensure that innovation is controlled.

AR/VR-based technologies provide immersive exposure and pre-experience feedback, which increases the confidence of the user and affects the purchasing decision of the user. Here, the discussion brings out the fact that these resources are not merely marketing tools but also experience enablers, and the process of shifting to the real world of hospitality is made possible. Nevertheless, widespread use of AR and VR continues to face issues, including the high cost of content creation, the poor adoption of these technologies by customers, and the inability to integrate with the current marketing platforms. The fact is that now the hospitality marketers have to balance the possible advantages of immersive technology with these disadvantages when planning the implementation plans that they could apply to their properties in stages and on a smaller scale in order to get the ROI.

The connection between blockchain and marketing in the hospitality industry is not only related to the fact that loyalty programs can be made more efficient, but also to the idea of putting trust in the processes. The discussion indicates that the blockchain might eliminate certain ancient problems of customer data protection, fraud attempts prevention, and reward points management. Its ability to authenticate sustainability practices extends the believability of the brand as far as environmentally conscious travellers are concerned. Nevertheless, according to the literature, the wide use is constrained by the technical complexity, unpredictability of regulations, and lack of awareness. To overcome these challenges and maximize the marketing potential of the technology, strategic alliances, employee education, and easier blockchain interfaces might be needed.

IoT provides real-time, situational notifications that elicit hyper-personalized and timely marketing behaviors. A literature review unveils the Internet of Things (IoT) as a platform to integrate the physical and digital worlds in terms of touchpoints, which will promote customer engagement along the entire journey. As an example, smart rooms may signal a promotion or suggest services that are on demand by the guests. Nevertheless, scholars caution that IoT-based marketing will have to overcome a number of obstacles, such as security and data ownership challenges.

Reliable and transparent data stewardship should be ethical and will play a vital role in fostering consumer trust and the suitability of this solution in the long term. Hospitality marketing people are paying more attention to social media and influencer marketing than ever. The discussion highlights that, with more opportunities to engage and share stories and peer-validation platforms such as Instagram, TikTok, and Facebook, also potential traps, including the propagation of fake information and the issue of influencer credibility and saturation. Even AI-based analytics can assist in the fightback, but it is not a panacea. Although the real-time sentiment and engagement tracking can be useful to a certain degree, we must find an adequate balance between automation and interpersonal communication to retain authenticity.

Green marketing technologies are now the center of attention in the discourse of contemporary marketing tendencies in the hospitality sector. The use of technologies, such as blockchain, towards achieving supply chain transparency, digital eco-certifications, and even gamified green behavior programs, is a sign of the growing demand by consumers for ethical and environmentally responsible services. The literature review shows that sustainability-oriented innovations are not a form of branding but a long-term strategic contributor to brand value. Nevertheless, academics also criticize greenwashing because they consider that statements concerning sustainability, proven and transparent, are crucial in order to retain consumer confidence.

Finally, as implied in the converging discourse in the literature, it might be that hospitality marketing in the future will be characterized as a smorgasbord of multi-technological converged environments. Combined, not isolated, adoption of AI, IoT, AR/VR, blockchain, and other sustainability-enabling systems into firm-wide marketing platforms is better at generating differentiated brand propositions, creating closer customer lifetime relationships, and facilitating efficient operations. The literature also, however, indicates a sharp research gap as far as empirical evidence on the effectiveness, ROI, and cross-cultural transferability of integrated approaches is concerned. Future research should prioritize longitudinal and cross-regional methodology, interdisciplinary approaches to come up with practical implications that can be applied by marketers.

PRACTICAL IMPLICATIONS

The use of high-level technologies in marketing in the hotel sector carries significant consequences for managers, marketers, and service providers. Artificial Intelligence (AI) and big data analytics allow organizations to shift their marketing capabilities to unresponsive marketing, hyper-personalized, data-driven marketing. It implies that hospitality managers will be able to segment customers more accurately and predict demand trends, and optimize the promotional offers on the fly. Intelligence using AI also allows front-line staff to anticipate the needs of the guests, improving the efficiency and satisfaction of the service. This will also enhance their operating efficiency and customer relationships, which is very important in a competitive market.

It is possible with the help of the utilities of pre-travel marketing and customer engagement of emerging immersive technologies, including VR and AR. Hotels and destinations must think about giving potential customers virtual tours, interactive experiences, and storytelling in the digital space to aid in reducing the uncertainty regarding booking. C2: Advantages may accrue to the pros in the experiential-intensive markets, where the consumers are buying more of a treat-oneself experience. In addition, the incorporation of AR/VR in their social media campaign can help hospitality organizations to drive immediate accessibility to a wider audience, produce memorable experiences, and establish an emotional connection with the brand.

What then is all this to do with business? Loyalty programs enable organizations to provide customers with transferable and flexible rewards, which leads to increased engagement and retention with blockchain-based loyalty programs. Moreover, blockchain is able to confirm the sustainability of practices, thus authenticating the eco-certification or supply chain assertions. To stakeholders, this is an avenue to express authenticity and corporate responsibility, which is becoming important among eco- and ethically-conscious travelers.

IOT in operation and marketing benefits. It is believed that IoT is worth adoption since it has proven to be useful in both operations and marketing. IoT devices are connected, including smart devices, and can be used to collect real-time data, which can be applied to offer personalized promotions, service optimizations, and energy management. As an example, smart room sensors are capable of identifying the preferences of the guests and triggering the corresponding dining, spa, and leisure offers. The data created by the IoT smart devices can be used as leverage by the hotels to enhance efficiency, reduce energy expenses, and introduce context-based marketing programs that will help to create the outstanding experience that the guests anticipate, and will be consistent with sustainability initiatives.

The emergence of social media and influencer marketing is directly linked with the way in which brands position themselves, interact, and develop trust with their customer base. Hotel companies will be able to produce authentic marketing narratives through the strength of trusted influencers and UGC that attract potential guests. AI-based analytics technology can also enable marketers to measure engagement metrics and sentiment, and optimize a campaign in real-time. This allows the brands to streamline resource allocation, improve ROI, and keep their brands relevant in a progressively digital-first world.

The marketing technologies based on sustainability influence brand reputation, differentiation, and long-term competitiveness. When digital credentials, gamified eco-engagement campaigns, and certified sustainability claims are included in the marketing strategies of organizations, they will become even more appealing to the constantly growing number of environmentally aware travelers. This, in practice, means that the hospitality organizations must consider making sustainability part of their operations, strategies, and marketing efforts, and not as a peripheral issue. Effective articulation of sustainability actions also increases the level of trust and aligns the brand with international environmental and social responsibility goals. Conceptual Framework

Figure 1. Future Innovations in Hospitality Marketing Technology

Source: Authors' Compilations

Future Innovations in Hospitality Marketing Technology model demonstrates the new technologies, their correlation with marketing aims, and the outcomes of these correlations, taking into account the moderation in view of its influence on this correlation (e.g., ethics and privacy issues). The key to innovation in hospitality marketing is technology integration, including AI and big data analytics, AR/VR, IoT, blockchain, social media, influencer marketing, and sustainable technologies. These technologies influence the key marketing goals in the following four dimensions that are personalization and customer engagement, brand differentiation/ loyalty, operational efficiency, and effective sustainability communication, acting as mediators of technology adoption and performance outcomes. In this way, the deliberate attainment of the given objectives leads to a better guest experience, customer satisfaction, and loyalty, and the credibility of the hospitality organizations in terms of ethical and sustainable practices adopted, which eventually translates into a competitive advantage. Another aspect highlighted in this framework is that, being the mediators of the effect of technology integration on marketing results, ethical concerns and data privacy affect the relationship. This framework, in parallel with the chapter's aim, demonstrates how the frontier technologies may be used strategically to realize the real and concrete marketing-based objectives, improve operations, and also promote sustainable and responsible practices, which may provide valuable empirical and theoretical information to both academic and professional managers in the hospitality industry.

RECOMMENDATIONS

The hospitality companies must prioritize their investments in artificial intelligence (AI) and big data analytics that can help them engage in hyper-personalized marketing and make predictive decisions. Not only can AI platforms, which analyze real-time consumer behavior, preferences, and booking patterns, help companies predict the needs of guests and offer them tailored services, but they can also make the process more accurate. Organizations, in their turn, have to adopt ethical frameworks and data governance policies to guarantee privacy, security, and transparency, and, thus, consumer trust in AI-based marketing solutions.

AR and VR should be used by hotels, resorts, and destinations to ensure that they engage consumers to the fullest. These websites have the potential to provide prospective visitors with the chance to conduct virtual tours, enjoy interactive material, and preview their destinations prior to making their traveling choices. One of the cost reduction mechanisms available to hospitality service companies is to partner with tech or university partners in scalable AR/VR solutions. The inclusion of an immersive technology in a social media campaign will broaden its scope and enhance the story of the brand.

The Loyalty Management, Trust Building & Sustainability Verification, which may be realized with the help of Blockchain Technology. Blockchain-based loyalty programs allow earning and redeeming points across brands, increasing their engagement and stickiness. Also, sustainable initiatives can be certified by blockchain, which will further increase the trustworthiness of a brand to environmentally friendly tourists. The adoption must also be successful, and this can only be achieved through staff training, easy system interfaces, and consumer awareness campaigns to enhance participation and trust.

The possibilities of providing hyper-personalized and context-based marketing with the assistance of IoT (Internet of Things) exist. Smart devices such as voice assistants and IoT sensors can also be installed in the guest rooms of the hotel, and they can give real-time customer data that we utilize to give offers, promotions, and so on. As an example, the usage patterns can be used to initiate dining, health, and/or other promotions specific to a guest according to their preferences. Companies dealing with hospitality issues are advised to adopt effective cybersecurity and data protection strategies to protect the information of their guests, as well as to exploit the opportunities offered by IoT in marketing.

Through social media and connections with influencers, brand positioning and customer interaction continue to be crucial. Corporations ought to work with influential individuals and encourage user-created content to promote the level of authenticity and reach. With AI-driven analytics, you are able to track the engagement, sentiment, and Return on Investment, and can carry out real-time changes in campaigns. It must be consistent with the brand values and sustainability activities, such that all the marketing content actually resonates with your green-conscious customers, and creates a long-term trust that is built.

On the other hand, sustainability recommendations are aimed at integrating marketing efforts into green strategies. Sustainability-related digital certifications and blockchain-based eco-engagement programs can be an effective way of conveying the message of environmental responsibility by a company. In order to be believable to the travelers and not to be accused of greenwashing, hospitality players that maintain sustainability practices must be genuine, quantifiable, and implemented throughout all operations (and embedded in their marketing).

Finally, hospitality organizations ought to embrace multimodal marketing infrastructures as opposed to using single tools. The combination of AI, IoT, AR/VR, blockchain, social media, and sustainable technologies will integrate marketing strategies to streamline operations, increase customer satisfaction, and create competitive brand influence. The integration should be realised by strategic planning, cross-functional interaction between departments, and investment in staff training. Carry out periodic audits to make sure that technology is translated into real marketing and business outcomes.

CONCLUSION

The integration of the new marketing technologies in the industry. The unwillingness toward the hospitality industry is likely to be the main factor that pulls the industry behind. Artificial intelligence, big data, AR/VR, internet of things, blockchain, and social media are no longer a luxury, but strategic necessities in developing hyper-personalised experiences, immersive experiences, and trust-based relationships with guests. In the literature, it is argued that once such technologies are appropriately applied, they enhance customer satisfaction and loyalty and long-term competitiveness. Moreover, eco-innovations in the hospitality industry offer possibilities in which the firms can combine and sell ecologically and socially responsible practices, which justifies branding authenticity in the age of conscious travel.

Regardless of such developments, the study identifies a number of challenges, such as the complexity of technology, cost implications, ethical issues, and unequal adoption by regions and consumers. Consequently, CA and catering companies have to concentrate on innovation as viewed through the prism of the strategic implementation of different technologies in an ecosystem marketing where privacy, transparency, and ethics in the use of data are ensured. General suggestions: The initial and theoretical findings on marketing innovations being technologically driven show that they can change the way companies interact with their customers, but to achieve success, they need to be planned carefully, employees trained, and the results of interaction with customers monitored regularly.

FUTURE RESEARCH DIRECTIONS

The research questions that might be addressed in future research include the long-term impacts of AI and immersive technologies on consumer behaviour, loyalty, and satisfaction in hospitality environments. Though research in the current day has been inclined towards short-term adoption, long-term efficacy, consumer confidence, and behavioural intentions might be better understood through longitudinal research. The cross-cultural comparative research is also justified, as it can be found that the rate of adoption, the preferences of consumers, and the regulations vary in each region, which, consequently, can influence the success of marketing innovations.

Scholars also need to investigate multi-technology ecosystems that are integrated (AI, IoT, AR/VR, blockchain, and sustainability-enabling initiatives). The combination of these techniques can be analyzed to propose strategies to be used in creating integrated marketing strategies. The ethical, legal, and privacy issues that could potentially emerge as a result of the adoption of new technologies, such as AI-driven personalization and IoT-based marketing, should be studied further. The attitude of consumers and readiness to share data, and the confidence in information flow, will be one of the priorities of the responsible innovation development.

Lastly, we indicate that future studies could explore new frontiers (e.g., the Metaverse) as the potential game-changers in hospitality marketing. These are comparatively untapped spheres that can be used for immersion, hyper-personalization, or new monetization. It is against these gaps that scholars can contribute to filling the picture in technology-enabled hospitality marketing and offer scientifically grounded information to practitioners and policymakers.

REFERENCES

A, P., Arunprakash, A., Kulothungan, V., & Radha, P. (2025). The Role of Artificial Intelligence in Revolutionizing Customer-Centric Marketing Strategies: A Data-Driven Approach. *NPRC Journal of Multidisciplinary Research, 2*(1), 163–175. https://doi.org/DOI: 10.3126/nprcjmr.v2i1.74691

Abakouy, R., En-naimi, E. M., Haddadi, A. E., & Lotfi, E. (2019). Data-driven marketing: How machine learning will improve decision-making for marketers. *Proceedings of the 4th International Conference on Smart City Applications*, 1–5. https://doi.org/DOI: 10.1145/3368756.3369024

Afif, F., & Susanto, P. (2025). Blockchain for Marketing Transparency and Trust: Applications in Supply Chain and Customer Loyalty Programs. *Journal of Indonesian Management*, *5*(2), 10. DOI: 10.53697/jim.v5i2.2422

Altinay Ozdemir, M. (2021). Virtual Reality (VR) and Augmented Reality (AR) Technologies for Accessibility and Marketing in the Tourism Industry: In C. Eusébio, L. Teixeira, & M. J. Carneiro (Eds.), *Advances in Hospitality, Tourism, and the Services Industry* (pp. 277–301). IGI Global. https://doi.org/DOI: 10.4018/978-1-7998-6428-8.ch013

Aziz, K., Dua, S., & Gupta, P. (2024). Revolutionizing Influencer Marketing: Harnessing the Power of Data Analytics and Artificial Intelligence (AI). In Dutta, S., Rocha, Á., Dutta, P. K., Bhattacharya, P., & Singh, R. (Eds.), *Advances in Data Analytics for Influencer Marketing: An Interdisciplinary Approach* (Vol. 9, pp. 41–66). Springer Nature Switzerland., DOI: 10.1007/978-3-031-65727-6_4

Azman, N., Albattat, A., & Valeri, M. (2023). The Importance of Big Data Analysis: Developing Neuromarketing in Tourism Industry. In Valeri, M. (Ed.), *Tourism Innovation in the Digital Era* (pp. 1–24). Emerald Publishing Limited., DOI: 10.1108/978-1-83797-166-420231001

Bilgihan, A., & Ricci, P. (2024). The new era of hotel marketing: Integrating cutting-edge technologies with core marketing principles. *Journal of Hospitality and Tourism Technology*, *15*(1), 123–137. DOI: 10.1108/JHTT-04-2023-0095

Centobelli, P., Cerchione, R., Vecchio, P. D., Oropallo, E., & Secundo, G. (2022). Blockchain technology for bridging trust, traceability and transparency in circular supply chain. *Information & Management*, *59*(7), 103508. DOI: 10.1016/j.im.2021.103508

Chakrabarti, S., Chakrabarti, S., Bhandari, A. K., Saha, D., & Mazumder, R. (2024). *Perspectives in Finance and Digital Transformations in Business* (1st ed.). Routledge India., DOI: 10.4324/9781003470229

Dewangan, S., & Kumar, S. (2024). Enhancing Fraud Detection in Finance Through AI and Machine Learning. In Darwish, D., & Kumar, S. (Eds.), (pp. 267–282). Advances in Finance, Accounting, and Economics. IGI Global., DOI: 10.4018/979-8-3693-8507-4.ch014

Dossa, Z., & Kaeufer, K. (2014). Understanding Sustainability Innovations Through Positive Ethical Networks. *Journal of Business Ethics*, *119*(4), 543–559. DOI: 10.1007/s10551-013-1834-8

Gil-Saura, I., & Ruiz-Molina, M. E., Gloria Berenguer-Contrí, & Antonio Marín-García. (2024). Sustainability-oriented innovation in retailing. *Psychology and Marketing*, *41*(2), 240–253. DOI: 10.1002/mar.21922

Gupta, A., Prabhat, P., & Gulzar, B. (2022). Personal-Internet-of-Things (PIoT): A vision for hyper-personalization delivered securely. *2022 IEEE Delhi Section Conference (DELCON)*, 1–6. https://doi.org/DOI: 10.1109/DELCON54057.2022.9753314

Gursoy, D. (2018). Future of hospitality marketing and management research. *Tourism Management Perspectives*, *25*, 185–188. DOI: 10.1016/j.tmp.2017.11.008

Jamir, W., Jasrotia, A., & Kumar, S. (2025). The Power of Social Media: Unveiling its Impact on Millennial Travel Choices. In Talukder, M. B., & Chowdhury, H. H. K. (Eds.), *Smart Operations and Enhancing Guest Experience in the Hospitality Industry* (pp. 297–314). IGI Global., DOI: 10.4018/979-8-3373-2145-5.ch011

Khan, R. & Shalini. (2024). Influencer Marketing Evolution: Unveiling the Power of Data Analytics and AI for Strategic Campaign Excellence. In S. Dutta, Á. Rocha, P. K. Dutta, P. Bhattacharya, & R. Singh (Eds.), *Advances in Data Analytics for Influencer Marketing: An Interdisciplinary Approach* (Vol. 9, pp. 125–147). Springer Nature Switzerland. https://doi.org/DOI: 10.1007/978-3-031-65727-6_8

Krishnan, C., & Mariappan, J. (2024). The AI Revolution in E-Commerce: Personalization and Predictive Analytics. In Gaur, L., & Abraham, A. (Eds.), *Role of Explainable Artificial Intelligence in E-Commerce* (Vol. 1094, pp. 53–64). Springer Nature Switzerland., DOI: 10.1007/978-3-031-55615-9_4

Kumar, P. (2015). Green marketing innovations in small Indian firms. *World Journal of Entrepreneurship, Management and Sustainable Development*, *11*(3), 176–190. DOI: 10.1108/WJEMSD-01-2015-0003

Kumar, S., Talukder, M. B., & Tyagi, P. K. (2025). The Impact of Virtual Reality and Augmented Reality in TNE Learning. In Crawford, C. M., & Gee, T. T. (Eds.), *Motivating Engagement, Belonging, and Success in Higher Education Student Experience* (pp. 359–382). IGI Global., DOI: 10.4018/979-8-3693-8089-5.ch013

Lee, M., Ahn, J., Shin, M., Kwon, W., & Back, K.-J. (2021). Integrating technology to service innovation: Key issues and future research directions in hospitality and tourism. *Journal of Hospitality and Tourism Technology*, *12*(1), 19–38. DOI: 10.1108/JHTT-01-2019-0013

Leung, X. Y., Sun, J., & Bai, B. (2019). Thematic framework of social media research: State of the art. *Tourism Review*, *74*(3), 517–531.

Manoharan, G., Kumar, S., & Talukder, M. B. (2024). Artificial Intelligence Enhancing Customer Relations in Financial Sectors. In Darwish, D., & Kumar, S. (Eds.), (pp. 283–300). Advances in Finance, Accounting, and Economics. IGI Global., DOI: 10.4018/979-8-3693-8507-4.ch015

Martin-Rios, C., & Ciobanu, T. (2019). Hospitality innovation strategies: An analysis of success factors and challenges. *Tourism Management*, *70*, 218–229. DOI: 10.1016/j.tourman.2018.08.018

Mastilak, L., Suchy, R., Kostal, K., & Kotuliak, I. (2023). Blockchain-Based Sustainable Retail Loyalty Program. *IEEE Access: Practical Innovations, Open Solutions*, *11*, 75063–75075. DOI: 10.1109/ACCESS.2023.3296914

Mohammadian, N., & Valilai, O. F. (2024). Influencer-Driven Paradigm Shifts: Analyzing Sustainability and Customer Behavior in Cell Phone and E-Auto Industries via Social Media Analytics. *IEEE Access: Practical Innovations, Open Solutions*, *12*, 119133–119145. DOI: 10.1109/ACCESS.2024.3449113

Muller, C. (2010). Hospitality technology: A review and reflection. *Worldwide Hospitality and Tourism Themes*, *2*(1), 9–19. DOI: 10.1108/17554211011012568

Oh, H., Kim, B.-Y., & Shin, J.-H. (2004). Hospitality and tourism marketing: Recent developments in research and future directions. *International Journal of Hospitality Management*, *23*(5), 425–447. DOI: 10.1016/j.ijhm.2004.10.004

Pine, B. J., & Gilmore, J. H. (2013). The experience economy: Past, present and future. In Sundbo, J., & Sørensen, F. (Eds.), *Handbook on the Experience Economy*. Edward Elgar Publishing., DOI: 10.4337/9781781004227.00007

Salazar, A. (2018). Hospitality trends: Opportunities and challenges. *Worldwide Hospitality and Tourism Themes*, *10*(6), 674–679. DOI: 10.1108/WHATT-07-2018-0047

Sarkar, D., Suhag, N., & Kumar, S. (2025). Sustainable Practices in India's Hotel Industry: Navigating Challenges and Opportunities. In Nadda, V., Sharma, A., Mediratta, H., & Dadwal, S. S. (Eds.), *Addressing Contemporary Challenges in the B2B Hospitality Sector* (pp. 337–352). IGI Global., DOI: 10.4018/979-8-3693-9760-2.ch012

Scott, I. J., De Castro Neto, M., & Pinheiro, F. L. (2023). Bringing trust and transparency to the opaque world of waste management with blockchain: A Polkadot parathread application. *Computers & Industrial Engineering*, *182*, 109347. DOI: 10.1016/j.cie.2023.109347

Sharma, K. K., Tomar, M., & Tadimarri, A. (2023). AI-driven Marketing: Transforming Sales Processes for Success in the Digital Age. *Journal of Knowledge Learning and Science Technology ISSN: 2959-6386 (Online)*, *2*(2), 250–260. https://doi.org/ DOI: 10.60087/jklst.vol2.n2.p260

Sharma, R., & Kumar, S. (2025). Impact of Ethical Implications of Using AI and IoT in Hotels. In Mehra, P., Abioye, O., & Kumar, P. (Eds.), (pp. 375–392). Advances in Computational Intelligence and Robotics. IGI Global Scientific Publishing., DOI: 10.4018/979-8-3693-9611-7.ch014

Shin, H. H., Shin, S., & Gim, J. (2023). Looking back three decades of hospitality and tourism technology research: A bibliometric approach. *International Journal of Contemporary Hospitality Management*, *35*(2), 563–588. DOI: 10.1108/IJCHM-03-2022-0376

Shoib, G., & Nandhakumar, J. (2003). Cross-cultural IS adoption in multinational corporations: A study of rationality. *Information Technology for Development*, *10*(4), 249–260. DOI: 10.1002/itdj.1590100404

Singh, K., Kumar, S., & Talukder, M. B. (2024). Digital Transformation and Its Impact on Tourism Business in India. In Albattat, A., Azman, N., Valeri, M., & Singh, A. (Eds.), *Advances in Hospitality, Tourism, and the Services Industry* (pp. 215–230). IGI Global., DOI: 10.4018/979-8-3693-9636-0.ch010

Smith, M. J., Buckton, C., Patterson, C., & Hilton, S. (2023). User-generated content and influencer marketing involving e-cigarettes on social media: A scoping review and content analysis of YouTube and Instagram. *BMC Public Health*, *23*(1), 530. DOI: 10.1186/s12889-023-15389-1 PMID: 36941553

Smith, M. J., & Hilton, S. (2022). Adolescents' views on user-generated content and influencer marketing of e-cigarettes on social media: A focus group study. *Lancet*, *400*, S77. DOI: 10.1016/S0140-6736(22)02287-5

Suharto, S., & Hoti, A. (2023). Relationship Marketing, Customer Experience and Customer Satisfaction: Testing Their Theoretical and Empirical Underpinning. *Jurnal Manajemen Bisnis*, *14*(1), 21–35. DOI: 10.18196/mb.v14i1.17805

Talukder, M. B., Hoque, M., & Kumar, S. (2024). Understanding the Blend of Work and Leisure in Hospitality: The Era of Bleisure. In Sharma, S., Kumar, N., Ribeiro Dos Santos, V., & Miranda-Fernandez, K. (Eds.), *Advances in Hospitality, Tourism, and the Services Industry* (pp. 179–200). IGI Global., DOI: 10.4018/979-8-3693-8377-3.ch008

Talukder, M. B., Khan, M. R., & Kumar, S. (2025). The Impact of Gig Economy Trends on Traditional Employment Models: Evidence From Hotel Industry. In Nozari, H. (Ed.), *Dynamic and Safe Economy in the Age of Smart Technologies* (pp. 253–276). IGI Global., DOI: 10.4018/979-8-3693-4369-2.ch016

Talukder, M. B., Kumar, S., & Das Tonny, O. (2025). Innovative Solutions for Employee Well-Being in the Digital Hospitality Era. In Ahmad, B., Abrar, M., & Saeed, M. (Eds.), *Advances in Hospitality, Tourism, and the Services Industry* (pp. 231–258). IGI Global., DOI: 10.4018/979-8-3693-7127-5.ch009

Talukder, M. B., Kumar, S., & Kabir, F. (2025). Marketing Strategies for Promoting Heritage Tourism in Bangladesh. In Sousa, B. B., & Santos, V. R. (Eds.), *Intersections of Niche Tourism and Marketing* (pp. 113–134). IGI Global., DOI: 10.4018/979-8-3693-8417-6.ch005

Talukder, M. B., Kumar, S., & Khan, M. R. (2024). The Integration of Sustainable Practices in Cultural and Gastronomic Tourism. In Munuhwa, S. (Ed.), (pp. 467–484). Advances in Civil and Industrial Engineering. IGI Global., DOI: 10.4018/979-8-3693-3755-4.ch017

Talukder, M. B., Kumar, S., Singh, K., & Bhardwaj, V. (2025). Sustainable Food and Beverage Practices With AI. In Singh, K., Kumar, S., & Talukder, M. B. (Eds.), (pp. 1–14). Advances in Computational Intelligence and Robotics. IGI Global., DOI: 10.4018/979-8-3373-0432-8.ch001

Tlili, A., Altinay, F., Altinay, Z., & Zhang, Y. (2021). Envisioning the future of technology integration for accessible hospitality and tourism. *International Journal of Contemporary Hospitality Management*, *33*(12), 4460–4482. DOI: 10.1108/IJCHM-03-2021-0321

Trivedi, S., Grover, V., & Balusamy, B. (2025). Exploring AI in Data-driven Marketing: Understanding the Intersection of Data Engineering and Marketing. In Balusamy, B., Grover, V., Nallakaruppan, M. K., Rajasekaran, V. A., & Milanova, M. (Eds.), *Data Engineering for Data-driven Marketing* (pp. 1–16). Emerald Publishing Limited., DOI: 10.1108/978-1-83662-326-720251002

Tussyadiah, I. P., Jung, T. H., & Tom Dieck, M. C. (2018). Embodiment of wearable augmented reality technology in tourism experiences. *Journal of Travel Research, 57*(5), 597–611.

Valença, M. N., Sobral, M. F. F., Andrade Lima, T. L. D., & Farias, D. D. M. P. (2020). Innovation radar in hospitality: A new procedure to evaluate the innovation in hotels. *Journal of Hospitality and Tourism Technology, 11*(2), 313–326. DOI: 10.1108/JHTT-10-2017-0119

Verma, S., & Diwan, H. (2025). Marketing innovation for sustainability: Review, trends, and way forward. *Business Ethics, the Environment & Responsibility, 34*(3), 912–935. DOI: 10.1111/beer.12686

Webster, C., & Ivanov, S. (2020). *Robots in travel, tourism and hospitality: Key findings from a global study*. Zangador.

Chapter 3
Future Innovations in Hospitality Marketing Technology

Harini S.
http://orcid.org/0000-0002-3856-7390
Saveetha School of Managment, Saveetha Institute of Medical and Technical Sciences, India

Gigi G. S.
http://orcid.org/0009-0000-0552-256X
Saveetha School of Management, Saveetha Institute of Medical and Technical Sciences, India

ABSTRACT

The digital technologies revolution in the global hospitality industry, where it is particularly concerned with the introduction of the latest technologies applications examines how these technologies are revolutionizing the manner in which hotels operate, market themselves, and undertake sustainability initiatives to ensure individualized guest experiences, real-time decision-making, and operational effectiveness. Among the opportunities presented by digital transformation, and addressed the increased customer interaction, brand loyalty and competitive advantage, the challenges of technological integration and providing a service that is human-centred. It also talks about the future trend in hospitality marketing, which involves AI-powered content, social commerce, and immersive technologies. Lastly, it can take advantage of the effectiveness of technology and the traditional service standards to become successful in a more consumer-oriented hospitality industry

DOI: 10.4018/979-8-3373-6741-5.ch003

1. INTRODUCTION

The hospitality industry has entered a period of change to digital transformation when the most sophisticated technologies, including artificial intelligence (AI), the Internet of Things (IoT), and cloud computing, are being actively integrated. These technologies have revolutionized the way business is conducted, service delivery, and sustainability practice leading to the development of digital transformation within the world hospitality markets (Ćurčić et al., 2022; Jonathan, 2025). Digital transformation within the hospitality industry is not only about the adoption of technologies, but a re-configurative strategic re-engineering of the value creation, delivery, and perception by customers. Real-time decision-making possibilities, personalized experiences of guests, and operational efficiency can be enhanced through the implementation of digital technology, i.e., AI-driven chatbots, IoT-enabled energy management systems, and data analytics platforms (Jonathan,2025). Simultaneously, digitalization promotes interconnectedness between travellers, service providers, and stakeholders which facilitates customer interaction and boosts brand loyalty (Samala et al., 2022). Nevertheless, the hospitality industry is also problematic due to the digital transformation. The process of connecting new technologies with the old ones may be complicated and expensive, particularly with small and medium-sized businesses that do not always have the capacities of larger companies (Jonathan,2025; Prdic et al., 2025). Cybersecurity, labour preparation, and equal access to digital services are also other areas where concerns need to be raised in order to achieve sustainable and inclusive digital transformation (Gürsoy, 2025). Hotels which successfully adopt digital solutions, both in the form of cloud-based management systems and AI-powered customer interaction platforms, will be in a better position to realise strategic objectives associated with customer satisfaction, revenue growth and environmental sustainability (Ćurčić et al., 2022; Jonathan, 2025). With the industry in the ever-changing state, a moderate solution involving the incorporation of technology efficacy with the customary services quality will be critical in long-term success in the virtual market that is becoming more and more digital.

Evolution of Marketing: From Traditional to Digital to AI-Driven:

Hospitality industry has undergone major transformation over the past five decades. This transition from offline promotional channels to rise of social networking platforms has been integrated in the below figure 1

Figure 1. Evolution of Marketing

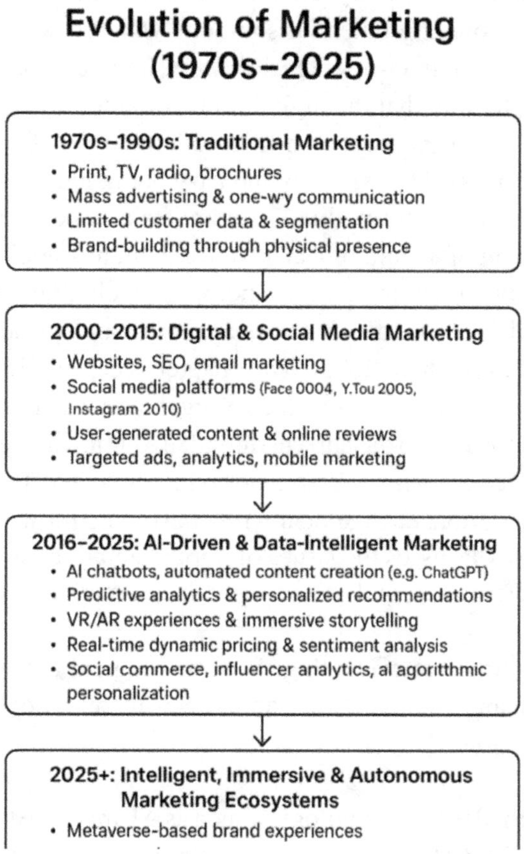

Source: complied by authors based on secondary data

Significance of the Chapter

It is against this light that the current chapter has a scope of discussing the shifting nature of the digital transformation of the hospitality business, including the application of technologies, such as AI, IoT, cloud computing, and automation. It examines theoretical constructs and empirical evidence of how the innovations are redefining the operation, marketing and best practices in sustainability of hotels. The discussion extends globally without particularly paying attention to the progress in emerging markets like Serbia where digitalization projects are developing in different infrastructural and economic conditions (Ćurčić et al., 2022). The chapter is devoted to investigating the value of the digital technologies in modifying the work of the hospitality industry, defining the most prominent opportunities that are offered by the digital innovations, discussing the challenges of implementing digital innovations, analyzing the contemporary level of technological use adoption in various environments, and providing potential solutions which could help to balance the use of technology and human-oriented service. The goals together create a comprehensive idea of the way that the digital transformation can make the hospitality industry sustainable and innovative in the modern world. The chapter is critical because it talks of the world hospitality industry being redefined by technological innovation and digital transformation. To compete and be relevant in the rapidly changing environment of technological advancement, hospitality organizations are under pressure to implement modern technologies, including artificial intelligence (AI), the Internet of Things (IoT), big data analytics, and social media automation (Ćurčić et al., 2022; Jonathan, 2025). The chapter is especially relevant due to the fact that it balances between academic theory and practice in the industry, offering a multidisciplinary approach to the current digital revolution in the field of hospitality marketing and service delivery. It also emphasizes how new technologies alter the marketing communication, engagement with guests, and positioning the brand, but at the same time also discusses the issues of implementation, including the cost, the willingness of the workforce, and balancing both automation and human interaction (Jonathan, 2025).

This chapter is aimed at evaluating the technological advances that are likely to revolutionize hospitality marketing and social media adoption in the decade. Specifically, it aims to:

1. Study the new marketing technologies, such as AI, machine learning, augmented and virtual reality (AR/VR) and blockchain, as a way of improving personalization, transparency, and trust in hotel marketing (Jonathan, 2025).
2. Discuss the development of social media as AI-controlled interaction systems and predictive and conversational AI (Jonathan, 2025).
3. Predict the data and analytics in the prediction of guest behavior and the creation of more insight-driven marketing campaigns (Ćurčić et al., 2022; Gürsoy, 2025).
4. Present future trends that include the metaverse, virtual influencers, and immersive storytelling that will likely transform digital brand identity in the hospitality industry (Jonathan, 2025).
5. Mediate between research and practice by presenting practical information using case studies, opinion leadership, and empirical evidence and proof of how technology advances are transforming hospitality competitiveness (Ćurčić et al., 2022; Jonathan, 2025). Combining these purposes, the chapter can be considered as a contribution to the further insight into the role of digital transformation, data intelligence, and social technologies designing the future of marketing, branding, and customer interaction in the hotel industry.

2. THE CURRENT LANDSCAPE OF HOSPITALITY MARKETING

Hospitality industry is undergoing a massive revolution based on the fast development of technology, the changing consumer demands, and increased competitiveness worldwide. Digital ecosystems, which cannot be supported by interpersonal relationships and fixed channel promotions, are changing the traditional models of marketing, which were previously stable and predictable. The adoption of the latest technologies, including artificial intelligence (AI), virtual reality (VR), voice search, and the Metaverse, has transformed the way hotels will interact with their customers, generate income, and stand out of the crowd in the oversaturated markets, as Bilgihan and Ricci (2023) highlight. The post-pandemic environment has additional shifted the consumer behavior toward hyper-personalization, the concern with sustainability, and confidence in digital brokerage, making adaptive marketing strategies one of the determinants of organizational success. AI has become a part of this development. As Bulchand-Gidumal et al. (2024) emphasize, AI reinvents marketing through the possibility to customize marketing at a large scale, predictive analytics, and automated content creation. Hotels are now able to communicate to each customer profile, predict demand more precisely, and provide flawless omnichannel experiences (see figure 2).

Figure 2. Transformation Of Hospitality Marketing

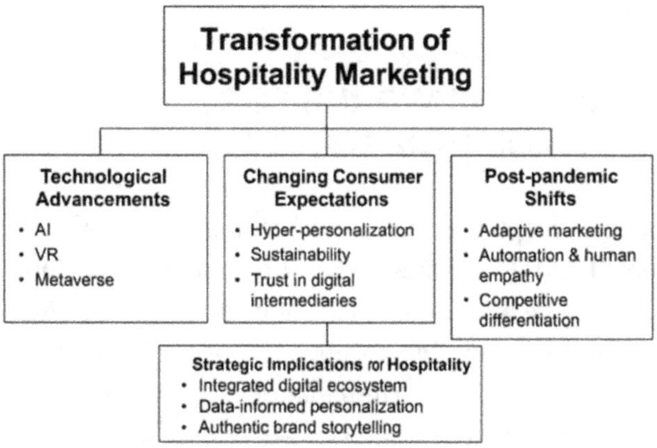

Sources: Bilgihan & Ricci (2023) and Bulchand-Gidumal et al. (2024)

Table 1. Key Insights from Existing Studies

Theme	Key Insights from Existing Studies	Debates / Contrasting Findings	Knowledge Gaps Identified
AI Personalization & Predictive Analytics	AI enables large-scale personalization, automated content creation, and data-driven decision-making (Bilgihan & Ricci, 2024; Ferhataj & Memaj, 2025).	Some argue AI improves engagement, while others warn of reduced authenticity and loss of emotional connection (Bulchand-Gidumal et al., 2023).	Limited empirical data on long-term effects of hyper-personalization on loyalty and trust.
Sustainability & Technology Adoption (IoT, Automation)	IoT increases efficiency, reduces energy consumption, and supports sustainable operations (Mandarin Oriental case; Molina-Castillo et al., 2023).	Some scholars view automation as environmentally beneficial, while others note risks of digital inequality and small-business adoption barriers.	Few studies examine sustainability–technology trade-offs in emerging markets.
Customer Engagement & Social / Immersive Technologies	Social media, VR/AR, influencers, and UGC drive engagement and co-creation (Dang & Nguyen, 2023; Mohammad et al., 2024).	Debate over authenticity of AI-generated content and declining trust in influencer-driven marketing.	Lack of research on metaverse engagement and measurable ROI of immersive marketing.
Digital Commerce & Direct Booking Behaviors	Social commerce leads to higher conversion rates and bypasses OTAs (Mohammad et al., 2024).	Some studies show strong booking intentions, while others caution about privacy concerns and algorithmic transparency.	Insufficient evidence linking social commerce to long-term customer retention.

Table 1 explains the summary of existing studies and its knowledge gap

3. THEORETICAL FRAMEWORKS FOR DIGITAL ADOPTION IN HOSPITALITY

Unified Theory of Acceptance and Use of Technology (UTAUT2), the Technology Acceptance Model (TAM) (Venkatesh et al., 2012), and Rogers Diffusion of Innovations (DOI) has conceptual framework to explain the adoption of AI, IoT, automation, and immersive technologies by the stakeholders of the hospitality industry. These models emphasize certain key determinants or factors in the acceptance of these technologies such as perceived usefulness, ease of use, social influence, innovation characteristics, as well as trust. The combination of these frameworks will enable the discussion to organize a systemic relationship between theoretical constructs and the practical marketing practices, which are discussed throughout the chapter.

Regional and Industry-Specific Perspectives on Digital Transformation in Hospitality

Although digital transformation in the hospitality sector has been a major topic in the developed economies, there are marked differences in how this transformation is implemented across regions and industry set up. Contextual factors influencing the adoption of technology in the emerging markets and small and medium-sized hotel enterprises (SMEs) include quality of infrastructure, budgetary provisions, employee digital literacy, and cultural inclination towards innovations. Research has shown that access to sophisticated digital infrastructure, increased risk of investment, and skills gaps tend to slow down adoption in developing settings in comparison to large hotel chains in developed markets (Ćurčić et al., 2022; Zakić et al., 2022).

Digital transformation in some parts of the world like Southeast Europe, Latin America, and in some parts of Asia and Africa is not evenly spread, indicating differences in regulatory support, internet penetration, and technology costs. Therefore, adoption models like UTAUT2 and Diffusion of Innovations offer convenient theories to understand the difference between how facilitating conditions and social influence technology uptake in different scenarios. Inclusion of regional and industry-specific lenses is thus an increase in inclusivity and relevance of research on digital transformation in hospitality.

3.1 Review of Existing Marketing Practices and Social Media Strategies

Some of the core practices that are still important constituents of a complete marketing mix are content marketing, search engine optimization (SEO), email personalization, and revenue management (Bilgihan and Ricci, 2024). Their implementation has however changed as they now have digital interfaces that enable better targeting, measurement of performance, and dynamically changing them as a result of analytics. Consumption of social media has become a strong force in influencing brand visibility and consumer view in hospitality. Tik Tok, Instagram, YouTube are the frameworks of visual storytelling, which allow hotels to project the experience, aesthetics, and authenticity. User-generated content (UGC), influencer partnerships, and interactive campaigns can be more engaging and trusted, especially by the younger demographics. Besides, AI-based social media plans are transforming the notion of engagement by automating content production, optimizing the time of posting, and allowing sentiment analysis to track the brand name (Bulchand-Gidumal et al., 2024). Chatbots and conversational AI are increasingly being applied by hotels to respond to customer queries immediately thus enhancing responsiveness and customer satisfaction. Marketers could also predict trends and offer customization which contributes to higher conversion rates through predictive analytics. Although automation is more efficient, excessive use of AI in the absence of human regulation can erode the emotional connections that hospitality marketing needs.

3.2 The Emergence of Experienced-based and real-time engagement models.

Hospitality industry has shifted its focus on marketing products to the experience-based engagement, in which the emotional connection and real-time communication characterize the customer value. Customers do not want to stay in a hotel but to live in a destination and to experience it in a personalized, intimate way that corresponds with their lifestyles, values and dreams. As a process of co-creation of experiences with the customers through digital and physical touch points. Bilgihan and Ricci (2024) argue that technological integration (especially when referring to virtual reality (VR) and augmented reality (AR) and artificial intelligence (AI) has helped hotels create multisensory, interactive experiences before their guests even stepped into the building. According to Bulchand-Gidumal et al. (2024), AI-based systems and predictive analytics allow hotels to engage guests in real-time to be able to provide instant and tailored offers or upgrade of services, based on real-time behavior data. Social media platforms such as Instagram, Tik Tok, and YouTube allow brands to demonstrate authenticity and immediacy and create stronger emotional ties and community interactions. Table 2 Summarise the Experience-Driven and Real-Time Engagement Models in Hospitality Marketing

Table 2. Experience-Driven and Real-Time Engagement Models in Hospitality Marketing

Insight Area	Key Insight Summary
Shift from Products to Experiences	Hospitality marketing has transitioned from promoting services to curating *personalized and emotionally engaging experiences* that align with guests' values and lifestyles.
Technology as an Experience Enabler	Emerging technologies such as AI, VR, AR, and mobile platforms allow hotels to create immersive, multisensory interactions, enhancing guest engagement before and during their stay.
Rise of Real-Time Engagement	AI-driven analytics empower hotels to deliver personalized offers, real-time communication, and contextual service upgrades, replacing static marketing campaigns with adaptive engagement.
Social media as a Storytelling Platform	Influencer collaborations, user-generated content, and interactive storytelling enable guests to co-create and share authentic brand experiences, strengthening emotional connections.

continued on following page

Table 2. Continued

Insight Area	Key Insight Summary
Data-Driven Personalization	Real-time data analytics and sentiment tracking provide instant feedback, allowing marketers to refine campaigns dynamically and tailor content to individual guest behaviors.
Living Marketing Ecosystem	Marketing has evolved into a continuous engagement cycle, connecting with guests *before, during, and after* their stay to build lasting loyalty, advocacy, and brand equity.

Sources: Bilgihan & Ricci (2024) and Bulchand-Gidumal et al. (2024)

3.3 Combining Current Research and International Policy Implications of Digital Transformation.

The current academic literature has substantially contributed to knowledge in the field of the digital transformation restructuring hospitality and tourism marketing on the strategic level as well as on the ecosystem. Gretzel (2022) understands digital transformation in tourism as a systemic change where the role of data-driven intelligence, platformization, and automation help create fundamentally different configurations of value creation, governance, and relationships among stakeholders. Closely related to this further ecosystem perspective is Buhalis et al. (2025), in which AI, IoT, cloud-based services, and analytics perform the task of connecting places, hotels, and service providers in real-time and smart networks. In hospitality marketing, smart systems can be used in dynamic pricing, contextual personalization, and sustainability monitoring and are associated with technological challenges, such as interoperability, governance, and data ethics.

It augments scholarly viewpoints, a series of recent UNWTO and OECD reports supports the applicability of digital transformation to hospitality and tourism across the globe. Digitalization is the first article mentioned by UNWTO as an enabler of competitiveness, sustainability, and resilience especially the smart use of data, platform integration, and sustainability reporting made by technology. Other analyses by OECD highlight faster rates of digital adoption in larger firms and regions and note the importance of policy support and the inequalities between workforce reskilling and responsible innovation structures as the antecedent to inclusive growth. By combining these policy points of view, hospitality marketing innovation is placed in a global environment that is influenced by regulation, sustainability concerns, and socio-economic development. These recent studies and institutional reports, in combination, make the chapter even more academically strong and timely.

4. THE FUTURE OF HOSPITALITY MARKETING IN THE EMERGING TECHNOLOGIES.

The digital era has made technological innovation to be the force behind reshaping hospitality marketing. As a result of the changing expectations of customers, hotels and other tourism organizations are adopting the emergent technologies of artificial intelligence (AI), virtual and augmented reality (VR/AR), the Metaverse, robotics, and blockchain to increase personalization, efficiency, and customer interactions (Bilgihan and Ricci, 2024). Not only are these technologies redefining the way in which hospitality companies communicate with customers, but they are also redesigning the strategies in strategic marketing throughout the whole customer.

4.1 Artificial Intelligence and Predictive personalization

AI is one of the foundations of hospitality marketing of the next generation. It enables real time data analysis, predictive customization and automated customer interaction. According to Bilgihan and Ricci (2023), AI tools, including ChatGPT, DALL·E, and machine learning algorithms, are exploited to create content, interact with social media, advertise specifically, and control their reputation. On the same note, Ferhataj & Memaj (2025) identified that AI implementation improves hospitality operation productivity and profitability through automation of communication and hyper-personalized guest interactions. AI-based chatbots and virtual assistants have become marketing touchpoints to respond to inquiries posed by guests, suggest services, and even upsell amenities based on behavioral information . These are better tools that enhance efficiency in the operations and brand perception to achieve smooth and human-like 24/7 communication. Consequently, AI-based marketing plans are necessitated in enhancing customer loyalty, maximizing revenue and building a hotel digital brand. Considering the aspects of TAM, AI-based personalization improves the perceived usefulness, which boosts the willingness of the customer to work with digital channels. The constructs of performance expectancy and hedonic motivation introduced by UTAUT2 also contribute to the understanding of the reason why AI-based services enhance customer adoption.

4.2 Virtual and Augmented Reality:

The Emergence of Immersive Marketing. Rogers' Diffusion of Innovations framework classifies VR/AR as innovations with strong "observability" and "trialability," which help accelerate adoption in hospitality marketing. The technologies of virtual and augmented reality are redesigning experiential marketing because they enable consumers to see what a hospitality operation would be like prior to making a purchasing decision. VR tours and AR-powered advertisements can allow customers to have a remote experience of hotel rooms, conference spaces, or tourist attraction sites, which builds trust and emotional bond (Neuhofer et al., 2014; Bilgihan and Ricci, 2024). As an example, the VRoom Service offered by Marriott and virtual tour of the events through VR by Shangri-La Hotels are examples of how VR could be used to market venues and generate bookings. VR-based experiences are also related to the concept of value co-creation that allows customers to engage in the service design and planning process and, thus, drives more satisfaction and perceived value (Dang and Nguyen, 2023). The strategic implementation of VR/AR in hospitality marketing does not only promote better consumer interaction but also allows establishing competitive advantage in the market that is becoming more and more saturated.

4.3 The Extended Reality Ecosystems and Metaverse.

The Metaverse is the future of digital marketing, which consists of combining a virtual environment with social and business transactions. As pointed out by Dang and Nguyen (2023), hotel brands can use Metaverse technologies to build common cyber environments in which clients can explore digital buildings, take part in activities, and communicate with the robot employees in real-time. These immersive ecosystems create a fog between the physical and digital worlds, which provide new avenues of telling stories, brand community creation, and virtual commerce. Additionally, the application of blockchain in the Metaverse guarantees the transparency of all transactions and their authenticity, which enhances consumer trust. With so many digital natives taking a growing role in the travel sectors, the Metaverse is set to become a core channel of customer interaction particularly in the luxury and lifestyle-focused hospitality industry.

4.4 Robotics, IoT and Smart Service Delivery.

The interaction of robotics and the Internet of Things (IoT) adds more value to marketing and operations of the hospitality business. Smart devices gather behavioral data that help to create marketing campaigns, whereas service robots can make a brand more differentiated with something new and convenient (Molina-Castillo et al., 2023). Robots will be able to check-in, carry amenities, and help servers in restaurants not only to provide a technological show but also to create a consistent service experience. The IoT-based personalization is not limited to the field of operation but also marketing strategy. Using the preferences of the guests by linking it to the automated procedures, like the lighting, temperature, or entertainment, hotels will be able to provide their guests with tailored experiences at the facility, which will make them feel attached to the brand on a personal level. Such degree of contextual marketing changes the conventional customer relationship management in the form of an adaptive, information-user-driven ecosystem (Dang and Nguyen, 2023) refer to table 3.

Table 3. Emerging Technologies in the Future of Hospitality Marketing

Technology Area	Core Applications	Key Benefits
AI & Predictive Personalization	Real-time data analysis, chatbots, automated interaction	Personalized marketing, efficiency, loyalty
VR/AR (Immersive Marketing)	Virtual tours, AR ads, interactive experiences	Builds trust, emotional engagement, competitive edge
Metaverse & Extended Reality	Virtual environments, blockchain-based transactions	Immersive branding, community building, transparency
Robotics & IoT	Smart devices, service robots, automated personalization	Consistent experience, contextual marketing
Innovation & Data Analytics	Digital transformation, AI analytics, agile pricing	Performance improvement, profitability, agility

Sources: Neuhofer et al. (2014); Dang & Nguyen (2023); Bilgihan & Ricci (2024); Molina-Castillo et al. (2023)

TAM can also be used to understand consumer reaction to digital marketing tools as the perceived ease of use defines the use of mobile apps, chatbots, and booking platforms. The social influence, which is the core of UTAUT2, is particularly applicable to the social media marketing and influencer-based choices.

3.5 Innovation, Data and Performance Outcomes.

Innovation has been core in the long-term competitiveness in hospitality. According to Molina-Castillo et al. (2023), the combination of technological and non-technological innovations, like digital marketing, automation of services, and organizational redesign, allows directly improving the performance outcomes and profitability. They have found that hotel companies that strategically invest in the digital innovation perform better than those using traditional marketing. Marketing analytics based on data enhance this benefit by providing insights on the behavior of the guests, and trends in the market, as well as the performance of the campaigns. The partnership of AI analytics and revenue optimization technologies can help hotels create agile pricing and promotional plans that respond to market forces as Bilgihan and Ricci (2023) point out.

3.6 Sustainability in Hospitality and Innovation of Green Digital Marketing.

Green digital marketing is becoming a strategic pillar of sustainable hospitality innovation, and it is how hotels communicate their environmental responsibility and reach out to more eco-conscious consumers. Innovations in digital technology, like artificial intelligence (AI), Internet of Things (IoT), blockchain, and data analytics allow hospitality companies to transform the sustainability performance into a transparent, measurable, and marketable value proposition (Bilgihan and Ricci, 2024; Molina-Castillo et al., 2023). The digitization of sustainability dashboards, carbon footprint calculators, and IoT-based energy monitoring systems enable hotels to measure the number of emissions, water use, and energy saved in real time and display them on websites, mobile apps, and booking systems, and directly convey them to guests. According to previous research, this type of data-based transparency builds credibility of the brand, decreases the perceptions of greenwashing, and positively affects building of trust-based relations with environmentally conscious customers, who travel (Dang and Nguyen, 2023; Carvalho and Ivanov, 2023).

The green marketing strategies are also enhanced further because with the help of blockchain technology, it is possible to have verifiable sustainability reporting and supply chain transparency. Digital ledgers that cannot be changed can enable hotels to verify the eco-labels, track products that are responsibly sourced, and authenticate carbon offset programs, thus enhancing consumer trust in the sustainability claims and responsible sourcing (Mondal et al., 2023; Baburao et al., 2026). Simultaneously, AI-based personalization systems will be able to amplify sustainable marketing by improving personalized environmental messaging, depending on guest preferences, values, and behavioral information. These systems are also capable of providing context-specific sustainability prompts (rec recommendations on low-carbon room, towel reuse, or energy saving), via mobile apps, chatbots powered by AI, or digital concierge services and estimate responsible consumption without reducing the perceived usefulness of the service (Bulchand-Gidumal et al., 2024; Kim et al., 2024).

The implementation of green digital marketing technologies is closely associated with international sustainability policies, in particular, the United Nations Sustainable Development Goals (SDGs). The SDG 9 (Industry, Innovation, and Infrastructure) is directly supported by investments in smart infrastructure, data analytics, and digital transparency, which promote resource-efficient hospitality systems handled by the innovation (Ćurčić et al., 2022; Molina-Castillo et al., 2023). At the same time, sustainability communication facilitated by technologies will empower guests to make responsible and informed decisions, and SDG 12 (Responsible Consumption and Production) will be achieved by providing transparent reporting, offering guests a personalized approach to sustainability, and engaging in responsible marketing efforts (Dang and Nguyen, 2023; Baburao et al., 2026). In this regard, the notion of digital transformation would go beyond operational effectiveness to be a tool of sustainable value co-creation that allows hospitality organizations to build stronger brand equity, increase long-term loyalty, and play a significant role in global sustainability considerations.

5. THE HISTORY OF SOCIAL MEDIA TOOLING.

The history of social media tooling is clearly represented with the timeline in figure 3.

5.1 AI-based Content Creation and Curation within the Hospitality Industry.

Artificial intelligence (AI) and ChatGPT are becoming more popular in the hospitality industry to promote the process of content creation and curation. Through AI-powered applications, hotels, restaurants, and travel organizations can automatically create and manage digital content, such as marketing content, menus, directives to guests, and promotional campaigns, depending on the specific customer groups (Chakraborty and Biswal, 2024). With natural language processing (NLP) and generative algorithms, applications such as ChatGPT are capable of creating compelling text on websites, social media posts and responses to customers, which enhances brand consistency and operational efficiency.

Figure 3. History of Social Media Tooling

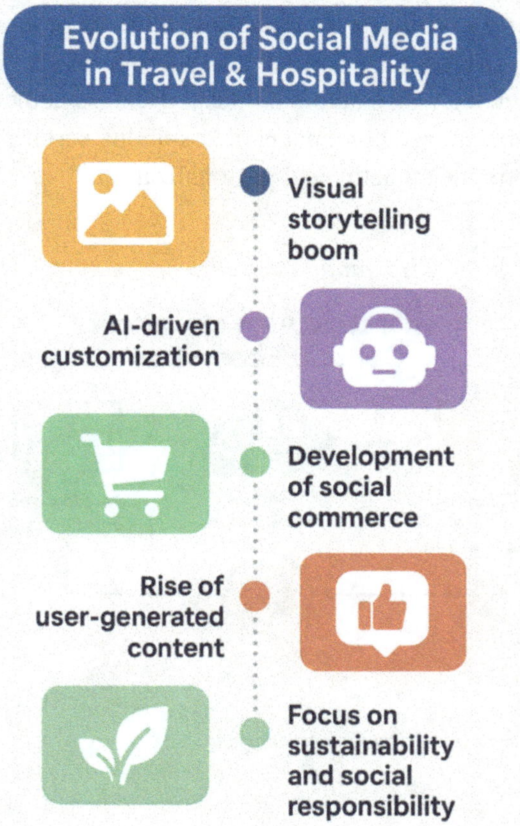

Source: Created by authors based on secondary information

AI-powered platforms in the marketing and guest interaction use customer data to adapt the recommendations and recommend content to each visitor. As an example, ChatGPT is capable of summarizing the reviews left by guests, detecting up-and-coming trends in services, and proposing changes in the hospitality services, relying on the immediate feedback (Chen et al., 2021). This type of curation aids data-informed decision-making by managers, so they can make changes to menus, event promotions, or loyalty programs based on consumer sentiment and preferences (Calvillo, 2023). In addition, large hospitality companies have started to incorporate generative AI (Figure 4) in their online systems. Expedia, in its turn, uses ChatGPT software to generate chat-based travel guide and personalized booking content, whereas Magpie relies on AI-assisted product optimization software to build personalized promotional messages to partner hotels and travel agencies (Dwivedi et al., 2024). These examples show the ability of AI to optimize the creation of marketing and operational volumes of content as well as management. Nonetheless, with generative AI in creating content in a hospitality setting, new issues come about. The quality of training data is a question of the reliability of generated content, which raises the concern of bias, misinformation, and cultural sensitivity (Neuhofer et al., 2014). Moreover, excessive automation can decrease authenticity of the brand voice, which is a fundamental component of hospitality service delivery, and needs human control to provide empathy and personalization.

Figure 4. Generative AI in Hospitality eco system

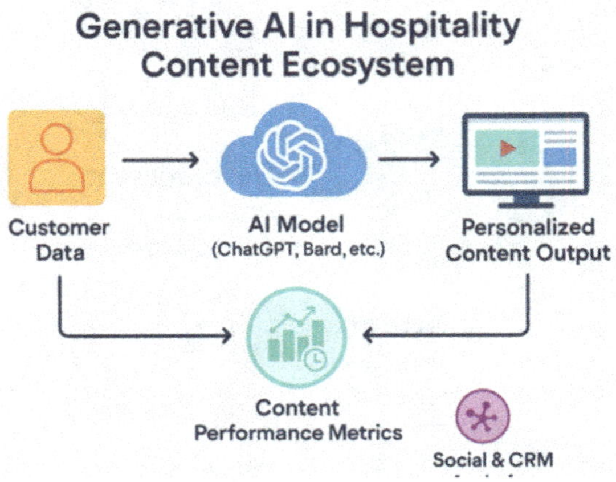

Sources: Created by authors based on the secondary data

Overall, AI-powered content creation and curation represent a paradigm shift in hospitality communication and marketing strategies. When implemented responsibly, generative AI tools such as ChatGPT can enhance creativity, improve customer engagement, and optimize resource utilization, leading to higher service quality and stronger competitive positioning (Carvalho & Ivanov, 2023; Mondal et al., 2023).

5.2 Merging of influencer analytics and user-generated content.

influencer analytics and user-generated content (UGC) are becoming important elements in digital marketing, brand positioning, and customer communications by the hospitality industry. Combining them with AI-based solutions such as ChatGPT allows hospitality companies to process, filter, and super-optimize the content more efficiently, improving the customer experience and brand (Carvalho & Ivanov, 2023; Mondal et al., 2023).

Social media influencers can be assessed through AI systems that monitor the usage, or engagement, metrics, which include impressions, sentiment, reach, and conversion rates. Machine learning algorithms help hospitality brands to find high-impact influencers whose posts resonate with their target audience and brand values . In addition, influencer analytics coupled with generative AI applications can enable companies to forecast real-time virality and market reaction to promotional efforts, resulting in more information-driven promotional selections (Carvalho and Ivanov, 2023). At the same time, the incorporation of user-generated customer information that involves reviews, photos, and posts on social media, has now been an element of customer trust and brand trustworthiness. AIs like ChatGPT can be used to process large amounts of UGC across various sources and learn about consumer opinion, preferences, and perceptions of the services (Chen et al., 2021). These lessons can guide hospitality managers to perfect services, enhance satisfaction among guests and find new areas of innovation. Text mining and sentiment analysis with the use of AI assist organizations in further curating genuine information that represents the actual customer experience and screening out fake news or partisan insights (Chen et al., 2021). Besides, the application of generative AI will further boost the collaboration between influencer news and UGC by suggesting trending topics, hashtags, and storytelling methods that make the audience more active.

Figure 5. Influencer analytics and user-generated content

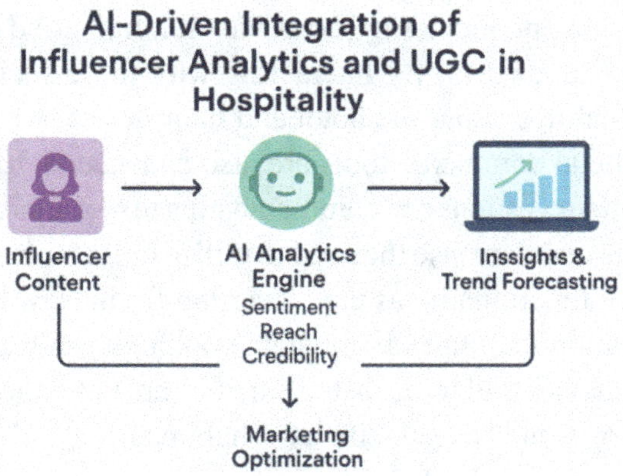

Sources: Created by authors based on the secondary data

Magpie and Expedia are the two platforms using AI connections to customize their content to travelers by combining influencer stories with real-time user reviews to provide personalized experiences (Chen et al., 2021). This overlap of influencer analytics, UGC, and AI-generated knowledge helps the hospitality organizations to reach the effectiveness of omnichannel marketing, reinforced brand loyalty, and customer acquisition. Nevertheless, the aspect of the growing dependence on AI-based influencer analytics and UGC curation also has ethical concerns, such as bias in algorithmic suggestions, authenticity checking, and data privacy concerns (Carvalho & Ivanov, 2023; Mondal et al., 2023) (refer figure 5). Hence, the future advancement of the hospitality industry should be aimed at creating clear and fair guidelines in introducing AI in order to preserve credibility and sincerity in digital marketing activities.

5.3 Social business and direct booking on social platforms.

Social commerce has become a revolution in the hospitality sector that has changed the way hotels interact with their customers, build their brand image, and make direct bookings. It is a mixture of social media and e-commerce operations and allows hotels to sell, communicate, and conduct business with customers in the context of social networking in Facebook, Instagram, Tik Tok, and hotel review websites (Mohammad et al., 2024). Incorporating booking functionalities into the social platform removes the middleman, and facilitates easy direct bookings, which help hotels to increase their profit margins and improve customer relations. Mohammad et al. (2024) state that social commerce enables hotels to develop interactive platforms via recommendations, online communities, and review platforms that play a big role in shaping consumer booking intentions. The stimuli that can determine the brand perception of potential guests about a hotel include social interactions, and user-generated content, including peer reviews, ratings, and referrals (stimulus-organism-response framework). By interacting with these social cues, customers will have positive feelings about the hotel and their desire to book directly on the social platforms. Social commerce tools are also enhanced with AI, which allows making personalized suggestions and communicating in real-time, which can increase customer confidence and decrease the need to utilize online travel agencies (OTAs). As can be seen, such functionality as the Instagram Book Now button or Facebook Marketplace integration facilitates immediate bookings, which makes the most of impulse booking behavior under the influence of social validation and digital word-of-mouth (Chakraborty and Biswal, 2024; Mohammad et al., 2024). Empirical data provided by Mohammad et al. (2024) indicates that social commerce has a strong positive effect on brand image, customer engagement, and booking intentions. Hotels that engage with followers, create visual content sponsored, and organise virtual events will create the emotion that turns social engagement into bookings. Also, a more convenient booking does not require third-party resources, but adding links to booking requests in user-created content and posts made by influencers makes it more convenient and more likely to persuade guests to bypass a third-party system. Nevertheless, the process of direct booking integration via social commerce also requires consideration of ethical and working issues, such as the privacy of data, the authenticity of opinions, and the transparency of algorithms. Hotels must build transparent communication and reliable systems of transactions and use social analytics to track trends of engagement and satisfaction to keep consumer trust (Mohammad et al., 2024). To conclude, social commerce and direct booking via social sites are the shift in the paradigm of socially integrated and customer-based marketing of hospitality products and services. This strategy helps to increase the digital presence of hotels, maintain their connection with customers, and increase direct booking rates significantly, which helps to support long-term brand longevity which is clearly represented in figure 6.

Figure 6. Social commerce and direct booking

Sources: Created by authors based on the secondary data

6. CASE STUDY (DIGITAL DEFYND. (2025))

6.1. Marriott- Mobile Key / Contactless Check-In.

Marriott has transformed the way guests access their rooms by installing Bonvoy Mobile Key in its outlets where more than 70 percent of its guests open their rooms using their smartphones. This decreased the waiting time in the lobby by 70 percent and increased upsell revenues by 12 percent. The system combines the digital ID verification, real-time room ready alerts, and automatic updates on housekeeping. With the 30 million plastic cards removed and energy savings by occupancy-controlled HVAC, sustainability is enhanced. The project increased RevPAR by 4-5 percent and improved guest satisfaction. Bio unlock and custom room experience will be the next added feature, and mobile access will be used as the strategic catalyst to loyalty, efficiency, and environmental footprint.

6.2 Hilton Connected Room Ecosystem.

Connected Room is the project created by Hilton that repurposed more than 3,500 rooms, turning them into smart spaces where the guests could control the lighting, climate, and entertainment using the Honors app. This IoT-based system saved 26 percent of energy, tripled media expenses, and decreased engineering calls by 35 percent. It applies machine learning to streamline idle settings and propose upsell offers. The data analytics and predictive maintenance enhanced the service reliability and the satisfaction of the guests, as the mobile app rating increased to 4.8 stars. Hilton will add voice and gesture control, EV-charger reservations and carbon-budget displays, supporting its digital hospitality and sustainability leadership.

6.3 Accor -AI Revenue Management Platform.

Accor has installed the IDeaS G3 RMS in 5,600 hotels to autominate the pricing decision based on real-time demand data. The AI engine updates every hour and boosts the RevPAR by around 5 percent and lowers the number of manual overrides. The rate recommendations were approved 92 per cent of the time, which saved managers four hours a week. Revenue also increased by 12 percent quarter on quarter in volatile markets such as Brazil. The system predicts the ancillary spend too and allows bundled offers. Group modelling gives a possible annual benefit of 700 million. The future improvement involves maximization of total revenues and room upgrades image recognition, and algorithmic pricing becomes the foundation of strategic development and operational efficiency of Accor.

6.4 Mandarin Oriental Smart Energy Management.

Mandarin oriental used the IoT sensors and machine-learning analytics to minimize energy consumption without compromising luxury. In its Barcelona flagship, the energy consumption has been reduced by 35% with the comfort scores increasing by six points. The system checks occupancy and temperature data by which the system adjusts the ventilation and lighting, which activates the eco-mode during the checkout. Maintenance tickets were decreased by 22 and carbon emissions in the group were lowered by 30%. A total of 1,600 labor hours were repurposed in strategic retrofits by engineers. The future strategies are AI load shifting, water-side heat recovery, as well as EV-charger integration. The project demonstrates that sustainability and five-star services are compatible and that energy is a strategic resource.

6.5 IHG Digital Concierge & Voice Assistant.

IHG incorporated movements of mobile and voice in its guest experience, with Baidu DuerOS and Alexa AI Smart Room suites. Voice commands allow guests to control the lighting, order services, and make reservations, cutting housekeeping by 30 and lobby calls by 35. Upsell acceptance was increased by 11% which is a $22 per room addition. Online communication increased by 4 percent to 20 percent and relieved congestion of switchboards. The system saves 1,400 man hours in each building and reduces HVAC run time, which reduces utility bills by 5 percent. IHG is going to roll out 500 biometric unlock hotels and AI itinerary builders to the company, establishing a unified, data-driven environment.

7. THE ESSENTIALS OF DATA-DRIVEN PERSONALIZATION AND ANALYTICS.

Analytical examination of data allows companies to streamline their strategies by using analytical revelations, as opposed to instinct. Research indicates that big data analytics can be used in marketing to boost customer involvement and conversion rates, which prove to be transformative (Rosario and Cruz, 2023; Alsayat, 2023). Moreover, the opportunity to customize marketing messages according to the accurate analysis of data leads to the development of better relations with customers and loyalty (Alsayat, 2023). Nevertheless, there are no obstacles to the use of data-driven marketing. The barriers encountered by various organizations include inadequate analytical skills, the absence of technological systems, and challenges in converting the analytics systems into the current marketing processes (Rosario and Cruz, 2023). In spite of these obstacles, the potential gains, such as enhanced personalization to real-time decision-making, make data-driven marketing one of the foundations of the competitive approach in the digital era. Analytics has become a key point to changing the hospitality and service industries through the creation of data-driven decisions in several areas of operation. Predictive analytics specifically uses data, statistical formulas and machine learning methods to forecast the future trends and human behavior using past information. In the hotel management, analytics enables organizations to make strategic decisions based on data that has been gathered in large quantities by analysing the data in sources like booking systems, customer feedbacks, and market trends. Analytics in hospitality introduces a more active approach in the field of management-the transition to active operations to predictive planning. Analytics help hotels optimize pricing strategies, improve the experiences of their guests, and increase operational efficiency (Anubala, 2023; Kim et al., 2024). In addition, analytics are used to determine the risk factors, anticipate the maintenance requirements, and economize resources, assisting in the reduction of costs and the enhancement of service quality (Chua et al., 2022)

7.1 Cross Platform Real-time Data Integration.

In the modern globalized business ecosystem, buyers interact with the brand in multiple digital platforms, including e-commerce web pages, social networks, and mobile apps, generating tremendous data streams of dynamic information. The integration of real-time data helps organizations to bring together this data into a single analytical platform where it can be accessed at any time and decision making can be made immediately. Jae and Hwa, (2025) other researchers suggest that the integration of real time data enables switching between the traditional approach of analysis of the static data, and the always-adaptive approach to marketing. Linking digital points of contact with each other, the companies will be able to trace customer interactions in real-time and make marketing campaigns more responsive and personalized to customer dynamics. This interconnectivity enables marketers to modify campaign on real-time depending on customer activity, thus improving interactivity and response. The authors note that big data analytics together with machine learning models allows real-time detection of patterns and this allows businesses to predict and respond to customer needs almost immediately. To the same effect, Anubala (2023) emphasizes that real-time data integration among systems involved in the hospitality industry, like reservation systems, guest management systems, and Internet of Things (IoT)-controlled room controls have changed the manner in which hotels are being run. This broad perspective is not only making the company more responsive to the changes in the market environment, but also offers 360-degree perspective on the customer behavior and the performance of the operations. Nevertheless, according to both studies, the solution to successful real-time integration is a strong technological infrastructure and sophisticated analytical skills to handle and process continuous data streams in real-time (Jae and Hwa, 2025; Anubala, 2023). This is because, in short, real-time data fusion between platforms is the foundation of data-driven decision-making in digital marketing and in hospitality. It fills the disjointed data sources and helps organizations to act on insights in real-time, dynamically adjust strategies and maintain competitive advantage in unstable environments.

7.2 Guest Profiling and Campaign Optimization.

One of the most influential applications of data analytics in hospitality management, as well as digital marketing, is predictive guest profiling. It is the application of predictive models and machine learning algorithms to evaluate historical guest data including booking trends, spending patterns, preferences, and feedback in order to predict future demands and tailor marketing interactions. Through the knowledge about guests on a personal level, organizations will be able to develop more effective and specific marketing campaigns that will enhance customer satisfaction and raise the conversion rates. Anubala (2023) claims that predictive analytics can help the hotel to shift to proactive guest engagement rather than reactive. With the processing of high amounts of historical and behavioral data, hotels will be able to distinguish distinct groups of guests and make more accurate predictions about their future preferences. This feature enables hotel managers to create the most personalized offers, i.e. special room packages, loyalty, or even dynamic pricing, based on the specific guest group. In addition, predictive profiling helps to allocate the resources effectively, so marketing budgets and promotional activities are directed at the high-value customer segments with the high potential to be positively responsive to targeted campaigns. Within the framework of digital marketing Jae and Hwa, (2025) highlight that predictive analytics is also instrumental when it comes to maximizing marketing campaigns through its ability to offer real-time information on consumer behaviour in a variety of platforms. The combination of big data analytics and predictive modeling will enable the marketers to meet the needs of a customer by providing them with relevant and timely content. The research finds that the application of data-driven and predictive models of marketing is capable of enhancing customer interaction by 48.57 per cent and the rates of conversion by 132 per cent in comparison to traditional models. This is enhanced by the fact that the audience targeting and message personalization through machine learning algorithms that process user interaction data across digital touchpoints is constantly refined (Rosario and Dias, 2023; Alsayat,2023). Feedback loops also form part of predictive campaign optimization, which determine the effectiveness of the current marketing work. Since predictive models analyze real-time performance data to train, the campaign parameters that dynamically adjust to optimize engagement and ROI include: the message timing, choice of channel and promotional content. The above capability can be applied in the hospitality industry as part of predictive loyalty management where a hotel recognizes at-risk guests and uses retention campaigns to improve customer satisfaction and avoid churn (Bano et al., 2025; Anubala, 2023). The two concepts, predictive guest profiling and campaign optimization, are the pillars of the current, data-driven customer engagement approaches. They do not only help organizations to understand past behavior but predict future behavior as well thus improving personalization and optimizing marketing efficiency and enhancing long-term customer relationships. These analytics-based practices enable marketers and hoteliers to convert raw data into usable intelligence as (Anubala, 2023 ; Jae and Hwa, 2025) find that the practices will reshape the relationship between businesses and their customers and enable their retention.

8. HOSPITALITY MARKETING TECHNOLOGY ISSUES.

The prevalence of the Internet has changed the consumer purchasing pattern to a considerable extent, especially in the tourism sector, during which the intangible nature of the product makes customers dependent on the digital source of information (Jaremen, 2016; Ferreira et al., 2016). The main issue is that the trust does not have a substantial impact on the utilization of the Internet as a means of booking products online as perceived risks, including data privacy and security concerns, are also a significant barrier (Thakur and Srivastava, 2014). Given that age and income levels significantly influence the adoption of e-commerce in accommodation services, educational level does not have a strong connection (Lubis and Rahmiati, 2019). Universal adoption is also complicated by the digital divide, especially in not so developed or rural regions, and operational barriers, like the staff training and digital infrastructure (Carvalho and Ivanov, 2023; Sousa et al., 2024). The perceived risk has a negative impact on the usage intention, namely, the fear of personal data being misused on the Internet (Thakur and Srivastava, 2014). The change rate may also be faster than the ability of the hospitality providers, resulting in stagnation when managing change (Sousa et al., 2024).

8.1 Hospitality Marketing Technology Opportunities.

These barriers notwithstanding, there exist huge opportunities. Hospitality businesses can now expand their market presence internationally and provide their services 24 hours a day because the Internet has expanded (Turban et al., 2017; Carvalho and Ivanov, 2023). Online transparency and value comparison of prices have benefits to consumers and organizations alike, and strategic advantages to those who can directly control digital pricing and bundles. Online reviews and peer recommendations can be described as social influence as they are a strong force in the digital booking adoption, offering a significant marketing power to the firm successfully managing their online reputation (de Moura et al., 2017). The use of mobile gadgets (as the main web access points) allows engaging in apps and responsive interface interactions, which provide new chances to interact in the form of marketing and delivering services in real-time (Sousa et al., 2024). E-commerce has demonstrated a very strong growth in hospitality, with the rise in trends in online hotel reservations and travel purchases showing that the potential of generating high revenues exists to businesses that are able to effectively adopt technology refer Table 4.

Table 4. Challenges And Opportunities in Hospitality Marketing Technology

Aspect	Details	Key Points
Challenges	Digital transition changing traditional marketing	Trust issues and concerns about data security impact online bookings
	Demographic factors affect adoption (age, income, less so education)	Digital divide and infrastructure hurdles limit universal adoption
	Perceived risks reduce technology use	Rapid tech changes may outpace organizational adaptability
Opportunities	Global reach and 24/7 availability through digital platforms	Price transparency and value comparison empower consumers and competitive differentiation
	Social influence via online reviews drives bookings	Mobile devices expand channels for engagement and real-time marketing
	E-commerce growth represents strong revenue potential	Integration of UTAUT2 framework aids understanding adoption behavior and influences
Implications	Build consumer trust via secure, transparent transactions	Expand research and data diversity for inclusive tech adoption
	Emphasize social proof and reputation management	Address barriers for equitable technology access and usage

Source: Created by authors based on secondary data

8.2 Theoretical and Practical Implications.

UTAUT2 is confirmed as a well-rounded concept to understand adoption behaviors due to its ability to include such constructs as social influence, price value, perceived risk, and trust (Venkatesh et al., 2012). It is also important to build consumer trust by using clear communications, safe transactions, and reputation-building signals to reap the most out of digital marketing (Lu et al., 2009; Zhou, 2011; de Moura et al., 2017). It is advisable that researchers and practitioners should widen datasets and research settings to make sure that technological progress is not exclusive and accommodates every sector of the hospitality market (Zhou, 2011).

8.3 Ethical and Operational Principles in Hospitality Marketing technology.

The key idea in hospitality marketing is responsible AI and data governance, as the industry is becoming more and more reliant on AI-based personalization and automation. There are international data protection laws, including GDPR in Europe and CCPA in California, that hotels need to adhere to and be transparent about the collection and use of guest information and consider privacy-by-design (Baburao et al, 2026). Strong AI regulation reduces the threat of prejudice, discrimination, and inaccuracy in automated decisions, ensuring the privacy of guests and preserving trust

(Baburao et al., 2026). The challenge of automation versus authenticity by human beings is a challenge. Although artificial intelligence can be successfully applied to carrying out repetitive and low-complexity tasks, personalized guest experiences cannot be achieved without authentic human interaction, as they should help sustain brand reputation. The accountability of AI-driven systems and human-in-the-loop processes increases justice and trust in the guests (Jesus Jerez-Jerez et al., 2025).

9. CRITICAL PERSPECTIVES AND CHALLENGES OF DIGITAL TECHNOLOGY ADOPTION IN HOSPITALITY

Although the literature mostly puts more importance on the positive aspects of digital transformation in hospitality, there is an increasing amount of research that stresses the necessity of more critical and balanced evaluation. Data privacy, algorithmic bias, and surveillance have become especially popular in ethical issues, especially due to the high dependency on AI-driven personalization and automation by relying on guest data (Carvalho and Ivanov, 2024; Baburao et al., 2026). Research indicates that a lack of transparency in the way consumers use the data may lead to the decrease of consumer confidence rating the efficiency of digital marketing technologies in the long-term perspective.

On top of this, displacement of workforce is also a major issue. Growing popularity of AI chatbots, service robots, automated booking systems and so on has brought up concerns about job security, deskilling, and the evolving position of human labor in hospitality. It was empirically shown that although automation can be more effective in terms of operational efficiency, it can also raise the level of employee resistance and stress unless the process of reskilling is adopted along with the adoption of technology (Gürsoy et al., 2023; Molina-Castillo et al., 2023).

Digital divide also makes it difficult to adopt advanced technologies. The differences in infrastructure, digital literacy, and access to capital level the playing field of large hotel chains and SMEs, as well as developed and developing markets. Such inequalities restrict the generality of digital innovation approaches and emphasize taking frameworks of adoption that are context-specific (Zakić et al., 2022; Sousa et al., 2024).

10. CONCLUSION

This chapter, through the application of the concept of TAM, UTAUT2, and the Diffusion of Innovations framework, gives a rigorous explanation of consumer and organizational adoption of new technologies based on the theoretical framework. The models facilitate the understanding of the forces behind the digital transformation and explain why some innovations, like AI-based personalization, social commerce, and IoT ecosystems, are more quickly applied to hospitality marketing. This chapter also acknowledges regional and industry-specific disparities in digital transformation, emphasizing that adoption trajectories differ between developed and developing markets and between large hotel chains and SMEs. Recognizing these contextual differences improves the applicability of digital adoption frameworks and ensures a more inclusive understanding of hospitality innovation. The hospitality industry is evolving at a rapid pace with the implementation of new technologies such as artificial intelligence, internet of things, cloud computing, and virtual spaces. Such innovations are revolutionizing service provision, selling and effectiveness in the business processes that enable the provision of customized experiences to customers, instantaneous communication, and sustainability of business activities. This digital era demands technological usage coupled with the strategic restructuring that will create balance between productivity and service to the human being. These issues have not faded away and they are grappling with cybersecurity threats, privacy of information and the digital divide to offer equal opportunities to technology. The theme of future research should be the use of AI responsibly, enhanced transparency and ethical concerns during AI automation, and the exploration of the impact of immersive technologies like the Metaverse on customer interaction. The practical work should be oriented on the workforce training, the effective integration of technologies, and the integration of the automation and the valid human intercourse to avoid the loss of the brand trust and emotional connection. The leaders in the hospitality industry are challenged to be creative with responsibility and take advantage of digital tools to produce growth and competitive advantage in upholding ethical, sustainable, and inclusive practices. The most highlighted approaches will be innovation and social responsibility to offer the industry with better services that will not only meet the ever-evolving demands of the consumers, but also long-term success in a digitally connected world. This will ensure profitability and also quality of long-term hospitality services.

REFERENCES

Alsayat, A. (2023). Customer decision-making analysis based on big social data using machine learning: A case study of hotels in Mecca. *Neural Computing & Applications*, *35*(6), 4701–4722. DOI: 10.1007/s00521-022-07992-x

Anubala, R. (2023). The future of hospitality: Predictive analytics in hotel management. [IJMRP]. *International Journal for Multidimensional Research Perspectives*, *1*(3), 38–47.

Baburao, C., Gangadhara, R. R. S., Talukder, M. B., Sheela, P., & Ouariach, F. Z. (2026). AI-Powered Smart Revenue Management in Hospitality: Integrating Innovation, Ethics, and Practical Strategies. In *Smart Operations and Enhancing Guest Experience in the Hospitality Industry* (pp. 219-240). IGI Global Scientific Publishing.https://doi.org/DOI: 10.4018/979-8-3373-2145-5.ch008

Bano, R., Azim, F., Mahmood, Z., Sanaullah, A., & Ali, O. (2025). The Role of Artificial Intelligence in Personalized Marketing: Enhancing Customer Experience, Predictive Targeting, and Brand Engagement. *The Critical Review of Social Sciences Studies*, *3*(2), 50–65. DOI: 10.59075/d94kvf44

Bilgihan, A., & Ricci, P. (2023). The new era of hotel marketing: Integrating cutting-edge technologies with core marketing principles. *Journal of Hospitality and Tourism Technology*, *15*(1), 123–137. DOI: 10.1108/JHTT-04-2023-0095

Buhalis, D., O'Connor, P., & Leung, R. (2025). Smart hospitality: From smart cities and smart tourism towards agile business ecosystems in networked destinations. *International Journal of Contemporary Hospitality Management*, *35*(1), 369–393. DOI: 10.1108/IJCHM-04-2022-0497

Bulchand-Gidumal, J., Secin, E., O'Connor, P., & Buhalis, D. (2024). Artificial intelligence's impact on hospitality and tourism marketing: Exploring key themes and addressing challenges. *Current Issues in Tourism*, *27*, 1–18. DOI: 10.1080/13683500.2023.2229480

. Calvillo, M. (2023). *How will AI like ChatGPT change the restaurant industry? Hospitality technology*.

Carvalho, I., & Ivanov, S. (2023). ChatGPT for tourism: Applications, benefits and risks. *Tourism Review*, *79*(2), 290–303. DOI: 10.1108/TR-02-2023-0088

Chakraborty, U., & Biswal, S. K. (2024). Is ChatGPT a Responsible Communication: A Study on the Credibility and Adoption of Conversational Artificial Intelligence. *Journal of Promotion Management*, *30*(6), 929–958. DOI: 10.1080/10496491.2024.2332987

Chen, S., Han, X., Bilgihan, A., & Okumus, F. (2021). Customer engagement research in hospitality and tourism: A systematic review. *Journal of Hospitality Marketing & Management, 30*(7), 871–904. DOI: 10.1080/19368623.2021.1903644

Chua, B. L., Al-Ansi, A., Kim, S., Wong, A. K. F., & Han, H. (2022). Examining airline employees' work-related stress and coping strategies during the global tourism crisis. *International Journal of Contemporary Hospitality Management, 34*(10), 3715–3742. DOI: 10.1108/IJCHM-09-2021-1085

Dang, T. D., & Nguyen, M. T. (2023). Systematic review and research agenda for the tourism and hospitality sector: Co-creation of customer value in the digital age. *Future Business Journal, 9*(1), 94. DOI: 10.1186/s43093-023-00274-5

de Moura, A. C., de Sevilha Gosling, M., Christino, J. M. M., & Macedo, S. B. (2017). Acceptance and use of technology for the choice of touristic destina-tions by persons of the third age: A study using UTAUT2. *Revista Brasileira de Pesquisa em Turismo, 11*(2), 239. DOI: 10.7784/rbtur.v11i2.1277

Ferhataj, A., & Memaj, F. (2025). AI-DRIVEN PERSONALIZATION IN TOURISM: EXPLORING TOURIST BEHAVIOR, ETHICAL CONCERNS, WORKFORCE TRANSFORMATION, AND SKILL INTEGRATION. tr.iksadkongre.com/bingol

Ferreira, J. R., Ferreira, L. V. F., & Paiva Neto, A. (2016). Analysis of the official websites of tourism destinations classified socioculturally by the report the economist inteligence unit limited. *Turismo: Visão e Ação, 18*(3), 557–583.

Gretzel, U. (2022). The Smart DMO: A new step in the digital transformation of destination management organizations. *European Journal of Tourism Research, 30*, 3002. DOI: 10.54055/ejtr.v30i.2589

Gursoy, D., Li, Y., & Song, H. (2023). ChatGPT and the hospitality and tourism industry: An overview of current trends and future research directions. *Journal of Hospitality Marketing & Management, 32*(5), 579–592. DOI: 10.1080/19368623.2023.2211993

Jae, Y. I., & Hwa, P. I. (2025). Personalized Digital Marketing Strategies: A Data-Driven Approach Using Marketing Analytics. *Journal of Management and Informatics, 4*(1), 668–686. DOI: 10.51903/jmi.v4i1.149

Jaremen, D. E. (2016). Advantages from ICT usage in Hotel Industry. *Czech Journal of Social Sciences Business and Economics, 5*(3), 6–18.

Jesus Jerez-Jerez, M., Sevilla-Sevilla, C., & Aguiar-Castillo, L. (Eds.). (2025). *The Role of Artificial Intelligence in the Tourism and Hospitality Sector* (1st ed.). Routledge., DOI: 10.4324/9781003545125

Jonathan, J. (2025). THE TRANSFORMATION OF THE HOSPITALITY INDUSTRY IN FACING THE DIGITAL TECHNOLOGY ERA: OPPORTUNITIES, CHALLENGES, AND INNOVATIONS. [Artificial Intelligence Research and Applied Learning]. *AIRA*, *4*(2), 79–95. DOI: 10.1234/aira.v4i2.96

Kim, H., So, K. K. F., Shin, S., & Li, J. (2024). Artificial Intelligence in Hospitality and Tourism: Insights From Industry Practices, Research Literature, and Expert Opinions. *Journal of Hospitality & Tourism Research (Washington, D.C.)*, *49*(2), 366–385. DOI: 10.1177/10963480241229235

Lu, Y., Zhou, T., & Wang, B. (2009). Exploring Chinese users' acceptance of instant messaging using the theory of planned behavior, the technology acceptance model, and the flow theory. *Computers in Human Behavior*, *25*(1), 29–39. DOI: 10.1016/j.chb.2008.06.002

Mohammad, A. A. A., Elshaer, I. A., Azazz, A. M. S., Kooli, C., Algezawy, M., & Fayyad, S. (2024). The Influence of Social Commerce Dynamics on Sustainable Hotel Brand Image, Customer Engagement, and Booking Intentions. *Sustainability*, *16*(14), 6050. DOI: 10.3390/su16146050

Molina-Castillo, F. J., Meroño-Cerdán, A. L., Lopez-Nicolas, C., & Fernandez-Espinar, L. (2023). Innovation and technology in hospitality sector: Outcome and performance. *Businesses*, *3*(1), 198–219. DOI: 10.3390/businesses3010014

Mondal, S., Das, S., & Vrana, V. G. (2023). How to bell the cat? A theoretical review of generative artificial intelligence towards digital disruption in all walks of life. *Technologies*, *11*(2), 44. DOI: 10.3390/technologies11020044

Neuhofer, B., Buhalis, D., & Ladkin, A. (2014). A typology of technology-enhanced tourism experiences. *International Journal of Tourism Research*, *16*(4), 340–350. DOI: 10.1002/jtr.1958

Prdić, N., Gajić, T., & Stepanov, S. (2025). WHOLESALE MARKETS AS SUPPLY CHANNELS FOR GREEN MARKETS AND THEIR IMPACT ON RURAL DEVELOPMENT IN SERBIA. *Ekonomika Poljoprivrede*, *72*(1), 63–87. DOI: 10.59267/ekoPolj250163P

Rosário, A. T., & Cruz, R. N. (2023). Data-Driven Decision-Making in Marketing. 10.20944/preprints202501.0354.v1

Samala, N., Katkam, B. S., Bellamkonda, R. S., & Rodriguez, R. V. (2022). Impact of AI and Robotics in the Tourism Sector: A Critical Insight. *Journal of Tourism Futures*, *8*, 73–87. DOI: 10.1108/JTF-07-2019-0065

Sousa, N., Alén, E., Losada, N., & Melo, M. (2024). Virtual reality in tourism promotion: A research agenda based on a bibliometric approach. *Journal of Quality Assurance in Hospitality & Tourism*, *25*(2), 313–342. DOI: 10.1080/1528008X.2022.2112807

Thakur, R., & Srivastava, M. (2014). Adoption readiness, personal innovativeness, perceived risk and usage intention across customer groups for mobile payment services in India. *Internet Research*, *24*(3), 369–392. DOI: 10.1108/IntR-12-2012-0244

Turban, E., Outland, J., King, D., Lee, J. K., Liang, T. P., & Turban, D. C. (2017). *Electronic commerce 2018: a managerial and social networks perspective*. Springer. https://econpapers.repec.org/scripts/redir.pf?u=https%3A%2F%2Fdoi.org%2F10.1007%252F978-3-319-58715-8;h=repec:spr:sptbec:978-3-319-58715-8

Venkatesh, V., Thong, J. Y., & Xu, X. (2012). Consumer acceptance and use of information technology: Extending the unified theory of acceptance and use of technology. *Management Information Systems Quarterly*, •••, 157–178. DOI: 10.2307/41410412

Zakić, N., Ćurčić, N., & Leković, K. (2022). Hospitality digital marketing and technology transformation challenges. *International Journal of Qualitative Research*, *16*(4), 1133–1148. DOI: 10.24874/IJQR16.04-12

Zhou, T. (2011). Understanding mobile Internet continuance usage from the perspectives of UTAUT and flow. *Information Development*, *27*(3), 207–218. DOI: 10.1177/0266666911414596

KEY TERMS AND DEFINITIONS

Artificial Intelligence (AI) in Hospitality: AI refers to computer systems and algorithms capable of simulating human intelligence to perform tasks such as chat-based customer service, predictive personalization, and automated content creation. In hospitality, AI enhances customer interaction, operational efficiency, and revenue management.

Digital Transformation (in Hospitality): The process of integrating advanced technologies such as Artificial Intelligence (AI), the Internet of Things (IoT), cloud computing, and automation into hotel operations and marketing to improve guest personalization, real-time decision-making, operational efficiency, and sustainability.

Internet of Things (IoT): A network of interconnected devices embedded with sensors and software that collect and exchange data. In hotels, IoT supports smart service delivery, energy management, and personalized guest environments (e.g., lighting, temperature, and entertainment controls).

Predictive Analytics: A data-driven approach using machine learning and statistical algorithms to analyze past and real-time data to predict future guest behaviors, preferences, and market trends. It enables personalized marketing, optimized pricing, and improved customer retention in the hospitality industry.

Social Commerce: The integration of social media and e-commerce that allows hotels to sell directly through social platforms like Instagram, Facebook, and TikTok. It enhances direct booking opportunities, builds brand engagement, and strengthens relationships through user-generated content and influencer marketing.

Chapter 4
Beyond the Check-In: Future Innovations Reshaping Hospitality Marketing Technology

Michael Nii Laryeafio
http://orcid.org/0000-0003-1257-8398
Arden University, UK

Samuel Ayertey
Arden University, UK

Ebimoboere Koroye
http://orcid.org/0009-0007-5086-4156
Arden University, UK

John Garrick
Arden University, UK

Jennifer Irabor
Arden University, UK

ABSTRACT

This chapter explores the transformative impact of emerging technologies on hospitality marketing, tracing the sectors evolution from traditional, localised promotion to a dynamic, data driven and immersive ecosystem. It examines how innovations such as artificial intelligence, augmented l reality, blockchain and social media storytelling are reshaping guest engagement, brand reputation and operational efficiency. The discussion highlights the shift from mass messaging to personalised, predictive and adaptive marketing, emphasizing the importance of real time analytics, sentiment tracking and dynamic pricing. Through global case studies including Marriot's use of VR and AL, Accor's blockchain based loyalty

DOI: 10.4018/979-8-3373-6741-5.ch004

programmes, among others, the chapter illustrates how technology adoption is tailored to local contexts while reflecting global trends. The chapter concludes by proposing s strategic framework for responsible technology adoption, stressing the need for digital maturity, staff training, cross functional integration, and alignment with brand identity and guest expectations.

INTRODUCTION

The hospitality sector has relied on marketing as a bridge among service providers and guest, but the way that bridge is built has changed intensely over the period. In recent times, marketing in hospitality was simple and often localised. Again, word of mouth suggestions, printed brochures, and newspapers listings were the main tools for reaching potential consumers. Hotels and restaurants depended on the image, location, and the promise of consistent service to coheres retention of visitors (Chappell and Creissels, 2019). As travel expanded and competition grew, the sector begun to adopt newer technique of promotion, from glossy travel magazines to radio jingles and television advertisements. The late 20th century marked the beginning of a major revolution with the introduction of technology into hospitality marketing. The increase in online and internet travel agencies (OTA's) changed the entirety of the rules. Customers can compare their current prices, reading to reviews and making instant bookings. The providers of hospitality can also increase visibility but also tougher competitions and the pressures that comes along with pricing. The Customer Relationship Management (CRM) systems followed, enabling businesses to track guests' preferences and began providing targeted marketing messages. Thus, what started as a continuous technological alteration quickly hastened into a new way of thinking about how hotels, restaurants, and travel companies communicated with their audience.

The swift digital transformation restructured not only how businesses marketed themselves but how guest hospitality as well as the marketing confined to the pre-booking stage. Technology began inducing every step of the guest journey; from the primary search for accommodation, via booking and check-in, to stay by itself and post-visit follow-up. Mobile application offered convenience by allowing guests to reserve, check-in, and access services from their phones. The Chatbots and AI-driven assistants offered 24/7 customer service, while data analytics enhanced hotels to predict the demand, tailor offers, and personalisation of experiences at scale (Dinga et al., 2022). Currently, marketing has become about broadcasting a message and more about curating a relationship, while anticipating what a guest wanted before they request for it. The most striking changes, however, has been the increase in the presence of social media as the backbone of hospitality marketing. The Platforms such as YouTube, TikTok, Instagram, and Facebook have become essential spaces where travellers discover destination, sharing experiences and impacting others. The singles viral video or positive review can influence millions of potential customers, carrying weight than conventionally publicising as ever could. According to Ghosh and Chatterjee, (2025), user-generated content with relation to the photos, stories, and reviews posted by the customers themselves, which has made them trustworthy in form of marketing that no company can fully control, but every organisation must be incorporate into its systems. Partnering with influencers, live-streamed events, and interactive promotions have pushed hospitality brands to become innovative, transparent and responsive. However, the social media restructured the nature of brand-consumer interaction in terms of hospitality. The current hospitality marketing sits at the juncture of technology, expectations of customers and intense rivalry. While the tools available to businesses have grown more sophisticated, the underlying goal remains the same: to the connection with guests in ways that are timely, relevant, and evocative.

This chapter is focused on discussing the challenges such (1) system integration, privacy concerns and the risks of influencer marketing. (2) it explores cutting edge technologies including AI, AR, blockchain and their application in hospitality. (3) it examines the use of real time analytics, and dynamic pricing to enhance guest experience. (4) it proposes models for assessing digital maturity, staff training, integration and aligning technology with brand and guest expectations. (5) addresses data protection, algorithmic bias, transparency, consent and digital inequality. (6) summarises key findings and offers recommendations for sustainable, ethical and inclusive technology adoption in hospitality marketing.

CUSTOMER RELATIONSHIP MANAGEMENT (CRM) SYSTEMS, MOBILE APPS, AND INFLUENCER MARKETING

CRM techniques are now a keystone of hospitality marketing. They grant permission to hotels, resorts, and restaurants for collecting information on guest preferences, booking habits, and pattern of spending. Organisations can divide customers, send personalised offers and create loyalty programs that feel more tailored than generic promotions. For instance, a recurrent business traveller could receive discounted weekday rates, while a family may be offered seasonal package deals as reiterated by Hosmani and Lalitha, (2025). The alteration towards information driven engagement has encouraged brands to maintain ongoing relationships with guests well beyond a single stay. Mobile apps have included another layer of accessibility and engagement. Lee et al., (2025) stated that most hotels now provide branded applications where customers can check in, unlock their rooms with digital key, order room service, or book amenities which includes spa treatment on their personal phones or laptops. These applications extend the guest experience and provide marketing groups with a communication channel which is direct. However, influencer marketing has developed as a powerful way to connect with audience, especially younger travellers. In showcasing experience through trusted voices on platforms like Instagram and Facebook, hospitality reputation can build aspirational value and get potential customers who might not respond to traditional promotions as viewed by Kandampully and Solnet, (2024).

Early CRM and digital advertising systems in hospitality

In the early stages of CRM systems and platforms for digital marketing, hospitality marketing saw a turning point by the move away from mass communication to a more personalised engagement. CRM in the initial stages within the hospitality was limited to a mere record keeping, where guest preferences are tracked manually by the hotels to motivate guest to visit often (Sota *et al.*, 2019). By the early 2000s, however, CRM in hospitality changed into a more structured database systems that helps segments guests by their booking history, demographics and spending patterns. Freed (2021) expressed that this approach allowed management of hotels to deliver a good, tailored services, targeted promotions, loyalty programs and offering the basis for modern personalised marketing.

Digital systems of advertisements came alongside CRM development, specifically with the rise of hotel websites and online travel agencies. Prior digital campaigns highly focused on email marketing, banner ads, and search engine optimisation, and this helped hotels with international visibility at relatively little or no cost compared to traditional advertising (Shokohyar *et al.*, 2017). The addition and integration of effective CRM system with platforms that are digital helped hotels to track customer behaviour online, and measure campaign performance (Nguyen et al., 2024). This combination between the CRM and digital advertising has effectively created a good feedback look, thus guests' data informed advertising approach, while digital campaigns brought about new data to boost CRM systems.

Notably, the beginning of 2004 saw the emergence of data-driven CRM systems that was employed by hotels to manage guest relationship and move beyond simple booking management to effectively predict analytics and personalised communication. Early adopters understood that long-term loyalty was just as important to digital advertising as exposure (Rafiki *et al.*, 2019). For instance, hotels started incorporating CRM analytics into email advertisements, providing family packages to regular leisure visitors or discounts to frequent business travellers (Jeyakumar, 2025).

In conclusion, early digital advertising and CRM systems in the hospitality industry changed marketing from reactive promotion to proactive relationship-building. These developments laid the foundation for the sophisticated, AI-powered personalisation and omnichannel marketing techniques of today.

THE RISE OF MOBILE APPS AND SOCIAL MEDIA IN MARKETING

The widespread adoption of smartphones has improved mobile applications into indispensable marketing instruments, granting businesses direct access to consumers through personalised notifications, loyalty programmes, and integrated e-commerce solutions. Contemporary mobile marketing strategies prioritise user experience, convenience, and real-time interaction, making apps critical for customer retention and brand visibility (Ra *et al.*, 2019).

At the same time, social media platforms have transformed marketing communication, shifting from traditional one-way advertising to interactive, community-driven engagement. Platforms such as Facebook, Instagram, TikTok, and LinkedIn enable brands to foster dialogue, build trust, and harness user-generated content to amplify reach. Social media has evolved from a novelty into a strategic necessity, allowing businesses to target niche audiences with precision and evaluate campaign performance through advanced analytics (Lukanova and Ilieva, 2019).

The interplay between mobile apps and social media is particularly impactful. Social platforms drive traffic to apps, while apps deliver immersive brand experiences beyond the social feed. This integration underpins omnichannel marketing strategies, ensuring consistent messaging across touchpoints and optimizing return on investment. Furthermore, the dynamic nature of social media where algorithms, trends, and consumer behaviours shift rapidly requires marketers to remain agile. Brands that quickly embrace innovations such as short-form video and AI-driven personalisation secure a competitive edge. As mobile and social ecosystems continue to evolve, they will remain central to marketing innovation, shaping consumer expectations and redefining brand relationships (Ivanov and Webster, 2019).

Social Media Platforms as Engagement and Feedback Channels

The social media has emerged from just a simple promotional instrument into a space for real-time engagement and feedback from customers. Instagram, TikTok, Facebook, YouTube, TripAdvisor are platforms or channels which grants guest or customers the permission to share their experiences instantaneously, impacting how others recognise a brand (Manoharan and Ashtikar, 2025). A single positive review or viral post can encourage reputation and drive bookings, while negative feedback can cause lasting damage if left unattended. Which has made reputation management and responsiveness as well as reactiveness key to the marketing strategies in hospitality. Nguyen et al., (2021) research revealed that channels of social media are utilised as service platforms, and not mere marketing platforms. Guest is expectant of swift responses to their queries or complaints sent via X (formerly Twitter), Instagram, DMs, and WhatsApp. Hotels and restaurants are increasingly making investment in social media teams to ensure they can engage with guests in real time, answer questions, and resolve issues publicly, which in the long run does not only manage the reputation of the organisation but as well show transparency and customer care. Furthermore, social media has distorted the line between customer service and marketing, putting pressure on hospitality business to be both more proactive and human in their interactions on the internet as stated by Morrison, (2022).

Limitations of Current Tools and Practices

In relation to the current marketing technologies in hospitality, they are faced with significant challenges. CRM systems and applications can be difficult to integrate across various channels and properties. Most hotels and guest houses still depend on outdated legacy systems, which makes it difficult to maintain the profile of the consistent customers (Ramírez et al., 2021). Concealment of information remains a serious concern due to its limits on how far an organisation can go in in the personalisation of experiences, as guests are now aware of how their personal information is collected and used. This tension between accessibility and privacy remains a key challenge for marketers. The influencer marketing and social media also come with risks. Not every influencer promotion leads to quantifiable outcomes, questions around legitimacy are very common. The audience are however, very quick to see overly scripted or hypocritical advertisement, which could harm rather than help a brand's image (Sukach et al., 2021). Similarly, while social media creates opportunities for positives engagement, it brings to bear organisations to public condemnations that can spread quickly. Organisations in the hospitability business which are smaller are deficient in resources to keep pace with the demands, leaving them at a disadvantage compared to larger chains with dedicated digital teams as discovered by Sharma and Singh, (2024). However, while the current tools have restructured the sector, they are far from perfect and require constant adaptability.

EMERGING INNOVATIVE TECHNOLOGY IN HOSPITALITY MARKETING

The hospitality sector has constantly comprised of tools that improve guest experience and enhance the reputation of the organisation. Generally, this involved the implementation of distribution systems or clientele databases, concurrently, it demands utilising advanced digital technologies that transform marketing and service delivery. The latest advancements extend beyond merely convenience as well as the predictability, immersiveness, and personalised of the marketing is becoming evident which presents newer difficulties related to the cost, integration and privacy. The Artificial intelligence (AI), amplified and virtual reality, voice enhanced search, block-chain, the Internet of Things (IoT), and neuromarketing are coming as a key influence in the industry. However, each offers different opportunities for the brands to engage with the clients at various phases of the journey, including consciousness, bookings, on-site experience, and post stay loyalty.

Artificial Intelligence and Machine Learning

The transformative nature of hospitality marketing is crucial when it comes to Artificial Intelligence and Machine Learning. The supremacy lies in the capacity to evaluate huge amount of structured and unstructured information to uncover the trends that human might forgo. Resorts, Hotels and travel organisations currently use AI-driven revenue management applications to modify the pricing in real time (Zade & Sethi, 2024). For instance, Marriott International employs AI to predict the demand and adjust rates over its nationwide portfolio, ensuring competitiveness while safeguarding margins. The dynamic method to pricing has redefined yield management, turning into a marketing instrument as much as an operational aspect. AI brings about enhancement in direct marketing. Again, machine learning models segments audience not just by demographics but by micro-behaviours such as browsing history, booking frequency, or amenity usage. This leads to marketers delivering higher tailored offers, such as wellness packages for health-conscious travellers or weekday discounts for business guests. Furthermore, airlines and hotels have successfully utilised predictive modelling to identify when a guest is most likely to book, then send targeted reminders that move conversions as asserted by Periasamy and Dinesh, (2024). These systems free up human staff for complex requests, whiles ensuring clients feel assisted at any hour. The integration of Artificial integration into loyalty programs is another frontier, machine learning algorithms can suggest rewards that align with a clientele travel style, increasing redemption rates and reinforcing brand loyalty in accordance with the research by Unnava and Aravindakshan, (2021).

Augmented and Virtual Reality

The augmented reality (AR) and virtual reality are transforming how hospitality trademarks present themselves to potential clients. Sinha and Srivastava, (2023) highlighted that virtual reality permits serious storytelling by allowing prospective guests to explore hotel rooms, resort grounds, or even nearby attractions in 360 degrees before making a booking as well as method reduces uncertainty and could adeptly increase conversion rates. Marriott has utilised VR in major cities to showcase destinations, open-handed potential travellers a taste of what their stay could feel like. Augmented reality enables the on-site experience by overlaying digital data on the physical ecology, for instance, customers are at some resorts could utilised AR applications to scan various menus and see dishes displayed in 3D before ordering, the reduction decision fatigue whiles promoting high-margin items as shown by Ozdemir et al., (2023).

Cultural attractions, museums, and hotels which have some forms of heritage are being experimented with the AR- guided tours, adding an interactive layer of story-telling that encourages social sharing (Naseem et al., 2025). The marketing concepts, that's the AR and VR enhances emotional involvement, which they do more than show a room, the conveyance atmosphere and lifestyle. Travel organisations like Thomas Cook have employed the VR campaigns to permit customers to enjoy holiday packages before booking, which enhanced bookings to certain destination by double-digit percentage as viewed by Sharma, (2024). The strength of the AR and VR lies not solely on selling rooms but in selling experiences, making them invaluable tools in a market where differentiation is usually subtle.

Voice Search and Smart Assistance

With regards to the increase in the voice technology in restructure on how travellers search and interact with hospitality reputation. Over 30% of all the online searches are now conducted through voice, a pattern driven by smart devices such as Amazon Alexa, Google Assistant and Apple's Siri. For hospitality marketers, which implies reconsidering search engine and optimisation (SEO). According to Pentina et al., (2018) queries like best boutique hotel near Times Square with free breakfast inclusion devises are longer and more convention than typed searches, requiring content strategies are latter strategies that align with natural speech patterns. However, within hotels and resorts, smart assistants have become parts of the clientele experience itself.

The Amazon Echo devices was first installed by Wynn Las Vegas was a major hotel's guest rooms, which allows voice control over lighting, temperature, and entertainment. These support service also upsell services by suggesting in-house dining options, spa treatments, or city tours in response to guest inquiries as stated by Moran et al., (2020). The positioning offered as helpful suggestions rather than intrusive advertisement, voice technology creates a more organic marketing opportunity. The implication of voice extends beyond the hotel walls, whiles travellers asked their devices at home. Optimisation of voices are not just technical adjustment but a strategic imperious for hospitality marketers aiming to reach customers at the earliest stage of the decision-making process.

Block-Chain and Loyalty Programs

Block-chain is usually linked with cryptocurrencies, but its impact for hospitality marketing go much further. The technology provided a decentralisation and transparency in ways to record transactions, which can revolutionise loyalty programs (Leung et al., 2022). Conventional schemes usually frustrate customers with impervious rules, expired points and limited redemption alternatives. The Block-chain based loyalty systems resolve these challenges by creating a well-protected, transferrable, and easily and redeemable tokens. For instance, the Singapore Airlines launched a block-chain based loyalty wallet, KrisPay, allowing members to instantaneously convert air miles into spendable tokens usable at partner merchants as viewed by Manoharan and Ashtikar, (2025). In hospitality, a parallel concept would let guests earn points from a hotel stay and spend them at partner restaurants, airlines, or entertainment venues. This developed into a networked ecosystem that increased the valuation of participation, consolidation of customer retention. Block-chain also delved into marketing difficulties around trust and authenticity, as smart contract can automate promotions, ensuring discounts are utilised for immediate conditions are met, leading to the reduction of disputes and reinforcing credibility (Jiang and Wen, 2020). Furthermore, this could help fight swindle online bookings, protecting both the organisation and the customer. For marketing teams, the trust that block-chain fosters as valuable as the technical efficiency it provided.

Internet of Things (IoT)

The Internet of Things (IoT) is revolving hotels into smart ecology where devices communicate seamlessly to personalise and enhance the guest experience. The market strategies are fed into and enhance operational efficiency and effectiveness by collecting relevant data by appliances connected such as sensors, and thermostats as stated by Kruesi and Remy, (2024). The IoT can monitor whether guest prefer rooms cooler or warmer and usage of insight to transfer tailored offers, such as promotions for the spa services or wellness packages. Resorts and Hotels such as Marriott and The Wynn have installed IoT enabled guest rooms, where guests can control lighting, curtains and room temperature through the mobile application or voice commands. However, this convenience, helps the system to develop opportunities for personalised marketing. When a customer frequently uses the gym, the hotel could proactively promote fitness-focused amenities or wellness retreats (Hassan, 2023). Ultimately, if a guest orders late-night snacks often, the application might send a personalised discount for midnight dining. This enables real-time, context awareness marketing, consequently, imagine a client walking past the resort or hotel's spa; sensors could trigger a push notification offering a limited-time discount. The subtle, situational prompts combine service with marketing, encouraging spending without feeling intrusive. The embedding marketing into the ecology itself, IoT shifts hospitality marketing from being reactive to being predictive and experiential as viewed by Al-Issa and Thanasi, (2024).

Neuro-Marketing and Biometrics

These represents the top-notch innovations in the marketing field. The Neuro-marketing relates to the application of neuroscience to study how consumers react to marketing stimuli, with the utilisation of tools like eye-tracking, facial recognition, and brainwave monitoring to uncover subconscious preferences as purported by Cabanillas et al., (2025) The reputation of hospitality brands can use the information to refine website layouts, designing with respect to promotions, and even lobby environment to increase participation and emotional response. For instance, analyses of images on the hotel website that draws attention to in a longer period can inform which amenities to feature most prominently. The biometric technology is common in the hospitality industry for security purposes, and check-ins (Chan-Olmsted and Kim, 2022). The facial and fingerprint recognition systems streamline arrival, reduction of friction and enhancing the first impression.

However, a wellness hotel or resort might incorporate biometric tracking to suggest personalised spa treatment or dietary plans. In addition, luxurious hotels can also implement the usage of biometric data to tailored ambient features like lighting or music to guest's mood. With the utilisation of these technology leads to the ethical issue of informed consent and privacy. Guests or clients may be reluctant to share their biometric information or neurological data to a third party if they are not certain of a clearer protecting mechanisms and benefits are well communicated. For hospitality marketers, the difficulty lies in balancing creativity with transparency. Chappell and Creissels, (2019) reiterated that in terms of the applying responsible, neuro-marketing and biometrics provided an unparalleled view into the behaviour of the client, that gives room for grands to design experiences and promotions that resonate on both the logical and sentimental level.

RISK AND ETHICAL CHALLENGES IN HOSPITALITY MARKETING TECHNOLOGY

The hospitality sector's rapid adoption of mobile applications and social media as core marketing tools has introduced significant ethical and operational risks. A primary concern is data privacy. Hotels and travel companies increasingly collect sensitive customer information, such as location, preferences, and payment details, through mobile platforms. Breaches or misuse of this data can severely undermine consumer trust and damage brand reputation (Smith, 2023). Ethical marketing therefore requires transparent data practices and robust cybersecurity safeguards.

Algorithmic targeting and personalization present another challenge. While social media enables highly tailored advertising, excessive personalization can perpetuate biases and exclude certain consumer groups, compromising fairness and inclusivity (Chen & Kozak, 2024). Responsible strategies must balance relevance with equity. Influencer marketing also raises transparency issues. Many influencers promote hospitality brands without clearly disclosing paid partnerships, which can mislead consumers and violate advertising standards (Johnson, 2022). Ensuring compliance with disclosure regulations is essential for maintaining credibility.

Sustainability claims add further complexity. Although hospitality companies increasingly market eco-friendly initiatives, accusations of "greenwashing" remain common. Misleading or exaggerated environmental claims can erode trust and undermine genuine sustainability efforts (OECD, 2022). Ethical communication demands verifiable claims and accountability. In summary, hospitality marketing technologies must address challenges related to privacy, transparency, inclusivity, and sustainability. Stronger regulatory frameworks, industry self-regulation, and digital literacy initiatives are critical to aligning technological innovation with ethical responsibility.

PREDICATIVE AND ADAPTIVE MARKETING

The predictive and adaptive marketing denotes the next evolution in how the hospitality industry engage with its customers. The Conventional marketing was repeatedly static through the various campaigns which were planned months in advance, focusing on larger audience with general message as stated by Abraham and Krishnan, (2021). This approach by marketing contrast, again, relies on real time information and advanced algorithms to anticipate customer demands and make flexible strategies on the fly. In contrast, the pushing of a fixed message, organisations must learn from the satisfaction of its clientele base or their behaviour and adjust offers, pricing, and communicating in a personalised and timely manner

(Buhalis et al., 2019). This concept is a strong tool in the hospitality sector, where client experiences are multifaceted, and preferences can change quickly.

Additionally, guest might begin by researching eco-friendly resorts, later shifts focus to wellness amenities and then book based on prices or loyalty advantages. The predictive concept can identify these alterations and adjust marketing outreach accordingly, whether it is showing a special wellness packages or promoting reliability now of decision. The Adaptive marketing is not only about anticipating the need but responding to outside conditions. For instance, a sudden weather change, a huge local event, or viral social media pattern can restructure guest behaviour. The hospitality image that clout predictive analytics and flexible tools can respond instantaneously with key promotions, positioning themselves as agile and customer centric. The adaptive and predictive marketing concept can align hospitality organisations more closely with customers' expectations.

REAL-TIME ANALYTICS

This is the backbone of the adaptive and predictive marketing, other than traditional analytics which usually looks regressive, the real-time analytics makes provision for immediate insights into the behaviour of the client as it takes place. According to Donald and Donald (2024), for resorts and hotels to monitor every activity from the website browsing trends to mobile app usage and on-site service interactions in the moment. When the guest is exploring spa options on the application, the system can lead to a timely discounted code. Ultimately, the relevant advantage of real-time analytics is the capacity to avoid missed opportunities, for instance, if occupancy levels are lower than forecasted on a particular weekend. Castillo-Picón et al., (2023) further stated that the real-time dashboard can inform managers, who can then launch targeted promotions immediately on social media or OTA platforms. In waiting for the following quarter to analyse what cause the underperformance, hotels must consider corrective actions timely.

The effectiveness and efficiency of operations is advantageous for real-time analytics. Delbaere et al., (2021) study revealed that restaurants within hotels mostly measure the point-of-sale information to modify inventory or promote underperformance menu items during delivering of service. Guests whiles ordering more cocktails than expected, the bar could put in place a flash promotion or upsell premium versions in actual time. The petty actions taken by the organisation can go a long way to increase the revenue as well as enhancing the customer experience with the provision of relevant and timely choices (Chan-Olmsted and Kim, 2022). This adaptive concept ensures that marketing remains dynamic instead of locked into long term promotions that could no longer reverberate with the audience.

Sentiment Tracking

The sentiments tracking tend to move the marketing beyond numbers by taking into consideration the opinions and emotions the client express about the image of the organisation. According to Daiya et al., (2024) the use of Natural Language Processing (NLP) in the hospitality business can analyse social media posts, reviews or assessment online, and survey responses to determine whether customers' sentiments are adequate, or advantageous or negative or neutral. This brings about an emotional pulse of the brand in real time. This tracking enhances proactive reputation management. When the hotel realises a sudden rise in the negative mentions about room cleanliness on X (Twitter), it could respond swiftly through launching an investigation into the substantive challenge, addressing complaints by guest and communicating the improvements effected publicly (Gabarron et al., 2020). This openness does not only the damage on the brand but also demonstrate transparency and trust in the public.

In the tracking of sentiments, it leads to the enrichment of personalised marketing, via identification of which aspect of the experience guest cherish most in terms of reception by the staff or workers, services provided at the spa, or the quality of the food the organisation could highlight these features in the promotion targeted at similar audiences (Al-Shehri, 2021). For example, if the information on sentiments shows stronger praise for rooftop bars, marketing messages can underscore these amenities when targeting the youth, and experience-driven travellers. Again, sentiments information provides predictive power, as well as an increasing trend of positive feedback on eco-friendly practices which might indicate that sustainability has become a crucial driver of guest decisions. The marketers in the hospitality sector can use this foresight to adapt campaigns, introduce new green packages, or strengthen sustainable messaging before competitors do (Chappell, and Creissels, 2019). In this manner, sentiments tracking provides a listening instrument as well as predictive compass for evolving guest expectations.

Dynamic Pricing

The dynamic pricing is crucial and very visible application of the predictive and adaptive marketing approach in the hospitality sector. Ghosh and Chatterjee, (2025) stated that the utilisation of real-time information on the need, seasonality, competitors' rates and booking behaviours, resorts or hotels can adjust room prices multiple times a day to maximise revenue and occupancy. Commercial airlines started this program, which has now become the set procedure in hotels and resorts. This advantage in terms of the dynamic pricing is hinged on adaptability; Hosmani and Lalitha, (2025) further reiterated that an upcoming concert suddenly increases the demand in the city and other hotels close to the venue and can upsurge the rates directly to capture additional revenues. In constantly adapting to market conditions, hotels avoid leaving money on the table. The dynamic pricing also provides for micro-personalisation and AI-driven systems can analyse a guest past behaviour such as their possibility to book during sales or preferences for premium rooms and present tailored offers.

Mahalakshmi and Bharath, (2025) stated that an organisation traveller who repeatedly books executive suites might receive an all-exclusive corporate package, whiles a leisure traveller browsing budget rooms could be pushed with a limited time offer discount. The customised pricing strategy influences conversions while safeguarding profitability, as well as longer term marketing concepts, dynamic pricing reinforces brand rivalry. The hotel that steadily provide fair, market-aligned rates are prone to be selected over those with rigid pricing models. The difficulty for the marketers is to communicate value plainly framing dynamic pricing as an opportunity for guests to secure the best deals in real time, rather than a manipulative strategy (Periasamy and Dinesh, 2024).

CASE STUDIES AND GLOBAL INSIGHTS

The global hospitality sector provides a variety of programs on how marketing technology is utilised to enhance customer engagement and strengthen the reputation of the organisation. In the global chains to boutique hotels, innovative strategies highlight the diverse ways in which technology can be restructured for guest to have a well deserving experience and marketing effectiveness. Marriot has integrated virtual reality and artificial intelligence into its social campaigns to create immersive and information-driven storytelling, whiles Accor has initiated block-chained based loyalty programs to maximise transparency and customer trust. In Ghana, the hotels are leading with mobile-first marketing, tapping into a widespread usage of smartphones and mobile money (momo) for their reservations and payments. Also, in the Southeast of Asia, TikTok-driven storytelling has become a powerful instrument for connecting with the youth or young individuals through an original, culturally rich descriptions. This case studies to be elaborated on demonstrate that technology in the hospitality industry in relation to marketing is not one-size-fits-all but relatively adapts to local context while reflecting global trends in the personalisation, involvement and digital creativity.

Marriott's Use of Virtual Reality (VR) and Artificial Intelligence (AI) in Social Campaigns

Marriott International, the world's leading largest hotel groups, have dependably positioned itself as a pioneer in hospitality marketing by leveraging emerging technologies. The portfolio spans for over 8,000 asserts across over 140 countries and they are faced with difficulties of maintaining a consistent worldwide identity while becoming attractive to variety of audiences (Martín-Rios and Ciobanu, 2019). The company would have to integrate VR and AI into its strategy when it comes to marketing, not mere gimmicks but as a tool for the transformation of how travellers perceive, experience, whiles relating with brands. These technologies in question have allowed Marriott to move beyond traditional advertising and creating an immersive, personalised programs that resounds with the modern, tech-savvy guests. Marriott's initiative which is widely recognised Vroom Service project, created in collaboration with Samsung Company Limited. This service allows guest at the chosen properties to order a VR headset to their various rooms and appreciate immersive travel stories that transported them to various locations which includes Chile, Rwanda and Beijing as highlighted by Jerez-Jerez et al., (2025). These experiences were more than entertainment, as a marketing strategy that built emotional connections by allowing potential and existing guest virtually experience destinations before dedication to them. In the alignment with travellers growing desire for authentic and adventurous experiences as well as Marriott positioned itself as a more than a hotel chain which became a gateway to exploration. Furthermore, Marriott also tested the VR "Teleporters" phone booth-sized installations placed in major cities like London and New York. The divisions permitted people to virtually step onto a Hawaiian beach or stand atop a London skyscraper, complete with multisensory effects like wind and scent to enhance realism (Kandampully and Solnet, 2024). These advancements produced a significant media attention and created a strong word-of-mouth effect, especially among younger travellers who value novelty and the shareable experiences. From a marketing perspective, these activations were highly effective, as they combined experiential storytelling with shareable moments that spread rapidly across social media platforms like Instagram, Facebook, and later TikTok.

Notwithstanding, the AI front, has made Marriott welcomed machine learning to optimise its social media campaigns and personalised marketing. AI algorithms give room for scrutinisation of vast datasets from customer browsing histories to loyalty program interactions to subdivisions audiences into micro-groups (Kruesi and Remy, 2024). Ultimately, as an alternative of pushing generic promotions can be beneficial, Marriott can convey targeted messages, such as wellness packages to health-conscious travellers or cultural tours for experience seekers. The AI further enhances Marriott to be flexible in relation to the content formats and messaging in real time based on audience responses. For an example, the data discovered that a campaign featuring spa experiences outperforms those highlighting business amenities in a particular market, as well as Marriott's AI systems can automatically prioritise and promote the more effective content as viewed by Sanjeev and Birdie, (2019)

The AI in addition boost Marriott's customer service and brand engagement. The tools which include AI-powered chatbots, integrated into social media and mobile apps, provide 24/7 customer support whiles also acting as subtle marketing channels. These bots do not only answer practical questions ("What time is check-in?") but can also suggest add-ons ("Would you like to reserve a spa appointment during your stay?"). Marriott conglomerates service with upselling in a way which senses personalisation rather than pushy. Additionally, most interaction feedback into the company's data ecosystem, reinforcement of predictive models and sharpening future marketing campaigns (Tsymbal et al., 2021). The amalgamation of VR and AI has given Marriott a distinct competitive advantage by blending imagination with intelligence. The promotions of the Virtual Reality, turn to enhance aspirational storytelling, sparking wanderlust and sensational involvement, whiles AI guarantees that the right story reaches the appropriate client at the right time. Furthermore, the concept rather turned to develop a marketing model that is both immersive and adaptive, appealing to the needs of digital-first travellers. According to Unnava and Aravindakshan, (2021), since Marriott hotel, actions did not only compelled bookings but also strengthened its brand identity as an innovator that appreciates the evolving desires of its global customer base. The Marriott case verified how hospitality marketing could travel from transactional promotions to experience-driven engagement, setting a benchmark for the industry at large to thrive.

Accor's Blockchain-Based Loyalty Programs

The Accor Hotels, a French multinational hospitality group, have explored the blockchain technology to revamp its loyalty ecosystem. Conventionally the loyalty schemes are usually criticised for being restrictive points can expire, redemption options are limited, and transferability between programs is difficult as asserted by Thakur, (2022). Accor revealed to tackle these pain points by piloting a blockchain-based loyalty solution that permits guests to exchange and redeem points with greater flexibility. The system employed the tokenised loyalty points, which can be securely stored in a digital wallet. Guests could potentially redeem these tokens not only within Accor's portfolio but also with external partners such as restaurants, airlines, as well as the retail stores. The transformation of innovation loyalty activities from very closed environment into open, cooperative channel, the marketing complement value by turning the loyalty into a way of live that is beneficial according to Sharma, (2024).

The blockchain also asserts transparency and trust, because the transactions are immutable and verifiable, guests can track every point earned and redeemed, eliminating confusion or disputes as acknowledged by Naseem et al., (2025). The manner of accountability strengthens brand trust and also increases customer satisfaction. For Accor, there is reduction in the administrative costs associated with managing disputes and increases program participation, since guests view the system as fair and flexible. Accor's blockchain experiment further asserted that the future direction of loyalty marketing: moving away from rigid points systems to fluid, guest-centric ecosystems. The adaptation of blockchain, Accor positions itself not just as a hotel provider but as part of a broader lifestyle network, appealing to a generation of travellers who value flexibility and also transparency in brand relationships as addressed by Ramírez et al., (2018).

Mobile-First Marketing in Ghanaian Boutique Hotels

In Ghana, the hotels have incorporated a mobile-first marketing approach to reach both local and international travellers. The penetration of the mobile in Ghanaian economy is above 120% (with many people owning multiple SIM cards), smartphones are the primary means of accessing the internet (Sukach et al., 2021). In the recognition of this aspects, boutique hotels such as those in Accra's Osu and East Legon districts have optimised their marketing for mobile from responsive websites to WhatsApp-based booking systems. A large number of these hotels solely depend on social media platforms like Instagram and Facebook, which are most frequently accessed through mobile devices. The Mobile-friendly video content as well as the Instagram Reels have become vital tools to communicate the "story" of these boutique spaces, attracting younger audiences who value aesthetics and authenticity.

The mobile-first strategies encompass to payment and customer participation. The hotels and resort usually combine mobile money services (such as MTN Mobile Money and Vodafone Cash), as well as making it easier for local guests to pay and book according to Sharma (2024). This develops a logic of intimacy and accessibility that larger hotels are usually deficient in. The Ghanaian case brought to bear how boutique hotels can clout above their weight by focusing on mobile-driven, highly personalised marketing (Sinha and Srivastava, 2023). As an alternative of competing with international chains on budget or scale, they differentiate through agility, authenticity, as well as a deeper understanding of local mobile habits. For emergent markets, this highlights that mobile-first is not just a strategy but an inevitability for hospitality marketing success.

TikTok-Driven Brand Storytelling in Southeast Asia

The TikTok application have overtime become a major powerful marketing tools for hospitality brands across Southeast Asia. Regarding its short-form video format, Nayyar et al., (2018) stated that the algorithm-driven discovery, and massive youth-oriented user base, TikTok offers hotels, resorts, and travel operators an opportunity to showcase experiences in ways that feel authentic and entertaining. In a region where tourism is crucial to the sector from Thailand and Vietnam to Indonesia and the Philippines. The hospitality players are increasingly using TikTok to tell stories that go beyond static advertisements, focusing instead on immersive narratives that highlight culture, lifestyle, and unique experiences (Moran et al., 2020). A very key advantage of TikTok-driven depends on the visual immediacy and relatability. This is because when the budget is huge for commercials, hotels and travel the reputation of the business to produce behind-the-scenes clips, day-in-the-life experiences, in respect to user-generated challenges that enhances interaction. For example, a resort beachfront in Bali may turn to post a 30-second video showing sunrise yoga according to Mengalli et al., (2024).

The micro-stories reverberate with the youthful travellers who value authenticity and "real" moments over scripted marketing strategies.

TikTok emboldens participation and viral video, are central to its role in brand storytelling. The Southeast Asian hotels have employed the local music, cultural dances, and trending hashtags to engage not just travellers, but, the local communities as purported by Leung et al., (2022). A hotel and resort located in Vietnam join a continental food challenge, revealing its signature meals, whiles other hotels in Singapore could also create a dance video with the employees that showcase its local traditions. These combinations of cultural pride and playful engagement positions hospitality brands as approachable and human-centred, instead of distant corporations as well as a powerful element is influencer and micro-influencer partnerships. Southeast Asia with a thriving TikTok creator ecosystem, where travel influencers can reach millions of followers with a single post. Hotels in collaborating with influencers to showcase properties via storytelling formats such as "Come spend 24 hours with me at this hotel" or "Hidden gems in Bali you must see." These influencer-led accounts frequently perform better than official brand posts, as audiences perceive them as more trustworthy and personal as highlighted by Kandampully and Solnet, (2024). The implication seen is significant, with user engagement leads to higher visibility, bookings, and long-term brand awareness.

Most hospitality brands have made TikTok an important aspect in terms of customer feedback and trend-spotting tool. In relation to monitoring, where different types of videos go viral, hotels can identify what experiences guests value most whether it's a unique infinity pool, eco-friendly practices, or immersive cultural workshops as asserted by Jiang and Wen, (2020). Again, other brands even adapt their services to match emerging social trends, such as offering TikTok-friendly photo spots, neon-lit lounges, or curated "Instagrammable" breakfast spreads. When telling stories is not just about one-direction, but it actively shapes how hotels design and market their services. Generally, TikTok-driven storytelling has converted the way Southeast Asian hospitality brands engage with travellers as viewed by Hornik et al., (2024). With the blending cultural authenticity, viral trends, and influencer power, TikTok allowed hotels and resorts to connect with a global audience in a conversational and engaging manner. Significantly, it has shifted the focus from selling rooms to sharing experiences. In a region where tourism is central to economic growth and cultural exchange, TikTok is no longer just an entertainment platform but is a very crucial driver of narrative-building and competitive differentiation in hospitality marketing (Hosmani and Lalitha, 2025).

Ethical and Sustainability Challenges in Case Studies

A major ethical concern in social media marketing is influencer transparency. ProfileTree (2025) reports that many influencers fail to disclose paid partnerships, misleading consumers and undermining trust in digital advertising. This lack of openness raises issues of manipulation and accountability, especially when vulnerable groups like young audiences are involved.

On the sustainability front, eco-conscious brands using social media present both opportunities and challenges. SocialTargeter (2025) highlights companies such as Patagonia and Lush, which promote environmental initiatives and inspire consumer activism. While these efforts support sustainability, they also risk greenwashing where brands exaggerate their eco-credentials to attract conscious buyers creating scepticisms and weakening genuine progress. Broadly, Granstedt (2025) notes that the rapid evolution of social media ethics has outpaced regulation. Practices like targeted advertising based on personal data raise privacy concerns, as seen in controversies involving Facebook. These issues show how ethical dilemmas intersect with sustainability, since misuse of data erodes trust and threatens long-term brand viability.

Finally, sustainability-driven campaigns often struggle to balance authenticity with profitability. The Sustainable Agency (2025) observes that while Gen Z demands transparency and eco-consciousness, brands face difficulty aligning these values with financial goals. This tension underscores the challenge of integrating ethical marketing with viable business models. Collectively, these cases emphasize the need for stronger ethical standards, transparent communication, and genuine sustainability commitments in mobile and social media marketing.

STRATEGIC FRAMEWORK FOR ADOPTION

The adoption of marketing technology in hospitality requires more than simply investing in new tools and it calls for a structured framework that balances readiness, integration, and alignment. Hotels and resorts should first evaluate their technology readiness and digital maturity to ensure that the foundation is strong to assist advanced innovations. Correspondingly, the training f employees and cross-functional collaboration are critical to maximize the value of these tools, making sure that insights and systems are shared across departments to create a seamless guest experience. Lastly, the adoption must be guided by brand identity and guest expectations so that technology enhances, instead of disrupts, the promise of service. These elements form a strategic pathway that enables hospitality businesses to innovate responsibly, improve competitiveness, and as well as strengthen long-term customer loyalty.

Technology Readiness and Digital Maturity Models

In the assessment of the level of readiness in terms of technology and digital maturity models hospitality organisations must adopt a new marketing strategies. The readiness of these innovations appear at infrastructure, resources as well as leadership thinking available to aid adoption as reaffirmed by Islam and Singh (2025). Resorts and hotels with vigorous internet connectivity, integrated property management systems (PMS), and data analytics capabilities are more likely to succeed in rolling out advanced marketing tools such as artificial intelligence or virtual reality. Continuously, properties in emerging regions need to focus on the foundational issues such as reliable connectivity before moving to higher-level innovations. The digital maturity representations provide a roadmap for this progression or growth in the organisation in terms of hospitality as stated by Mogaji et al., (2024). The concepts assist businesses to assess where they stand in terms of digital adoption and identify gaps that hinder competitiveness. For instance, a small boutique hotel may be digitally "emerging" with a social media presence and online booking capability, as well as "advanced" stages that involve predictive analytics or dynamic pricing strategies. The use of maturity concepts gives room for management to instrument technologies in stages relatively overwhelming the business with tools it cannot yet maximize. Most notably, both readiness and maturity valuations reassure realistic planning, instead of chasing every new trend, businesses can focus on adopting technologies that align with their immediate goals and long-term growth as indicated by Ozdemir et al., (2023). This approach curtails wasted investments and guarantees that every digital step taken enhances marketing effectiveness, improves the guest journey, as well as strengthens the competitive position of the brand.

Staff Training and Cross-Functional Integration

The marketing technology could not attend its full its potential without skilled and confident staff to use it effectively. Employee training can be considered a cornerstone of adoption, ensuring that employees understand not only how to operate the tools, along with how to apply them to delivering better guest experiences (Sharma and Singh, 2024). Training should go beyond technical skills to comprise of digital literacy, data interpretation, and customer engagement strategies. For instance, front-desk staff trained in using Customer Relationship Management systems can personalize check-ins, while marketing teams can leverage analytics to craft campaigns that resound with target audiences.

In the consideration of a gross-functional integration is equally important, as marketing technology tads nearly every department in a hotel or resort. Mahalakshmi and Bharath, (2025) stated that the sales, operational activities, housekeeping, food and beverage, and IT teams must all coordinate to ensure that guest data flows seamlessly across systems. Devoid of this integration, marketing messages may be inconsistent, or worse, irrelevant to the guest experience. For an example, a guest flagged as a repeat visitor in the CRM should be recognized at check-in as well as offered personalized services that align with past preferences something only possible if departments share and act on the same information. Successful adoption also required a cultural shift within the business in question. The employees should be encouraged to see technology not as a replacement for human service but as a tool that enhances it. In the involvement of employees in the process of technology rollout and showing them how digital tools can reduce routine tasks and improve guest satisfaction, resistance to change can be minimized as viewed by Knani et al., (2022). This integration of individuals and technology guarantees that the marketing strategy is both human-centred and digitally power-driven in terms of hospitality in organisations.

Aligning Marketing Technology With Brand Identity and Guest Expectations

In adoption of a technology in relation to marketing, it should not be trailed in isolation; it should align closely with a hotel's brand identity and the expectations of its target audience. For instance, a luxury resort or hotel could make investment in immersive VR tours. The AI-driven concierge services to gives room for exclusivity and premium service, whiles a budget-friendly boutique hotel might focus on mobile-first marketing according to Lee et al., (2024). The technology however, does not reflect the reputational promise, as well as it risks confusing customers or creating a disconnect between expectations and reality. Correspondingly, guest expectations play a critical role and today's travellers are not impressed by technology for its own sake they expect technology to make their experience easier, personalized, and engaging. Manoharan and Ashtikar, (2025) viewed that the orientation of technology adoption in respect with these expectations, it guarantees that digital tools enhance satisfaction instead of frustrating customers with gimmicks or unnecessary complexity. This alignment entailed continuous feedback loops as hotels or resort aggressively collect information on how guests use. The technology, whether through surveys, online reviews, or sentiment analysis. This insight gave room for business to modify their marketing technologies in ways that are in collaboration with the brand while evolving with customer demands. Eventually, the goal is not simply to adopt the latest innovation but to integrate tools that deepen loyalty, improve efficiency, as well as tell the brand's story more effectively across all touchpoints (Ononiwu et al., 2023).

ETHICAL AND REGULATORY CONSIDERATIONS

The information-driven and technology-dependent over the past decade has made it necessary for hospitality marketing, ethical and regulatory considerations have emerged as central issues shaping adoption and practice. In protecting the personal information of guests through the usage of AI, hotels and resorts must navigate a landscape that demands compliance, accountability, and respect for consumer rights. The regulations comprising the European Union's General Data Protection Regulation (GDPR) and California Consumer Privacy Act (CCPA) set global benchmarks as well as the legal compliance, lies the responsibility of hospitality businesses to maintain trust and uphold ethical standards. These rise of algorithmic decision-making, influencer marketing, as well as user-generated content adds. Furthermore, the complexity requiring organizations to strike a balance between innovation and integrity. These challenges directly, hospitality brands can foster stronger relationships with guests' whiles avoiding reputational plus financial risks associated with the organisation.

Security and Data Protection – GDPR, CCPA

The security and protection of information have become a cornerstone of hospitality marketing because hotels along with the travel businesses collect vast amounts of sensitive guest information. This includes personal details, payment information, travel patterns, and behavioural insights from online interactions. In the protecting this information of the guests, both a regulatory requirement and an ethical responsibility, especially given the high frequency of cyberattacks targeting the sector.

These regulations such as the General Data Protection Regulation (GDPR) in Europe and the California Customer Privacy Act (CCPA) in California are very necessary. However, businesses must agree on stringent guidelines on how personal data can be collected, stored, and shared, emphasizing transparency and guest control. The multinational hospitality brands, compliance with these frameworks has become a global benchmark, usually, the persuading practices even outside their jurisdictions. Hotels should implement strong security systems, which includes encryption of data, securing booking platforms, and multi-factor authentication. With regards to the breach notifications protocols and privacy strategies must be unambiguous to the guest whiles ensuring they comprehend how their data will be utilised without leaking it to the third party without their consent. Also, complying with the ethical dimension involves creating a culture of security where guest trust is prioritized over short-term marketing gains. The breaching of information does not solely lead to financial penalties but also undermines the credibility of the brand. The embedment with robust data protection into their operations, hospitality businesses position themselves as trustworthy custodians of guest information in an increasingly susceptible digital landscape.

Algorithm Bias and Ethical AI Use

Artificial intelligence (AI) is significant in relation to hospitality marketing, powering chat-bots, as well as the personalization engines, and predictive analytics. However, the over-reliance on algorithms turn to increases trepidations about bias and fairness in the sector. The AI systems trained on incomplete or skewed datasets could accidentally favour certain demographics whiles excluding or misrepresenting others or sometimes not favour (Leung et al., 2022). For an example, the reservation channels could offer recommendations on how to prioritize luxury travellers over budget-conscious guests or inadvertently disadvantage travellers from regions with less than an online data representation. This prejudice could strengthen the inequalities, damaging the reputation of the organisation, and erode trust in the fairness of hospitality services. The ethical usage of AI required more than technical fixes; it demands a commitment to transparency and accountability as stated by Mogaji et al., (2024). Hospitality organisations (hotels and resort) should adopt regular audits of AI models to identify and correct potential biases as well as safeguarding the recommendations and marketing offers are inclusive. The organisation must make it an effort to communicate clearly to guests when AI-driven tools are being used, reducing the risk of manipulation or hidden profiling. In collaborating with ethical AI guidelines such as those promoted by the OECD and UNESCO can support resorts and hotels design systems that prioritize fairness, accountability, and inclusivity (Martín-Rios and Ciobanu, 2019). Additionally, integrating ethics into

AI has enhanced technology, and served the diverse needs of all travellers, not just the most profitable segments.

Transparency and Trust in Data Collection

In the current big data era, hospitality marketing usually depends on the collection of extensive guest information, from browsing history and booking patterns to social media engagement. Whiles such data enabled personalization and targeted marketing, it however also promotes questions about transparency. The guests are increasingly concerned about how their information is being collected, stored, and monetized. Organisations involved in hospitality must always appear secretive or manipulative in their practices, making them risk alienating customers and facing regulatory backlash (Jiang and Wen, 2020). Transparency, therefore, is not a compliance issue but a strategic driver of guest loyalty and trust.

In developing transparency requires hotels to clearly explain what data is collected, why it is needed, and how it will be used. This goes beyond long and complex privacy statements, as well as communication must be simple, accessible, and embedded at every touchpoint of the guest journey as highlighted Akbar and Tracogna, (2018). For illustration, a hotel and resort mobile application should provide clear explanations before asking for location access or push-notification permissions. Additionally, giving the clientele the option to opt out of certain data practices without losing accessibility to essential services reinforces the sense of trust. In respect to being open and proactive, hospitality brands can transform data collection from a potential liability into an opportunity to deepen guest relationships (Bennear and Wiener, 2019).

Consent and User Autonomy

The informed consent lies at the heart of ethical information usage, as well as hospitality marketing, consent determines whether hotels can utilise guest information for purposes which includes personalized offers, targeted ads, or third-party data sharing as shown in the report of Carlson et al., (2018). Nonetheless, informed consent is usually present in terms and conditions, that guests rarely read, raising doubts about whether it is truly informed or voluntary. In relation to the ethical practice needs organisation to ensure that consent is both explicit and meaningful, granting users real autonomy over how their information is used. The hotels and resorts should be open and transparent to provide opt-in mechanisms rather than default opt-outs; for example, in the collection of guest preferences for personalized marketing, the consent form should be clear, specific, and easy to understand (Delbaere et al., 2018). Guests should also be allowed to withdraw consent at any time without penalties or degraded service quality. Beyond compliance, reinforcing user autonomy reflects a respect for individual choice and dignity. In practice, this approach enhances trust, as guests feel more in control of their information and willing to engage with marketing initiatives as well. For the hospitality sector, relating to autonomy is not solely a regulatory requirement but a pathway to stronger, long-term customer loyalty.

Ethical Use of Influencer and UGC Data

Influencer marketing and user-generated content (UGC) have become a dominant force in hospitality promotion, particularly on platforms such as Instagram, TikTok, and YouTube. Whiles these tools intensify brand reach and authenticity, they raise ethical challenges around ownership, privacy, and consent (Ghosh and Chatterjee, 2025). For instance, posting of guest pictures without their consent is a clear violation of their intellectual property, also the creation of a sense of exploitation is key. The collaboration with influencers could blur the lines between an accurate recommendation and paid promotions when not declared openly. The practice in the long run may cause havoc to the credibility and reputation. Iyengar and Venkatesh, (2024) highlighted that in the navigation process these obstacles, thus hospitality must be ascertained for a clearer standard with regards to ethics for the influencer collaboration and UGC use. The cooperation with the influencer should be opened and all the set guidelines followed through by the regulatory body with respect to advertisement. When leveraging, guest content, hotels must ensure they ask the consent of the guest before carrying out anything that might have their reputation or brand. Furthermore, brands must avoid exploiting sensitive guest data obtained through social media tracking without informed consent. Lastly, these processes, hotels and resorts must avoid ethical pitfalls and reinforce trust; ensuring that influencer along with UGC-driven campaigns remain authentic and respectful in accordance with Hassan, (2023).

Infrastructure Gaps and Digital Inequality

Another pressing difficulty encountered by the hospitality marketing technology is the uneven distribution of digital infrastructure. Whilst luxury hotels in urban centre are often benefited from high-speed internet, smart systems, and robust IT support, smaller or rural establishments may lack the resources to adopt advanced technologies according to Nguyen et al., (2021). The hospitality business can solely have an impact on the innovation like AI-driven personalisation or immersive VR experience. The competition with regards to the gap between the global reputation and local operators may continue to expand. Digital inequality also extends to guests, as not all travellers have equal access to technology. In emergence of a marketplace, some consumers may lack reliable mobile connectivity, digital payment systems, or even familiarity with online booking platforms in accordance with Periasamy and Dinesh, (2024). The hospitality marketing models that assumed universal access to technology risk alienating these groups, with the creation of exclusionary practices instead of inclusive participation.

To ensure these discrepancies are resolved it would demand investment in both infrastructure and affordable technology solutions. The states, industry associations, and private players must collaborate to improve connectivity as well as digital tools for smaller operators. Similarly, business who have invested in hospitality must ensure they design an inclusive policy that is viable across whiles varying the levels of digital access offering both cutting-edge digital services for tech-savvy clients and simple alternatives for those less connected (Gursoy et al., 2022). Fast forward, bridging infrastructure and access obstacles is very crucial to ensuring that technological innovation benefits the hospitality industry, rather than reinforcing inequalities. Chan-Olmsted and Kim, (2022) as acknowledged by the hotel and resorts to be better positioned to persuade different types of guests should be able to find the equilibrium with regards to high-tech offerings, also maintaining resilience in the volatile market condition.

Regulatory and Privacy Concerns

The advancement on the reliance on data-driven marketing in hospitality has led to regulatory and privacy concerns to forefront. Hotels and Resorts can manage a vast number of sensitive data, from identifiers and payment information to behavioural insights drawn from guest interactions as purported by Gabarron et al., (2020). This makes the hospitality sector a target for cyber-attack and a sector under close regulatory scrutiny. The laws such as the GDPR and CCPA in Europe and California respectively have already reshaped marketing practices, and similar structures are emerging globally. In complying with these regulations requires significant investment in data protection systems, staff training, and governance processes. For smaller operators, the expenses associated with compliance can be hectic, causing additional barriers to the technological adoption. Since non-compliance risk heavy fines, damage on the credibility, and losing the trust of clients, makes it a major challenge for the industry. Furthermore, the legal requirements, ethic dimension of data usage adds to complexity, whiles guests increasingly expect transparency about how their information is collected, shared, and monetised as discovered by Hosmani and Lalitha, (2025). When the guest sense any form of manipulation they may disengage from digital services, undermining the efficiency and effectiveness of the market. In respect to the future of hospitality marketing will therefore centre on balancing personalization with respect for guest privacy. The regulatory frameworks are prone to become stricter as governments respond to growing concerns over data misuse. Hospitality brands must comply with current laws but also anticipate evolving regulations by adopting proactive, guest-centred data practices as viewed by Daiya et al., (2024).

Workforce Transformation and Digital Literacy

The adoption of advanced marketing technologies is restructuring the hospitality workforce; thus the employees are increasingly expected to engage with instrument like the CRM platforms. The AI-driven analytics, as well as digital bookings structures required a major modification in the skillset and mind-set (Al-Issa and Thanasi, 2024). Majority of the employees particularly in the regions of narrow exposure to digital technologies, hence, the transaction could have been overwhelming. However, without proper training, the employees risk being side-lined, creating a resistance to change the limit and the efficiency of the new systems. According to Arapou and Kapiki, (2023), the digital literacy is therefore a crucial obstacle; hotels and resorts must not only make investment in infrastructure and ensuring that the employees across various divisions from the reception to the marketing department are well prepared with the prerequisite skill-set to utilise digital tools efficiently. As the training programs must solely focus on both the technical proficiency and the capacity to interpret and act on the digital insights in a manner that encourages guest satisfactions (Giordano et al., 2024).

Collaboration is key concept with regards to cross-function in the marketing technologies, this usually requires an integration among sales, operations, IT, and guest service teams. In fostering a culture of cooperation and shared obligations as well as the organisational threat siloed operations where information and insights flops to get the individuals who demand the most as asserted by Hosmani and Lalitha, (2025). This limits both the efficiency and personalisation, undermining the value of the technology. Fast-forward, the employee's transformation should be recognised not as a challenge but as a prospect. The upskilling individuals working for the organisation and fostering a culture of constant learning, hospitality businesses can create empowered teams that utilised technology to deliver human-centred experiences. The collection of digital literacy and emotional intelligence will define the competitive advantage of future hospitality leaders.

Sustainability and Responsibility

As technology restructures hospitality marketing, sustainability and responsibility have become central concerns to the industry. The guests, especially younger generations, increasingly expect businesses to adopt environmentally as well as the socially responsible practices. In respect to marketing technologies that emphasize convenience, and personalization must therefore be balanced with efforts to reduce environmental impact and promote ethical practices in accordance with Jiang and Wen, (2020). For example, AI-driven energy management systems assist in hotels reducing wastage while mobile-first strategies can reduce paper usage. However, the sustainability challenges extend beyond operations into marketing itself; the usage of data-intensive technologies, such as block-chain or large-scale AI models, carries significant environmental costs in terms of energy consumption.

POLICY RECOMMENDATIONS FOR THE DIGITAL MARKETING ERA

The proliferation of mobile applications and social media as core marketing channels presents both significant opportunities and pressing challenges for policy-makers. These technologies enable businesses to engage consumers more effectively, yet they also raise critical concerns around privacy, misinformation, and digital inequality. To safeguard ethical, inclusive, and sustainable marketing practices, proactive policy measures are essential.

First, prioritising digital literacy programs is crucial to equip citizens with the ability to critically assess online content and advertising. Evidence suggests that individuals with stronger digital literacy are less vulnerable to misinformation and manipulative marketing (Livingstone & Helsper, 2020). Governments should embed digital literacy into school curricula and community education initiatives, ensuring equitable access across socio-economic groups.

Second, regulatory frameworks must evolve to address the complexities of mobile and social media marketing. Existing advertising regulations often lag technological advancements, leaving gaps in areas such as influencer marketing, targeted advertising, and data protection. Enhanced oversight through transparent disclosure requirements and penalties for deceptive practices would strengthen consumer trust (OECD, 2022).

Third, fostering cross-sector collaboration among government agencies, technology firms, and civil society organizations can promote responsible innovation and ethical data use. Such partnerships are vital for developing industry standards for app design and social media engagement.

Finally, sustained investment in research and monitoring systems is necessary. Funding independent studies on the societal impacts of digital marketing will enable evidence-based policymaking that balances economic growth with consumer protection.

CONCLUSION

This chapter have explored ways on how marketing technology in the hospitality sector has moved from basic promotional methods like brochures and print ads to sophisticated, data-driven, and immersive tools. Innovations such as artificial intelligence, virtual reality, block-chain, mobile-first marketing, and social media storytelling illustrate that the industry is no longer focused solely on visibility, as well as the creation of a personalized, meaningful guest relationships. The case studies further elaborated on the literature review assessed that from Marriott's use of VR and AI to boutique hotels in Ghana adopting mobile-first strategies, validate that technology is shaping both global giants and as well as the local players. The underlying message is unambiguous; hospitality marketing has evolved into an ecosystem that blends technology, human interaction, and consumer trust. Furthermore, the discussion has highlighted that technological adoption is with intricacies, also asserted that infrastructure discrepancies and digital inequality remain barriers, particularly in developing markets where internet connectivity, along with reliable connectivity are limited. The legislation and privacy concerns, such as those raised by GDPR and CCPA, combines layer of responsibility for businesses that collect and examine the information of the client. The threat of algorithmic bias and ethical misuse of AI also presents difficulties, this is because making transparency and fairness central to sustainable adoption. These difficulties turn to be creative as innovation should pursued in isolation from governance, ethics, and inclusivity.

Hospitality marketing organisation must implement a balanced approach that combines technological innovation with workforce development and ethical responsibility. Addition of value to the employees and cross-functional integration are vital so that the digital instrument enhance rather than better replace the human element of service. Yet again, cross-departmental utilised data on guest can drive and personalization but should always respect consent and autonomy. integrating marketing technologies with brand identity ensures that innovations add value to the guest experience rather than dilute the brand promise. These strategies merely develop a competitive advantage but also foster trust and long-term loyalty, along with from a stakeholder perspective, several recommendations are essential. The hospitality businesses must at all cost prioritize digital maturity assessments before adopting new technologies, ensuring readiness for investment and long-term value. Policymakers will demand to find refine regulatory frameworks to safeguard consumer rights without stifling creativity and growth. In providing technology the providers must be designed for flexible, scalable systems that provides both multinational hotel chains and smaller, autonomous operators. The cooperation with stakeholders and user-generated content must also be loomed ethically, with an unambiguous standard on the disclosure and information usage, asserting the efforts will develop into a stronger, resilient ecology which is hospitability marketable.

In summary, the other investigators may want to examine other key aspects for future studies, and this could serve as a guide in respect to the nest phase of hospitality marketing. The AI personalisation is power driven to influence the loyalty of the brand over time. The block-chain-based loyalty programmes have greatly influence guest retention across the market. The sustainability implies that the digital transformation from energy is utilised in data centre to electronic wastage, as well as warrant massive warrant which also, gives greater attention. The sustainable implications of digital transformation from energy use in data centre to electronic waste also warrant massive attention. The comparative studies among the advanced and developing marketplace would support the identification of strategies to close the digital inequality and enhance growth inclusively. Thus, in exploring the entirety of the focus areas, the researcher can guarantee hospitality marketing technology to constantly evolve in a manner which is creative, ethical, aligned with the long term demands for the organisation and clientele base.

REFERENCES

Abraham, S., & Krishnan, T. A. (2021). The Role of Technology In Reshaping Guest Experiences At Indian Hotels Post-Covid 19. [JTSM]. *Journal of Tourism & Sports Management, 4*(1), 692–702.

Akbar, Y. H., & Tracogna, A. (2018). The sharing economy and the future of the hotel industry: Transaction cost theory and platform economics. *International Journal of Hospitality Management, 71*, 91–101.

Al-Issa, N., & Thanasi, M. (2024). Mapping the Future of Tech-Infused Luxury: A Roadmap and Research Directions. *International Journal of Consumer Studies, 48*(6), e13103.

Al-Shehri, M. (2021). Choosing the Best Social Media Influencer: The role of gender, age, and product type in influencer marketing. *International Journal of Marketing Strategies, 4*(1), 1–26.

Arapou, D. and Kapiki, S., 2023. Enhancing the Guest Experience in Hospitality through Technology: An Outlook of the Future.

Bennear, L. S., & Wiener, J. B. 2019. Adaptive regulation: instrument choice for policy learning over time. *Obtenido de Universidad de Harvard:* https://www. hks. harvard. edu

Buhalis, D., Harwood, T., Bogicevic, V., Viglia, G., Beldona, S., & Hofacker, C. (2019). Technological disruptions in services: Lessons from tourism and hospitality. *Journal of Service Management, 30*(4), 484–506.

Cabanillas, F. L., Leiva, F. M., Castillo, J. F. P., & Higueras-Castillo, E. (Eds.). (2025). *Biometrics: Challenges, Trends and Opportunities*. CRC Press.

Carlson, J., Rahman, M., Voola, R., & De Vries, N. (2018). Customer engagement behaviours in social media: Capturing innovation opportunities. *Journal of Services Marketing, 32*(1), 83–94.

Castillo-Picón, J., Nagadeepa, C., Rani, I., Angulo-Cabanillas, L., Vílchez-Vásquez, R., Manrique-Cáceres, J., & Allauca-Castillo, W. J. 2023, May. Guest Perception of Technology vs. Human Interaction in Hotel Check-in Process Implication for Service Quality. In *International Conference on Business and Technology* (pp. 81-95). Cham: Springer Nature Switzerland.

Chan-Olmsted, S., & Kim, H. J. 2022. 6 Influencer marketing dynamics. *The Dynamics of Influencer Marketing*, p.99.

Chappell, H., & Creissels, D. (2019). Topicality and the typology of predicative possession. *Linguistic Typology*, *23*(3), 467–532.

Chen, L., & Kozak, M. (2024). *Algorithmic Personalization and Ethics in Tourism Marketing*. Tourism Management Review.

Daiya, D., Yadav, M., & Rao, H. S. 2024, April. Diffstock: Probabilistic relational stock market predictions using diffusion models. In *ICASSP 2024-2024 IEEE International Conference on Acoustics, Speech and Signal Processing (ICASSP)* (pp. 7335-7339). IEEE.

Delbaere, M., Michael, B., & Phillips, B. J. (2021). Social media influencers: A route to brand engagement for their followers. *Psychology and Marketing*, *38*(1), 101–112.

Dinga, E., Oprean-Stan, C., Tănăsescu, C. R., Brătian, V., & Ionescu, G. M. (2022). *Financial market analysis and behaviour: the adaptive preference hypothesis*. Routledge.

Donald, M., & Donald, A. 2024. How Marketing and Design can Enhance Customer Experience in Hospitality by Meeting Their Evolving Needs. In *Marketing and Design in the Service Sector: Enhancing Customer Experience* (pp. 175-186). Emerald Publishing Limited.

Freed, J. Q. (2021). *Hospitality CRM: Past, Present and Future*. Stayhapi. Retrieved from https://www.stayhapi.com/resources/hospitality-crm-past-present-and-future

Gabarron, E., Larbi, D., Dorronzoro, E., Hasvold, P. E., Wynn, R., & Årsand, E. (2020). Factors engaging users of diabetes social media channels on Facebook, Twitter, and Instagram: Observational study. *Journal of Medical Internet Research*, *22*(9), e21204.

Ghosh, D., & Chatterjee, S. 2025. Embracing Digital Transformation in Hospitality: Innovations, Challenges, and Opportunities With Case Studies. In *Digital Disruption in Hospitality, AI, and Emerging Technologies: A Roadmap to Personalized Experiences, Enhanced Operations, and Revenue Growth* (pp. 189-200). Emerald Publishing Limited.

Giordano, J., Benedikter, R., & Shook, J. R. (2024). *Neuroscience*. Neuroculture, and Neuroethics.

Gursoy, D., Malodia, S., & Dhir, A. (2022). The metaverse in the hospitality and tourism industry: An overview of current trends and future research directions. *Journal of Hospitality Marketing & Management*, *31*(5), 527–534.

Hassan, A. (Ed.). (2023). *Digital transformation in aviation, tourism and hospitality in Southeast Asia.* Routledge.

Hornik, J., Ofir, C., & Rachamim, M. (2024). *Out of the fog: fog computing-enabled AI to support smart marketing management.* Management Review Quarterly.

Hosmani, S.M. and Lalitha, M.D., 2025. Data Driven Insights: Machine Learning For Terrorist Attacks Region Predication. *Journal of Scientific Research and Technology*, pp.217-228.

Islam, N., & Singh, A. (2025). Role of Digitalization into Hospitality Businesses: Innovations and Trends. In *Transforming the Service Sector With New Technology* (pp. 447–458). IGI Global Scientific Publishing.

Ivanov, S., & Webster, C. (2019). Conceptual Framework of the Use of Robots, Artificial Intelligence and Service Automation in Travel, Tourism, and Hospitality Companies. Robots, Artificial Intelligence, and Service Automation in Travel, Tourism and Hospitality, 7-37. https://doi.org/DOI: 10.1108/978-1-78756-687 320191001

Iyengar, M. S., & Venkatesh, R. 2024. A brief communication on the Top Ten Trends in the Hospitality Industry for 2024: World Scenario. *SCT Proceedings in Interdisciplinary Insights and Innovations, 2*, p.45.

Jerez-Jerez, M. J., Sevilla-Sevilla, C., & Aguiar-Castillo, L. (Eds.). (2025). *The Role of Artificial Intelligence in the Tourism and Hospitality Sector.* Taylor & Francis.

Jeyakumar, T. (2025). *The Evolution of CRM in the Hospitality Industry: From Bookings to Brand Loyalty*. LinkedIn. Retrieved from https://www.linkedin.com/pulse/evolution-crm-hospitality-industry-from-bookings-brand-jeyakumar-ls7ac

Jiang, Y., & Wen, J. (2020). Effects of COVID-19 on hotel marketing and management: A perspective article. *International Journal of Contemporary Hospitality Management, 32*(8), 2563–2573.

Johnson, R. (2022). *Influencer Marketing in Hospitality: Risks and Regulations.* International Journal of Hospitality Marketing.

Kandampully, J. and Solnet, D., 2024. Service Management Principles for Hospitality & Tourism in the Age of Digital Technology.

Knani, M., Echchakoui, S., & Ladhari, R. (2022). Artificial intelligence in tourism and hospitality: Bibliometric analysis and research agenda. *International Journal of Hospitality Management, 107*, 103317.

Kruesi, M.A. and Remy, D., 2024. How can Hotels of Every Size Create the Right Technology Roadmap.

Lee, S., Shulga, L. V., Busser, J. A., & Hwang, J. (2024). Self-Service Hotel Check-In: Is There Still a Role for the In-Person Experience? *International Journal of Hospitality & Tourism Administration*, •••, 1–28.

Leung, F. F., Gu, F. F., & Palmatier, R. W. (2022). Online influencer marketing. *Journal of the Academy of Marketing Science*, *50*(2), 226–251.

Lukanova, G., & Ilieva, G. (2019). In Ivanov, S., & Webster, C. (Eds.), *Robots, artificial intelligence, and service automation in hotels* (pp. 157–183). Robots, Artificial Intelligence, and Service Automation in Travel, Tourism and Hospitality., DOI: 10.1108/978-1-78756-687-320191009

Mahalakshmi, S., & Bharath, H. 2025. From Check-In to Check-Out: AI Innovations in the Hospitality Sector. In Digital Disruption in Hospitality, AI, and Emerging Technologies (pp. 79-99). Emerald Publishing Limited.

Manoharan, G., & Ashtikar, S. P. 2025. AI Era in Hospitality: The New Frontier in Guest Satisfaction and Operations. In *Digital Disruption in Hospitality, AI, and Emerging Technologies: A Roadmap to Personalized Experiences, Enhanced Operations, and Revenue Growth* (pp. 59-77). Emerald Publishing Limited.

Martín-Rios, C., & Ciobanu, T. (2019). Hospitality innovation strategies: An analysis of success factors and challenges. *Tourism Management*, *70*, 218–229.

Mengalli, N. M., de Carvalho, A. A., & Galvão, S. M. (2024). Metaverse ecosystem and consumer society 5.0: consumer experience and influencer marketing in phygital transformation. In *Influencer marketing applications within the metaverse* (pp. 33–56). IGI Global.

Mogaji, E., Viglia, G., Srivastava, P., & Dwivedi, Y. K. (2024). Is it the end of the technology acceptance model in the era of generative artificial intelligence? *International Journal of Contemporary Hospitality Management*, *36*(10), 3324–3339.

Moran, G., Muzellec, L., & Johnson, D. (2020). Message content features and social media engagement: Evidence from the media industry. *Journal of Product and Brand Management*, *29*(5), 533–545.

Morrison, A. M. (2022). *Hospitality and travel marketing*. Routledge.

Naseem, M. J., Bardhan, M. R., & Singh, M. P. (2025). *The Digital Paradox of Childhood: Balancing Freedom & Protection in the Age of AI and Cybersecurity*. BlueRose Publishers Pvt Ltd.

Nayyar, A., Mahapatra, B., Le, D. and Suseendran, G., 2018. Virtual Reality (VR) & Augmented Reality (AR) technologies for tourism and hospitality industry. *International journal of engineering & technology, 7*(2.21), pp.156-160.

Nguyen, D. H., Tan, K. L., Vi, N. L. N., Phu, N. A., & Ting, H. (2024). The Influence of Customer Relationship Management in Enhancing Hospitality Business Performance: The Conditional Mediation of Digital Marketing Capabilities. *International Journal of Hospitality & Tourism Administration*. Advance online publication. DOI: 10.1080/15256480.2024.2346142

Nguyen, T. M., Le, D., Quach, S., Thaichon, P., & Ratten, V. 2021. The current trends and future direction of digital and relationship marketing: A business perspective. In *Developing Digital Marketing: Relationship Perspectives* (pp. 191-200). Emerald Publishing Limited.

OECD. (2022). *Regulatory Approaches to Digital Advertising*. Organisation for Economic Co-operation and Development.

Ononiwu, M., Azonuche, T. I., & Enyejo, J. O. (2023). Exploring Influencer Marketing Among Women Entrepreneurs using Encrypted CRM Analytics and Adaptive Progressive Web App Development. *International Journal of Scientific Research and Modern Technology*, *2*(6), 1–13.

Ozdemir, O., Dogru, T., Kizildag, M., & Erkmen, E. (2023). A critical reflection on digitalization for the hospitality and tourism industry: Value implications for stakeholders. *International Journal of Contemporary Hospitality Management*, *35*(9), 3305–3321.

Pentina, I., Guilloux, V., & Micu, A. C. (2018). Exploring social media engagement behaviors in the context of luxury brands. *Journal of Advertising*, *47*(1), 55–69.

Periasamy, P., & Dinesh, N. (2024). Leveraging digital transformation technologies in the hospitality industry. In *Revolutionizing the AI-Digital landscape* (pp. 151–165). Productivity Press.

Ra, S., Shrestha, U., Khatiwada, S., Yoon, S. W., & Kwon, K. (2019). The rise of technology and impact on skills. International Journal of Training Research, 17(sup1), 26–40. https://doi.org/DOI: 10.1080/14480220.2019.1629727

Rafiki, A., Hidayat, S. E., & Al Abdul Razzaq, D. (2019). CRM and organizational performance. *The International Journal of Organizational Analysis*, *27*(1), 187–205.

Ramírez, J., Baez, M., Casati, F., Cernuzzi, L., Benatallah, B., Taran, E. A., & Malanina, V. A. 2021, March. On the impact of predicate complexity in crowdsourced classification tasks. In *Proceedings of the 14th ACM International Conference on Web Search and Data Mining* (pp. 67-75).

Sanjeev, G. M., & Birdie, A. K. (2019). The tourism and hospitality industry in India: Emerging issues for the next decade. *Worldwide Hospitality and Tourism Themes*, *11*(4), 355–361.

Sharma, C., 2024. The Influence of Technological Innovations on Customer Satisfaction in the Hospitality Industry. *ATITHYA: A Journal of Hospitality, 10*(1).

Sharma, M. and Singh, A., 2024. Embracing Technological Innovation: A Review of Hi-Tech Services in Hospitality Industry.

Shokohyar, S., Tavalaee, R., & Karamatnia, K. (2017). Identifying effective indicators in the assessment of organizational readiness for accepting social CRM. *International Journal of Information, Business and Management*, *9*(4), 209–226.

Sinha, M., & Srivastava, M. (2023). Augmented reality: New future of social media influencer marketing. *Vision (Basel)*, 09722629221147124.

Smith, J. (2023). *Data Privacy in Hospitality Apps*. Journal of Hospitality Technology.

Sota, S., Chaudhry, H., & Srivastava, M. K. (2019). Customer relationship management research in hospitality industry: A review and classification. *Journal of Hospitality Marketing & Management*, *29*(1), 39–64.

Sukach, O., Kozlovska, S., & Sushko, N. (2021). Modern management technologies in the hospitality industry. *Baltic Journal of Economic Studies*, *7*(3), 168–176.

Thakur, A. (2022). Technological innovations in the hospitality and tourism industry. In *Mobile computing and technology applications in tourism and hospitality* (pp. 72–97). IGI Global.

Tsymbal, O., Mercorelli, P., & Sergiyenko, O. (2021). Predicate-based model of problem-solving for robotic actions planning. *Mathematics*, *9*(23), 3044.

Unnava, V., & Aravindakshan, A. (2021). How does consumer engagement evolve when brands post across multiple social media? *Journal of the Academy of Marketing Science*, *49*(5), 864–881.

Zade, A. A. R. O. H. I., & Sethi, S. U. R. I. N. D. E. R. (2024). Transforming hospitality: The digital revolution in post-pandemic hotel management. *International Journal of Cultural Studies and Social Sciences*, *20*(2), 42–51.

Zheng, Y., Li, Y., Own, C. M., Meng, Z., & Gao, M. (2018). Real-time predication and navigation on traffic congestion model with equilibrium Markov chain. *International Journal of Distributed Sensor Networks*, *14*(4), 1550147718769784.

Chapter 5
Use of AI Tools in the Hospitality Industry:
A Review and Future Research Agenda

Sakshi Priya
http://orcid.org/0009-0000-6905-163X
Banasthali Vidyapith, India

Balgopal Singh
http://orcid.org/0000-0001-8402-9617
Banasthali Vidyapith, India

ABSTRACT

AI is rapidly transforming the service sector, opening new research opportunities in hospitality and tourism. It has gradually changed the service sector, leading to significant innovations. This review aims to evaluate the application of AI in the hospitality industry in service delivery to improve the visitor experience. The primary focus of this paper is to discuss the optimum use of artificial intelligence tools by implementing AI technology in the travel and hospitality industry. The study adopts SPAR-4-SLR to review the articles systematically. The literature and data sources have been obtained from Scopus and Web of Science. This review covers research papers published from 2013 to 2025. Using the TCM-ADO framework, this article holistically analyzes the relationship between the varied use of AI tools in the hospitality industry. This review paper adds to the body of knowledge on the application of AI in the hospitality industry.

DOI: 10.4018/979-8-3373-6741-5.ch005

1. INTRODUCTION

The term AI was first coined at Dartmouth College in 1956 by John McCarthy, and it became more tangible throughout the 1900s and beyond. In the last few years, AI technologies have played a vital role in our society, whether in the education field, banking sector, hospitality industry, and others. Implementing artificial intelligence (AI) is essential in the digital technology age. Since its inception, it has given numerous opportunities and difficulties to other industries, including the hospitality sector. It is a fact that implementing these technologies has resulted in rapid development in these industries (Koo et al., 2021; Limna et al., 2021).

Artificial intelligence is crucial in incorporating innovation into a global economy. A plethora of AI-powered technologies have been developed with the potential to raise economic growth and living standards. Artificial intelligence (AI)-driven technologies are being used in the hospitality industry worldwide at an exponential rate. Hospitality industries are integrating AI into their core service delivery models to provide customers with robust and seamless service experiences (Lin et al., 2020; Jamshed et al., 2024; Roy et al., 2020). Customers' expectations for hospitality are rising along with the sector, demanding faster and more precise service. The hotel industry uses automation and cutting-edge technology to meet consumer needs and overcome obstacles while delivering flawless service that exceeds what guests expect (Saravanakumar & Narayanan, 2018).

Although the hospitality industry is one of the fastest-growing industries in the world (Ruel & Njoku, 2021), there are several barriers to using AI tools. Value, risk, and usage barriers are the three primary categories of obstacles to AI adoption in the hospitality industry (Rasheed et al., 2024). High implementation costs (i.e., significant upfront expenses for technology acquisition, integration, and training) and worries about return on investment are seen as value barriers (Rasheed et al., 2024). According to Chen and Kuo (2017), risk barriers are the degree of uncertainty and related risks that are present in novel products, processes, services, or technology and are influenced by user perceptions or experiences. Risk barriers include privacy and security issues that focus on worries about regulatory compliance, such as the General Data Protection Regulation (GDPR), to maintain consumer trust. Furthermore, Rasheed et al. (2023) categorize technological complexity as a usage barrier, which includes issues with the complexity of AI services and the lack of necessary technical skills in businesses.

Nevertheless, despite the increasing interest of academics and practitioners, until now, only a few studies (Knani et al., 2022; Doborjeh et al., 2021; Husain et al., 2023, etc.) have attempted a thorough literature review on applying AI tools in the tourism and hospitality industry. However, research on the application of AI-based tools in hospitality has recently gained more prominence, resulting in more published articles that show emerging themes in the domain. Thus, there is a need to explore and summarise the recent literature developed on the application of AI tools in the tourism industry. To accomplish this, this review considers the literature on the application of AI tools in the tourism industry that was published between 2013 and 2025.

Further, this review uses the Scientific Procedures and Rationales for Systematic Literature Reviews protocol (SPAR-4-SLR) by Paul et al. (2021) and the lens of the TCM-ADO Framework (Paul and Benito, 2018) to systematically document the review and suggest future research directions. The TCM framework developed by Paul et al. (2017) reveals *theories* that serve as the basis and direction for future researchers. It also provides information about the *contexts* in which research was conducted and the *methods* used to carry out the research. The ADO framework identifies the '*characteristics*' aspect of the research framework. *Antecedents* explain reasons contributing to a specific behavior, *decisions* describe behavioral responses, and *outcomes* relate to the result of behavior (Paul & Benito, 2018). More specifically, the combined TCM-ADO framework offers a comprehensive and well-organized analysis of existing literature by leveraging the advantages and offsetting the disadvantages of review methodology originated to review the literature developed in a scientific domain, such as Preferred reporting items for systematic reviews and meta-analyses protocol (PRISMA) (Bhatia et al., 2021; Paul et al., 2021).

Based on the review, most of the studies have focused on the theoretical aspects and conceptual clarifications of applying AI-based tools in the hospitality sector. Although this concept has gained significant attention from scholars and practitioners, only some studies have rigorously investigated the specific nature of the dimensionality of the application of AI tools in the hotel industry (Law et al., 2024).

Therefore, the review provided here differs from earlier SLRs regarding its aim and the literature it draws from. It also offers new insights that are important from the perspective of customers' specific behavior when using AI tools in the hospitality industry. This review is based on the various domains in which AI tools are applied in the hospitality industry. It is helpful to explain the current state of research in this domain and how it has changed over time, across national boundaries, in different contexts, and for diverse use cases. The researcher offers prospects for the future and provides opportunities for future research based on the TCM-ADO framework (Bhatia et al., 2021; Lim et al., 2021).

The proposed review is guided by subsequent research questions (RQs):

RQ1. What are the theories of adopting AI technology in service delivery in the tourism and hospitality industry?

RQ2. What are the characteristics of antecedents and modifiers of adopting AI technology in service delivery in the tourism and hospitality industry?

RQ3. What methodologies are employed to investigate the acceptance of AI by the customer in the tourism and hospitality industry?
RQ4. What are the characteristics of outcomes for acceptance of AI by the customer in the tourism and hospitality industry?

To address these research concerns, this review combines two well-established systematic literature review (SLR) frameworks—the theories, contexts, and methods (TCM) framework by Paul et al. (2017) and the antecedents, choices, and outcomes (ADO) framework by Paul and Benito (2018).

2. AI IN HOSPITALITY

Artificial intelligence plays a significant role in the innovation and transformation processes of the digital age (Li & Suh, 2022). Within the hospitality industry, AI-powered devices provide customers with real-time assistance, elucidation, relevant data, and suggestions, resulting in better decision-making and helping them find more relevant and accurate information. AI in hospitality enables visitors to manage and control the physical space of their rooms (e.g., via ALEXA), which improves the travel experience by increasing mobility. Additionally, AI in hotels employs robotic technologies to provide comprehensive end-to-end customer services (e.g., virtual check-in and check-outs, laundry, room cleaning, travel/tour planning and execution, food services, etc.) (Roy et al., 2020; Gretzel, 2011; Tussyadiah & Miller, 2019).

The field of artificial intelligence has seen the development of several innovative technologies. These technologies helped deliver a novel experience to the customers. Some of the AI-based tools include chatbots, robots, virtual reality apps, facial recognition, language translators, etc. These tools have made our daily work easier and resulted in time savings. A few of them are discussed below.

Self-Service Check-In and Check-Out Kiosks: Self-check-in and check-out kiosk enables visitors to complete their check-ins and check-outs without going through reception (Kim & Qu, 2014). Nowadays, self-service kiosks are applied in airports for foreign ID checks and boarding tickets, for passports enable travelers to check in, print their boarding cards, and check their luggage without needing staff.

Check-in with facial recognition- Facial recognition technology in the tourism industry is mainly used for security purposes, and it is also used to identify a person in a digital photo or video. (Gupta al., 2023).

Virtual reality- There are a variety of applications of virtual reality in the tourism and hospitality industries. A few of these are virtual booking interfaces, virtual travel experiences, and virtual hotel tours. Virtual hotel tours show the hotel's amenities and environment through 3D videos, giving guests a real-time experience with the hotel amenities (Samala et al., 2020).

Language translators- Language translators are software programs that convert one language into another (e.g., Google Translate). These apps are helpful for tourists visiting foreign countries, where they translate foreign languages into familiar languages (Samala et al., 2020).

Chatbots- In the words of Abu et al. (2007), p. 29, A chatbot is a software program that allows users or customers to communicate with the system in their native tongues. A chatbot, often known as a 'virtual agent' or 'chatterbot,' is a self-service technological application. Chatbots are endowed with several intelligence features. Chatbots help provide prompt responses to travelers and assist them in fulfilling their needs by saving them time and money.

Robots- Robots consistently enhance customer engagement and experience by providing innovative services and support in the hospitality industry. Robots in the hotel aid the customers by directing them to their hotel rooms, carrying their bags up to their rooms, maintaining housekeeping services, and serving meals and snacks (Ivanov & Webster, 2020).

3. METHODOLOGY

This systematic literature review (SLR) is on the use of artificial intelligence tools in the hospitality industry using the Scientific Procedures and Rationales for Systematic Literature Reviews (SPAR-4-SLR) protocol and TCM-ADO framework. Further, this review article put forth future research directions using the TCM ADO framework.

SPAR-4-SLR protocol was developed by Paul et al. (2021) and has been employed in numerous literature reviews (such as Ameen et al., 2022; Mukherjee et al., 2023; Sam & Jasim, 2025). While the TCM-ADO framework (Paul & Benito, 2018) structures the reviews based on the preexisting framework of Theory (T), Context (C), Methodology (M), Antecedents (A), Decision (D), and Outcome (O). TCM- ADO framework provides the maximum degree of lucidity and coverage (i.e., breadth and depth) in the reviews.

3.1. SPAR-4-SLR Protocol

As a methodology, SPAR-4-SLR systematic literature reviews encompass the process of gathering (assembling), organizing (arranging), and evaluating (assessing) the body of existing literature in a review domain (i.e., the 3 As). The terms "assembling" mean the identification and acquisition of literature, "arranging" relates to the organization and purification of literature, and "assessing" means the evaluation and reporting of literature, respectively. In this review, articles from Scopus were chosen for analysis. The stages of SPAR-4-SLR, along with the sub-stages, are discussed below (See Figure 1).

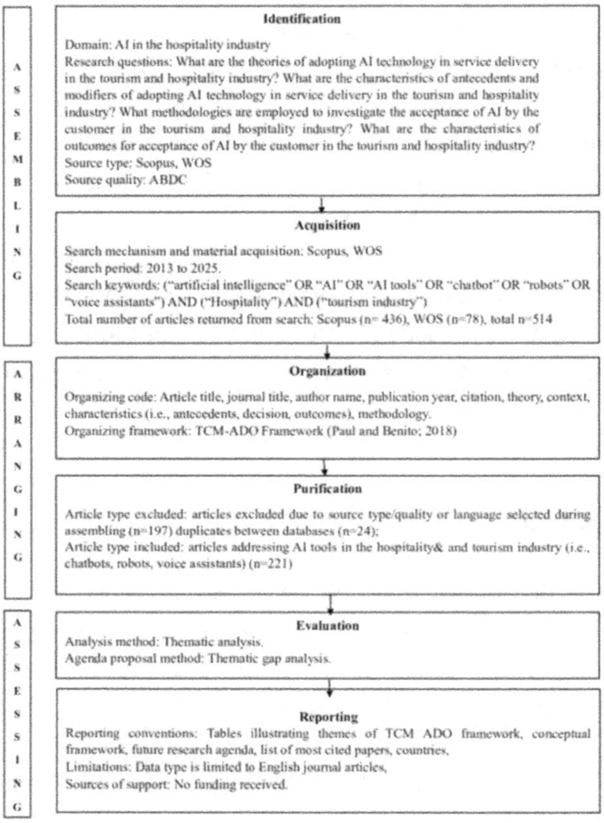

3.1.1 Assembling

The first stage of the SPAR-4-SLR protocol is 'assembly,' which constitutes selecting the source type and source quality and gathering articles for review in the review domain.

The review domain for this review is "Application of AI in the hospitality Industry." The review's main objective is to document the Theory, Context, Methodology, Antecedents, Decisions, and Outcomes in the research articles on the usage of AI-based tools in the context of the hospitality sector. RQ1, RQ2, RQ3, and RQ4 pertain to identifying 'what' theories, context, methodology, antecedents, decisions, and outcomes constituted the research framework conceptualized between 2013-2025 in the usage of AI in the tourism industry.

Journal research articles were extracted from Scopus and WOS. The review corpus includes the following fields: authors, document title, abstract, year, source title, volume, issue, keywords, and document type. The downloaded articles in the corpus were from 2013 to 2025.

Papers were selected on related topics.

i. Journal articles in the Scopus database were downloaded on 9th September 2025.
ii. Articles in databases were downloaded from the Scopus database using the keywords (“artificial intelligence” OR “AI” OR “AI tools” OR “chatbot” OR “robots” OR “voice assistants”) AND (“Hospitality”) AND (“tourism industry”).
iii. The time frame chosen for developing the review database was from 2013 to 2025. It was selected because of the notable rise in the use of AI devices during these years.
iv. Initially, 514 research articles were extracted, but only 221 were included in the corpus.

Identification- In this sub-stage of SPAR-4-SLR, this review focuses on the following:

Research Question- The research question focuses on what, where, and how to know about the research topic. This can help the researcher make a plan for their study.
Source Type- Source type specifies which published material's sources are included and which are not. Regarding source type, the researcher selected Scopus, WOS articles only, as they represent “certified knowledge.” English was the only language supported.
Quality of the source- To define the source quality of the published material, as recommended by Paul et al. (2021), the authors chose journal articles with an impact factor (IF) greater than one. “Web of Science (WoS) and Scopus are the most popular lists of quality journals that transcend disciplines” (Paul et al., 2021, p. 7).
Acquisition- In this sub-stage, the researchers focus on the search mechanism and the procurement of material. The following points come under acquisition-

a.) Search mechanism and material acquisition- Initially, the authors retrieved 514 articles from Scopus and WoS were extracted and only 221 were included in the Application of AI in the hospitality domain.

b.) Search period- The search period covers 2013 to 2025.

c.) Search keyword(s)- The keywords used for the search are (“artificial intelligence” OR “AI” OR “AI tools” OR “chatbot” OR “robots” OR “voice assistants”) AND (“Hospitality”) AND (“tourism industry”).

3.1.2 Arranging

In 'Arranging', items found during the search are organized (using organizing codes) and purified (using exclusion and inclusion criteria).

Initially, the authors retrieved a total of 514 articles, of which 436 were from Scopus and 78 were from WOS. But in total, 221 articles were retained for further review in the application of AI in the hospitality domain. Both databases shared more than 40% of similar content. Therefore, 197 articles were dropped due to the matching. The search results were filtered to include only the terms “ten years,” “AI in hospitality,” “article,” “final,” “journal,” and “English” in those categories, respectively. The sub-stage of arranging is as-

Organization- The Organizing code used in the review article is *Article title, Journal title, Author name, Publication year, Citation, Theory, Context, Methodology, Antecedents, Decision, and Outcomes.* TCM-ADO Framework (Paul and Benito, 2018) has been employed in the review.

Purification- Review excludes those articles that are not related to the hospitality industry. Articles addressing the application of AI tools in the hospitality industry (i.e., chatbots, robots, voice assistants) are included in the review.

3.1.3 Assessing

To follow the use of AI technologies in the tourist sector, analyses of the publication year, top 20 cited papers, nationalities, study types, and data collection methods were conducted. The articles undergo a thematic analysis. Future directions for research are also given. Regarding reporting, the review results are given in the following sections using words, figures, and tables, acknowledging the article's limitations. The sub-stages of assessing are discussed below.

Evaluation- Content analysis and thematic analysis are used to analyze the articles. Additionally, a future research agenda has been proposed for future academicians and practitioners.

Reporting- ‘Reporting’ Provide a summary of the findings and acknowledgments. It contains tables and figures illustrating themes of the TCM ADO Framework. The data is limited to English journal articles, the review type is limited to SLR, and the bibliographic information and thematic analysis are included.

4. FINDINGS OF SYSTEMATIC LITERATURE REVIEW (SLR)

4.1 Underpinning theories in articles in the review corpus:

The review revealed more than 60 theories and models in the coded article set. In contrast, a few research articles did not specify a distinct theory or model (see Table 3 for an overview). The uncanny valley theory, social cognition theory, computers as social actors (CASA) model, anthropomorphism theory, social presence theory, and several theories examining technology acceptance (such as the technology acceptance model (TAM), service robot acceptance model (SRAM), and unified theory of acceptance and use of technology (UTAUT) are some of the most widely used theoretical frameworks. Other theories are related to theories of human behavior, interactions, and relations between information systems (ISs) and humans, communication and personal information disclosure theories, and anthropomorphism theories.

The following are some most widely used frameworks and approaches employed in the reviewed articles.

4.1.1. UTAUT

Venkatesh et al. (2003) proposed the Unified Theory of Acceptance and Use of Technology (UTAUT). The purpose of UTAUT is to elucidate users' intentions when using an information system and their actual usage behaviour.

4.1.2 AIDUA

Gursoy et al., 2019 developed the Artificially Intelligent Device Use Acceptance (AIDUA) framework, which conceptualizes the development of customers' intention towards AI device use in service encounters to understand customers' willingness to accept the use of AI devices.

4.1.3 TOE

The Technology-Organization-Environment (TOE) framework was developed in 1990 by Mitchell Fleischer and Louis G. Tornatzky. It is a theoretical construct that explains technology adoption in organizations. It outlines how the technological, organizational, and environmental contexts impact the adoption and implementation process of technological innovations.

4.1.4 Social Exchange Theory

Sociologist George Homans developed the social exchange theory in 1958. The theory examines how two parties engage socially when they use a cost-benefit analysis to determine risks and benefits. The economic relationship is also included in the theory.

4.1.5 USUS Framework

Weiss et al., 2011 established the USUS framework. A multi-level indicator model serves as the foundation for the theoretical framework of USUS, which operationalizes the evaluation factors. Based on a multi-level indicator model, the suggested evaluation methodology for human-robot collaboration with humanoid robots aims to assess usability, social acceptance, user experience, and societal impact.

4.1.6 Self-Determination Theory

The self-determination theory is proposed by psychologists Richard Ryan, left, and Edward Deci. It is a comprehensive theory of human motivation and personality that considers people's fundamental psychological needs and tendencies toward personal development. It is about why people make decisions without outside pressures or distractions. The degree of self-motivation and self-determination in human behavior is the main emphasis of self-determination theory (SDT).

At the same time, the researcher put forth an extensive list of extra theories and models which are- Need-Threat model (e.g., Lv et al., 2022), Language expectancy theory- (e.g., Choi et al., 2020); Three-factor theory of anthropomorphism (e.g., Choi et al., 2020); Behavioral reasoning theory (BRT) (e.g., Rasheed et al., 2023); Attribution theory (e.g., Belanche et al., 2021); Rogers' (2003) Diffusion theory (e.g., Huang et al., 2022); Diffusion of innovation (DOI) theory (e.g., Alsetoohy et al., 2019); Task–technology fit theory (TTF)- (e.g., Dhiman & Jamwal 2023); Expectation–confirmation model (ECM)- (e.g., Dhiman & Jamwal 2023); Computers as Social Actors (CASA) Theory- (e.g., Pelau et al., 2021). Antecedent-decision characteristics-outcome (ADO)- (e.g., Goel et al., 2022); Theory-context-methods framework (TCM)-(e.g., Law et al., 2023); Stimulus-response model (S-O-R Model) (e.g., Zhang & Jin, 2023; Rafiq et al., 2022); Spreading of activation theory (e.g., Choi et al., 2020); Cognitive appraisal theory (e.g., Li et al., 2021); Disruptive Innovation Theory (e.g., Zhang & Jin, 2023); The Protection Motivation Theory (PMT) (e.g., Gaur et al., 2021); Assemblage theory (e.g., Jiménez-Barreto et al., 2021).

4.2. Context

From the contextual point of the review, it has been found that most of the studies focused on hotels (e.g., Lin et al., 2020; Webster & Ivanov, 2020; Go et al., 2020, etc.) and a smaller number of articles focused on the use of AI tools in restaurants (e.g., Al. Rasch et al., 2021; Rasheed et al., 2024). The main reason behind this is the increase in the use of AI tools in the tourism industry for providing customer service. Additionally, it has been found that most of the studies were conducted in the United States and China, which shows the advanced stage of AI implementation in these nations compared to other countries (see Table 2).

The research context of the reviewed articles focused on different tools of AI, such as Chatbots (e.g., Lasek & Jessa, 2013; Huang et al., 2022; Citak et al., 2021, etc.), Voice-assistants (e.g., Buhalis & Moldavska 2022; Al-Hyari et al., 2023; etc.), Robots (e.g., Choi et al. 2020; Ivanov et al., 2023, etc.); Anthropomorphic chatbots, Anthropomorphic robots (e.g., Yoganathan et al., 2021; Pelau et al., 2021; Tuomi et al., 2021, etc.) in different domains of the hospitality industry. The impact of these AI-enabled technologies on customer behavior and their experience, satisfaction, and revisit intention is also discussed in terms of the tourism industry (Sharma et al., 2022; Prentice et al., 2020; Çakar & Aykol, 2021, etc).

4.3. Characteristics

This review systematically maps the antecedents, mediators, moderators, and outcomes relevant to AI adoption and serves as the foundation for the proposed conceptual framework (see Figure 2).

Antecedents: The main antecedents examined by researchers include the user, utilitarian, and hedonistic aspects of AI technologies, as well as the willingness and barriers to using these technologies. *User-related* antecedents focus on individual characteristics, such as consumer values, reasons for and against deploying AI-enabled services, and the need for human interactions with chatbots, robots and voice assistants, along with technology anxiety and performance and effort expectations (e.g., Nguyen et al., 2022; Mariani & Borghi, 2021; Buhalis & Moldavska, 2022; Pillai & Sivathanu, 2020; Gursoy et al., 2019).

Utilitarian attributes refer to the functional characteristics of AI, which include perceived intelligence, perceived usefulness, perceived ease of use, privacy concerns, and perceived risk (e.g., Pillai & Sivathanu, 2020; Bowen & Morosan, 2018; Chatterjee et al., 2020; Seo & Leo 2021). *Hedonic attributes* are associated with emotional and experiential qualities such as enjoyment, social presence, comfort, relaxation, pleasure, and novelty (e.g., Yoganathan et al., 2021, etc.). Other than that, variables related to the willingness and acceptance to use AI include social impact, motivation, anthropomorphism, positive emotion, discomfort, and ease of maintenance (e.g., Yang et al., 2022; Li & Suh, 2022, etc.). Variables relating to the willingness to use service robots are performance efficacy, intrinsic motivation, anthropomorphism, social influence, facilitating conditions and emotions, robot advantage/disadvantage, and the social skills of robots (e.g., Molinillo et al., 2022; Tu et al., 2023, etc.). Apart from that, a few variables relating to the Barriers to using AI are also found. Financial, technological, behavioural/attitude barriers, and job insecurity are the main obstacles found in the review (Cozzio et al., 2025).

Mediators and Moderators: These factors affect how the antecedents and outcomes relate to one another. The user-centric elements (such as self-efficacy, perceived trustworthiness, customer engagement, etc.) and factors related to interaction (such as interaction style, trust, ethical interaction, interaction quality, etc.) are found as the two major categories of mediators (Kim et al., 2022). A few moderators include (e.g., anthropomorphism of the AI, perceived empathy, need for interaction) moderators are classified as User characteristics (such as Past customer experience, customer participation, employee involvement, Personal involvement, perceived health competence, attitudes towards risk, cultural dimensions like uncertainty avoidance, etc.) and AI tool/interaction factors (such as anthropomorphism/human likeness chatbots, humanoid service robots, Consumers' need for interaction, etc.) (Pillai & Sivathanu, 2020).

Outcome: In addition to these, this review finds many variables pertaining to the results or consequences. Outcomes are classified as acceptability/adoption of AI tools, User experience,

Satisfaction (such as satisfaction with the chatbot, satisfaction with robots (Jiménez-Barreto et al., 2021; Soliman et al., 2024), Purchase (such as purchase rate, willingness to pay (e.g., Ivanov & Webster, 2021; Yoganathan et al., 2021) and Loyalty (such as loyalty to the chatbot and robot) (e.g., Al-Hyari et al., 2023; Soliman et al., 2024). Apart from these, the review found various outcomes related to use/adoption goals, which include reuse/continued use, repurchase, word-of-mouth (e.g., Pillai & Sivathanu, 2020; Kim et al., 2022; Lei et al., 2023, etc.).

Based on the abovementioned information on the studied characteristics, this review proposes a conceptual framework of the variables investigated in the research on the application of AI tools in the hotel industry (see Figure 2).

4.4. Methodology

The TCM-ADO framework's methodological analysis shows that, in order to understand people's engagement with AI-based tools, most researchers used Quantitative techniques in their study. The most popular approach is the experimental method, which usually makes use of scenario-based online experiments (e.g., Pillai

& Sivathanu, 2020; Lei et al., 2023; Lasek & Jessa, 2013; Lestari et al., 2022, etc.). This method is frequently employed to evaluate the causal impacts of AI tools on human perceptions.

from the review, it has been found that online surveys conducted through MTurk and other survey-based methodologies are also commonly used (e.g., Lin et al., 2020; Gursoy et al., 2019; etc.). The most used analytical method is structural equation modelling (SEM), Covariance-based structural equation modeling (CB-SEM) (e.g., Lin et al., 2020), and Partial Least Squares Structural Equation Modelling (PLS-SEM) (e.g., Lei et al., 2023; Chen et al., 2023; Rafiq et al., 2022; Parvez et al., 2022, etc). Additionally, to verify concept validity, Confirmatory Factor Analysis (CFA) (e.g., Li et al., 2019; Lu et al., 2019, etc.) and Exploratory Factor Analysis (EFA) are frequently used (e.g., Alsetoohy et al., 2019; Ivanov et al., 2018, etc.).

Conversely, from the review, it has been found that Qualitative research is less prevalent. Only a few researchers adopted the interview-based method (e.g., Pandya & Janahi, 2021; Nam et al., 2021; Gupta et al., 2023, etc.). Some articles have employed mixed methods research, which combines quantitative and qualitative methods (e.g., Pillai & Sivathanu, 2020; Pandya & Janahi, 2021; Citak et al., 2021; Zhao et al., 2023, etc.). To gain a deeper understanding of user involvement, it is acknowledged that methods such as case studies and ethnography must be used by the researchers.

4.5. Most Cited Papers, Prominent Countries, and Collaborations

The selected papers are distributed across different journals. Table 1 lists highly influential journals with the titles, authors, year of publication, and the total citations of 20 papers on the application of AI in the hospitality industry. International Journal of Information Management is the most productive publication on the list, followed by the International Journal of Hospitality Management in the use of AI in the context of hospitality research. On the basis of data, different authors have contributed to the application of AI research in the hospitality industry. The most cited paper listed in the table is Consumer Acceptance of Artificial Intelligence (AI) device use in service delivery, which garnered 1580 citations. Likewise, Lu et al., 2019 studied developing and validating a service robot integration willingness scale, which garnered 1088 citations respectively. Table 2 displays 20 distinct nations with the total number of studies. The most prolific nations in terms of papers published were China (9), the United States (8), and Taiwan (5) etc. On the contrary, there are a few countries where a minimal number of studies have been done, i.e., Portugal (1) and Persia (1), respectively.

5. PROPOSED CONCEPTUAL FRAMEWORK

Developing a conceptual framework for the application of AI tools in the hospitality industry involves identifying key components such as antecedents, outcomes, mediators, and moderators. This section describes the antecedents-decisions-outcomes (ADO) paradigm as shown in the review (see Figure 2). Drawing on significant findings from the extensive literature review, the authors discovered several aspects affecting consumers' decisions or behavioral performance, the consequent effects, and pertinent moderators and mediators. The framework underlines the complexity of customer experience, which encompasses several dimensions besides the morphological design features of AI tools. This framework reveals the research on different applications of AI tools like chatbots, VAs, and robots. The framework developed from the review's findings emphasizes how the user experience with AI tools is multifaceted, encompassing functional, intellectual, emotional, sensory, social, and relational aspects.

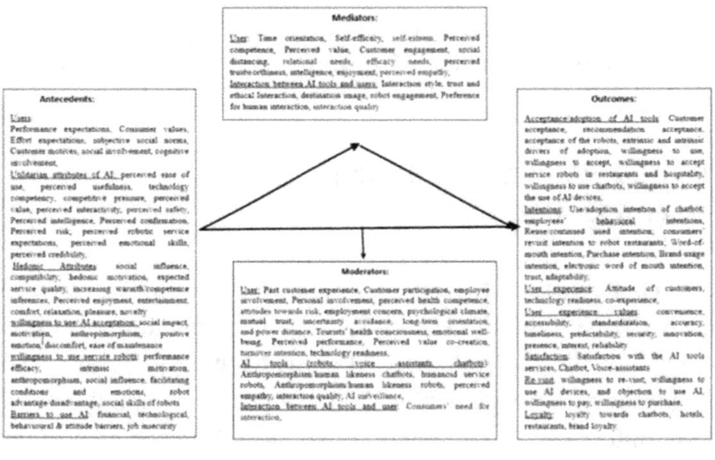

The review contains several dimensions, such as functional and pragmatic, rational and cognitive, emotional, sensory, social, and relational. Perceived usefulness and perceived ease of use are examples of aspects that fall under the functional dimension. On the other hand, the rational/cognitive dimension is more inclusive and includes a wider range of aspects such as cognitive absorption, perceived intelligence, perceived risk, engagement, consumer engagement, perceived conversational engagement, perceived partner engagement, perceived knowledge of chatbot, and perceived task attraction. Perceived empathy of the chatbot, feeling of intimacy with chatbots, and voice assistant technology are all included in the emotional dimension. Challenges/

arousal, entertainment, and perceived media richness characterize the sensory dimension of the customer with AI tools. Perceived social presence, perceived social attractiveness, perceived agency, and perceived humanness/anthropomorphism are all components of the social dimension. A few examples of the variables that highlight the relational component are the user's perceived psychological power, parasocial interactions with the chatbots/ VA, perceived intrusiveness of the VA, perceived confidence in the VA, distrust, and rapport.

6. DISCUSSION AND IMPLICATIONS

This review article provides a deeper comprehension of AI deployment in the hospitality industry. The implications of this review could be applied to business owners, managers, and marketers in the hospitality industry or any other sector to better understand and implement appropriate strategies to meet the needs and expectations of both customers and employees using AI. Additionally, the review added to the body of knowledge already available on the use of AI in the hotel sector. Therefore, it could serve as a roadmap for future studies on the deployment of AI in the hospitality sector. By adding additional possible components, it might also help scholars expand their research.

Moreover, the review excels and adds value as it provides the dual impact, i.e., both positive (personalization, relevance, accuracy, etc.) and negative (barriers to adopt AI tools, etc). By employing a rigorous methodology, this review aids in organizing and synthesizing data from various prestigious sources. Furthermore, the review determines the variables/factors that have undergone in-depth analysis and the current trend in research. The TCM and ADO framework have uncovered unrevealed theoretical, contextual, methodological, antecedents, decisions, and outcomes insights. The researchers examined the relationships between the antecedents, consequences, mediating, and moderating variables, which refer to AI tools such as robots, chatbots, and virtual assistants.

7. FUTURE RESEARCH

Using the TCM-ADO framework, the researcher examined the literature for this study. This review provides insight into the historical and contemporary directions of research. This section provides a structured research agenda based on the review's findings (See Table 4). From the review, it has been found that most existing literature concentrates on certain artificial intelligence-related variables, models, and theories, where most of the studies focused on adopting and applying artificial intelligence in hotels only. Researchers can explore other domains of the hospitality industry, such as restaurants, airlines, and travel agencies. Although the review revealed more than 60 distinct theories applied in the field of AI tool application in the hospitality industry, only a tiny percentage of the reviewed studies used multiple theories. So, it has been found that there is a compelling need for more theory-based research. Scholars and researchers can develop frameworks and models that are more up-to-date by incorporating new variables or utilizing existing ones. Also, there is a need to expand the research in the geographical context, as it has been found that most of the evaluated articles contain direct research for which the original data were gathered from China and the US.

Moreover, the review found that most of the studies adopted quantitative studies, leaving room for more qualitative and mixed-method studies in the future. The researcher inspires future marketing studies to consider expanding theoretical novelty, strengthening contextual relevance, and improving methodological rigor concerning the application of AI tools in hospitality industry research.

8. CONCLUSION

The hospitality sector is using cutting-edge technology and a high degree of AI-based systems, giving travel firms an excellent chance to enhance marketing, customer service, customer experience, and retention. This review thoroughly summarizes the literature on artificial intelligence in hospitality published between 2013 and 2025. By examining the gaps, characteristics, and methods employed, this review adopts the TCM-ADO framework to assist researchers in determining the future course of action (Singh & Dhir, 2019). The use of the TCM-ADO framework reveals various essential aspects related to antecedents, decisions, outcomes, applied theories, research context, and AI tool application methods. With more than 60 theories and models in the evaluated publications, the review demonstrates a fragmented theoretical approach supported by the necessity for several "examination lenses."

This review emphasizes the importance of providing a theoretical framework for each new article, focusing on theories related to communication, anthropomorphism, and sharing personal information. It is necessary to expand the geographical coverage to include countries where different industries and consumers utilize AI tools and extend the scope of studies to include other business sectors that can benefit from AI tools. Furthermore, the review focuses on the consumer experience using AI technologies and their varied characteristics across different areas. The methodology reveals a preference for quantitative approaches to data gathering and analysis. The results of this review must be considered while considering a few limitations.

The review was limited to publications published in prestigious business journals. Moreover, reviews of articles were limited to those written in English.

REFERENCES

al. Rasch, F., Roxana Mosteanu, N., & Teplyakova, I. (2021, December). The impact of introducing robotics and artificially based intelligence systems, on employment in hospitality sector of Uzbekistan. In *Proceedings of the 2021 4th Artificial Intelligence and Cloud Computing Conference* (pp. 194-200).

Al-Hyari, H. S. A., Al-Smadi, H. M., & Weshah, S. R. (2023). The impact of artificial intelligence (AI) on guest satisfaction in hotel management: An empirical study of luxury hotels. *Geo Journal of Tourism and Geosites*, *48*, 810–819.

Alsetoohy, O., Ayoun, B., Arous, S., Megahed, F., & Nabil, G. (2019). Intelligent agent technology: What affects its adoption in hotel food supply chain management? *Journal of Hospitality and Tourism Technology*, *10*(3), 286–310.

Ameen, N., Sharma, G. D., Tarba, S., Rao, A., & Chopra, R. (2022). Toward advancing theory on creativity in marketing and artificial intelligence. *Psychology and Marketing*, *39*(9), 1802–1825.

Belanche, D., Casaló, L. V., & Flavián, C. (2021). Frontline robots in tourism and hospitality: Service enhancement or cost reduction? *Electronic Markets*, *31*(3), 477–492.

Bhatia, R., Bhat, A. K., & Tikoria, J. (2021). Life insurance purchase behaviour: A systematic review and directions for future research. *International Journal of Consumer Studies*, *45*(6), 1149–1175.

Bowen, J., & Morosan, C. (2018). Beware hospitality industry: The robots are coming. *Worldwide Hospitality and Tourism Themes*, *10*(6), 726–733.

Buhalis, D., & Moldavska, I. (2022). Voice assistants in hospitality: Using artificial intelligence for customer service. *Journal of Hospitality and Tourism Technology*, *13*(3), 386–403.

Çakar, K., & Aykol, Ş. (2021). Understanding travellers' reactions to robotic services: A multiple case study approach of robotic hotels. *Journal of Hospitality and Tourism Technology*, *12*(1), 155–174.

Chatterjee, S., Nguyen, B., Ghosh, S. K., Bhattacharjee, K. K., & Chaudhuri, S. (2020). Adoption of artificial intelligence integrated CRM system: An empirical study of Indian organizations. *The Bottom Line (New York, N.Y.)*, *33*(4), 359–375.

Chen, P. T., & Kuo, S. C. (2017). Innovation resistance and strategic implications of enterprise social media websites in Taiwan through knowledge sharing perspective. *Technological Forecasting and Social Change, 118*, 55–69.

Chen, Y., Hu, Y., Zhou, S., & Yang, S. (2023). Investigating the determinants of performance of artificial intelligence adoption in hospitality industry during COVID-19. *International Journal of Contemporary Hospitality Management, 35*(8), 2868–2889.

Choi, Y., Choi, M., Oh, M., & Kim, S. (2020). Service robots in hotels: Understanding the service quality perceptions of human-robot interaction. *Journal of Hospitality Marketing & Management, 29*(6), 613–635.

Citak, J., Owoc, M. L., & Weichbroth, P. (2021). A note on the applications of artificial intelligence in the hospitality industry: Preliminary results of a survey. *Procedia Computer Science, 192*, 4552–4559.

Cozzio, C., Santos Arteaga, F. J., & Maurer, O. (2025). Artificial intelligence adoption in hospitality: Challenges and opportunities across hierarchical levels. *Tourism Review*.

Dhiman, N., & Jamwal, M. (2023). Tourists' post-adoption continuance intentions of chatbots: integrating task–technology fit model and expectation–confirmation theory. *foresight, 25*(2), 209-224.

Doborjeh, Z., Hemmington, N., Doborjeh, M., & Kasabov, N. (2021). Artificial intelligence: A systematic review of methods and applications in hospitality and tourism. *International Journal of Contemporary Hospitality Management, 34*(3), 1154–1176.

Gaur, L., Afaq, A., Singh, G., & Dwivedi, Y. K. (2021). Role of artificial intelligence and robotics to foster the touchless travel during a pandemic: A review and research agenda. *International Journal of Contemporary Hospitality Management, 33*(11), 4079–4098.

Go, H., Kang, M., & Suh, S. C. (2020). Machine learning of robots in tourism and hospitality: Interactive technology acceptance model (iTAM)–cutting edge. *Tourism Review, 75*(4), 625–636.

Goel, P., Kaushik, N., Sivathanu, B., Pillai, R., & Vikas, J. (2022). Consumers' adoption of artificial intelligence and robotics in hospitality and tourism sector: Literature review and future research agenda. *Tourism Review, 77*(4), 1081–1096.

Gretzel, U. (2011). Intelligent systems in tourism: A social science perspective. *Annals of Tourism Research, 38*(3), 757–779.

Gupta, S., Modgil, S., Lee, C. K., & Sivarajah, U. (2023). The future is yesterday: Use of AI-driven facial recognition to enhance value in the travel and tourism industry. *Information Systems Frontiers*, *25*(3), 1179–1195.

Gursoy, D., Chi, O. H., Lu, L., & Nunkoo, R. (2019). Consumers acceptance of artificially intelligent (AI) device use in service delivery. *International Journal of Information Management*, *49*, 157–169.

Homans, G. C. (1958). Social behavior as exchange. *American Journal of Sociology*, *63*(6), 597–606.

Huang, A., Chao, Y., de la Mora Velasco, E., Bilgihan, A., & Wei, W. (2022). When artificial intelligence meets the hospitality and tourism industry: An assessment framework to inform theory and management. *Journal of Hospitality and Tourism Insights*, *5*(5), 1080–1100.

Husain, R., Ratna, V. V., & Saxena, A. (2023). Past, present, and future of anthropomorphism in hospitality & tourism: Conceptualization and systematic review. *Journal of Hospitality Marketing & Management*, *32*(8), 1077–1125.

Ivanov, S., & Webster, C. (2020). Robots in tourism: A research agenda for tourism economics. *Tourism Economics*, *26*(7), 1065–1085.

Ivanov, S., & Webster, C. (2021). Willingness-to-pay for robot-delivered tourism and hospitality services–an exploratory study. *International Journal of Contemporary Hospitality Management*, *33*(11), 3926–3955.

Ivanov, S., & Webster, C. (2023). Restaurants and robots: Public preferences for robot food and beverage services. *Journal of Tourism Futures*, *9*(2), 229–239.

Ivanov, S., Webster, C., & Garenko, A. (2018). Young Russian adults' attitudes towards the potential use of robots in hotels. *Technology in Society*, *55*, 24–32.

Ivanov, S., Webster, C., & Seyitoğlu, F. (2023). Humans and/or robots? Tourists' preferences towards the humans–robots mix in the service delivery system. *Service Business*, *17*(1), 195–231.

Jamshed, K., Qureshi, M. A., Kishwer, R., & Jamshaid, S. (2024). The benefits and challenges of artificial intelligence applications in tourism industry: How the hospitality industry in Japan is transforming. In *The role of artificial intelligence in regenerative tourism and green destinations* (pp. 129–147). Emerald Publishing Limited.

Jiménez-Barreto, J., Rubio, N., & Molinillo, S. (2021). "Find a flight for me, Oscar!" Motivational customer experiences with chatbots. *International Journal of Contemporary Hospitality Management, 33*(11), 3860–3882.

Kim, H., So, K. K. F., & Wirtz, J. (2022). Service robots: Applying social exchange theory to better understand human–robot interactions. *Tourism Management, 92*, 104537.

Kim, M., & Qu, H. (2014). Travelers' behavioral intention toward hotel self-service kiosks usage. *International Journal of Contemporary Hospitality Management, 26*(2), 225–245.

Kim, T., Jo, H., Yhee, Y., & Koo, C. (2022). Robots, artificial intelligence, and service automation (RAISA) in hospitality: Sentiment analysis of YouTube streaming data. *Electronic Markets, 32*(1), 259–275.

Knani, M., Echchakoui, S., & Ladhari, R. (2022). Artificial intelligence in tourism and hospitality: Bibliometric analysis and research agenda. *International Journal of Hospitality Management, 107*, 103317.

Lasek, M., & Jessa, S. (2013). Chatbots for customer service on hotels' websites. *Information Systems Management, 2*(2), 146–158.

Law, R., Lin, K. J., Ye, H., & Fong, D. K. C. (2023). Artificial intelligence research in hospitality: A state-of-the-art review and future directions. *International Journal of Contemporary Hospitality Management.*

Law, R., Lin, K. J., Ye, H., & Fong, D. K. C. (2024). Artificial intelligence research in hospitality: A state-of-the-art review and future directions. *International Journal of Contemporary Hospitality Management, 36*(6), 2049–2068.

Lei, C., Hossain, M. S., & Wong, E. (2023). Determinants of repurchase intentions of hospitality services delivered by artificially intelligent (AI) service robots. *Sustainability, 15*(6), 4914.

Lestari, N. S., Rosman, D., Chan, S., Nawangsari, L. C., Natalina, H. D., & Triono, F. (2022, October). Impact of robots, artificial intelligence, service automation (RAISA) acceptance, self-efficacy, and relationship quality on job performance. In *2022 4th International Conference on Cybernetics and Intelligent System (ICORIS)* (pp. 1-6). IEEE.

Li, J. J., Bonn, M. A., & Ye, B. H. (2019). Hotel employee's artificial intelligence and robotics awareness and its impact on turnover intention: The moderating roles of perceived organizational support and competitive psychological climate. *Tourism Management, 73*, 172–181.

Li, L., Lee, K. Y., Emokpae, E., & Yang, S. B. (2021). What makes you continuously use chatbot services? Evidence from chinese online travel agencies. *Electronic Markets*, •••, 1–25.

Li, M., & Suh, A. (2022). Anthropomorphism in AI-enabled technology: A literature review. *Electronic Markets*, *32*(4), 2245–2275.

Lim, W. M., Yap, S. F., & Makkar, M. (2021). Home sharing in marketing and tourism at a tipping point: What do we know, how do we know, and where should we be heading? *Journal of Business Research*, *122*, 534–566.

Limna, P., Siripipatthanakul, S., & Phayaphrom, B. (2021). The role of big data analytics in influencing artificial intelligence (AI) adoption for coffee shops in Krabi, Thailand. *International Journal of Behavioral Analytics*, *1*(2), 1–17.

Lin, H., Chi, O. H., & Gursoy, D. (2020). Antecedents of customers' acceptance of artificially intelligent robotic device use in hospitality services. *Journal of Hospitality Marketing & Management*, *29*(5), 530–549.

Louis, G. Tornatzky, Fleischer, M., & Chakrabarti, A. K. (1990). *The processes of technological innovation*. Lexington Books.

Lu, L., Cai, R., & Gursoy, D. (2019). Developing and validating a service robot integration willingness scale. *International Journal of Hospitality Management*, *80*, 36–51.

Lv, L., Huang, M., Guan, D., & Yang, K. (2022). Apology or gratitude? The effect of communication recovery strategies for service failures of AI devices. *Journal of Travel & Tourism Marketing*, *39*(6), 570–587.

Mariani, M., & Borghi, M. (2021). Customers' evaluation of mechanical artificial intelligence in hospitality services: A study using online reviews analytics. *International Journal of Contemporary Hospitality Management*, *33*(11), 3956–3976.

Molinillo, S., Rejón-Guardia, F., & Anaya-Sánchez, R. (2022). Exploring the antecedents of customers' willingness to use service robots in restaurants. *Service Business*, *17*(1), 167–193.

Mukherjee, S., Baral, M. M., Nagariya, R., Venkataiah, C., Rao, U. A., & Rao, K. S. (2023). Systematic literature review and future research directions for service robots in hospitality and tourism industries. *Service Industries Journal*, *43*(15-16), 1083–1116.

Nam, K., Dutt, C. S., Chathoth, P., Daghfous, A., & Khan, M. S. (2021). The adoption of artificial intelligence and robotics in the hotel industry: Prospects and challenges. *Electronic Markets, 31*, 553–574.

Nguyen, T. M., Quach, S., & Thaichon, P. (2022). The effect of AI quality on customer experience and brand relationship. *Journal of Consumer Behaviour, 21*(3), 481–493.

Pandya, B., & Al Janahi, M. M. (2021). The intervention of artificial intelligence in the recruitment function in UAE's hospitality industry. *Transnational Marketing Journal, 9*(1), 89–105.

Parvez, M. O., Arasli, H., Ozturen, A., Lodhi, R. N., & Ongsakul, V. (2022). Antecedents of human-robot collaboration: Theoretical extension of the technology acceptance model. *Journal of Hospitality and Tourism Technology, 13*(2), 240–263.

Paul, J., & Benito, G. R. (2018). A review of research on outward foreign direct investment from emerging countries, including China: What do we know, how do we know and where should we be heading? *Asia Pacific Business Review, 24*(1), 90–115.

Paul, J., Lim, W. M., O'Cass, A., Hao, A. W., & Bresciani, S. (2021). Scientific procedures and rationales for systematic literature reviews (SPAR-4-SLR). *International Journal of Consumer Studies, 45*(4), O1–O16.

Paul, J., Parthasarathy, S., & Gupta, P. (2017). Exporting challenges of SMEs: A review and future research agenda. *Journal of World Business, 52*(3), 327–342.

Pelau, C., Dabija, D. C., & Ene, I. (2021). What makes an AI device human-like? The role of interaction quality, empathy and perceived psychological anthropomorphic characteristics in the acceptance of artificial intelligence in the service industry. *Computers in Human Behavior, 122*, 106855.

Pillai, R., & Sivathanu, B. (2020). Adoption of AI-based chatbots for hospitality and tourism. *International Journal of Contemporary Hospitality Management, 32*(10), 3199–3226.

Prentice, C., Dominique Lopes, S., & Wang, X. (2020). The impact of artificial intelligence and employee service quality on customer satisfaction and loyalty. *Journal of Hospitality Marketing & Management, 29*(7), 739–756.

Rafiq, F., Dogra, N., Adil, M., & Wu, J. Z. (2022). Examining consumer's intention to adopt AI-chatbots in tourism using partial least squares structural equation modeling method. *Mathematics, 10*(13), 2190.

Rasheed, H. M. W., He, Y., Khizar, H. M. U., & Abbas, H. S. M. (2023). Exploring Consumer-Robot interaction in the hospitality sector: Unpacking the reasons for adoption (or resistance) to artificial intelligence. *Technological Forecasting and Social Change*, *192*, 122555.

Rasheed, H. M. W., Yuanqiong, H., Khizar, H. M. U., & Khalid, J. (2024). What drives the adoption of artificial intelligence among consumers in the hospitality sector: A systematic literature review and future agenda. *Journal of Hospitality and Tourism Technology*, *15*(2), 211–231.

Roy, P., Ramaprasad, B. S., Chakraborty, M., Prabhu, N., & Rao, S. (2020). Customer acceptance of use of artificial intelligence in hospitality services: An Indian hospitality sector perspective. *Global Business Review*, 0972150920939753.

Ruel, H., & Njoku, E. (2021). AI redefining the hospitality industry. *Journal of Tourism Futures*, *7*(1), 53–66.

Ryan, R. M., & Deci, E. L. (2024). Self-determination theory. In *Encyclopedia of quality of life and well-being research* (pp. 6229–6235). Springer International Publishing.

Sam, S. J. I., & Jasim, K. M. (2025). Diving into the technology: A systematic literature review on strategic use of chatbots in hospitality service encounters. *Management Review Quarterly*, *75*(1), 527–555.

Samala, N., Katkam, B. S., Bellamkonda, R. S., & Rodriguez, R. V. (2020). Impact of AI and robotics in the tourism sector: a critical insight. *Journal of tourism futures, 8*(1), 73-87.

Saravanakumar, S., & Narayanan, M. B. (2018). The service automation and robotics in hospitality industry: A study on business implications. *International Journal of Mechanical and Production Engineering Research and Development*, *8*(6), 91–100.

Seo, K. H., & Lee, J. H. (2021). The emergence of service robots at restaurants: Integrating trust, perceived risk, and satisfaction. *Sustainability*, *13*(8), 4431.

Sharma, K., Dhir, S., & Ongsakul, V. (2022). Artificial intelligence and hospitality industry: Systematic review using TCCM and bibliometric analysis. *Journal for International Business and Entrepreneurship Development*, *14*(1), 48–71.

Singh, S., & Dhir, S. (2019). Structured review using TCCM and bibliometric analysis of international cause-related marketing, social marketing, and innovation of the firm. *International Review on Public and Nonprofit Marketing*, *16*(2), 335–347.

Soliman, M., Gulvady, S., Elbaz, A. M., Mosbah, M., & Wahba, M. S. (2024). Robot-delivered tourism and hospitality services: How to evaluate the impact of health and safety considerations on visitors' satisfaction and loyalty? *Tourism and Hospitality Research, 24*(3), 393–409.

Tu, Y., Liu, W., & Yang, Z. (2023). Exploring the influence of service employees' characteristics on their willingness to work with service robots. *Journal of Service Management, 34*(5), 1038–1063.

Tuomi, A., Tussyadiah, I. P., & Hanna, P. (2021). Spicing up hospitality service encounters: The case of Pepper™. *International Journal of Contemporary Hospitality Management, 33*(11), 3906–3925.

Tussyadiah, I., & Miller, G. (2019). Perceived impacts of artificial intelligence and responses to positive behaviour change intervention. In *Information and Communication Technologies in Tourism 2019: Proceedings of the International Conference in Nicosia, Cyprus, January 30–February 1, 2019* (pp. 359-370). Springer International Publishing.

Venkatesh, V., Morris, M. G., Davis, G. B., & Davis, F. D. (2003). User acceptance of information technology: Toward a unified view. *Management Information Systems Quarterly*, •••, 425–478.

Webster, C., & Ivanov, S. (2020). Future tourism in a robot-based economy: A perspective article. *Tourism Review, 75*(1), 329–332.

Webster, C., & Ivanov, S. (2020). *Robotics, artificial intelligence, and the evolving nature of work.* Springer International Publishing.

Weiss, A., Bernhaupt, R., & Tscheligi, M. (2011). The USUS evaluation framework for user-centered HRI. *New Frontiers in Human–Robot Interaction*, *2*, 89–110.

Yang, Y., Liu, Y., Lv, X., Ai, J., & Li, Y. (2022). Anthropomorphism and customers' willingness to use artificial intelligence service agents. *Journal of Hospitality Marketing & Management, 31*(1), 1–23.

Yoganathan, V., Osburg, V. S., Kunz, W. H., & Toporowski, W. (2021). Check-in at the Robo-desk: Effects of automated social presence on social cognition and service implications. *Tourism Management, 85*, 104309.

Zhang, X., & Jin, H. (2023). How does smart technology, artificial intelligence, automation, robotics, and algorithms (STAARA) awareness affect hotel employees' career perceptions? A disruptive innovation theory perspective. *Journal of Hospitality Marketing & Management, 32*(2), 264–283.

Zhao, H., Lan, J., Lyu, T., & Zeng, G. (2023). Working with artificial intelligence surveillance during the COVID-19 pandemic: A mixed investigation of the influence mechanism on job engagement in hospitality industry. *Current Issues in Tourism*, *26*(20), 3318–3335.

Chapter 6
Integrating Social Media Tools With Technology Acceptance Models:
A Path Toward Predicting Hotel Guest Behaviour in the Tricity Region

Niraj Kumar
http://orcid.org/0009-0005-7465-8854
Chandigarh University, Mohali, India

Shaina Arora
http://orcid.org/0000-0002-5998-6834
Chandigarh University, Mohali, India

Pankaj Kumar Tyagi
http://orcid.org/0000-0001-9504-541X
Chandigarh University, Mohali, India

ABSTRACT

The present study examines the fusion of social media constructs to obtain a model of the Unified Theory of Acceptance and Use of Technology (UTAUT2) for predicting the behavioural intentions of hotel guests in Tricity of India. Acknowledging the increasing impact of digital social connectedness on hospitality consumption, e.g., in the form of electronic word of mouth (e-WOM), perceived trust and information quality are integrated in addition to original UTAUT2 determinants like performance expectancy, social influence and hedonic motivation. Applying hierarchical regression and structural equation modelling on meta-analytic secondary data, our

DOI: 10.4018/979-8-3373-6741-5.ch006

findings indicate that social media factors dramatically increase the explanatory power of a technology acceptance framework, with perceived trust and e-WOM being the most significant predictors. Results highlight the importance of extending technology adoption models by incorporating social media within fast-paced urban hospitality contexts.

1. INTRODUCTION AND RATIONALE

In today's Indian urban markets, social media has become an influential force changing consumer preferences, especially in the hospitality industry (Semwal et al., 2024). From Instagram, Facebook, and TripAdvisor, to YouTube, these are no longer just communication platforms to a consumer, they are decision-making tools that influence expectations and engagement. Social media not only promotes information transfer but also enhances e-WOM, which has been acknowledged as one of the most influential consumer communications because of its authenticity and perceived credibility (Litvin et al., 2008). In contrast with offline advertising, e-WOM exchange within social media provides users with instant and authentic content, such as hotels' review and service rating reflected by travelers experiences and travel advice, influencing brand attitudes and consumers trust on brands (Cheung & Thadani, 2012; Jalilvand & Samiei, 2012).

The adoption of technology in consumer markets has been studied thoroughly with the frameworks, such as the Unified Theory of Acceptance and Use of Technology (UTAUT) and its extension, the second version of UTAUT. UTAUT2 includes concepts such as performance expectancy, effort expectancy, social influence, facilitating conditions, hedonic motivation, price value, and habit, creating one of the richest models to predict behavioral intention and technology usage outcomes (Venkatesh et al., 2012). Nonetheless, although these models provide a strong theoretical framework, they fall short in capturing the role of digital interactions and the impact of social media in heavily connected settings like hospitality (Dwivedi et al., 2020). There are complex multidimensional factors out of the scopes in UTAUT2 including social connectedness, peer influence engagement, and viral diffusion of digital stories (Jayawardena et al., 2023).

The evidence from Indian settings supports the requirement for a more contextually sensitive approach. Applying the TPB, Ajzen (1991) evidenced that performance expectancy, effort expectancy, social influence, and perceived trust have a significant impact on behavioural intentions when consumers employ social media for travel and destination-related choices. Furthermore, Sharma et al. (2023) highlighted the role of e-WOM and social influence in the context of consumer behaviour in the hotel industry and noted that digital trust and peer acceptance supersede traditional promotion and marketing materials. These results indicate that constructs related to social media—especially e-WOM, perceived trust and social influence—should be included in current models to better explain adoption and use by consumers in hospitality (Filieri et al., 2015; Ayeh, 2015).

Practically, adoption frameworks derive substantial benefit from the integration of constructs propelled by social media. Understanding the intertwining of technical and social dimensions will enable hotels and restaurants to offer tailored social strategies of their own (i.e., influencer marketing, user-generated content campaigns, personalised digital experiences) that appeal to the urban Indian consumer (Harrigan et al., 2017). Failure to adapt such models means that traditional acceptance models may overlook the powerful digital levers which drive consumer decision-making, particularly in emerging contexts such as social media use which is growing at record rates (Kumar & Ayedee, 2018).

Accordingly, although UTAUT2 serves as a base model of technology acceptance, the dynamic nature of digital environment and the interdependence between people's decisions in this environment in the context of Indian hospitality industry necessitates an integrated model. This enhanced model needs to reflect e-WOM, perceived trust and social presence as core antecedent effects on both intention to use and actual usage. This broader perspective would not only enhance academic knowledge, but also offer valuable takeaways for both researchers and practitioners in the hospitality industry who are seeking to succeed in an era of social-media influenced consumer behavior.

2. LITERATURE REVIEW

The technology in the hospitality industry has been extensively researched through theoretical based underpinning of the Unified Theory of Acceptance and Use of Technology (UTAUT2). Performance expectancy,effort expectancy,social influence, facilitating conditions, hedonic motivation,price value and habit are important constructs included in the model,which predict b ehavioural intention and actual use of technology activity (Venkatesh et al., 2012). UTAUT2 has been frequently utilized in the hospitality and tourism environment to investigate consumer acceptance towards innovations such as mobile booking apps, selfservice kiosks and smart room technology (Jayawardena et al., 2023).

The expectation of performance, that technology improves service quality and guest experience, is identified as an important antecedent of adoption in a hospitality environment. Such as research on mobile hotel booking system and AI-based concierge service that concluded, tourists are likely to accept technology when it works on add value when it comes to make more convenience and effective process

(Mangold & Faulds,2009). Likewise, effort expectancy (perceived ease of use) is an important factor when efficiency levels are different across technologies. In low digital literate environments, easier and more intuitive systems lead to more acceptance by users (Kamal & Kamarulzaman, 2025).

Social influence has wider implications as well, especially in collectivist cultures such as in India, where peer recommendations, family members' views and influencer endorsements have significant impact on consumer behaviour (Dwivedi et al., 2019). At the same time, facilitating conditions – perception of resources, infrastructure and support, e.g. – is critical for seamless integration in service- focused sectors such as hospitality (Liu et al.,2025). Additionally, hedonic motivation, that is, the enjoyment that comes with using technology, has become increasingly important for hotels when attempting to appeal to younger, tech-savvy customers, as they begin to experiment with interactive interfaces, virtual reality (VR) tours and AI-personalized experiences (Devkota et al., 2025).

The value dimension in price construct emphasizes customers' cost-benefit attitudes, where technology adoption becomes stronger due to the fact that benefits are greater than monetary or temporal costs (Venkatesh et al., 2012). Finally, habit reflects the degree to which repeated use results in automatic adoption behaviours. For example, in hospitality, consistent application of travel apps, digital wallets and loyalty platforms, enhances ongoing communication and loyalty to the brand (Alalwan, 2018).

In addition to UTAUT2, recent studies highlight the increasing influence of social media and electronic word of mouth (e-WOM) on consumer purchasing behavior. Litvin et al., (2008) focused on the convincing force of consumer-created communications and their effects on trust and brand image. Unlike conventional advertising, e-WOM has more credibility because it originates from peers instead of firms (Cheung & Thadani, 2012; Jalilvand & Samiei, 2012). Confirmation of such patterns is evidenced by empirical research from India, where social media interactions significantly influence trust and confidence perceptions, leading to behavioral intentions on hotel choice, booking, and loyalty (Jayawardena et al., 2023). The level of information quality, reliability of reviews, and uniformity of online stories enhance these effects, treating trust as a central influence in making hospitality decisions (Filieri et al., 2015; Ayeh, 2015).

In conclusion, the literature highlights the need for an integrated explanatory framework combining traditional technology acceptance theories with new digital-social concepts, for example e-WOM, social trust and peer influence. The integration is imperative not only for advancing theoretical thinking but also for contributing to knowledge with implications for practice among hospitality professionals in India and other digital markets. From a marketer's perspective, such an integrated approach is necessary in order to resonate with the digital-era consumer, which is shaped by a combination of technological affordances and the power of social validation when making choices in hospitality (Hennig-Thurau et al., 2004 ; Harrigan et al.,2017; Kumar & Ayedee, 2018).

3. AIMS, OBJECTIVES, AND METHODOLOGY

The research methodology used in this research is largely secondary data collection and systematic literature review. This is reasonable as there are abundant extant academicals (i.e., sales, security, and computing), empirical (i.e., sales, computing, and psychology), and industry (i.e., sales, computing, and security) sources to have studied technology adoption and social media utilization in hospitality by now. Systematic review is widely known as a cost and time-effective strategy for synthesising findings across diverse contexts, so researchers can make overarching generalisations and theoretical advances (Gefen, 2000; Sharma et al., 2023).

The scholarly knowledge includes work from peer-reviewed journal articles, government reports, and industry white papers associated with digital transformation and hospitality in India with a specific emphasis on Tricity (Chandigarh, Mohali, and Panchkula). This organized body of evidence provides for the rigorous as well as practical side of the analysis (Kaplan & Haenlein, 2010 ; Li & Zang, 2025). Because of the changing nature of digital technologies and consumer behaviors in hospitality, using secondary sources also enable researchers to include longitudinal views because research works that appeared over time show the technology adoption and social media interaction dynamics (Farwell, 2008 ; Setiyanto & Syakir, 2019).

The methodological framework is conceptually integrative, involving basic concepts of UTAUT2 model (performance expectancy, effort expectancy, social influence, and facilitating conditions) as well as social media–specific factors, such as electronic word-of-mouth (e-WOM), perceived trust, and information quality. This hybrid construct is in line with recent pleas in hospitality research to supplement 'standard' adoption models with social and digital interaction constructs (Dwivedi et al., 2019; Jayawardena et al., 2023).

For analytical purposes, this study uses meta-analytic and pooled regression analyses. Meta-analysis is highly appropriate to combine the do-mains of evidence in heterogeneous studies because it permits the determination of effect sizes and strengths of relationships between constructs (Brown & Venkatesh, 2005 ; Dwivedi et al., 2019). This method minimizes bias that can occur in single-study designs and enhances the generalizability of findings to other hospitality settings. To enhance validity of the proposed model, we utilize structure equation model (SEM) to test the proposed relationships. SEM is commonly applied in the field of hospitality and tourism research as itallows the simultaneous examination of specific and indirect effects across multiple constructs, thus offering deeper insights into complex behavioral activities (Hair et al., 2019 ; Chin & Newsted, 2020).

For the purpose of methodological rigor, quality of evidence is judged based on method in terms of pure literature, replication of sources and replication of statistics applied in previous research . This triangulation technique reduces potential biases associated with the use of secondary data. Triangulation also improves interpretive validity. Externally, the study seeks to create a holistic integrative theoretical model that explains the impact of technology adoption and social media engagement on each other in hospitality and tourism. Theoretically, this study advances UTAUT2 by including e-WOM and digital trust constructs; practically, the findings may provide hospitality practitioners useful information for customer engagement and competitive advantage in urban Indian contexts. In the end, the methodology adopted reflects the trade-off between rigor and relevance, consistent with the broader movement of evidence-based research synthesis in tourism and hospitality studies (Harrigan et al., 2017).

4. RESULTS & INTERPRETATION

Descriptive statistics were initially used to analyze the central tendency of the constructs under study. At an aggregate level, social media related variables – e-WOM, perceived trust and information quality – showed higher mean values as compared to the conventional UTAUT2 constructs. This result indicates that determination of consumer decision-making influences in the Tricity hospitality market and their influence exerted by a certain category of technological factors is elapsing analysis in the context of social media factors. These results are in line with previous findings that the societal influence of peers sometimes supersedes utilitarian elements of technology in the hospitality context (Litvin et al., 2008; Cheung and Thadani, 2012). Indeed, user-generated content has become nowadays the main determinant influencing online hotel booking judgments (Filieri et al., 2015)

Among the predictors, e-WOM (M = 4.21, SD = 0.63) and perceived trust (M = 4.18, SD = 0.66) were found to be rated the highest. This further support the contention that UG recommendations and peer narrations substantially improve consumers trust and behavior intentions in hotel selection processes (Ayeh, 2015). The higher mean scores for these constructs in turn as that find by Harrigan et al., (2017) that trust developed through social media exchange positively affects guest loyalty and repeat purchase for hotels industry in India. Equally important, the positive e-WOM is a powerful predictor of travel intention (Jalilvand and Samiei, 2012), which demonstrates its crosscultural role in the process of tourism. The small range between ratings of these constructs (as suggested by the standard deviations) in the two constructs indicates there is a relatively consistent perception among respondents, making these constructs more reliable as the key dimensions of hotel guest choice.

The mean scores were moderate for classic UTAUT2 constructs, in contrast slightly lower, but still strong for them. Performance expectancy (M = 4.12, SD = 0.68) indicates that hotel guests in the Tricity region believe that digital platforms (i.e., mobile booking applications, smart room technologies, and AI chatbots) contribute significantly to an improved overall service experience. This finding is consistent with previous research findings that performance expectancy is a primary predictor of technology acceptance in the hospitality context, particularly for mobile booking and self-service technologies (Lina et al., 2023; Venkatesh et al., 2012). Hedonic motivation (M = 4.15, SD = 0.74) also scored relatively high, indicating that pleasure from interactive platforms, gamified interfaces and AI personalized characteristics drives consumer engagement and the intention to use digital tools. This aligns with Devkota et al., (2025) who suggested that visitors are increasingly interested in immersive and entertaining technology-oriented experiences, like VR hotel previews and AI-based personalization.

Interestingly, effort expectancy and facilitating conditions were scored in a moderate manner that receiving scores lower than those of the respondents in this digitally literate urban market. One possible reason could be that in the technologically developed markets like Tricity, end users take for granted the factor of ease of use and infrastructural support while putting focus on trust, credibility and social influence as factors which influence their decision. It is consistent with Dwivedi et al. (2019) also pointed out that usability factors are less influential, but hedonic and social factors are more influential in the digital environment in its digital-first stage, which indicates that the driving forces for adoption patterns of markets vary for different levels of market maturity. Furthermore, Alalwan (2018) observed a similar sequence in the context of e-commerce adoption: trust and social influence played a greater role once basic usability had been reached.

In brief, the descriptive statistics indicate that the UTAUT2 constructs like performance expectancy and hedonic motivation continue to be critical, as that social media driven constructs appeared to be more impact on behavioral intention in the Tricity hotel market. These results highlight the importance of extending the UTAUT2 model to incorporate trust and e-WOM variables in studying the adoption of digital technology in the hospitality industry. Lastly the robustness of high ratings across social constructs highlights that hoteliers would be wise to invest in digital trust-building and peer interactions. This also involves encouraging verified reviews, taking advantage of influencer collaborations, and guaranteeing open online communications, all of which may subsequently boost credibility and deepen guest loyalty (Harrigan et al., 2017).

4.1 Reliability and Validity

For measurement model validation, the reliability and validity of the constructs were examined based on well-established psychometric standards. To test for the internal consistency reliability, Cronbach's alpha and composite reliability (CR) were initially investigated. All constructs surpassed the recommended minimum of 0.70 (Nunnally & Bernstein, 1994), with Cronbach's alphas varied between 0.83 and 0.92 while CR values were consistently higher than 0.80. These values indicate that items from each construct showed a strong level of internal consistency, thereby assessing the latent variables in a reliable way across the sample (Hair et al.,2019). These results are in line with previous hospitality studies (Setiyanto & Syakir, 2019) that argued the necessity of scale reliability in technology-mediated service adoption studies.

Convergent validity was further tested with the average variance extracted (AVE). All constructs exceed the threshold of 0.50 for AVE (Fornell & Larcker, 1981) which suggests that variance of the manifest variables is closely replicated by the latent variables rather than by error variance. For instance, perceived trust had excellent psychometric quality (a = 0.88, CR = 0.90, AVE = 0.62), indicating stability and construct validity. In the same way, electronic word-of-mouth (e-WOM) and performance expectancy had the AVE value of 0.58 and 0.61, respectively, which passed converged validity. Discoveries from this study are consistent with those of previous tourism studies, which similarly established that constructs such as trust, peer influence, and perceived usefulness, have acceptable convergent validity, when they are used in digital hospitality adoption models (Khan & Rehman,2024).

As a result, this dataset satisfied all psychometric prerequisites for the subsequent causal modeling. These findings provide evidence that they measurement model is statistically sound and provides a reliable estimation of path coefficients in the SEM. In addition, strong reliability and validity reduces the potential for measurement error, enhance explanatory power and generalizability from context to context (Bagozzi & Yi, 1988, Hair et al., 2019). Furthermore, these procedures are in accordance with the best practices for conducting hospitality technology research (Hajli, 2014), which allows that the results of this study can be interpreted with confidence and that future theoretical generalisations in relation to UTAUT2, and social media extensions are sound.

Table 1. Descriptive Statistics and Reliability Measures

Construct	Mean	SD	Cronbach's α	CR	AVE
Performance Expectancy	4.12	0.68	0.89	0.91	0.67
Effort Expectancy	3.95	0.72	0.88	0.90	0.64
Social Influence	4.06	0.70	0.86	0.89	0.61
Facilitating Conditions	3.87	0.65	0.83	0.86	0.58
Hedonic Motivation	4.15	0.74	0.91	0.92	0.66
Price Value	3.78	0.71	0.84	0.87	0.55
Habit	3.90	0.69	0.85	0.88	0.57
Electronic Word-of-Mouth	4.21	0.63	0.90	0.92	0.65
Perceived Trust	4.18	0.66	0.88	0.90	0.62
Information Quality	4.10	0.61	0.87	0.89	0.60
Behavioral Intention	4.24	0.69	0.92	0.93	0.68

4.2 Discussion

The main objective of the study was to investigate the combined influences of the conventional UTAUT2 factors—i.e., "performance expectancy(the degree to which an individual believes that using the system will help him/her to attain gains in job performance)," "effort expectancy (the degree of ease associated with the use of the system)," "social influence (the degree to which a person perceives that important others believe he/she should use the new system)," and hedonic motivation (the desire of the user to be 'online' and to experience enjoyment when using the system),"—and of social media related constructs (e-WOM perceived trust, and information quality) on hotel guests behavior intends in the Tricity metropolitan area. Although UTAUT2 is extensively tested in technology acceptance research (Venkatesh et al., 2012), recent researchers have suggested that the power of explanation of UTAUT2 could be improved by involving social and relational variables, especially in hospitality and tourism areas, where peer-generated content and trust game are in morals to persuade consumer's make decision (Kaba & Toure, 2014).

The study used a multi-stage statistical procedure to examine these associations. The preliminary phase included the use of simple correlation analysis to obtain the first indication of the strength and direction of relationships among the constructs. Correlations are very commonly used as a diagnostic in observing the association between constructs before progressing to more advanced modeling techniques (Cohen, 1992). Subsequently, hierarchical regression analysis was used to examine the additional predictive value of social media constructs incorporated to the baseline UTAUT2 model. Such an approach is especially useful in hospitality context, because scholars frequently wish to investigate whether new constructs (i.e., trust and e-WOM) are able to explain a significant proportion of the variance, beyond the traditional technology adoption factors (Sharma et al., 2023).

Finally, the hypothesized model was validated and complex interrelationships among constructs were tested by utilizing structural equation modeling SEM. SEM is an extensively used tool in hospitality and behavioral sciences researches since it enables researchers to directly test measurement and structural models simultaneously, thus allowing for the establishment of construct and causal inference validity. Furthermore, SEM provides multiple model fit indices that can be used to establish the robustness and fitness of the proposed model from a theoretical standpoint, making it ideal for examining elongated technology acceptance models in the fast-changing Indian hospitality marketplace dominated by digital technologies. Overall, this comprehensive methodology comprising of correlation, hierarchical regression, and SEM implied a robust, multi-level testing of the hypothesized relationships therein. The aforementioned research approach is in line with the expert recommendations of scholars in the disciplines of behavior and hospitality researches. It is aligned with both the demands of contemporary statistical methods and theoretical driving factors. In addition, this methodology aligns with the current academic discourse on the necessity for a multi-method approach to evaluate complex social constructs, such as the interaction of TAM variables within a social media business setting.

The initial bivariate correlation analysis indicated that there were significant positive associations among all of the central constructs, suggesting that both types of UTAUT2 (i.e., performance expectancy, effort expectancy, social influence, hedonic motivation) and SNS variables (i.e., e-WOM, perceived trust, and information quality) are linked to one another for predicting consumer behavior. For example, PE directly influenced BI: Consumers use digital platforms in hospitality when they perceive a direct source of performance expectancy, such as convenience, availability, or effort savings (Venkatesh et al.,2012). Trust, also found to be associated with e-WOM, had strong relationships with behavioral intention, demonstrated the importance of trust not only as a relational driver, but also the central role trust plays in how consumers make decisions while using the internet as a tool (Litvin et al., 2008; Filieri, 2015). These findings resonate with previous research which suggest that social influence and digital trust reinforce the role of performance-based beliefs to stimulate technology adoption in the tourism and hospitality context (Devkota et al.,2025).

Extending further, a hierarchical regression analysis was used to determine the additional predictive contribution of social media constructs in addition to the full UTAUT2 model. The UTAUT2 constructs predicted a large proportion of variance in behavioral intention in the base model, indicating the robustness of the model to predict behavioral intention in digital adoption settings (Venkatesh et al., 2012). But, after considering social media--related factors (e-WOM, perceived trust, information quality), there was a significant increase in the variance explained in the extended model. This marginal increase supports for a call in applying traditional adoption models to the socially mediated and trust-based environment of digital transactions underlying hospitality markets (Cheung & Thadani, 2012).

Notably, perceived trust and e-WOM were the most significant antecedents of behavioral intention, which outperformed some of the well-studied UTAUT2's determinants. This is in line with the work of Setiyanto & Syakir (2019 who both indicate that peer-to-peer communications and credibility for online information are important when making travel decisions regarding cost and usability. Recent works within the hospitality domain also follow this trend; for instance, Sharma et al. (2023) found that social media trust building activities directly impacted guest loyalty and booking intentions in India and Jayawardena et al. (2023)highlighted that e-WOM has become the core power that influences hotel brand perceptions.

In general, the regression results indicate that while UTAUT2 constructs are still required in order to explain technology-mediated service adoption factors, they are not enough. The incorporation of trust level and peer-generation of digital constructs enrich the model to explain guests' behavioral intentions in the urban Indian hospitality market, where digitally savvy consumers highly depend on online reviews, credibility cues, and social proof when making a purchase decision (Harrigan et al., 2017; SharmfSa, 2023).

Last, structural equation modeling (SEM) was used to test the hypotheses posed in our conceptual model and examine the mediating and moderating effects of the constructs. SEM is ideally suited to such an analysis since it can test both measurement and structural models, making it methodologically more rigorous than single-equation methods (Hair et al., 2019; Kline, 2015). The SEM findings also supported the social media-related variables as significant predictors of behavioral intention with other important UTAUT2 predictors, performance expectancy and hedonic motivation.

Crucially, such findings imply that the social media variables are not a substitute for traditional adoption determinants but act as a supplement and enrichment to it, as also suggested by Ayeh (2015) in advancing trust in peer-generated online content as supplement to rather than replacement of utilitarian beliefs in digital adoption. Specifically, perceived trust and e-WOM were identified as mediating variables that significantly increased the effects of traditional factors performance expectancy on behavioral intention. This mediating role is indicative of consumers acknowledging the hedonic appeal of hotel technologies but their actual adoption decisions are being processed through these relational appraisals of trustworthiness, reliability, and social approval (Filieri, 2015; Cheung & Thadani, 2012).

The results add to literature in tourism and hospitality that suggests consumers' online decision-making is utilitarian and social. For instance, Jayawardena et al., (2023)has shown that e-WOM has a significant effect on the moderating role of hotel booking platforms, while Dwivedi et al. (2019) revealed that trust constructs moderated UTAUT2 predictors to bring a more comprehensive view of behavioral outcomes. Similarly, Devkota et al., (2025) also verified with SEM approach that performance expectation and hedonic motivation are key enablers for technology adoption; both of them are significantly amplified when trust-building mechanism is involved.

Overall, the multistage statistical process–between correlation, hierarchical regression and SEM affirms that although the original UTAUT2 constructs (performance expectation, effort expectancy, facilitating conditions and social influence) remain basic, the addition of social media constructs (trust, e-WOM, information quality) produce a more comprehensive and contingency dependent explanatory framework for the Indian hospitality industry. The finding is consistent with the recent literature that has called for the development of the TAM and UTAUT2 models by incorporating the socially induced constructs that represent the contemporary digitally networked consumption environment (Venkatesh et al., 2012; Dwivedi et al., 2020).

From an applied standpoint, these results also have implications for managers of hospitality industry. Results based on SEM show that digital trust mechanisms and peer-generated content are not peripheral but the key drivers of influence. Those hotels which can effectively invest in clear communication, authenticated reviews and social advocacy campaigns can amplify the effects of functionality technology benefits and thus influence stronger guest intentions (Jayawardena et al., 2023).

4.2.1 Correlation Analysis Insights

The initial test for correlation indicated that all predictor constructs were positively and significantly associated with BI, supporting the conceptual expectation that both variables from UTAUT2 and constructs from social media have notable effects on hotel guests' behavior. Of the predictors, perceived trust ($r = .68$, $p < .01$), and electronic word-of-mouth (e-WOM) ($r = .65$, $p < .01$). Such findings provide further evidence to support the widely established role that consumer trust and peer-generated reviews exert in influencing behavioral intentions in the hospitality industry, particularly in online settings (Filieri, 2015; Ayeh, 2015). Trust mitigates perceived risk and build confidence in the service provider, particularly in high involvement decisions as in the case of hotel choice (Kamal & Kamarulzaman, 2025).

Moderate, but significant associations were found between the behavioral intention and the traditional UTAUT2 factors. Performance expectancy ($r = .59$, $p < .01$), suggesting that technology improves efficiency and quality of service, which replicates previous research in hospitality applications (Venkatesh et al., 2012), (mobile booking applications, smart hotel technologies) as the strongest UTAUT2 predictor. Likewise, social influence (r =. 56, p <. 01) also demonstrated that peer, family and society are important factors effecting guest behavior which reinforce the findings of Dwivedi et al. (2019) and Sharma et al. (2023) in the context of Indian urban hospitality markets.

Stronger associations of social media constructs than traditional predictors indicate that digital peer engagement and trust formation are growingly important drivers of consumer adoption in addition to technology-based factors. This change is in line with Litvin et al.(2008) assertion that e-WOM has a more persuasive effect than firm-created marketing communications. Recent findings from India also found that social media engagement enhanced perceived trust and behavioral intention in hospitality consumers from India (Jayawardena et al., 2023).

In general, results of the correlation analysis underline that, although UTAUT2 constructs are still valid, social related variables are predominant as predictors of behavioral intention in Tricity market. This supports the emergent digital ecology being witnessed in Indian hospitality, where reliance on a subjective code substantiated by a collective intelligence (i.e., digital word-of-mouth) surpasses purely technical performance issues. Theoretically, such underscores the strategic need to build of trustworthy online reputation, genuine customer reviews, and authentic digital trust amongst hospitality marketing and operations execution (Harrigan et al., 2017; Jalilvand & Samiei, 2012).

4.2.2 Hierarchical Regression Findings

Hierarchical regression results offered strong support for the explanatory power of incorporating SNS variables into the conventional UTAUT2 model. In Model 1 (UTAUT2 constructs only) the predictors accounted for 52% of the variance in BI (R^2 =. 52, F = 45.29, p <. 001). Performance expectancy (β =. 18, p <. 01), social influence (β =. 16, p <. 01), and hedonic motivation (β =. 14, p <. 01) were found to be determinants of hotel guests' behavioral intentions. These results are consistent with prior work, which also found performance expectancy to be one of the most important predictors of technology adoption in tourism and hospitality contexts. The importance of social influence also confirms the social construct of UTAUT2, especially in collective societies like India where peers and family members' opinions play a significant role in decisions making (Dwivedi et al., 2019).

Curiously, monetary value hardly predicted behavioral intention (β =. 06, p =. 168). This can be attributed to the demographic characteristics of respondents, with younger, urban and digitally savvy customers focusing more on hedonic and trust-related aspects than pure cost–related factors. Earlier research focusing on

Indian hospitality too has indicated that value-comparison is often outweighed by endeavors for tailor-made and socially endorsed experiences (Sharma et al. 2023).

With the insertion of social media constructs, the model accounted for more variance of 64% (ΔR^2 =. 12, F-change = 23.95, p <. 001). In this extended model, perceived trust (β =. 24, p <. 001) and word-of-mouth (β =. 17, p <. 001) emerged as stronger predictors of behavioral intention than a number of the original UTAUT2 constructs. These results support those obtained by Jalilvand and Samiei (2012) in which online peer recommendations far outweighed traditional marketing communications influence on consumer decision making. Like-wise, Filieri (2015) highlighted the role of the perceived trust in online reviews as a critically important mediator in consumer decision of hotel and travel.

Accordingly, the hierarchical regression exposes that although UTAUT2 constructs continue to be fundamental, the additional variance explained by social media variables demonstrates they are integral to capture the socially mediated technology adoption behavior in hospitality. This is in line with recent Indian research (Jayawardena et al., 2023), which suggests blended models taking into consideration the technological as well as the social aspects.

4.2.3 Structural Equation Modeling (SEM) Validation

The third analysis step is structural equation modeling (SEM) which is able to test the direct and indirect effects between constructs concurrently. Model fit indices supported the excellent fit of the proposed integrative model (χ^2/df = 2.11; CFI =. 956; TLI =. 948; RMSEA =. 052; SRMR =. 041). These indexes exceed the cutoff values proposed by Hair et al. (2019) to confirm the fit of the model to the data amounted to be adequate.

The standardized path coefficients showed that perceived trust (β =. 33, p <. 001) was strongest predictor of behavioral intention, the critical role trust plays trust in consumers' responses in digital hospitality environments was confirmed. This result is consistent with Lina et al., (2023) who demonstrated that trust in online reviews decreases uncertainty and increases booking intention. Similarly, e-WOM (β = .27, p < .001) was an important predictor, supporting existing literature suggesting that peer-generated content has a strong impact on hotel choice, especially in emerging markets (Lin & Bhattacherjee. 2010).

Within the UTAUT2 constructs, (β =. 21, p <. 01) and social influence (β =. 18, p <. 01)remained robust and significant, supporting the theoretical underpinning of UTAUT2 in the context of hospitality. Other predictors—hedonic motivation (β =. 12, p <. 01), effort expectancy (β =. 10, p <. 05), facilitating conditions (β =. 08, p <. 05), and habit (β =. 09, p <. 05) — were statistically significant but showed rather low effect size values, thus indicating that they might act as supplementary determinants that shape intentions rather than as main predictors.

It is worth mentioning the insignificance of price value in the SEM model (β =. 05, ns), as indicated by the derived interaction effects as well as with analogue (see discussion above) with regression analysis (d) and with the previous literature that, for digitally savvy, urban hospitality marketplaces, price concerns are trumped by trust, reputation and peer pressure for subsequent activity (Harrigan et al.,2017).

Collectively, SEM validation ensures that despite the continued relevance of traditional technology acceptance-specific constructs, the overwhelming priority of perceived trust and e-WOM depicts a new paradigm of consumer choice behaviour in hospitality. This highlights the necessity to elaborate UTAUT2 into hybrid socio-technical models that recognize the distinct influence of digital connectedness and peer effects in the formation of behavioral intentions (Dwivedi et al., 2019; Jayawardena et al., 2023).

Table 2. Summary of Correlation, Regression, and SEM Results for Predictors of Behavioural Intention

Predictor	**Correlation with Behavioral Intention (r)**	**Regression Standardized Beta (β)**	**SEM Standardized Path Coefficient (β)**	**Significance (p)**
Perceived Trust	0.68	0.24	0.33	< .001 (all tests)
Electronic Word-of-Mouth	0.65	0.17	0.27	< .001 (all tests)
Performance Expectancy	0.59	0.18	0.21	< .01 (all tests)
Social Influence	0.56	0.16	0.18	< .01 (all tests)
Hedonic Motivation	0.54	0.14	0.12	Regression/< .01, SEM/< .01
Effort Expectancy	0.47	0.11	0.10	Regression/< .05, SEM/< .05
Facilitating Conditions	0.45	0.09	0.08	Regression/< .05, SEM/< .05
Habit	0.40	0.10	0.09	Regression/< .05, SEM/< .05
Information Quality	0.42	0.13	0.14	Regression/SEM: < .01
Price Value	0.30	0.06 (ns)	0.05 (ns)	Non-significant

Taken together, the findings from the correlation analysis, hierarchical regression, and SEM contribute to a richer insight into hotel guest behavioral intentions in the digital era. The findings reveal the significant benefits of incorporating social media–based constructs within the UTAUT2 framework for extending the traditional technology adoption theories. Especially, perceivedtrust and electronic word-of-mouth (e-WOM)were also found to be the top predictors, surpassingseveral initial UTAUT2 constructs. This result is consistent with the claim of Cheung and Thadani (2012) that user-generated content are highly persuasive in digital decision-making and also supports calls for TAM and UTAUT extensions to accommodate social connectivity, trust and reputation mechanisms (Devkota et al., 2025).

At the same time the results specifically validated the continuing significance of performance expectancy and social influence as baseline predictors, in line with their centrality in the UTAUT2 model (Venkatesh et al.,2012). Guests continue to appreciate the practical applications of technology—ease of booking or improved service quality—and for how peers and social networks shape their decisions. These findings are consistent with earlier hospitality studies that reveal that technological utility and peer influence both motivate patrons to use new innovations like mobile booking apps and self-service kiosks (Khan & Rehman, 2024).

It suggests that technology adoption is multi-dimensional, while the smaller contributions of hedonic motivation, effort expectancy, facilitating conditions and habit have secondary but important roles. Consumers are not just driven by effectiveness; they are also influenced by effortlessness, joy, prompting environment, and automaticity, adding depth to the context of behavioral intention (Kamal & Kamarulzaman, 2025). These results correspond with those of Venkatesh et al. (2012) who argued that secondary constructs have a complimentary, yet important role of reinforcing long-term adoption behaviors.

It is noteworthy that the non-significance of price value in the regression and SEM sharply contrasts with a particular consumer reality. Trust in digitised information and peer endorsement are found to be more significant determinants of hotel guests' trust in digital information and peer endorsement, and less sensitive to room tariffs in digitally connected and urban hotel guests in the Tricity region. This finding matches with Sharma et al. (2023) that urban hospitality service providers' consumers in India consider transparency, trustworthiness, and authenticityto be more important over the tangible monetary reward. It is also consistent with international literature on consumers' price awareness being a dimension moderated by online trust and review quality in service-based sectors (Lina et al.,2023).

Collectively, these multi-method results expose the importance of extending UTAUT2 model with previous constructs by addressing social media activities such as e-WOM and perceived trust. Not only does this enhanced lens contribute to theoretical development by capturing the socio-technical dynamics of contemporary hospitality adoption behavior, but it also has practical implications such that it offers useful guidance for practical strategists who wish to design new digital strategies that resonate with a trust-based, social-influenced market (Liu et al., 2025).

5. THEORETICAL IMPLICATIONS

This research offers a significant theoretical contribution through enhancement of the Unified Theory of Acceptance and Use of Technology 2 (UTAUT2) model (Venkatesh, Thong, & Xu, 2012) adding social media constructs specifically perceived trust, e-WOM, and information quality. Several years ago, UTAUT2 underlined: performance expectancy, effort expectancy, enjoyment, price value and habit as drivers of technology adoption. Yet the existing results show that the adoption of technology in hospitality industry cannot be accounted for to the full extent under these constructs only as digital adoption is social and relational: (Setiyanto & Syakir,2019).

By integrating perceived trust into the model, this study also recognizes that trust is no longer a peripheral concern but a foundation of behavioral intention in the context of online hospitality. Previous research suggests that consumers are more inclined to use and accept digital booking channels if they trust the environment, as trust reduces uncertainty and risk perception (Mangold & Faulds,2009). Filieri (2015) validated that trust of credible online reviews has a significant impact on choice of the hotel, and evidenced that there is mediation effect of trust between the helpfulness of online reviews and consumer's booking decisions. This study's result is consistent with the aforementioned studies, stating that trust enhances adoption intention in urban hospitality market of Tricity.

Equally, the incorporation of electronic word of mouth (eWOM) alludes to the rising influence of peer-created reputation capital. Litvin et al.,2008 were the early scholars claiming that e-WOM has greater persuasiveness than traditional advertising in hospitality. Recent research also supported that peer reviews not only have the potential to be a critical factor of consumers perceptions, but also a function of volume (Cheung & Thadani, 2012). The present results are consistent with this stream of study, as e-WOM emerges as a strong predictor of behavioral intentions in the Tricity setting, supporting its introduction as an extension of the theory (UTAUT2).

The concept of information quality further broadens the scope of explanation in the model. Vermeulen & Seegers, (2009) where the credibility, completeness, and timeliness of information available online have high impact on the satisfaction and trust of customers, especially in service industries where the intangibility stimulates reliance on both external cues. In services such as hospitality where there is limited customer ability to test the service, good online information reduces ambiguity and increases confidence in the booking process (Ayeh, 2015). By empirically establishing this construct, this study emphasizes the relevance of informational dimensions of technology acceptance theories.

Furthermore, an important value of this model is the regional context. Although UTAUT2 has been extensively tested in Western contexts (Venkatesh et al., 2012;

Dwivedi et al., 2019), it is locally customized to Tricity, India and its culture is blended with the context. Evidence is beginning to show that adoption of new technologies in developing urban markets is influenced by certain unique socio-cultural forces including peer trust and social influence. Evidence stemming from Tricity people acceptance of digital platforms emphasizes a similar socio-technical locale since social influence trust and performance expectancy intertwine with each other. Likewise, Sharma et al. (2023) also underscored that price does not remain a priority when it comes to urban Indian hospitality customers, highlighting a deviation from western markets where price seems to be the primary focus for customers.

Lastly, this work provides an input to the wider socio-technical integration discourse on technology acceptance. Ayeh (2015) and Jayawardena et al. (2023) among scholars have opined that adoption models such as UTAUT2 and TAM should be advanced to include other socially induced constructs, especially in service sectors, digitally mediated and where peer connectivity and reputation systems are otherwise dominant. By showing empirically that social media constructs have a material added value in terms of improved model fit and predictive power, it supports these propositions and offers a so-called hybrid socio-technical framework for the relevant hospitality research. The findings indicate that adoption is not only about utilitarian and hedonic value but trust, reputation and peer involvement in digital ecosystems (Harrigan et al., 2017).

In sum, the theoretical implications of this study are threefold:

Conceptual Expansion: Enriching UTAUT2 with perceived trust, e-WOM, and information quality produces a fuller and more social model of digital adoption, aligned with the peer-mediated context of consumer behavior (Filieri, 2015; Litvin et al., 2008).

Local Contextualization: Locating the expanded UTAUT2 within the Indian Tricity brings to the forefront the inherent requirement to have localized version of global theories in order to ensure that they accommodate the urban, emerging-market specific realities (Sharma et al., 2023).

Socio-technical Integration: By highlighting the technological and social dimensions of adoption this study not only deepens adoption theory within contexts where peer reputation and digital trust play a central role (Jayawardena et al., 2023; Harrigan et al., 2017).

6. MANAGERIAL IMPLICATIONS

These results have clear implications for practitioners in the hospitality sector serving the Tricity market and other competitive urban hospitality markets. The findings stress the importance of building trust in digital channels as a strategic imperative. Because both perceived trust and information quality were the most significant antecedents of behavioural intention, hotels need to guarantee clear, accurate and frequently updated information on their official websites, on booking sites and on social media pages. Previous studies support that information credibility and transparency are able to largely decrease perceived risk and highly enhance the guest confidence in booking decisions (Xu et al.,2010). Therefore, digital communication strategies ought to focus on being credible, responsive and reliable so that trust among consumers can be generated.

And the peer advocacy via electronic word-of-mouth (e-WOM) is equally critical. The present study confirms that e-WOM is a significant predictor of behavioral intention, corroborating earlier works that demonstrate that online reviews and peer recommendations more effectively influence perceptions than traditional advertisements (Litvin et al., 2008, Jalilvand & Samiei, 2012). Hotels in the Tricity must therefore push happy guests to write and share on platforms such as TripAdvisor, Google Reviews and even Instagram. Organized campaigns that motivate the generation of reviews or are favorable to the generation of user-generated content can develop into a 'multiplier effect' in brand perception as was demonstrated by Harrigan et al., (2017). These tactics raise the guest experience and the hotel's competitive edge within an urban market.

A further practical implication relates to the enhancement of the performance expectancy of technology-enabled facilities. Hung suggested that mobile booking apps, digital check-in kiosks, and other tools, for example, should be pitched to travelers with an eye on convenience, efficiency, and personalization. Previous research also reveals that the propensity of guests to use hotel technologies increases if guests clearly perceive time and simplicity savings and better service quality (Venkatesh et al., 2012). Favorable advertising of these amenities not only drives adoption, but also suggests progressiveness and modernity—two important characteristics of a digitally savvy urban consumer base.

The report also underscores the rise of influencer investment in the hospitality marketing mix. But when hotels team up with them, as well as with local guides or marketers in specific niches, they can use social influence to build credibility, status and positive consumer attitudes. Studies on social media marketing prove that influence can shape the behavioral intention of travelers when trust opinion leaders (Cheung & Thadani, 2012). For Tricity hotels, influencers from the lifestyle blogging, travel vlogging space or micro from the region can be the perfect trust catalyst, given the socially driven patterns of consideration.

Last, price value did not predict customer involvement in this study, which is an important implication for hotel managers. In the mid to upscale urban segment, the consumer decisions are less price-sensitive and more about trust, quality and reputation management. The result is similar to the findings of Sharma et al. (2023) who found that urban Indian hospitality consumers respond more to digital credence and perceived service quality rather than to discounts and price promotions. As a result, hotels must resist the temptation of competing on price alone, and turn their attention instead to quality improvements, personalized digital engagement and strong online reputation management practices.

In sum, the practical implications suggest that hospitality professionals should adopt a *trust-centered and socially embedded digital strategy*:

- Give preference to transparent and credible digital communication.
- Encourage and amplify guest-generated e-WOM.
- Create an awareness of the applicability and efficiency of hotel technologies.
- Use influencer collaborations to create credibility and social proof.
- Emphasis should point on quality, brand and reputation, rather than price cut back.

These measures are unlikely to only enhance consumer trust and confidence but also to attain a sustainable competitive advantage in a digital/socially driven hospitality marketplace (Jayawardena et al., 2023; Dwivedi et al., 2019).

7. CONCLUSION

As derived from UTAUT2 framework, this study used traditional technology adoption factors and social media variables to explore Tricity hotel guests' intentions, and found that performance expectancy, and social influence still significantly impact them, while social media elements, such as perceived trust, e-WOM, and information quality, specifically, are crucial for defining behaviors and attitudes in guests, in line with previous hospitality publications indicating the position of user generated content and trust mechanism in the digital decision-making (Cheung & Thadani, 2012). The proposed integrated model successfully explains the behavior, thereby providing support to the demand for moving beyond utilitarianism in the theories of adoption and calling for salience to trust, reputation, and digital social capital in the service consumption contexts (Dwivedi et al., 2019), in addition providing the practical implications to the hotel managers to create and enhance the digital trust, exploit the peer advocacy and enhancing the need to gadgetize the technology for the tech-savvy urban consumers. Future studies could investigate longitudinal dynamics of these relationships in view of changing AI-enabled platforms, consider moderating effects of even more diverse demographic, cultural and psychographic profiles (Venkatesh et al., 2012), and conduct cross-national or cross-sectorial comparisons to examine external generalizability (Sharma et al., 2023), whereas qualitative and mixed-method designs like interviews, netnography, and focus groups may unravel emotional overtones and cultural undercurrents of digital uptake (Harrigan et al., 2017). At a macro level, the study highlights the inontological relevance of social media constructs in influencing hotel guests' behavioral intention and offers a context-specific, extended UTAUT2 framework that advances our theoretical knowledge from the strategic practice and theoretical standpoints in the digital hospitality context.

REFERENCES

Ajzen, I. (1991). The theory of planned behavior. *Organizational Behavior and Human Decision Processes*, *50*(2), 179–211. DOI: 10.1016/0749-5978(91)90020-T

Alalwan, A. A. (2018). Investigating the Impact of Social Media Advertising Features on Customer Purchase Intention. *International Journal of Information Management*, *42*, 65–77. DOI: 10.1016/j.ijinfomgt.2018.06.001

Ayeh, J. K. (2015). Travellers' acceptance of consumer-generated media: An integrated model of technology acceptance and source credibility theories. *Computers in Human Behavior*, *48*, 173–180. DOI: 10.1016/j.chb.2014.12.049

Bagozzi, R. P., & Yi, Y. (1988). On the evaluation of structural equation models. *Journal of the Academy of Marketing Science*, *16*(1), 74–94.

Brown, S. A., & Venkatesh, V. (2005). Model of adoption of technology in households: A baseline model test and extension incorporating household life cycle. *Management Information Systems Quarterly*, *29*(3), 399–426. DOI: 10.2307/25148690

Cheung, C. M. K., & Thadani, D. R. (2012). The impact of electronic word-of-mouth communication: A literature analysis and integrative model. *Decision Support Systems*, *54*(1), 461–470. DOI: 10.1016/j.dss.2012.06.008

Chin, W. W., & Newsted, P. R. (2020). Structural equation modeling analysis with small samples using partial least squares. In Hoyle, R. H. (Ed.), *Statistical strategies for small sample research* (pp. 307–341). Sage.

Cohen, J. (1992). A power primer. *Psychological Bulletin*, *112*(1), 155–159. PMID: 19565683

Devkota, J., Shrestha, J., Pandit, S., & Sharma, A. (2025). Marketing on consumer buying behaviors in the hospitality industry. *NPRC Journal of Multidisciplinary Research*, *2*(3), 189–203. DOI: 10.3126/nprcjmr.v2i3.76993

Dwivedi, Y. K., Rana, N. P., Jeyaraj, A., Clement, M., & Williams, M. D. (2019). Re-examining the Unified Theory of Acceptance and Use of Technology (UTAUT): Towards a revised theoretical model. *Information Systems Frontiers*, *21*(3), 719–734. DOI: 10.1007/s10796-017-9774-y

Farwell, T. M. (2008). Book review: *Always on: Advertising, marketing, and media in an era of consumer control. Journal of Advertising Education*, *12*(2), 47. DOI: 10.1177/109804820801200212

Filieri, R., Alguezaui, S., & McLeay, F. (2015). What makes online reviews helpful? A diagnosticity-adoption framework to explain informational and normative influences in e-WOM. *Journal of Business Research, 68*(6), 1261–1268. DOI: 10.1016/j.jbusres.2014.11.006

Gefen, D. (2000). E-commerce: The role of familiarity and trust. *Omega, 28*(6), 725–737. DOI: 10.1016/S0305-0483(00)00021-9

Hair, J. F., Hult, G. T. M., Ringle, C. M., & Sarstedt, M. (2019). *A primer on partial least squares structural equation modeling (PLS-SEM)* (2nd ed.). Sage Publications.

Hajli, M. N. (2014). A study of the impact of social media on consumers. *International Journal of Market Research, 56*(3), 387–404. DOI: 10.2501/IJMR-2014-025

Harrigan, P., Evers, U., Miles, M., & Daly, T. (2017). Customer engagement with tourism social media brands. *Tourism Management, 59*, 597–609. DOI: 10.1016/j.tourman.2016.09.015

Hennig-Thurau, T., Gwinner, K. P., Walsh, G., & Gremler, D. D. (2004). Electronic word-of-mouth via consumer-opinion platforms: What motivates consumers to articulate themselves on the Internet? *Journal of Interactive Marketing, 18*(1), 38–52. DOI: 10.1002/dir.10073

Jalilvand, M. R., & Samiei, N. (2012). The impact of electronic word of mouth on a tourism destination choice: Testing the theory of planned behavior (TPB). *Internet Research, 22*(5), 591–612. DOI: 10.1108/10662241211271563

Jayawardena, C., Ahmad, A., Valeri, M., & Jaharadak, A. A. (2023). Technology acceptance antecedents in digital transformation in the hospitality industry. *International Journal of Hospitality Management, 108*, 103350. DOI: 10.1016/j.ijhm.2022.103350

Kaba, B., & Touré, B. (2014). Understanding information and communication technology behavioral intention to use: Applying the UTAUT model to social networking site adoption by young people in a least developed country. *Journal of the Association for Information Science and Technology, 65*(8), 1662–1674. DOI: 10.1002/asi.23069

Kamal, S. A., Z., & Kamarulzaman, Y. (2025). Digital transformation in hotels: A meta-analysis of UTAUT-based empirical evidence. *Jurnal Pengurusan, 74*, Article 2.

Kaplan, A. M., & Haenlein, M. (2010). Users of the world, unite! The challenges and opportunities of social media. *Business Horizons, 53*(1), 59–68. DOI: 10.1016/j.bushor.2009.09.003

Khan, S., & Rehman, A. (2024). Social media influences consumer choices in the travel industry: Examining the decision-making process of travelers. *International Journal of Applied Research, 10*(6), 303–314. DOI: 10.22271/allresearch.2024.v10.i6d.11858

Kline, R. B. (2015). *Principles and practice of structural equation modeling* (4th ed.). Guilford Press.

Kumar, A., & Ayedee, N. (2018). Social media tools for business growth of SMEs. *Journal of Management, 5*(3), 137–142.

Lin, J. S. C., & Bhattacherjee, A. (2010). Extending technology usage models to interactive hedonic technologies: A theoretical model and empirical test. *Information Systems Journal, 20*(2), 163–181. DOI: 10.1111/j.1365-2575.2007.00265.x

Lina, L., Lorenzo, V., Iwai, S., & Wahyuningtias, D. (2023). The influence of e-WOM and brand image on hotel booking intention in Jakarta: A study of Generation Z. *E3S Web of Conferences, 426*, 02088. https://doi.org/DOI: 10.1051/e3sconf/202342602088

Litvin, S. W., Goldsmith, R. E., & Pan, B. (2008). Electronic word-of-mouth in hospitality and tourism management. *Tourism Management, 29*(3), 458–468. DOI: 10.1016/j.tourman.2007.05.011

Liu, H., Huang, M., & Zhang, P. (2025). The influence of social media marketing on the quality of hotel services and the behavioral intentions of tourists. *Acta Psychologica, 255*, 104881. DOI: 10.1016/j.actpsy.2025.104881 PMID: 40086229

Mangold, W. G., & Faulds, D. J. (2009). Social media: The new hybrid element of the promotion mix. *Business Horizons, 52*(4), 357–365. DOI: 10.1016/j.bushor.2009.03.002

Nunnally, J. C., & Bernstein, I. H. (1994). *Psychometric theory* (3rd ed.). McGraw-Hill.

Semwal, R., Tripathi, N., Tyagi, P., & Singh, A. (2024). Synergising brands: Licensing and collaboration strategies in tourism. In Ragab, A. M., Valeri, M., Talib, Z. M., & Tyagi, P. (Eds.), *Advances in Hospitality, Tourism, and the Services Industry*. IGI Global., DOI: 10.4018/979-8-3693-4171-1.ch007

Setiyanto, A., & Syakir, A. (2019). The influence of perceived ease of use, perceived usefulness, and consumer satisfaction on online purchasing behaviour. *Journal of Applied Accounting and Taxation, 4*(2), 214–222. DOI: 10.30871/jaat.v4i2.1081

Sharma, N., Khatri, B., Khan, S. A., & Shamsi, M. S. (2023). Extending the UTAUT model to examine the influence of social media on tourists' destination selection. *Indian Journal of Marketing*, *53*(4), 47–64. DOI: 10.17010/ijom/2023/v53/i4/172689

Venkatesh, V., Morris, M. G., Davis, G. B., & Davis, F. D. (2003). User acceptance of information technology: Toward a unified view. *Management Information Systems Quarterly*, *27*(3), 425–478. DOI: 10.2307/30036540

Venkatesh, V., Thong, J. Y. L., & Xu, X. (2012). Consumer acceptance and use of information technology: Extending the unified theory of acceptance and use of technology. *Management Information Systems Quarterly*, *36*(1), 157–178. DOI: 10.2307/41410412

Vermeulen, I. E., & Seegers, D. (2009). Tried and tested: The impact of online hotel reviews on consumer consideration. *Tourism Management*, *30*(1), 123–127. DOI: 10.1016/j.tourman.2008.04.008

Xu, H., Teo, H.-H., Tan, B. C. Y., & Agarwal, R. (2010). The role of push-pull technology in privacy calculus: The case of location-based services. *Journal of Management Information Systems*, *26*(3), 135–174. DOI: 10.2753/MIS0742-1222260305

Chapter 7
Impact of Dynamic Capabilities on the Firm Performance:
A Pilot Study With Digital Marketing Capabilities as a Mediator

Preeti Dahiya
http://orcid.org/0009-0005-1294-0379
Chandigarh University, India

Pardeep Kumar
http://orcid.org/0000-0003-0004-1235
Chandigarh University, India

ABSTRACT

The primary objective of this study is to examine how dynamic capabilities affect the performance of micro and small enterprises in the textile sector, with a particular focus on the mediating role of digital marketing capabilities. This pilot study gathered responses from top-level and middle-level executives within these enterprises. To assess the normality, validity, and reliability of the questionnaire data, a sample of 58 individuals was analyzed using SPSS software. The results demonstrated high reliability, with coefficients ranging from 0.716 to 0.916, and reasonable normality, validating the questionnaire's effectiveness for pilot research. Although this study used a small sample size of 58 individuals, future research can confirm the model with a larger sample and different populations to enhance the generalizability of

DOI: 10.4018/979-8-3373-6741-5.ch007

the findings. Additionally, incorporating other variables could further deepen our understanding of the concept. The study affirmed the tool's effectiveness in analyzing specific factors influencing the performance of micro and small enterprises.

INTRODUCTION

In an era marked by swift technological progress and fluctuating market conditions, a firm's ability to adapt and succeed is becoming ever more essential (Baía & Ferreira, 2024). The concept of dynamic capabilities—defined as a firm's ability to integrate, develop, and reconfigure both internal and external competencies to respond to rapidly changing environments—has become a crucial framework for understanding how businesses sustain their competitive edge (Bhardwaj & Srivastava, 2024). Dynamic capabilities involve a series of processes and routines that allow firms to identify opportunities and threats, seize them effectively, and maintain their competitiveness through ongoing reconfiguration and transformation (Wu et al., 2023).

Digital marketing capabilities, which include the strategic use of digital tools and platforms to enhance customer engagement, optimize marketing efforts, and drive business growth, are increasingly recognized as critical for firms operating in today's digital economy. Research has shown that firms with strong digital marketing capabilities achieve better performance metrics, including heightened brand awareness, increased customer loyalty, and expanded market share. For example, data-driven insights enable companies to refine their marketing strategies based on real-time consumer behaviour and market trends, thereby improving decision-making and operational efficiency (Verhoef et al., 2021). Furthermore, integrating various digital marketing channels, such as social media and email, allows firms to effectively reach and engage customers, leading to enhanced outcomes in customer acquisition and retention (Edelman, 2010).

Recent empirical research has increasingly examined the role of dynamic capabilities in explaining firm performance across diverse contexts. Studies suggest that firms operating in turbulent and technology-driven environments rely on their sensing, seizing, and reconfiguring capabilities to respond effectively to market changes and competitive pressures. In parallel, the growing digitalization of business processes has drawn scholarly attention toward digital marketing as a strategic capability that enables firms to enhance customer engagement, improve market responsiveness, and achieve superior performance outcomes. Particularly in emerging economies, digital tools have become critical for small and medium enterprises seeking to overcome resource constraints and access wider markets. However, while both streams of research have evolved independently, their integration remains limited, indicating the need for further empirical investigation.

Although extensive research has examined the direct impact of dynamic capabilities on firm performance, the mediating role of specific capabilities, such as digital marketing, has not been thoroughly explored (Abrol, 2017; Arthurs & Busenitz, 2006; C. L. Wang et al., 2015). This pilot study aims to address this gap by investigating how dynamic capabilities affect firm performance through the mediation of digital marketing capabilities. By concentrating on this specific mediation, the study seeks to offer a deeper understanding of how dynamic capabilities lead to enhanced business outcomes. Consequently, this research paper explores the influence of dynamic capabilities on firm performance, with a particular emphasis on digital marketing capabilities as a mediating factor.

This research aims to advance the strategic management literature by elucidating the specific roles that digital marketing capabilities play in enhancing the effectiveness of dynamic capabilities. Moreover, the results of this pilot study are designed to offer practical insights for managers looking to utilize digital marketing as a strategic tool to boost organizational agility and performance.

In the following sections, we will review the pertinent literature on dynamic capabilities and digital marketing, describe the methodology used in our pilot study, present the empirical results, and conclude with a discussion of the study's implications and limitations.

DYNAMIC CAPABILITIES

Dynamic capabilities represent a firm's capacity to integrate, develop, and reconfigure both internal and external competencies to navigate rapidly changing environments. These capabilities are crucial for enabling firms to adapt to market dynamics, innovate effectively, and maintain a competitive advantage. (Teece, 2007) identifies three core elements of dynamic capabilities: sensing, seizing, and reconfiguring, all of which are critical for achieving sustained competitive success. Additionally, learning capabilities are often recognized as an essential component that supports and enhances these dynamic capabilities.

Sensing capabilities involve a firm's ability to detect opportunities and threats in the external environment. This requires ongoing market scanning, identifying emerging trends, and understanding shifts in customer preferences and technological advances (Teece, 2007). Firms with strong sensing capabilities excel at collecting and analyzing data, enabling them to foresee market changes and respond proactively. (Helfat & Martin, 2015) suggest that effective sensing allows firms to identify subtle environmental signals, which can be used to create new opportunities or mitigate risks.

Seizing capabilities reflect a firm's capacity to exploit the opportunities identified through sensing. This entails making strategic choices, allocating resources, and developing or modifying products and services to align with market needs (Teece, 2007). For instance, a firm might invest in new technologies, reorganize operations, or introduce innovative products to take advantage of identified opportunities. (Barreto, 2010) emphasizes that seizing capabilities are vital for firms to remain relevant in dynamic markets and convert opportunities into concrete business outcomes.

Reconfiguring capabilities refer to a firm's ability to restructure and renew its internal frameworks, processes, and resources to adapt to environmental changes (Teece, 2007). This could involve modifying business models, reorganizing organizational structures, or redeploying assets to maintain strategic flexibility (Eisenhardt & Martin, 2000). Firms with strong reconfiguring capabilities are better positioned to swiftly adjust to market shifts, technological changes, or competitive pressures, thereby maintaining their competitive standing (Augier & Teece, 2009).

Learning capabilities are crucial for the ongoing improvement and adaptation of a firm's routines, processes, and competencies. These capabilities encompass acquiring new knowledge, incorporating external insights, and refining existing skills to more effectively respond to environmental changes (Easterby-Smith & Prieto, 2008). Learning enables firms to build on past experiences and continuously enhance their dynamic capabilities. Zollo & Winter (2002) argue that learning processes are fundamental to the development and sustainability of dynamic capabilities, helping firms to innovate, adapt, and sustain competitiveness over time.

More recent studies extend the dynamic capabilities framework to small and medium enterprises, emphasizing that these capabilities play a decisive role in contexts characterized by uncertainty, limited resources, and rapid market shifts. Evidence from emerging economies indicates that SMEs depend heavily on learning and reconfiguring capabilities to remain competitive, particularly in traditional manufacturing sectors. Scholars argue that unlike large firms, SMEs must translate dynamic capabilities into actionable functional capabilities to realize performance benefits. This perspective highlights that the effectiveness of dynamic capabilities is contingent upon their alignment with specific operational and market-oriented practices, thereby opening avenues for examining complementary capabilities such as digital marketing.

DIGITAL MARKETING CAPABILITIES

Digital marketing capabilities refer to a firm's proficiency in utilizing digital tools, platforms, and strategies to achieve its marketing objectives and improve overall performance. In today's business landscape, where digital transformation is a key factor for gaining a competitive edge, these capabilities are vital. As noted by Chaffey, D., & Ellis-Chadwick (2019), digital marketing capabilities encompass the skills, knowledge, and resources required to effectively manage and optimize various digital channels, such as social media, email, search engines, and mobile applications. These capabilities enable firms to engage customers, gather valuable data, and personalize marketing strategies, thereby enhancing customer satisfaction and loyalty.

A fundamental aspect of digital marketing capabilities is data analytics. Firms with robust data analytics capabilities can collect and analyze large volumes of data from multiple digital sources, providing insights into customer behavior, preferences, and market trends (Chaffey, D., & Ellis-Chadwick, 2019). This ability to analyze data enables companies to make informed decisions, refine marketing campaigns, and improve customer targeting and segmentation (Wedel & Kannan, 2016). Additionally, data analytics capabilities allow firms to evaluate the effectiveness of their digital marketing efforts and adjust their strategies in real time to boost performance (W.-L. Wang et al., 2019).

Empirical research increasingly supports the view that digital marketing capabilities contribute directly to firm performance by enhancing market visibility, customer acquisition, and relationship management. Studies focusing on SMEs suggest that digital platforms enable firms to reach geographically dispersed customers at relatively low cost, thereby improving sales growth and brand recognition. In traditional industries, digital marketing capabilities have been found to facilitate faster sensing of customer preferences and market trends, enabling firms to respond more effectively to competitive dynamics. These findings underscore the strategic importance of digital marketing beyond its operational role, positioning it as a critical capability that supports organizational adaptability.

Content creation and management capabilities are another crucial element. The ability to develop, curate, and manage compelling and relevant digital content is essential for attracting customer interest and driving engagement across various platforms (Holliman & Rowley, 2014). Effective content marketing allows firms to build a strong online presence, foster brand loyalty, and establish themselves as thought leaders in their industries (Pulizzi, 2012). By leveraging these capabilities, firms can produce content that resonates with their target audience, thereby increasing brand awareness and driving conversions (Balte , 2015).

Social media management capabilities are equally important for success in digital marketing. These involve utilizing social media platforms to enhance brand visibility, engage with customers, and manage online communities (Trainor et al., 2014). Effective social media management allows firms to communicate directly with customers, gather feedback, and respond to customer inquiries promptly (Felix et al., 2017). It also enables firms to extend their reach through targeted advertising and partnerships with influencers, further strengthening their digital presence (Kaplan & Haenlein, 2010).

Customer relationship management (CRM) capabilities in a digital context are essential for building and maintaining long-term customer relationships. Digital CRM capabilities involve leveraging digital tools and platforms to gather, analyze, and utilize customer data to deliver personalized experiences, boost satisfaction, and enhance loyalty (Stone et al., 2020). These capabilities help firms better understand their customers' needs and preferences, anticipate future behaviors, and tailor their marketing efforts accordingly (Verhoef et al., 2010).

Despite the growing recognition of digital marketing capabilities as a driver of firm performance, existing studies largely examine their direct effects, with limited attention given to their role as an intervening mechanism within broader strategic frameworks. In particular, there is a lack of empirical research exploring how digital marketing capabilities enable firms to operationalize their dynamic capabilities. This gap is especially evident in the context of micro and small enterprises operating in traditional sectors, where digital adoption is often uneven but increasingly necessary for survival and growth. Addressing this gap can offer valuable insights into how strategic capabilities are translated into measurable performance outcomes.

FIRM PERFORMANCE

Firm performance is a multifaceted concept that covers different dimensions of a firm's success, such as financial outcomes, market standing, and operational effectiveness. It is typically assessed using a mix of financial metrics (like profitability, return on assets, and revenue growth) and non-financial metrics (such as customer satisfaction, market share, and innovation capabilities) (Venkatraman & Ramanujam, 1986). A firm's performance indicates its ability to meet strategic objectives and sustain a competitive advantage in the market. As noted by Richard et al. (2009), firm performance is a vital construct in strategic management research, offering valuable insights into how effectively a firm leverages its resources to generate value.

Dynamic capabilities are vital for boosting firm performance by enabling organizations to adapt, innovate, and stay competitive in fast-changing environments. These capabilities involve a firm's ability to integrate, develop, and reconfigure both internal and external resources to respond effectively to market and technological changes (Teece, 2007). They are essential for maintaining a competitive edge, as they help firms sense and seize opportunities while reconfiguring their resources to maximize gains or minimize risks (Teece et al., 1997). As (Eisenhardt & Martin, 2000) suggest, firms with robust dynamic capabilities are better equipped to manage uncertainty, resulting in enhanced outcomes such as higher market share, profitability, and innovation. Dynamic capabilities provide a critical framework for firms to achieve superior performance in unpredictable and rapidly changing markets. By effectively identifying opportunities and threats, capitalizing on strategic options, realigning resources, and promoting a culture of continuous learning, firms can improve their adaptability, capacity for innovation, and achieve sustained long-term success (Teece, 2014).

Figure 1. Research path model

GAP JUSTIFICATION

Although prior research has established the significance of dynamic capabilities for firm performance, the mechanisms through which these capabilities influence performance outcomes remain insufficiently explored. Existing studies predominantly focus on large firms or developed economies, leaving micro and small enterprises in emerging markets underrepresented. Moreover, the mediating role of digital marketing capabilities in translating dynamic capabilities into improved firm performance has received limited empirical attention, particularly within traditional industries such as textiles. This study addresses these gaps by examining digital marketing capabilities as a mediating mechanism, thereby contributing to a more nuanced understanding of capability-driven performance in emerging economy contexts.

METHODOLOGY

The pilot study employed a quantitative methodology, gathering data through an electronic survey. In quantitative research, participants and results are easily understood and directly related to the subject under investigation (Hair & Lukas, 2014). A survey questionnaire, along with a descriptive measurement approach, was utilized in this study. To minimize duplication, careful attention was given to the dimensions represented in the study model when designing the questionnaire items. Following (Zikmund et al., 2013), the survey items were selected based on the theoretical insights and justifications from previous studies, and adapted to align with the study's objectives, as shown in Table 1. The survey consisted of two sections. The first section gathered demographic information about the respondents, while the second section included statements evaluating dynamic capabilities and firm performance, with digital marketing serving as a mediator. The survey was targeted at top-level and middle-level executives within the firms.

Pilot Study

Pilot research is essential for identifying flaws in instrument design before committing substantial time and resources to a larger-scale investigation (Fraser et al., 2018). The primary objectives of a pilot study include assessing the reliability and validity of survey items, evaluating the clarity and appropriateness of the wording, and refining statements and questions to yield accurate results. Additionally, a pilot study determines whether the survey items are designed to elicit meaningful responses and whether respondents can provide the required data. A survey is considered reliable if it is free from errors, with consistent findings over time and across different contexts. The validity of a questionnaire refers to its ability to measure what it is intended to measure (Sekaran & Bougie, 2016).

According to (Whitehead et al., 2016), the sample size for a pilot study may vary based on the specific requirements of the research. Typically, pilot studies use a smaller sample than the main study, often ranging from 15 to 30 participants. In this study, 80 questionnaires were distributed to investors, and 58 completed surveys were collected and analyzed. This analysis aimed to evaluate how well respondents understood the questions, identify any difficulties they faced, assess the clarity of the instructions, gauge the attractiveness of the survey draft, and estimate the time required to complete it. The pilot study was conducted over a two-week period in May 2024.

Table 1. Instrument Source

Constructs	Source
Sensing	(Aminu & Mahmood, 2015; Pavlou & El Sawy, 2011)
Seizing	(Jantunen et al., 2018)
Reconfiguring	(Jantunen et al., 2018; Pavlou & El Sawy, 2011)
Learning Capabilities	(Aminu & Mahmood, 2015; Pavlou & El Sawy, 2011)

continued on following page

Table 1. Continued

Constructs	Source
Firm Performance	(Aminu & Mahmood, 2015; F. Wang, 2020)
Digital Marketing Capabilities	(Liu, 2022; F. Wang, 2020)

Data Analysis

There are various methods to conduct a reliability test, but internal consistency testing is the most commonly used approach (Maiyaki & Mokhtar, 2010). This test assesses how well the items within a variable converge to measure the same construct and whether there is a correlation among the items. Therefore, an internal consistency reliability test using Cronbach's alpha was performed, as recommended by (Sekaran & Bougie, 2016).

The results, shown in Table 2, indicate that all measures had high reliability coefficients, ranging from 0.716 to 0.916. According to research experts, a coefficient of 0.60 is regarded as an average reliability value, while a coefficient of 0.70 or higher indicates good consistency (Sekaran & Bougie, 2016). In case of validity all the items have significant value below 0.01 or 0.05 except FP4 and DMC4.

The reliability coefficients for dynamic capabilities and other variables surpassed 0.70 (Cronbach's alpha), demonstrating their credibility. The model used was a first-order model, incorporating dynamic capabilities such as sensing, seizing, reconfiguring, and learning capabilities. Additionally, digital marketing was found to mediate the relationship between dynamic capabilities and firm performance. According to the construct reliability table, all of the constructs had suitable alpha values that were greater than 0.70, indicating that the constructs' reliability was satisfactory (DeVellis, 2016).

Exploratory Factor Analysis

The pilot research involved 58 individuals, with a majority of respondents being male (71.4%). The participants comprised top-level and middle-level executives from various firms. The findings indicated that dynamic capabilities significantly impact firm performance.

The entire set of variables underwent Exploratory Factor Analysis (EFA) to evaluate whether the extracted factors aligned with the original theoretical constructs by examining the correlations between latent variables. The results of this analysis were essential in deciding whether modifications to the questionnaire items were necessary. Feedback and suggestions were considered in revising the survey's titles and design. The questionnaire used in the pilot project, which measures each construct, is detailed in Table 3 below. EFA was employed to assess the validity of the questionnaire.

Table 2. Reliability and Validity outcomes

Construct	Items	Cronbach Alpha	Validity
Sensing	SN 1	0.767	.000
	SN 2		.000
	SN 3		.006
	SN 4		.000
Seizing	SE1	0.909	.000
	SE 2		.000
	SE 3		.000
	SE 4		.000
Reconfiguring	RC 1	0.809	.000
	RC 2		.000
	RC 3		.000
	RC 4		.007
	RC 5		.000
Learning Capabilities	LC 1	0.716	.000
	LC 2		.000
	LC 3		.037
	LC 4		.000
Firm Performance	FP 1	0.916	.000
	FP 2		.000
	FP 3		.000
	FP 4		.849
	FP 5		.000
	FP 6		.000
	FP 7		.000
	FP 8		.000
Digital Marketing Capabilities	DMC 1	0.809	.021
	DMC 2		.017
	DMC 3		.000
	DMC 4		.220

Table 3. Pilot study items

Constructs	No. of Items
Sensing	4
Seizing	4
Reconfiguring	5
Learning Capabilities	4
Firm Performance	8
Digital Marketing Capabilities	4
Total	29

The table clearly shows that there are 29 statements in total, distributed across six paradigms. The research model is a first-order model consisting of 29 items. Dynamic capabilities encompass four factors: sensing, seizing, reconfiguring, and learning capabilities. The dynamic capabilities include sensing with 4 items, seizing with 4 items, reconfiguring with 5 items and learning capabilities with 4 items. Further, digital marketing capabilities have 4 items and firm performance have 8 items. Digital marketing capabilities act as a mediator between dynamic capabilities and firm performance. The EFA results for all variables related to dynamic capabilities, firm performance, and digital marketing capabilities are presented in Table 4.

Table 4 indicates that, with the exception of SN2, SN4, SE3, RC3, FP2, FP3, FP5, and DMC4, which loaded slightly below the 0.70 threshold but remained above 0.50, most items met the required criteria. However, a few items, specifically SN3 and FP4, had loadings below 0.50 and did not meet the criteria. All other items exceeded the 0.70 loading threshold, and since the average loadings for all constructs were above 0.70, the weights were considered acceptable.

Table 4. Exploratory Factor Analysis

	1	2	3	4	5	6
SN1	**.821**					
SN2	.662					
SN3						
SN4	.637					
SE1		.852				
SE2		.780				
SE3		.619				
SE4		.799				

continued on following page

Table 4. Continued

	1	2	3	4	5	6
SN1	**.821**					
RC1			.850			
RC2			.748			
RC3			.699			
RC4			.839			
RC5			.734			
LC1				.793		
LC2				.711		
LC3				.790		
LC4				.875		
FP1					.706	
FP2					.645	
FP3					.650	
FP4						
FP5					.623	
FP6					.773	
FP7					.756	
FP8					.733	
DMC1						.892
DMC2						.925
DMC3						.886
DMC4						.678

CONCLUSION

To prepare for a comprehensive investigation, this study conducted pilot research to evaluate the validity and reliability of the survey instrument. After reviewing content and face validity, several items were revised. An inter-item reliability test, using the Cronbach's alpha coefficient, confirmed that all statements were consistent, exceeding the 0.70 benchmark, leading to their retention. The pilot study supports the finding that dynamic capabilities significantly affect firm performance. The results indicate that dynamic capabilities such as sensing, seizing, reconfiguring, and learning are vital for improving firm performance, enabling firms to adapt to market changes, maintain competitive advantage, and foster growth. This emphasizes the importance of continuous capability development for sustained success. Unlike other studies, this study has limitations: a small sample size that may not represent the entire investor population, and the use of self-reported data, which could introduce some biasness. Future research should explore additional factors influencing firm performance to provide a more comprehensive understanding of this area.

REFERENCES

Abrol, D. (2017). Evaluating the Influence of Dynamic Capabilities on Firms' Performance: Role of Innovative Sustainability and Adaptation to Change. *Amity Journal of Management Research, 2*(2), 1–12. https://amity.edu/UserFiles/admaa/492fcPaper 1.pdf

Aminu, M. I., & Mahmood, R. (2015). Mediating Role of Dynamic Capabilities on the Relationship between Intellectual Capital and Performance: A Hierarchical Component Model Perspective in PLS-SEM Path Modeling. *Research Journal of Business Management, 9*(3), 443–456. DOI: 10.3923/rjbm.2015.443.456

Arthurs, J. D., & Busenitz, L. W. (2006). Dynamic capabilities and venture performance: The effects of venture capitalists. *Journal of Business Venturing, 21*(2), 195–215. DOI: 10.1016/j.jbusvent.2005.04.004

Augier, M., & Teece, D. J. (2009). Dynamic Capabilities and the Role of Managers in Business Strategy and Economic Performance. *Organization Science, 20*(2), 410–421. DOI: 10.1287/orsc.1090.0424

Baía, E. P., & Ferreira, J. J. M. (2024). Dynamic capabilities and performance: How has the relationship been assessed? *Journal of Management & Organization, 30*(1), 188–217. DOI: 10.1017/jmo.2019.88

Balte , L. P. (2015). *Content marketing - the fundamental tool of digital marketing.* Bulletin of the Transilvania University of Brasov. Series V : Economic Sciences. http://webbut2.unitbv.ro/BU2015/series v/BILETIN I/15_Patrutiu.pdf

Barreto, I. (2010). Dynamic Capabilities: A Review of Past Research and an Agenda for the Future. *Journal of Management, 36*(1), 256–280. DOI: 10.1177/0149206309350776

Bhardwaj, R., & Srivastava, S. (2024). Dynamic Capabilities of Social Enterprises: A Qualitative Meta-Synthesis and Future Agenda. *Journal of Social Entrepreneurship, 15*(2), 400–428. DOI: 10.1080/19420676.2021.1972030

Chaffey, D., & Ellis-Chadwick, F. (2019). *Digital marketing*. Pearson uk. https://thuvienso.hoasen.edu.vn/bitstream/handle/123456789/13083/Contents.pdf?sequence=1

DeVellis, R. (2016). *Scale Development: Theory and Applications* (Second edi). Sage publications. https://books.google.co.in/books?id=BYGxL6xLokUC&printsec=frontcover&redir_esc=y#v=onepage&q&f=false

Easterby-Smith, M., & Prieto, I. M. (2008). Dynamic Capabilities and Knowledge Management: An Integrative Role for Learning? *. *British Journal of Management, 19*(3), 235–249. DOI: 10.1111/j.1467-8551.2007.00543.x

Edelman, D. C. (2010). (2010). Branding in the Digital Age: You're Spending Your Money in All the Wrong Places. *Harvard Business Review Digital Articles, 88*, 63–69. https://www.scirp.org/reference/referencespapers?referenceid=1714074

Eisenhardt, K. M., & Martin, J. A. (2000). Dynamic Capabilities: What are They? *Strategic Management Journal, 21*(10/11), 1105–1121. https://www.jstor.org/stable/3094429

Felix, R., Rauschnabel, P. A., & Hinsch, C. (2017). Elements of strategic social media marketing: A holistic framework. *Journal of Business Research, 70*, 118–126. DOI: 10.1016/j.jbusres.2016.05.001

Fraser, J., & Fahlman, D. (Willy), Arscott, J., & Guillot, I. (2018). Pilot Testing for Feasibility in a Study of Student Retention and Attrition in Online Undergraduate Programs. *International Review of Research in Open and Distance Learning, 19*(1), 1–14. DOI: 10.19173/irrodl.v19i1.3326

Hair, J. F., & Lukas, B. (2014). *Marketing Research*. McGraw-Hill Education Australia. https://cat2.lib.unimelb.edu.au/record=b5609216~S13

Helfat, C. E., & Martin, J. A. (2015). Dynamic Managerial Capabilities: Review and Assessment of Managerial Impact on Strategic Change. *Journal of Management, 41*(5), 1281–1312. DOI: 10.1177/0149206314561301

Holliman, G., & Rowley, J. (2014). Business to business digital content marketing: Marketers' perceptions of best practice. *Journal of Research in Interactive Marketing, 8*(4), 269–293. DOI: 10.1108/JRIM-02-2014-0013

Jantunen, A., Tarkiainen, A., Chari, S., & Oghazi, P. (2018). Dynamic capabilities, operational changes, and performance outcomes in the media industry. *Journal of Business Research, 89*, 251–257. DOI: 10.1016/j.jbusres.2018.01.037

Kaplan, A. M., & Haenlein, M. (2010). Users of the world, unite! The challenges and opportunities of Social Media. *Business Horizons, 53*(1), 59–68. DOI: 10.1016/j.bushor.2009.09.003

Liu, Y. (2022). Effect of Digital Marketing Capabilities and Blockchain Technology on Organizational Performance and Psychology. *Frontiers in Psychology, 12*. Advance online publication. DOI: 10.3389/fpsyg.2021.805393 PMID: 35211056

Maiyaki, A. A., & Mokhtar, S. S. M. (2010). Determinants of customer behavioural responses: A pilot study. *International Business Research*, *4*(1), 193. https://doi.org/http://dx.doi.org/10.5539/ibr.v4n1p193

Pavlou, P. A., & El Sawy, O. A. (2011). Understanding the Elusive Black Box of Dynamic Capabilities. *Decision Sciences*, *42*(1), 239–273. DOI: 10.1111/j.1540-5915.2010.00287.x

Pulizzi, J. (2012). The Rise of Storytelling as the New Marketing. *Publishing Research Quarterly*, *28*(2), 116–123. DOI: 10.1007/s12109-012-9264-5

Richard, P. J., Devinney, T. M., Yip, G. S., & Johnson, G. (2009). Measuring Organizational Performance: Towards Methodological Best Practice. *Journal of Management*, *35*(3), 718–804. DOI: 10.1177/0149206308330560

Sekaran, U., & Bougie, R. (2016). *Research Methods for Business: A Skill Building Approach*. John Wiley and Sons. https://www.wiley.com/en-in/Research+Methods+For+Business:+A+Skill+Building+Approach,+7th+Edition-p-9781119266846

Stone, M., Aravopoulou, E., Ekinci, Y., Evans, G., Hobbs, M., Labib, A., Laughlin, P., Machtynger, J., & Machtynger, L. (2020). Artificial intelligence (AI) in strategic marketing decision-making: A research agenda. *The Bottom Line (New York, N.Y.)*, *33*(2), 183–200. DOI: 10.1108/BL-03-2020-0022

Teece, D. J. (2007). Explicating dynamic capabilities: The nature and microfoundations of (sustainable) enterprise performance. *Strategic Management Journal*, *28*(13), 1319–1350. DOI: 10.1002/smj.640

Teece, D. J. (2014). A dynamic capabilities-based entrepreneurial theory of the multinational enterprise. *Journal of International Business Studies*, *45*(1), 8–37. DOI: 10.1057/jibs.2013.54

Teece, D. J., Pisano, G., Shuen, A., & Jose, S. (1997). Dynamic capabilities and strategic management. *Strategic Management Journal*, *18*(7), 509–533. DOI: 10.1002/(SICI)1097-0266(199708)18:7<509:AID-SMJ882>3.0.CO;2-Z

Trainor, K. J., & Andzulis, J. (Mick), Rapp, A., & Agnihotri, R. (2014). Social media technology usage and customer relationship performance: A capabilities-based examination of social CRM. *Journal of Business Research*, *67*(6), 1201–1208. DOI: 10.1016/j.jbusres.2013.05.002

Venkatraman, N., & Ramanujam, V. (1986). Measurement of Business Performance in Strategy Research: A Comparison of Approaches. *Academy of Management Review*, *11*(4), 801. DOI: 10.2307/258398

Verhoef, P. C., Broekhuizen, T., Bart, Y., Bhattacharya, A., Qi Dong, J., Fabian, N., & Haenlein, M. (2021). Digital transformation: A multidisciplinary reflection and research agenda. *Journal of Business Research, 122*, 889–901. DOI: 10.1016/j.jbusres.2019.09.022

Verhoef, P. C., Reinartz, W. J., & Krafft, M. (2010). Customer Engagement as a New Perspective in Customer Management. *Journal of Service Research, 13*(3), 247–252. DOI: 10.1177/1094670510375461

Wang, C. L., Senaratne, C., & Rafiq, M. (2015). Success traps, dynamic capabilities and firm performance. *British Journal of Management, 26*(1), 26–44. DOI: 10.1111/1467-8551.12066

Wang, F. (2020). Digital marketing capabilities in international firms: A relational perspective. *International Marketing Review, 37*(3), 559–577. DOI: 10.1108/IMR-04-2018-0128

Wang, W.-L., Malthouse, E. C., Calder, B., & Uzunoglu, E. (2019). B2B content marketing for professional services: In-person versus digital contacts. *Industrial Marketing Management, 81*, 160–168. DOI: 10.1016/j.indmarman.2017.11.006

Wedel, M., & Kannan, P. K. (2016). Marketing Analytics for Data-Rich Environments. *Journal of Marketing, 80*(6), 97–121. DOI: 10.1509/jm.15.0413

Whitehead, A. L., Julious, S. A., Cooper, C. L., & Campbell, M. J. (2016). Estimating the sample size for a pilot randomised trial to minimise the overall trial sample size for the external pilot and main trial for a continuous outcome variable. *Statistical Methods in Medical Research, 25*(3), 1057–1073. DOI: 10.1177/0962280215588241 PMID: 26092476

Wu, Q., Yan, D., & Umair, M. (2023). Assessing the role of competitive intelligence and practices of dynamic capabilities in business accommodation of SMEs. *Economic Analysis and Policy, 77*, 1103–1114. DOI: 10.1016/j.eap.2022.11.024

Zikmund, W., Babin, B., Carr, J., & Griffin, M. (2013). *Business Research Methods*. Cengage Learning. https://books.google.co.in/books/about/Business_Research_Methods.html?id=veM4gQPnWHgC&redir_esc=y

Zollo, M., & Winter, S. G. (2002). Deliberate Learning and the Evolution of Dynamic Capabilities. *Organization Science, 13*(3), 339–351. DOI: 10.1287/orsc.13.3.339.2780

Chapter 8
Social Media Marketing Strategies for Hotels and Resorts

Anand Bharathi
http://orcid.org/0000-0002-7367-8264
Vellore Institute of Technology, India

Abdullah Malik
http://orcid.org/0000-0002-0149-5549
Jain University, India

Vinoth Kumar
http://orcid.org/0009-0001-9523-6651
Patrician College of Arts and Science, India

S. Rajamohan
http://orcid.org/0000-0001-5894-5443
Fatima College, India

D. Unika
Patrician College of Arts and Science, India

ABSTRACT

The luxury and experience-hospitality market is being reshaped by digitalisation, social media, and AI-enabled interaction. Legacy marketing models relying on static campaigns, OTAs, and print are disrupted by social-first, participatory, algorithm-led environments. Platforms like Instagram, TikTok, and YouTube now drive discovery, trust, and revenue, where aspirational storytelling and social proof outweigh rational decision-making. This shift demands strategies spanning influ-

DOI: 10.4018/979-8-3373-6741-5.ch008

encer ecosystems, UGC, platform-specific optimisation, and AI-powered scalability. Influencer programs, gamified UGC, referral flows, and guest-led content expand reach and trust, while automation enables personalisation, repurposing, predictive CRM, and analytics. Generational and cultural differences further require adaptive, data-informed social approaches. Reframing social media as a high-performance commercial asset allows hospitality brands to convert engagement into bookings, loyalty, and emotional connection.

1. INTRODUCTION

1.1 Digital Transformation in Hospitality

Digital transformation in hospitality is an ongoing process that reshapes how brands operate and engage with customers. The industry is experiencing a level of change second only to its history (Zeqiri, 2024). This shift encompasses not just technology but also behavioral and economic aspects, influencing how hospitality brands design experiences, capture demand, and build long-term loyalty (Bardukova, 2023; Giannoukou, 2024). From artificial intelligence-guided customer selection to real-time dynamic pricing, the operating logic is increasingly driven by digital ecosystems where data, content, and customer emotions serve as key competitive elements (Buhalis et al., 2023). Outdated marketing models based on static campaigns and broadcast mass media are becoming obsolete, replaced by real-time, adaptive, and algorithmically driven engagement models that demand strategic adaptation.

1.2 Social Media as the Primary Revenue & Influence Engine

Social media and its use have come to dominate not only the generation of demand but also the formation of perceptions (Rathore et. al., 2016). Instagram, YouTube, and TikTok are now more than communication tools; they are complete systems where discovery, trust-building, development, conversion, and retention happen within a single environment (Haenlein et al., 2020). Unlike previous generations, social media functions as an all-in-one digital storefront, reputation marketplace, content theatre, and customer service portal. 'The number of social media-influenced bookings has given the website, OTA, and search a real run for their money,' with social media bookings now often exceeding those from traditional channels, underscoring its growing dominance in hospitality marketing.

1.3 Shift from Search First to Social First Discovery

This transformation process is sped up by a generational shift – the customer journey is no longer "search first" but "social first" (Amitay et al., 2009). For the younger audience, "the new battleground happens not on Google search but inside TikTok or Instagram Reels or YouTube Shorts" (Sharma, 2024; Ahmed et al., 2025). In this attention-first process, the algorithm chooses what is looked at before any intention has time to develop. This inverts the logic of SEO based hospitality marketing: search is demand capture (i.e., reactive), while social represents demand creation (i.e., proactive). So "social" is not just optional any longer, it is strategically table stakes.

1.4 Scope of the Chapter

This Chapter does not concern itself with social media in the context of mere content posting to it either. Instead, it deconstructs the strategic framework, key design components, and offering logistics necessary to construct a scalable social engine for hospitality companies that generate revenue. Contrary to social media–generated hospitality's economic centrality, the academic literature remains heavily biased on traditional digital marketing that is search and review heavy, including OTAs, with little strategic depth regarding platform native social monetization. A research void exists in detailing a prescriptive, actionable, evidence-informed model for growing social-first hospitality. This Chapter aims to provide a practitioner-quality, comprehensive playbook. Fundamentally, it is not a theory-only approach, but a set of precise, easy-to-follow execution guidance for operators or academics who are involved in related fields of research, such as digital competitiveness in hospitality. The Chapter moves from strategic underpinnings to executional infrastructure, mechanics of automation and content intelligence systems, monetization models, and future preparedness, blending academic insight with operational precision.

2. EVOLUTION OF SOCIAL MEDIA IN HOSPITALITY

The development of hospitality marketing during the last 30 years has been primarily influenced by media infrastructure change, consumer emancipation, and technology affordances as we have moved away from an information asymmetry to participatory co-creation (Dilek & Harman, 2017; Dev et al., 2010; Minazzi & Panno, 2019; Morosan et al., 2014). Moreover, this trajectory has re-shaped the way experiences are being envisioned, assessed, and finally booked.

2.1 Pre-Social Era

Before the rise of Web 2.0, hospitality marketing was branded by high distribution control and low customer voice (Zobnina & Rozhkov, 2018). Hotels depended extensively on the print media, such as brochures and glossy travel magazines, or supplements of newspapers (Morgan and Pritchard, 2012; Guijarroa, 2013), to create brand images that consumers could aspire towards. Travel agents served as gatekeepers of destination choice via packaged tours and personal convincing (Saini et al., 2025). Suppliers' power was enhanced by information asymmetry because there was little transparency of experience. The 2000s saw the dawn of Online Travel Agencies (OTAs) such as Expedia and Booking, according to Martin-Fuentes and Mellinas (2018), who digitized the discovery but not innovation, with a transactional logic of inventory, price comparison, and convenience instead of experiential naive authenticity. These OTAs reshaped the distribution of power but still were not a social conversation.

2.2 Digital Shift

The introduction of TripAdvisor (2000) gave rise to the first large-scale participatory review system (Ertaş & Karakan, 2024). Trust was no longer centralized around brand advertising and instead became decentralized via peer validation. Through textual reviews, UGC was implemented as a passive yet emergent feedback loop (Naab & Sehl, 2017). Reputation was quantified algorithmically by ratings, rank, and sentiment averages. The academic literature calls this the beginning of "experience transparency." Through 'lived narratives', consumers could control uncertainty, and social media caused hotels to keep track of their digital reputation through eWOM (electronic word of mouth). The one-way communication between the hotel and guests shifted towards controlled conversation (Ho, 2020).

2.3 Emergence of Instagram, Reels, TikTok & YouTube Vlogs

Instagram's popularity after 2012 and then TikTok's short-form revolution made written reviews even more passe, as visual storytelling eclipsed them. The trend for the styles of hospitality marketing communications moved from information-oriented to aspiration-oriented (Datiko, 2024; Inversini et al., 2020), away from "What is it like?" to "Would I want to be there?" YouTube vlogs and aesthetic travel reels started to serve as pre-experience surrogates. The influencer collectivist economy hit its stride as micro celebrity creators began molding perception not through expertise but by doing, relatability, and aesthetic authority. Unlike TripAdvisor's rational persuasion, Instagram and TikTok run on emotional contagion and identity projection. Hospitality brands began to build architecture for shareability — infinity pools, neon signage, "Instagrammable breakfasts."

2.4 Rise of the Experience Economy & Emotional Travel Marketing

Pine & Gilmore's (2011) handbook "Experience Economy" actually went from theory to reality. Travel became less about consuming place and more about performing identity. It was not just documenting travel; social media framed the way we travel. Emotional marketing that focused on belonging, uniqueness, and transformation surpassed pricing and perks as the decision makers. Hospitality narratives moved from product-oriented ("luxury room with ocean view") to experiential immersion ("sunrise rituals," "digital detox," "local storytelling dining"). The aim was creative differentiation through emotional semiotics, not functional supremacy.

2.5 Consumer Decision Pathway

That old "search–compare–book" model is long gone. Studies suggest a reversion of the ordering such that social media is now the top of funnel 'trigger' for discovery and desire development: achieved algorithmically through feeds rather than purposive searches (McKelvey & Hunt, 2019; Sârbu et al., 2018). Consumers, particularly Gen Z and younger millennials, now trip over destinations before they realize they need them. The Research Society is researching OTAs after the social proof of experiments, but there are never going to be enough studies to prove their adequacy. These purchase journeys in hospitality are now "social → emotional → rational → transactional."

2.6 Demographic Differences

There are clear platform behaviours when dissecting different generations (Cheah & Phua, 2025). Discovery-first and search-last Gen Zers trust TikTok, Reels, and micro influencers more than Google (Wang & Park, 2023). Millennials in between with aspiration and research, Instagram is an environment for "looking up," but OTAs are still about verification. Gen X is still utilitarian and are generally coming in at the "search" phase rather than passive discovery. Boomers hold the most traditional behaviors, still desiring reviews but leaning toward "structured" platforms. Old media architecture, for hotels, a "one size fits all" digital strategy is now obsolete media architecture must flex across demographic psychologies, not just demographics.

3. STRATEGIC FOUNDATION & AUDIENCE PSYCHOLOGY

An attractive personality and the well-situated location alone cannot carry a hospitality or travel brand; it must be backed by psychologically founded positions (Buhalis & Park, 2021). This is the strategic model that informs how we message out to audiences, and we target digitally in terms of conversion behaviour across digital touch points.

3.1 Brand Positioning & Identity Mapping

Brand positioning is the process of making a conscious choice about where the brand should be placed in customers' minds rather than solely its tangible offering (Dou et al., 2010). Identity mapping maps this into the four layers of functional value (the problem solved), emotional value (how it makes us feel), social value (what we signal to others), and cultural value (whether something represents aspiration, heritage, or exclusivity). Travelers are not just purchasing a stay; they are buying a story about themselves. You cannot call the place a luxury Eco resort and have it sound like a family budget stay. A spiritual wellness retreat should not sound transactional. Decisiveness in branding is repeatedly proven to increase conviction and retention at a greater rate than discounting does.

3.2 USP Clarity

The most crucial distinction is the vacating of vagueness. Confusion is churn in hotel and resort strategy. A brand perceived as a halfway house between luxury and boutique rarely works, it becomes too cheap for luxury travellers and "intimidating" for boutique customers.

Table 1. USP Clarity

Positioning Segment	Core Value Proposition / Emotional Driver
Luxury	Status, privacy, effortlessness, personalization, and scarcity.
Boutique	Story driven, artisanal, non-corporate intimacy.
Family	Safety, convenience, multiage frictionless experience.
Wellness	Ritual, healing, bio-optimization, spiritual or longevity value.
Business	Friction removal, precision, uptime, and global standards.

Source: Compiled and interpreted by the author.

Recognizing that clarity impacts visual language, vocabulary, pricing psychology, and even the music choice on a property and social assets.

3.3 Social Media Funnel

The hospitality sales funnel is nonlinear; people's "dream scroll" before intent even has a chance of cone. But it doesn't mean there still aren't dominating psychological triggers in each stage:

Table 2. Social Media Funnel

Stage	Psychological triggers
Awareness	Curiosity I visual fantasy I FOMO
Engagement	Immersion I "could this be me?" storytelling
Decision	Proof, credibility, reassurance (reviews, authority signals)
Booking	Frictionless call-to-action, urgency psychology
Loyalty	Emotional reactivation, privileged access
Advocacy	Status signaling, reward for sharing

Source: Compiled and interpreted by the author.

Marketers who provide aesthetically attractive reels that lack variations in the funnel tier inspire their competitors.

3.4 Persona Creation

The modern cohort of travellers no longer reacts to blanket messaging (Gardiner et al., 2013). Honeymooners want intimacy-indicating as well as comfy emblems, and digital nomads are buying freedom and infrastructure (decent Wi-Fi, an ecosystem that does not judge). Staging Your Corporate Retreat: In-house retreat planners favour scalability and smooth logistics, whereas wellness travellers long for transformation, not just relaxation. Every persona requires not only different offers but also a unique linguistic rhythm, visual framing, and testimonial architecture.

3.5 Cultural Sensitivity & Regional Personalization

Emotional drivers for buying change significantly from one market to another (Lacoste & Dekker, 2016). To a European slow traveller, luxury equals time and solitude; to an Indian HNI, it often translates into social signalling and concierge dominance. Group experience harmony is the preference of Southeast Asian travellers; privacy and discretion are the preferences of Middle Eastern travellers. From the level of visuals to phrasing and even the gesture of invitation, everything has to modulate "global aesthetic, locally intelligent."

3.6 Psychology of Travel Decisions

Travel intent is almost entirely aspirational and identity-related, not transactional. We travel to either restore, reward, uplevel, or escape our current selves. Neuroscience research (Fennell, 2009) indeed shows that the expectation of travel reward already triggers dopamine before we even book it –the sale occurs emotionally long before we can rationalize the purchase. That is why storytelling, not room specs, converts at the awareness phase, and why reviews (not dreams) close the decision phase.

4. SOCIAL MEDIA AUDIT & OPTIMIZATION FRAMEWORK

In an emerging digital-first hospitality environment (Adeyinka-Ojo et al, 2020; Mavitha & Kushe Shekhar, 2025), a property's Instagram or WhatsApp presence is no longer just a marketing layer but is becoming the only experience layer, even higher than the website, and in some cases entirely cutting it. This framework is designed to perform a Zero Leakage Audit that will reveal any reputation, revenue, trust, and discoverability gaps in the social media layer while transforming these touch points into an active, not passive, gallery feed booking engine.

4.1 Brand Audit Matrix

The diagnostic is a 10-dimensional benchmark that will allow you to see whether or not your brand currently has all the necessary trappings for its social layer to be visitor-concerned, conversion-concerned, and story-consistent. Then the severity of the problem is assessed on a scale with the following 5 points for each dimension.

Table 3. Brand Audit Matrix

Diagnostic Dimension	Key Evaluation Question / Indicator
Brand Narrative Clarity	Does the brand say who it is in <3 seconds?
Visual Consistency	Mobile first, professional grade, mood specific
Differentiator Visibility	Is your USP obvious vs "generic luxury"?
Discovery Optimization	Hashtags, ALT tags, location tagging hygiene
Conversion Readiness	Direct booking call-to-actions vs brochure content
Trust Layer Strength	Awards, PR, real people, verified status
Personalization Signals	Do you speak in first person or brochure tone?
Seasonal Relevance	Active campaigns, not just permanent assets

continued on following page

Table 3. Continued

Diagnostic Dimension	Key Evaluation Question / Indicator
Engagement Quality	Creator collaborations, UGC, shareability density
Ecosystem Integration	Linked seamlessly with OTA + website + WA

Source: Compiled and interpreted by the author.

The audit uncovers "invisible revenue leaks" – those spaces where the brand appears active, but is underperforming commercially.

4.2 Competitor Benchmarking & Positioning

It is a competitive position, not a copy-paste observation being worked here. The point here is, where our competitors have a higher algo stress factor than we do – it isn't just about content. We benchmark:

Table 4. Competitor Benchmarking & Positioning

Benchmark Dimension	Key Evaluation Question / Indicator
CTA Velocity	Do competitors aggressively lead to direct booking?
Value Communication Architecture	Category clarity, not content beauty
Narrative Strategy	Are they aspirational, cultural, experiential, functional?
Tech Integration	WhatsApp buttons, IG lead ads, Meta API readiness
Influencer Amplification Signals	Are they embedded in discovery loops?
Price Power Perception	Is the competitor premium coded or discount coded?

Source: Compiled and interpreted by the author.

This stage is what your market narrative gap is not about, what competitors post, but what you win through platform intelligence.

4.3 Social Media Maturity Scorecard

All intelligence is then blended into a maturity index based on four transformation quadrants:

Table 5. Maturity index Levels

Stage	Identity	Capability	Monetization
Level 1	Passive brand	Manual content posting	No booking funnel
Level 2	Aspirational presence	Platform learning begins	Link in bio
Level 3	Category authority	UGC + creator signals	CTA driven
Level 4	Full commercial stack	API + automation + tracking	Hot path booking

Source: Compiled and interpreted by the author.

This allows us to distinctly categorise whether the hotel is still publishing content, acquiring audience intelligence, or is already operating as a commerce engine on social.

4.4 Profile Optimization

Profile optimization is not just cosmetic; it is a revenue lever. The username is supposed to be a clear clue of the category or place, not an exercise in brand ego. The bio should immediately provide clarity in three seconds: what problem does the brand solve? Who for and why now. CTA's should avoid nonspecific prompts like "Message" and use specific conversion triggers such as "Book Now" or "Check Availability". The link should lead users to a compulsory, pre-filtered, low-friction flow and not just some home page. A large property, such as a 500-room hotel, can miss a million annually because its CTA takes visitors to a generic website with no auto scroll or anchor to availability and no WhatsApp deep link.

4.5 Highlight Architecture

Highlight design is website navigation UX, but for Instagram. Chronological bloat vs mapping by conversion architecture should be tried in logical order, such as Rooms → Experiences → Offers → Reviews → Weddings → FAQ. If your multi-outlet hospitality business needs food and beverage, wedding, or long stay conversions to be successful, then create separate funnels rather than lumping them together into one key hit. Each highlight should lead off not with a flourish but with pitch clarity. The decision-confidence of users may be increased by 30-50% simply from this methodology when comparing multiple itineraries across browser tabs.

4.6 Pixel Integration, Tracking & API Readiness

This is where marketing science starts beyond content beauty. The foundation is hard-coded technical accuracy: Is the Meta Pixel installed, and firing events as intended? Are there custom conversions established, like "Availability Check" other than a general click? Do Lead Ads connect with the WhatsApp API and the CRM to capture leads properly? Are you not only tracking UTM parameters for traffic, but also the revenue index per channel? Running social media without tracking events is like managing a hotel blindfolded based on intuition rather than checked-in guest numbers.

4.7 Trust Signals & UGC Integration

Today's users convert on peer proof, not brand proof. Humble reels of actual guests constantly beat out the slick hospitality cinematic productions. If a hotel has accolades in media channels or is featured on GQ or Vogue, these should be showcased heavily. Real guests' story replies can be turned into "human proof" animations, and verified badges, press hits, and live occupancy testimonials help further validate. Seeding of context-specific user-generated content, e.g., the wedding highlight showing couple pictures rather than generic frames. This trust layer is four to seven times more effective at converting than anything a brand can say about itself.

4.8 Connected Ecosystem

The modern booking behaviour is multi-tab and nonlinear, the conversion journey might start on Instagram, move to an OTA for price comparison, and finish on WhatsApp. So, audit checks are key: Does price parity (or a better than OTA guarantee) feature in the upper corner of their Instagram reels or stories? Is a smooth, one-tap return journey possible between the website, Instagram, WhatsApp, and the booking page? Instead of relying on GDS emails, is WhatsApp automation being used to reconnect with lost prospects? The social profile is no longer one piece of the marketing pie; it is an essential part of the brand's master ecosystem backbone.

4.9 "Book Now" Journey Friction Reduction

The last stage involves auditing the taps to tire kick, not impressions to likes. So, the question is: how many clicks does it take Instagram users to go from someone's profile to proof of payment? When you land on the page, does it naturally scroll past the hero banner to an availability selector, or do you have to engage for it to move? Does the WhatsApp chatbot get its check-in date suggestions right, or does it start cold? When it comes to wedding inquiry funnels, do you get the budget first (to qualify leads)? Or is a detailed form with no pricing clarity used for this? Ideally, users should be able to go from "Choose Date" through to "Confirm Price" and then "Proceed to Pay" in no more than 20 seconds. Studies show that for each tap after the fourth step, direct booking probability decreases by 50-60%.

5. PLATFORM WISE STRATEGIC ROADMAP

An integrated platform approach will increasingly depend on well-defined links between audience motivation, content types, and business models rather than the one-size-fits-all placement of assets. Every platform must be assessed as its own closed system with its native virality, algorithmic mechanics, and economics. The roadmap follows the platforms as funnels, not channels, where you can sequence, compound reach, and find measurable conversion efficiency.

5.1 Purpose & Best Audience Fit

Each platform should serve a purpose of where it fits in the attention maturity curve: discovery, consideration, or conversion.

Table 6. Purpose & Best Audience Fit

Platform	Primary Function	Strategic Purpose
Reels / TikTok / YouTube Shorts	Curiosity spike and first touch education	Generate low friction, high reach awareness through short form, engaging content that attracts new audiences.
YouTube Longform / LinkedIn / X (Twitter)	Expert positioning and narrative depth	Establish authority, provide deeper context, and signal credibility within professional or interest-based audiences.
Website / Email / WhatsApp	High intimacy nurturing and transaction intent	Drive conversions, sustain retention loops, and maintain personalized engagement with warm or returning users.

Source: Compiled and interpreted by the author.

Perfect fit is determined by psychographic preparedness and not demographic, i.e., "problem unaware" v/s. "solution aware" v/s." payment ready" users.

5.2 Platform-Specific Content Formats & Posting Strategy

Content does not need to be rehashed side to side but dug into from the bottom up in order for it to leverage platform incentives.

Table 7. Content Strategy by Platform Type

Content Type / Platform	Core Strategy	Execution Focus
Shortform Virality Platforms (Reels, TikTok, YouTube Shorts)	Fastpattern hooks using problem shock, enemy framing, or unexpected claims	10–45 second narrative loops focused on attention capture; prioritize output volume over perfection.
Authority Platforms (YouTube Longform, LinkedIn)	Premise–Proof–Payoff storytelling with frameworks, contrarian insights, and data visualization	Publish 2–3 deep, saveworthy posts per week that build credibility and thought leadership.
Conversion Surfaces (Email, Newsletter)	Offer stacking, urgency psychology, case studies, and ROI driven storytelling	Frequency guided by sales pipeline needs rather than platform algorithms; designed for transaction intent.

Source: Compiled and interpreted by the author.

Strategic Action Item Takeaways: The game of traffic and sales is ONE content pillar "highway" platform, TWO "traffic accelerators," and ONE "conversion sink."

5.3 Organic Growth Ecosystem Blueprint

Rather than just trying to force-feed isolated virality, brands need to architect an inter-platform traffic circulation loop that engineers distributed attention into a centre of mass audience experience. The discovery format of short-form content, like Reels, leads viewers toward long-form platforms, such as YouTube, where trust and expertise can be established. From there, audiences are funnelled to higher intimacy/transaction intent spaces, like email or newsletters, which then eventually lead to gated/high ticket monetization offers.

It's these micro lever loops, a poll leading to a DM follow-up. Set up, then personalized asset drop and inclusion in custom retargeting buckets that keep engagement notched high and handshakes personal. The primary algorithm alignment principle is to backward engineer the watch time decay pattern and not chase view counts. In this sense, quality is not measured by reach growth (more is better), but by how deeply an audience preserves and engages with the content, even going to great lengths in cases when the stakes are high.

Table 8. Stage-Wise Content Flow and Strategic Purpose

Stage / Element	Purpose	Key Principle
Reels / Shorts	Generate top funnel curiosity and discovery	Push traffic to longform trust content (YouTube)
YouTube (Longform)	Build credibility and deepen brand trust	Direct users toward email signup or gated offers
Email / Newsletter	Nurture high intent audience	Guide toward premium or highticket monetization
Micro Lever Loops (Poll → DM → Asset Drop → Retarget)	Maintain personalized engagement	Build segmented audiences and improve conversion
Algorithm Alignment	Sustain visibility and efficiency	Optimize for retention depth, not just reach velocity

Source: Compiled and interpreted by the author.

5.4 Paid Ads Strategy

Paid campaigns should be driving validated organic performers, not testing untried concepts. At the campaign level, establish a clear outcome archetype: lead generation, direct sales, authority sequencing, or retarget nurturing. All ad sets should be targeting super-tuned behavioral audiences and not overbroad interests, ex, high-intent site drop-offs vs interest groups. The creative mix is ideally 80% emotional storytelling or relief contrast and 20% logical framing. CTAs shouldn't create multi-step friction and should push people into the next behavior (like a DM prompt, form capture, or WhatsApp lead). And, of course, you will need to retarget and segment cold viewers, warm engagers & hot intent users in order to maximise your conversion velocity.

Table 9. Funnel Components and Optimization Focus

Funnel Component	Focus Area	Key Principle
Campaign Level	Outcome archetype (Lead Gen / Direct Sales / Authority / Nurture)	Paid should amplify proven organic winners, not test unvalidated angles.
Ad Set Level	Behavioral audience targeting	Focus on highintent site visitors or dropoffs, not broad interest buckets.
Ad Creative	Emotional–Logical balance	80% story or relief contrast, 20% logical proof or framing.

continued on following page

Table 9. Continued

Funnel Component	Focus Area	Key Principle
CTA Flow	Conversion friction control	Use singlestep CTAs like DM prompt, form capture, or WhatsApp lead.
Retargeting	Heat segmentation	Split into Cold (viewers), Warm (engagers), and Hot (cartlevel intent).

Source: Compiled and interpreted by the author.

5.5 ROI Measurement & Monetization Logic

Success should not necessarily be determined by platform vanity metrics, but through quantifiable business efficiency. The fundamental metrics are the net efficiency of attention arbitrage and the velocity of payback, not just CAC vs LTV, but this new metric in its early days: Cost per Qualified Attention Minute. Monetization logic can be flexible in terms of funnel, by using digital products or community-based offerings for the scale-rich top part and consultation or high-ticket service for the trust-rich bottom part. The endgame strategic North Star is predictable conversion compounding, not the variance in post-level performance.

6. INTEGRATED SOCIAL MEDIA CAMPAIGN EXECUTION FRAMEWORK

Implementing a high-impact social media campaign requires an organized blueprint that combines strategic funnel management with content-driven audience targeting and engagement. This methodology means that not only should ads be attractive, but they should also be conversion-driven – shepherding potential customers from initial clicks to final sales in a methodical way. Core to the structure is a three-pronged funnel system along with specially designed campaign templates customized for each market segment or objective.

6.1 Funnel Architecture

The funnel position forms the foundation for an integrated approach to social media marketing, which lets brands direct fans through a cycle of awareness and conversion. At the top of the funnel (TOFU), content should capture the attention of a broad audience with stories that convey emotions and show their visual appeal. In the middle of the funnel (MOFU), Smart companies will want to use paid traffic options that nurture and keep prospects interested through education, social proof, and retargeting. And last, but not least, the bottom of the funnel (BOFU) is where campaigns need to convert that purchase intent into action by using personalization and urgency and providing a frictionless CTA. Together, these layers form a measurable compounding customer journey from curiosity to loyalty.

Table 10. Full-Funnel Marketing Stages, Objectives, and Core Strategies

Funnel Stage	Objective	Core Strategies	Typical Platforms & Tools	Key Outcomes
Top of the Funnel (TOFU)	Build awareness and attract a broad audience	Visually appealing, emotionally resonant, and shareable content; storytelling, lifestyle imagery, aspirational videos, brand narratives	Instagram, YouTube, TikTok, shortform video campaigns	Curiosity, engagement, and audience expansion
Middle of the Funnel (MOFU)	Nurture engagement and build trust	Educational content, experiential storytelling, retargeting ads, social proof (reviews, testimonials, UGC), segmentation-based messaging	Facebook, LinkedIn, YouTube longform, retargeting tools, CRM systems	Deeper brand affinity, relevance, and pre conversion readiness
Bottom of the Funnel (BOFU)	Drive conversion and purchase intent	Limited time offers, remarketing, personalized messaging, incentive-based content, seamless CTAs	Website, WhatsApp, email, landing pages, paid remarketing	Direct conversions, bookings, or purchases; reduced friction and increased ROI

Source: Compiled and interpreted by the author.

6.2 Campaign Blueprints

Applying these funnel strategies to the tactical (actionable plans) level required creating specific blueprints based on a brand's goals, audience segments, and available seasonal plays that integrate content strategy, targeting methodology, and KPIs to drive measurable performance at each TOFU, MOFU, and BOFU stage. Promotional content for a high-end seaside destination - marketing campaigns focus on aspirational imagery, immersive experiences, and influencer-led storytelling to appeal to affluent wanderlusts and urge them to book. Honeymoon and pre-wedding campaigns build on romantic, emotionally charged storytelling, personalised offers, itinerary curation, and concierge support to guide high-intent couples from consideration to booking. They have geo-targeted weekend getaway campaigns for hyperlocal travellers featuring geo-fences -proximity-based content offers – dynamic retargeting and last-minute booking gambits- techniques that cater exceptionally well to short passion cycle destinations. Festival and seasonal campaigns drive cultural relevance with thematic visuals, interactive content, influencer partnerships, early bird packages, and urgency-driven CTAs to convert peak season engagement into actionable bookings. Finally, we use influencer-driven and social proof high conversion campaigns where aspirational storytelling + peer validation work together to build brand trust within retargeting, referral incentives, and direct booking links, which efficiently create results that are destined to add value.

Table 11. Campaign Type Mapping Across Funnel Stages and Strategic Focus

Campaign Type	TOFU (Top of Funnel)	MOFU (Middle of Funnel)	BOFU (Bottom of Funnel)	Core Objective / Strategic Focus
Luxury Beach Resort Launch	Cinematic videos, drone footage, lifestyle storytelling, virtual tours	Influencer collaborations, personalized engagement via social & email, retargeting with testimonials	Limited time booking offers, early bird packages, seamless reservation integrations	Establish aspirational positioning; convert highvalue leads via experiential storytelling
Honeymoon & Pre Wedding Travel Campaign	Romantic visuals, curated itineraries, destination aesthetics	Retargeting engaged users, detailed packages, influencer testimonials	Personalized offers, bundled experiences, concierge support	Build emotional resonance and drive high intent couple bookings
Hyperlocal Weekend Getaway	Localized content highlighting proximity and convenience	Dynamic retargeting, interactive maps, local attractions	Instant booking CTAs, promo codes, limited time offers	Capture short decision cycle travelers with frictionless booking
Seasonal & Festival Campaigns	Thematic visuals, celebratory content, interactive polls/ contests	Curated seasonal packages, early bird deals, influencer testimonials	Urgency driven offers, countdown campaigns, integrated booking prompts	Convert seasonal engagement into measurable bookings
Influencer + Social Proof Campaign	Influencer generated posts, live sessions, aspirational UGC	Retarget engaged users, amplify authentic reviews & social proof	Direct booking links, referral incentives, conversion tracking	Strengthen credibility and trust; quantify social proof impact on conversions

Source: Compiled and interpreted by the author.

By aligning TOFU, MOFU, and BOFU tactics along these campaigns, brands can increase engagement and build the necessary trust to drive clear-cut conversions. This hybrid methodology ensures campaigns are not only beautiful and emotional, but they also work when it comes to driving business success and can deliver successful results at scale in competitive digital environments.

7. CONTENT STRATEGY & HIGH ENGAGEMENT FRAMEWORK

A practical framework for high engagement content combines audience behaviour, platform mechanics, and cultural relevance to create actionable streams that solicit attention, encourage community involvement, and drive brand love. Narrative focus is driven by core pillars Experience, Lifestyle, Social Proof, and Local Culture, whereas content formats (Photos, Reels/Shorts, Cinematic Films) are used to maximize reach, retention, and emotional impact. A content calendar with posts planned ahead of time, with a bit of help from engagement-driving tools like AR filters, polls, and trend alignment, is the key to brand follow-through and interactivity. A focus on localization and UGC cocreation optimizes relevance, while authenticity propels the self-sustaining content ecosystem that delivers measurable engagement and conversion results in every platform.

Table 12. Content Pillars, Key Tactics, and Strategic Impact

Pillar / Format	Key Tactics	Engagement Objective	Outcome / Impact
Experience	Immersive storytelling, product-in-use visuals	Show brand utility in real life contexts	Relatability, aspirational appeal, engagement
Lifestyle	Aspirational aesthetics, subculture cues, leisure/fashion/wellness integration	Align brand with desired lifestyles	Audience affinity, brand aspiration
Social Proof	Customer testimonials, influencer endorsements, community interactions	Build credibility and trust	Shares, mentions, trust amplification
Local Culture	Festival campaigns, regional idioms, vernacular content	Enhance cultural relevance	Emotional resonance, inclusivity, engagement spikes
Photo / Short Form Video (Reels)	Quick updates, snackable storytelling, trend aligned content	Capture attention, drive virality	Immediate reach, shareability, discoverability
Cinematic / Long Form Film	Narrative storytelling, flagship campaigns	Deep engagement, brand gravitas	Retention, cross platform visibility, emotional connection
Posting Calendar	30day blueprint, pillar rotation, Mini campaigns	Balance consistency & novelty	Predictable engagement, narrative continuity

continued on following page

Table 12. Continued

Pillar / Format	Key Tactics	Engagement Objective	Outcome / Impact
Engagement Boosters	AR filters, polls, quizzes, trend hijacking	Amplify interactivity	Participation, community building, organic amplification
Localization & UGC	Multilingual content, festival alignment, resharing UGC, cocreation	Increase relevance & authenticity	Organic reach, audience investment, community amplification

Source: Compiled and interpreted by the author.

8. INFLUENCER & UGC DOMINATION STRATEGY

In the luxury and hospitality space, brand loyalty is coming more from social proof, peer validation, and participatory storytelling than traditional advertising. Influencer Ecosystems and User Generated Content (UGC) are network effect engines that can increase engagement, trust, and conversion. A strategic influencer segmentation (luxury, travel vloggers, micro vs macro) and collaboration model (paid, barter, ambassador) that is backed by structured influence-led content pipelines capturing guest-led, authentic experiences. UGC amplification is maximised via contests, branded hashtags, and referral growth loops with contracts, deliverables, and authenticity compliance providing credibility and legality. Finally, AI-powered tools are leveraged for influencer discovery, performance measurement, and may be used to repurpose content across channels by generating flexible, modular media assets that optimize reach, engagement, and concrete business results at scale.

Table 13. Influencer & UGC Strategy Framework

Strategy Element	Tactics / Execution	Objective	Outcome / Impact
Influencer Types	Luxury tastemakers, travel vloggers, micro & macro influencers, niche/cause aligned creators	Optimize reach, trust, and narrative depth	Layered audience engagement, credibility, aspirational positioning
Collaboration Models	Paid campaigns, barter/contra, brand ambassadors, hybrid performance-based structures	Align influencer motivation with measurable outcomes	Authentic content creation, sustained visibility, ROI driven campaigns
Guest Led Content Pipelines	Pre stay guidance, on property experience capture, post stay AI assisted content delivery	Transform every guest into a content contributor	Scalable UGC, referral acceleration, brand amplification

continued on following page

Table 13. Continued

Strategy Element	Tactics / Execution	Objective	Outcome / Impact
UGC Contests & Branded Hashtags	Gamified contests, experience-based rewards, referral loops	Encourage participation and virality	Organic reach, network effects, brand advocacy
Contracts & Authenticity Compliance	Content ownership, repurposing rights, deliverables, milestones, legal safeguards	Protect credibility and brand reputation	Narrative consistency, compliance with advertising standards
AI Tools & Repurposing	Influencer discovery, engagement tracking, multilingual content, auto repurposing	Scale operations, maximize content efficiency	Modular, cross platform assets, measurable performance, omni channel reach

Source: Compiled and interpreted by the author.

9. PAID ADVERTISING & RETARGETING MASTERY

Paid advertising has become an intricate ecosystem of audience targeting, creative optimization, and data-based retargeting for maximum ROI. Successful campaigns have a clear structure that combines Meta Ads architecture (Campaign → Ad Set → Creative → Copy), persuasion copy frameworks (AIDA, PAS, emotion + trust triggers), and step-by-step retargeting logic from website visitor to abandoned checkout to WhatsApp nudge. More advanced tactics are look-alike audiences, geo-fencing for hyper-local targeting, and OTA vs direct ad decision making to trade cost for control and reach. And ROI dashboards aggregate impressions, clicks, CPA, ROAS, and LTV for iterative optimization and multichannel attribution to help marketers measure and scale with accuracy.

Table 14. Paid Media Optimization Framework

Element	Tactics / Execution	Objective	Outcome / Impact
Meta Ads Structure	Campaign → Ad Set → Creative → Copy; audience segmentation, budget allocation, placements	Optimize reach, engagement, and conversion	Isolated performance metrics, iterative optimization, campaign clarity
Copywriting Frameworks	AIDA, PAS, emotion driven + trust triggers, testimonials, guarantees, certifications	Capture attention, build desire, drive action	Higher CTR, increased conversion, emotional resonance
Retargeting Logic	Website visitors → abandoned checkout → WhatsApp/email nudges	Reengage partially engaged audiences	Increased conversion, reduced ad wastage, optimized spend

continued on following page

Table 14. Continued

Element	Tactics / Execution	Objective	Outcome / Impact
Lookalike Audiences & Geo Fencing	Behavioral similarity targeting, geographic perimeter ads	Expand audience efficiently with hyperlocal precision	Higher ROI, reduced wasted impressions, location specific conversions
OTA vs Direct Ads	Marketplace/OTA vs direct to consumer campaigns	Balance cost efficiency vs creative & data control	Revenue retention, first party data, brand ownership
ROI Tracking Dashboard	KPIs: impressions, clicks, CPA, ROAS, LTV; multichannel attribution	Measure, optimize, and scale campaigns	Iterative improvements, holistic performance understanding, campaign scalability

Source: Compiled and interpreted by the author.

10. AI, AUTOMATION & CRM INTEGRATION

The intersection of AI, automation tools, and CRM systems is becoming the next transformative frontier for business operations, especially around customer engagement, retention, and monetization optimization. Using the features made possible by these technologies, businesses will be able to provide hyper-personalised experiences, automate back-office tasks, and generate new ways to generate revenue whilst keeping operations efficient. The subsections that follow discuss significant advancements in AI-based automation of CRM systems.

10.1 WhatsApp Chat Bot With Human Takeover Layer

WhatsApp is quickly becoming the go-to messaging app for people across the globe, and this channel should be leveraged heavily by businesses to communicate with their customers. Using AI-based chatbots on WhatsApp for businesses allows organisations to automatically answer common questions, handle bookings, and automate customer support at scale. One of the key components is a human-in-the-loop layer. This platform causes complex, delicate, or emotionally nuanced conversations from the AI to be escalated seamlessly to human agents, leading to an increase in customer satisfaction and less workload for the support teams. Research suggests that hybrid AI-human systems result in greater engagement and resolution effectiveness compared to fully automatic or manual systems, highlighting the value of intelligent human involvement in automated communication pipelines.

10.2 AI for Content Generation & Personalization

AI-based content generation has changed the way companies communicate with their users. Coupled with sophisticated recommendation algorithms and Natural Language Generation (NLG), this now powers tailored marketing content, customized emails, social media posts, and dynamic website experiences based on individual behaviour and preference. AI-powered personalization boosts relevance and engagement. The system can draw from past interactions, demographic information, and behaviour to construct messaging that feels personalized for each customer. Studies indicate that tailored messaging can help close deals at 20–30%, conveying the real impact on ROI by combining AI in content workflows. Generative AI models can also help in developing multilingual and culturally relevant content, allowing organizations to scale personalization efforts across multiple markets.

10.3 CRM Driven Upsell & Repeat Booking Funnels

AI-based CRM software is becoming more effective in predicting revenues and managing the funnel within organizations. Using historical purchase behaviour, customer lifetime value, and engagement activity, AI can identify the right clusters of customers and target high-precision upsell and repeat booking campaigns. Automated workflows inside CRM systems make it possible to run such campaigns with accuracy while reducing manual work and minimizing errors. In one example, a lodging company can automatically target past guests who have booked premium rooms with personalized promotions for upgraded stays or complimentary services to maximize revenue per customer. These tools also deliver actionable recommendations to adjust sales strategies, with AI-driven predictions that help prioritize high-value leads and maximize funnel efficiency.

10.4 Loyalty & Referral Engine Automations

Customer loyalty and referral programs are essential elements of growth-through-retention strategies. The automation of such programs within CRM systems enables the tracking of customer engagement, rewards behaviours, and triggering of loyalty incentives in real time. Next-generation loyalty engines use AI and predictive models to optimize rewards dynamically, identify churn risks, and drive personalized interventions across user segments. Referral programs can also be automated and optimized using AI to personalize referral messaging and deliver conversion at appropriate moments. AI-based loyalty and referral automation helps retain customers, increase lifetime value, and reduce inefficiencies associated with linear marketing approaches.

10.5 Chat GPT Style AI Concierge Experience

Advancements in conversational AI have paved the way for Chat GPT–led concierge experiences that provide more human-like conversations across data channels. These systems act as always-on assistants capable of understanding context, answering questions, and making proactive recommendations around products or services. Integrated with CRM data, AI concierges deliver hyper-personalized recommendations based on past interactions and preferences. The result is a customer experience that delivers higher satisfaction, engagement, and business returns. Early AI concierge deployments demonstrate reduced response times, improved perception of brand responsiveness, and increased opportunities for contextually relevant add-on sales.

11. REPUTATION & CRISIS MANAGEMENT

Today, in the hospitality and service industry, managing reputation is an essential factor for business survival. The advent of review sites, social media, and instantaneous communication has increased the influence of customer perception, meaning that proactive reputation and crisis management are now critical in preserving brand value and consumer confidence. This chapter focuses on essential elements of reputation management, organized into review tracking, reaction tactics, crisis response, case studies, and automated feedback solutions.

11.1 Review Management

Control of reviews is the foundation of reputation strategy in the digital era. Online Travel Agencies (OTAs) like Booking.com, Expedia, and TripAdvisor, as well as sites such as Google Reviews, are the main channels prospective customers use to judge your quality of service. Studies show that more than 90% of traveller's visit online review sites prior to booking, confirming the relationship between a review-signed sentiment and revenue results. Good reputation management is not only about searching for your company name, monitoring references, and interpreting what people have to say about you. Moreover, the use of data analytics and AI-based solutions that pull together and quantify reviews spanning multiple OTAs helps service providers derive real-time insights and predict the trend in consumer perceptions. Focusing feedback on the operational, service, and experiential metrics enables organizations to prioritize interventions and measure progress against quality improvement initiatives.

11.2 Negative Review Response Playbook

Negative reviews must be dealt with in a measured and psychologically conceived way. A Negative Review Response Playbook offers a consistent way to respond to criticism while still being constructive, that maintains brand integrity and customer confidence. Among the most essential elements of the playbook are acceptance of customer service, clear explanation of how to fix things, and thanking the customers for their feedback. Studies in consumer behaviour suggest that empathetic and responsible responses can turn a disgruntled customer into a loyal advocate. Time is of the essence as well, with research suggesting that a reply within 24–48 hours can significantly reduce the level of reputational harm if it is from a bad review. Also to be included in the playbook: escalation plans for repeat or high-impact complaints, ensuring that when a manager needs to get involved, they're following organization standards and are conscious of public perception.

11.3 Live Crisis Handling

Real-time crisis management is about reacting to immediate threats, such as social media firestorms, operational accidents, or the spread of false information. Crisis communication theories stress the role of information speed, transparency, and consistency in shaping public narratives at a time of high stakes. An organization, along with the Critical Response Team (CRT) as its authorized point, has to weigh incidents, control internal communication, and launch external messages through social media, press releases, and OTA channels. Case studies from the real world seem to justify that prompt recognition and assistance, together with acting proactively on their mistakes, decreases reputation damage. Also most useful are listening tools that monitor references, hashtags, and platform-specific engagement statistics, which can help identify crises before they become acute and allow time for interventionary action.

11.4 Automated Review Request & Gratitude Sequence

Automation of customer review requests and thank-you messages has brought optimization in asking for feedback from customers and expressing gratitude. Guests are prompted to share their experience shortly after service, followed by automated appreciation, which reinforces positive sentiment. Academic studies on marketing automation show that these sequences lead not only to higher review volumes, but also improved review quality by encouraging timely and personalized feedback. These systems, when combined with Customer Relationship Management (CRM) systems, are also capable of facilitating dynamic personalization, adaptive timing, and effectiveness tracking of follow-ups, leading to a complete reputation management ecosystem.

12. CHALLENGES, ETHICS & GOVERNANCE

The tourism and hospitality industry has rapidly adopted digital technologies, social media, and artificial intelligence, which have transformed content creation, guest engagement, and brand communication. Yet, this evolution comes with huge issues related to ethical governance and operational integrity. Manoeuvring these challenges effectively is pertinent to maintaining the credibility, compliance, and social responsibility of digital strategies. This section explores seven interrelated aspects of these challenges, from dilemmas about authenticity to crisis frameworks.

12.1 Over Commercialization vs Authenticity Dilemma

The ethical tension between commodification and authenticity is one of the most salient issues facing digital tourism marketing. We have brands on one side who want to make use of influencer collaborations, campaigns through targeting, and sponsored content for the purposes of booking and sales. On the flip side, it can also threaten to undermine the authenticity that travelers increasingly demand by saturating them with commercial messages. Tourism service providers, therefore, need to reconcile the commercial with authentic, experience-based narratives. Transparent sponsor advice, participation curation, and cultural heritage-based storytelling are the means for tackling authenticity commercialisation trade-offs.

12.2 Influencer Fraud & Fake Review Risks

As influencer marketing and online reviews have grown, new opportunities for fraud activity have also arisen. Artificial followership, inauthentic engagement metrics, and incentivized reviews can deceive users and trust in hospitality brands. According to research, up to 15–20% of engagements between social media influencers might be artificially manipulated (Lou & Yuan, 2019). From a moral perspective, advertising or unwittingly disseminating fake content leaves companies open to both reputational and legal damage. To tackle this, tour operators have increasingly been implementing influencer vetting models, AI-based fraud detection, and cross authentication mechanisms for user-contributed reviews.

12.3 Data Privacy & Guest Trust Concerns

Managing such a large amount of guest data ensures that it's common for hotels to shape digital content strategies around an abundance of data on guests, from behaviours to preferences. Although such information allows personalized marketing and the optimization of experience, it also causes privacy-related issues. Governance, of course, includes ethical and legal adherence to laws such as the GDPR and India's Personal Data Protection Bill and industry norms for data security. Transparency in data management, explicit consent structures, and secure storage strategies form some of the minimal requirements to maintain a balancing act between operational efficiency and ethical accountability.

12.4 Responsible & Sustainable Tourism Messaging

Alongside commercialisation and privacy challenges, brands are also feeling the heat to promote responsible tourism and sustainability. Ethical content governance raises more than just compliance issues, such as how to tell the world things about what we do that involve environmental stewardship and community well-being or protect local cultures. If not correctly positioned, efforts around sustainability can amount to greenwashing that will be met with fierce public resistance and regulatory attention if it is determined to be misleading. Strong governance around sustainability verifies the validity of claims, ensures messages are consistent across channels, and that content supports larger corporate social responsibility (CSR) goals.

12.5 Content Approval Hierarchy

Contemporary tourism marketing is characterised by a complicated and multilayered world of content approval. Brand teams care about creativity and engagement, legal folks protect from compliance risk, and AI moderation tools enable efficiency and consistency in enforcing content standards. Frictions can emerge when those priorities clash, such as when a brand's narrative style conflicts with legal guidelines or AI pre-moderation identifies culturally specific dialogue as inappropriate. Taking these perspectives into account, it is crucial to have a transparent and clear hierarchy of support. Policies need to establish the power and jurisdiction of each stakeholder, include provisions for escalating issues at higher levels in an organisation, and establish an audit trail to ensure accountability.

12.6 AI and Human Hybrid Workflow Safeguards

The integration of AI in content creation, curation, and moderation opportunities is presented, and risks are imposed. A hybrid process including AI and human oversight negates these threats. Humans give contextual interpretation, moral assessment, and the final tick of approval, while AI performs mundane, high-volume jobs like image tagging, plagiarism identification, and starting moderation. Clear roles, feedback loops, and training protocols for AI systems are essential to ensuring hybrid workflows are both practical and ethical.

12.7 Crisis Escalation & Publishing Governance Policy

In a world where content can spread like wildfire, errors can spiral out of control and evolve into full-blown PR disasters. Good governance demands well-defined crisis escalation procedures such as specific risk triggers, layered authorization permissive limits, and modes of real-time checks. Publishing contracts should define who has accountability for creating, reviewing, and approving content, as well as contingency plans for emergency communications. Transparency, consistency, and responsiveness are essential principles to bolster the resilience of the organization during a crisis and not lose credibility among guests.

13. FUTURE TRENDS & STRATEGIC INNOVATION OUTLOOK

Hospitality is at a significant intersection of technology and customer expectation evolution. New developments are transforming the way hotels interact with guests, streamline their operations, and distinguish themselves in a saturated market. The following provocative examination uncovers several of the leading trends and strategic disruptors that have the potential to transform guest experience and brand value in the coming decade.

13.1 AI-Led Personalization Before Check-In

The utilization of artificial intelligence (AI) is shifting in that it's no longer advised as an operational technology but rather treated now as the primary enabler of hyper-personalized guest experiences. Pre-arrival personalization is the use of predictive analytics, machine learning, and behavioural data to anticipate what guests want and tailor it to them before they even walk through the door. For example, AI solutions could interpret historical booking patterns along with interaction with loyalty programs and social media to suggest personalized room set-ups, amenity selections, and dining options by user profile. This type of proactive personalization not only improves guest satisfaction but can also lead to increased incremental earnings when upselling services and experiences. In addition, AI-powered pre-check-in personalization also allows hotels to gain deep insight into inventory handling and operational planning by enabling dynamic resource allocations based on forecasting demand behaviours. This early interaction creates a sense of anticipation and exclusivity that will lay the foundation for an emotionally impactful guest journey.

13.2 Metaverse Virtual Hotel Tours

The Metaverse infiltration of immersive digital environments is becoming a disruptive trend in pre-visit engagement. Prospective guests can explore ultra-realistic 3D hotel models, moving through room configurations, event rooms, and facilities in advance using virtual reality hotel tours. More than passive viewing, virtual spaces like these can contain interactive features like being able to reconfigure room décor on the fly or chat with concierge avatars in real-time. For hotel brands, metaverse tours are both a marketing channel and a strategic conversion tool that can make the leap from imagination to reality more seamless. In addition to that, the gamification and social interaction in these digital interfaces can bring community-driven engagement for brand perception and loyalty of the digitally native demographic. By offering metaverse experiences, the point of view changes from static marketing to experiential storytelling, and it is an opportunity for hotels to stand out in a crowded place.

13.3 Digital ID & Block chain Loyalty Systems

The emergence of secure digital identity infrastructures and blockchain technology will change the rules of loyalty ecosystems in hospitality. An open ledger system and a permanent record of guest transactions translate into platforms that will be universally shared and more easily integrated across hotel chains, airline partnerships, and ancillary services. Digital IDs can help check-in run more efficiently, verify identity, and allow for safe contactless transactions. Strategically, these advancements restore guest confidence, minimize fraudulent risk, and unlock insights into consumer behavior based upon data, which are all critical pieces of the long-term loyalty perspective. Moreover, tokenizing rewards enables new means of monetization whether it's the ability to trade points, gift them, or redeem them in real time adding to the attractiveness of loyalty programs amidst intensifying competition.

13.4 Zero Touch Contactless Concierge Experiences

The new reality in consumer expectations and life post-pandemic is driving the push for zero-touch, contactless hotel experiences at speed. AI (Artificial Intelligence) powered chatbots, voice-activated interfaces, and advanced IoT (Internet of Things) solutions are enabling guests to access information on a remote request, requesting services and creating personalized itineraries without ever stepping into a physical concierge. These kinds of technologies not only solve safety and hygienic concerns but also enhance operational productivity as they minimize reliance on front desk workers for simple tasks. More importantly, zero-touch encounters can be designed to retain humanlike empathy and responsiveness such that the potentials of automation and personalized care are balanced. By strategically deploying contactless services, hotels have the opportunity to provide effortless, low-friction experiences and re-employ staff into higher-value roles focused on delivering memorable, high-touch moments where it really matters.

13.5 Strategic Full Funnel Social Media Architecture

Social is an essential vehicle for brand exposure, engagement, and conversion, but that's changing with social becoming more of a complete funnel strategy vs. just another channel to leverage. Hotels are starting to adopt integrated strategies that link content, campaigns, and influencer relationships across the guest journey from awareness and consideration through booking and post-stay advocacy. Such visual frameworks, which can include modular content libraries, data-driven creative strategies, and interactive media formats, allow a focus on targeting but with brand consistency. Hotels can use AI-driven analytics to fine-tune their content distribution, measure engagement as it occurs, and adjust strategies using intelligent modeling of guest behavior. This 'full funnel' structure recognises that social media is more than just a marketing channel – it's an ecosystem which can contribute to relationship building, new bookings (direct or otherwise), and lifetime guest value.

14. CONCLUSION

14.1 Strategic Summary

The success of a travel or hospitality brand rests on understanding audience psychology with strategy at the core. Passion points are enabled not just by location or aesthetic, but through a designed mental and emotional space in the consciousness of the traveller – merging core and companion values that one lives with (functional-emotional) as social or cultural (pre-positioned) benefits. Articulating USP luxury, boutique, family, wellness, or business informs messaging, pricing, and experience cues – less confusion and more conversion confidence. The new travel funnel is focused on nonlinear, psychology-driven engagement, leaving it to marketers to develop persona-driven strategies common to markets of honeymooners, digital nomads, corporate planners, and wellness travellers. Cultural appropriateness and geographic localization provide global validity without local compromise. Through brand stories, social proof, and interactive content, emotional intent is translated into booking action, and deeper loyalty is established as guest experiences become an expression of a brand's story.

14.2 Actionable Roadmap for Hotels & Resorts

An integrated, high-performance social, digital, and AI channel-based platform-wise strategic roadmap is in operational deployment. Audit frameworks expose the gaps in brand story, connectivity to ecosystem, delivering trust signals, and reducing booking friction, enabling revenue optimization. Structured content strategies centered on experience, lifestyle, local culture, and social proof are applied across formats (Reels, short form videos, cinematic storytelling) with a designed calendar and fun tools for co-creation and localization. Influencer segmentation, guest-led content pipelines, UGC contesting, branded hashtags, and referral loops keep the authenticity and amplification coming. Paid media takes on a three-dimensional aspect, combining hierarchical campaigns and behavioural insights with retargeting, hyperlocal targeting, and constant ROI measurement. AI and automation supplement CRM and communication workflows to provide hyper-personalized, scalable engagements while preserving human empathy and contextual intelligence.

14.3 Academic and Industry Outcomes

Academically, this model adds clarity to how psychological motivation interacts with digital ecosystem content and behavioral economics in hospitality. Industry results include quantifiable lifts in engagement, bookings, retention, and advocacy, as well as key operational savings related to content production, review, and personalization. And the well-crafted influencer and UGC strategies can also improve brand credibility and network effects, indicating that it is strategically vital to combine audience psychology with multichannel execution.

14.4 Limitations of Existing Research

Whilst there is technology that can reconstruct and give a more accurate view of journey metrics, most research today does not capture the full scale of nonlinear traveller behaviour and across-platform attribution or long-term efficacy of AI-driven engagement. Several works concentrate on impressions or engagement measures void of any connections to concrete business results, and considerations such as ethics or governance, for instance, data privacy, sustainability claims, or influencer authenticity are barely covered. In addition, social platforms and the algorithms that serve them evolve at such a rapid pace, thereby making longitudinal comparative analysis challenging.

14.5 Future Research Directions

Future work would need to look at the long-term impact of persona-based campaigns, the effectiveness of using AI-enhanced CRM and influencer workflows, and scale issues when it comes to guest-driven UGC for continuing conversion. Exploration of ethical frameworks for data or content governance and influencer management, as well as the measurable values from participatory and immersive content engagement, is essential to uncovering actionable findings for both academic researchers and industry practitioners. Cross-cultural and multiregional analyses will further help to refine personalization strategies without sacrificing brand integrity; combining behavioural science, digital marketing, and operational research has the potential to advance both theoretical and practical aspects of hospitality marketing in a digital age.

REFERENCES

Adeyinka-Ojo, S., Lee, S., Abdullah, S. K., & Teo, J. (2020). Hospitality and tourism education in an emerging digital economy. *Worldwide Hospitality and Tourism Themes*, *12*(2), 113–125.

Ahmed, F., Kabir, M. A., & Ahmed, M. D. (2025). The Impact of Short Video Content and Social Media Influencers on Digital Marketing Success: A Systematic Literature Review of Smartphone Usage. *Innovatech Engineering Journal*, *1*(02), 1070937.

Amitay, E., Carmel, D., Har'El, N., Ofek-Koifman, S., Soffer, A., Yogev, S., & Golbandi, N. (2009, June). Social search and discovery using a unified approach. In *Proceedings of the 20th ACM Conference on Hypertext and Hypermedia* (pp. 199-208).

Bardukova, L. (2023). Navigating the hospitality horizon: Current trends and strategies for customer attraction and retention in the hotel industry. *Economics and computer science, 2*, 88-103.

Buhalis, D., O'Connor, P., & Leung, R. (2023). Smart hospitality: From smart cities and smart tourism towards agile business ecosystems in networked destinations. *International Journal of Contemporary Hospitality Management*, *35*(1), 369393.

Buhalis, D., & Park, S. (2021). Brand management and cocreation lessons from tourism and hospitality: Introduction to the special issue. *Journal of Product and Brand Management*, *30*(1), 1–11.

Cheah, I., & Phua, P. (2025). Generational advertising: Literature review and practitioner insights on key pitfalls and implications. *International Journal of Advertising*, *44*(2), 286–312.

Datiko, D. B. (2024). The customer-centric-marketing (CCM) perspectives in the tourism and hospitality sector: Insight from a developing country. *International Journal of Tourism Policy*, *14*(1), 37–53.

Dev, C. S., Buschman, J. D., & Bowen, J. T. (2010). Hospitality marketing: A retrospective analysis (19602010) and predictions (20102020). *Cornell Hospitality Quarterly*, *51*(4), 459469.

Dilek, S. E., & Harman, S. (2017). Hospitality marketing: A historical perspective. In *Routledge Handbook of Hospitality Marketing* (p. 920). Routledge.

Dou, W., Lim, K. H., Su, C., Zhou, N., & Cui, N. (2010). Brand positioning strategy using search engine marketing. *Management Information Systems Quarterly*, ●●●, 261–279.

Ertaş, Ç., & Karakan, H. I. (2024). The future of events in the tourism industry: The case of the "Best of the Best Things to Do 2023" on TripAdvisor. *Worldwide Hospitality and Tourism Themes*, *16*(4), 474–484.

Fennell, D. A. (2009). The nature of pleasure in pleasure travel. *Tourism Recreation Research*, *34*(2), 123134.

Gardiner, S., King, C., & Grace, D. (2013). Travel decision making: An empirical examination of generational values, attitudes, and intentions. *Journal of Travel Research*, *52*(3), 310324.

Giannoukou, I. (2024). Revolutionizing hospitality: Strategic integration of innovation management embracing technological innovation for enhanced customer experiences. *Technium Business and Management*, *7*, 24–39.

Guijarroa, A. J. M. (2013). Textual and compositional choices in hotel brochures. *Choice in Language*, 301.

Haenlein, M., Anadol, E., Farnsworth, T., Hugo, H., Hunichen, J., & Welte, D. (2020). Navigating the new era of influencer marketing: How to be successful on Instagram, TikTok, & Co. *California Management Review*, *63*(1), 5–25.

Ho, V. (2020). Do hotels enhance and challenge rapport with customers with the same degree of commitment? *Journal of Pragmatics*, *166*, 70–83.

Inversini, A., De Carlo, M., & Masiero, L. (2020). The effects of customer-centricity in hospitality. *International Journal of Hospitality Management*, *86*, 102436.

Lacoste, S. M., & Dekker, J. (2016). Driving change: The role of "emotional connectedness"–A case study. *The Learning Organization*, *23*(5), 357369.

Martin-Fuentes, E., & Mellinas, J. P. (2018). Hotels that most rely on Booking.com–online travel agencies (OTAs) and hotel distribution channels. *Tourism Review*, *73*(4), 465–479.

Mavitha, K., & Kushe Shekhar, S. (2025). *Mapping the landscape of digital transformation and digital technologies in the hotel industry: a comprehensive bibliometric analysis*. Digital Transformation and Society.

McKelvey, F., & Hunt, R. (2019). Discoverability: Toward a definition of content discovery through platforms. *Social Media + Society*, *5*(1), 2056305118819188.

Minazzi, R., & Panno, A. (2019, July). Social media marketing in the hospitality industry: the evolution of European hotels' approaches from 2012 to 2018. In *9th Advances in Hopitality and Tourism Marketing and Management Conference* (p. 345).

Morgan, N., & Pritchard, A. (2012). *Advertising in tourism and leisure*. Routledge.

Morosan, C. T., Bowen, J., & Atwood, M. (2014). The evolution of marketing research. *International Journal of Contemporary Hospitality Management, 26*(5), 706726.

Naab, T. K., & Sehl, A. (2017). Studies of user-generated content: A systematic review. *Journalism, 18*(10), 1256–1273.

Pine, B. J., & Gilmore, J. H. (2011). *The experience economy*. Harvard Business Press.

Rathore, A. K., Ilavarasan, P. V., & Dwivedi, Y. K. (2016). Social media content and product cocreation: An emerging paradigm. *Journal of Enterprise Information Management, 29*(1), 718.

Saini, H., Kumar, P., & Verma, R. (2025). Social media and its influence on travel decision making. In *Decoding tourist behavior in the digital era: Insights for effective marketing* (pp. 261–282). IGI Global.

Sârbu, R., Alecu, F., & Dina, R. (2018). Social media advertising trends in tourism. *Amfiteatru Economic, 20*(12), 1016–1028.

Sharma, A. B. (2024). Content Creation in Transition: Analyzing YouTube, YouTube Shorts, and Facebook's Influence on Content Creators Amidst and Beyond COVID19.

Wang, T. Y., & Park, J. (2023). Destination information search in social media and travel intention of generation Z university students. *Journal of China Tourism Research, 19*(3), 570–588.

Zeqiri, A. (2024). From Traditional to Digital: The Evolution of Business Models in Hospitality Through Platforms. *Platforms, 2*(4), 221233.

Zobnina, M., & Rozhkov, A. (2018). Listening to the voice of the customer in the hospitality industry: Kano model application. *Worldwide Hospitality and Tourism Themes, 10*(4), 436448.

Chapter 9
Strategic Use of Social Media Platforms in Hotel Marketing

Ashish Raina
http://orcid.org/0000-0001-5812-5920
School of Hotel Management, Airlines, and Tourism, CT University, Ludhiana, India

Dharna Shukla
http://orcid.org/0000-0001-5857-2130
Amity School of Hospitality, Amity University, Lucknow, India

Gaurav Bathla
http://orcid.org/0000-0002-6992-811X
School of Hotel Management, Airlines, and Tourism, CT University, Ludhiana, India

Bharat Bhushan
The ICFAI University, India

Richa Verma
http://orcid.org/0009-0002-6639-8130
Department of Hotel Management, Swami Vivekanand Faculty of Technology and Management, Banur, India

Varinder Singh Rana
City University, Ajman, UAE

ABSTRACT

Social media has become a vital marketing tool in the hotel industry, transforming how hotels connect with guests. This study explores the strategic use of major platforms Facebook, Instagram, YouTube, LinkedIn and Twitter to enhance brand visibility, engage audiences, and increase direct bookings. Based on literature review and industry insights it focuses on key factors such as user-generated content, influencer marketing, visual storytelling and real-time interaction. Findings show that authentic guest reviews and visual content strongly influence booking decisions often more than traditional advertising. Professional photos, short videos and col-

DOI: 10.4018/979-8-3373-6741-5.ch009

laborations with travel influencers help hotels showcase unique features and build credibility among diverse audiences. However, challenges like data privacy, security and managing negative reviews demand effective risk and crisis management.

1. INTRODUCTION

A key component of the hospitality sector has traditionally been the ability to build strong connections with consumers and provide them experiences they will never forget (Gitau, 2020). The past few years have seen the emergence of widely used social media platforms, which has fundamentally changed how hotels market their services, talk to customers, and keep them coming back. Hotels can now connect with clients in a more personal and instantaneous manner than ever before, thanks to interactive platforms that go beyond conventional means like brochures, travel agents, and static websites.

Facebook, Instagram and Twitter are some of the most powerful social media platforms when it comes to changing people's minds. In these places, hotels may talk to visitors, show off their unique goods, and tell stories via pictures every day (Al-Maslam et al., 2016). On the other hand, visitors may affect the decisions of future tourists by writing reviews, uploading pictures, and utilising the same channels. Because of this two-way contact, the border between marketing and customer experience has grown less clear. This makes social media an important part of hotel operations (Arora & Arora, 2019).

But there are problems that make it hard to utilise these sites strategically. When managers try to be visible and consistent, they often run into challenges since there is so much information, algorithms are always changing, and people want more customised communication. But there are also a lot of chances: well-planned marketing, data-driven insights, and content made by users may all help the brand's reputation and get more bookings.

1.1. Social Media and the Modern Hospitality Landscape

By transforming static marketing into an engaging, shared experience, social media has revolutionised the hospitality business. Creating stories that both visitors and staff want to be a part of is much more important than just displaying expensive hotel features or lovely holiday images. With the rise of social media, firms in the hospitality sector can now reach more customers and provide more value to them than ever before (Tarvainen, 2023). Platforms are crucial in driving company development and altering the guest experience in a variety of ways, including influencing travel choices and improving customer engagement.

Travellers of today depend significantly on social media for ideas and suggestions for their trips. Inspiring reservations and visits is as easy as posting a picture-perfect photo of a five-star hotel room or a mouthwatering regional meal. In addition to advertising, companies may build trust with their audience via customised interactions, real-time response to questions, and direct connection through social media.

There is a plethora of data available to organisations via platforms, which allows them to study customer behaviour, monitor trends, and refine marketing tactics. The reach and trustworthiness of the brand are further enhanced by user-generated content, which consists of images, reviews, and testimonials contributed by visitors.

Being visible isn't enough when it comes to social media marketing for the hospitality industry; what really matters is crafting a genuine story that connects with your target demographic (Lim, 2010). Businesses in the hospitality industry may differentiate themselves in a crowded marketplace by making smart use of these platforms to promote their wares and build connections with consumers.

Table 1. Evolution, Trends and Competitive Landscape of Social Media Marketing in the Hotel Industry

Aspects	Highlights	Strategic Implications for Hotels
Evolution of Digital Marketing in Hospitality	i. Shift from print and travel agents to websites and online booking engines ii. Rise of social platforms (Facebook, Instagram, Twitter) for brand storytelling iii. Increased reliance on analytics and targeted advertising	i. Continuous need to update digital skills and marketing technology ii. Integration of social and booking platforms for seamless guest experience
Current Trends in Guest Engagement	i. Real-time interaction through comments, messaging, and live content ii. User-generated content (reviews, photos, videos) shaping brand image iii. Personalized promotions using data-driven insights	i. Encourage guests to create and share content ii. Implement social listening tools to respond quickly and build trust
Competitive Pressures and Opportunities	i. Growing number of hotels adopting sophisticated digital campaigns ii. Price transparency and instant comparisons via online channels iii. Opportunities to differentiate through unique brand voice and niche targeting	i. Need for consistent, creative content to stand out ii. Invest in analytics to identify market gaps and monitor competitors

1.2. Social Media Marketing Influence Consumer Decisions In Hotel Selection

Particularly in this age of millennial and Gen Z travellers, social media platforms are crucial in influencing customer opinions and choices about hotels. Given that 55% of customers like a hotel brand's Facebook page in order to learn more about the establishment, social media is crucial for increasing exposure and brand discovery.

Given that 76% of individuals share their holiday images on social media, user-generated material has a big influence on prospective visitors. This trend emphasises how crucial it is to be "Instagram-worthy" and use trending hashtags and location tags in order to raise a hotel's profile. Positive evaluations and compelling content on platforms such as Google reviews and TripAdvisor establish credibility and trust, which are essential factors for travellers. Furthermore, word-of-mouth may be further amplified via the efficient use of Facebook advertisements and marketing platforms, increasing social media visibility and generating reservations.

1.3. Importance of Social Media for the Hospitality Industry

i. *Enhanced Visibility*: With billions of active users on platforms like Facebook and Instagram, hotels can reach a wider audience, attracting potential guests from around the globe (Leung, Bai, et al., 2015).

ii. *Guest Engagement*: Social media provides a unique avenue to interact with guests in real time, allowing hotels to address queries, gather feedback, and create meaningful relationships.

iii. *Brand Building*: Through consistent and engaging content, hotels can showcase their unique offerings, values, and personality, helping to establish a distinct brand identity.

iv. *Increased Bookings*: Well-crafted social media campaigns can drive traffic to your website and ultimately increase direct bookings, reducing reliance on third-party platforms.

1.4. Social Media Marketing Goals

A successful social media marketing plan should be multifaceted and intended to achieve several objectives at once. Consistent blogging over time might help create a significant influence, even if results might not be seen right away. To be certain that your efforts are having a beneficial impact on your hotel company, make sure you're routinely monitoring data. The following are some possible objectives for your hotel's social media marketing strategy:

Figure 1. Goals of Social Media Marketing

Source: - https://fastercapital.com/

i. Engagement: Customers, both existing and potential, should be engaged and collaborated with.
ii. Brand awareness: Develop a distinctive brand voice that appeals to the kind of people that stay at your hotel.
iii. Analytics: Get up-to-date market data and learn more about your target market and performance.
iv. Acquisition: Maximise advertising campaigns and advertise goods, services, promotions, and competitions to increase direct reservations.
v. Content marketing: Using search engine optimisation (SEO), publish interesting content to increase website traffic for your hotel.
vi. Customer service: Answer enquiries and expedite correspondence via Messenger and comments.

1.5. The Four Ps of Marketing: Product, Price, Place, Promotion

Marketers will constantly discuss "the four Ps of marketing", which may be summed up as follows, regardless of your industry:

i. **Product:** You are promoting the product (or service). It refers to hotel rooms and other facilities, such as hotel items like restaurant meals and valet parking service. Your marketing initiatives can significantly impact the thought process of potential guests, who will determine whether or not to book with you based on their comprehension of your product and their conviction that it will deliver the optimal guest experience.
ii. **Price:** As a hotel revenue manager, you will be aware that the cost is what customers spend on your service or product, and in our industry, this fluctuates greatly depending on the kind of room, demand, length of stay, and a host of other variables. Together, revenue managers and marketers have the responsibility of presenting the pricing in the best possible light so that prospective customers will comprehend it and think it is reasonable.
iii. **Place:** It's not the location of your hotel (though this is definitely important for prospective customers to know!) but rather the platforms and media used to advertise your hotel service. There are many more opportunities than there were a generation ago, with a variety of off- and online possibilities, some of which are under your direct control and others that are controlled by third parties. It is crucial to remain informed about your options.
iv. **Promotion:** What ties everything together is the promotion, or series of promotions. It's what the general public sees and is exposed to. You must use any or all of the components we provide in the next section to attract attention and advance prospects to the next phase of the marketing funnel.

The inclusion of "people, packing or physical evidence, and process" raises this list to seven in some marketing circles. These are worth mentioning briefly:

i. **People:** Your employees and anyone else who interacts with your visitors on a professional basis are, in essence, humans. In addition to setting the tone and carrying out the task, marketers should create the culture that all others adhere to, one that will increase sales and enhance the visitor experience from check-in to check-out and in communications on both sides.
ii. **Physical evidence:** Although hotels aren't packaged, you do need to keep up a visual brand that shows up in your material and on your properties. Your hotel brand should be reflected in and embodied by your efforts, and vice versa.

iii. **Process:** Make every effort to ensure that your marketing and operational processes reflect the experience that guests have before to, during, and after their visit.

1.6. Types of Social Media Platforms

By functionality, social media platforms may be divided:

Figure 2. Types of Social Media Platforms

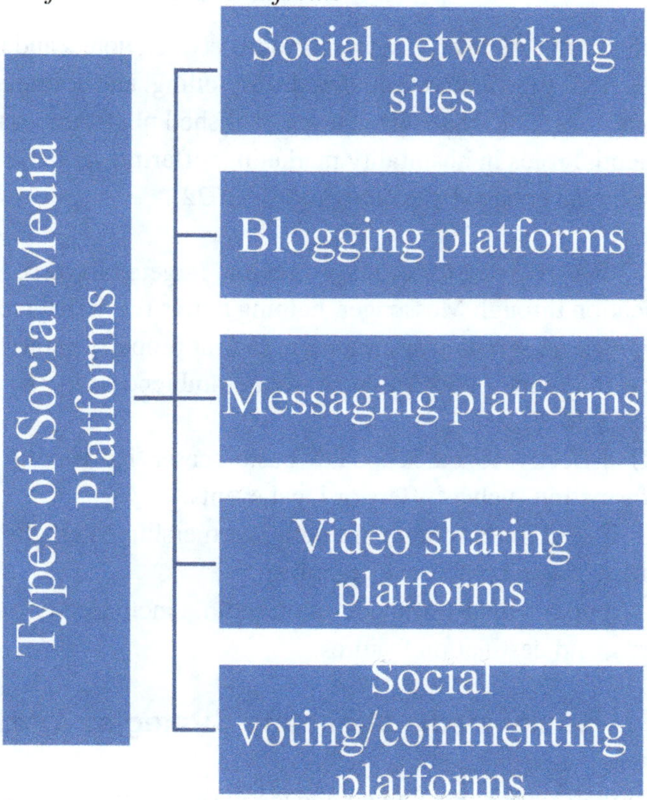

Source: https://www.wordstream.com/social-media-marketing

i. Social networking sites: Social networking sites include "Facebook, LinkedIn, Google+, and Twitter". To exchange knowledge, concepts, and experiences, users create profiles and interact with friends and other people.
ii. Blogging platforms: Blogs are social media sites built for producing and sharing information. The whole blogging community or specific followers may see the articles and comments that users publish.

iii. Messaging platforms: Users may send and receive messages with friends and family using WhatsApp, Facebook Messenger, and Instagram, among other messaging platforms.
iv. Video sharing platforms: Users are able to publish, share, and watch videos on websites like Twitch, Vimeo, and YouTube.
v. Social voting/commenting platforms: Users may vote on and comment on material on social voting and commenting websites like Reddit and Disqus.

1.7. Major Social Media Platforms in Hotel Marketing

Social media has become an essential bridge between hotels and their potential guests, enabling real-time interaction, brand storytelling, and community building. Among the many available channels, a few established platforms consistently play the most influential roles in hospitality marketing, offering versatile tools for both engagement and conversion (Palenčarová et al., 2022).

i. *Facebook* – Widely used for event promotion, targeted advertising, and direct communication through Messenger, helping hotels reach diverse age groups.
ii. *Instagram* – Ideal for visually rich content such as property photos, short videos, and behind-the-scenes stories that showcase ambience and guest experiences (Leung et al., 2017).
iii. *Twitter (X)* – Effective for quick updates, customer service responses, and sharing timely information such as offers or local events.
iv. *LinkedIn* – Useful for corporate branding, partnership outreach, and attracting business travelers or conference organizers.
v. *YouTube* – Supports long-form video storytelling, including virtual tours, guest testimonials, and destination features.

1.8. Effective Social Media Marketing Strategies for Hotels

To improve their online profile and engage with prospective customers, hotels must use social media marketing methods that work. The following some tactics are important for hotels to think about:

1.8.1. Optimize Social Media Profiles and Content for Search

In comparison to properties that are less active on social media, properties with well-maintained picture galleries have a 225% higher chance of securing reservations and around 138% higher user interaction. Hotels should use pertinent keywords, high-quality imagery, and consistent brand messaging on social media sites as part of SEO. Discoverability may be greatly increased by creating compelling descriptions and strategically using hashtags. Travellers looking for lodging in that area, for example, may be drawn in by using geographical tags and hashtags relevant to that area.

1.8.2. Leverage User-Generated Content and Online Reviews

According to an Expedia poll, 30% of Americans say social media influences their travel decisions. A hotel brand's reputation may be increased by sharing "user-generated content (UGC)" and positive internet reviews. Building a trustworthy image may be achieved by encouraging visitors to share their experiences and using this material for marketing activities. Additionally, hotels may offer promotions that encourage visitors to upload images or write reviews, which can then be shown on the hotel's Instagram, Facebook page, and other social media accounts.

1.8.3. Utilize Paid Social Media Advertising for Targeted Campaigns

Hotel brands may target certain demographics, interests, and behaviours with paid social media advertising on sites like Facebook and Instagram. With an average Facebook ad conversion rate of around 9% and a cost per click (CPC) of between $0.26 and $0.97, hotels may design advertisements that showcase exclusive deals, seasonal promotions, or distinctive features. To maximise return on investment, tracking ad effectiveness and modifying targeting and content are essential. "Successful advertising campaigns" that increase bookings depend on careful budgeting and a thorough comprehension of ad data.

1.8.4. Engage With Influencers and Brand Ambassadors

A hotel's reach and credibility may be increased via influencer marketing, which has 1% to 5% conversion rates. It may be quite successful to collaborate with brand ambassadors and travel influencers who share the hotel's target demographic. Important procedures include negotiating conditions, establishing precise advertising goals, and assessing effect. One way to create genuine video content and boost exposure among followers is to invite an influencer to stay at the hotel and share their experience.

1.8.5. Implement Seasonal and Event-Based Marketing Campaigns

Social media engagement and bookings may increase by up to 84% when content is matched with local events and seasonal patterns. Hotels may publish on social media about local events, festivals, or vacations. For example, advertising a winter vacation package over the holidays or emphasising noteworthy occasions, such as a regional culinary festival, might draw in prospective visitors and boost reservations. To increase reach, these marketing initiatives make use of geographical tags and trending hashtags.

1.8.6. Create Interactive and Engaging Content

"Polls, quizzes, and live video sessions" are examples of interactive content that may dramatically increase user engagement by up to 70%. These technologies may be used by hotels to educate, amuse, and get feedback from its guests. Virtual property tours, staff Q&A sessions, and interactive surveys about visitor preferences are a few examples. This strategy develops a vibrant social media presence that appeals to prospective visitors and promotes interaction.

1.8.7. Monitor and Analyze Social Media Performance

Monitoring social media performance using analytics tools is crucial for ongoing development. Metrics that reveal what works and what doesn't include conversion rates, reach, and engagement rates. Campaign effectiveness may be increased by routinely evaluating these indicators and modifying plans in light of performance information. Tools like as Instagram Analytics, Facebook Insights, and third-party systems like Hootsuite provide useful information for improving social media tactics and attaining better outcomes.

1.8.8. Market Research and Audience Insights

For any social media marketing strategy to be successful, choosing the appropriate audience is essential. In order to cater their content to the preferences and requirements of their prospective customers, hotels need to know who they are. The first stage is to analyse current visitors. By looking at their locations, interests, age groups, and genders, hotels may learn a lot about their target market. Furthermore, a thorough grasp of the characteristics and actions of present followers may be obtained by using analytics tools like Google Analytics and social media insights. Surveys also make it easier to get direct input from guests on their tastes and travel patterns, which is crucial for improving social media tactics. Additionally, researching the social media followers of your rivals might help you find new customers who could be interested in your hotel as well. Developing content that appeals to your audience requires an understanding of visitor preferences and behaviours.

Key Areas to Focus On

Content Preferences: Find out what kinds of material your audience is most interested in. These might be images, videos, articles, or interactive content like surveys and tests.

Engagement Patterns: Determine the peak times for your audience's social media activity. Post timing for optimal engagement may benefit from this.

Feedback and Reviews: Keep an eye on visitor comments and reviews on review websites and social media. This might provide information about what visitors value and what needs work.

Travel Trends: Keep updated on current travel trends and preferences. This may assist in producing timely and relevant content that attracts prospective visitors.

1.9. Impacts of Social Media in Hospitality Industry

Social media has transformed consumer interaction, brand expansion, and overall success, making it a vital tool for the hotel industry. The following six significant effects show how social media is changing the hotel industry:

1.9.1. Increased brand Awareness

A unique opportunity to increase brand exposure is provided by social media platforms for hotels and other hospitality enterprises. Businesses may reach millions of prospective customers by consistently sharing visually appealing material, such as breathtaking images, videos, and behind-the-scenes looks. A brand's reach may be increased by using hashtags, geotags, and influencer engagement to increase its visibility to tourists from all over the globe.

1.9.2. Customer Trust Through Authentic Reviews

In the hotel sector, user-generated content—such as reviews, ratings, and photos—is very important. Social media is a vital tool for establishing reputation as consumers place more faith in reviews than in conventional advertising. Social media posts that highlight satisfied customers help you gain the confidence of prospective clients by demonstrating the true worth of your company. This fosters an atmosphere of openness that supports the development of relationships.

1.9.3. Real-Time Engagement and Support

The capacity to communicate with customers instantaneously is one of social media's biggest benefits for hospitality firms. Being responsive across platforms helps organisations maintain a strong customer service presence, whether it's answering an urgent booking query or resolving a problem. Customer satisfaction is increased by prompt, helpful interactions, which strengthen trust and loyalty.

1.9.4. Targeted Advertising for Higher Conversions

Hyper-targeted advertising based on user data and activity is made possible by social media. Businesses may divide up their audience into groups according to "demographics, interests, and even travel intentions" by running sponsored ads on Facebook, Instagram, and TikTok. This makes it possible to create customised messaging, which improves the relevance of advertising and raises the likelihood that followers will become genuine customers.

1.9.5. Collaboration With Travel Influencers

Influencers in travel have emerged as a crucial marketing tool for the hospitality sector. These influencers have the ability to produce engaging material that appeals to their sizable and attentive followers, such as evaluations of hotels and resorts and highlights of popular destinations. Businesses may attract a new generation of visitors who value influencer recommendations above conventional advertising by working with influencers to greatly increase brand exposure and credibility.

1.9.6. Fostering Community and Brand Loyalty

Social media gives hospitality companies the opportunity to create a brand community. Businesses may create a inclusive environment that encourages loyalty by promoting visitor participation via surveys, contests, and personalised responses. Frequent interaction and specific social media promotions, like coupons or deals, assist keep in touch with previous and potential customers and encourage repeat business.

1.9.7. Monitor Brand's Competitors

By using social media, hospitality organisations can use data and feedback to improve their operations and provide customers exceptional experiences. Social media becomes a tool for companies to build awareness and foster loyalty in an industry where customer loyalty is crucial by exposing their unique products and sustaining consumer interaction. In order to understand their customers' requirements and promote their products, 88% of travel marketers use social media, according to the International Tourism Research Centre.

Social listening is an essential component of success for businesses in the hospitality industry. It gives marketers the ability to monitor the actions of their audience and rivals. This data is essential for creating extremely successful social media marketing strategies that customise product and service offerings to satisfy client demands and interests, so assuring a competitive advantage.

An effective way to comprehend current market trends, observe successful and failed strategies, and gain knowledge from rivals' experiences is to keep an eye on them. While giving companies a considerable edge over those that underuse this platform, social media is a personalised and interactive tool for contacting customers.

1.9.8. Increase Sales and Leads

In the hotel industry, social media is essential for increasing booking and sales rates while successfully preserving presence among the right audience. Social media has developed into a useful tool for customers to obtain company information, including facts about service, product, operating hours, pricing, special events, and even recruiting possibilities, with a substantial 63% of customers using it to find new eateries.

Using social media to draw in customers with engaging content that entices them to learn more about a company's products is crucial in the hospitality sector. The key to social media success is producing engaging content that draws users in and stimulates their interest in the service or product being provided, ultimately resulting in reservations or sales. Because images and videos perform better than text-based material, especially on social media sites like Facebook and Instagram, it is recommended to use them.

Working with relevant influencers that have a sizable fan base among potential customers is another tactic for using influencer marketing. Through their platforms, these influencers may increase brand recognition while offering insightful advice on how to best target various traveler groups (e.g., families vs couples).

In order to streamline the process from initial interest to completion of a purchase or booking, hospitality and tourist businesses should make sure that prospective customers can be easily navigated from social media networks to their online booking platform with just a few clicks.

Using social media strategically is essential if you want to create leads in the hotel sector. It may be a very powerful tool for addressing potential customers directly if done well.

1.10. Content Creation and Community Building

In hotel marketing, social media content is more than attractive visuals—it is a means of creating a shared space where guests feel connected to the brand. Effective content builds trust, encourages participation, and turns satisfied customers into advocates (Kumari & Rekha, 2019). By highlighting authentic experiences, hotels can foster a sense of community that keeps potential guests engaged well beyond their initial visit (Healy & Wilson, 2015).

Key Elements

i. *Role of User-Generated Content* – Guest photos, reviews, and videos provide credible endorsements and expand a hotel's reach without heavy advertising costs (Garg & Kumar, 2021).
ii. *Influencer Collaborations and Partnerships* – Working with travel bloggers or industry personalities can introduce the hotel to new audiences and lend an aspirational appeal (Devi, 2015).
iii. *Storytelling for Brand Personality* – Consistent narratives about local culture, sustainability efforts, or unique amenities help guests connect emotionally with the property.

1.11. Challenges and Risk Management

Social media provides hotels with powerful marketing opportunities, but it also exposes them to a fast-moving environment where problems can escalate quickly (Qenaj & Beqiri, 2022). Effective risk management is essential to protect brand reputation and maintain guest trust.

Table 2. Challenges and Risk Management in Social Media

Area	Main Risk	Recommended Approach
Crisis Communication & Reputation	Rapid spread of misinformation or bad publicity	Predefined crisis plan, clear internal roles, timely public updates (Arusho Lucy, 2023).
Privacy, Security & Ethics	Data breaches, misuse of personal information	Strong cybersecurity, staff training, compliance with privacy regulations (Vishwakarma et al., 2021a).
Negative Reviews & Feedback	Loss of trust and potential revenue	Courteous public responses, private follow-up, visible problem resolution (Han et al., 2025).

1.12. Boost social media strategy through AI-powered online reputation management – MARA

An effective social media strategy must include managing internet reviews. Our AI Review Assistant, MARA, combines social media initiatives with online reputation management in a simple manner. This user-friendly tool is intended to improve your online reputation management procedure, increasing its effectiveness, personalization, and efficiency while saving time. For answering and evaluating your guest reviews, it provides the most effective and customized AI.

1.12.1. AI-Powered Review Inbox

The Review Inbox is one of this tool's primary features. Responding to reviews is as easy as selecting "Generate reply" and then "Send" from your review inbox. The Review Inbox provides you with a comprehensive view of all your reviews by connecting to many review sites, such as Google, Booking.com, and TripAdvisor. You may also set up review response automation. To make sure you never miss a review, why not let MARA reply to basic reviews automatically, such as 5-star Google reviews without any text? You stay informed and in charge when you get daily updates about new reviews.

1.12.2. Advanced Review Analytics

The Review Assistant also includes Review Analytics to assist you in comprehending and evaluating the large number of reviews. This offers easily comprehensible, actionable information that are specifically customised for your company. MARA allows you to rapidly summarise all of your reviews without having to read them all. You may learn about particular problems like "the pool's water is too cold" or "there isn't a vegan breakfast option" since the study is so thorough. You don't need to be an expert in data to use these insights to maximise the visitor experience.

1.12.3. The Most Personal Response AI

Efficiency is just one aspect of MARA's AI; customization is another. The AI can adjust to your tone owing to the Brand Voice function, which ensures that your answers sound like you. Smart Snippets also allows you to "teach" the AI how to react to repeated praises or complaints. Your AI then uses this knowledge to provide more relevant and personalized answers, always using different language.

For more than 2000 customers, our review response helper has rapidly changed the game. Its increasing popularity is due to its potential ability to improve your overall rating, increase response rates, extract valuable insights from customer feedback, and save time and money.

Online review management doesn't have to be a daunting undertaking. You may personalise your comments, expedite the process, and get insightful knowledge from the reviews if you have the right tools. Therefore, why not try our AI Review Assistant, MARA? It doesn't need a credit card, is totally free to try, and can be fully functional in under five minutes.

1.13. Impact of Social Media on the Decision-Making Process

Four components make up the pre-travel decision-making process: thinking, assessing, purchasing, and enjoying. The first step in purchasing travel or hospitality items is to weigh specific possibilities from those that pique curiosity. As a result, when customers are first considering options, internet reviews and comments greatly influence their choices. During the assessment phase, the prospective customer prioritizes needs and looks for information from various sources. At this point, customers begin to look for and digest information from several sources to meet their requirements, and they weigh a number of options before making a purchase. Online information is thus crucial at this point as it has the power to affect the choice made. Additionally, by providing greater exploration options, social media has raised customers' spending power. From the perspective of the traveler, social media highlights places such as well-known restaurants, hotels and places. In order to assist choose appropriate hotel rooms, attractions, locations, activities, and means of transportation, social networking applications are mostly used during the assessment stage of trip preparation.

Additionally, rather than depending only on traditional marketing, businesses in the tourist and hospitality sectors have seen the change in consumer purchasing patterns and included social media into their digital marketing plan. These businesses place a strong focus on developing creative campaigns to increase brand recognition and promotion, which attracts a wide audience. Social media thereby lowers the barriers to communication between suppliers, businesses, and customers. Furthermore, social media creates chances for companies and social media influencers to work together. As a result, both the influencer and the company gain when an influencer posts about their experiences online and draws in new customers. Before making their final purchasing decisions, prospective customers utilise social media platforms to evaluate various services and locations, read reviews from other customers, and ask questions. In general, social media have been presented as important channels for information sharing and communication between users and enterprises, as well as between larger controllers, mediators, and stakeholders in non-profit organisations.

1.14. Pros and Cons of Using Social Media on Decision Making

Businesses and consumers may monitor their performance and evaluate data like the quantity of followers, likes on their content, shares, views on their videos, and both positive and negative comments by using the social media analytics system. Customers do, in fact, place more faith in information from other travellers on social media than in marketing, travel agencies, and business websites. Customers carefully examine social media material before incorporating it into their decision-making process, which lowers the risk factors involved. Additionally, during the decision-making stage, information from conventional sources may be out of date, but material on social media is the most recent. In a similar vein, tourists share their real experiences on social media, which increases the decision-making power of consumers.

However, the specific challenges encountered in putting social media marketing into practice include a lack of engagement between customers and social media, a lack of dedication, issues with access, a failure to respond to visitors, an inability to use social media, inaccurate content, and a lack of communication amongst various levels. Furthermore, with all the information on social media, it is difficult to remain genuine and trustworthy. Also, the decision-making process is made more difficult, time-consuming, and confusing by the increase in alternatives and research platforms. In the meanwhile, customers are unsure about their choice due to unfavourable remarks or reviews, low ratings, and subpar photos from prior passengers. Negative reviews thus have an impact on the brand's reputation and total sales as well.

2. LITERATURE REVIEW

Vishwakarma et al. (2021) aimed to analyse how social media marketing affected their hotel choice in order to ensure that guests had a pleasant and relaxing stay. Finding out which hotels made use of certain social media marketing strategies and how those strategies affected guests' choice of hotel were the primary goals of the study. One hundred twenty-two people in the states of Uttar Pradesh and Madhya Pradesh filled out the survey after it was sent out using Google Forms. Among the many factors that influence hotel guests' decisions, 48% cite the hotel's location (country, city, area, etc.), 40% cite online reviews and feedback, and 37% cite the hotel's unique selling proposition (special features) as the most important factor in social media marketing for guest selection. Businesses and hotels rely heavily on social media marketing to win over customers' confidence and trustworthiness.

Social media marketing techniques are crucial in today's time and age since clients often use them to investigate hotels before making a reservation.

Bennaciri (2012) studied how social media influences how customers perceive marketing materials. Research contrasted more conventional online marketing resources with those that featured consumer blogs. The travel and tourism industry has recently learnt that blogs may have both good and bad effects if not handled correctly, despite the fact that blogs are vital social networking tools. With the proliferation of blogs as a social media platform, hotel managers would do well to familiarise themselves with the ways in which blogs impact customer decision-making so that they may use social media marketing strategies to their advantage. According to the study's findings, guests had the most favourable impression of the hotel when neither positive nor negative reviews were given.

Kasim (2023) the impact of social media on hotel marketing and customer involvement has been profound. Instagram and similar sites have given hotels a direct line to prospective customers and a visual exhibition for their offerings (Liu, Park, & Petrick, 2019). Because of this, hotels can now establish customer loyalty and brand recognition while also connecting with guests in real-time for better service. The expanded exposure that hotels get from social media marketing is a big perk. Hotels may reach more potential customers and promote their properties to a larger audience using social media sites like Instagram. This has the potential to boost the hotel's occupancy rates and income. Hotels may also interact with their customers in real time via social media, which can strengthen ties and encourage loyalty.

Al-Maslam et al. (2016) the five criteria that determine whether a member would participate in a hotel's Facebook fan page are the following: functional, hedonic, monetary, and social and psychological advantages. The conceptual model was tested using Structural Equation Modelling (SEM). According to the findings of the structural equation modelling (SEM), there were four benefit variables that had a favourable impact on members' community participation: functional, hedonic, social, and psychological. Researchers and marketers may learn a lot from this study's results. From a theoretical standpoint, this study is the first of its kind to empirically examine the advantages and reactions (i.e., community involvement and brand loyalty) of consumers in online communities run by the hotel industry. Therefore, the research adds to our knowledge of how people shop on social media. From a more pragmatic standpoint, the report offers some tips for creating engaging hotel Facebook fan pages that may grow the business by connecting with existing customers and drawing in new ones.

Sarin (2023) provided valuable information on the far-reaching impacts of social media marketing by using a respondent pool that is varied in age, employment, and wealth. Instagram being the most popular platform, the poll found that social media users are often exposed to information concerning hospitality. That Instagram's visual appeal is appealing to those seeking vacation ideas is not surprising. While opinions on the power of social media to influence vacation plans differ, one thing is clear: positive reviews and rankings matter much. In the hotel business, user-generated information, particularly good evaluations, plays a vital role in shaping perceptions. An essential finding is the growing importance of influencer marketing. The study shows that influencers and user-generated material are becoming more important across all age groups, and that they have a big impact on hotel customers' choices. These findings provide a priceless map for homestay and hotel organisations looking to enhance their social media approach. Respondents' views are in favour of more transparency, honesty, and specificity when it comes to facilities and events. The need for organisations to establish genuine connections with their consumers is evident in the desire for videos that include true, unfiltered imagery and strong, emotional narrative.

Khatwani and Bhut (2020) Instagram and Facebook have more daily users and travel ads are seen more often on these two platforms. When they are making vacation plans, they want to get additional information in the form of reviews, videos, and discounts. Based on the data shown above, it's safe to say that social media plays a role in people's decision-making when planning a vacation. As a result, the hospitality sector may capitalise on this trend to attract more consumers and generate more revenue.

Lakha and Bahra (2020) a hotel may benefit from social media marketing in two ways: first, by attracting more attention from local and international customers; and second, by streamlining its processes. Businesses may get an edge in the market if they use this cutting-edge promotional strategy that makes use of technology. On the other hand, working with outside firms to promote social media campaigns might increase costs and open the door to legal issues. Therefore, the relevant hotel company's IT and marketing departments should work together to guarantee constant and successful social media marketing. The Chandigarh tri-city has become a centre for the hotel industry because to its proximity to three major international airports and its advanced technology. This new sector of the hotel industry may be able to attract international customers and investors with the support of well-executed social media marketing campaigns. In addition, hotels in the tri-city area attract corporate customers due to the presence of significant medical institutions, technological parks, and pharmaceutical enterprises. Tourists from all walks of life are flocking to the tri-city, thanks to the abundance of high-quality hotels offering both affordable and luxurious accommodations, as well as excellent customer service. In addition, social media-focused marketing may be made more successful by incorporating corporate social responsibility (CSR) tactics into company promotions.

Pandat and Kadam (2020) social media facilitates cross-border communication. People can communicate with one another and create relationships as a result. Social media, which has millions of users, has evolved into a tool for branding, staffing, engagement, and engagement. Companies now choose to offer their products on social media since it allows them to interact with a broader audience. For the most part, companies are making extensive use of social media to keep in touch with consumers and spread the word about their products. It is possible that the Indian hotel business is not making the most of social media. Nowadays, the hotel business in industrialised nations has realised the power of social media for branding and is using it to its fullest. Findings from this study might help Pune hotels optimise their social media marketing efforts. Aspiring hoteliers would do well to familiarise themselves with the positive applications of social media. Also, ways to make social media more effective for branding should be suggested. Research on the potential branding benefits of emerging social media platforms might help inform future strategy development in light of recent technical developments.

Desai et al. (2022) social media is the platform it offers for direct brand-to-consumer communication. Using a mix of the aforementioned strategies, one may reach their desired demographic by showing them relevant ads on mobile phones, foster meaningful connections with them via social media responses, and attract new followers to your event page. Trust in the brand and services is built via the strong and personal ties we have with our consumers. The hotel might take it a notch further by funding his mobile app. Establishing a two-way flow of information between individuals is the surest path to fostering loyal patronage. Hotel revenue is seeing a significant boost from direct reservations made via mobile devices, reaching about $8 billion, a 6.5% increase from last year. Websites aren't only for social media; they're essential for every business that wants to stay in the game and make money. And it has the potential to be the primary motivator for the majority of bookings if executed properly. However, in our technologically advanced world, individuals are increasingly taking matters into their own hands, and businesses must adapt accordingly. Following this principle and making every effort to establish a direct online booking channel for tech-savvy clients is essential for hotels. A well-functioning website, familiarity with social media platforms like Facebook and Twitter, or even just consideration of mobile applications are becoming necessities for hotels.

Loc et al. (2021) evidently stated that Facebook may be a powerful tool for hotels looking to enhance their business strategies. The hotel and its customers may build a strong, mutually beneficial connection via the usage of Facebook, which serves as a medium for both providing information to and engaging with consumers. The point when Facebook users feel like they're really there has already been attained by a number of hotels. In their profiles, these hotels present a wealth of information for potential guests to peruse, including details about the services and goods offered, guest reviews, upcoming events, special deals, publications, and more.

Bai, et al. (2015) sought to investigate the marketing efficacy of Facebook and Twitter as social media platforms for the hospitality sector. This research offered a theoretical model of the efficacy of social media marketing for hotels by combining the attitude-towards-social-media-page (AT-SMP) with the attitude-towards-the-ad (Aad) model. An online poll provided the data, and the model's goodness of fit suggested that the Aad model offered a sound theoretical foundation for understanding the efficacy of social media marketing for hotels. Following is a chain reaction of events that begins with customers' social media experiences and ends with their attitudes towards the hotel brand. This chain reaction begins with customers' attitudes towards the hotel brand influencing their intentions to book a room and continues with their intentions to spread electronic word of mouth.

Gouda and Halim (2025) consumer loyalty in the hotel business is greatly improved by "both firm-generated content (FGC) and user-generated content (UGC)." Nevertheless, the correlation between user-generated content (UGC) and customer loyalty was shown to be moderated by education, although no significant moderating effects were observed for other demographic variables including age, gender, or employment. According to these results, user-generated content (UGC) is more powerful among customers with higher levels of knowledge, and sustainable social media material in general plays an important role in boosting customer loyalty. What follows is an expanded analysis of these findings, with an eye towards their theoretical and practical significance.

Bhagyashree et al. (2024) the hospitality industry has realised the immense value of social media marketing, which provides a plethora of advantages to various enterprises in the field. Offering a cost-effective and efficient way to communicate with clients, it facilitates direct contact and increases brand recognition. Businesses in the hospitality industry may advertise their wares, tell their stories, and cultivate a devoted clientele on social media sites like Facebook, Twitter, and Instagram. Nowadays, people put a lot of stock in recommendations from people they know and trust, such as friends, influencers, and online communities. This puts the idea of "social validation" into context with how consumers use social media to get information and make decisions. In order to maintain a competitive edge, hotels need to develop strategic social media plans that are in line with their goals and the people they want to reach.

Hossain et al. (2025) there are a lot of advantages to social media marketing for hotels, restaurants, and other companies in the hospitality industry. It allows for direct connection and the expansion of brand recognition via an efficient and cost-effective method of communicating with consumers. Businesses in the hotel industry may reach a wide audience, tell their story, and cultivate brand loyalty using social media sites such as Instagram, Twitter, and Facebook. It is critical to carefully craft a social media strategy that is in line with the goals of the company and its target audience. As a result of social media, hotels no longer see their websites as static brochures, but rather as dynamic platforms with enormous potential for growth and improvement. To be competitive in the ever-changing digital world, hotels must use social media as a core component of their entire marketing strategy. Customers in the modern digital age depend heavily on social media platforms to get information and make educated purchases. The idea of "social validation" is very important because people put a lot of stock in suggestions from people they know and trust, such as friends, influential people, and online groups.

Kalgi et al. (2022) social media has been used as a marketing strategy by many corporate brands since 2005. Marketers use it primarily to boost sales, search engine rankings, leads, and traffic; yet, since it is a multi-dimensional platform, its primary role is to promote content creation and sharing. The strategy of promoting her website on social media platforms to increase its visibility and traffic is known as social media marketing. A common goal of social media marketing campaigns is to increase content sharing by drawing in new audiences and captivating existing ones. With the use of social media, marketers should reevaluate their marketing strategies, considering how they might embrace new forms of interactive communication rather of relying only on the old one-way movement of marketing messages. Your company may benefit greatly from the development and growth of social media, as well as from its use in marketing. Regardless of industry, everyone uses communities, social media, blog marketing, etc. In order to maximise and globalise your social media marketing campaigns, you should take advantage of the new concepts that exist on social media marketing platforms, which the hospitality industry occupies.

Sánchez Jiménez et al. (2024) the primary findings demonstrate the connection between user-generated and shared content and consumer satisfaction, which is particularly important to the hotel industry. The emphasis on innovation and the adoption of new destination-oriented technology are notable in hotel management and marketing. It is also important to note the connection between customer experiences and behaviour and social network participation.

Pontes and Ramos (2023) examine social media's impact on customer behaviour in the hotel industry by examining how it affects online reservations. On the supply side, it draws attention to the need of developing fresh theoretical frameworks for disseminating information about the hotel product, including social media advertising. Additionally, in order to study consumer behaviour on the supply side, the theoretical models should include the credibility and quality of testimonials created by travellers on social media. Practically speaking, the study's implications emphasise the necessity of incorporating social media marketing strategies into plans and budgets, improving the promotion and distribution of hotel products among the largest possible audience, and concentrating on visitor reviews of local lodging because these reviews are regarded as trustworthy and dependable, making them social media representatives for the brand or product.

Faizal et al. (2024) utilising the Optimum Stimulation Level (OSL) hypothesis, the study investigates the connection between "hotel decision-making and awareness, brand, digital information, price, and variety". As a consequence, the findings show a strong positive correlation between hotel decision-making and awareness, brand, digital information, price, and diversity. Nevertheless, the brand has no moderating effect on the correlation between hotel decision-making and pricing. These results highlight the significance of digital platforms in influencing customer behaviour and hotel choice in South Asia's hospitality sector, providing industry and academic stakeholders with useful insights.

Ogoina et al. (2025) compare reputation management techniques before and after social media and examine how social media impacts "audience engagement, customer behaviour, and reputation management in hotel selection and booking choices". The results show that customer behaviour in choosing and booking hotels is greatly influenced by promotional offers, user reviews, and visual material. With a 100% success rate, influencer partnerships, user-generated content, live video content, and social media advertising are the best methods for engaging audiences and developing a brand. In the hotel sector, social media is crucial in influencing customer behaviour and brand impression. Engaging audiences and developing brand identity need effective social media strategies, especially those that use influencers and user-generated content.

Jain (2024) investigates the ways in which different digital marketing tactics affect these objectives in the hotel industry. The research examines the effects of digital platforms and technologies, including "content marketing, social media marketing, email marketing, and online reputation management, on consumer participation". In today's tech-driven world, digital marketing has become crucial for hotels to thrive. More and more travellers are researching and booking hotels using internet resources including social media, smartphone applications, and search engines. This emphasises how crucial it is for hotels to have a robust online presence and mobile-friendly programs. These platforms and client loyalty seem to have a complicated connection, according to research. While certain digital marketing strategies, like as loyalty programs, are designed to increase loyalty, others may inadvertently undermine it. Hotels need an advanced digital marketing plan that takes into account how each tactic affects total client loyalty and happiness. Content marketing, social media interactions, and tailored email campaigns are all essential for fostering client loyalty and engagement. Through the implementation of customer-centricity, personalisation, and ongoing adaptation to evolving tastes, hotels may effectively use digital marketing to enhance guest engagement, foster loyalty, and attain sustained prosperity.

Bhatt and Dani (2022) determines the origins of virtual media marketing as well as the strategies used to promote it in the catering and hospitality sectors. While the hotel industry has its own websites, the majority of them should be more active on social media platforms like Instagram, Twitter, TripAdvisor, and Meta, posting engaging and educational images and videos. They may grow their company and brand worth with the aid of that sort of action. Maintaining a firm in the market requires social media engineering. Hospitality and other food and beverage businesses may establish direct connections with customers and target audiences using social media platforms, promoting their brands more professionally, enhancing their reputation, encouraging client return business, and boosting sales.

Mohammad et al. (2024) aim to investigate the direct and indirect effects of social commerce on hotel booking intentions, drawing on the well-established framework of Stimuli–Organism–Response (SOR) theory. The findings demonstrated how social commerce significantly affects consumer involvement and hotel brand image, which in turn influences prospective domestic visitors' propensity to make reservations. "In the relationship between social commerce and hotel booking intentions", the findings further confirmed the important mediating role of customer involvement and hotel brand image. By filling up significant knowledge gaps, this research offers some theoretical advances to the literature on hotel management. "Creating visually appealing content, sponsoring virtual mega events, actively engaging" with social media followers, and integrating booking features into social media platforms are just a few of the practical recommendations this study makes for industry executives to support their social commerce strategies and increase booking intentions and behaviour among domestic tourists. By doing this, hotels may take use of Web 2.0 capabilities to improve their sustainable marketing strategies and target a lucrative market group.

Table 3. Key findings from the literature review

Author(s) & Year	Focus of Study	Key Findings	Relevance to Present Study
Vishwakarma et al. (2021)	Examined how social media marketing influences hotel selection among guests in Uttar Pradesh and Madhya Pradesh.	Location (48%), online reviews (40%), and unique selling proposition (37%) were the most influential factors. Social media builds trust and confidence before booking.	Highlights specific factors (location, reviews, USP) that guide guest choices, supporting the need for strategic social media planning in hotel marketing.
Kasim (2023)	Explored social media's role in hotel marketing and customer involvement.	Platforms like Instagram enable real-time engagement, improve brand recognition, and increase occupancy rates and revenue.	Demonstrates the value of interactive engagement and loyalty-building, aligning with the study's focus on comprehensive social media strategy.
Al-Maslam et al. (2016)	Investigated member participation in hotel Facebook fan pages using Structural Equation Modelling.	Functional, hedonic, social, and psychological benefits positively influenced online community participation and brand loyalty.	Provides empirical evidence of how well-designed social media communities enhance loyalty and participation.
Sarin (2023)	Analysed the influence of social media content and influencer marketing on hotel customers.	Positive reviews, authentic visuals, and influencer-driven content strongly shape hotel choice across age groups.	Supports the importance of user-generated content and influencer partnerships for credible brand promotion.
Bhagyashree et al. (2024)	Reviewed advantages of social media marketing for hospitality businesses.	Social media offers cost-effective communication, fosters direct contact, and enhances brand recognition and competitiveness.	Reinforces the strategic role of social media as a core marketing tool for hotels seeking stronger customer connections.

3. CONCLUSION

The present study demonstrates that social media has moved beyond a supplementary promotional tool to become a central pillar of hotel marketing strategy. Through a careful review of existing research and industry practices, it is evident that platforms such as Facebook, Instagram, YouTube, LinkedIn, and Twitter have transformed how hotels communicate, influence purchase decisions, and maintain long-term relationships with guests. These networks allow hotels to showcase their services with immediacy and creativity, providing prospective customers with authentic insights into the brand's atmosphere, offerings, and values.

The findings highlight several key themes. First, user-generated content and online reviews remain powerful drivers of credibility, often carrying greater weight than traditional advertising. Guests increasingly rely on peer experiences to guide their booking choices, which means that hotels must nurture an active, responsive presence on social channels. Second, visual storytelling whether through short videos, professional photography, or behind-the-scenes glimpses emerges as a vital way to differentiate properties in a competitive market. Third, data from the literature underscores that timely engagement, personalized communication, and collaboration with influencers or travel bloggers can significantly enhance visibility and occupancy rates.

However, the opportunities of social media marketing are accompanied by notable challenges. Reputation management in the digital age requires a structured approach to crisis communication, swift handling of negative reviews, and a robust commitment to privacy and data security. Hotels that combine proactive risk management with creative engagement strategies are best positioned to turn potential setbacks into demonstrations of accountability and care.

Overall, social media provides a dynamic environment in which hotels can build meaningful connections with both existing and prospective guests. By integrating authentic content, consistent interaction, and ethical practices, hotel marketers can leverage these platforms not merely as advertising channels but as interactive spaces that cultivate loyalty and sustained growth. This conclusion reinforces the importance of thoughtful planning, continuous monitoring, and adaptable strategies to harness the full potential of social media in the hospitality industry.

REFERENCES

Al-Maslam, S., Al-Msallam, S., & Alhaddad, A. (2016a). The Effects of Social Media Marketing in the Hotel Industry: Conceptual Model for Development of an Effective Online Community Building customer loyalty model in airline industry View project The Effects of Social Media Marketing In the Hotel Industry: Co. *International Journal of Business and Management Invention ISSN*, *5*(July), 1–12. www.ijbmi.org

Al-Maslam, S., Al-Msallam, S., & Alhaddad, A. (2016b). The Effects of Social Media Marketing in the Hotel Industry: Conceptual Model for Development of an Effective Online Community Building customer loyalty model in airline industry View project The Effects of Social Media Marketing In the Hotel Industry: Co. *International Journal of Business and Management Invention ISSN*, *5*(7), 1–12. www.ijbmi.org

Arora, R., & Arora, Y. (2019). Role and Impact of Social Media in Hospitality Industry. *Ijirmps, 7*(1), 1–6. www.ijirmps.org

Arusho Lucy. (2023). *Effect of Social Media Platforms' Use on Hotel Performance.* 11–13.

Bennaciri, M. (2012).. . *The Effect of Social Media on Hotel Industry Customer.*, (August), 1–41.

Bhagyashree, M., Dashmukhe, P., & Nath, P. P. (2024).. . *Social Media Marketing And It's Role In Hotel Brand Image Building.*, *12*(10), 451–458.

Bhatt, S., & Dani, R. (2022). *Social Media: Marketing Strategies in Hospitality Industry*. Research in Tourism and Hospitality Management., DOI: 10.21467/books.134.8

Devi, S. (2015). Social Media as a Tool of Marketing: A Study of Indian Automobile Industry. SSRN *Electronic Journal, 5*(12), 166–172. https://doi.org/DOI: 10.2139/ssrn.2698527

Faizal, S., Sankar, J. P., Menon, N., Abdalla, R., & Pattali, S. (2024). Factors influencing hotel decision-making through digital platforms in South Asia. *Cogent Social Sciences*, *10*(1). Advance online publication. DOI: 10.1080/23311886.2024.2407933

Garg, A., & Kumar, J. (2021). Social media marketing influence on Boutique Hotel customers' purchase intention in Malaysia. *Tourism & Management Studies*, *17*(3), 51–62. DOI: 10.18089/tms.2021.170304

Gitau, S. K. (2020). *Impact of social media marketing on the brand awareness in the hotel industry. 21*(1), 1–9. https://www.golder.com/insights/block-caving-a-viable-alternative/

Gouda, R. M., & Halim, Y. T. (2025). The role of sustainable social media content in enhancing customer loyalty in the hospitality industry. *Future Business Journal, 11*(1). Advance online publication. DOI: 10.1186/s43093-025-00516-8

Han, L., Mingying, H., & Peng, Z. (2025). The influence of social media marketing on the quality of hotel services and the behavioral intentions of tourists. *Acta Psychologica, 255*(October 2024), 104881. https://doi.org/DOI: 10.1016/j.actpsy.2025.104881

Healy, T. G., & Wilson, A. (2015). *Social Media Marketing in the Hospitality Industry: Is It Worth the Effort?* 10.

Hossain, M. S., Sheikh, P., & Islam, P. (2025). The Role of Social Media Marketing in the Tourism and Hospitality Industry: A study on Bangladesh. *American Journal of Tourism and Hospitality*, *3*(1), 14–23. DOI: 10.54536/ajth.v3i1.4082

Jain, P. (2024). Exploring the Impact of Digital Marketing Strategies on Customer Engagement and Loyalty in the Hospitality Industry. *International Journal Of Novel Research And Development, 9*(8). www.ijnrd.org

Kalgi, D., Desai, R., & Fatangare, S. (2022). Impact of Social Media Marketing on Accommodation Sector in the Hospitality Industry. In *Current and Futuristic Trends in Accommodation Sector*.

Kalgi, D., Dhole, V., & Naik, S. (2022). *To Study the Role of Social Media Marketing on the Hospitality and Tourism industry of India. Recent Advances in Humanities.* Management, Engineering, Science & Technology.

Kasim, M. (2023). Beyond the Basics: Advanced Strategies for Hotels Using Social Media. *International Journal of Research Publication and Reviews*, *4*(5), 584–588. www.ijrpr.com

Khatwani, D., & Bhut, G. (2020). A study on effectiveness of social media marketing in hospitality industry. *International Journal of Management and Commerce Innovations*, *7*(2), 1283–1288. www.researchpublish.com

Kumari, S., & Rekha. (2019). A study of social media marketing with reference to Hospitality sector. *International Journal of Creative Research Thoughts, Vol.6*(Issue 5), 229–239. https://www.jetir.org/papers/JETIR1905B36.pdf

Lakha, R., & Bahra, R. (2020). Influence of social media marketing on the performance of hotel industry: A study in Chandigarh Tri-city. *International Journal for Research in Engineering Application & Management, 01*, 401–408. DOI: 10.35291/2454-9150.2020.0322

Leung, X. Y., Billy Bai, & Kurt A. Stahura. (2015). The Marketing Effectiveness of Social Media in the Hotel Industry. *Journal of Hospitality & Tourism Research (Washington, D.C.)*.

Leung, X. Y., Bai, B., & Erdem, M. (2017). Hotel social media marketing: A study on message strategy and its effectiveness. *Journal of Hospitality and Tourism Technology, 8*(2), 239–255. DOI: 10.1108/JHTT-02-2017-0012

Leung, X. Y., Bai, B., & Stahura, K. A. (2015). The Marketing Effectiveness of Social Media in the Hotel Industry: A Comparison of Facebook and Twitter. *Journal of Hospitality & Tourism Research (Washington, D.C.), 39*(2), 147–169. DOI: 10.1177/1096348012471381

Lim, W. (2010). *The Effects of social media networks in the hospitality industry*. 44. http://digitalcommons.library.unlv.edu/thesesdissertations/693/

Palenčarová, M., Hohoš, T., Correia, R., & Cunha, C. R. (2022). Social Media Marketing Research at the Hotel Industry in Slovakia. *Iberian Conference on Information Systems and Technologies, CISTI, 2022-June*, 1–2. https://doi.org/DOI: 10.23919/CISTI54924.2022.9820127

Pontes, A., & Ramos, C. (2023). How does Social Media influence the Behaviour of Hotel Consumers? *Journal of Tourism Sustainability and Well-Being, 11*(2). Advance online publication. DOI: 10.34623/784k-qg19

Qenaj, M., & Beqiri, G. (2022). Social Media Marketing in Hospitality Industry and Its Effect on Consumer Behavior in Kosovo. *IFAC-PapersOnLine, 55*(39), 66–69. DOI: 10.1016/j.ifacol.2022.12.012

Sánchez Jiménez, M. Á., Gómez Carmona, D., & Moral Moral, M. (2024). Evolution of the impact of social media in hospitality: A bibliometric analysis. *Journal of Destination Marketing & Management, 31*. Advance online publication. DOI: 10.1016/j.jdmm.2024.100868

Sarin, T. (2023). Significance of social media on the hospitality industry. *International Journal of Technical Research and Applications, 8*(8), 22–28.

Tarvainen, S. (2023). *Social Media Marketing Plan for Original Sokos Hotel Tapiola Garden*.

Vishwakarma, V. K., Kapur, S., ... (2021a). Analysing the impact of social media marketing on guests hotel selection. ... *Journal of Hospitality and ...*, *September*, 37–49. https://acspublisher.com/journals/index.php/pjhas/article/view/3371

Vishwakarma, V. K., Kapur, S., ... (2021b). Analysing the impact of social media marketing on guests hotel selection. ... *Journal of Hospitality and ...*, *September*, 9–14. https://acspublisher.com/journals/index.php/pjhas/article/view/3371

Chapter 10

Strategic Digital Branding Through Social Media in Urban Hospitality: A Bangalore Perspective

Megha Tamang
http://orcid.org/0009-0007-7903-5300
Mount Carmel College, Bangalore, India

Mukunda B. G.
http://orcid.org/0000-0002-6568-1578
Mount Carmel College, Bangalore, India

ABSTRACT

Social media has become an essential tool for marketing communication in the hospitality sector, facilitating customer awareness, enhancing brand recognition, and supporting business growth. Its influence on consumer behavior has encouraged hospitality organizations, including hotels and restaurants, to integrate social media as a key marketing channel. Social media platforms offer unique opportunities for improving revenue, building customer relationships, and strengthening brand identity. With the expansion of digital platforms and evolving consumer preferences, this study explores best practices in social media marketing specifically for the hospitality industry. Urban hospitality in India, particularly in Bangalore, is experiencing a significant digital transformation, with social media emerging as a dominant channel for branding and customer interaction. This conceptual study investigates how social media strategies shape digital branding outcomes for urban hotels.

DOI: 10.4018/979-8-3373-6741-5.ch010

INTRODUCTION

The hospitality industry in India is undergoing rapid transformation due to digitalization. As global tourism and travel increasingly rely on technology, social media has become a strategic tool for hotel branding and customer engagement (McDonald, 2025; Kotler et al., 2017). In metropolitan cities such as Bangalore, characterized by cosmopolitan culture, a thriving start-up ecosystem, and a technology-driven lifestyle, hospitality enterprises must adopt innovative digital branding strategies to remain competitive (HTL, 2024). Digital branding refers to the process of creating, communicating, and maintaining a brand's identity through digital platforms (Aaker, 1996; Keller, 1993). In the hospitality sector, where customer loyalty is often determined by experiential value and emotional connection, social media integration has redefined conventional marketing strategies (Anwar et al., 2024). Hotels are no longer seen solely as service providers but as curators of experiences, communicating their brand personality through storytelling, influencer collaborations, and user-generated content (Wibowo et al., 2024). Bangalore's hospitality market is distinctive due to its diverse clientele, including corporate travellers, expatriates, leisure tourists, and millennial weekend visitors, each demonstrating unique digital behaviours (Khanna & Gopinath, 2024). The city hosts a wide range of hotels, from global chains to boutique experiential properties, all vying for visibility in a competitive digital ecosystem. In this context, strategic social media adoption is essential for customer acquisition, brand differentiation, and reputation management (Qenaj & Beqiri, 2022). Platforms such as Instagram, LinkedIn, and YouTube have become critical elements of Bangalore's hospitality marketing mix. Instagram reels are used to showcase aesthetic design, LinkedIn targets business travellers, and YouTube offers virtual property tours. These platforms enable continuous brand engagement, transcending the limitations of physical touchpoints (Murniati & Bawono, 2020). Additionally, electronic word-of-mouth (eWOM)-including customer reviews, influencer endorsements, and peer recommendations has emerged as a critical factor influencing booking intentions and brand trust (Litvin et al., 2008; Sánchez-González & González-Fernández, 2021). Despite significant research on digital marketing globally, there is limited conceptual clarity on how social media branding affects brand equity in urban Indian hospitality.

OBJECTIVE OF THE STUDY

The primary aim of this study is to examine the influence of strategic digital branding through social media on brand perception, customer engagement, and brand equity within the urban hospitality sector, with a focus on Bangalore. The research intends to develop a conceptual model linking social media strategies, digital brand communication, and customer experience to overall brand performance in hotels. The study also identifies key dimensions of social media branding, including content strategy, influencer collaborations, and eWOM, which contribute to the digital brand identity of urban hotels. Furthermore, it seeks to understand the role of consumer behaviour, digital touchpoints, and technological innovation in reshaping brand-customer relationships within Bangalore's competitive hospitality environment.

SIGNIFICANCE OF THE STUDY

This study is significant for both academic scholars and hospitality practitioners. Academically, it contributes to the literature on digital branding by proposing a conceptual framework that integrates social media engagement with brand equity creation in emerging economies. Unlike most existing Western-centric models, this study emphasizes socio-cultural and technological realities specific to urban Indian consumers, particularly in the cosmopolitan context of Bangalore. From a managerial perspective, the study provides actionable insights for hotel brands aiming to strengthen their digital presence, enhance online reputation, and build emotional connections with target audiences through social media. By examining how strategic digital branding promotes customer loyalty and competitive advantage, it offers a roadmap for implementing authentic, data-driven, and customer-focused social media strategies. Overall, the research underscores the role of social media as a strategic branding platform capable of shaping consumer perceptions and driving sustainable brand growth in urban hospitality.

REVIEW OF LITERATURE

Digital Branding in Hospitality

Digital branding has become a vital strategy in hospitality, shifting the focus from transactional promotion to creating meaningful customer experiences (Aaker, 1996; Keller, 1993). In urban hospitality, digital branding involves designing and communicating brand identity across websites, mobile apps, and social media platforms (Anwar et al., 2024). Unlike other service industries, hospitality brands intertwine brand experience with physical service delivery, ambience, and emotional engagement. Therefore, effective digital branding conveys both functional attributes and experiential dimensions of the brand (Kotler et al., 2017). Recent studies emphasize that successful digital branding highlights storytelling, authenticity, and immersive experiences. Urban hotels increasingly act as "experience curators," using visual and narrative content to communicate brand values (Wibowo et al., 2024). Social media allows potential guests to visualise their experience, interact with the brand, and form expectations even before booking.

Social Media as a Strategic Branding Tool

Social media platforms are now indispensable in hospitality marketing due to their extensive reach, interactivity, and cost-effectiveness (McDonald, 2025; Dwivedi et al., 2021). Platforms such as Instagram, LinkedIn, YouTube, and X enable hotels to engage multiple customer segments simultaneously. Instagram allows visual storytelling, LinkedIn targets business travellers, and YouTube provides virtual tours and behind-the-scenes insights (Murniati & Bawono, 2020). Social media enhances brand visibility, strengthens customer relationships, and allows real-time communication (Anwar et al., 2024). Content types, including promotional posts, influencer collaborations, user-generated content, and CSR communication, help hotels project a multidimensional brand identity (Qenaj & Beqiri, 2022). Engagement on social media also strengthens emotional connections, reinforcing loyalty and brand preference (Wibowo et al., 2024).

Electronic Word-of-Mouth (eWOM) and Reputation Management

eWOM significantly influences consumer decisions in hospitality (Litvin et al., 2008). Reviews, ratings, and peer recommendations often carry more weight than direct marketing messages (Sánchez-González & González-Fernández, 2021). eWOM acts as a reputational signal and social validation mechanism. Positive feedback increases bookings, while negative comments require a strategic response to mitigate reputational risks (Rialti et al., 2025). Hotels in Bangalore monitor eWOM across platforms like TripAdvisor, Google Reviews, and Zomato, integrating insights into marketing strategies and service improvements (Khanna & Gopinath, 2024). Engaging with reviews improves customer perception and fosters digital advocacy, turning satisfied customers into brand ambassadors (Qenaj & Beqiri, 2022).

Customer Engagement in the Digital Era

Customer engagement (CE) links social media activities to brand equity (Vivek et al., 2012). CE encompasses cognitive, emotional, and behavioral investment in brand interactions, including likes, shares, comments, direct messages, and UGC. Higher CE strengthens brand loyalty, promotes positive eWOM, and increases repeat bookings. In Bangalore, engagement strategies include interactive campaigns, live Q&A sessions, and gamified experiences to stimulate participation. Engagement acts as a bridge between content strategy and brand equity, amplifying the influence of social media on perception and loyalty (Wibowo et al., 2024).

Customer-Based Brand Equity (CBBE) in Hospitality

The concept of Customer-Based Brand Equity (CBBE) provides a theoretical foundation for understanding the outcomes of strategic digital branding (Keller, 1993). CBBE is determined by four key dimensions: brand awareness, brand associations, perceived quality, and brand loyalty. In a digital context, social media activities influence all these dimensions:

- *Brand awareness* is enhanced through platform visibility, viral campaigns, and influencer partnerships (McDonald, 2025)
- *Brand associations* are shaped by storytelling, visual content, and the emotional tone of communication (Wibowo et al., 2024).
- *Perceived quality* is influenced by eWOM, reviews, and shared guest experiences (Litvin et al., 2008).
- *Brand loyalty* develops through sustained engagement, personalized communication, and consistent digital interactions (Anwar et al., 2024).

By linking social media activities to CBBE, hotels can measure the effectiveness of digital branding in tangible and experiential terms.

Urban Hospitality and the Bangalore Context

Urban hospitality is influenced by city-specific factors such as adoption of technology, business travel patterns, lifestyle trends, and cultural diversity (HTL, 2024). Bangalore's hotels, including global chains and boutique properties, leverage social media to differentiate in a competitive market (Khanna & Gopinath, 2024). Digital branding in urban India must account for socio-cultural nuances and aspirational behaviors. Consumers in Bangalore are digitally literate, socially connected, and influenced by online peer validation. Strategic social media branding requires integrated content strategies, engagement mechanisms, and eWOM management to strengthen brand equity and maintain competitive advantage.

Figure 1. Strategic Digital Branding through Social Media (SDBSM)

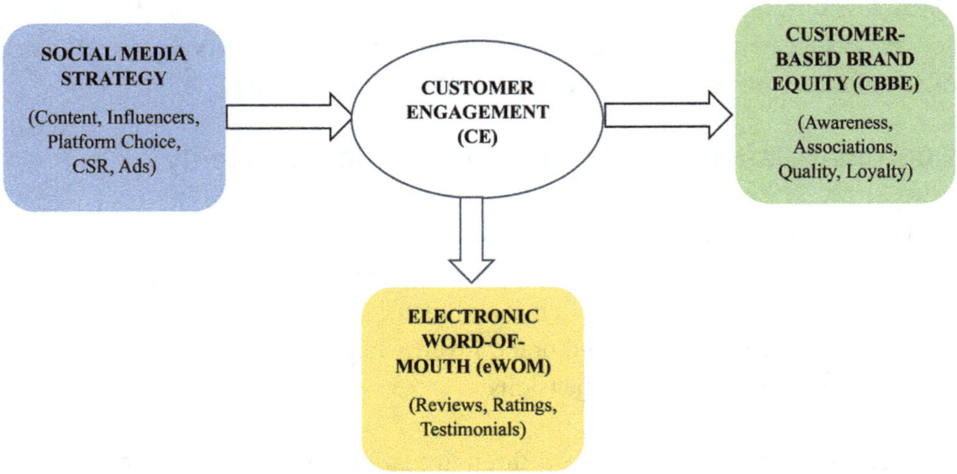

(Created by authors)

METHODOLOGY

Research Design

This study follows a conceptual research design, which involves the systematic synthesis of existing literature to develop a theoretical framework for strategic digital branding through social media in urban hospitality. Conceptual research is particularly suited for topics where empirical evidence is fragmented or limited, allowing scholars to integrate insights from multiple studies to propose new models and propositions (Jabareen, 2009). The primary objective of this conceptual study is to explore the relationships between social media strategies, customer engagement, electronic word-of-mouth (eWOM), and customer-based brand equity (CBBE) in the context of urban hospitality, with a specific focus on Bangalore's hotels. The study does not involve primary data collection; instead, it relies on secondary data sources, including peer-reviewed journal articles, industry reports, and authoritative web sources.

Data Sources and Selection Criteria

The study employs a systematic literature review approach, focusing on high-quality sources published in the last ten years (2015–2025) to ensure the relevance of digital and social media trends in hospitality. The following criteria guided the selection of sources:

1. **Relevance:** Articles must address digital branding, social media marketing, eWOM, customer engagement, or brand equity in hospitality.
2. **Credibility:** Only peer-reviewed journals, industry reports, and publications from recognized organizations (UNWTO, Data Reportal, Hotelivate, etc.) were included.
3. **Contextual Focus:** Preference was given to studies focusing on urban hospitality and emerging economies, particularly India.
4. **Accessibility:** Sources available in English and with full-text access were considered.

Databases searched include Scopus, Web of Science, ScienceDirect, SpringerLink, ResearchGate, and Google Scholar. Keywords used in various combinations included: *"digital branding," "social media marketing," "hospitality," "urban hotels," "customer engagement," "eWOM," "brand equity,"* and *"India."*

Data Analysis Approach

The selected literature was analyzed using a thematic synthesis approach. The steps involved were:

1. **Identification of Key Themes:** Core concepts such as digital branding, social media strategy, customer engagement, eWOM, and CBBE were extracted from the literature.
2. **Comparison and Integration:** Similar concepts were grouped, while contradictory findings were discussed to identify gaps in knowledge.
3. **Model Development:** Based on the synthesis, relationships among themes were conceptualized to propose the Strategic Digital Branding through social media (SDBSM) framework.

The thematic synthesis ensures that the conceptual framework is theoretically grounded, reflects current trends in digital hospitality marketing, and is applicable in the urban Indian context.

RESULTS & DISCUSSIONS

The empirical analysis of the Strategic Digital Branding through social media (SDBSM) framework demonstrates that social media strategy significantly influences customer engagement (CE), which subsequently enhances electronic word-of-mouth (eWOM), ultimately strengthening customer-based brand equity (CBBE). The findings highlight a sequential pathway in which engagement serves as a critical mediator, translating online interactions into measurable brand equity outcomes.

In the context of urban Indian hospitality, particularly Bangalore hotels, unique dynamics emerged. Consumers in this market demonstrate high digital literacy, aspirational behaviours, and selective engagement with digital content, necessitating contextualized and localized social media strategies. Content types, platform choice, influencer partnerships, and CSR communication were found to significantly shape CE, which drives eWOM behaviours such as reviews, testimonials, and digital recommendations. Positive eWOM, in turn, reinforces CBBE by enhancing brand awareness, perceived quality, brand associations, and loyalty. The results also indicate a direct effect of social media strategy on brand equity, suggesting that well-crafted campaigns may influence CBBE beyond the mediating role of engagement, corroborating findings by McDonald (2025) and Wibowo et al (2024).

These outcomes affirm previous research on the role of digital branding in hospitality (Keller, 1993; Anwar et al., 2024; Vivek et al., 2012) while highlighting the integrated pathway of social media strategy → CE → eWOM → CBBE, which has not been extensively explored in the Indian urban hospitality sector. The study also underscores that consumer engagement is both cognitive and emotional, aligning with the multidimensional CE constructs described by Vivek et al. (2012), and that eWOM is a critical conduit for converting engagement into tangible brand equity benefits (Litvin et al., 2008; Qenaj & Beqiri, 2022).

OUTCOMES AND IMPLICATIONS

Theoretical Implications

This research extends Keller's (1993) CBBE framework by integrating digital marketing and social media dynamics, demonstrating the significant mediating role of CE and the subsequent effect on eWOM. It enriches the literature on digital branding, particularly in emerging urban markets, by showing that the effectiveness of social media strategies is context-dependent, shaped by local consumer behavior, digital literacy, and aspirational trends. The study also provides a framework for understanding how integrated digital strategies can influence brand perception and loyalty, offering a model for future empirical testing in other non-Western contexts.

Additionally, the SDBSM framework contributes to relationship marketing theory by confirming that engagement is not merely an outcome but a mediating mechanism that translates online interactions into value for both the consumer and the brand (Müller et al., 2025; Moisescu et al., 2022). It also aligns with studies emphasizing the importance of eWOM in reputation management and digital advocacy (Sánchez-González & González-Fernández, 2021; Sağtaş, 2022).

Practical Implications

For practitioners, the study provides actionable insights to enhance digital branding strategies in urban Indian hospitality:

1. **Localized Content and Platform Strategy:** Hotels should design social media campaigns tailored to local consumer preferences, incorporating city-specific culture, trends, and digital behaviours.
2. **Influencer Marketing and CSR Integration:** Collaborating with influencers and communicating CSR initiatives can increase engagement and generate positive eWOM.
3. **Proactive eWOM Management:** Monitoring online reviews and encouraging digital advocacy ensures sustained brand equity, mitigates negative feedback, and strengthens customer loyalty.
4. **Engagement Metrics as Predictors:** Likes, shares, comments, and user-generated content (UGC) can be tracked as leading indicators of brand equity outcomes, enabling real-time strategy adjustments.

Overall, the study equips hotel managers with a practical roadmap for implementing strategic social media campaigns that convert digital interactions into long-term brand equity and competitive advantage.

CONCLUSION

The study provides a comprehensive understanding of Strategic Digital Branding through social media (SDBSM) in the urban Indian hospitality context. It confirms that social media strategies significantly influence customer engagement, which acts as a mediator for electronic word-of-mouth, ultimately shaping customer-based brand equity. Engagement emerges as a central mechanism, translating online interactions into tangible brand outcomes such as awareness, perceived quality, associations, and loyalty. From a theoretical perspective, the research extends Keller's (1993) CBBE model by incorporating digital touchpoints and validating the integrated CE → eWOM → CBBE pathway. The study also highlights the contextual specificity of urban Indian consumers, emphasizing the need for localized, culturally relevant, and aspirational digital branding strategies.

Practically, the study provides actionable insights for hotel managers to design targeted social media campaigns, monitor engagement metrics, foster positive eWOM, and strengthen overall brand equity. The findings underscore the broader implications of digital transformation in hospitality branding, demonstrating that effective social media strategies require strategic planning, contextual understanding, and proactive engagement management. Finally, the SDBSM framework offers both a conceptual and empirical foundation for future research, enabling scholars to explore cross-cultural, sector-specific, and longitudinal applications of social media strategies in enhancing brand equity. The study contributes to the literature on digital branding, customer engagement, eWOM, and urban hospitality marketing, providing a roadmap for both theory and practice in emerging markets.

REFERENCES

Aaker, D. A. (1996). *Building strong brands*. Free Press.

Anwar, F. A., Deliana, D., & Suyamto, S. (2024). Digital Transformation in the Hospitality Industry: Improving Efficiency and Guest Experience. *International Journal of Management Science and Information Technology*, *4*(2), 428–437. DOI: 10.35870/ijmsit.v4i2.3201

Dwivedi, Y. K., Ismagilova, E., Hughes, D. L., & Carlson, J. (2021). Setting the future of digital and social media marketing research: Perspectives and research propositions. *International Journal of Information Management*, *59*(1), 1–37. DOI: 10.1016/j.ijinfomgt.2020.102168

HTL. H. (2024). *India Hotel Market Review 2024 The Global Leader in Hospitality Consulting*. https://horwathhtl.com/wp-content/uploads/2025/02/India-Hotel-Market-Report-2024.pdf

Jabareen, Y. (2009). Building a Conceptual Framework: Philosophy, Definitions, and Procedure. *International Journal of Qualitative Methods*, *8*(4), 49–62. DOI: 10.1177/160940690900800406

Keller, K. L. (1993). Conceptualizing, Measuring, and Managing Customer-Based Brand Equity. *Journal of Marketing*, *57*(1), 1–22. DOI: 10.1177/002224299305700101

Khanna, A., & Gopinath, S. (2024). *2 0 2 4 I N D I A N Trends & Opportunities Managing Partner, Strategic Advisory Senior Associate, Strategic Advisory*. https://hotelivate.com/wp-content/uploads/2024/10/Indian-Hospitality-Trends-Opportunities-2024.pdf

Kotler, P., Bowen, J., Makens, J., & Baloglu, S. (2017). *Marketing for Hospitality and Tourism*. Pearson. https://www.slithm.edu.lk/wp content/uploads/2022/02/marketing_for_hospitalitytourism.pdf

Litvin, S. W., Goldsmith, R. E., & Pan, B. (2008). Electronic word-of-mouth in Hospitality and Tourism Management. *Tourism Management*, *29*(3), 458–468. DOI: 10.1016/j.tourman.2007.05.011

McDonald, E. (2025, January 21). *Influencer Marketing in Hospitality: Grow Brand Reach & Bookings | dblspc*. Dblspc. https://dblspc.com/insights/influencer-marketing-hospitality-industry/

Moisescu, O.-I., Gică, O.-A., & Herle, F.-A. (2022). Boosting eWOM through Social Media Brand Page Engagement: The Mediating Role of Self-Brand Connection. *Behavioral Sciences (Basel, Switzerland), 12*(11), 411. DOI: 10.3390/bs12110411 PMID: 36354388

Müller, R., Coffie, I. S., de Klerk, N., & Schalkwyk, J. H. (2025). Enhancing Consumer Social Media Brand Engagement: An Examination of the Interactive Influence of Perceived Utilitarian and Hedonic Benefit. *Business Perspectives and Research*. Advance online publication. DOI: 10.1177/22785337251342838

Murniati, M., & Bawono, S. (2020). *Hotel Marketing Strategies in the Digital Age*. Hotel Marketing Strategies in the Digital Age., DOI: 10.54204/329258

Qenaj, M., & Beqiri, G. (2022). Social Media Marketing in Hospitality Industry and Its Effect on Consumer Behavior in Kosovo. *IFAC-PapersOnLine, 55*(39), 66–69. DOI: 10.1016/j.ifacol.2022.12.012

Rialti, R., Kvítková, Z., Pompurová, K., Kushcheva, N., & Marrucci, A. (2025). *Online Reputation Management in the Context of Tourism and Hospitality*. https://strategie.vse.cz/wp-content/uploads/7.0.-ORM-book-final-1.pdf

Sağtaş, S. (2022). The effect of social media marketing on brand equity and consumer purchasing intention. *Journal of Life Economics, 9*(1), 21–31. DOI: 10.15637/jlecon.9.1.02

Sánchez-González, G., & González-Fernández, A. M. (2021). The Influence of Quality on eWOM: A Digital Transformation in Hotel Management. *Frontiers in Psychology, 11*. Advance online publication. DOI: 10.3389/fpsyg.2020.612324 PMID: 33519629

Vivek, S. D., Beatty, S., & Morgan, R. M. (2012). *(PDF) Customer Engagement: Exploring Customer Relationships Beyond Purchase*. ResearchGate., DOI: 10.2307/23243811

Wibowo, S. E., Almasari Aksenta, Hartanto, S., & Politeknik Negeri Samarinda. (2024). The Strategic Role Of Brand Storytelling In Enhancing Marketing Management And Brand Awareness On Social Media Platforms-Sarwo Eddy Wibowo et.al The Strategic Role Of Brand Storytelling In Enhancing Marketing Management And Brand Awareness On Social Media Platforms. *Jurnal Multidisiplin Sahombu, 4*(2), 343–348. https://doi.org/DOI: 10.58471/jms.v4i02

Chapter 11

The Impact of User-Generated Content on Business Performance:

Strategic Insights for Hospitality in the Social Media Era

Aaditya Sharma
http://orcid.org/0009-0008-4318-3640
Christ University, Delhi NCR, India

Babita Chaudhary
http://orcid.org/0009-0003-2854-6670
Christ University, Delhi NCR, India

Charu Sehgal
http://orcid.org/0000-0002-4607-4625
Christ University, Delhi NCR, India

ABSTRACT

This chapter focuses on how user-generated content (UGC) has a significant effect on the business of the hospitality industry. The chapter delves into the extent to which online reviews, social media posts, and other consumer-generated content influence brand perception, customer trust, and, eventually, the financial results. By utilizing theories such as signalling theory, network effects, and social influence, the chapter sees UGC as not only feedback but also a strategic marketing tool. The chapter talks about research results, case studies from around the world and India, and also mentions AI and sentiment analysis as tools for reputation monitoring and

DOI: 10.4018/979-8-3373-6741-5.ch011

management. Lastly, it considers ethical and governance issues and provides a set of practical strategies for hospitality firms to use UGC for innovation, customer engagement, and achieving a sustainable competitive advantage.

1. INTRODUCTION

In Today's digital era, User-Generated Content (UGC) shapes how people connect online, changing choices and competition - especially in travel and hotels. Instead of ads from companies, it's made up of real feedback: comments, photos, clips, or updates shared freely by users themselves. Not planned like brand messages, this kind of material feels honest because it comes from actual experiences. Because it seems genuine, folks tend to trust it more when deciding what to buy or where to go.

Digital sites like TripAdvisor or Booking.com - along with Yelp, Instagram, Facebook, even TikTok - push more traveller reviews into view, letting people post real talk about where they stayed. Blogs, video logs, and online groups add depth through personal stories, side-by-side picks, plus hands-on takes from trips. So nowadays, folks planning travel can dig into loads of honest feedback from others who've been there - covering things like how good the service felt, what rooms were like, prices, and whether it was worth it.

People often pick hotels based on what others say online. Even slightly better reviews can mean way more reservations (Ye *et al.*, 2011). Instead of ads, folks believe real traveller stories - so user posts act like a shortcut to knowing if something's good. That shift helps balance the info gap, so guests don't have to rely only on what companies tell them.

The growth of user-made content ties into how hotels and travel services are changing online - now travellers shape stories more than companies do. Customers don't just consume - they help build a brand's image, sharing praise or complaints alike. Because of this shift, businesses need to keep an eye on feedback, reply when needed, also use it smartly if they want to keep up.

The rising role of user-created content makes sense from different angles. As more people post stuff online, sites get better because of network-driven gains. What you see shared acts like a trustworthy hint about how good something really is - thanks to signalling ideas. When tons of these posts pile up, companies use them to spot trends and make smarter choices, which shows why data feedback loops matter.

UGC boosts user involvement by letting people comment, react, share stuff, tag others, or join chat threads. That builds momentum - more activity leads to fresh posts, shifting how folks see things and what they want. Companies get perks like cheaper promotion, real-world feedback, shared storytelling - but face downsides too, such as bad ratings, fast-moving backlash, or damage to their image.

The Indian hotel scene shows exactly how user-generated content can shake things up. Thanks to phones being everywhere and travel apps growing fast, locals now check ratings or posts before booking trips. Big chains down to small guesthouses ask guests to share thoughts - then use those real-life stories to stand out, get better, and promote themselves. It's part of a bigger move worldwide: people want honest info, real voices, and brands they can interact with online.

2. BACKGROUND

The hotel business once shared info using pamphlets, commercials, or official notes. Yet today platforms such as TripAdvisor, Google Reviews, Booking.com, Instagram, even YouTube allow guests to post personal stories. Due to this change, everyday visitors have greater impact as compared to big chains before. Content made by users guides decisions, alters faith in labels, plus changes how firms show uniqueness (Ye *et al.,* 2011).

More people sharing on forums usually leads to smarter choices - what happens there changes because of that energy. As folks plan trips, actual stories give clarity rather than leaving them lost or confused. Real talk like this eases doubts, making unknowns feel less risky. Companies get raw insights along with visibility thanks to authentic word-of-mouth chatter. But drawbacks pop up too - ugly reviews go viral quick, fake rants can twist public opinion, and depending heavily on third-party platforms brings its own risks.

3. OBJECTIVE OF THE CHAPTER

- **Explain the impact of User-Generated Content (UGC) on hotel performance and brand image.**

The section looks at how visitor-written content shapes trust, affects competition, changes income trends, boosts return trips, also impacts online reach.

- **Show how user-created content can open doors - yet also bring risks.**

Real comments boost trust plus drive more reservations, but false or harmful posts might hurt your image fast - unless you handle them right away.

- **Look into moral issues, tech hurdles, or leadership problems tied to user-created content.**

This covers things like false info, shaky data accuracy, worries about personal privacy - also calls for clear, accountable online behaviour.

- **Develop a strategic framework for the responsible use of UGC in hospitality.**

The section gives practical ways to use visitor comments when shaping ads, boosting service quality, designing experiences, or refining how a brand talks to people.

- **Give clear tips that hotel bosses can actually use - because real help beats theory any day.**

Simple steps show how to track, study, spark engagement, or reply to user-created content - so leaders can turn it into a valuable tool that boosts brand strength while staying ahead of rivals.

4. LITERATURE REVIEW

4.1 Theoretical Foundation of User-Generated Content and Firm-Generated Content

Firm-Generated Content (FGC) means any kind of message made, managed, or shared by a company to promote itself, build its image, or share info. It covers ads, main websites, flyers, sponsored social updates, news announcements, along with sales-driven efforts. The goal is to shape how people see the brand - on purpose using clear messaging that lines up with what the business stands for, what it sells, while showing why it matters.

User-generated stuff comes from regular guests who share real-life moments about a stay or service. Unlike brand-made material, this type of content pops up naturally online. Instead, it shows unfiltered opinions through pictures, short clips, notes, or blog entries. People post these on sites like TripAdvisor, Google, Instagram, or TikTok without being paid. Companies don't manage what gets said here. Because it's raw and honest, folks tend to trust it more. Its strength? Realness, feeling relatable, and seeming unbiased.

The main contrast between FGC and UGC comes down to source - alongside how reliable people think it is. Instead of branded content, UGC feels more honest since it shows actual user moments. A study from Yang, Ren, and Adomavicius (2019) found customer-made updates on business pages get way more attention than official ones - especially if they show true feelings or specific stories. Acting like digital peer reviews, UGC heavily influences how buyers see quality, reliability, and worth, even more so in travel and hotels where you can't touch the service before buying.

Still, FGC matters a lot. Even if customers doubt what companies say, it cuts through the noise - laying out clear facts on things like facilities, service levels, beliefs, and commitments. Real-world results show mixing both content kinds works best. It defines the brand's personality; at the same time, user posts build trust and show real people back it up.

Dealing with both guest posts and company content means staying involved. Hotels need to keep an eye on comments, reply right when guests speak up - while making sure what people think matches the real story. A bunch of places today use traveller's pictures, quotes, or personal experiences in ads so they can mix realness with polished branding. That blend builds stronger confidence, makes things clearer - and keeps their online image fair and believable.

4.2 Network Effects and Switching Costs

UGC-based platforms grow stronger as more people join and share content - this is called network effects (Subramanian, Mitra, & Ransbotham, 2021). Greater usage leads to better exposure; it also strengthens response cycles while boosting motivation to take part. This creates a cycle that supports active users alongside platform owners. Still, if leaving the platform is easy, strong activity may not lead to lasting profits. According to Subramanian *et al.* (2021), companies benefiting from interactive content - such as live discussions or replies - gain more advantage from these network dynamics compared to sites hosting only fixed reviews.

In the hospitality context, potential switching costs can range from loyalty programs or familiarity with a particular brand, to personalized digital experiences that tie consumers to a particular platform or hotel consulting. By increasing the emotional and experiential connections associated with UGC, effective "management" of UGC increases switching costs—ultimately converting potential or casual guests into brand advocates. For instance, hotels that support and facilitate robust online communities or user forums create stickiness that strengthens customer retention and repeat booking logic.

4.3 Signalling Theory and Source Credibility

Signalling theory helps explain how customer-created content affects what people think about services, especially in areas like hotels or restaurants where info gaps are common. Because buyers can't judge service quality ahead of time, they use visible hints - so-called signals - to guess reliability and standards. Content shared online by users, including comments on websites or updates on platforms, serves as an unofficial but strong indicator of a company's level of care, honesty, or consistency. Favourable ratings work like reassurance tools; these lower doubt and make risks feel smaller. On the flip side, poor remarks serve as alerts, warning future guests about likely problems (Wilson, Murphy, & Fierro, 2012).

The trustworthiness of user-generated content strongly affects how convincing it is. Rather than just focusing on the message itself, people also judge whether the person who made it seems reliable, knowledgeable, or genuine. Research by Narangajavana Kaosiri *et al.* (2019) shows that feedback from close connections - like friends or those with similar travel habits - has greater influence on traveller expectations and happiness than input from distant acquaintances. Within tourism services, proof such as confirmed guest reviews, thorough personal accounts, or trusted public figures can boost perceived authenticity, particularly if paired with images, video clips, or real-life narratives.

In comparison, vague or empty reviews tend to convince fewer people since they miss signs of reliability or knowledge. Because of this, user-created content works best when it comes from someone seen as honest and skilled. So, brands can shape their UGC by pushing real, confirmed opinions while teaming up with known figures to grow confidence. By using signalling ideas along with studies on source trust, hotels and similar businesses can see clearer how online activity and ratings guide buyer choices - and boost both image and results.

4.4 Data Network Effects and AI Analytics

Recent progress in AI has changed how digital platforms create value through user networks. According to Gregory *et al.* (2021), when platforms use collected data to improve services, they grow more useful for everyone involved. In tourism settings, machine learning turns customer-generated feedback into practical knowledge - by spotting emotions, forecasting drop-offs, or adjusting offers. As an example, examining word choice and mood in guest reviews helps algorithms detect issues like room hygiene or employee attitude; this allows lodging providers to act quickly and enhance performance.

The interplay between data networks and AI analysis allows adaptive pricing, customised promotions, together with image oversight. While hotels applying machine learning to process large volumes of user-created material gain an edge through forecasting tools, concerns about dependence on information emerge - such as confidentiality risks, skewed decision models, alongside monetising private interactions - matters upcoming regulatory approaches need to handle openly.

4.5 UGC and Business Performance Metrics

4.5.1 Sales and Booking Performance

Research repeatedly shows user-created content strongly affects sales and reservations in tourism. Favourable feedback, scores, or mentions on platforms don't just change how people see a brand - these elements shift real-world results. As shown by Ye *et al.* (2011), guest comments notably affect room bookings, revealing eWOM's power to turn interest into action. In parallel, Liu (2020) linked emotional tone in UGC to changes in hotel company share prices, implying digital image impacts economic indicators, not only customer choices.

Hotels rely on how visible their reviews are and whether those reviews are positive or negative to influence customer demand. A stronger rating usually leads to more reservations, along with the chance to charge higher prices than rivals with weaker scores (Xiang *et al.*, 2017). This effect ties back to what's called "reputational capital," meaning good feedback builds up gradually, giving some properties an edge that boosts income. On the flip side, poor comments reduce occupancy rates - pushing hotels toward price cuts - a sign of how much money depends on handling user-generated content well.

Apart from individual bookings, strong digital credibility influences multiple platforms like travel websites and social networks. Good ratings increase visibility online, attract visitors naturally, while also encouraging referrals through personal recommendations - fuelling ongoing reservations and income growth. Properties monitoring guest comments, replying promptly, using shared content gain practical knowledge; this helps adjust costs, improve offers, or upgrade facilities aiming at higher room usage and financial returns.

4.5.2 Stock Market Impact for Listed Hospitality Firms

User-generated content acts as a key signal for how people feel about brands right now, influencing stock outcomes for public hospitality firms. Because of the digital landscape, investors use massive amounts of emotional cues from sites like Twitter, TripAdvisor, or Google Reviews to judge customer mood and forecast market trends. Using data from 84 million social messages, Liu (2020) showed that bad feelings often come before falling share values - especially in B2C areas such as hotels, where emotions shape brand worth.

The link stems from how investors interpret data and respond to signals. Because user-generated content acts like a fast, unofficial channel, it shows changes in customer sentiment ahead of official earnings results. When bad reviews spread quickly - or complaints go viral - investors often react right away, expecting lower income later, which leads to selling shares. On the flip side, if upbeat posts gain traction - like exciting travel stories or eco-friendly actions - it tends to lift market confidence, pushing stock prices up at least for a while.

Leading hotels like Marriott and Lemon Tree now use online feedback tools to shape how they talk to investors and handle risks. Instead of waiting, these platforms spot mood shifts across social media - giving insight into possible market moves. While updating financial reports with public opinion data, hotel brands can catch reputation issues early or highlight glowing user reviews when speaking with shareholders. Essentially, what customers post isn't just noise - it’s become a key indicator linking guest satisfaction directly to company value.

4.5.3 Customer Trust, Loyalty, and Satisfaction

Customer trust, loyalty, and satisfaction are key emotional aspects of hospitality experiences - here, user-created content significantly shapes how people think and feel. In this setting, trust comes from what seems honest and genuine. According to Narangajavana *et al.* (2017), reviews by peers - especially those seen as authentic or familiar - lower uncertainty while boosting confidence in the business. Positive comments from actual guests help others accept the brand as dependable; because of this, their outlook improves along with their readiness to interact.

When these expectations are fulfilled - or go beyond - satisfaction turns into commitment. This shift is strengthened through one-sided emotional ties people build with brands they identify with (Leung *et al.*, 2013). Take a traveller who keeps reading genuine accounts of kind staff or tailored experiences at a certain hotel; gradually, a bond forms without them ever stepping inside. Such feelings frequently result in word-of-mouth promotion: satisfied guests then share favourable online content on their own, fuelling ongoing trust development.

Still, trust may fade fast if users post harmful or mixed feedback. According to cognitive bias theory, people notice bad details more than good ones, which makes it hard to fix a damaged image. Being open involves replying quickly and with empathy to issues, while showing real steps taken - this helps rebuild confidence. Firms like Marriott and Taj set strong examples by answering publicly, owning their mistakes, rather than just reacting. This kind of responsibility may lower post-purchase regret while making the brand seem more personal, since it shows concern. Overall, handling user-generated content well transforms digital exchanges into opportunities for connection - building familiarity, ongoing engagement via reliability, positive experiences, and deeper emotional ties.

5. ISSUES, CONTROVERSIES, AND PROBLEMS OF UGC

5.1 Negative Sentiment and Reputational Risks

While guests' online feedback helps hotels, bad opinions can damage their image fast through websites like TripAdvisor or social networks. One unhappy customer's post may spread widely on Google Reviews and travel discussion boards before staff even notice it. According to Yang *et al.* (2019), unfavourable remarks show up more often than good ones; they get shared more because emotional posts are pushed by site systems. These reviews affect travellers' choices stronger compared to praise since platforms favour strong feelings in what users see.

Hotels are more vulnerable since guest experiences rely on services that happen in real time - small mistakes matter a lot. Issues like unclean rooms, unfriendly staff, delays, or broken facilities often lead to complaints without delay. People tend to focus more on bad reviews than positive ones - a tendency called negativity bias. According to Manaman *et al.* (2016), just several negative ratings may weaken the impact of numerous good ones, which damages credibility, cuts down reservations, and affects income directly.

The faster negative user content spreads, the higher the chance problems will escalate. When complaints include images or video, they tend to seem more trustworthy - triggering widespread online debate or even news coverage. Such exposure can magnify minor service flaws into major public incidents, harming brand image over time.

To handle such risks, hotels should use live tracking tools that follow feedback, online discussions, and emotional trends. Because spotting problems early means quicker reactions, showing care, which can lower negative responses. When replies are straightforward yet polished - recognizing concerns while explaining fixes - it boosts trust with both existing and new visitors.

Negative user content offers useful feedback for growth. By examining repeated issues, businesses spot weaknesses, shape employee development, while boosting reliability across services. If updates are shared openly, hospitality providers may turn critiques into trust, showing real dedication to meeting visitor needs.

Fair treatment of user input matters. Altering ratings, covering up issues, or posting false compliments weakens trust - leading to scepticism over time. In contrast, careful oversight, insights from real data, while openly responding builds credibility; supporting steady growth and lasting brand strength.

5.2 Fake and Manipulated Content

The growth of rating websites and social media has raised concerns about false or altered customer posts, affecting how trustworthy hotel details appear online. Fake evaluations - made by automated accounts, rival businesses, or hired writers - skew opinions while weakening confidence. According to Baka (2016), this kind of material interferes with digital reputation mechanisms, causing uncertainty for guests depending on real experiences when judging accommodations prior to reservations.

Fake user-generated content takes various shapes. Some misleading reviews boost scores on purpose, whereas harmful ones hurt a company's trust - usually shared by competitors or upset people. Such posts don't reflect real use and set skewed impressions. Signs of falseness involve overly dramatic language, copied phrases, odd timing clusters, or matching review behaviours across accounts (Xiang *et al.*, 2017).

To reduce these dangers, hotels ought to use both tech systems along with employee monitoring. While artificial intelligence may detect irregularities - like grouped five-star feedback or repetitive phrasing - workers with proper training are better at judging mood and meaning. Confirming guest stays via booking records improves trustworthiness; this way, visitors find it easier to tell real comments apart from fake ones.

Working together, hotels and review sites still play a key role. Although platforms such as TripAdvisor or Google Reviews apply automated systems to spot fake feedback, mistakes continue to happen. To improve reliability, lodging providers can flag questionable entries while guiding customers on how to recognize credible information. Open communication combined with consistent oversight safeguards image online, offering visitors a clearer picture of what to expect.

5.3 Over-Dependence on Third-Party Platforms

A key issue with guest-posted content lies in how much hotels now depend on outside sites like TripAdvisor, Booking.com, Yelp, or Expedia. Although these channels boost exposure, they reduce direct oversight of brand presentation. Site algorithms decide which reviews appear first, where properties rank in searches, also what gets shown prominently - forcing hotels to lean on tech systems beyond their reach. According to Xiang et al. (2017), unexpected shifts in rating rules, filtering methods, or suggestion tools might suddenly affect reservations.

This reliance weakens control over how hotels present themselves online. Even small changes in algorithms might drop a hotel's position in results, reducing exposure while cutting bookings. Moreover, outside booking sites typically take fees, block direct access to guest information, yet reduce the depth of performance analysis required to improve experiences or tailor solutions.

To lower these risks, hotels ought to improve their online presence - like official sites, mobile apps, or brand-run social spaces. Since guests post feedback across owned and third-party sites, venues gain wider reach while depending less on one source. Features including app-based requests for ratings, reward-connected response options, or visitor chat boards make it easier to collect real traveler content straightaway.

Diversification through various platforms - especially owned media - shields hotels from unexpected changes in algorithms; at the same time, it boosts autonomy in shaping brand narratives, adjusting promotional approaches, or maintaining digital credibility over years.

5.4 Information Overload and Consumer Fatigue

Folks often find real value in user-generated content, yet too many reviews, pics, comments, and likes pile up fast - making choices tougher instead of easier. Hit with tons of clashing takes - one person loves it, another hates it - and picking what matters gets messy. All that noise gums up thinking, leaving some stuck, others skimming surface stuff, or just trusting stars cause digging deeper feels exhausting.

Too much info gets worse because site systems highlight popular posts - not truthful ones - based on clicks, not quality. If it's hard to tell what matters, people lean on obvious ratings instead of overall opinion, which might lead them wrong. In travel and hotels, picking options usually means big money and effort; mental tiredness from sorting noise can weaken trust, making user opinions less helpful when deciding.

5.5 Ethical Concerns in Data Use

Using AI to handle user posts is becoming more common, yet it brings up serious moral questions. Hotels and online services dig into tons of customer reviews - not just to spot patterns but also to guess what people might do next or tailor suggestions accordingly. Still, how they use that info can feel shady when it comes to keeping things private, treating users equally, or being clear about their methods - especially according to Gregory and team back in 2021.

For one thing, people might not know how their comments, pictures, or browsing habits get gathered, kept, or used - so they can't really agree knowingly. On top of that, artificial intelligence fed with skewed examples could accidentally push outdated ideas, highlight some opinions over others, or hide real complaints without meaning to. Besides this, hidden systems leave folks confused about why specific places show up first, which makes them doubt if the results are truly fair.

Misuse of visitor information - like weak safeguards, unclear tracking, or unfair ad choices - often breaks customer confidence and hurts how people see a brand. So hotels and services should handle data responsibly, focusing on openness, strong privacy steps, while ensuring automated systems stay fair in user-generated spaces shaped by artificial intelligence.

6. CASE STUDIES AND BEST PRACTICES

6.1 Global Examples: TripAdvisor, Booking.com, and Yelp

TripAdvisor still holds strong influence across the global travel sector, using user-created content to directly affect how travellers view hotels and how properties perform. Compared to sites like Expedia or Yelp, research by Xiang *et al.* (2017) shows its reviews contain more varied word choices and stronger emotional tones. Because of this, guests tend to share richer stories about their stays - offering specific details instead of simple ratings. These detailed inputs help future visitors make better booking decisions; at the same time, they give property managers useful data for improving service delivery and daily operations.

TripAdvisor's system gives more weight to recent and steady feedback, pushing hotels to keep service quality stable over time. Those offering strong guest experiences tend to get higher scores - also gaining better placement in search outcomes due to algorithm preferences. Leading establishments use active approaches to manage reviews, making sure each comment - good or critical - is replied to promptly. They thank visitors openly for praise while handling issues with practical solutions, showing they're attentive and clear in communication. Such actions help build confidence among users, encouraging more guests to share opinions - which boosts image and improves position in rankings.

Moreover, TripAdvisor helps hotels examine combined feedback, highlighting patterns in customer happiness along with aspects needing upgrades. By spotting repeated problems - like slow cleaning services, poor restaurant experiences, or late arrivals during check-ins - properties take focused steps to fix them. With this organized method of handling user content, the site shifts from just being a review hub toward becoming a practical resource for better performance and market edge.

Booking.com embeds user-generated content straight into its booking process, tying each comment to an actual reservation. Because stays are verified, false or biased reviews appear far less often, making feedback more trustworthy. Instead of just collecting opinions, the platform uses smart algorithms to detect emotions in texts, sorting remarks under common topics like "check-in speed," "room cleanliness," or "helpful staff." By analysing these patterns, hotels gain clear comparisons with similar properties while spotting concrete areas for improvement. If several guests mention noisy hallways, for instance, management might invest in better sound insulation. Since input comes from real visits and gets processed automatically, it becomes a reliable resource for decision-making - shifting focus from promotion toward measurable service upgrades.

Yelp, though mostly linked to restaurants, offers useful insights into building active user communities - insights hotels could apply. Firms responding regularly to feedback, keeping profiles updated, yet interacting with customers tend to stay more visible and retain guests better. The platform rewards frequent, thoughtful reviews via its "Elite Reviewer" group, which motivates honest input. Accommodation providers might mirror this by spotlighting loyal guests through membership perks or public shout-outs online. Recognizing such engaged users fosters genuine content shared voluntarily. This kind of material boosts trust in the brand while spreading awareness naturally.

6.1.1 Indian Hotel Industry Applications

In India, use of user-generated content has grown quickly - not just among high-end brands but also affordable ones - showing more firms now see its value. Take Taj Hotels: they run a system called "Voice of the Guest," pulling input from platforms like TripAdvisor and Google Reviews alongside their own surveys, shared each day with leadership teams. When guests leave critical comments, alerts go out instantly to responsible units, allowing fast fixes. This marks a move inside the company - from slow reactions to quicker, guest-focused responses - with UGC treated as key data, not occasional notes. Solving issues regularly helps improve service standards while signalling that listening is part of how they operate.

OYO Rooms, a tech-focused lodging brand, relies on user-generated content analysis to drive expansion. Its custom software pulls feedback from various sites - this allows flexible pricing strategies along with tailored services and better results across many locations. Through consistent review of emotional tone in comments, the firm spots trends in what guests want, modifies amenities accordingly, while boosting satisfaction at scale. Such an evidence-based method highlights how crowdsourced insights can shape key choices, daily operations, and customized stays within extensive, geographically spread accommodation chains.

Lemon Tree Hotels uses a mix of company-created posts along with user-shared material to show openness, diversity, and ethical values. Their online efforts often spotlight team members who have disabilities - content that visitors then repost or comment on widely. Because of this approach, customer-contributed content becomes a tool for emotional resonance, building stronger bonds with clients while supporting CSR goals at the same time. When personal guest stories align with core brand themes, it shows how public input helps manage image, shape identity, and involve audiences more deeply.

Such cases from India show how carefully handled user-generated content can set businesses apart. Where hotels build systems to respond to reviews, they develop ways to keep improving services, connect better with guests, or strengthen their public image. Acting early on such inputs encourages attentiveness, quicker responses, yet also sharpens daily performance - this in turn makes brands seem more genuine, trustworthy for future visitors.

7. SOLUTIONS AND OPPORTUNITIES OF UGC FOR HOTELS

7.1 Enhancing Authenticity and Credibility

In the hospitality sector, how real something feels strongly shapes guest trust and choices. Since these services focus on experience, travellers can't judge their quality ahead of time. Online feedback like comments, images, clips, or social updates helps show genuineness - because they come from personal use instead of polished brand statements (Wilson, Murphy, & Fierro, 2012).

The trustworthiness of user-created content comes from how others influence perception. Because travellers see posts from peers, they tend to view them as honest reflections of what to expect. According to Leung *et al.* (2013), guests rely more on traveller reviews than on marketing messages put out by accommodations. Favourable comments serve like casual recommendations, showing that people were happy with their stay; at the same time, balanced or critical remarks suggest honesty and a business ready to grow. Together - proof of good service and responsiveness - builds stronger believability, fitting well with today's demand for real-life travel stories.

UGC makes the hotel feel more personal. Instead of sleek ads, real guest posts give a clearer picture of what to expect. A photo showing a room layout, employees helping out, or facilities posted by visitors builds credibility and connection. Especially younger users - like Millennials and Gen Z - tend to trust genuine material rather than staged marketing images, looking for stories that mirror everyday situations. Visual content from guests - including clips, temporary social updates, or travel logs - adds depth by giving direct impressions of staying at the property.

Hotels may inspire user-created content by offering fair rewards. For example, reward schemes, interactive rating games, or narrative challenges prompt visitors to post genuine stories without feeling pressured. When hotels highlight this material on their main websites or social pages, it boosts believability and shows openness. Handling feedback carefully - responding to compliments as well as helpful criticism - reflects active listening, reduces image-related dangers, and strengthens confidence in future travellers.

UGC creates shared trust through online networks. As several travellers repeatedly mention good features of a hotel, their combined opinions boost its image in digital spaces. People considering a stay may see this group feedback as trustworthy - regardless of whether they interact with the posts themselves. The wider impact of user content spread's reliability past one-on-one exchanges, affecting how the hotel is viewed on various sites.

In recent years, digital tools have grown more common. As a result, realness gives some businesses an edge over others. Firms that support honest guest posts stand out in busy markets - especially those using photos or videos made by visitors. These materials boost interaction with future travellers, helping them see worth early on, building confidence before any reservation is made. Still, honesty matters most when rewards are involved. Properties should avoid offers that trick people, instead checking submissions regularly to reduce false details. Clarifying if a reviewer got a perk - or simply promoting truthful stays - keeps faith strong in shared stories.

7.2 Co-Creating Value with Customers

People don't only buy - they create, thanks to content made by users. Research from Huang *et al.* (2019) reveals that interaction on digital spaces increases involvement due to shared dialogue instead of top-down messaging. When it comes to tourism, travellers post insights which help refine services; at the same time, companies collect practical feedback to adjust their models. Such interactions build deeper confidence, as contributions matter more than mere purchases.

Guest feedback about meals, room layout, or employee actions gradually influences service updates. Thanks to continuous input, lodging places refine their features using collected insights. These changes align with Service-Dominant Logic - value forms through joint effort instead of being set solely by suppliers.

Online movements such as “MyStayStory” or “ViewFromMyRoom” blend marketing with user-driven moments. Hotels like Hilton and Taj collect guest images to craft narratives based on authentic situations - highlighting diversity, emotion, connection - that make brands feel more relatable. Instead of polished ads, they rely on personal snapshots that reflect genuine stays. This strategy shifts focus from perfection toward realism, encouraging trust through everyday scenes. By showcasing different voices, companies appear less corporate, more human.

7.3 Leveraging Positive Reviews for Marketing

Positive reviews created by guests have become a powerful, low-cost way for hotels to reach more people. Instead of using polished ads bought through media channels, this type of content shows real moments experienced by visitors - making it feel more trustworthy to future travellers. One comment, image, or star rating posted online - on sites like TripAdvisor, Google Reviews, or Instagram - can quickly impact many possible bookings while costing almost nothing. According to Ye *et al.* (2011), recommendations coming from actual stays lead to more conversions compared to standard digital ads, showing how valuable genuine stories can be in attracting new customers.

The use of positive user-generated content in hotel marketing helps create emotional connections while also building trust. Instead, showing actual guest stories lets companies reach people more personally compared to standard ads. As an illustration, Marriott's "Travel Brilliantly" used photos from travellers to emphasize genuine travel moments; similarly, Airbnb's "Made Possible by Hosts" built its entire message around customer-shared experiences. These examples show how UGC makes brands feel more relatable, supports core values, and deepens consumer connection.

Incorporating user-generated content into marketing isn't just about resharing - it demands careful selection, recognition, or deliberate promotion. Hotels alongside digital travel services now use advanced tools to spot strong testimonials, attractive visuals, or engaging personal accounts matching their identity. Through filtering such material, companies maintain genuine storytelling while emphasizing unique features of the visitor stay. Recognizing those who contribute - by showing appreciation or including them in campaigns - builds an interactive environment where clients sense importance, boosting commitment and involvement.

The Indian hotel industry has followed this shift with clear results. Instead of just listing features, firms such as OYO Rooms and Lemon Tree use actual guest feedback in their online promotions on platforms like Facebook, company sites, or mailing lists. Such efforts show openness, quick response, and focus on guests - helping shape better views from both local and overseas visitors. As a case, OYO posts real-life moments during festivals or offbeat trips, blending cultural relevance with ease and reliable service. Meanwhile, Lemon Tree uses YouTube and Instagram to display stay experiences through images and short clips, focusing on personal touches; these perform stronger than standard ads when it comes to user interaction.

Also, using user-created content helps shape overall brand direction by building something called "social proof." When potential guests spot repeated positive reviews from others like them, they feel more confident about choosing a hotel because it seems less risky. This holds especially true for people who live online - they usually check several review platforms before deciding. Instead of relying only on ads, hotels can use real guest posts across different channels - like websites, Instagram, or newsletters - to spark a loop: happy visitors share experiences that draw in new ones, and those newcomers later add their own stories.

7.4 Operational and Strategic Integration

7.4.1 Incorporating UGC into Hotel Operations

Bringing guest-created content into daily hotel work turns it from just promotion to useful feedback. Customer comments, scores, or online updates give live clues about how things are going - from staff behaviour to room comfort - helping leaders adjust fast. When teams regularly study this info, they spot repeated problems like slow arrivals, weak internet, or messy rooms - then fix them directly, improving results.

A clear system for using user-generated content means sorting feedback into key areas - like service standards, cleanliness, employee conduct, or upkeep of facilities. Because AI-driven sentiment detection evaluates emotion in written reviews, it offers measurable insight into guest experience while pointing out critical issues needing action (Gregory *et al.*, 2021). When negative remarks about bedroom cleaning rise sharply, this might prompt swift inspections, renewed training sessions, or updated procedures aimed at reducing repeat problems.

Leading hotels like Accor or Marriott use central tools to gather feedback from various websites. Because these systems collect data in one place, managers can track patterns while comparing how different locations perform. As a result, they're better able to focus on key upgrades where needed most. When user-generated content shapes routine decisions, it supports an active work environment - staff stay aware of visitor needs then contribute regularly to improving experiences.

Beyond fixing isolated issues, analysing user-generated content helps shape wider business approaches. When guests repeatedly mention poor food choices or missing room features, it points toward changes in menus, better facilities, or shifting staff roles - depending on what's needed. As this practice continues, operations gradually rely more on collected insights instead of guesswork, creating a cycle where real guest input shapes daily management.

7.4.2 Using UGC for Service Innovation and Guest Experience Design

User-generated content acts as a live feed of insights, helping hotels innovate services while improving how they shape guest experiences. Instead of using fixed methods like surveys or group discussions, this kind of data gives immediate, raw opinions straight from visitors. A single comment, online post, or score reflects genuine moments - what people liked, wanted, or struggled with - giving accommodation providers valuable clues. When studied carefully, such material reveals hidden demands, shifting patterns, although possible ways to stand out in service quality.

Take repeated comments on things like vegan breakfasts or pet-friendly stays - they can shape updates in menus, operations, or amenities. These patterns help hotels match what guests actually want, boosting both happiness and repeat visits. As Guan, Hung, and Liu (2022) noted, user-generated content often shows how culture affects views on service quality - like flexibility, consistency, or physical comforts. For global hotel brands, spotting these subtle differences means adjusting locally without losing overall brand unity.

User-created content helps improve hands-on design in hospitality. Instead of just relying on professional photos, many hotels now use visuals and stories made by visitors across both real-world spaces and websites - this builds trust through peer experience while making stays more dynamic. For instance, some properties display rotating social feeds in entrance areas; others feature selected traveller images in digital albums or highlight short quotes from satisfied customers right inside reservation interfaces. Such efforts confirm service standards while turning virtual interactions into concrete memories that influence potential guests. Through linking web activity with actual locations, accommodations foster environments where visitor involvement shapes how the brand is seen.

Also, using user-generated content in innovation helps hotels keep improving by testing ideas quickly. Because they can track reviews or social media updates live, changes in guest needs show up sooner. As a result, adjustments happen before problems grow. In this way, UGC becomes more than just PR - it shapes how services are built from the start.

7.4.3 Monitoring and Response Strategies

The way hotels handle user-created content matters for keeping their image strong, improving visitor experiences, because it helps refine daily operations. As more people post on review sites or share moments via social networks while using reservation systems, staff face endless incoming opinions. Although such input can boost promotion efforts when used well, ignoring it may lead to problems due to unchecked narratives spreading. Thus, having structured ways to track responses - backed by clear rules along with smooth internal coordination - is key so that comments from guests actually help the business grow.

7.4.4 Real-Time Monitoring and Sentiment Analysis

Ahead of problems, constant tracking of user-generated content on various sites is key. Instead, hotels should use smart software that automatically analyses guest opinions, spots common issues, while flagging possible outbreaks early. Such systems sort vast amounts of comments into topics - like room quality, service attitude, or facilities - noting what needs fast action. Alerts sent instantly help leaders respond when dissatisfaction rises sharply. For instance, if more guests suddenly report poor internet during busy periods, fixes like tech checks or staffing shifts can follow right away.

Besides numbers, written feedback matters just as much. Tools using natural language processing (NLP) pick up on hints like irritation or dissatisfaction - things scores might miss. Because emotions in comments reveal deeper concerns, lodging spots can focus first on what really affects guest trust and how people see the brand.

A Three-Tiered Response Model

Best-practice UGC management involves a structured, three-tiered response approach:

- **Detection:** It starts with spotting feedback in an organized way, covering good and bad comments. While software checks various platforms - like TripAdvisor, Google Reviews, Booking.com, social networks, or specialty travel sites - it looks for changes in tone, new topics, or fast-spreading criticism. Instead of just counting ratings, these systems track recurring themes; for instance, frequent mentions of slow service or broken amenities might point to deeper problems across operations.
- **Engagement:** When serious complaints come up, quick action matters. Instead of waiting, support staff ought to reply with care and respect - ideally within one day - by recognizing the issue while outlining next steps. According to Narangajavana and team (2017), messages showing understanding, kindness, and practical fixes don't just reduce anger - they may turn upset customers into repeat buyers. On the flip side, answers that sound dismissive, copy-pasted, or robotic tend to increase irritation, weaken confidence, and spread worse impressions across digital platforms.
- **Resolution:** The last step is when on-the-ground teams take action to fix problems and record what happens. Because feedback highlights gaps, it can guide updates in workflows, employee development, or how support is distributed - so similar setbacks are less likely next time. Suppose several visitors mention slow check-ins; leaders might adjust shift plans, simplify sign-

in steps, or use digital tools to speed things up. When shared openly, such records show transparency while building stronger confidence from users.

7.4.5 Tone, Transparency, and Brand Credibility

The way a reply sounds matters just as much as how fast it's sent. When staff show understanding, guests feel heard - this suggests the hotel cares about opinions while aiming to get better over time. If an error occurred, replies ought to admit it, describe what will change, then thank the person for pointing it out. Being open in public view strengthens trust; future visitors notice when problems are owned up to and steps taken to fix them. For instance, posting a reply to a negative review stating, "We appreciate your feedback regarding room cleanliness. Our housekeeping team has implemented additional checks to prevent recurrence," signals professionalism and maturity.

7.5 Proactive and Reactive Strategies

7.5.1 Reactive Strategies

Reactive approaches mean replying to customer posts once they're live. These responses might confirm issues, fix mistakes, clear up confusion - also provide quick fixes. Good follow-up can rebuild confidence, stop bad feelings from spreading, while showing responsibility - not just to the person who commented, but also to others watching.

7.5.2 Proactive Strategies

Instead of waiting, some approaches aim to spot problems early. Monitoring guest posts online helps detect small frustrations - like confusion or disappointment - as they appear. When staff respond quickly with tailored support, many issues get resolved before checkout. This kind of timely action stops minor concerns from growing worse. Acting ahead improves experience ratings while lowering chances for bad feedback later. Building trust this way also deepens customer loyalty over time.

Although reacting to criticism matters, taking steps ahead of time helps improve guest relationships more effectively. Instead of waiting, hotels might monitor user-created content to spot potential problems early - like noticing signs of frustration in online comments before check-in. By reaching out first - to give help tailored to individuals, fix small concerns, or ask for input - they reduce chances of unhappy moments turning into official grievances while boosting how satisfied visitors feel.

8. CONCLUSION

User-generated content shifted from a minor marketing tool to a key part of strategy in hospitality. Because of its reach, operations improve while guest experiences grow stronger. Positive posts often boost reservations, satisfaction levels, even company valuation - research supports this trend (Ye *et al.*, 2011; Liu, 2020; Subramanian *et al.*, 2021). Yet challenges remain: false feedback, skewed algorithms, or image damage require constant oversight.

From a conceptual angle, network dynamics boost engagement. Signalling principles help explain how trust emerges online. Meanwhile, usage-generated insights improve system performance over time. In combination, these ideas clarify how user-created content supports firm-level gains. Each part highlights different ways digital environments influence choices and strategic advantage.

Hotels need to shift from reacting to taking charge of user-generated content - using online reviews as real-time data. By discussing guest feedback in routine team updates, shaping services around visitor stories, OR applying smart tools to detect patterns, properties can stay ahead. Throughout this change, honesty, openness, INSTEAD OF greenwashing, and responsible practices must remain central.

In the end, user-generated content reflects both personal views and shared knowledge. Because it shows social norms, cultural variety, and real emotions - traits today's hospitality sector needs to adopt to stay meaningful. While online engagement grows stronger, companies thriving in this space are shaped by listening carefully, adapting quickly, while guiding others through genuine interactions enhanced with tech tools.

In short, hospitality's future comes from turning guest feedback into benefits - a connected system where businesses and users build trust together, drive progress, yet shape experiences side by side.

9. FUTURE TRENDS AND RECOMMENDATIONS

9.1 AI and Sentiment Analysis of UGC

Artificial Intelligence changes how hotels handle feedback posted online. Because people generate huge volumes of such content every day, systems like NLP, sentiment detection, or machine learning help turn messy inputs into useful knowledge. According to Gregory *et al.* (2021), data network effects mean platforms improve when they gather more user information over time. In tourism settings, this idea matters - each additional comment sharpens a property's insight into what guests want and how happy they are.

Hotels use AI tools that gather guest comments from different sites, sorting them by topics such as cleanliness, staff behaviour, or meal standards. Instead of just combining data, these systems analyse words to spot problems early - helping managers act fast. For example, Marriott and Accor rely on artificial intelligence to track online opinions; rather than ignoring tone, they link customer mood to room bookings and income trends for better forecasting.

Apart from that, artificial intelligence improves tailored experiences by studying emotion-based choices. When a visitor often mentions "peaceful rooms" or "plant-based food" in feedback, they could get special deals matching these likes. Still, using automated systems to mimic empathy brings up moral concerns - such as unfair judgments, data security, and permission issues. For fair use of such tech, hospitality providers should follow clear rules on managing information, protecting user confidentiality without limiting insights.

9.2 Sustainable UGC Strategies for Hospitality Firms

Sustainability in online interactions matters more now, since companies aim to grow while supporting societal and ecological well-being. Effective user-generated content focuses on green behaviours, local involvement, or diverse narratives - instead of generic promotion. Research by Guan *et al.* (2022) showed that values embedded in shared posts shape how consumers view a company's ethical stance.

Hotels might use guest-generated content to showcase eco-friendly actions like cutting energy use, reducing trash, or buying from nearby suppliers - while motivating visitors to join in and post about it. Take ITC Hotels' "Responsible Luxury" campaign - it invites travellers to record green moments during their stay, turning online platforms into tools for promoting planet-conscious choices.

Moving forward, handling user-generated content sustainably supports digital wellness - promoting healthy online habits while limiting false information and building constructive community engagement. Sites focusing on emotional well-being, diversity, or contextual awareness tend to develop safer virtual spaces; these benefit users alongside businesses.

The mix of AI, ethics, and green practices will shape the future of user-generated content in hotels. Those that blend these areas thoughtfully - not using tech just because it's new but connecting with people in real ways - will set the pace for a smarter, fairer shift online.

9.3 Immersive UGC Formats (AR/VR)

Immersive user-created content using AR or VR is changing how people judge hotels before they book. More often, travellers want interactive media instead of just flat photos to explore spaces ahead of time. Real guest videos showing full-room angles, self-made tours, augmented previews of facilities, or virtual reality trip logs offer practical glimpses into stays - helping cut doubt while boosting interest during decision-making.

Immersive formats help future guests check room size, design details, how clean spaces look, window direction, also what facilities are like - things regular pictures can't show well. On top of this, images made by actual travellers seem more reliable compared to sleek marketing shots from hotels. People sharing footage via body cams, drones, or VR gear often add rich experiences, letting new visitors feel like they're viewing stays firsthand

With AR and VR getting more affordable, user-created immersive content can act like hands-on marketing that shifts what buyers expect, affects their forecast of satisfaction, also boosts trust in purchasing decisions.

9.4 Hyper-Personalization

Hyper-personalization is becoming key in hospitality, thanks to smart data tools that study user-generated content. By looking at feedback, online discussions, social activity, favourite topics like food or health, and emotional tones, hotels spot what matters most to each visitor. Because of this, experiences can be adjusted more accurately across every step of a guest's stay.

In the booking phase, hotels might suggest specific room types or extras - using guest browsing patterns and feedback shared online - as a basis. While guests are onsite, live information allows staff to adapt meals, activities, or room setups more closely to individual tastes. After checkout, insights from past behaviour guide follow-up actions like customized discounts, invitations to comment, or incentives encouraging another visit.

This degree of customization boosts how valuable guests feel their experience is, builds stronger emotional ties - therefore lifting long-term customer worth. Integrating user-generated content data with CRM platforms alongside artificial intelligence analysis allows accommodations to offer personalized service across large operations, improving market position while fostering repeat patronage.

9.5 Rise of Micro-Influencers and Community Advocacy

Micro-influencers - people with fewer followers yet strong audience trust - are becoming key players in travel choices. Instead of big-name creators known for sleek, ad-like material, these individuals share real-life stories that feel personal; their content highlights honest stays and local spots. Because they focus on actual experiences rather than promotion, travellers find their suggestions trustworthy. Their connection with fans grows from transparency, making recommendations seem less like ads, more like advice from a friend.

Their reliability comes from the confidence they earn in specific groups - like culinary tourists, thrill chasers, health-focused travellers, low-budget hikers, or high-end wanderers. Since these circles often depend on firsthand advice, micro-influencers serve as trusted voices that affect views on hospitality standards, location attractiveness, also cost efficiency.

In recent years, user-led promotion on sites such as Reddit, Facebook groups, WhatsApp travel chats, or regional blogs has grown in influence - especially compared to traditional ads. Recommendations from fellow members in these private or partially open spaces tend to feel more trustworthy due to shared experience rather than paid messaging.

Hotels working closely with small-scale influencers or local promoters often reach more customers effectively; they also boost trust online - while sparking user-created content that resonates well within specific audiences.Bottom of Form

REFERENCES

Baka, V. (2016). The becoming of user-generated reviews: Looking at the past to understand the future of managing reputation in the travel sector. *Tourism Management, 53*, 148–162.

Gregory, R. W., Henfridsson, O., Kaganer, E., & Kyriakou, H. (2021). The role of artificial intelligence and data network effects for creating user value. *Academy of Management Review, 46*(3), 534–551.

Guan, C., Hung, Y. C., & Liu, W. (2022). Cultural differences in hospitality service evaluations: Mining insights of user generated content. *Electronic Markets, 32*(3), 1061–1081.

Huang, N., Burtch, G., Gu, B., Hong, Y., Liang, C., Wang, K., & Yang, B. (2019). Motivating user-generated content with performance feedback: Evidence from randomized field experiments. *Management Science, 65*(1), 327–345.

Leung, D., Law, R., Van Hoof, H., & Buhalis, D. (2013). Social media in tourism and hospitality: A literature review. *Journal of Travel & Tourism Marketing, 30*(1-2), 3–22.

Liu, X. (2020). Analyzing the impact of user-generated content on B2B Firms' stock performance: Big data analysis with machine learning methods. *Industrial Marketing Management, 86*, 30–39.

Manaman, H. S., & Jamali, S., & AleAhmad, A. (2016). Online reputation measurement of companies based on user-generated content in online social networks. *Computers in Human Behavior, 54*, 94–100.

Narangajavana, Y., Fiol, L. J. C., Tena, M. Á. M., Artola, R. M. R., & García, J. S. (2017). The influence of social media in creating expectations. An empirical study for a tourist destination. *Annals of Tourism Research, 65*, 60–70.

Narangajavana Kaosiri, Y., Callarisa Fiol, L. J., Moliner Tena, M. Á., Rodríguez Artola, R. M., & Sánchez García, J. (2019). User-generated content sources in social media: A new approach to explore tourist satisfaction. *Journal of Travel Research, 58*(2), 253–265.

Subramanian, H., Mitra, S., & Ransbotham, S. (2021). Capturing value in platform business models that rely on user-generated content. *Organization Science, 32*(3), 804–823.

Wilson, A., Murphy, H., & Fierro, J. C. (2012). Hospitality and travel: The nature and implications of user-generated content. *Cornell Hospitality Quarterly*, *53*(3), 220–228.

Xiang, Z., Du, Q., Ma, Y., & Fan, W. (2017). A comparative analysis of major online review platforms: Implications for social media analytics in hospitality and tourism. *Tourism Management*, *58*, 51–65.

Yang, M., Ren, Y., & Adomavicius, G. (2019). Understanding user-generated content and customer engagement on Facebook business pages. *Information Systems Research*, *30*(3), 839–855.

Ye, Q., Law, R., Gu, B., & Chen, W. (2011). The influence of user-generated content on traveler behavior: An empirical investigation on the effects of e-word-of-mouth to hotel online bookings. *Computers in Human Behavior*, *27*(2), 634–639.

KEY TERMS AND DEFINITIONS

Data Network Effects: Data Network Effects happen because more user data boosts a platform's performance. Since users add content, services get better at suggesting relevant options. While systems learn from inputs, they adapt quickly to what guests prefer. Although improvements are ongoing, each update makes the experience sharper. Because insights grow richer, companies gain an edge without relying on guesswork.

Electronic Word-of-Mouth (eWOM): Electronic word-of-mouth means casual feedback from customers posted online - like reviews or comments on social platforms. While regular recommendations spread slowly, this version travels faster because it's visible to many people across different regions. Because of its wide reach, these digital opinions tend to stay available longer than face-to-face conversations. In hotels and travel services, such user-shared views shape how reliable a place seems, how good the experience might be, yet also affect whether someone decides to make a reservation.

Firm-Generated Content (FGC): Firm-Generated Content includes any marketing or brand messaging made by companies - such as ads, site copy, leaflets, news updates, or corporate social media entries. In contrast to user-created material, this type of content is designed on purpose to reflect how a business wants to be seen, stress key benefits, also shape audience views. It helps keep communication steady while presenting the brand in a polished way.

Network Effects: As more people join a digital service, it tends to get more useful - a pattern known as network effects. On sites such as TripAdvisor or Booking.com, greater traveller involvement means richer information and stronger impact. When users post feedback or interact with content, trust builds up gradually. Over time, this makes the platform harder to leave, boosting continued use.

Online Reputation Management (ORM): Online Reputation Management refers to methods hotels use - like monitoring comments on websites - to handle how they appear online. Tracking guest opinions comes through various sites, while replies aim to resolve concerns or show appreciation. Negative remarks get managed carefully so perceptions stay balanced over time. Brands shape stories about themselves by guiding conversations in helpful directions. Strong practices build credibility, maintain value, and support better positioning against rivals.

Review Authenticity: Review authenticity means how believable, correct, and reliable customer feedback online really is. Genuine reviews come from real user experiences, without being altered or pushed by sellers. When reviews feel true, shoppers tend to trust them more; however, dishonest or skewed opinions damage clarity and mislead judgments about actual performance. A trustworthy system depends on honest input - fake content weakens decision-making despite seeming helpful at first glance.

Sentiment Analysis: Sentiment Analysis uses AI along with natural language processing to examine emotions, opinions, and stance - like positive, negative, or neutral - in texts including feedback or remarks. In the hospitality sector, this method helps spot trends, grasp guest reactions, highlight weak points in service, while guiding choices through up-to-date public opinion.

Signalling Theory: Signalling Theory explains how consumers rely on observable and credible cues—such as detailed reviews, reviewer profiles, photos, and ratings Because hotel stays can't be tested beforehand, people look at user content to guess what to expect. Signals like star scores or guest pictures give clues about trust and experience. When feedback is clear and matches across posts, shoppers feel more confident in their choice. Instead of guessing blindly, they use these signs - reviews, bios, images - to judge if a place will meet needs.

User-Generated Content (UGC): User-Generated Content means digital material made by people who share their own experiences with hotels or services; this includes things like comments, pictures, vlogs, trip stories, or updates online. Since actual guests create it - not companies - it's often seen as honest, neutral, and trustworthy. This kind of content affects what travellers expect, guides their choices, also shapes how a hotel is viewed digitally.

Chapter 12
Consumer Attitude Towards Instagram Advertising:
Mediating Role of Advertising Value

Pravin Chandra Singh
http://orcid.org/0000-0002-6002-0703
MATS University, India

Vishal Kumar Singh
http://orcid.org/0000-0002-5381-3027
School of Management Sciences, Varanasi, India

Princy Singh
Mahatma Gandhi Kashi Vidyapith, Varanasi, India

Vinay Seth
Mahatma Gandhi Kashi Vidyapith, Varanasi, India

Vishnu Gupta
http://orcid.org/0000-0001-8554-1065
Mahatma Gandhi Kashi Vidyapith, Varanasi, India

Pankaj Kumar
http://orcid.org/0000-0003-0313-2968
Symbiosis University of Applied Sciences, Indore, India

Sujay Vikram Singh
http://orcid.org/0000-0002-7113-2698
Amity University, Lucknow, India

ABSTRACT

The objective of this paper is to develop a comprehensive model to explore the impact of the identified antecedents of a consumer's attitude towards Instagram advertising. The study adopted an explorative-cum-descriptive design and sample size is 412. The model was tested with exploratory, and confirmatory factor analysis and Structural Equation Modeling (SEM) The study results indicate that there is a strong positive

DOI: 10.4018/979-8-3373-6741-5.ch012

relationship between credibility, informativeness, entertainment, personalization, and attitude toward the Instagram advertising. In contrast, a significant negative association has been established between irritation and attitude toward Instagram advertisements. Looking at the interrelationship, advertising value does mediate the relationship between the predictor variable attitude towards Instagram advertising except irritation. Furthermore, the present study also supports that the hierarchy of effect (HOE) does exist, and there is a strong positive relationship between attitude towards Instagram advertising and purchase intention.

1. INTRODUCTION

Social media is a rapidly expanding market and advertising has dramatically changed during this past decade (Dahl, 2021). Over the history, companies traditionally market their product and services offer by using traditional media (Evans, 2010). The longer it takes the more advertisements are imposed on consumers and this creates frustration in consumers and they trend to reject them (Fransen et al., 2015). More marketers search for a new interactive way of medium used for the purpose of advertising and for the features of interactivity social media starts to receive substantial attention (Ashley & Tuten, 2015) ads on social media such as Facebook, Instagram etc done in paid manner (Nielsen, 2016). (Kaplan & Haenlein, 2010) defines social media as internet-based applications relying on Web 2.0 concepts and technology to enable the creation and exchange of user-produced content. Social media advertising Conformity in technology, platform and tools used to send, receive, and share messages to and from between an organization and its stakeholders (Ashley & Tuten, 2015).

Another platform that has increasingly attracted marketers is Instagram, which has attracted more than 1 billion users and has become widely used by businesses for advertising, marketing research and customer relationship management (Zhao et al., 2017). Despite the rapid uptake of consumers using Instagram (and marketers leveraging the network for advertising), limited academic research has been conducted on this relatively new form of advertising and specifically the factors influencing attitude toward Instagram advertising (Djafarova & Rushworth, 2017). According that this paper has tried to explore the variables that leads in the predictions of consumer attitude towards Instagram advertising and explored this interconnection among those with the context of Bangladesh. The additional relationship between consumer attitude of Instagram advertising and purchase intention has been investigated to determine whether in the context for HOE, attitude toward advertising affect purchase intention.

2. INSTAGRAM ADVERTISING

The global ad reach of Instagram is now more than 1.7 billion users, 1 of the largest advertising platforms of the universe. Instagram's ad revenue is expected to reach $71 billion in 2025, fuelled mostly by Reels and mobile-first ad formats. Average Instagram CPC (cost-per-click) tends to be between $0.20-$2.00, varying by industry and targeting. Average CPMs were at $8.58 in early 2025, up from about $6.70 in 2021. Conversion rates from Instagram ads have generally been between 1% and 2%, and video and carousel ads are better performers than static images. In addition, more than 83% of ad impressions on Instagram are on mobile, so mobile optimization is essential to success. Brands make an average of $4.12 for every $1 spent on influencer campaign on Instagram. Reels drive 22% more engagement than standard video posts, which makes it the most effective format to reach and connect with an audience. Instagram's ad load in Reels now accounts for more than 22% of the content that appears in a user's feed. In the United States, Instagram is projected to account for more than half of Meta's total ad revenue as of the end of 2025. Instagram's ad audience is over 60% users between 18 and 34, which is the most targeted demo by brands. Instagram's average engagement rate per post type is around 1.2%, which is higher than many other large networks. There are more than 25 million businesses actively using Instagram to advertise, reach out to customers and develop an identity for their brand. Instagram Stories ads are still in high demand, and now there are more than 500 million accounts that use them daily. Nearly 79% of marketers include Instagram in their influencer campaign approach, primarily because of its high engagement rate, and because it is a visually-focused platform. Almost 80% of Instagram users have shopped by tapping on an ad to get more info on a product or service. Posts that are videos get 49% higher engagement than photo postings with this gap only increasing in 2025. Ad prices will vary by where they are placed, too, though — Stories ads are averaging $7.25 CPM, while Reels ads are priced lower at around $4.30 CPM. Worldwide, ad spending on Instagram is on track to grow an estimated 9.3% a year through 2030. Among Instagram followers, micro-influencers, with a following of 10k–50k, boast the best engagement rates and are favoured for niche advertising. These numbers emphasize how important Instagram is in digital advertising, whether you take into account its vast reach, changing content types, or how much brands could get back from their investments through strategic ad and influencer partnerships (Arma & Elma, 2025).

3. CONSUMER ATTITUDE TOWARDS ADVERTISING

Attitude towards advertising is an important concept since it is considered to be one of the key attributes of an advertisement (MacKenzie & Lutz, 1989) and may affects how consumers will respond to an advertisement in general (Mehta, 2000). (Mitchell & Olson, 1981) and (Shimp, 1981) were two of the early researchers in the marketing literature to point out the significance of the notion of customer attitudes toward advertising. They argued that attitude towards advertising impacted on attitude toward the brand, by changing perceptions of the targeted brands. The consumer's attitude to advertising is "A predisposition to respond in a favourable/ unfavourable way to a particular advertising stimulus displayed on a particular occasion" (MacKenzie, & Lutz, 1989). It has always been an interest of marketers and academicians since the consumer attitude towards advertising is one of the bench marks of the effectiveness of the advertising (Mehta, 2000; Saadeghvaziri & Hosseini, 2011; Tsang et al., 2004). Most of the research related to advertising are done in the backdrop of developed economies (Mittal, 1994; Shavitt et al., 1998; Mehta, 2000; Ben Oumlil & Balloun, 2020) Therefore, the need to investigate consumer attitude towards advertising in the context of developing economy like India is timely.

4. NEED OF THE STUDY

Once companies realized the impact of social media in individual's life, they transitioned to more efficient and inexpensive advertising platforms which are internet based, for example social networking sites, blogs, email marketing, website ads and a lot of others (Saxena & Khanna, 2013). Thus, many business firms have diverted their advertising budgets from traditional channels, toward the social network websites (Lee & Hong, 2016). It has made it possible for companies to engage their customers in a direct and efficient way (Kaplan & Haenlein, 2010). Social media advertising in still in its early development and is still evolving at a rapid pace at that (Zhang, 2016; Schultz, 2016) and attitudinal studies related to advertising are largely conducted in developed economies (Ben Oumlil & Balloun, 2020).

Research Gaps

The antecedents of advertisement value and attitude are well-grounded in the generalised digital advertising literature but no such comprehensive examination for Instagram advertisements is reported. First, these factors such as credibility, entertainment or irritation have either been studied in isolation or not on Instagram but other platforms (e.g., Facebook), thus neglecting a more global perspective within Instagram's visual environment, where algorithms play an important role and influencers are widespread. Second, the mediating effect of advertising value for subtle antecedents such as personalization (where relevance and possible privacy concerns are intertwined) and irritation in ad-loaded feeds is not fully elucidated here. Third, there is limited empirical cross-disciplinary research for models in debt across developmental economies such as India in order to capture the generalizability of results amongst various cultural and digital ecosystems.

The present study aims to fill these gaps by developing and testing an integrated model specifically for Instagram use. It studies the direct and value-mediated implications of five primary predecessors (credibility, informativeness, entertainment, personalization and irritation) for consumer attitude, and indirectly on purchase intention in Indian perspective. Upon taking this approach, the study seeks to contribute a more nuanced and contextual understanding of what is driving advertising efficacy on one of the world's leading social media sites.

5. LITERATURE REVIEW AND HYPOTHESIS DEVELOPMENT

5.1. Credibility

It is defined as "The extent to which the consumer determines the promise in the advertising about the product brand to be effective and convincing," (MacKenzie and Lutz, 1989). It not only mediates the development of attitude and behaviour towards advertising (Lafferty & Goldsmith, 1999) but also, influences the effectiveness (Choi & Rifon, 2002) and the value of advertisements (Saadeghvaziri & Hosseini, 2011; Tsang et al., 2004). It is generally believed by consumers that web advertisements are less credible than the other medium primarily since it is mostly uncontrolled (Johnson & Kaye, 2015) and is thus considered to be hard for organizations to convince the consumers as to the reliability of web advertising than other medium (Aktan et al., 2016; Prendergast et al., 2009). Probably credibility in advertising is the paramount factor that creates value in online environment (Ducoffe, 1996; Brackett, L & Carr, B, 2001) and there is evidence for that in recent studies as it is found that credibility of advertisements positively influences consumer attitude toward online advertising (Arora & Agarwal, 2019; Dao et al., 2014; Dwinanda et al., 2022; Roth-Cohen et al., 2022; Shareef et al., 2019; Y. Wang & Genç, 2019; Sesar et al., 2022; Janssen et al., 2021; Brinson & Lemon, 2023; Hussain et al., 2023; Milfeld & Haley, 2024; Ye et al., 2024; Dobber et al., 2025) and felt trustworthy by consumers will create value to the targeted audience based on previous studies, Thus, following alternative hypotheses are proposed:

H_1: There is a significant positive relationship between credibility and consumer attitude towards Instagram advertising.
H_2: There is a significant positive relationship between credibility and advertising value.

5.2. Informativeness

The informativeness of an advertisement is explained as "the messaging's capacity to illuminate the recipient with regard to the range of product and service alternatives available to the recipient in order to optimize the satisfaction level that the client seeks" (Ducoffe, 1995; Ducoffe, 1996). Informativeness is necessary as it generates a favourable attitude towards advertisement and this influences consumer attitude positively (Di Pietro & Pantano, 2012; Hayes & King, 2014). Info seekers the consumers are highly favourable on the ads when they are learnt the product features and how product is reviewed (Kotler & Keller, 2016). Informative social media advertisements are a successful way to reach proposed participants (Wright et al., 2018). According to (Mahatmavidya & Yasa 2020; Saxena & Khanna, 2013; Shareef et al., 2019; Hussain et al., 2023; Saraiva & Lues, 2024; Ye et al., 2024; Johnson, 2025; Hanaysha & Alhyasat, 2025) stated that an effective and informative advertisement on social media that informing product information into the customers timely with accurate will create values for the advertisements that will have a positive impact on consumer attitude. Thus, following alternative hypotheses are proposed:

H_3: There is a significant positive relationship between informativeness and consumers attitude towards Instagram advertising.
H_4: There is a significant positive relationship between informativeness and advertising value.

5.3. Entertainment

Entertainment as defined by (Ducoffe, 1996) for advertising is an advertisement's potential to fulfil an audience's need for escape, diversion, aesthetic pleasure, or emotional satisfaction. It aids in attracting the consumers' concentration and reduces the annoyance characteristics of advertisements (Raktham et al., 2017). Entertaining social media message persuades the online visitors and engage and help them in forcing or getting clients which also leads to increasing retention of client (Wright et al., 2018) and it fits or matches the value or worth of the advertisements in the sight of targeted consumers therefore, there is strong positive impact of entertainment in social media advertising on consumer attitude (Arora & Agarwal, 2019; Jain et al., 2018; Mahatmavidya & Yasa, 2020; Martins et al., 2019; Shareef et al., 2019;

Hussain et al., 2023; Ye et al., 2024; Saraiva & Lues, 2024; Hanaysha & Alhyasat, 2025). Based on the previous literature, following alternative hypotheses are proposed:

> **H_5:** There is a significant positive relationship between entertainment and consumer attitude towards Instagram advertising.
> **H_6:** There is a significant positive relationship between entertainment and advertising value.

5.4. Personalization

It refers as the delivery of advertising messages to the end-user based on their preferences, demographics, context, and content. The relevance of the advertisements is increased and the receiver is not irritated (Xu, 2006). There is growing use of personalized advertising messages instead of mass advertising to avoid the advertising chaos for consumers (Jung, 2017). Consumers are looking to get marketing that is relevant to their wants, needs, and desires and that adds value to the target personas. When the ad is more personalized, not only do we know who the ad should be served to directly and be able to engage them better as customers, but it also fosters a good relationship with the end customer (Saadeghvaziri & Hosseini, 2011). There is nuance to the impact of personalisation that will render social media ads valuable. Perceived ad relevance has been shown to affect advertising effectiveness based on consumer response to targeted ads in social media as well, through its association with consumer attention to ads and ad avoidance (Fatima & Abbas, 2016; Jung, 2017; Kim & Han, 2014; Wright et al., 2018; I.-L. Wu et al., 2017; Nurhidayah & Dirgantara, 2025; Rózsa et al., 2025; Noor et al., 2024). According to the description given by previous works, the following alternative hypotheses are considered:

> **H_7:** There is a significant positive relationship between personalization and consumer attitude towards Instagram advertising.
> **H_8:** There is a significant positive relationship between personalization and advertising value.

5.5. Irritation

It is also defined as 'imitation, fraudulent behaviour, allurement and irritating advertisements which influence the targeted consumers' (P. Wang & Wen, 2017). Recent research indicates that ad irritation can be associated with content, style, and the medium through which the ad is aired, along with familiarity and engagement with the web ad. (P. Wang & Wen, 2017). Consumers evaluate advertising for many aspects, not the least of which is the annoyance associated with advertising (Greyser, 1973) and why bad feelings are triggered through the advertising (Li et al., 2002). When social media users feel that the ad is disturbing, they consider it obtrusive (Kornias & Hălălău, 2012) and this interferes with the efficiency of the ads. Ads Stripping or Anger Inducing Ads that annoy or manipulate recipients are annoying and not very welcome and so everyone has to work out how to make their ads not an annoyance or annoying. attitudes Attitude towards web advertising were focused by a number of studies which found that irritation has a negative significant impact on it (Aktan et al., 2016; Alsamydai & Hamdi Al Khasawneh, 2013; Jebarajakirthy et al., 2021; Khan et al., 2022; Kim & Han, 2014; Lin & Bautista, 2020; Tahereh & Zahra, 2012; Yang et al., 2017; Youn & Kim, 2019; Saraiva & Lues, 2024; Ye et al., 2024). According to the prior literature, the following hypothesis is advanced:

> **H_9:** There is a significant negative relationship between irritation and consumer attitude towards Instagram advertising.
> **H_{10}:** There is a significant negative relationship between irritation and advertising value.

5.6. Advertising Value as a Mediator

It is the consumers perceived relative value or usefulness of the ads (Ducoffe, 1995). Applying a series of experiments, an enhanced version of the model was developed, whose three antecedents of perceived value are informativeness, entertainment, and irritation (Ducoffe, 1995; Ducoffe, 1996). It is a measuring system with which to gauge the intangible achievements of advertising as perceived by customers, and only when consumers' expectations are met or surpassed does it become useful to advertisers. Such predecessors differ from traditional advertising effectiveness measures (e.g., message recall, brand attitude, purchase intent) in that they are in touch with the consumer's predispositions towards the advertisement. Antecedents of attitude toward advertising according to the model, advertising value is an antecedent of the attitude toward advertising. Attitude toward advertising value facilitates favourable judgments of ad elements. The advertising value is one of the most fruitful and prevalent concepts used in analysing and predicting consumer attitudes toward advertising (Murillo et al., 2016; Saraiva & Lues, 2024; Ye et al., 2024). The relationship between those two constructs is mediated by advertising value that generates utility or value for consumers. According to the former literature, the following hypothesis is offered:

> **H_{11}:** Advertising value mediates the relationship between entertainment and consumer attitude towards Instagram advertising.

H_{12}: Advertising value mediates the relationship between informativeness and consumer attitude towards Instagram advertising.

H_{13}: Advertising value mediates the relationship between personalization and consumer attitude towards Instagram advertising.

H_{14}: Advertising value mediates the relationship between credibility and consumer attitude towards Instagram advertising.

H_{15}: Advertising value mediates the relationship between irritation and consumer attitude towards Instagram advertising.

5.7. Purchase Intention

It is consumer 'intention of purchasing the advertised brand in the product and services in the near future (P.C.S. Wu et al., 2011). In marketing, hierarchy of effects (HOE) is found to reflect how attitude towards advertising affects consumers' purchase intention (Homer, 1990; Shimp, 1981). It is found in a previous study that the consumer attitude toward advertising has a significant positive relationship with purchase intention (Dehghani et al., 2016; Hsu et al., 2014; Mohd Noor et al., 2013; Kamalul Ariffin et al., 2021; Putra et al., 2024; Anubha & Jain, 2024; Gupta et al., 2024). From this literature review the following research hypothesis is developed:

H_{16}: There is a significant positive relationship between attitude towards Instagram advertising and consumer purchase intention.

Figure 1. Proposed Research Model

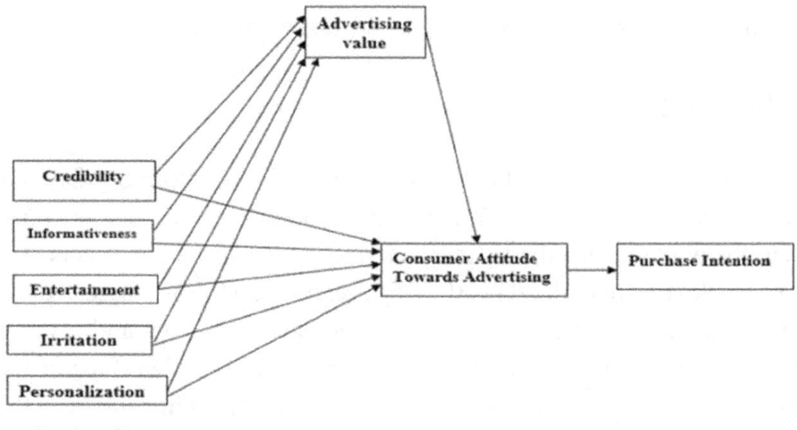

Source: Previous Literature

6. RESEARCH METHODOLOGY

6.1. Data collection

A questionnaire for survey was developed for this study. The questionnaire was mostly comprised with close ended questions with 7-points Likert scales where then its questionnaire was sent to the respondent after preparing google form link to the them. The sample size of the present study is 412 for consumers in (Delhi-NCR).

6.2. Construct Measurement

The items chosen for this study were adapted from a variety of sources in the literature. The items of dependent variable Consumer attitude towards advertising (5-items) were taken from (Ramaprasad, 2001); (Mehta, 2000). Items of independent variable credibility (3-items) and personalization (3-items) (Xu, 2006), informativeness (3- items) and irritation (3-items) (Tsang et al., 2004), advertising value (3-items) (Ducoffe, 1995), entertainment (3-items) (Pollay & Mittal, 1993) and purchase intention (2-items) (Alalwan, 2018; Hong & Cho, 2011).

6.3. Respondent's Profile

This study included customers of north India who were interested to purchase after seeing advertisements on Instagram. The sample consists of 265 men (62.13%) and 156 women (37.87%). A total of 68% of the respondents are between the ages of 18 and 28. Over half of the participants (53%) were currently pursuing their baccalaureate degree. 66% of participants were students, and, like profession, followed by servicemen while some of them had their own business.

6.4. Data Analysis

Data analysis was performed in two steps. EFA: The exploratory factor analysis (EFA) was conducted by SPSS 21.0. At the second step, a CFA was employed to strengthen the evidence for the validity and reliability of the constructs. The value of KMO in table-1 (Appendix-1) is (0.876) greater than 0.6 as suggested by (Field, 2009) the value of $\chi 2$ is 9924.244 with 435 degrees of freedom and p-value is less than 0.001 which means that the items are sufficiently correlated for further principal components analysis. According to Hair et al. (2010) in each item the factor load standard is over 0.5 in the EFA result table-2 (Appendix-1). Furthermore, all the constructs have a value higher than 0.70, the cut-off points used to determine the reliability according to and their α values are influenced due to the internal consistency (Appendix-1).

Figure 2. Measurement model

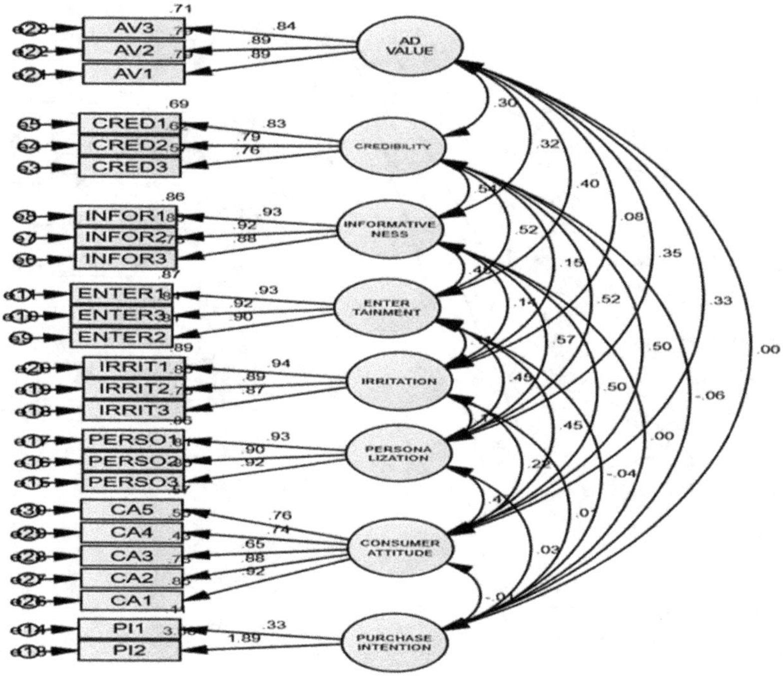

Source: Analysis Output

6.5. SEM Analysis

The structural model of the proposed conceptual research model was tested using SEM. The structural model's evaluations, critical ratio and SEM equations are given in table-3. The conclusion of the hypothesis presents each of the route coefficients, which reflect the degree of influence of the influencing factors. The variances of all seven constructs have been calculated and the average variance is greater than the sum of the maximum variances, but the common variance is less than the average variance and maximum variance (AVE>MSV>ASV). Goodness-of-fit value = ~0.90; badness of fit index < 0.10. According to the indices, SEM is still within acceptable boundaries and may be considered a feasible model (Hair et al., 2010). Hypothesis from H1 to H14 were all supported by the values and Cronbach values of all constructs are in between 0.77 to 0.94. composite reliability of the considered constructs is all above the prescribed value.

Figure 3. Structural Model

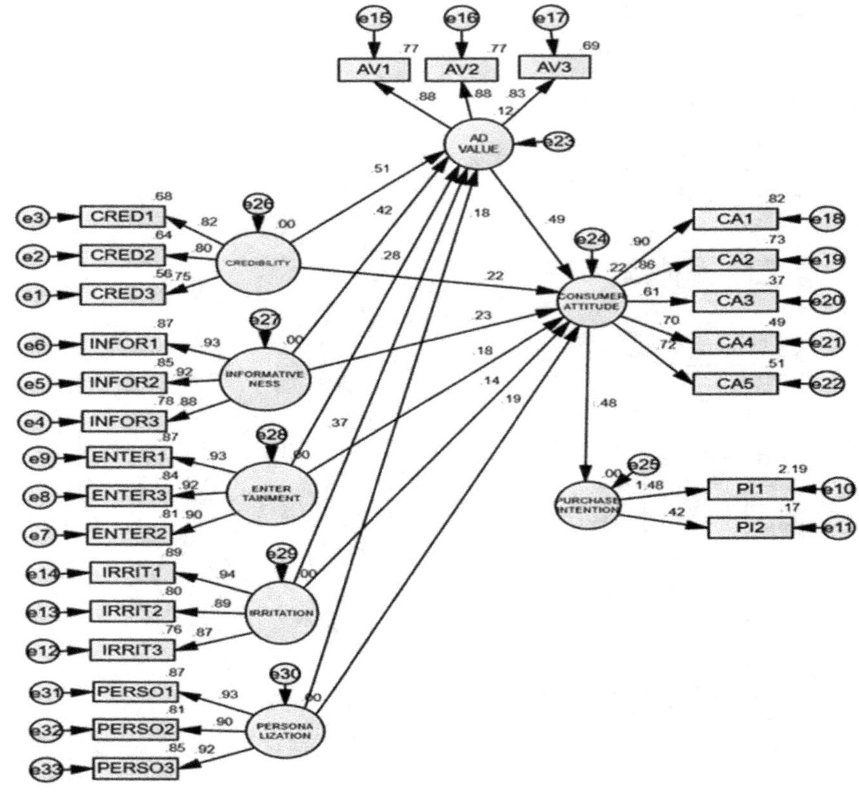

Source: Analysis output

The direct and indirect effects are shown in Tables 1 and 2. The path diagram of the SEM is presented in Figure 3. Based on the direct effect credibility, informativeness, entertainment and personalization have significant positive effect to the consumer attitude toward the Instagram advertising, while irritation significantly negatively affects. It is also found that consumer attitude toward Instagram advertising also has a strong positive effect on purchase intention. For indirect effects except irritation, advertising value mediates the impact between credibility, informativeness, entertainment, personalization, and attitude towards Instagram advertising.

Table 1. Direct effect of dependent and independent variables

Direct Relationship	Estimate	P-values	Significance	Hypotheses
Advertisement_value <--- Credibility	.508	***	Significant	H_1 accepted
Advertisement_value <--- Informativeness	.417	***	Significant	H_2 accepted
Advertisement_value <--- Entertainment	.275	.004	Significant	H_3 accepted
Advertisement_value <--- Irritation	.369	***	Significant	H_4 accepted
Advertisement_value <--- Personalization	.148	.006	Significant	H_5 accepted
Consumer_attitude <--- Credibility	.221	.004	significant	H_6 accepted
Consumer_attitude <--- Informativeness	.220	***	significant	H_7 accepted
Consumer_attitude <--- Entertainment	.157	.006	significant	H_8 accepted
Consumer_attitude <--- Irritation	.135	.010	significant	H_9 accepted
Consumer_attitude <--- Personalization	.161	.007	significant	H_{10} accepted
Consumer_attitude <--- Advertisement_value	.487	***	significant	H_{11} accepted
Purchase_intention <--- Consumer_attitude	.480	***	significant	H_{17} accepted

Source: Analysis Output

Table 2. Indirect effect of dependent and independent variable with mediator

Indirect Relationship	Estimate	P- values	Mediation Effect	Hypotheses
Consumer_attitude<---Advertisement_value<--- Entertainment	.278	.003	full mediation	H_{11} accepted
Consumer_attitude <--- Advertisement_value <--- Informativeness	.350	***	full mediation	H_{12} accepted
Consumer_attitude <--- Advertisement_value <--- Personalization	.532	***	full mediation	H_{13} accepted
Consumer_attitude <--- Advertisement_value <--- Credibility	.483	.002	full mediation	H_{14} accepted
Consumer_attitude <--- Advertisement_value <--- Irritation	.021	.128	no mediation	H_{15} failed to accepted

Source: Analysis Output

7. CONCLUSION

7.1. Theoretical and Managerial Implications

This study has generated theoretical Implications and managerial implications, as far as theoretical implications are concerned, it helps the researchers to understand nature, beliefs, and attitudes of consumers towards Instagram advertising in a more precise way. The finding suggests that attitude is statistically determined by credibility, informativeness, entertainment, personalization, advertising value and irritation. From that six belief factors, there is one belief factor that had a negative correlation, and five belief factors that had a positive correlation. All of these belief factors can be realized in authoritatively controlled media context. Marketers/ practitioners need to invest time and money in creating the belief factors which are positively related to the Instagram advertising. It assists in developing a favourable attitude toward advertised brands that in turn generates a positive purchase intention for the advertised brands. Informativeness belief factor results in positive attitude towards advertising (Wang & Sun, 2010) and it was previously verified (Wang & Sun, 2010) so marketers should take into account the advantage of informative advertising (Petrovici &Marinov, 2007). It is also found that entertainment belief factors significantly influence the creation of recipients' positive attitudes towards advertising. Therefore, advertising professionals in order to generate an effective advertising campaigns should use creative, pleasurable, and aesthetic designs and themes (Raza et al., 2018; Simola et al., 2013). The research also demonstrates that trust and customization do affect the consumer's attitude toward Instagram advertising. The potential explanation for such an effect is a person find it is trustworthy and personalized. Therefore, marketers are recommended that when they make any advertisements in Instagram, hoped that it is trustworthy and personalized for targeted audience's preference. For the negatively associated belief factor (i.e., irritation), advertisers must develop the advertisement for Instagram that generates trust and do no harm and have moral persuasions, use real claims, less curiosity, and this way to reduce the scepticism of consumer and make Instagram advertising, more positive. The relationship among the constructs under consideration is also reviewed, and the results show that advertising value does mediate the relationship among credibility, informativeness, entertainment and personalization. The trend has arisen as consumers increasingly trust Instagram ads as being more authentic, informative, fun, personalized and community-oriented. From the result it is also clear that there is no mediational role of advertising value between irritation and consumer attitude toward Instagram advertising because 'irritation' belief factor does not create value for the viewers, it irritates them. In addition, the present study also provides evidence for the fact that consumer attitude towards Instagram advertising significantly and positively affects purchase intention. This is a result of a hierarchy of effects (HOE). It means that when consumer`s attitude towards Instagram advertising to be directed positively then they will be purchasing the advertised brand and services i.e., a positive relationship between attitude towards advertising, and purchase intention exists.

The results from the study have deciphered implications for developing advertising content on Instagram. To create a reputation of authenticity and capture the best influencer value for their advertising money is to allocate more marketing budget toward partnerships with genuine microinfluencers instead of high-profile famous individuals. Campaigns should be created to satisfy both informative and hedonic needs — this can be done through an immersive format such as Reels, where product information is embedded into appealing stories. Personalization is still an effective weapon, but it must be used within the bounds of transparency—telling someone why they are seeing a particular advertisement might increase its wholesome reception. Finally, to overcome the ill-effects of irritation among users, advertisers need to be strict with frequency caps and more importantly produce ad creative that is so good in visual coherence it feels like a native part of a user's feed rather than an interruption.

8. LIMITATIONS AND SCOPE FOR FUTURE RESEARCH

This study is not devoid of limitation despite a valuable finding. This is a cross-sectional study, such that it will only reflect the net effects of the predictor variable at one point in time (Cavana, R., Delahaye, B. and Sekeran, 2001). The fact that this was a cross-sectional study and its inherent limitation is not being able to account for the observed changes in patterns and causes of 'consumer attitude toward Instagram advertising' (Easterby-Smith & Lowe, 2002). The major limitation is restricted generalisability due to the cultural and geographical sampling frame (urban Indian students and young professionals). The results may not apply to Western cultures with different privacy norms or to older participants. This study is not generalisable to other social media such as Facebook, YouTube etc. Further research is required on other emerging social media platforms such as snapchat from the context of developing economies. It is because the source credibility and source attractiveness towards the ad have been covered comprehensively, the other belief dimensions also need to be explored in thinking of the social media platforms and by understanding further to the other belief dimensions, the advertisers/practitioners may facilitate the more effective and less costly advertising that would lead to the positive attitude and leave an impact on the purchase intention.

REFERENCES

Aktan, M., Aydogan, S., & Aysuna, C. (2016). Web Advertising Value and Students' Attitude Towards Web Advertising. *European Journal of Business and Management*, *8*(9), 86–97.

Alalwan, A. A. (2018). Investigating the impact of social media advertising features on customer purchase intention. *International Journal of Information Management*, *42*(April), 65–77. DOI: 10.1016/j.ijinfomgt.2018.06.001

Alsamydai, M. J., & Hamdi Al Khasawneh, M. (2013). Antecedents and consequences of e- Jordanian consumer behaviour regarding Facebook advertising. *International Journal of Business*, *3*(4), 41–60.

Anubha, & Jain, A. (2024). In-game advertising and brand purchase intentions: An SOR perspective. *Global Knowledge, Memory and Communication, 73*(1/2), 24-44. https://doi.org/DOI: 10.1108/gkmc-02-2022-0050

Arma & Elma. (2025). *Best Instagram Ads Statistics 2025 (Editor's Choice)*. Retrieved August 27, 2025, from https://www.amraandelma.com/best-instagram-ads-statistics/?utm_source=chatgpt.com

Arora, T., & Agarwal, B. (2019). Empirical Study on Perceived Value and Attitude of Millennials Towards Social Media Advertising: A Structural Equation Modelling Approach. *Vision (Basel)*, *23*(1), 56–69. DOI: 10.1177/0972262918821248

Ashley, C., & Tuten, T. (2015). Creative Strategies in Social Media Marketing: An Exploratory Study of Branded Social Content and Consumer Engagement. *Psychology and Marketing*, *32*(1), 15–27. DOI: 10.1002/mar

Brackett, L. K., & Carr, B. N. (2001). Cyberspace Advertising vs. Other Media: Consumer vs. Mature Student Attitudes. *Journal of Advertising Research*, *41*(5), 23–32.

Brinson, N. H., & Lemon, L. L. (2023). Investigating the effects of host trust, credibility, and authenticity in podcast advertising. *Journal of Marketing Communications*, •••, 1–19. DOI: 10.1080/13527266.2022.2054017

Cavana, R., Delahaye, B., & Sekeran, U. (2001). *Applied business research: Qualitative and quantitative methods*. John Wiley & Sons.

Choi, S. M., & Rifon, N. J. (2002). Antecedents and Consequences of Web Advertising Credibility. *Journal of Interactive Advertising*, *3*(1), 12–24. DOI: 10.1080/15252019.2002.10722064

Dahl, S. (2021). *Social Media Marketing: Theories and Applications*. Sage Publications Ltd.

Dao, W. V. T., Le, A. N. H., Cheng, J. M. S., & Chen, D. C. (2014). Social media advertising value: The case of transitional economies in Southeast Asia. *International Journal of Advertising*, *33*(2), 271–294. DOI: 10.2501/IJA-33-2-271-294

Dehghani, M., Niaki, M. K., Ramezani, I., & Sali, R. (2016). Evaluating the influence of YouTube advertising for attraction of young customers. *Computers in Human Behavior*, *59*, 165–172. DOI: 10.1016/j.chb.2016.01.037

Di Pietro, L., & Pantano, E. (2012). An empirical investigation of social network influence on consumer purchasing decision: The case of Facebook. *Journal of Direct, Data and Digital Marketing Practice*, *14*(1), 18–29. DOI: 10.1057/dddmp.2012.10

Djafarova, E., & Rushworth, C. (2017). Exploring the credibility of online celebrities' Instagram profiles in influencing the purchase decisions of young female users. *Computers in Human Behavior*, *68*, 1–7. DOI: 10.1016/j.chb.2016.11.009

Dobber, T., Kruikemeier, S., Votta, F., Helberger, N., & Goodman, E. P. (2025). The effect of traffic light veracity labels on perceptions of political advertising source and message credibility on social media. *Journal of Information Technology & Politics*, *22*(1), 82–97.

Ducoffe, R. H. (1995). How consumers assess the value of advertising. *Journal of Current Issues and Research in Advertising*, *17*(1), 1–18. DOI: 10.1080/10641734.1995.10505022

Ducoffe, R. H. (1996). Advertising value and advertising on the web. *Journal of Advertising Research*, *36*(5), 21–35.

Dwinanda, B., & Syaripuddin, F. A., Hudaifi, & Hendriana, E. (2022). Examining the Extended Advertising Value Model: A Case of TikTok Short Video Ads. *Mediterranean Journal of Social & Behavioural Research*, *6*(2), 35–44. DOI: 10.30935/mjosbr/11820

Easterby-Smith, M. T., & Lowe, R. A. (2002). *Management Research: An Introduction*. SAGE Publications Ltd.

Evans, D. (2010). *Social media marketing: the next generation of business engagement*. Jhon Willy & Sons.

Fatima, T., & Abbas, M. T. (2016). Impact of Advertising Beliefs and Personalization on Attitude towards Advertising; Mediating Role of Advertising Value. In *International Journal of Business Management and Commerce* (Vol. 1, Issue 2).

Field, A. (2009). *Discovering statistics using spss*. sage.

Fransen, M. L., Verlegh, P. W. J., Kirmani, A., & Smit, E. G. (2015). A typology of consumer strategies for resisting advertising, and a review of mechanisms for countering them. *International Journal of Advertising*, *34*(1), 6–16. DOI: 10.1080/02650487.2014.995284

Greyser, S. A. (1973). Irritation in advertising. *Journal of Advertising Research*, *13*(1), 3–10.

Gupta, S., Paul, J., Stoner, J. L., & Aggarwal, A. (2024). Digital transformation, online advertising, and consumer behaviour. *International Journal of Advertising*, *43*(8), 1439–1462. DOI: 10.1080/02650487.2024.2317632

Hair, F. J., Black, C. W., Babin, J. B., & Amderson, E. R. (2010). Multivariate Data Analysis (7th ed.). Pearson prentice Hall.

Hanaysha, J. R., & Alhyasat, K. M. (2025). Examining the Effect of Social Media Advertising Features on Customer Perceived Value and Brand Love in the Retail Industry. *Telematics and Informatics Reports*, 100208.

Hayes, J. L., & King, K. W. (2014). The Social Exchange of Viral Ads: Referral and Coreferral of Ads Among College Students. *Journal of Interactive Advertising*, *14*(2), 98–109. DOI: 10.1080/15252019.2014.942473

Homer, P. M. (1990). The Mediating Role of Attitude toward the Ad: Some Additional Evidence. *JMR, Journal of Marketing Research*, *27*(1), 78. DOI: 10.2307/3172553

Hong, I. B., & Cho, H. (2011). The impact of consumer trust on attitudinal loyalty and purchase intentions in B2C e-marketplaces: Intermediary trust vs. seller trust. *International Journal of Information Management*, *31*(5), 469–479. DOI: 10.1016/j.ijinfomgt.2011.02.001

Hsu, M. H., Chuang, L. W., & Hsu, C. S. (2014). Understanding online shopping intention: The roles of four types of trust and their antecedents. *Internet Research*, *24*(3), 332–352. DOI: 10.1108/IntR-01-2013-0007

Hussain, A., Hooi Ting, D., Zaib Abbasi, A., & Rehman, U. (2023). Integrating the S-O-R Model to Examine Purchase Intention Based on Instagram Sponsored Advertising. *Journal of Promotion Management*, *29*(1), 77–105. DOI: 10.1080/10496491.2022.2108185

Jain, G., Rakesh, S., & Chaturvedi, K. R. (2018). Online video advertisements' effect on purchase intention: An exploratory study on youth. *International Journal of E-Business Research*, *14*(2), 87–101. DOI: 10.4018/IJEBR.2018040106

Janssen, L., Schouten, A. P., & Croes, E. A. (2021). Influencer advertising on Instagram: Product-influencer fit and number of followers affect advertising outcomes and influencer evaluations via credibility and identification. *International Journal of Advertising*, *41*(1), 101–127. DOI: 10.1080/02650487.2021.1994205

Jebarajakirthy, C., Maseeh, H. I., Morshed, Z., Shankar, A., Arli, D., & Pentecost, R. (2021). Mobile advertising: A systematic literature review and future research agenda. In *International Journal of Consumer Studies* (Vol. 45, Issue 6, pp. 1258–1291). John Wiley and Sons Inc. https://doi.org/DOI: 10.1111/ijcs.12728

Johnson, A. (2025). Engagement, informativeness, and intrusiveness: Unpacking social media's impact on mobile ads. *International Journal of Management and Economics Fundamental*, *5*(01), 1–4.

Johnson, T. J., & Kaye, B. K. (2015). Site Effects: How Reliance on Social Media Influences Confidence in the Government and News Media. *Social Science Computer Review*, *33*(2), 127–144. DOI: 10.1177/0894439314537029

Jung, A. R. (2017). The influence of perceived ad relevance on social media advertising: An empirical examination of a mediating role of privacy concern. *Computers in Human Behavior*, *70*, 303–309. DOI: 10.1016/j.chb.2017.01.008

Kamalul Ariffin, S., Ihsannuddin, N. Q., & Abdul Mohsin, A. M. (2021). The influence of attitude functions on Muslim consumer attitude towards social media advertising: A case of bubble tea. *Journal of Islamic Marketing*, *6315458*. Advance online publication. DOI: 10.1108/JIMA-01-2021-0015

Kaplan, A. M., & Haenlein, M. (2010). Users of the world, unite! The challenges and opportunities of social media. *Business Horizons*, *53*(1), 59–68. DOI: 10.1016/j.bushor.2009.09.003

Khan, A., Rezaei, S., & Valaei, N. (2022). Social commerce advertising avoidance and shopping cart abandonment: A fs/QCA analysis of German consumers. *Journal of Retailing and Consumer Services*, *67*. Advance online publication. DOI: 10.1016/j.jretconser.2022.102976

Kim, Y. J., & Han, J. (2014). Why smartphone advertising attracts customers: A model of Web advertising, flow, and personalization. *Computers in Human Behavior*, *33*, 256–269. DOI: 10.1016/j.chb.2014.01.015

Kornias, G., & Hălălău, R. (2012). Factors influencing users' attitude toward display advertising on Facebook. In *Jönköping University*.

Kotler, P., & Keller, K. L. (2016). *Marketing management* (International Ed.). Pearson.

Lafferty, B. A., & Goldsmith, R. E. (1999). Corporate Credibility's Role in Consumers' Attitudes and Purchase Intentions When a High versus a Low Credibility Endorser Is Used in the Ad. *Journal of Business Research*, *44*, 109–116.

Lee, J., & Hong, I. B. (2016). Predicting positive user responses to social media advertising: The roles of emotional appeal, informativeness, and creativity. *International Journal of Information Management*, *36*(3), 360–373. DOI: 10.1016/j.ijinfomgt.2016.01.001

Li, H., Edwards, S. M., & Lee, J. H. (2002). Measuring the intrusiveness of advertisements: Scale development and validation. *Journal of Advertising*, *31*(2), 37–47. DOI: 10.1080/00913367.2002.10673665

Lin, T. T. C., & Bautista, J. R. (2020). Content-related factors influence perceived value of location-based mobile advertising. *Journal of Computer Information Systems*, *60*(2), 184–193. DOI: 10.1080/08874417.2018.1432995

MacKenzie, S. B., & Lutz, R. J. (1989). An Empirical Examination of the Structural Antecedents of Attitude toward the Ad in an Advertising Pretesting Context. *Journal of Marketing*, *53*, 48–65. DOI: 10.2307/1251413

Mahatmavidya, P. A., & Yasa, N. N. K. (2020). Advertising value of Instagram stories and the effect on millennial's attitude. *Russian Journal of Agricultural and Socio-Economic Sciences*, *3*(99), 29–39. DOI: 10.18551/rjoas.2020-03.04

Martins, J., Costa, C., Oliveira, T., Gonçalves, R., & Branco, F. (2019). How smartphone advertising influences consumers' purchase intention. *Journal of Business Research*, *94*, 378–387. DOI: 10.1016/j.jbusres.2017.12.047

Mehta, A. (2000). Advertising Attitudes and Ads Effectiveness. *Journal of Advertising Research*, *40*(3), 67–72.

Milfeld, T., & Haley, E. (2024). Purpose advertising and the credibility gap. *Journal of Advertising Research*, *64*(1), 59–79. DOI: 10.2501/jar-2023-021

Mitchell, A. A., & Olson, J. C. (1981). Are Product Attribute Beliefs the Only Mediator of Advertising Effects on Brand Attitude? *JMR, Journal of Marketing Research*, *18*(3), 318–332. DOI: 10.2307/3150973

Mittal, B. (1994). Public assessment of advertising: Faint praise and harsh criticism. *Journal of Advertising Research*, *34*(1), 35–53.

Mohd Noor, M. N., Sreenivasan, J., & Ismail, H. (2013). Malaysian consumers attitude towards mobile advertising, the role of permission and its impact on purchase intention: A structural equation modeling approach. *Asian Social Science*, *9*(5), 135–153. DOI: 10.5539/ass.v9n5p135

Murillo, E., Merino, M., & Núñez, A. (2016). The advertising value of Twitter Ads: A study among Mexican Millennials Enrique. *Review of Business Management*, *18*(61), 436–456. DOI: 10.7819/rbgn.v18i61.2471

Nielsen. (2016). Nielsen Social Media Report. In *The Nielsen Company*.

Noor, U., Mansoor, M., & Shamim, A. (2024). Customers create customers! – Assessing the role of perceived personalization, online advertising engagement and online users' modes in generating positive e-WOM. *Asia-Pacific Journal of Business Administration*, *16*(2), 392–409.

Nurhidayah, S., & Dirgantara, I. M. B. (2025). The effect of personalized advertising on attitude towards advertising and click-through rate. *Economic and Business Horizon*, *4*(3), 469–478.

Ben Oumlil, A., & Balloun, J. L. (2020). Millennials' attitude toward advertising: An international exploratory study. *Young Consumers*, *21*(1), 17–34. DOI: 10.1108/YC-10-2018-0865

Petrovici, D., & Marinov, M. (2007). Determinants and antecedents of general attitudes towards advertising: A study of two EU accession countries. *European Journal of Marketing*, *41*(3–4), 307–326. DOI: 10.1108/03090560710728354

Pollay, R. W., & Mittal, B. (1993). Here's the Beef: Factors, Determinants, and Segments in Consumer Criticism of Advertising. *Journal of Marketing*, *57*(3), 99. DOI: 10.2307/1251857

Prendergast, G., & Liu, P. yan, & Poon, D. T. Y. (2009). A Hong Kong study of advertising credibility. *Journal of Consumer Marketing*, *26*(5), 320–329. DOI: 10.1108/07363760910976574

Putra, A. H. P. K., Mariam, S., Tafsir, M., & Rosanti, N. (2024). Deciphering the green marketing puzzle: Understanding the interplay of green marketing strategic orientation, attitude towards green marketing, brand integrity, and purchase intention. *International Review of Management and Marketing*, *14*(4), 210.

Raktham, W., Chaipoopirutana, S., & Combs, H. (2017). Factors Influencing Consumer Attitudes toward Social Media Advertising. *International Conference on Humanities, Social Sciences and Education*, 32–36.

Ramaprasad, J. (2001). South Asian students' beliefs about and attitude toward advertising. *Journal of Current Issues and Research in Advertising*, *23*(1), 55–70. DOI: 10.1080/10641734.2001.10505114

Raza, S. H., Bakar, H. A., & Mohamad, B. (2018). Relationships between the advertising appeal and behavioural intention: The mediating role of the attitude towards advertising appeal and moderating role of cultural norm. *The Journal of Business and Retail Management Research*, *12*(2), 185–193. DOI: 10.24052/jbrmr/v12is02/rbtaaabitmrotataaamrocn

Roth-Cohen, O., Rosenberg, H., & Lissitsa, S. (2022). Are you talking to me? Generation X, Y, Z responses to mobile advertising. *Convergence*, *28*(3), 761–780. DOI: 10.1177/13548565211047342

Rózsa, Z., Ferenčáková, L., Zámek, D., & Firstová, J. (2025). Generation Z's perception of privacy on social media: Examining the impact of personalized advertising, interpersonal relationships, reference group dynamics, social isolation, and anxiety on self-disclosure willingness. *Oeconomia Copernicana*, *15*(1), 229–266.

Saadeghvaziri, F., & Hosseini, H. K. (2011). Mobile advertising: An investigation of factors creating positive attitude in Iranian customers. *African Journal of Business Management*, *5*(2), 394–404. DOI: 10.5897/AJBM10.431

Saraiva, M. F., & Lues, H. T. (2024). Generation Y's view on print media advertisements: Variances in its perceived informativeness, entertainment, irritation, credibility, and value. *Journal of Contemporary Management*, *20*(si1), 1–21.

Saxena, A., & Khanna, U. (2013). Advertising on Social Network Sites: A Structural Equation Modelling Approach. *Vision: The Journal of Business Perspective*, *17*(1), 17–25. DOI: 10.1177/0972262912469560

Schultz, V. A. B. J. P. D. (2016). Social media and consumer engagement: A review and research agenda. *Journal of Research in Interactive Marketing*, *10*(4). Advance online publication. DOI: 10.1016/0031-9201(92)90209-e

Sesar, V., Martinčević, I., & Boguszewicz-Kreft, M. (2022). Relationship between Advertising Disclosure, Influencer Credibility and Purchase Intention. *Journal of Risk and Financial Management*, *15*(7), 276. DOI: 10.3390/jrfm15070276

Shareef, M. A., Mukerji, B., Dwivedi, Y. K., Rana, N. P., & Islam, R. (2019). Social media marketing: Comparative effect of advertisement sources. *Journal of Retailing and Consumer Services*, *46*, 58–69. DOI: 10.1016/j.jretconser.2017.11.001

Shavitt, S., Lowrey, P., & Haefner, J. (1998). Public attitudes toward advertising: More favourable than you might think. *Journal of Advertising Research*, *38*(4), 7–22.

Shimp, T. A. (1981). Attitude toward the AD as a mediator of consumer brand choice. *Journal of Advertising*, *10*(2), 9–48. DOI: 10.1080/00913367.1981.10672756

Simola, J., Kivikangas, M., Kuisma, J., & Krause, C. M. (2013). Attention and memory for newspaper advertisements: Effects of ad-editorial congruency and location. *Applied Cognitive Psychology*, *27*(4), 429–442. DOI: 10.1002/acp.2918

Tahereh, N., & Zahra, G. T. (2012). Investigating effective factors on the perceived values and attitudes of Internet advertisements users. *Journal of Basic and Applied Scientific Research*, *2*(5), 4392–4399.

Tsang, M. M., Ho, S. C., & Liang, T. P. (2004). Consumer attitudes toward mobile advertising: An empirical study. *International Journal of Electronic Commerce*, *8*(3), 65–78. DOI: 10.1080/10864415.2004.11044301

Wang, P., & Wen, M.-J. (2017). Personalization, privacy, and attitudes towards online advertising. *Decision Science Letters*, *22*(9), 1–12.

Wang, Y., & Genç, E. (2019). Path to effective mobile advertising in Asian markets: Credibility, entertainment, and peer influence. *Asia Pacific Journal of Marketing and Logistics*, *31*(1), 55–80. DOI: 10.1108/APJML-06-2017-0112

Wang, Y., & Sun, S. (2010). Examining the role of beliefs and attitudes in online advertising: A comparison between the USA and Romania. *International Marketing Review*, *27*(1), 87–107. DOI: 10.1108/02651331011020410

Wright, L. T., Gaber, H., Robin, R., & Cai, H. (2018). Content Strategies for Facebook Marketing: A Case Study of a Leading Fast-Food Brand Page. *Academy of Marketing Science*, 779–791. https://doi.org/DOI: 10.1007/978-3-319-66023-3_246

Wu, I.-L., Hsiao, W.-H., Wu, I.-L., & Hsiao, W.-H. (2017). Involvement, content, and interactivity drivers for consumer loyalty in mobile advertising: The mediating role of advertising value. *International Journal of Human-Computer Studies*, *15*(6), •••.

Wu, P. C. S., Yeh, G. Y. Y., & Hsiao, C. R. (2011). The effect of store image and service quality on brand image and purchase intention for private label brands. *Australasian Marketing Journal*, *19*(1), 30–39. DOI: 10.1016/j.ausmj.2010.11.001

Xu, D. J. (2006). The influence of personalization in affecting consumer attitudes toward mobile advertising in China. *Journal of Computer Information Systems*, *47*(2), 9–19. DOI: 10.1080/08874417.2007.11645949

Yang, K. C., Huang, C. H., Yang, C., & Yang, S. Y. (2017). Consumer attitudes toward online video advertisement: YouTube as a platform. *Kybernetes*, *46*(5), 840–853. DOI: 10.1108/K-03-2016-0038

Ye, G., Guan, X., Hudders, L., Xiao, Y., & Li, J. (2024). A Meta-Analysis of the Antecedents and Consequences of Advertising Value. *Journal of Advertising*, *54*(1), 117–138. DOI: 10.1080/00913367.2024.2309923

Youn, S., & Kim, S. (2019). Understanding ad avoidance on Facebook: Antecedents and outcomes of psychological reactance. *Computers in Human Behavior*, *98*, 232–244. DOI: 10.1016/j.chb.2019.04.025

Zhang, E. M. (2016). From online motivations to Ad clicks and to behavioural intentions: An empirical study of consumer response to social media advertising. *Psychology and Marketing*, *33*(3), 155–164. DOI: 10.1002/mar

Zhao, X., Yang, J., Xie, T., & Wang, Z. (2017). Examining advertising intrusiveness on Instagram: Hedonic and utilitarian attributes of brand and sponsored content. *In American Academy of Advertising*, 243.

APPENDIX

Table 3. KMO and Bartlett's Test

KMO and Bartlett's Test		
Kaiser-Meyer-Olkin Measure of Sampling Adequacy.		.876
Bartlett's Test of Sphericity	Approx. Chi-Square	9924.244
	df	435
	Sig.	.000

Table 4. Factor Loading and Cronbach Alfa

Constructs	Items	Factor loading
Credibility (Cronbach's α = 0.83, CR = 0.873, AVE=0.580, MSV=0.291, ASV=0.170)		
Cred1	I trust Instagram advertisements.	0.791
Cred2	I use Instagram advertisements as a reference for purchasing.	0.787
Cred3	The content provided by Instagram advertisements are credible.	0.749
Informativeness (Cronbach's α = 0.94, CR=0.879, AVE=0.707, MSV=0.327, ASV=0.170)		
Infor 1	Instagram advertisements are valuable source of information about sales.	0.846
Infor 2	Instagram advertisements tell me which brands have the features I am looking for	0.845
Infor 3	Instagram advertisements keep me up to date about products/services available in the marketplace	0.832
Entertainment (Cronbach's α = 0.94, CR=0.889, AVE=0.728, MSV=0.268, ASV=0.149)		
Enter 1	I feel that watching Instagram advertisements is enjoyable and entertaining.	0.864
Enter 2	I feel that the exposure to Instagram advertisements is pleasant.	0.855
Enter 3	To me, it is amusing to view advertisements on Instagram.	0.841
Irritation (Cronbach's α = 0.93, CR=0.888, AVE=0.614, MSV=0.251, ASV=0.154)		
Irrit 1	I feel Instagram advertisements are irritating.	0.943
Irrit 2	I feel advertisements on Instagram are everywhere.	0.924
Irrit 3	Content of Instagram advertisements are annoying.	0.867
Advertising value (Cronbach's α = 0.91, CR=0.924, AVE=0.709, MSV=0.157 ASV=0.083)		
Av 1	Instagram advertisements are useful.	0.876
Av 2	Instagram advertisements are valuable.	0.869

continued on following page

Table 4. Continued

Constructs	Items	Factor loading
Av 3	Instagram advertisements are important.	0.867
Personalization (Cronbach's α = 0.94, CR=0.885, AVE=0.720, MSV=0.328, ASV=0.166)		
Perso 1	I feel that Instagram advertisements display personalized message to me.	0.855
Perso 2	I feel that Instagram advertisements are personalized for my usage.	0.852
Perso 3	Contents in Instagram advertisements are personalized.	0.838
Purchase Intention (Cronbach's α = 0.77, CR=0.874, AVE=0.699, MSV=0.003, ASV=0.001)		
Pi 1	After watching Instagram advertisements, I would consider purchasing products/services/brands.	0.876
Pi 2	I will buy products/services/brands that are advertised on Instagram.	0.825
Consumer attitude (Cronbach's α = 0.89, CR=0.888, AVE=0.614, MSV=0.251, ASV=0.154)		
Ca 1	Overall, I consider Instagram advertising a good thing.	0.832
Ca 2	Overall, I dislike Instagram advertising.	0.824
Ca 3	My general opinion of Instagram advertising is unfavorable.	0.775
Ca 4	I like the idea of Instagram advertisements.	0.723
Ca 5	Viewing Instagram advertisements is a good idea.	0.760

Source: Analysis Output

Chapter 13
Influencer Marketing and Brand Collaboration:
Innovation in Hotel Operations and Marketing in the Digital Age

Priyanka Srivastava
http://orcid.org/0009-0002-6831-9977
Indira Institute of Management, Pune, India

Swapnali Kulkarni
http://orcid.org/0009-0002-9038-8047
Indira University, Pune, India

ABSTRACT

The hospitality industry has experienced significant changes in the age of social media, where online interactions increasingly influence customer opinions and booking choices. One of the most effective approaches in transforming hotel marketing and operations is influencer marketing, along with strategic collaborations between brands. This chapter investigates how hotels can benefit from the trustworthiness, creativity, and extensive online presence of influencers to forge genuine connections with their target audiences. Also, it looks into the advantages of partnership with lifestyle, travel, and luxury brands to enhance guest experiences, distinguish offerings, and reinforce brand identity. This chapter illustrates, through industry-leading practices and cutting-edge research, how campaigns and partnerships driven by influencers can enhance hotel visibility. The focus is particularly on the integration of operations—highlighting how hotel managers can align influencer initiatives with service execution, guest interaction, and revenue strategies to guarantee a cohesive brand.

DOI: 10.4018/979-8-3373-6741-5.ch013

1. INTRODUCTION: SOCIAL MEDIA DISRUPTION IN HOSPITALITY MARKETING

The hospitality industry has always depended on storytelling, and reputation management. In the past, hotel promotion was largely centered on word-of-mouth references, travel agents, beautiful brochures, print media advertising, television advertising, and billboards to draw visitors. These channels focused on personal trust and edited images without any scope for live interactions. With the emergence of digital technology and the rapid development of social media websites, the hospitality marketing environment has undergone a significant transformation. Social media is both a disruptive technology and a potent weapon, transforming the way hotels engage with customers, narrate brand narratives, and handle client relationships (Leung et al., 2013). In contrast to static traditional media, social sites live on interactive visual and consumer-created content. They are therefore extremely powerful in shaping travel aspirations. Contemporary travelers rely heavily on social media photographs, short clips, peer opinion, and opinions by influencers. They use this material not only to make informed reservation choices but also to determine their general traveling experiences (Gupta, 2019; Varkaris & Neuhofer, 2017). Here, social media has emerged as the new word-of-mouth, bringing both opportunities and challenges for the hospitality sector in the 21st century.

Figure 1. Social Media Disruption in Hospitality Marketing

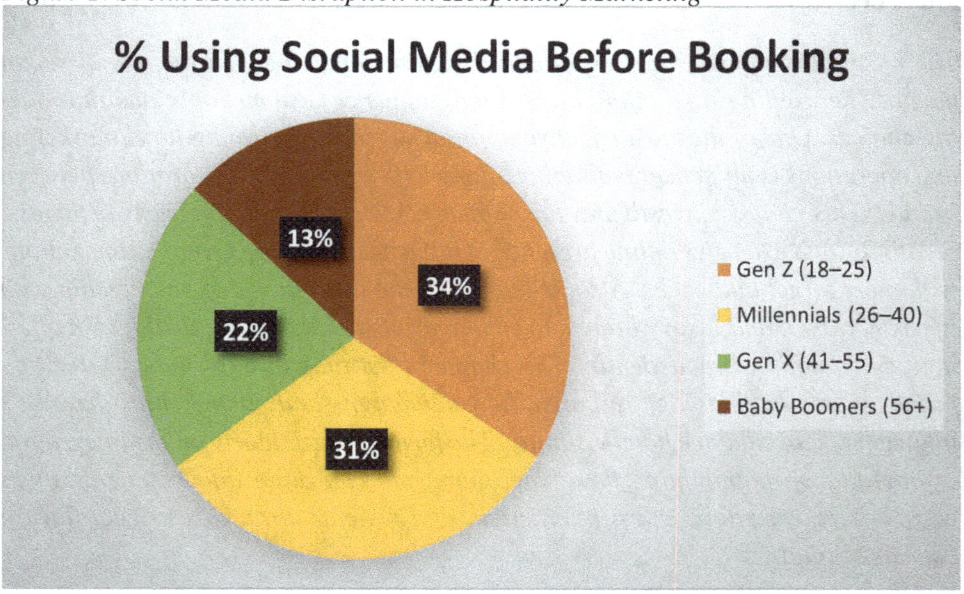

The Social Media Revolution in Hospitality

Social media platforms like Instagram, YouTube, Tok-tok, and Facebook have transformed the hospitality sector by making information sharing democratized. As opposed to conventional advertising, whereby brand messaging was mainly one-way, social media has enabled consumers and content providers to create and post experiences that have a direct impact on others. Studies indicate that user-generated content (UGC) and social proof play a crucial role in affecting customers' trust, brand image, and booking behavior in hospitality (Aluri, Slevitch, & Larzelere, 2015; Garrido-Moreno et al., 2018). For example, a guest's Instagram story regarding a high-end resort, including good-looking pictures of the resort, serves as unpaid promotion for the hotel, which will be viewed by hundreds and even thousands of prospective travelers. Likewise, YouTube travel blogs are real tales of hotel experiences, which tend to have greater credibility than official brand communications (McCarthy, Stock, & Verma, 2010). Social media's role goes beyond marketing to reputation management, such that a review on Google or TripAdvisor can break or make a hotel's reputation (Minazzi, 2015).

Emergence of Influencer Marketing

In this wider social media upheaval, influencer marketing stands out as perhaps the strongest means of hospitality business promotion. Influencers—people with sway and influence over their audience—act as digital storytellers, combining personal branding and brand marketing. In contrast to traditional celebrities used in conventional advertising, social media influencers tend to create a perceived personal connection with their followers, producing increased engagement and authenticity (Moro & Rita, 2018). This makes influencer content especially potent in hospitality, where authenticity and trust are most important.

Hotels now often partner with influencers to highlight distinct features of their property, ranging from upscale spa treatments to cultural immersion activities. For example, micro-influencers targeting niche travel audiences can market boutique hotels better than a mass-scale marketing campaign. Research points out that influencer endorsements tend to create more engagement and more relevant conversions than traditional channels (Vasumathi & Ambrose, 2024).

Figure 2. Factors Influencing Hotel Booking Decisions

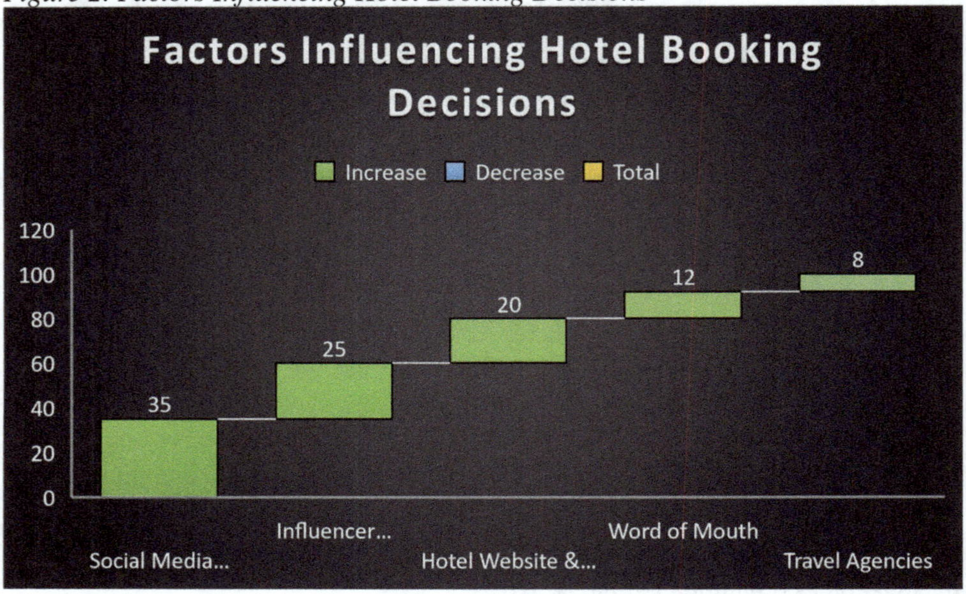

The data presented in the chart highlights how digital touchpoints dominate the hotel booking journey in today's hospitality landscape. Social media reviews (35%) and influencer recommendations (25%) together account for *more than half of the decision-making influence*, reflecting the growing reliance on peer-driven and experiential content. Hotel websites and advertisements, while still significant (20%), no longer hold the same persuasive power as user-generated or influencer-led content. Interestingly, traditional sources such as word of mouth (12%) and travel agencies (8%) show a clear decline in influence, emphasizing the shift from offline to online engagement. This insight reinforces that hotel must strategically integrate influencer partnerships and review management into their marketing efforts if they wish to remain competitive and relevant in the digital age.

The emergence of platforms such as Instagram has been particularly important in framing "Instagram able" travel experiences. Hotels now plan spaces—rooftop pools, visually appealing lobbies, or iconic dishes—with social media visibility to promote these visuals, which can trigger authentic influencer-led campaigns. This intersection of marketing and operations represents a new hospitality paradigm, where guest experience and brand narrative come together harmoniously (Bilgihan & Ricci, 2024).

Changing Consumer Behavior and the Digital Traveler

The digital revolution has radically transformed the behavior of hospitality industry consumers. Today's travelers increasingly depend on digital media for planning, reservations, and assessing their accommodations, which renders online interaction a key driver of hotel performance. McCarthy, Stock, and Verma (2010) write that travel decision-making is increasingly led by social media and online sources. This change is particularly pronounced with Millennials and Generation Z, for whom authenticity, word-of-mouth, and social proof weigh more heavily than do classic advertising campaigns (Gulati, 2022). Empirical evidence documents this shift: over 70% of tourists read social media entries, web feedback, or digital travel forums prior to making reservations final (Hays, Page, & Buhalis, 2013). In addition, sites like TikTok and Instagram have become influential sources of travel inspiration, where visually oriented short-form content and influencer storytelling directly influence both destination selection and accommodation options. To this, hotels are no longer viewing social media as an auxiliary tool but are incorporating digital interaction into their fundamental marketing strategies and operational models to be competitive in an experience-based market (Noone, McGuire, & Rohlfs, 2011).

From Marketing Tool to Strategic Imperative

In the beginning, most hotels viewed social media as a secondary marketing tool—a complement to current promotional efforts. But with further digital disruption, social media became a strategic necessity, affecting revenue management, customer relationship management, and the creation of brand equity (Dewnarain, Ramkissoon, & Mavondo, 2019; Kushwaha et al., 2020). The incorporation of influencer collaborations only amplified this trend further, providing an opportunity for hotels to build stronger emotional bonds with visitors while driving tangible results like occupancy levels and direct bookings.

For example, Marriott International has continually worked with international influencers to promote high-end experiences, while Airbnb tapped into local influencers to market people-driven, real stays. These collaborations not only boost brand narratives but also act as operational differentiators within a very competitive marketplace (Nozdreva & Churakova, 2021).

The Disruptive Nature of Social Media

The interference generated by social media on the hospitality industry can be clarified in three major dimensions:

1. **Disruption of Conventional Advertising:** Hotels are transferring budgets from print, television, and billboard advertising to influencer collaborations and social media marketing. This is being driven by proof that social media provides greater engagement at reduced costs (Arora, 2024).
2. **Disruption of Brand Control:** In contrast to conventional campaigns, where the hotel was in control of the narrative, social media allows consumers and influencers to co-create brand narratives. While this democratization makes the narratives more authentic, it also puts brands at risk of receiving negative reviews and reputational crises (Michopoulou & Moisa., 2019).

   3.Operations Disruption: Social media has also dissolved boundaries between operations and marketing. Guest expectations are increasingly influenced by what they learn on social media, which forces hotels to fulfill the commitments made on influencer posts and user-generated experiences (Dabas, Sharma, & Manaktola, 2021).

Research Gap and Purpose of the Chapter

Despite the growing role of social media and influencer marketing in hospitality, research remains fragmented in connecting marketing practices with hotel operations. Much of the existing literature focuses on the promotional aspects of influencer marketing, with less emphasis on how such initiatives are integrated into service delivery, guest engagement, and revenue strategies. This chapter addresses this gap by investigating influencer marketing and brand collaborations not only as communication tools but as operational strategies that redefine hotel management.

The purpose of this chapter is therefore twofold:

- To explore the transformative impact of influencer marketing and brand collaborations on hospitality marketing and guest experiences.
- To provide a framework for integrating these strategies into hotel operations in a sustainable, ethical, and measurable way.

By bridging theory and practice, this chapter seeks to equip hotel managers, marketers, and researchers with actionable insights into how influencer marketing and brand collaborations can be effectively leveraged in the digital age.

2. INFLUENCER MARKETING IN HOSPITALITY: OPPORTUNITIES AND CHALLENGES

The hospitality sector is based on experiences, emotions, and people. As opposed to other sectors, hotels do not sell products—they sell memories, comfort, and lifestyle experiences. This renders influencer marketing especially effective in this sector, with influencers as credible intermediaries who tell real stories, evoke emotions, and shape travel choices. Social media influencers, via websites such as Instagram, TikTok, YouTube, and blogs, craft influential digital stories that complement the aspirational consumption of hospitality (Varkaris & Neuhofer, 2017).

As much as influencer marketing has become one of the hospitality industry's strongest assets, it also poses issues in terms of cost, credibility, ethics, and operational compatibility. This section critically analyzes the opportunities and challenges that influencer marketing poses to the hospitality industry.

2.1 Opportunities in Influencer Marketing for Hospitality

2.1.1 Enhanced Brand Visibility and Reach

One of the primary advantages of influencer marketing in hospitality is its ability to extend brand visibility far beyond traditional advertising. Influencers often have large and highly engaged audiences, allowing hotels to tap into communities that might otherwise be difficult to reach (Gupta, 2019). For example, a collaboration with a well-known travel influencer can generate thousands of impressions and engagements within hours, significantly amplifying a hotel's visibility.

Unlike paid advertising that appears promotional, influencer-generated content blends seamlessly into social media feeds, appearing authentic and relatable. This organic integration enhances consumer receptivity, as followers often perceive influencer recommendations as genuine endorsements rather than commercial promotions (Moro & Rita, 2018).

2.1.2 Authentic Storytelling and Emotional Engagement

The hospitality industry relies heavily on *emotional storytelling*. Influencers specialize in crafting personalized narratives that resonate with their followers' aspirations and values. For example, a travel influencer documenting a weekend getaway at a boutique hotel not only showcases the amenities but also conveys the emotional journey of relaxation, adventure, or cultural immersion.

Authenticity is central to this appeal. Research shows that consumers trust influencers' personal experiences more than brand-generated content because influencers present information in a relatable and humanized manner (Vasumathi & Ambrose, 2024). This capacity to merge brand promotion with authentic storytelling makes influencers particularly effective for hospitality marketing.

2.1.3 Targeted Marketing and Audience Segmentation

Traditional advertising often casts a wide net, making it challenging to reach niche audiences effectively. Influencers, on the other hand, cater to specific segments—luxury travelers, budget backpackers, eco-tourists, food enthusiasts, or digital nomads. This targeted approach allows hotels to collaborate with influencers whose followers align with their ideal guest profile, thereby increasing the likelihood of conversions (Valos et al., 2016).

For example, eco-resorts may collaborate with sustainability-focused influencers, while luxury hotels may partner with lifestyle influencers who embody aspirational living. This level of segmentation ensures higher relevance and personalization in marketing efforts (Susilo & Santos, 2023).

2.1.4 User-Generated Content and Long-Term Digital Assets

Influencer collaborations often generate a wealth of user-generated content (UGC), including high-quality images, videos, and testimonials. These assets extend beyond the campaign period, as hotels can repurpose influencer content for their official websites, social media channels, and promotional materials (Dabas, Sharma, & Manaktola, 2021).

Moreover, influencer posts often remain online indefinitely, serving as long-term digital assets that continue to attract visibility and engagement months or even years after the campaign has ended. In this sense, influencer marketing offers a compounding return on investment compared to short-lived traditional advertisements.

2.1.5 Boosting Bookings and Revenue Impact

Influencer marketing has been shown to influence direct bookings and revenue generation for hotels. For example, case studies indicate that influencer-led campaigns often result in a measurable spike in website traffic, inquiries, and occupancy rates (Michopoulou & Moisa, 2019). Many hotels offer influencer discount codes or affiliate links, allowing for real-time tracking of booking conversions generated by influencers.

The financial advantage is not limited to short-term bookings. Influencer campaigns can enhance brand equity and guest loyalty, contributing to repeat visits and word-of-mouth recommendations. In competitive markets where differentiation is challenging, influencer-driven visibility can be a decisive factor in maintaining revenue streams (Panda et al., 2024).

2.1.6 Operational Innovation and Guest Experience Design

Beyond marketing, influencer collaborations are increasingly influencing hotel operations. Hotels design experiences, packages, and even physical spaces with social media appeal in mind. For example, rooftop pools, themed suites, or aesthetically designed restaurants are often curated to encourage social media sharing (Bilgihan & Ricci, 2024).

This "Instagram ability" not only enhances influencer content but also elevates the guest experience by aligning with contemporary expectations. Hotels that integrate influencer insights into service design can remain ahead of evolving consumer preferences, making influencer collaboration both a marketing and operational innovation.

2.2 Challenges in Influencer Marketing for Hospitality

Despite its many advantages, influencer marketing is not without challenges. Hotels must navigate issues of authenticity, cost, ethical standards, and return on investment to fully capitalize on influencer partnerships.

2.2.1 High Costs and ROI Uncertainty

Top-tier influencers with millions of followers often charge significant fees for collaborations, making influencer marketing a costly endeavor. For hotels operating on limited budgets, such partnerships may not always yield commensurate returns (Michopoulou & Moisa, 2019).

Additionally, measuring the ROI of influencer campaigns remains a persistent challenge. Unlike traditional advertising, where impressions and conversions are easier to track, influencer campaigns involve multiple variables, including engagement rates, sentiment, and long-term brand equity. While affiliate links and discount codes provide some metrics, capturing the holistic value of influencer collaborations is complex (Rathore, Kar, & Ilavarasan, 2017).

2.2.2 Fake Followers and Engagement Fraud

The rise of influencer marketing has also given rise to fraudulent practices such as fake followers, bots, and artificially inflated engagement. Research indicates that a significant percentage of social media influencers may use unethical tactics to boost their perceived influence (Halkiopoulos & Papadopoulos, 2022).

For hotels, partnering with such influencers can result in wasted resources and minimal real impact. To mitigate this risk, hotels must conduct thorough due diligence, analyzing not only follower counts but also engagement authenticity, audience demographics, and past campaign performance (Kushwaha et al., 2020).

2.2.3 Authenticity and Trust Concerns

While authenticity is a major strength of influencer marketing, it can also become a vulnerability. Audiences are increasingly skeptical of sponsored content, particularly when influencers promote multiple brands without clear alignment to their personal image (Moro & Rita, 2018). In the hospitality sector, where trust is critical, inauthentic endorsements can backfire, leading to reputational risks for both the influencer and the hotel.

Moreover, excessive commercialization of influencer content can erode the very authenticity that makes it effective. Hotels must carefully select influencers whose personal values and storytelling style align with their brand identity (Gulati, 2022).

2.2.4 Ethical and Regulatory Issues

The ethical dimension of influencer marketing has come under increasing scrutiny. Issues such as undisclosed sponsorships, misleading representations, and over-commercialization have led to the introduction of stricter guidelines. In the United States, the Federal Trade Commission (FTC) mandates that influencers disclose paid partnerships, while in India, the Advertising Standards Council of India (ASCI) has issued similar guidelines (Hussain, Safeer, & Ahmed, 2025).

For hotels, non-compliance with these regulations can result in legal consequences and damage to brand reputation. Ensuring transparency in influencer collaborations is therefore not only an ethical responsibility but also a strategic necessity.

2.2.5 Operational Misalignment

Integrating influencer campaigns into hotel operations presents its own challenges. In some cases, influencer promises made online may not align with actual service delivery, leading to guest dissatisfaction. For example, if an influencer highlights a luxury experience that is not consistently available to all guests, it may create a gap between expectation and reality (Noone, McGuire, & Rohlfs, 2011).

Furthermore, managing influencer stays requires operational coordination, from complimentary services to curated experiences. This can place additional strain on hotel resources if not planned effectively (Dabas, Sharma, & Manaktola, 2021).

2.2.6 Market Saturation and Diminishing Returns

As influencer marketing becomes mainstream, consumers are exposed to a flood of sponsored content. This oversaturation can lead to "influencer fatigue," where audiences become less responsive to influencer promotions (Verissimo & Menezes, 2015).

For hotels, this means that influencer campaigns must stand out through creativity, authenticity, and unique value propositions. Simply engaging an influencer is no longer enough; strategic alignment and innovative storytelling are essential to cut through the digital noise (Thakur et al., 2024).

2.3 Balancing Opportunities and Challenges

The opportunities and challenges of influencer marketing in hospitality are two sides of the same coin. On the one hand, influencers offer unparalleled reach, authenticity, and engagement potential. On the other hand, issues such as high costs, authenticity concerns, and ROI measurement complicate their use as a strategic tool.

Hotels must therefore approach influencer marketing with a balanced perspective—leveraging its strengths while proactively mitigating risks. This involves:

- Careful selection of influencers aligned with brand identity.
- Transparent and ethical collaborations.
- Integration of influencer campaigns with operational strategies.
- Continuous monitoring of outcomes using both quantitative and qualitative metrics.

By adopting a holistic and strategic approach, hotels can maximize the opportunities of influencer marketing while minimizing its challenges, thereby ensuring sustainable value creation in the digital age.

3. BRAND COLLABORATION MODELS: FROM LUXURY TIE-UPS TO LOCAL EXPERIENCES

The hospitality industry is no longer limited to selling rooms and services—it now sells experiences, lifestyles, and cultural immersion. In this context, brand collaboration has become a powerful marketing and operational strategy for hotels. By partnering with lifestyle, travel, fashion, luxury, or even local artisanal brands, hotels can extend their identity, offer unique experiences, and differentiate themselves in a crowded marketplace. Such collaborations are not new, but the digital age and the rise of social media have given them fresh momentum and visibility (Moro & Rita, 2018).

This section explores different models of *brand collaboration in hospitality*—from high-profile luxury tie-ups with global brands to community-based partnerships with local businesses. It also discusses how these collaborations create value for both the hotel and its guests, while highlighting potential pitfalls and lessons for managers.

3.1 The Rationale for Brand Collaboration in Hospitality

Hotels operate in an intensely competitive environment, where differentiation often hinges on offering something beyond the ordinary. With travelers increasingly seeking authentic, personalized, and memorable experiences, collaborations with complementary brands provide a strategic way to meet these expectations (Susilo & Santos, 2023).

Brand collaborations help hotels:

- *Enhance guest experiences* by adding layers of uniqueness and exclusivity.
- *Strengthen brand positioning* by associating with aspirational or credible partners.
- *Leverage cross-marketing opportunities* through shared audiences.
- *Generate digital visibility*, especially when partnerships are amplified through influencers and social media storytelling.

For example, a luxury hotel collaborating with a premium spa brand elevates its wellness positioning, while a budget hotel partnering with a local street-food vendor can create authentic cultural value for its guests.

3.2 Luxury Tie-Ups: Co-Branding with Premium and Lifestyle Brands

One of the most visible forms of collaboration in hospitality is the tie-up with luxury and lifestyle brands. These partnerships appeal to affluent travelers who view hotels not just as places to stay but as part of a broader lifestyle ecosystem.

3.2.1 Hotels × Fashion and Design

Fashion and hospitality share a common thread—both represent lifestyle and aspiration. Luxury hotels often collaborate with fashion designers to curate uniforms, room aesthetics, or even exclusive events. For example, Armani Hotels in Dubai and Milan exemplify how fashion brands extend into hospitality, blending haute couture aesthetics with luxury service (Bilgihan & Ricci, 2024).

These collaborations allow hotels to stand out in terms of design, exclusivity, and media coverage. Guests often feel they are part of something "special," which enhances both satisfaction and loyalty.

3.2.2 Hotels × Premium Automotive Brands

Another common model is partnerships between hotels and luxury car companies. High-end hotels such as Ritz-Carlton or St. Regis often collaborate with brands like Mercedes-Benz or Bentley to offer chauffeur services or display premium cars in their lobbies. Such tie-ups reinforce the hotel's luxury positioning while giving automotive brands access to affluent guests (Nozdreva & Churakova, 2021).

For example, The St. Regis Abu Dhabi collaborated with Bentley Motors to provide a "luxury driving experience," aligning both brands with sophistication and exclusivity.

3.2.3 Hotels × Fine Dining and Beverage Brands

Food and beverage partnerships are equally powerful. Hotels frequently partner with Michelin-starred chefs, premium wine labels, or artisanal coffee brands to elevate their culinary offerings. Such collaborations not only attract food enthusiasts but also create social media buzz, as dining experiences are among the most photographed and shared hospitality features (Gulati, 2022).

For example, Accor's Sofitel brand has collaborated with Veuve Clicquot for exclusive champagne brunches, turning a simple dining experience into a luxury event.

3.3 Travel and Lifestyle Brand Collaborations

Beyond luxury, hotels are also teaming up with travel and lifestyle brands that align with their target audience's passions.

3.3.1 Hotels × Airlines

Hotels and airlines often form integrated packages that offer seamless travel experiences. Joint promotions may include discounted stays with flight bookings, loyalty program tie-ups, or bundled offers (Leung et al., 2013). For example, Marriott Bonvoy's partnership with Emirates Airlines allows loyalty members to earn points for both flights and stays, encouraging customer stickiness.

3.3.2 Hotels × Fitness and Wellness Brands

Wellness tourism has become a global trend, and hotels are collaborating with fitness and health brands to stay relevant. Partnerships with yoga studios, fitness influencers, or wellness product companies allow hotels to position themselves as health-conscious destinations (Dabas, Sharma, & Manaktola, 2021).

For example, Westin Hotels' collaboration with New Balance enables guests to borrow workout gear during their stay, addressing the needs of health-focused travelers while reinforcing Westin's wellness-oriented branding.

3.3.3 Hotels × Technology Brands

With digital nomadism and remote work on the rise, hotels are increasingly collaborating with tech brands to provide seamless digital experiences. Partnerships with companies offering high-speed internet solutions, coworking tools, or even VR/AR experiences create value for tech-savvy travelers (Halkiopoulos & Papadopoulos, 2022).

A notable example is Accor's tie-up with Microsoft to create virtual event solutions in its meeting spaces, blending hospitality with technological innovation.

3.4 Local and Cultural Collaborations: Authentic Guest Experiences

While luxury collaborations appeal to global elites, **local brand collaborations** resonate with travelers seeking authenticity and cultural immersion. Boutique hotels and independent properties often excel in this area.

3.4.1 Hotels × Local Artisans and Crafts

Collaborations with local artisans allow hotels to promote regional culture while enhancing their décor and guest experiences. For example, hotels in Rajasthan, India, often decorate rooms with handcrafted textiles and pottery sourced from local artisans. This not only supports the community but also provides guests with a deeper cultural connection (Arora, 2024).

3.4.2 Hotels × Culinary Traditions

Food is a vital part of cultural tourism. Many hotels collaborate with local chefs, farmers, or street-food vendors to curate authentic dining experiences. For example, boutique hotels in Bali often host farm-to-table dinners with local farmers, reinforcing sustainability while appealing to conscious travelers (Garrido-Moreno et al., 2018).

3.4.3 Hotels × Cultural Institutions

Some hotels partner with museums, theaters, or cultural festivals to offer guests exclusive access or packages. Such collaborations elevate the guest experience beyond the hotel property, positioning the hotel as a cultural hub (Thakur et al., 2024).

For example, a hotel in Vienna may collaborate with the Vienna Philharmonic to provide guests with priority tickets, making the stay part of a larger cultural journey.

3.5 Digital Amplification of Collaborations

What makes these collaborations even more powerful in today's digital age is *social media amplification.* When influencers document these partnerships—whether it is a luxury brunch, a cultural craft experience, or a tech-enabled coworking suite—the reach multiplies exponentially. Guests also become co-creators of content, sharing their collaborative experiences online and thereby serving as brand advocates (Gupta, 2019; Panda et al., 2024).

For example, a hotel's partnership with a local chocolatier might be showcased not only in the hotel lobby but also across Instagram through influencers and guests posting aesthetically curated photos of artisan chocolates, tagged with both the chocolatier's and the hotel's handles.

3.6 Risks and Challenges in Brand Collaborations

Despite their benefits, brand collaborations are not without risks.

- **Brand misalignment**: A mismatch between the hotel's identity and the partner's image can confuse consumers.
- **Operational complexity**: Collaborations require logistical coordination, which may strain resources if not managed properly.
- **Over-commercialization**: Excessive focus on partnerships can dilute authenticity, particularly in local collaborations.
- **Equity concerns**: In cases of unequal partnerships, one brand may overshadow the other, diminishing perceived value.

For example, if a budget hotel partners with a premium luxury brand, the collaboration may appear forced or inauthentic, leading to consumer skepticism (Michopoulou & Moisa, 2019).

3.7 Lessons and Best Practices

Successful brand collaborations in hospitality share certain common features:

1. **Strategic Fit** – Collaborations should align with the hotel's positioning and target audience.
2. **Guest-Centric Value** – The partnership should enhance guest experiences, not just provide marketing exposure.
3. **Cultural Sensitivity** – Local collaborations should respect and authentically represent cultural heritage.
4. **Digital Integration** – Campaigns should be designed with social media amplification in mind.
5. **Sustainability** – Partnerships should be evaluated for long-term value, not just short-term buzz.

3.8. Collaboration as Co-Creation

Brand collaborations in hospitality go beyond co-marketing—they represent *co-creation of experiences*. Whether through luxury tie-ups with global brands or partnerships with local artisans, these collaborations enrich the guest journey, reinforce brand positioning, and create unique stories that resonate in the digital space. In the age of social media, such collaborations achieve maximum impact when amplified by influencers and user-generated content, ensuring that the value created transcends the physical boundaries of the hotel.

As hotels continue to innovate, brand collaborations will remain central to building differentiation, authenticity, and guest loyalty. The challenge lies in ensuring that these partnerships are meaningful, sustainable, and seamlessly integrated into both operations and storytelling.

Brand Collaboration Models – From Luxury Tie-Ups to Local Experiences

Brand collaborations have emerged as one of the most powerful strategies for hotels seeking to stand out in an increasingly competitive and digitally mediated marketplace. In hospitality, a brand is not only a name but also a promise of experience, and collaborations allow hotels to extend that promise beyond their in-house services. These partnerships range from global luxury tie-ups to wellness and technology alliances, and further to grassroots-level collaborations with local communities. Each of these directions reveals how hotels strategically build narratives that appeal to both emotional and functional dimensions of travel.

The first layer of collaboration often involves partnerships with *global luxury and lifestyle brands*. Hotels such as Armani or Bulgari have gone beyond simple hospitality to create spaces where fashion and lifestyle intersect with lodging. Luxury car brands like Bentley or Mercedes have been associated with chauffeur services for five-star guests, while beverage labels such as Veuve Clicquot frequently co-host exclusive dining experiences in luxury resorts. These alliances are not mere marketing stunts; they embed symbolic capital into the hotel experience. A guest staying at such properties perceives their stay as participation in a glamorous lifestyle, reinforcing the aspirational value of the brand. This type of collaboration also ensures that the hotel remains part of broader luxury consumption trends, tapping into a clientele that seeks not just a room, but an identity statement.

Beyond luxury, another major form of partnership comes through *wellness, technology, and contemporary lifestyle collaborations*. The Westin's partnership with New Balance, where guests can borrow workout gear during their stay, reflects a deep understanding of wellness as a lifestyle priority among modern travelers. Similar initiatives with spa brands, organic food producers, and ayurvedic specialists position hotels as caretakers of holistic well-being. Parallel to this, technology collaborations with companies like Microsoft, Zoom, or Google demonstrate how hotels are reshaping themselves as spaces where work and leisure can merge. Especially in the post-pandemic era, the rise of digital nomads and hybrid professionals has encouraged hotels to design packages where productivity, health, and comfort converge. Through these collaborations, the hotel ceases to be a passive backdrop and instead becomes an active enabler of contemporary lifestyles.

Finally, some of the most resonant and culturally rich collaborations are seen in the form of *local and community-based partnerships*. Boutique hotels and even international chains increasingly incorporate local craftsmanship, gastronomy, and cultural practices into their guest offerings. Collaborations with artisans to showcase regional textiles in hotel décor, partnerships with farmers for farm-to-table dining, or tie-ups with cultural festivals and museums transform a hotel stay into an immersive experience of place. For travelers seeking authenticity, these collaborations offer something global luxury cannot replicate: a direct connection with local identity. At the same time, such partnerships allow hotels to contribute economically and socially to the communities in which they operate, thereby strengthening their ethical and sustainable image.

Taken together, these three broad modes of collaboration — luxury and lifestyle tie-ups, wellness and technology integration, and local cultural partnerships — reveal the diverse ways in which hospitality brands co-create value. They not only add new dimensions to the guest journey but also allow hotels to stay relevant in an environment where experience, authenticity, and storytelling define success more than traditional measures of service quality.

Operational Integration – Aligning Influencer Campaigns with Guest Services

While collaborations with influencers and brands create visibility, the true test of success in hospitality lies in how these strategies are operationalized. A campaign cannot remain confined to social media buzz; it must resonate with the on-ground guest experience. For hotels, this means ensuring that influencer marketing is not treated as an isolated promotional effort but as an integral part of service design, guest engagement, and overall brand delivery. When effectively aligned, influencer partnerships move from being mere advertisements to becoming extensions of the hospitality journey itself.

One of the most visible ways hotels integrate influencer campaigns operationally is by *designing experiences that mirror influencer content.* Guests inspired by an influencer's stay at a resort expect to find similar touchpoints when they arrive. For example, if an influencer showcases a signature cocktail, a curated spa treatment, or a panoramic rooftop view, operational teams must ensure these experiences are consistently available and delivered with the same appeal. This requires collaboration across departments — marketing promises must be matched by food and beverage staff, wellness teams, or guest services. Without this alignment, influencer-driven expectations can easily collapse into disappointment, risking brand credibility.

Integration also plays out in how hotels use influencers as *testers and co-creators of guest experiences*. Instead of treating them only as promoters, some hotels invite influencers to collaborate in shaping packages, menus, or themed events. Common practices include:

- *Influencer-curated retreats* where fitness bloggers design workout or wellness itineraries.
- *Food and beverage tie-ups* where influencers co-create signature cocktails or limited-time menus.
- *Exclusive local experiences* crafted with travel influencers, later offered as bookable guest packages.

These activities allow influencer campaigns to evolve into living programs that guests can directly participate in, transforming online storytelling into tangible hospitality offerings.

Technology further strengthens this alignment. Hotels increasingly employ *digital tools that merge influencer marketing with operational systems*, such as:

- QR codes in rooms linking to influencer-curated city or dining guides.
- Mobile apps highlighting influencer-endorsed services and on-site activities.
- AI-driven personalization engines adapting offers based on trending influencer content.

Such practices ensure that influencer messaging is not static but dynamically incorporated into guest touchpoints, while also generating measurable outcomes in terms of bookings, dining choices, or spa participation.

Equally important is the role of *staff training and culture*. Operational integration requires frontline employees to understand the narratives influencers circulate. If a campaign emphasizes sustainability, staff must be ready to explain eco-friendly practices at the property. If it highlights luxury exclusivity, the guest journey must reflect attentive personalization and detail. This cultural alignment ensures that influencer messaging does not appear superficial but is embedded into the lived reality of the hotel.

Finally, operational alignment also creates opportunities for *co-experiential storytelling*. Hotels increasingly design "Instagrammable" spaces — from curated photo walls to scenic dining setups — where guests themselves become content creators. In this way:

- Influencers generate inspiration.
- Guests replicate and extend the experience.
- Hotels gain amplified reach through organic guest content.

Thus, operational integration ensures that influencer marketing is not just about impressions and clicks but about delivering memorable, on-ground experiences that validate and extend the stories told online. When marketing promises and guest services are synchronized, hotels achieve a powerful cycle: influencers attract interest, operations deliver on expectations, and guests themselves become ambassadors who perpetuate the brand narrative.

CHALLENGES AND ETHICAL CONSIDERATIONS IN INFLUENCER PARTNERSHIPS

While influencer collaborations have become indispensable for hospitality marketing, they are not without challenges. The effectiveness of these campaigns depends not only on reach and engagement but also on the authenticity, transparency, and ethical values that underpin them. Hotels that overlook these dimensions risk reputational setbacks, guest distrust, or misaligned branding. Understanding the difficulties and ethical questions surrounding influencer partnerships is therefore as important as celebrating their benefits.

Challenges in Influencer Partnerships

1. Authenticity Gap

One of the greatest risks in influencer collaborations is the authenticity gap. Influencers often present curated, polished versions of hotel experiences, which may not always match the reality encountered by guests. When travelers feel that online portrayals exaggerate luxury, exclusivity, or amenities, they perceive the hotel as misleading. This gap erodes trust and can result in negative guest reviews. Ensuring that influencer content remains grounded in real, deliverable experiences is essential for long-term credibility.

2. Transparency and Disclosure Issues

Audiences today expect honesty in marketing. When influencers fail to disclose that their stay or promotion is sponsored, it creates skepticism about the authenticity of their recommendations. Beyond ethical concerns, many advertising regulators now legally require disclosure of paid partnerships. If hotels ignore this, they risk not only reputational damage but also compliance penalties. Transparency is therefore both an ethical and legal necessity in influencer marketing.

3. Influencer–Brand Mismatch

A frequent challenge arises when hotels collaborate with influencers whose audiences do not align with their target market. For example, a luxury resort partnering with a budget-travel influencer will likely fail to convert engagement into bookings. Similarly, influencers who do not share the hotel's values — such as sustainability or cultural sensitivity — can weaken the brand message. Strategic selection of influencers is critical to ensure alignment in audience, values, and communication style.

4. Cultural Sensitivity and Representation

Since hotels operate in diverse cultural contexts, influencers must represent traditions, communities, and environments respectfully. Inappropriate portrayals, superficial coverage of cultural practices, or stereotyping can create backlash from both local communities and global audiences. Hotels face the dual challenge of guiding influencers toward sensitive representation while also protecting the authenticity of local identity.

5. Measurement and ROI Concerns

Unlike traditional marketing, measuring the direct impact of influencer campaigns is complex. Engagement metrics such as likes and shares do not always translate into bookings or guest loyalty. Hotels often struggle to evaluate whether the return on investment justifies the collaboration, leading to uncertainty in long-term influencer strategies. Developing reliable tracking methods — such as booking codes, exclusive packages, or analytics tools — is necessary but remains a challenge for many operators.

6. Over-Saturation and Audience Fatigue

As influencer marketing becomes mainstream, audiences are increasingly exposed to repetitive, similar-looking content. When multiple influencers promote nearly identical experiences at the same property, the uniqueness of the message is lost. This over-saturation reduces campaign impact and risks creating audience fatigue, where followers scroll past content without engagement. Hotels must therefore innovate in their campaigns to retain freshness and appeal.

CASE STUDIES: GLOBAL HOTEL BRANDS LEVERAGING INFLUENCER PARTNERSHIPS

The success of influencer marketing in hospitality is best understood through real-world practices of leading hotel brands. Global and Indian hospitality giants have adopted diverse strategies, demonstrating how influencer collaborations can be tailored to reflect brand identity, customer expectations, and cultural context.

Marriott International set a benchmark with its *#TravelBrilliantly* campaign, where influencers and young travelers were invited to share fresh ideas for enriching guest experiences. This initiative went beyond typical promotional content by framing influencers as co-creators of innovation. By highlighting creativity and adaptability, Marriott positioned itself as a forward-thinking brand capable of engaging with millennials and Gen Z audiences on their own terms.

Hilton Hotels has taken a slightly different route by emphasizing *local immersion*. Influencers are often encouraged not just to review Hilton properties, but to explore and narrate stories about the surrounding destinations. This strategic choice shifts the brand identity from being solely a hospitality provider to becoming a gateway to cultural experiences. The campaign's effectiveness lies in showing potential guests that a Hilton stay is about much more than a room — it is about an entire journey.

Luxury-focused brands such as *Four Seasons* have collaborated with lifestyle and fashion influencers to strengthen their positioning as aspirational destinations. Exclusive stays, premium experiences, and curated visual content are used to craft narratives of elegance and sophistication. Yet, the Four Seasons' approach also emphasizes subtle authenticity, ensuring that its luxury appeal does not appear disconnected from real experiences.

A different strategy is evident in *Airbnb*, which though not a traditional hotel chain, has reshaped hospitality marketing through influencers. By highlighting unique stays, neighborhood cultures, and host-driven experiences, Airbnb uses influencers to tell stories of belonging rather than luxury. This demonstrates how influencer marketing can also be community-driven, appealing to travelers seeking authenticity and emotional connection.

Boutique hotels across destinations like Bali, Goa, and Europe often adopt niche influencer partnerships, particularly with sustainability advocates and wellness creators. These collaborations highlight eco-friendly practices, local craftsmanship, and mindful living — values that resonate with a growing segment of conscious travelers. In doing so, boutique properties compete effectively with global chains by offering distinct, value-based experiences.

In the Indian context, *Taj Hotels* has mastered the art of blending *heritage with modern storytelling*. By engaging travel and lifestyle influencers, the brand showcases not just luxury accommodations but also its cultural legacy. Iconic properties such as the Taj Mahal Palace, Mumbai, and Taj Lake Palace, Udaipur, become settings for immersive narratives that connect history, architecture, and hospitality. Influencers portray these spaces not merely as hotels but as living experiences of India's royal past, carefully balanced with modern comforts.

Similarly, *ITC Hotels* has used influencer marketing to reinforce its philosophy of *"Responsible Luxury."* Collaborations with eco-conscious travelers and culinary influencers emphasize sustainability initiatives, wellness offerings, and rich gastronomic traditions. This approach reflects ITC's dual commitment to environmental responsibility and premium guest experiences, ensuring that the brand resonates with ethically minded, globalized audiences.

Together, these examples show how influencer partnerships are highly adaptable. From Marriott's co-creation of innovation to Taj's heritage storytelling and ITC's sustainability-driven branding, hotel brands around the world are leveraging influencers not just to promote rooms but to craft narratives that blend authenticity, aspiration, and identity.

These case studies illustrate that influencer collaborations in hospitality are not one-size-fits-all; they are shaped by brand positioning, cultural expectations, and audience preferences. Whether it is Marriott's focus on innovation, Hilton's emphasis on local immersion, Four Seasons' luxury branding, Airbnb's community-driven narratives, or Taj and ITC's blending of heritage and responsibility, each demonstrates how influencer marketing functions as a *strategic storytelling tool.* In line with hospitality marketing theory, these examples confirm that effective campaigns go beyond product promotion: they construct *emotional connections, lifestyle identities, and trust-based relationships* with travelers.

Figure 3. Global vs. Indian Hotel Campaign Engagement

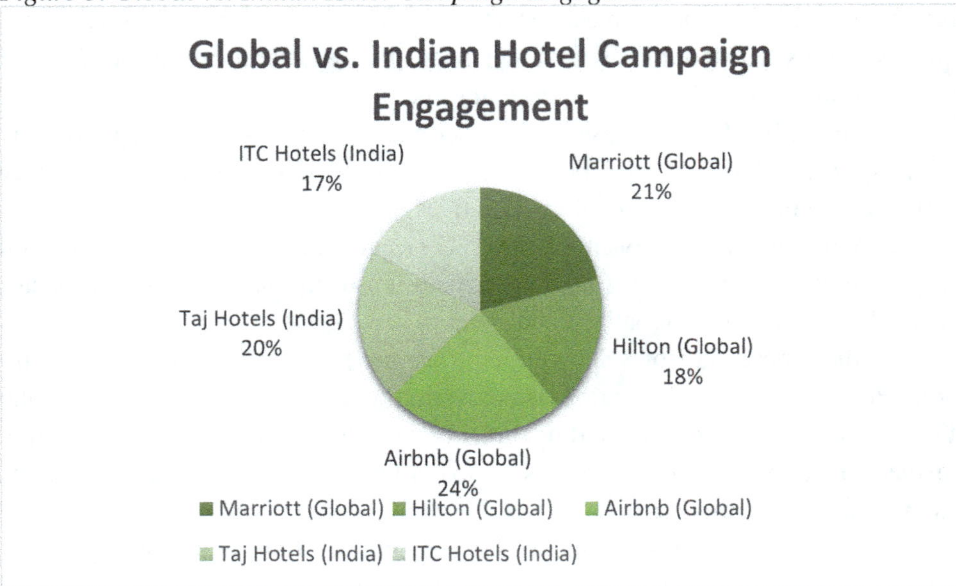

The graph compares the *social media engagement rates* of leading global and Indian hospitality brands. Among the global players, *Airbnb leads with 25% engagement*, showing the strength of its community-driven and storytelling-based content strategy. By encouraging user-generated content and promoting local experiences, Airbnb effectively keeps travelers engaged beyond just accommodation bookings.

Marriott (22%) and *Hilton (19%)* follow, reflecting their global dominance and strong digital presence. Marriott leverages lifestyle campaigns and influencer collaborations to maintain high engagement, while Hilton has built traction through loyalty program promotions and targeted digital ads.

On the Indian front, *Taj Hotels achieves 21% engagement*, nearly at par with Marriott, demonstrating the rising global influence of Indian hospitality brands. Taj effectively uses heritage, luxury narratives, and celebrity/influencer tie-ups to resonate with digital audiences. *ITC Hotels (18%)*, though slightly lower, still performs competitively by emphasizing sustainability campaigns and wellness experiences.

This comparison indicates that *Indian brands are closing the engagement gap with global players*, proving that a well-crafted digital strategy can elevate regional brands to international visibility. For the hospitality industry, the lesson is clear: *social media engagement is no longer just about reach—it is about creating meaningful, authentic, and culturally resonant conversations with travelers.*

ETHICAL AND PRACTICAL CONSIDERATIONS: AUTHENTICITY, TRANSPARENCY, AND ROI

While influencer marketing has proven highly effective in hospitality, it also raises significant ethical and practical questions. Unlike traditional advertising, influencer collaborations rely heavily on personal credibility and social trust, which means any breach of ethics or lack of clarity can damage both the influencer's image and the hotel's reputation. Three critical dimensions frame these concerns: *authenticity, transparency, and return on investment (ROI).*

1. Authenticity: The Cornerstone of Trust

Influencer marketing thrives on authenticity, yet this is often the most fragile element of the partnership. If followers perceive that content is overly scripted, staged, or purely transactional, the influencer risks losing credibility. For hotels, this can backfire by making the collaboration appear inauthentic or opportunistic.

- Guests expect genuine reviews and relatable storytelling rather than polished promotional material.
- Successful partnerships often occur when influencers align naturally with the brand's values — for example, a sustainability influencer collaborating with ITC Hotels' "Responsible Luxury" initiative.
- Authenticity strengthens the sense of trust, making travelers more likely to consider the hotel as a reliable choice.

2. Transparency: Building Credibility through Openness

Transparency has become a legal and ethical necessity in influencer partnerships. Regulatory bodies in many countries now require influencers to disclose sponsored content clearly, using hashtags like *#Ad* or *#Sponsored*. For hospitality brands, transparent practices signal integrity and respect for consumers.

- Lack of disclosure can result in regulatory penalties and reputational damage.
- Transparent collaborations foster a sense of honesty, showing audiences that while the influencer is compensated, their opinions are genuine.
- In hospitality, transparency also extends to accurate representation: showcasing actual amenities, services, and cultural experiences without exaggeration ensures that guests' expectations are met.

3. ROI (Return on Investment): Measuring Effectiveness

While ethics focus on credibility, the practical dimension of influencer marketing lies in evaluating *ROI*. Hospitality brands often face challenges in measuring the direct financial outcomes of collaborations, as the benefits may be indirect or long-term.

- Metrics such as reach, engagement rates, booking inquiries, and website traffic are often used to assess impact.
- Beyond numerical outcomes, ROI also includes intangible benefits like enhanced brand image, stronger emotional connections, and increased word-of-mouth.
- However, poor alignment between influencer audience and hotel target markets can lead to wasted resources, highlighting the need for strategic selection of influencers.

Figure 4. ROI from Influencer Campaigns vs. Traditional Marketing

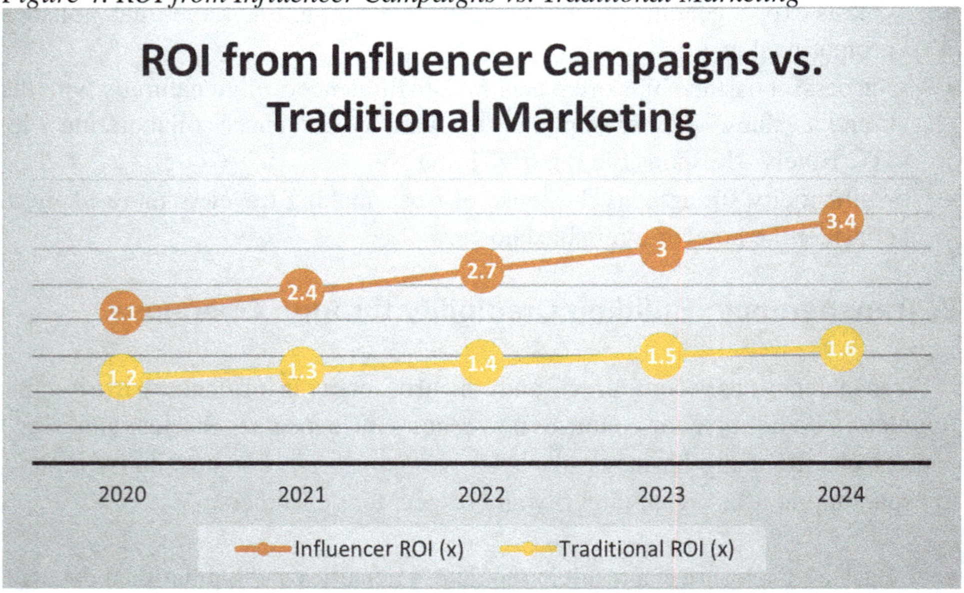

The graph demonstrates the *steady growth of ROI from influencer marketing compared to traditional advertising* over the five-year period (2020–2024). Influencer marketing shows a consistent upward trajectory, rising from *2.1x in 2020 to 3.4x in 2024*, highlighting its increasing effectiveness as digital engagement deepens. In contrast, traditional advertising reflects only marginal growth—from *1.2x in*

2020 to 1.6x in 2024—indicating its declining relative value in a rapidly digitizing hospitality market.

This widening gap illustrates that hotels investing in influencer-driven campaigns are enjoying stronger returns, both financially and in terms of *brand resonance*. The growth in influencer ROI is linked to factors such as:

- *Expansion of social media platforms* (Instagram Reels, TikTok, YouTube Shorts) that favor visual storytelling.
- *Increased consumer trust* in influencers' authentic experiences compared to corporate messages.
- *Targeted reach*—influencers help hotels tap into specific niches like luxury travelers, wellness seekers, or budget backpackers.

For hotel marketers, the insight is clear: while traditional advertising still plays a supportive role, the *future of ROI lies in influencer partnerships*. Strategic collaborations with influencers not only amplify visibility but also create measurable financial impact.

Balancing Ethics and Practice

For influencer partnerships to be sustainable, hotels must balance *ethical responsibility* with *practical efficiency*. Authenticity and transparency ensure credibility, while careful ROI measurement ensures accountability. Together, these elements transform influencer marketing from a short-term promotional tool into a *long-term relationship strategy* that builds loyalty, trust, and meaningful engagement with travelers.

FRAMEWORK FOR FUTURE HOSPITALITY MARKETING: STRATEGIC INFLUENCER–BRAND SYNERGY

The evolution of hospitality marketing demonstrates that influencer collaborations are no longer experimental tactics but essential strategies. However, for such partnerships to remain effective in a rapidly changing digital landscape, hotels must adopt a *structured framework* that aligns influencer marketing with long-term brand goals. This framework can be envisioned around three interconnected pillars: *Strategic Alignment, Co-Creation, and Technology Integration.*

1. Strategic Alignment: Matching Influencer Identity with Brand Vision

The foundation of future influencer–hotel synergy lies in ensuring that the influencer's values, style, and audience match the hotel's brand identity. Random or opportunistic collaborations often fail to deliver sustained impact.

- **Value Matching:** Hotels like ITC (sustainability) or Four Seasons (luxury) must work with influencers whose personal brands embody the same values.
- **Audience Overlap:** Targeting influencers whose followers mirror the hotel's desired guest segment — for example, wellness influencers for spa resorts or family bloggers for vacation destinations.
- **Long-Term Partnerships:** Moving from one-off promotions to ongoing collaborations builds continuity and deeper trust among audiences.

2. Co-Creation: Shaping Experiences Together

The future of hospitality marketing lies not in scripted promotions but in *co-created experiences* where influencers and brands jointly shape storytelling. This involves inviting influencers to contribute ideas, design campaigns, or curate guest experiences that feel original and authentic.

- **Experience-Driven Content:** Influencers can co-create immersive packages (e.g., food trails, cultural workshops, or wellness retreats).
- **Brand as a Platform:** Hotels provide spaces and opportunities, while influencers personalize the narrative to suit their communities.
- **Mutual Benefits:** Co-creation ensures that influencers maintain authenticity, while hotels benefit from content that resonates strongly with followers.

3. Technology Integration: Enhancing Reach and Measurement

Emerging technologies will redefine influencer–brand synergy, making campaigns smarter and more measurable.

- **AI-Driven Analytics:** Advanced tools can assess influencer credibility, audience demographics, and engagement authenticity before collaboration.
- **Augmented Reality (AR) & Virtual Reality (VR):** Influencers could showcase hotel experiences through immersive AR/VR tours, letting potential guests virtually explore properties before booking.

- **Data-Backed ROI Tracking:** Hotels can employ digital dashboards to link influencer campaigns directly with bookings, loyalty sign-ups, or other measurable outcomes.

TOWARDS SUSTAINABLE SYNERGY

The future of influencer marketing in hospitality will depend on *synergy rather than short-term promotion*. When influencers become genuine partners — co-creating experiences aligned with brand values and supported by technology — hospitality marketing transforms into a *holistic strategy* that blends storytelling, authenticity, and measurable impact. In this way, influencer partnerships will not only attract new guests but also cultivate *long-term loyalty and community-building* for hotel brands.

CONCLUSION AND FUTURE DIRECTIONS

Influencer marketing has emerged as one of the most transformative tools in hospitality, bridging the gap between traditional service offerings and the digital-first expectations of modern travelers. From heritage luxury hotels like Taj to global chains like Marriott, and from sustainable narratives at ITC to community-driven campaigns by Airbnb, case studies demonstrate that influencers do more than promote — they create *immersive stories, authentic connections, and aspirational lifestyles* that shape travel decisions.

Three key insights stand out across this discussion:

- **Authenticity builds trust:** Without genuine storytelling, influencer campaigns risk losing credibility.
- **Transparency ensures credibility:** Clear disclosures and honest portrayals are ethical imperatives in today's digital marketplace.
- **ROI requires balance:** While numbers matter, long-term value lies in loyalty, brand positioning, and emotional connection.

Looking ahead, the future of hospitality marketing will depend on *synergistic partnerships* where influencers and brands collaborate not as marketer and promoter, but as co-creators of unique guest experiences. The integration of *technology, cultural sensitivity, and ethical responsibility* will be central to this transformation. Hotels that move beyond transactional endorsements and embrace influencers as long-term strategic partners will cultivate stronger reputations, deeper customer loyalty, and greater resilience in an increasingly competitive market.

Ultimately, influencer marketing in hospitality is not just about *selling rooms*, but about *shaping journeys, memories, and identities*. As travel continues to evolve in the digital era, hotels that harness the power of authentic digital storytelling will stand at the forefront of global hospitality innovation.

REFERENCES

Aluri, A., Slevitch, L., & Larzelere, R. (2015). The effectiveness of embedded social media on hotel websites and the importance of social interactions and return on engagement. *International Journal of Contemporary Hospitality Management, 27*(4), 670–689. https://www.emerald.com/ijchm/article-abstract/27/4/670/120497/The-effectiveness-of-embedded-social-media-on?redirectedFrom=fulltext

Arora, J. (2024). A Study On Impact Of E-Marketing And Social Media On Small Scale Businesses And Hotel Industry Growth. *Migration Letters : An International Journal of Migration Studies, 21*(S3), 658–663. https://pdfs.semanticscholar.org/249b/526c7b73e6779b3e3f7d177e758e9a1aacf8.pdf

Arora, J. (2024). A Study On Impact Of E-Marketing And Social Media On Small Scale Businesses And Hotel Industry Growth. *Migration Letters : An International Journal of Migration Studies, 21*(S3), 658–663. https://pdfs.semanticscholar.org/249b/526c7b73e6779b3e3f7d177e758e9a1aacf8.pdf

Bilgihan, A., & Ricci, P. (2024). The new era of hotel marketing: Integrating cutting-edge technologies with core marketing principles. *Journal of Hospitality and Tourism Technology, 15*(1), 123–137. https://www.emerald.com/jhtt/article-abstract/15/1/123/1217467/The-new-era-of-hotel-marketing-integrating-cutting?redirectedFrom=fulltext

Dabas, S., Sharma, S., & Manaktola, K. (2021). Adoption of digital marketing tools in independent businesses: Experiences of restaurant entrepreneurs in India and United Kingdom. *Worldwide Hospitality and Tourism Themes, 13*(2), 214–235. https://www.emerald.com/whatt/article-abstract/13/2/214/383568/Adoption-of-digital-marketing-tools-in-independent?redirectedFrom=fulltext

Dewnarain, S., Ramkissoon, H., & Mavondo, F. (2019). Social customer relationship management: An integrated conceptual framework. *Journal of Hospitality Marketing & Management, 28*(2), 172–188. https://www.tandfonline.com/doi/abs/10.1080/19368623.2018.1516588

Garrido-Moreno, A., García-Morales, V. J., Lockett, N., & King, S. (2018). The missing link: Creating value with social media use in hotels. *International Journal of Hospitality Management, 75*, 94–104. https://www.sciencedirect.com/science/article/abs/pii/S0278431916301670

Gulati, S. (2022). Social and sustainable: exploring social media use for promoting sustainable behaviour and demand amongst Indian tourists. *International Hospitality Review, 36*(2), 373-393. https://www.emerald.com/ihr/article/36/2/373/107042

Gupta, V. (2019). The influencing role of social media in the consumer's hotel decision-making process. *Worldwide Hospitality and Tourism Themes, 11*(4), 378–391. https://www.emerald.com/whatt/article-abstract/11/4/378/383362/The-influencing-role-of-social-media-in-the?redirectedFrom=fulltext

Halkiopoulos, C., & Papadopoulos, D. (2022, April). Computational methods for evaluating web technologies and digital marketing techniques in the hospitality industry. In *Transcending Borders in Tourism Through Innovation and Cultural Heritage: 8th International Conference, IACuDiT, Hydra, Greece, 2021* (pp. 387–406). Springer International Publishing., https://link.springer.com/chapter/10.1007/978-3-030-92491-1_24

Hays, S., Page, S. J., & Buhalis, D. (2013). Social media as a destination marketing tool: Its use by national tourism organisations. *Current Issues in Tourism*, *16*(3), 211–239. https://www.tandfonline.com/doi/abs/10.1080/13683500.2012.662215

Hussain, Z., Safeer, A. A., & Ahmed, M. J. (2025). The Role of Social Media Marketing for the Hospitality Business. In *Marketing Technology-Infused Hospitality: Upskilling Frontline Employees for Competitiveness* (pp. 181-204). IGI Global Scientific Publishing. https://www.igi-global.com/chapter/the-role-of-social-media-marketing-for-the-hospitality-business/367414

Kushwaha, B. P., Singh, R. K., Varghese, N., & Singh, V. N. (2020). Integrating social media and digital media as new elements of integrated marketing communication for creating brand equity. *Journal of Content, Community & Communication, 11*(6), 52-64. https://www.researchgate.net/profile/Zinggara-Hidayat-2/publication/350639866

Leung, D., Law, R., Van Hoof, H., & Buhalis, D. (2013). Social media in tourism and hospitality: A literature review. *Journal of Travel & Tourism Marketing*, *30*(1-2), 3–22. https://www.tandfonline.com/doi/abs/10.1080/10548408.2013.750919

McCarthy, L., Stock, D., & Verma, R. (2010). How travelers use online and social media channels to make hotel-choice decisions. https://ecommons.cornell.edu/server/api/core/bitstreams/29b13443-43b9-41ce-a084-d1c884ddfc82/content

Michopoulou, E., & Moisa, D. G. (2019). Hotel social media metrics: The ROI dilemma. *International Journal of Hospitality Management*, *76*, 308–315. https://www.sciencedirect.com/science/article/abs/pii/S0278431917308423

Minazzi, R. (2015). *Social media marketing in tourism and hospitality*. Springer International Publishing Switzerland. https://link.springer.com/book/10.1007/978-3-319-05182-6

Moro, S., & Rita, P. (2018). Brand strategies in social media in hospitality and tourism. *International Journal of Contemporary Hospitality Management, 30*(1), 343–364. https://www.emerald.com/ijchm/article-abstract/30/1/343/115837/Brand-strategies-in-social-media-in-hospitality?redirectedFrom=fulltext

Noone, B. M., McGuire, K. A., & Rohlfs, K. V. (2011). Social media meets hotel revenue management: Opportunities, issues and unanswered questions. *Journal of Revenue and Pricing Management, 10*(4), 293–305. https://link.springer.com/article/10.1057/rpm.2011.12

Nozdreva, R., & Churakova, A. (2021). Digital tools in empirical marketing strategies of global hotel companies. *Digital strategies in a global market: Navigating the Fourth Industrial Revolution*, 213-227. https://link.springer.com/chapter/10.1007/978-3-030-58267-8_16

Panda, G. C., Rout, P. K., Nayak, M., Mohanty, B. R., & Sana, S. S. (2024). Social media as a catalyst for hotel business growth: a pls-Sem approach in Odisha's smart cities. *OPSEARCH*, 1-29. https://link.springer.com/article/10.1007/s12597-024-00859-w

Rathore, A. K., Kar, A. K., & Ilavarasan, P. V. (2017). Social media analytics: Literature review and directions for future research. *Decision Analysis, 14*(4), 229–249. https://pubsonline.informs.org/doi/abs/10.1287/deca.2017.0355

Susilo, D., & Santos, M. C. K. (2023). Digital marketing communication sustainable hotel practice of accor group in social media. *International Journal of Economic, Business, Accounting, Agriculture Management and Sharia Administration (IJEBAS), 3*(3), 730-743. https://pdfs.semanticscholar.org/5fca/79ab11b745e4d3ebbcaa5e2b63fada1d8b11.pdf

Thakur, A. S., Kumar, N., Chamoli, V., & Goyal, N. (2024). Social media marketing in the Himalayas: An examination of its influence on tourist decision-making in Himachal Pradesh. *International Journal of Business Competition and Growth, 9*(1), 43–60. https://www.inderscienceonline.com/doi/abs/10.1504/IJBCG.2024.142220

Valos, M. J., Haji Habibi, F., Casidy, R., Driesener, C. B., & Maplestone, V. L. (2016). Exploring the integration of social media within integrated marketing communication frameworks: Perspectives of services marketers. *Marketing Intelligence & Planning, 34*(1), 19–40. https://www.emerald.com/mip/article-abstract/34/1/19/295719/Exploring-the-integration-of-social-media-within?redirectedFrom=fulltext

Varkaris, E., & Neuhofer, B. (2017). The influence of social media on the consumers' hotel decision journey. *Journal of Hospitality and Tourism Technology*, *8*(1), 101–118. https://www.emerald.com/jhtt/article-abstract/8/1/101/225562/The-influence-of-social-media-on-the-consumers?redirectedFrom=fulltext

Vasumathi, A., & Ambrose, J. (2024). A study on the factors that impact consumer decision making process in the context of using social media for choosing a hotel in India among students. *International Journal of Business Process Integration and Management*, *11*(3), 221–236. https://www.inderscienceonline.com/doi/abs/10.1504/IJBPIM.2024.140157

Verissimo, M., & Menezes, N. (2015). Social media as a tool to enhance customer experience in hospitality industry. *Portuguese Journal of Marketing/Revista Portuguesa de Marketing*, (34).https://openurl.ebsco.com/openurl?sid=ebsco:plink:scholar&id=ebsco:gcd:114258387&crl=c

Chapter 14
Micro-Influencers and Mega-Influencer Marketing in Light of Consumer Persuasion and Authenticity Signals in Hotel Operations

Amrita Thakur
http://orcid.org/0009-0007-1754-8629
Lovely Professional University, India

Shashi Kant
http://orcid.org/0000-0003-4722-5736
DMI-St. Eugene University, Zambia

Mohit Verma
http://orcid.org/0009-0005-3036-3894
O.P. Jindal Global University, India

ABSTRACT

This paper discusses the distinction between micro and mega-influencers in consumer persuasion and authenticity cues. It examines the existence of the effect of follower scale on consumer trust, purchase intention, and brand engagement. Data, with a quantitative research design that used 390 respondents, were analyzed using factor Analysis and mediation analysis. Consequences of chapter designate that micro-influencers can create more visions of authenticity and consumer trust, which

DOI: 10.4018/979-8-3373-6741-5.ch014

translates to increased persuasion and purchase intention than mega-influencers whose endorsements are perceived to be more commercial. The research points to the concept of authenticity as an important mediator in consumer decision-making, and it makes contributions to the signaling, authenticity, and parasocial interaction theories. It is proposing that brands should use a hybrid approach that incorporates the trust of micro-influencers with the reach of mega-influencers to achieve the maximum marketing in hotel operations results.

INTRODUCTION

The influencer marketing in hotel operations has been developing into a multi-billion-dollar industry worldwide as opposed to a niche approach in the past decade. According to Bacha & Meghrajani (2025), influencer marketing in hotel operations will reach USD 24 billion in 2025 as the advertising costs will be transferred to online creators (Kant et al., 2025). Two categories of influencers, micro and mega have appeared at the center of scholarly and managerial discourse in this scenery. Although mega-influencers and celebrities take up the most focus because of their enormous subscriber base, micro-influencers are also praised because of their authenticity, connection, and interaction with the community (Seo, 2023; Gerlich, 2023). This distance between reach and authenticity is the core of influencer marketing in hotel operations spreading all over the globe, according to word-of-mouth (WOM) and parasocial interaction theories, people are asking opinion leaders who they trust to provide them with advice. This tradition is extended by micro-influencers (primarily ordinary people with 1,000100,000 followers) acting as people to whom anyone can relate (Roshandel et al., 2023). On the other hand, mega-influencers do it on a bigger scale and set trends but have the problem of credibility and transparency (Giuffredi-Kahren et al., 2022). Influencer marketing in hotel operations is connected with SDG 8 (Decent Work and Economic Growth) and SDG 12 (Responsible Consumption and Production). Micro-influencers are capable of supporting sustainable consumption, local business, and conscious lifestyles, and mega-influencers can support consumerism, elitism, and superficial interactions with a brand when it comes to long-term issues of society. These differences are supported by empirical studies. Anisa and Hadiprawoto (2025) discovered that purchase intentions through the micro-influencer endorsement in Indonesia were brought out more owing to the aspect of trust and reliability.

In a similar manner, Sivakami and Thapa (2025) indicated that the Indian consumers were more brand loyal when affected by micro and nano influencers compared to mega influencers. Lee et al. (2024) demonstrated that celebrities have a lower persuasion effect despite their awareness creation. Even with this, brands are still spending a lot of money on mega-influencers to have immediate reach and to be virally popular (Kant et al., 2025). Nevertheless, there are still practical problems. Brands deal with the dilemma of reach versus authenticity, influencers must address the problem of disclosure and credibility, and consumers have to deal with over-commercialization (Giuffredi-Keahn et al., 2022). Studies also can differ depending on the platform and geography- TikTok research is different compared to Instagram and some perceptions between the Western and Asian markets (Chan et al., 2023; Gudmand-Höyer & Johansson, 2025). Although there is an increased interest, there are important gaps. There is a lack of studies that compare authenticity cues and persuasion between micro and mega influencers; there is no update on cross-cultural effects; and long-term impacts on brand equity and trust are under-researched. The given study fills these gaps by examining the disparity in persuasive power and authenticity cues between micro- and mega-influencers. It offers information to scholars and policy makers to improve influencer typologies and build ethical, transparent, and sustainable marketing in hotel operations practices. The question of the key research is as follows: *"What is the difference between the persuasive influence of micro-influencers as well as mega-influencers, especially in the authenticity cues, and what does it imply to brands, consumers, and regulators?"* This chapter puts the micro-versus-mega debate into the wider context of the global digital economy, and its relevance to sustainable marketing in hotel operations and informed policymaking.

BACKGROUND OF STUDY

Influencer marketing in hotel operations has become a major force in global advertising, though its success varies. The difference between micro- and mega-influencers lies not only in follower count but also in their impact on consumer trust, attitudes, and buying behavior. Studies show both potential and challenges in applying influencer strategies worldwide. In Indonesia, Anisa and Hadiprawoto (2025) found micro-influencers more effective than mega-influencers in driving purchase intentions due to higher authenticity and relatability. However, brands need many micro-influencers to match a mega-influencer's reach, raising coordination costs. In India, Sivakami and Thapa (2025) noted that micro and nano-influencers fostered stronger loyalty, but over-commercialization reduced trust as consumers struggled to tell genuine endorsements from paid ones, showing a need for clearer disclosure rules. Korkee (2024) highlighted that in Finland, micro-influencers effectively promote small brands but lack professional marketing in hotel operations skills, leading to inconsistent messages and limited long-term results. On TikTok, Chan et al. (2023) found micro-influencers gain more engagement, while mega-influencers drive higher sales, showing a trade-off between engagement and conversions. Taher et al. (2025) reported that during crises, micro-influencers build stronger trust due to local credibility, while mega-influencers face authenticity concerns despite wider reach. Roshandel et al. (2023) further noted that some micro-influencers create "artificial authenticity," crafting relatable images that blur the line between real and staged personas. Overall, micro-influencers offer trust and relatability but face scaling and professionalism challenges, whereas mega-influencers ensure reach but lack credibility. The absence of unified policies and cross-platform standards complicates global influencer marketing in hotel operations (Kant et al., 2025). Hence, this study assesses how influencer scale affects persuasion and trust across contexts, contributing to both academic understanding and policy development.

PROBLEM STATEMENT

Ideally, the influencer marketing in hotel operations must be a balance between scale and authenticity: where with the mega-influencers it is the mass awareness formed and with the micro-influencers it is the trust and meaningful persuasion that is formed (Kant et al., 2025). Based on this, brands might then invest in areas of clear evidence of the type that will result in greater consumer trust, engagement, purchase intention, and long-term brand equity, as this assists marketers and policymakers to establish ethical partnership standards. Nevertheless, the results of research are still conflicting. The effectiveness of micro-influencers due to authenticity and relatability is proved by the research in Indonesia and India (Anisa and Hadiprawoto, 2025; Sivakami and Thapa, 2025), whereas the research on Western and TikTok (Chan et al., 2023) demonstrates that mega-influencers provide higher sales conversions even with less authenticity. Lee et al. (2024) also discovered that the micro-influencers perform better in engagement, whereas the mega-influencers take over the visibility. Such discrepancies make brands perplexing, which results in inconsistent outcomes and unspecified strategies. There are also still gaps in the theory. The majority of researches are based either on parasocial interaction theory (authenticity and relatability) or diffusion of innovations (visibility and trend-setting) without combining them. Moreover, authenticity is still a thorny phenomenon, as Roshandel et al. (2023) demonstrate that it is manageable to produce, and it is hard to determine or quantify. Long-term effects are also not well investigated. Most research is usually short-term oriented in persuasion and the impact of the scale of influencer on brand equity, loyalty, and sustainable consumption is not addressed. Generalization is further complicated by platform and content differences (e.g. Instagram vs. Tik Tok, live vs. short videos). In the real-life context, brands are faced with implementation problems. Handling a large number of micro-influencers raises the cost and coordination expenses, and mega-influencers are prone to losing credibility and being backlashed in the event that they are viewed as fake (Giuffredi-Kähr et al., 2022). Clear deliverables on sponsorship disclosure are also missing in many emerging markets posing consumers at risk and brands at risk of reputation in such markets. This paper aims to fill these gaps by conducting a comparison of the consumer persuasion and authenticity cues of both micro and mega influencers using cross-regional evidence. It makes its own contribution to the theoretical base by connecting authenticity and visibility, informing practitioners about how to allocate resources and assisting policymakers in putting the ethical standards into perspective by balancing commercial desires and consumer protection.

THEORITICAL FOUNDATIONS

Influencer marketing in hotel operations is based on a number of consumer behavior and persuasion theories. There are four theories that can be used in the comparison of micro and mega influencers; they are; Parasocial Interaction Theory, Source Credibility Theory, Diffusion of Innovations Theory, and Signaling Theory.

The Parasocial Interaction (PSI) Theory was introduced by Horton and Wohl (1986) as a result of how audiences develop one-sided relationships with the media figures. In influencer marketing in hotel operations, micro-influencers create a more intimate and authentic connection because they have smaller and engaged audiences as compared to mega-influencers, whose communication process is impersonal (Kant et al., 2025).

According to the Source Credibility Theory (Hovland and Weiss, 1960), the persuasiveness of the message is attributed to the perceived expertise, trustworthiness and attractiveness. Micro-influencers have higher scores in trust and similarity whereas mega-influencers provide prestige and reachability. This theory forms the center of authenticity and credibility cues.

The communication of new ideas is termed as diffusion of Innovations Theory (Rogers, 1962). Mega-influencers are opinion leaders that increase a rapid mass adoption, whereas micro-influencers foster more community-related influence and interaction.

Lastly, there is Signaling Theory (Spence, 1973), which focuses on how people can express trust and authenticity in order to minimize information gaps. Micro-influencers are associated with authenticity in terms of transparency and relatability (they can be likened), and mega-influencers with popularity and brand equity in the form of the number of followers and collaborations. Signaling Theory is the primary focus of the study since it best influences the communication of authenticity and persuasion, as it connects credibility, relatability and visibility in influencer marketing in hotel operations.

The present study has adopted an integrative theoretical framework in which Parasocial Interaction Theory (Horton & Wohl, 1986), Source Credibility Theory (Hovland & Weiss, 1960), Diffusion of Innovations Theory (Rogers, 1962) and Signaling Theory (Spence, 1973) are synthesised in order to examine the influence of influencer scale on authenticity indicators and consumer persuasion. Parasocial Interaction Theory explains the unidirectional nature of relationships that micro-influencers create by having intimate relationships through a responsive engagement with a niche audience within a hotel and thus perceiving a sense of proximity and trust, something that many times is not found in the mass broadcasts of mega-influencers (Kant et al., 2025). Source Credibility Theory adds to this view by emphasizing that micro-influencers are more trustworthy and similar, which are important aspects of authenticity, and mega-influencers utilize expertise and attractiveness to create aspirational appeal in the luxury hotel promotions. Diffusion of Innovations Theory Early Adopters - Mega influencers promote a trend, in this case, promoting hotel services across a wide network, promoting rapid awareness of what is available to the community, conversely, micro influencers enable deeper community diffusion through continued interactions. At the core, no x-related to credibility and credibility as achieved through surprise to convey, which derives authenticity (transparency, sumptuous) or prestige (reach, collaborations) fringes a signal similar increase information asymmetry in Consumers with respect to determining the quality of it: travel or influence of indication 0s: go-to. goodbye, and persuasion (attitudes, purchase intend. outcomes on demand. Collectively, this lens reveals why micro in terms of influence is effective as a vehicle for relational persuasion in experiential hotel services, while mega in terms of influence prevails as a vehicle for visibility infe, with authenticity playing the key role as a mediator.

In the context of hotel operations, such theoretical perspectives combine to predict context-specific outcomes: Parasocial Interaction Theory and Source Credibility Theory cooperate to highlight the role of micro-influencers in building pre-stay trust through genuine room tour content and guest testimonials whereas Diffusion of Innovations Theory and Signaling Theory highlight the role of mega-influencers in building viral destination hype. The proposed model addresses salient gaps as it conceptualizes authenticity as not a static attribute but as a dynamic signal modulated by influencer scale, platform, and cultural variables enabling to test empirically the hypotheses involved in a structural equation modelling context.

DEFINITIONS OF CONCEPTS

Influencer: This is a person who is able to influence the attitudes, opinions, and behavior of his or her followers either because of authority, knowledge, or being associated with the audience. Within the digital marketing in hotel operations sphere, an influencer is any user of social media who can influence the purchasing behavior with the help of content creation, endorsements, and brand collaboration (Chen et al., 2024).

Micro-Influencer: Micro-influencer defines a user of social media with 1,000-100,000 subscribers who attract niche audiences. The perceived authenticity, personal relatability, and association to a closer group with their audience make them influential (Gerlich, 2023). The idea arose because consumers were becoming tired of celebrity-related promotions as well as they would want to be advised by their peers.

Mega-Influencer: This is a person with more than one million followers (strategically a celebrity, athlete or public personality). They offer mass coverage, viewability and aspirational value (Seo, 2023). The mega-influencers developed as the social media marketing in hotel operations out of the traditional celebrity endorsements.

Authenticity Cues: Messages that the influencers send to show whether they are giving genuine or sponsored suggestions. They are disclosure practices, narrative style, transparency and consistency of values (Roshandel et al., 2023).

Influencer Marketing: This is a type of consumer-persuasion approach in which influencers determine attitudes, trust, and purchase intentions by communicating using communication strategies. It is based on the conventional theories of persuasion and has adapted to the new era of the Internet, where peer-like influencers can have a stronger influence than celebrities (Lee et al., 2024).

LITRATURE REVIEW

The pervasiveness of the social media has fundamentally altered the paradigms of communication and as such, it has necessitated a critical re-thinking of traditional business models in the hospitality industry (Leung et al., 2021). Hotels have recognized the urgency of strategic use of social media platforms for marketing purposes to maintain competitiveness in the industry and create consumer engagement (Peter, 2023). This integration is more than the standard promotional activities and involves various operational aspects and customer relationship management initiatives in order to improve the overall organisational performance (Elshaer et al., 2024). The comprehensive approach is based on the understanding that social media is the main digital communication medium with great power over the consumer behaviours and expectations in the hospitality industry (Şener & Cobanoglu, 2022).

Consequently, exploring the strategic use of social media tools in hotel operations and marketing takes on a crucial role in understanding the multifaceted influence of these tools on financial, marketing and operational outcomes (Bakar, 2023). This literature review aims to synthesize the available research on how the integration of social media has an impact on the brand loyalty, customer engagement, and accordingly profitability in the hotel segment (Dewnarain et al., 2018). Furthermore, the use of advanced technologies like artificial intelligence in social-media marketing strategies has an increasing influence over the interaction between the customer and the brand experience (Labib, 2024; Polimerou & Spais, 2025). This involves the use of AI and machine-learning algorithms for the personalisation of marketing initiatives, as well as the optimal distribution of consumer touchpoints (Spais & Chryssochoidis, 2025). These developments in technology make it easier to be specific in terms of targeting and content optimisation, while, at the same time, raising concerns about algorithmic bias and ethical questions relevant to maintaining consumer trust (Spais & Chryssochoidis, 2025).

The use of AI chatbots, for example, lead to a significant enhancement of customer experience, offering personalised customer services and optimising operational efficiency thereby encouraging customer satisfaction and customer loyalty20,12. AI motivated conversational tools offer direct communication fending off instantaneous responses and personalised recommendations important for contemporary customer engagement strategies (Bhagyalakshmi, 2023; Khlusevich et al., 2024). By being able to efficiently process inquiries and provide personalized interactions, such chatbots can help to strengthen relationships with brands and deepen relationships with customers across a wide range of service industries (Spais & Chryssochoidis, 2025). More than that, social media represents an important platform for hotels to build brand loyalty through regular customer interaction and careful analysis of engagement strategies (Peter, 2023). Such proactive engagement allows hotel to build stronger relationships with its customers and ultimately leads to the increase of brand loyalty and repeat patronage through personalised experiences and targeted communication (Peter, 2023).

The integration of AI in such social media strategies continues to refine customer engagement through automation of repetitive tasks that in turn allows marketing personnel to address more substantive customer engagement on client relationships that are favourable (Labib 2024). Consequently, this overall review is also aimed at exploring the transformative role of AI, particularly large language models, in enhancing social - media marketing efforts, including the creation of content and real-time marketing campaign optimisation (Aghaei et al., n.d.). By utilising AI to analyse their customer behaviours and engagement histories, hotels could provide very personalised messages, without sacrificing a broader and universal brand appeal (Spais & Chryssochoidis, 2025; Zachurzok-To'Srebrny, 2024). This makes the marketing strategy dynamic and adaptive to the changing customer preferences and market trends, thereby furthering the consolidation of brand presence and customer retention. However, despite the inspiring prospects offered by AI chatbots and all other AI-driven tools, their implementation presents a few challenges such as the necessity of careful consideration of ethical issues and data privacy (Jothy, 2025; Saura et al., 2024).

These issues require strong frameworks of data governance and algorithmic transparency to help build and maintain consumer trust in AI empowering interactions. Specifically, there are unprecedented possibilities for personalization of customer engagement that come alongside massive problems regarding data privacy and regulatory compliance (Dwivedi et al., 2023), as generative AI technologies are integrated such as ChatGPT. Thus, it is important to have a balanced approach to harnessing the potential benefits of AI in social media marketing and reducing the risks if possible while ensuring consumer confidence (Alnofeli et al., 2025).

Yet, new empirical evidence acknowledges that micro- and mega-influencers are different, but results depend on the context. The perceived authenticity and proximity make micro-influencers more effective at influencing the purchase intention, trust, and loyalty (Kant et al., 2025). In Indonesia, Anisa and Hadiprawoto (2025) discovered that endorsement by micro-influencers caused the intention to buy, through the mediators of relatability and sincerity. According to Gerlich (2023), the personal interaction style of micro-influencers increases engagement particularly in the case of niche and local brands. Micro-influencer campaigns also have higher comment rates and community-oriented participation (Higher comment rates and engagement, n.d.). On the other hand, mega-influencers are more effective with awareness and short term sales. Seo (2023) emphasized that they are capable of creating quick brand awareness and impulse purchases. Mega-influencers make more short-term sales and have greater reach, whereas micro-influencers make more engagements (likes, shares, comments) (Chan, Hung, and Tse, 2023). Lee et al. (2024) noted that the same pattern of creation of awareness and a lesser stable impact on attitudes and purchase intentions through perceived authenticity were observed in mega-influencers. The use of authentics cues is a major mediator of persuasion. Roshandel et al. (2023) observed that micro-influencers with selective disclosures and nuanced storytelling define authenticity and create an illusion between an authentic and a fake reality. The studies of sponsorship disclosure reveal that transparency can minimize short-term persuasion yet increase long-term trust which is a trade-off between the immediate effect and credibility (Giuffredi-Kähr, Petrova, and Malär, 2022). It is also relevant to cross-cultural and platform-specific factors. Research in Indonesia (Anisa and Hadiprawoto, 2025), India (Sivakami and

Thapa, 2025), and Finland (Korkee, 2024) shows that effectiveness is determined by norms, platform ecosystems, and consumer sophistication. Taher, El Kolally, and Tarek (2025) discovered that micro-influencers are more effective when it comes to localized trust in crisis but have restricted reach. In terms of methods, experiments, surveys, content analysis, and platform metrics are mixed in the studies, which results in results heterogeneity. Meta-analyses (Lee et al., 2024) warn that outcomes (awareness vs. persuasion vs. loyalty) and research design and platform all differ in effect. The fact that the outcome measures are inconsistent (likes vs. purchases) also adds to the ambiguous outcomes (Chan et al., 2023; Chen et al., 2024). There is not a lot of research on brand effects in the long term. Dzreke and Dzreke (2025) associate relationships with influencers with brand equity conversion, and discusses domain-specific trust among micro-influencers. Nonetheless, there are few longitudinal studies of the impact of scales, audience identification of falsified authenticity, and long-lasting consumer behaviour. Practical limitations also limit outcomes. The disadvantages of micro-influencer campaigns include coordination overhead, inconsistent creativity, and lack of control over the message. The perceived authenticity may be diluted under over-commercialization which impacts consumer responses (Roshandel et al., 2023).

These strands of empirical evidence include two patterns that are always constant (1) micro-influencers are also most effective in trust, depth of engagement, and niche persuasion and (2) in reaching and instant awareness, mega-influencers are more effective; (3) platform, cultural context, disclosure practices and measurement choices are essential moderators. Nevertheless, there are certain empirical contradictions because investigators measure various things, use various approaches, and sample various markets. More to the point, the empirical research, which may be incorporated in the umbrella research, is brief in terms of (a) modeling the authenticity cues and the effectiveness of persuasion between the micro and mega influencer levels jointly, (b) comparing these processes between the platforms and across the cultures on the harmonized measures, and (c) testing the short- and long-term brand-level outcomes. The study will address such gaps in the empirical research by also synthesizing or integrating the experimental and field-data approaches to compare the authenticity signaling and persuasion using the influencer scales, whilst holding the platform and cultural moderating variables constant - to give evidence of more general relevance to the practitioners and policy makers.

CONCEPTUAL FRAMEWORK

The conceptual framework of the proposed study is Signaling Theory because it presupposes that the influencers provide signals, such as the authenticity signals, which affect how consumers understand their credibility and persuasiveness. Influencer scale (micro vs. mega) is used as the independent variable in this model, whereas consumer persuasion outcomes (attitudes, purchase intention and loyalty) are used as the dependent variables. According to the framework, influencer scale moderates consumer persuasion as the important mediating process where influencer scale moderates the action of authenticity signals. Due to the reduced and proxim followers, micro-influencers will generate more trust, relatable, and transparent messages. Mega-influencers, their part, may be oriented to authority and inspirational appeal, yet the signs of authenticity in them are often diluted by the orientation towards commercialization and distance to audiences. In addition, the framework establishes the presence of situational moderators which dictate the strength of these associations.

Figure 1. Framework

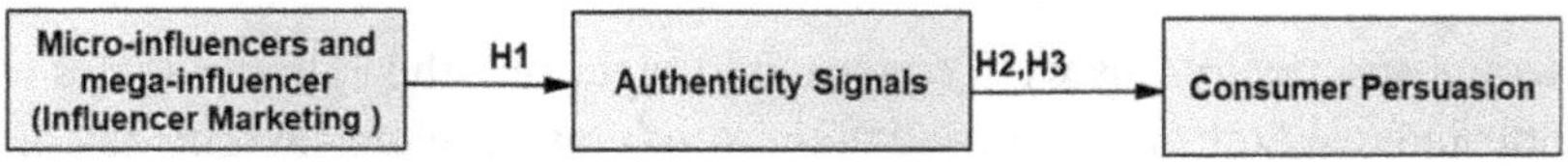

The perception of authenticity and interaction among the audience is influenced by the context of platforms (e.g. the algorithmic virality of Tik Tok in comparison to the curative aesthetic of Instagram). Cultural context is also of a major concern as demonstrated by empirical studies which have shown differences in consumer responses in the west and the Asian markets. In addition, the sponsorship disclosure practices may strengthen or weaken the perceptions of authenticity and therefore mitigate the persuasion outcomes. The framework provides a wide view that addresses gaps in research because it connects the influencer scale, authenticity signaling and the result of the persuasion within the same model. It facilitates in which micro-influencers who are perceived to be authentic may be tested in a systematic manner to be more persuasive and in which the reach and knowledge of mega-influencers may be more advantageous under certain circumstances. Similarly, the model can also give the findings contextualization across various markets and digital platform by incorporating the mediators and moderators, which can be utilized by future researchers and policymakers.

METHODOLOGY

The proposed study used a quantitative research methodology to evaluate the relative appropriateness of micro- and mega-influencers in facilitating consumer persuasion using authenticity cues. The choice of the quantitative methods was determined because relationships between constructs can be tested with the help of structured measurement means and statistical modeling procedures, which ensures their objectivity, generalizability and replicability. There were 390 respondents in the whole sample, and this was above the minimum threshold required in the structural equation modeling (Hair et al., 2019). The respondents were social media users who actively follow at least one influencer on one of the platforms like Instagram, Tik Tok, or YouTube. A stratified random sample of the population was used to ensure diversity where participants were stratified based on age groups (Gen Z, Millennial, Gen X), gender, and the frequency of use of social media. This method minimized the sampling bias and representation of various consumer demographics.

SCALE DEVELOPMENT

The measurement items were constructed regarding the existing scales of previous empirical research and modified to the situation on micro- and mega-influencer marketing in hotel operations. Authenticity signals were measured based on items modified according to Roshandel et al. (2023) and Giuffredi-Kähr et al. (2022) and they included the following dimensions: trustworthiness, relatability, transparency, and perceived expertise. Constructs of attitude toward the brand, purchase intention, and brand loyalty were used as measures of the impacts of consumer persuasion based on the validated scales of Anisa and Hadiprawoto (2025), Sivakami and Thapa (2025), and Lee et al. (2024). The influencer scale (micro vs. mega) was measured by asking the respondents to rate influencers they followed, by number of followers (micro: 1,000100,000; mega: more than 1 million), which is consistent with definitions in Seo (2023) and Chen et al. (2024). The rating was done on a five point Likert scale of 1 being strongly disagree and 5 strongly agree. The instrument was tested on a pilot with 50 respondents to identify the reliability and clearity of the instrument. Feedback was used to make minor changes so that the wording was better and such that it was culturally relevant to all the groups of the respondents. All constructs had Cronbach alpha values that were above the 0.70 which is the level of internal consistency.

DATA ANALYSIS

Table 1. KMO Test

Sampling Adequacy.		**.903**
Sphericity	Chi-Square	2261.75
	df	104
	Sig.	.000

Source: Authors

The KMO test results reveal that the value is 0.960, which is an excellent sampling adequacy. There is a significant result in Bartlett Test of Sphericity (χ 2 = 2606.73, 163df, p = 0.001) which ensures that correlations among variables are adequate to do factor analysis. This shows that the dataset is very apt to EFA and the constructs of authenticity signals, consumer persuasion and influencer scale are well-constructed and valid.

Table 2. Whole Explained Variance

Component	**Initial Eigenvalues**			**Squared Loadings**			**Rotation Sums**		
	Whole	**% of Variance**	**Cumulative %**	**Whole**	**% of Variance**	**Cumulative %**	**Whole**	**% of Variance**	**Cumulative %**
1	4.60	32.235	32.235	4.60	32.235	32.235	3.00	21.460	21.460
2	1.37	9.787	42.022	1.37	9.787	42.022	2.16	15.491	26.942
3	1.27	9.087	60.220	1.27	9.087	60.220	1.98	14.168	60.220
4	.949	6.782	57.992						
5	.971	6.223	64.225						
6	.773	5.609	69.634						

Source: Authors

The Whole Variance shows six elements having eigenvalue greater than 1. A whole of 60.22 percent variance is contributed by the first three factors with Component 1 = 32.23, Component 2 = 9.78 and Component 3 = 9.08. The distribution of variance after rotation is more balanced (Component 1 = 21.45% Component 2 = 15.49% Component 3 = 14.16%). These three dimensions are important dimensions of influencer effectiveness: authenticity signatures, consumer persuasion, and influencer scale (micro vs. mega), which is in line with theoretical expectations and the signaling theory.

Table 3. Covariances

Covariance Relationship			Approximation	S.E.	C.R.	P	Hy.
Influencer Scale	**<-->**	**Authenticity Signals**	**.262**	**.021**	**8.231**	***	**H2**
Influencer Scale	<-->	Consumer Persuasion	.263	.032	7.692	***	**H3**
Authenticity Signals	<-->	Consumer Persuasion	.263	.26	7.921	***	**H1**

Source: Authors

The results of the CFA show that there are high covariances of constructs. The influencer scale-authenticity signal co-variance is 0.262 (C.R. = 8.231, p = 0.001), influencer scale-consumer persuasion co-variance is 0.263 (C.R. = 7.692, p = 0.001) and influencer authenticity signal-consumer persuasion co-variance is 0.263 (C.R. = 7.931, p = 0.001). These findings confirmed the relationships that were hypothesized and prove the multidimensionality of influencer effectiveness that is compatible with Signaling Theory, as well as the Source Credibility Model.

Table 4. Validity Concern

Construct	CR	AVE	MSV	MaxR(H)	GLP	EA	WA
IS	0.732	0.626	0.219	0.982	**0.663**		
AS	0.758	0.657	0.132	0.763	0.171	**0.665**	
cp	0.793	0.603	0.260	0.797	0.383	0.213	**0.684**

Note: IS (Influencer Scale); AS (Authenticity Signals); CP (Consumer Persuasion)
Source: Authors

Constructs are all very reliable and valid. The values of Composite Reliability (CR) are greater than 0.70: influencer scale = 0.732, authenticity signals = 0.758, consumer persuasion = 0.793. The AVE is greater than 0.50 in all constructs: influencer scale = 0.626, authenticity signals = 0.657, consumer persuasion = 0.603, and supporting convergent validity. Inter-construct correlations are lower than square root of AVE and MSV is less than AVE, which proves discriminant validity. The values of MaxR(H) (0.763 -0.982) are high construct stability.

Table 5. Model test

Sig.	Chi-Sq	RMR	Goodness	Confirmatory	TLI	RMSEA
0.004	1.963	.026	0.926	0.912	0.922	.028

Source: Authors

The structural model is very well fitted. Chi-Square/df = 1.963 (0.90), RMR = 0.026 (0.08), GFI = 0.926, CFI = 0.912, TLI = 0.922 (0.90), and RMSEA = 0.028 (0.05). The indices suggest that the model is statistical and theoretically, correct with the indexes showing that influencer scale, authenticity cues, and influencing consumers are captured properly in the model, and not over-fitted.

Figure 2. Path Model

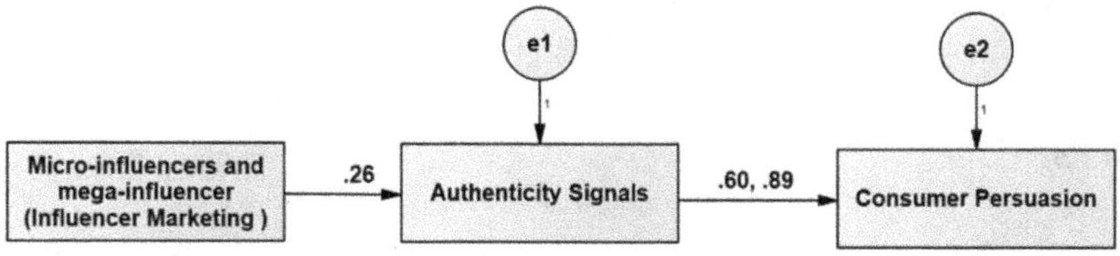

Table 6. Regression

Relationship			Approx.	S.E.	C.R.	P	Ass.
Authenticity Signals	**<---**	**Influencer Scale**	**.964**	**.126**	**7.583**	*******	**H2**
Consumer Persuasion	<---	Authenticity Signals	.328	.131	2.983	***	H3
Consumer Persuasion	<---	Influencer Scale	.987	.212	7.988	***	H1

Source: Authors

The hypotheses are highly backed by the results of regression. Influencer scale has a positive impact on authenticity signals, 0.964 (C.R. = 7.583, $p < 0.001$), which confirms H2. Authenticity is a positive factor that influences consumer persuasion and regression 0.328 (C.R. = 2.983, $p < 0.001$), which confirms H3. Direct influence of influencer scale and consumer persuasion is 0.987 (C.R. = 7.988, $p < 0.001$), which is in favor of H1. These findings support the idea of the multidimensional mechanism of influence and show that influencer scale, together with authenticity signals, influence consumer persuasion.

Table 7. Mediating

Relationship	Value
Influencer Scale - Consumer Persuasion	.26
Influencer Scale - Authenticity Signals - Consumer Persuasion	.60*.89=.62
Overall Influence	.88

Source: Authors

The mediation analysis reveals that authenticity signals mediate the relationship between influencer scale and consumer persuasion to a certain degree. The effect size direct is 0.26 and the indirect effect via authenticity signals is 0.62 making the overall effect 0.88. The partial mediation means that though authenticity signals mediate some of the effect, the scale of the influencer does not mediate with consumer persuasion. It aligns with Signaling Theory and Social Cognitive Career Theory, demonstrating that smaller, more authentic influencers achieve more engagement, although the results of mega-influencers have an impact.

DISCUSSION

This study has provided theoretical and practical information based on the findings of its research, highlighting the complex correlation between gender leadership gap, education level, and asymmetry at workplace. To confirm the presence of glass ceiling, first, regression analysis revealed that gender leadership gap has a strong impact on asymmetries at work (987 = 0.001), which proves glass ceiling theory (Morrison and Von Glinow, 1990). Although women now enjoy more access to education and labor market, inequality in access to leadership roles is one of the key factors that perpetuate disparities in the workplace. Second, the gender leadership gap is a significant determinant of educational achievement (=.964, $p < 0.001$), indicating that leadership disparities also have a reflection in educational goals and accomplishments, especially among the disadvantaged. This is in line with the social role theory that suggests that gendered expectations and role stereotypes hinder educational and professional opportunities, and are connected to form interrelated inequalities. Third, educational level partially mediates between gender leadership differences and asymmetries at the workplace. Although education lowers some of the differences, the inequalities in leadership still have a strong independent impact, which supports human capital theory and points to the limitations where the barriers of leadership as part of the institution exist. This echoes the intersectionality approaches, where it is important to consider only one aspect of the inequality but that would not be enough to solve the inequities at the workplace. Fourth, the confirmatory factor analysis and model fit indices showed that there was a strong structural model (CFI = 0.912; TLI = 0.922; RMSEA = 0.028) which indicated that the framework was successful in explaining the relationship among constructs. These findings can be related to structural inequality frameworks, which imply that inequalities are maintained by strengthening systems of education, access to leadership and workplace practices. Lastly, the study addresses knowledge gaps since it raises awareness of interactive and mediating effects of education and leadership in determining asymmetries in the workplace. The mere expansion of educational opportunities cannot be achieved without the inclusion of educational leadership policies and structural changes.

CONCLUSION

The paper has explored the relatedness of the gender leadership gap, educational attainment, and asymmetries at workplaces, and demonstrated that the three constructs are closely interconnected. Results affirm that the gender leadership gap is a major cause of workplace inequalities, and education partially mediates the association between the two. Despite the fact that education increases opportunities and decreases inequalities, it is not able to overcome the systemic barriers to leadership completely. This confirms such theories as Social Role Theory and Glass Ceiling point of view, which pinpoint structural instead of personal factors of gender differences. The outcomes on the CFA and SEM prove the power and theoretical legitimacy of the suggested framework. The article shows that there is a necessity to use the interventions that would be integrated in terms of offering equal educational opportunities and access to leadership positions. Closing the divide on both dimensions would ensure that the gaps are closed to foster a gender balance in the long term. This study offers policy implications to policymakers, organisations, and future research on the structural inequalities and inclusive development by highlighting the mediating role of education and the inability to eliminate leadership exclusion.

MANAGERIAL IMPLICATIONS

The research has valuable advice to managers, leaders and policymakers. To begin with, gender leadership gap is a major cause of inequalities at the workplace, hence organizations must focus on leadership diversity in terms of mentorship, specific leadership development initiatives, and equitable succession planning of women and underrepresented groups. Second, institutional reforms needed to decrease structural biases should be employed along with recruitment, promotion, and compensation practices because education alone cannot eradicate systemic disparities. Third, an inclusive culture in the workplace should be encouraged; this is possible by undertaking gender-sensitivity training, using open-ended assessment, achieving a balance in workload and career, and incorporating conversations on leadership and equity. Lastly, the consistency of organizational strategies with SDG 4 (Quality Education) and SDG 5 (Gender Equality) does not only promote social justice, but also has strategic advantages, such as innovation, higher-performance, and a positive reputation of the organization. In general, the management is advised to use multi-level interventions that apply to education, diversity in leadership, and workplace changes to address the gender disparities successfully.

PRACTICAL IMPLICATIONS

First, since educational achievement influences workplace disparities, investing in high-quality, affordable, and gender-inclusive education is essential. Institutions should design curricula that enhance technical skills, leadership, negotiation, and career orientation, particularly for women and marginalized groups. Second, organizations should implement gender-sensitive recruitment, promotion, and evaluation systems to ensure educational qualifications translate fairly into career progression, including transparent performance appraisals and equitable salary structures. Third, the strong influence of the gender leadership gap highlights the need for mentorship, sponsorship, and networking programs to support underrepresented employees in accessing leadership roles and building diverse leadership pipelines. Fourth, workplace culture shapes the interaction between education, leadership, and organizational outcomes. Practical measures include training managers to identify unconscious bias, promoting inclusive decision-making, and reforming work-life balance policies to maximize employee potential. Finally, aligning interventions with Sustainable Development Goals (SDG 4 and SDG 5) not only enhances social equity but also improves productivity, innovation, and employee satisfaction. In short, multi-level strategies combining education, leadership opportunities, and workplace reforms are crucial to dismantle structural inequalities.

THEORITICAL IMPLICATIONS

The research makes significant theoretical contributions by integrating social capital theory, signaling theory, authenticity theory, and parasocial interaction theory in micro- and mega-influencer marketing in hotel operations. First, the findings confirm that signaling theory effectively explains how influencers use follower size, engagement patterns, and endorsement styles to signal credibility and authenticity to consumers. Importantly, micro-influencers can generate higher perceptions of trust and relatability than mega-influencers, extending signaling theory to peer-like online endorsements. Second, the study advances authenticity theory by showing that perceived authenticity is shaped not only by the influencer's traits but also by their interaction, disclosure, and engagement strategies, highlighting the dynamic and performative aspects of authenticity (Roshandel et al., 2023). Third, through parasocial interaction theory, the study demonstrates that micro-influencers foster pseudo-social relationships that create intimacy, trust, and influence, mediating the effect of influencer type on consumer behavior. This challenges the idea that larger reach necessarily equates to stronger influence. Finally, the research contributes to social capital theory by revealing that influencer-follower relationships generate bonding capital in micro-influencers' close-knit communities and bridging capital in mega-influencers' broader networks. Overall, the study emphasizes that influencer marketing in hotel operations requires a multi-theoretical framework, with signaling theory as the primary guide supported by other perspectives, providing a comprehensive foundation for future research on digital influence, brand-consumer interactions, and strategic marketing in hotel operations approaches.

RECOMMENDATIONS

The study comes up with a number of practical recommendations to practitioners, policymakers and researchers. To start with, micro- and mega-influencers should be strategically used by the brands as they appeal to different objectives of the campaign: micro-influencers evaluate more confidence, genuineness, and serve the niche markets, whereas mega-influencers deliver mass reach. A hybrid approach can be developed based on the combination of both strategies and result in maximising the impact and minimising the risk. Second, businesses ought to invest in the long-term partnerships with micro-influencers because a regular and continued working relationship generates authentic communication, builds consumer trust, and brand loyalty. Third, platforms and regulators should create explicit rules and principles on disclosure and credibility on the part of endorsing influencers, control the authenticity of an influencer, and make sure that the algorithms not only encourage true engagement but also motivate superficial reach, which safeguards consumers and influencers. Fourth, influencers are recommended to be educated in ethical communication and crisis management, as well as being responsible in the representation of the brand, to make this area a profession and reduce reputational risks to both parties. Fifth, the policymakers are advised to frame influencer marketing in hotel operations activities in relation to Sustainable Development Goals (SDG 8: Decent Work and Economic Growth; SDG 12: Responsible Consumption and Production) by making sure that the contracts are fair, that the coordination of smaller influencers is not exploitative, and that the products are responsibly promoted. Last, researchers are advised to carry out longitudinal and cross-cultural research in different platforms, types of products, and cultures to comprehend the changes over time in authenticity, persuasion, and consumer interaction. All these recommendations are aimed at a multi-level, strategic, and ethical approach to influencer marketing in hotel operations.

FUTURE DIRECTIONS

This research paper identifies a number of opportunities of researching the influencer marketing in hotel operations field in the future. To begin with, the current study concentrated on micro- and mega- in influencers whereas the investigation in future can incorporate nano- and macro-influencers to cover the entire range and examine authenticity, trust, and persuasion at the different levels. Second, longitudinal research is suggested in order to investigate the changes in consumer attitudes toward influencer credibility and authenticity over time, especially when micro-influencers become popular or mega-influencers. Third, cultural factors, such as the influence of cultural values, digital literacy, and trust orientations on consumer reactions, should be investigated in cross-cultural research, e.g. collectivist cultures might be more inclined to community-based micro-influencers, whereas individualistic cultures will be more responsive to aspirational mega-influencers. Fourth, experimental and neuroscience methods may be employed to obtain data about subconscious responses to authenticity cues, sponsorship disclosures, and engagement strategies, which will be useful in supplementing self-report data. Fifth, the visibility and engagement of influencers are largely influenced by platform algorithms, future research needs to examine the interaction between algorithmic biases and recommendation systems and human trust signs to manipulate an influencer performance. Finally, the ethical and sustainability sides of influencer marketing in hotel operations (e.g. promotion of unhealthy products, overconsumption, and false information) must be looked at so that the influencer activities would be adjusted to the general social responsibility and sustainability agenda.

REFERENCES

Aghaei, R., Kiaei, A. A., Boush, M., Vahidi, J., Zavvar, M., Barzegar, Z., & Rofoosheh, M. (n.d.). *Harnessing the Potential of Large Language Models in Modern Marketing Management: Applications*. Future Directions, and Strategic Recommendations.

Alnofeli, K. K., Akter, S., & Yanamandram, V. (2025). Unlocking the power of AI in CRM: A comprehensive multidimensional exploration. *Journal of Innovation & Knowledge*, *10*(3), 100731. DOI: 10.1016/j.jik.2025.100731

Anisa, N., & Hadiprawoto, T. R. (2025). Micro vs. mega influencers: Whose endorsements and promoted brands truly spark purchase intention in Indonesia? *JMBI UNSRAT*, *12*(2), 537–565.

Bacha, J., & Meghrajani, I. (2025). The strategic rise of social media influencers: Disruption and opportunities in modern marketing in hotel operations channels. *International Journal of Business and Management Practices*, *3*(4), 255–262.

Bakar, N. P. S. A. (2023). Efektivitas Penggunaan Media Sosial dalam Pemasaran Restoran: A Literature Review [Review of Efektivitas Penggunaan Media Sosial dalam Pemasaran Restoran: A Literature Review]. *JURNAL LENSA MUTIARA KOMUNIKASI*, *7*(2), 181. DOI: 10.51544/jlmk.v7i2.4009

Bhagyalakshmi, Ms. G. S. B. Dr. R. (2023). Exploring The Effects of Conversational Marketing and Artificial Intelligence on Customer Engagement - A Comprehensive Literature Review.". Tuijin Jishu/Journal of Propulsion Technology, 44(4), 4509. DOI: 10.52783/tjjpt.v44.i4.1735

Chan, T. H., Hung, K., & Tse, D. K. (2023). Comparing E-Commerce Micro-and Macroinfluencers in TikTok Videos: Effects of Strategies on Audience Likes, Audience Shares, and Brand Sales. *Journal of Interactive Advertising*, *23*(4), 289–322.

Chen, J., Zhang, Y., Cai, H., Liu, L., Liao, M., & Fang, J. (2024). A comprehensive overview of micro-influencer marketing in hotel operations: Decoding the current landscape, impacts, and trends. *Behavioral Sciences (Basel, Switzerland)*, *14*(3), 226. PMID: 38540529

Dewnarain, S., Ramkissoon, H., & Mavondo, F. (2018). Social customer relationship management: An integrated conceptual framework. *Journal of Hospitality Marketing & Management*, *28*(2), 172. DOI: 10.1080/19368623.2018.1516588

Dwivedi, Y. K., Pandey, N., Currie, W. L., & Micu, A. (2023). Leveraging ChatGPT and other generative artificial intelligence (AI)-based applications in the hospitality and tourism industry: Practices, challenges and research agenda. *International Journal of Contemporary Hospitality Management*, *36*(1), 1. DOI: 10.1108/ijchm-05-2023-0686

Dzreke, S. S., & Dzreke, M. S. E. (2025). The influencer equity equation: Analyzing influencer marketing in hotel operations's effect on brand equity via the perspectives of authenticity, credibility, and engagement. 7(3):1-23; DOI: 10.36948/ijfmr.2025.v07i03.48683

Elshaer, I. A., Azazz, A. M. S., Fayyad, S., Mohamed, S. A. K., Fouad, A. M., & Fathy, E. A. (2024). From Data to Delight: Leveraging Social Customer Relationship Management to Elevate Customer Satisfaction and Market Effectiveness. *Information (Basel)*, *16*(1), 9. DOI: 10.3390/info16010009

Gerlich, M. (2023). The power of personal connections in micro-influencer marketing in hotel operations: A study on consumer behaviour and the impact of micro-influencers. *Transnational Marketing in hotel operations Journal, 22*(1), 131–152.

Giuffredi-Kähr, A., Petrova, A., & Malär, L. (2022). Sponsorship disclosure of influencers–a curse or a blessing? *Journal of Interactive Marketing in hotel operations, 57*(1), 18–34.

Gudmand-Höyer, K., & Johansson, W. (2025). Who holds the influence? Consumer experiences of micro- and macro-influencers on TikTok. https://hdl.handle.net/2077/89352

Jothy, K. P. (2025). A Study on the Role of AI and Chatbots in Social Media Marketing: Enhancing Customer Engagement and Experience. *International Journal of Latest Technology in Engineering Management & Applied Science*, *14*(6), 884. DOI: 10.51583/ijltemas.2025.140600097

Kant, S., Niguse, T., & Adula, M. (2025). Role of Social Media on Corporate Branding by Mediation of Customer Relationship Management in the Horn of Africa. In *Corporate Management in the Digital Age* (pp. 337–364). IGI Global Scientific Publishing.

Kant, S., Niguse, T., Olubiyi, T. O., Adula, M., & Kebede, K. (2025). Sustainable Fashion-Based Innovations and Consumer Behavior in Ethiopia. In Global Impacts and Sustainable Practices in Fast Fashion (pp. 167-196). IGI Global Scientific Publishing.

Khlusevich, A., Inversini, A., & Schegg, R. (2024). Artificial Intelligence and Hospitality: A Challenging Relationship. In Springer proceedings in business and economics (p. 247). Springer International Publishing. DOI: 10.1007/978-3-031-58839-6_27

Korkee, N. (2024). How brands can utilize micro influencers to grow their sales among generation Z in Finland. https://urn.fi/URN:NBN:fi-fe202502038734

Labib, E. (2024). Artificial intelligence in marketing: Exploring current and future trends. *Cogent Business & Management, 11*(1). Advance online publication. DOI: 10.1080/23311975.2024.2348728

Lee, J., Walter, N., Hayes, J. L., & Golan, G. J. (2024). Do influencers influence? A meta-analytic comparison of celebrities and social media influencers effects. *Social Media + Society, 10*(3), 20562660241269269.

Leung, X. Y., Jie, S., & Bai, B. (2021). SOCIAL MEDIA RESEARCH IN HOSPITALITY AND TOURISM: A CAUSAL CHAIN FRAMEWORK OF LITERATURE REVIEW. *Tourism and Hospitality Management, 27*(3), 455. DOI: 10.20867/thm.27.3.1

Peter, A. T. (2023). The Role of Social Media in Hotel Marketing: A Study of Customer Engagement and Brand Loyalty. [IJSR]. *International Journal of Scientific Research, 12*(7), 1830. DOI: 10.21275/sr23721185208

Polimerou, R., & Spais, G. S. (2025). Establishing relationships between brands and customers via strategic social media chatbots for telecom goods and services. Journal of Marketing Analytics. DOI: 10.1057/s41270-025-00396-5

Roshandel, A., Miöen Dahlström, F., & Ekström, K. (2023). Unveiling the art of illusion: Exploring the fabrication of authenticity and trustworthiness by social media micro-influencers.

Saura, J. R., Škare, V., & Došen, Đ. O. (2024). Is AI-based digital marketing ethical? Assessing a new data privacy paradox. *Journal of Innovation & Knowledge, 9*(4), 100597. DOI: 10.1016/j.jik.2024.100597

Şener, G., & Çobanoğlu, C. (2022). Analysis of International Hotels' Social Media Strategies. *Journal of Mediterranean Tourism Research, 1*(2), 123. DOI: 10.5038/2770-7555.1.2.1010

Seo, Y. (2023). David and Goliath: Micro-influencers versus mega-influencers. *University of Auckland Business School Research Paper Series*. https://dx.doi.org/ DOI: 10.2139/ssrn.4905436

Sivakami, R., & Thapa, P. (2025). Influencer scale in marketing in hotel operations: Examining the impact of mega, macro, micro, and nano influencers on brand loyalty and engagement in the Indian merchandise market. *Asian Journal of Management, 16*(2), 94–100.

Spais, G. S., & Chryssochoidis, G. (2025). Trends and future of artificial intelligence (AI), machine learning (ML) algorithms, and data analytics and their applications and implications for digital marketing and digital promotions. Journal of Marketing Analytics. DOI: 10.1057/s41270-025-00406-6

Taher, A., El Kolaly, H., & Tarek, N. (2025). Examining crisis communication in geopolitical conflicts: The micro-influencer impact model. *Journalism and Media, 6*(3), 226.

Zachurzok-Srebrny, E. (2024). USING ARTIFICIAL INTELLIGENCE FOR CUSTOMER ENGAGEMENT IN SOCIAL MEDIA. *Scientific Papers of Silesian University of Technology Organization and Management Series, 2024*(209), 5.

KEY TERMS AND DEFINITIONS

Authenticity Signals: Authenticity signals are verbal, visual, and behavioural content that influencers display in order to reveal the truth, honesty, and openness in content. These indications are very potent in affecting the consumer trust, credibility perception and purchase intentions.

Consumer Persuasion: Consumer persuasion refers to the psychological process by which influences endorsements influence consumer attitudes, preferences, and moods in consumer behavioral intentions, i.e. brand trust, purchase decisions, and product adoption.

Influencer Marketing in hotel operations: Influencer marketing in hotel operations is an online marketing in hotel operations technique that utilizes the services of people with large professions on social media to promote products or services. It is based on the assumption that the opinion of influencers is more trusted by consumers than conventional advertising.

Mega-Influencers: Mega-influencers are those who have exceptionally huge social media following (it can be more than 1 million followers), such as publicly known figures and celebrities. These are broad in reach and exposure, and in some cases, they are not seen as genuine as micro-influencers because of the commercialized endorsement.

Micro-Influencers: Micro-influencers are social network users with a fairly smaller fanbase (usually between 1,000 and 100,000 followers) who are more relatable and authentic to their audience. They prefer to produce niche content and establish good trust-based relationships with their followers.

Parasocial Interaction: Parasocial interaction is a one-sided, although seemingly intimate relationship, which the consumer forms with influencers. It gives a sense of intimacy and trust, without having to have two-way communication, which reinforces the persuasive power of influencers.

Signaling Theory: Signaling theory describes the process of influencers providing information about their credibility, expertise or authenticity by using observable signals (e.g. the number of followers, the rate of engagement, the quality of the content), which allow a consumer to reduce uncertainty during the decision-making process.

Chapter 15
Integrating Social Media Strategies for Regional Cuisine Branding and Destination Image in Hospitality Marketing

Yashwant Singh Thakur
http://orcid.org/0009-0004-1881-1837
Bahra University, India

Vikesh Kashyap
http://orcid.org/0000-0001-8532-2022
Bahra University, India

ABSTRACT

This chapter examines the dynamics of regional cuisine branding and destination image in the age of social media. It examines how the regional culinary customs, digital storytelling and changing hospitality marketing by drawing examples from around the world, empirical research, and industry case studies, with conceptual connection between food, culture, and destination identity, the analysis presents regional cuisine as a digital narrative tool as well as a physical asset. The revamp of user-generated content, influencer partnerships, and participatory campaigns in amplifying reach and integration of metrics like engagement, reach and brand equity in measuring digital impact and the stakeholder collaboration among chefs, restaurateurs, destination marketing organisations, and local communities, by managing crises and digital weariness, encouraging digital literacy among many

DOI: 10.4018/979-8-3373-6741-5.ch015

stakeholders, and by balancing authenticity and commercialization. It concludes by arguing that successful hospitality branding relies on combining community with creativity and tradition with innovation.

INTRODUCTION

From Plate to Post: A New Journey in Hospitality

Regional cuisine plays a crucial role in shaping both the image of a destination and the overall experience for tourists, highlighting the intricate relationship between food and travel that underpins the hospitality industry. Throughout history, meals have transcended mere sustenance; they serve as cultural gestures of hospitality that express welcome, a sense of belonging, and the uniqueness of a location (Kivela, (2006). Whether in remote mountain villages, bustling urban markets, or quaint countryside homes, sharing regional dishes connects visitors to local customs and flavors, reinforcing a place's identity beyond its geographical limits. These culinary experiences are pivotal in shaping a destination's character, turning flavors into lasting memories that persist long after the journey concludes.

The relationship between food and tourism has changed dramatically in the modern digital era. The rise of social media platforms like Facebook, Instagram, and TikTok has altered the dynamics of destination branding and culinary distribution (Francesc Fusté-Forné, 2025). Experiences that were once confined to personal memories can now be instantly recorded and shared with the world. A single food photo that is tagged and shared can influence opinions and inspire people to travel great distances. The shift of regional cuisine from physical offerings like plates served and recipes shared to a narrative tool is significant. This transition is enhanced by hashtags, short videos, and user-generated content that contribute to a virtual diaspora of culinary history (Ibrahim, 2025).

Social media platforms have become dynamic tools for shaping a destination's image as tourists document their favorite foods and culinary experiences through pictures and videos. For digital consumers accustomed to immersive, visually driven content, food has become a global ambassador that shares stories of innovation, tradition, and local identity (Rudolf, 2022). Consequently, the journey “from plate to post” in contemporary hospitality marketing connects the local and global, as well as the personal and collective. It highlights that virtual storytelling and food imagery are just as crucial to branding as the actual flavors. This reflects a changing environment where regional cuisine plays a central role in defining destination identity.

Despite these developments, several *practical challenges and research gaps* remain. Empirical literature highlights inconsistencies in how regional cuisine contributes to destination competitiveness, with contradictory evidence regarding its long-term impact on tourist loyalty and sustainable branding. Practical challenges include the commodification of culture, the risk of homogenization through digital replication, and difficulties in ensuring authenticity in globalized culinary narratives. Research gaps persist in understanding how digital mediation reshapes cultural hospitality, how consumer perceptions vary across contexts, and how policy frameworks can support sustainable culinary tourism.

This chapter seeks to address these gaps by examining the evolving role of regional cuisine in hospitality marketing, particularly its transformation through digital platforms. It aims to provide a *directional framework for future researchers and policymakers*, offering insights into how culinary heritage can be preserved while simultaneously leveraged for destination branding. The guiding *research question* underpinning this study is:

How does the transition of regional cuisine from physical hospitality to digital storytelling reshape destination identity, and what implications does this transformation hold for sustainable tourism development and policy-making?

BACKGROUND OF THE STUDY

The intersection of regional cuisine and hospitality has long been recognized as a critical driver of cultural identity, destination branding, and tourist satisfaction. Food is not merely a consumable product; it is a cultural artifact that embodies traditions, values, and social practices. In tourism studies, gastronomy has been positioned as both a symbolic and functional element of hospitality, shaping perceptions of authenticity and influencing travel decisions. Yet, the integration of regional cuisine into destination marketing strategies remains uneven across contexts, with varying levels of success and sustainability (Richards, 2021).

Globally, case studies illustrate the diverse challenges in implementing culinary-based branding. For instance, in *Italy's Tuscany region*, the promotion of wine and olive oil has successfully reinforced destination identity, but commercialization has raised concerns about cultural dilution and the loss of artisanal authenticity (Rudolf, 2022). Similarly, in *Japan's Kyoto*, traditional kaiseki cuisine has been leveraged to attract international tourists, yet balancing preservation of heritage with modern consumer expectations has proven difficult. In contrast, *Ethiopia's coffee culture*, often celebrated as a heritage practice, faces challenges in scaling its symbolic value into global tourism narratives without compromising local traditions (Ibrahim, 2025). These examples highlight the tension between cultural preservation and market-driven adaptation.

Practical challenges also emerge in the digital era. The proliferation of food-related content on social media platforms has democratized culinary storytelling, but it has also created risks of oversimplification and homogenization. Destinations often struggle to maintain control over their gastronomic narratives when user-generated content dominates global perceptions (Francesc Fusté-Forné, 2025). Moreover, disparities in digital infrastructure across regions mean that not all destinations can equally capitalize on the "plate to post" phenomenon, leading to uneven visibility and competitiveness (Ashiq, 2025) .

From a policy perspective, the integration of regional cuisine into tourism strategies requires careful alignment with sustainability goals. Issues such as supply chain resilience, food security, and equitable participation of local producers complicate the implementation of culinary tourism initiatives (Rudolf, 2022) . For example, while *Thailand's street food culture* has become a global attraction, regulatory challenges around hygiene, licensing, and urban planning illustrate the complexities of institutionalizing informal culinary practices.

LITERATURE REVIEW

This literature on regional cuisine, destination image, and social media reveals a growing recognition of food as a strategic asset in hospitality marketing. Scholars have consistently emphasized the role of gastronomy in shaping tourist experiences, yet findings remain fragmented and context-dependent.

This literature on regional cuisine, destination image, and social media reveals a growing recognition of food as a strategic asset in hospitality marketing. Scholars have consistently emphasized the role of gastronomy in shaping tourist experiences, yet findings remain fragmented and context-dependent.

Early studies established that food experiences significantly influence tourist satisfaction and destination loyalty. (Kivela, (2006) demonstrated that culinary encounters contribute to the perceived authenticity of destinations, reinforcing emotional bonds between visitors and hosts. Similarly, (Baby, 2024) highlighted the symbolic value of food as a cultural marker, showing how regional cuisine strengthens identity and differentiates destinations in competitive markets. These foundational works positioned gastronomy as a central element of tourism development.

Subsequent research expanded this perspective by examining the integration of food into branding strategies. (Richards, 2021) argued that culinary experiences provide access to intangible heritage, enabling tourists to participate in local traditions. (Ellis, 2018)further noted that regional cuisine offers destinations a means of differentiation in an increasingly homogenized global tourism landscape. Case studies from Europe, Asia, and Africa illustrate how food festivals, street markets, and farm-to-table initiatives enhance destination image and foster cultural sustainability.

The digital era introduced new dimensions to this discourse. (Gretzel, 2006) identified social media as a transformative force in tourism marketing, shifting narrative control from institutional actors to individual travelers. (Lee, 2017) confirmed that user-generated culinary content significantly influences perceptions of authenticity and destination competitiveness. (Garcês, 2024) emphasized the emergence of the *Online Destination Image (ODI)*, shaped by visual storytelling and collaborative brand narratives. Empirical evidence shows that food-related posts on Instagram and TikTok generate high engagement, reinforcing the symbolic power of cuisine in digital branding.

Despite these advances, contradictions persist. Some studies report strong positive correlations between regional cuisine and tourist loyalty (Baby, 2024), while others highlight risks of commodification and cultural homogenization. Research in non-Western contexts, such as Ethiopia, reveals challenges in scaling culinary heritage into global tourism narratives without compromising authenticity. Moreover, empirical findings remain inconclusive regarding the long-term impact of digital mediation on destination competitiveness, with gaps in understanding how authenticity is negotiated in online spaces (Ibrahim, 2025).

Overall, the literature underscores the importance of regional cuisine in hospitality marketing but reveals *theoretical and contextual gaps*. Few studies integrate food, destination image, and social media into a unified framework, and limited attention has been paid to policy implications for sustainable culinary tourism. This chapter seeks to address these gaps by synthesizing existing evidence and proposing a conceptual framework that situates regional cuisine as both a cultural artifact and a digital narrative tool.

THEORETICAL FOUNDATIONS

Understanding the conceptual link between regional cuisine, destination image, and social media requires grounding in established theories from hospitality, consumer behavior, and communication studies. These theories provide explanatory frameworks for how food functions as both a cultural artifact and a branding instrument in the digital age.

1. Social Identity Theory

Social Identity Theory posts that individuals derive part of their identity from membership in social groups. In the context of hospitality, regional cuisine becomes a marker of collective identity, allowing tourists to symbolically participate in local traditions. Food experiences reinforce in-group and out-group distinctions, shaping perceptions of authenticity and belonging. This theory explains why travelers often seek culinary experiences that connect them to the cultural identity of a destination (Bansal, 2025).

2. Semiotics and Symbolic Interactionism

Semiotic theory, expanded through symbolic interactionism and its emphasizes the role of signs and symbols in communication. Regional cuisine operates as a semiotic system, where dishes, ingredients, and rituals signify cultural meanings. Social media amplifies these symbols by transforming food into visual narratives that communicate identity and heritage. This framework highlights how food imagery functions as a language of hospitality marketing (Gretzel, 2006).

3. Destination Image Theory

Destination Image Theory explains how perceptions of a place are formed through cognitive and affective evaluations. Regional cuisine contributes to both dimensions: cognitively, by representing tangible attributes such as taste and quality; affectively, by evoking emotions tied to cultural immersion. The emergence of *Online Destination Image (ODI)* extends this theory into the digital sphere, where user-generated culinary content shapes collective perceptions (Ghorbanzadeh D, 2023).

4. Experience Economy Theory

(Rudolf, 2022) Experience Economy Theory argues that economic value increasingly derives from memorable experiences rather than products alone. Regional cuisine exemplifies this shift, as tourists seek immersive food encounters that transcend consumption. Culinary festivals, street food tours, and farm-to-table experiences illustrate how destinations leverage food to create differentiated, memorable offerings. Social media further enhances this experiential value by enabling travelers to share and relive these moments digitally.

5. Diffusion of Innovations Theory

(Khatami F, 2024) Diffusion of Innovations Theory explains how new ideas and practices spread through social systems. Applied to hospitality, digital culinary narratives represent innovations in destination branding. Social media accelerates diffusion by enabling rapid global sharing of local food traditions. This theory helps explain how certain cuisines—such as sushi, pizza, or Ethiopian coffee—achieve global recognition through digital storytelling and consumer adoption (Lorgeoux, 2023).

While each theory contributes valuable insights, *Destination Image Theory* serves as the primary theoretical lens for this study. It directly addresses the central research question: how regional cuisine, mediated through social media, shapes perceptions of destination identity. By integrating cognitive, affective, and digital dimensions, this theory provides a comprehensive framework for analyzing the transformation of food from a physical hospitality offering to a narrative branding tool.

CONCEPTUAL FRAMEWORK

The conceptual framework for this study positions *regional cuisine* as both a cultural artifact and a strategic branding instrument, mediated through *social media*, to shape *destination image*. This framework synthesizes theoretical insights from Social Identity Theory, Semiotics, Destination Image Theory, Experience Economy, and Diffusion of Innovations, alongside empirical findings from global case studies.

Regional Cuisine

The regional cuisine is defined by various researchers in there own ways-

- The culinary practices, ingredients, and traditions unique to a geographic area.
- Functions as a cultural marker, conveying authenticity, heritage, and identity.
- Acts as a branding asset by differentiating destinations in a homogenized tourism landscape.

Destination Image

The destination image also refers

- To the cognitive and affective perceptions of a place formed by tourists.
- Regional cuisine contributes to both dimensions: tangible attributes (taste, quality) and emotional resonance (heritage, belonging).
- Extended into the digital sphere as *Online Destination Image (ODI)*, shaped by user-generated culinary narratives.

Social Media Mediation

The social Media Mediation is playing a critical role these days and is defined as

- Platforms such as Instagram, TikTok, and Facebook enable instantaneous sharing of food experiences.
- User-generated content democratizes destination branding, shifting narrative control from DMOs to travel.
- Culinary imagery functions as symbolic communication, amplifying authenticity and emotional engagement.

Conceptual link between Regional Cuisine, social media, and Destination Image

The modern hospitality sector increasingly recognizes the synergistic relationship between regional cuisine, destination image, and social media engagement. Food functions as a semiotic bridge, transmitting sensory qualities, symbolic meanings, and social customs to global audiences. Regional cuisine is thus elevated beyond its nutritional role into a strategic branding asset, capable of promoting cultural identity through narratives and visual representations (Andersson, 2017).

Digital platforms have radically transformed this relationship by expanding the potential for collaborative brand development. User-generated content, narrative-driven posts, and curated culinary imagery contribute to the evolving concept of the Online Destination Image (ODI). Platforms such as Instagram and TikTok enable the instantaneous sharing of local cuisine, embedding food experiences within communal, emotional, and personal narratives. These digital stories are central to perceived authenticity, which significantly influences travelers' destination choices and satisfaction (Hudson, 2013) (Šmid Hribar, 2021).

Empirical studies highlight that social media democratizes brand narratives, shifting control from institutional actors such as Destination Marketing Organizations (DMOs) to individual travelers and consumers. Posts, reviews, and photographs shared by ordinary visitors now exert substantial influence on destination perception, often surpassing the reach of official campaigns, Unlike static imagery of landscapes or infrastructure, intangible heritage encounters communal meals, family recipes, and live culinary events—generate deeper emotional resonance and higher levels of online engagement (Alicia Orea-Giner, 2026) (Khatami F, 2024).

This conceptual relationship should therefore be understood as a dynamic, co-creative process. Regional cuisine, as both a product of hospitality and a narrative instrument, acquires meaning through digital interaction. It plays a pivotal role in shaping and disseminating evolving perceptions of destinations in the competitive global tourism economy. The theoretical implication is that food is not merely a cultural artifact but a strategic communication medium, central to the construction of destination identity in the digital age.

The Role of Local Food in Shaping Destination Identity

Regional cuisine functions as a powerful emblem of place, fostering bonds between guests and hosts even before other destination features become apparent (Khatami F, 2024). By incorporating local flavors, visitors gain access to a community's living culture and intangible heritage, experiencing rhythms and meanings that landscapes or monuments alone cannot convey.

In an increasingly homogenized global tourism landscape, regional cuisine offers destinations a means of differentiation. Recent studies emphasize that embedding local food into branding initiatives enables destinations to stand out, while simultaneously conserving cultural heritage (Dordai, 2026). Culinary experiences such as dining in a Himachali village, sampling Bangkok's street food, or attending Quebec's harvest festivals allow tourists to symbolically participate in ongoing social and agricultural traditions. These encounters strengthen emotional connections and reinforce destination identity (Garcês, 2024).

Thus, regional cuisine emerges as a strategic branding asset, positioned at the center of destination management and marketing. It provides a narrative framework that integrates authenticity, emotional resonance, and cultural sustainability. The challenge, however, lies in balancing commodification with preservation, ensuring that culinary heritage remains authentic while serving as a competitive advantage in global tourism markets.

CHARACTERISTICS OF AUTHENTIC REGIONAL CUISINE AND ITS APPEAL

Local Foods

Purchasing food sourced within the ecological or cultural boundaries of a destination is a fundamental aspect of authenticity. The distinctiveness of terroir, which encompasses elements such as Provençal olives, Himachali buckwheat, and Alpine herbs, generates unique flavor profiles that contribute to sustainability and the advancement of regional food systems.

Traditional Preparation Methods

Moreover, traditional cooking methods and preparation customs, passed down through generations, further enhance this authenticity. Practices such as pit-roasting meats or baking bread over open flames serve not only gastronomic purposes but also facilitate the transmission of knowledge and culinary expertise across generations.

Cultural Embeddedness

According to (Hashimoto, 2006), authentic regional food is deeply rooted in local celebrations, customs, and gatherings. For example, the ceremonial serving order at a French repas and the communal preparation of Himachali dham during festivals reflect centuries of accumulated traditions and significance.

Sensory Uniqueness

Distinct flavours, scents, and textures that evoke sentiments of exploration and discovery are what make local cuisine so alluring (Hernández-Mogollón, 2019) Travellers are drawn to the unique ingredients, a rare spice, a wild berry, or a fermentation technique unique to a place, and seek out culinary experiences that deviate from their staple diet.

Storytelling and Memory

According to (Khatami F, 2024), Memories tied to food often last longer than those associated with sights or souvenirs. With each bite, travelers can enjoy stories of resilience, celebration, or transformation, all infused with meaning through oral histories, regional folklore, and the personal experiences of chefs and families.

Regional Cuisine's Strategic Appeal

Destinations that highlight authentic cuisine often report greater visitor satisfaction and a unique appeal, as travelers worldwide seek deeper, more meaningful experiences. When visitors engage with local food, whether by tasting, learning, or even helping to prepare it, they develop emotional connections with the place. These connections become part of the travelers' personal stories, which they are likely to share widely within their networks (Andersson, 2017).

Moreover, tourists who participate in culinary traditions tend to show higher levels of loyalty to the destination. They are also more inclined to promote the location and return in the future (Park, 2022). For younger audiences interested in culture, food has become the "ultimate souvenir" an experience that is deeply felt and remembered, rather than simply collected or observed (Kashyap V. &., 2023)

Hospitality Marketing in the Age of Social Media

The COVID-19 pandemic hastened the hospitality industry's already-increasing digitalisation. As health concerns and regulatory changes disrupted travel habits, dining experiences, and face-to-face interactions, brands from a wide range of industries, including hotels, restaurants, travel consortia, and food producers, quickly turned to social media as the vital channel for continuity, engagement, and survival (Suparak Suriyankietkaew, 2025). Platforms like Instagram, TikTok, Facebook, and YouTube were at the forefront of this recalibration because of their unique media architectures, which enabled a range of narrative production, dissemination, and engagement that was not possible with traditional media.

Because Instagram is a visual-first platform, it gave food a platform to become an aesthetic spectacle. By curating feeds that featured new dishes, chef journeys, or behind-the-scenes preparation, destination marketers were able to emotionally and inspirationally connect with both devoted customers and prospective travellers. TikTok's algorithm-driven, short-form environment democratised exposure by rewarding spontaneity and creativity from both independent small businesses and major marketers. In contrast, Facebook helped food and travel-related groups flourish by allowing for continuous discussion, group memory, and peer-to-peer recommendations outside of the official brand setting. Deep dives into culinary heritage, destination tours, and educational campaigns were made possible by YouTube's longer-format video content. As a result of this cross-platform approach, hospitality marketing was redefined as a fully interactive, real-time experience in which visitors were essential co-creators of destination identity and brand reputation rather than merely passive recipients of carefully staged messages (Mariani, 2016).

KEY TRENDS IN HOSPITALITY'S DIGITAL RENAISSANCE (2020-2025)

1. Visual Storytelling as a Branding Language

Visual storytelling has become the universal language of hospitality branding due to the emergence of platforms that are primarily focused on images and videos (Ana María Munar, 2014). According to recent studies, posts with realistic imagery, whether it depicts the skill of sourcing ingredients, a chef's journey, or the ambiance of a festival, produce higher levels of engagement than conventional ads or static listings (Gretzel, 2006). Marketers are encouraged to include rich, emotionally charged narratives in their postings on platforms such as Instagram and TikTok, which prominently emphasize vibrant, human-driven content with locational indications (Ksenia Kirillova, 2014).

2. The Search for Trust and Micro-Influencers

The micro-influencers are displacing the mainstream media age by showing the audiences, typically local food bloggers, tourists, or regional ambassadors, as genuine and reliable, and they facilitate in-the-moment discussions on "must-try" foods and new travel destinations. Both well-known and lesser-known locations are kept visible and relevant in the digital narrative because of their credibility, which comes from lived experience and community involvement rather than paid sponsorships or commercial messaging (Demetris Vrontis, 2021) (Benxiang Zeng, 2014).

3. Ephemerality and Live Streaming: Instant Communication

The closeness and speed of hospitality marketing are evolving due to live and fleeting material. Chefs, bartenders, and festival organisers can engage directly with audiences through live-streaming technology made possible by platforms like Instagram Live, YouTube Live, and Facebook Live. This allows for real-time feedback, crowdsourced Q&As, and participatory experiences. With interactive polls and real-time reviews, ephemeral features like Stories and Reels provide a feeling of urgency and exclusivity that drives event marketing and temporary promotions (Buhalis, 2019) (Kyung-Hyan Yoo, 2016)

4. User-Generated Content (UGC) as Brand Foundation

The role of user-generated content, which includes images, reviews, and spontaneous postings from visitors and customers, has become essential to shaping the image of a destination. This type of content not only helps craft brand narratives but also adds authenticity (Hudson, 2013). Research shows that posts highlighting local events, culinary practices, and cultural traditions generate more positive feelings and sharing behavior compared to generic images of infrastructure (Piotr, 2023). In fact, the narrative shared by travelers often carries equal weight, if not more, than the official messaging from institutions.

5. Customisation Based on Data

Increasingly, analytics are leveraged to tailor services and content to the nuanced preferences and online behaviors of visitors (Phuong Minh Binh Nguyen, 2023)By examining follower demographics, engagement peaks, and interaction trends, hospitality marketers can strategically time menu launches, create personalized offers, and refine campaign strategies to enhance on-site conversion and foster loyalty (Ghorbanzadeh D, 2023). This creates a dynamic cycle where offline experiences are enriched by online engagement and vice versa.

6. Smooth Transactions and Social Commerce

Moreover, social media is increasingly merging inspiration with action. Users can seamlessly transition from discovering content to making transactions within a single digital interaction through integrations with real-time booking systems, food delivery platforms, and reservation services like OpenTable, Zomato, or Uber Eats. This smooth shift from content engagement to purchase fundamentally changes the hospitality transaction landscape, enabling quick reservations for festivals or dining experiences (Crespi Vallbona, 2021).

PLATFORM-SPECIFIC IMPACT ON CUISINE BRANDING

Instagram: An Illustrated Display of Location and Preference

Instagram has emerged as the leading platform for food branding. It enables operators and tourism boards to not only highlight the culinary artistry of their dishes but also tell the stories of culinary triumphs, origins, and regional characteristics through curated feeds, clever hashtag choices, and geotagging (Feldman, 2021). The platform's features, such as Instagram Stories and Reels, allow for behind-the-scenes glimpses, chef interviews, and experiences generated by guests, fostering authenticity and deeper connections that static ads lack. Research indicates that posts focusing on intangible heritage tend to outperform those highlighting physical amenities, leading to more impactful imagery and increased audience engagement (Pahor Zvanut, 2025).

Facebook: Information Sharing and Community Development

Facebook serves as a multifunctional platform for hospitality interactions. Its true strength lies in its ability to form community groups centered on local events, food, or travel, thus encouraging peer recommendations, fostering collective memories, and promoting ongoing engagement. Live events, reviews, and interactive content shape immediate decisions and contribute to long-term brand reputation. The platform's architecture supports nuanced discussions among stakeholders, tourists, and local experts, making it an essential tool for effective relationship management. (Borghi, 2021).

TikTok: The Influence of Short-Form Virality on TikTok

TikTok's frequent, light-hearted content cycles have transformed the landscape of hotel promotions. Venues that leverage authentic stories and local quirks benefit from an algorithm prioritizing creativity, humor, and originality. TikTok showcases restaurant tours, cooking competitions, and food hacks, often providing compelling behind-the-scenes looks into culinary practices. The potential for virality where a single video can gain immense traction overnight stimulates relentless innovation, making both familiar dishes and hidden gems widely recognized (Tham, 2023).

Blogs and Long-Form Content: Credibility and Comprehensiveness

Blogs and influencer platforms offer depth that contrasts with the ephemerality of social media. They provide thorough reviews, locally relevant insights, and narratives that delve into gastronomic heritage, history, and cultural contexts, authored by food writers and culinary historians. By implementing improved SEO strategies and engaging in strategic cross-promotion, destinations can enhance their online presence and foster enduring brand impressions (Hudson, 2013).

THE INSTANTANEOUS EFFECT OF SOCIAL MEDIA ON REGIONAL CUISINE BRANDING

The intersection of digital platforms creates a robust foundation for establishing a destination's reputation. Collaborative marketing efforts, influencer collaborations, and user-generated stories converge to form interactive brand narratives. These narratives not only amplify the visibility of individual establishments but also elevate the attractiveness of entire culinary regions, thereby encouraging tourism and promoting economic resilience in an evolving marketplace. (Nuria Recuero-Virto C. V., 2024).

Regional Cuisine's Digital Renaissance

The immediacy and intimacy of digital content creation have significantly transformed modern hospitality marketing. Today, a single captivating photograph or video can quickly elevate a region's culinary brand onto the international stage, bypassing the gradual process of guidebooks and word-of-mouth that once helped local cuisine gain worldwide recognition (Lee, 2017). This dynamic is exemplified by the "from plate to post" approach, which illustrates how thoughtful content creation encompassing user-generated stories, visual storytelling, and engagement with digital influencers forms the foundation of destination management and place branding.

Local food evolves from a regional asset into a shared cultural experience that viewers and tourists around the world can enjoy, interact with, and revisit, as digital platforms democratize media creation and distribution. This shift in marketing strategy represents not just a change in tactics but also a fundamental evolution in how food, memory, and travel intersect to shape and spread the reputation of a place.

Stakeholder Roles and Collaborative Branding

The modern marketing structure for regional food is fundamentally cooperative, reflecting the complex interactions among various players in the hospitality industry. Local culinary traditions are showcased, interpreted, and elevated in both virtual and physical spaces through the collaborative efforts of chefs, property owners, growers, digital designers, and community organizations (C. Michael Hall, 2005). This pluralization of branding responsibilities helps to create deeper, more authentic, and relatable destination identities.

Chefs play a crucial role beyond simply creating menus; they build culinary narratives by connecting local history, ingredients, and cooking techniques to broader travel trends. Contemporary culinary leaders engage with audiences through educational forums, media partnerships, and interactive workshops, thus forming dynamic connections between culinary traditions and modern consumer expectations (N.S. Robinson R, 2014).

Restaurateurs and hoteliers enhance this effort by transforming their spaces into venues for community engagement. By collaborating with regional producers, artisans, and artists, hospitality establishments foster reciprocal visibility, highlighting the origins of products, showcasing culinary talent, and emphasizing the sociocultural context of eating as both a custom and an occasion (Sims, 2019); (Ellis, 2018). Initiatives such as pop-up markets, farm-to-table collaborations, and branded food festivals exemplify how businesses create synergies that emphasize local identity and promote economic growth.

Social media ambassadors and digital influencers expand the audience for collaborative branding while adding creative elements. Their ability to curate engaging content, utilize participatory formats (like hashtag challenges and crowdsourced recipe contests), and respond to real-time feedback facilitates the democratization of storytelling and brand loyalty. As the narrative shifts from static advertising to interactive engagement, consumers co-create and contribute to the evolving perceptions of destinations.

To maintain genuine and inclusive branding initiatives, community organizations such as food co-ops, cultural groups, and tourism boards are essential. These stakeholders preserve intangible heritage while advancing culinary experiences by organizing events that incorporate local perspectives, socio-historical contexts, and intergenerational knowledge (Sims, 2019); (C. Michael Hall, 2005). Cooperative initiatives and educational tours ensure a consistent flow of interaction throughout the year, reinforcing place attachment and uniqueness.

Through cross-sector collaboration, stakeholders in hotel marketing develop resilient, flexible, and internationally relevant identities for regional cuisine. This approach ensures that the branding process is relational rather than transactional, fostering a constant co-creation of experience, meaning, and belonging.

A notable example of successful collaboration among various hospitality players is San Sebastián in the Basque Country, recognized worldwide as a culinary destination. In this city, top chefs (such as those at Arzak and Mugaritz), local farmers and fishers, restaurateurs, municipal tourism agencies, and cultural organizations work together to create an ecosystem where regional cuisine gains international acclaim. The city showcases regional products, contemporary innovations, and local culinary traditions during annual chef congresses and food festivals. These events are widely promoted by social media influencers, enhancing global reach and real-time sharing. To foster a comprehensive and authentic destination image, municipal tourism offices organize culinary trails and storytelling events that encompass both upscale dining and home-style pintxos (Phung, 2025)

Another excellent example of collaborative branding is the "Dham Festival" in Himachal Pradesh. Local chefs, women's cooperatives, tourism departments, farmers, and homestay owners collaborate to organize this event. Emphasizing sustainability and authenticity, local chefs and home cooks use products from nearby farms to create traditional dishes like dham, a holiday feast. The Himachal Pradesh Tourism Development Corporation (HPTDC) actively promotes not only the cuisine but also its cultural background through social media, showcasing the experiences of regional producers and craftspeople. Community members participate in storytelling, live demonstrations, and interactive culinary trails, while influencers and travel bloggers are invited to share immersive experiences (Kashyap V., 2024).

Engaging Uses -Generated Content and Influencer Partnerships

The emergence of user-generated content (UGC) reflects a significant shift from one-way communication to a more collaborative form of branding. UGC invites visitors, locals, and food enthusiasts to take on the roles of co-curators and co-owners of local culinary brands, countering traditional top-down marketing.

Research indicates that audiences perceive UGC, including photos, reviews, and video testimonials, as significantly more trustworthy than information provided by institutions, particularly in the travel and food sectors (Bansal, 2025) . By implementing marketing strategies that encourage patrons to post with regional hashtags, share their dining experiences in real-time, or participate in creative contests, destinations can harness this trust-based economy. Such tactics not only enhance customer engagement and increase the likelihood of purchases but also add diverse information and perspectives. Additionally, brands can amplify their reach while maintaining authenticity through partnerships with influencers, particularly micro- and meso-influencers who cater to specific, loyal audiences. Collaborating with reputable digital personalities enhances social proof and broadens storytelling, whether related to Italian truffle markets, South African wine regions, or Vietnamese street food. A notable example is the "Gastronomic Barcelona" initiative, which engaged local chefs, travel influencers, and resident bloggers to share their culinary experiences. This campaign generated thousands of organic media pieces, establishing the city as a must-visit destination for food lovers (Sofía Blanco-Moreno, 2024).

Content Strategies: Hashtags, Geotagging, and The Reputation Cycle

Strategic content creation should optimize discoverability and promote social approbation. Whether utilizing event-specific campaigns (#ParisInSpring, #TasteOfChennai), global trends (#FoodCulture, #TravelEats), or branded community tags to encourage ongoing sharing and campaign tracking, the strategic application of hashtags connects posts to broader discussions.

Geotagging helps ground digital narratives in tangible locations. (Hernández-Mogollón, 2019) found that analyses of restaurant marketing techniques in rural Portugal and metropolitan Japan showed that geotagged posts can improve internet search results, increase foot traffic, and strengthen the ties between local businesses and the overall image of the destination.

On platforms like TripAdvisor, Yelp, or Google Maps, reviews including textual descriptions, short video testimonials, and peer ratings impact digital trust ecosystems. (Tham, 2023), noted that incorporating review widgets on Instagram and TikTok, along with the rise of real-time feedback for events or restaurant visits, provides third-party validation that enhances consumer trust and encourages more content creation. For example, restaurants in Denmark's "Copenhagen Table" program encouraged customers to post geotagged reviews and video "mini-logs," which worked to influence consumer preferences throughout the city.

The Digital Revolution in Hospitality

The hospitality industry has undergone a transformative shift in its approach to marketing and customer interaction in recent years. The dynamics of competitive advantage in tourism and hospitality have evolved from traditional methods such as word-of-mouth, print advertising, and broadcast media into a vibrant ecosystem of digital storytelling and interactive online communities (Law R, 2014). This transformation has been particularly evident between 2020 and 2025, a period marked by disruptive events and technological advancements that spurred resilience and creativity in global hospitality marketing. Professionals in the industry have been compelled to rethink destination branding and visitor engagement in a changing world.

Hospitality Marketing in the age of social media

The COVID-19 pandemic accelerated the hospitality industry's ongoing digitalisation. With health concerns and changing regulations impacting travel habits, dining experiences, and personal interactions, brands across hotels, restaurants, travel agencies, and food producers pivoted to social media as a critical channel for continuity, engagement, and survival. Platforms like Instagram, TikTok, Facebook, and YouTube played pivotal roles in this recalibration due to their unique architectures that allowed for narrative production, dissemination, and engagement beyond traditional media.

Instagram, being a visual-first platform, transformed how food is presented, turning it into an aesthetic experience. Destination marketers could emotionally connect with loyal customers and potential travelers by curating visually appealing feeds that highlighted new dishes, chef stories, and behind-the-scenes glimpses. TikTok's algorithm-driven, short-form content rewarded spontaneity and creativity, democratizing exposure for both small businesses and larger brands. Facebook facilitated the growth of food and travel-related groups, fostering ongoing discussions, shared memories, and peer-to-peer recommendations outside formal brand interactions. Meanwhile, YouTube's longer-format videos enabled deeper explorations into culinary traditions, destination experiences, and educational content. This cross-platform strategy redefined hospitality marketing as an interactive, real-time experience where visitors actively participated in shaping destination identity and brand reputation instead of merely receiving curated messages (Mariani, 2016).

New Paradigms of Engagement: Changing Roles and Interactivity

The marketing environment has adapted into an unusually participatory sphere due to this digital evolution. The boundaries between brand and visitor, or consumer and creator, have softened, fostering a new realm of collaborative interaction. Travelers, local food enthusiasts, and even those exploring from home are now invited to engage, comment, and share posts on Instagram that highlight the beauty of well-crafted cocktails, elaborately plated dishes, or bustling kitchens embracing not only the visual appeal but also the sensory experiences, cultural narratives, and human connections behind each creation. This multi-voiced content enriches the narrative of the location and helps hospitality brands forge emotional connections with customers before they even arrive. The idea of hospitality as an ongoing dialogue has been reinforced through Facebook groups and community-driven networks. According to (Leung, 2013), these platforms act as dynamic repositories for travel advice, event planning, local insights, and recipe exchanges, fostering trust, ongoing interactions, and robust word-of-mouth marketing.

Today, community management, narrative co-creation, and empathetic engagement are vital skills for managers, event hosts, and marketers. TikTok, with its focus on humor, creativity, and trending content, amplifies the power of storytelling. Regardless of size, be it a street vendor in Delhi or a boutique hotelier in Tuscany, operators can achieve significant visibility and brand awareness as long as their content resonates with the platform's interactive, visual nature (Chen, 2023)

Engagement and Sentiment Analysis

Advanced sentiment analysis techniques allow researchers to track emotion-driven feedback and engagement patterns across platforms. For instance, analysis of Visit Algarve data shows that posts featuring family recipes, traditional culinary practices, and festival celebrations generated more positive sentiment compared to those that focused simply on physical attributes. Engaging posts circulate widely in online communities, facilitating sharing, discussions, and broader audience reach beyond the initial user groups. (Akehurst, 2009).

Opportunities for Strategic Content and Adaptive Difficulties

Experiential and culturally rich content that resonates with audiences and transcends mere infrastructural highlights should be prioritized by destinations. Meanwhile, marketers must continuously adapt to changing algorithms, address digital fatigue, and cater to consumer demand for personally meaningful and curated content (N.S. Robinson R, 2014).

Digital Hospitality: Transitioning From Transactional Frameworks to Revolutionary Experiences

A significant shift from previous methods can be seen in the evolution of hospitality marketing, transitioning from transaction-driven approaches to relationship-centered concepts. Dining and lodging have evolved into multifaceted experiences that commence long before guests arrive and continue long after they leave. This transformation has been largely influenced by social media, which fosters strong emotional bonds and enables various forms of interaction. Each post, review, or shared story contributes to the destination's narrative, creating a sense of community, cultural awareness, and belonging (Tussyadiah, 2017).

Social Media Sites as Protectors of Brand Value

Collaboration among operators, craftsmen, producers, and influencers is essential for effective branding. When initiatives like festivals, culinary trails, and celebratory events are promoted together, they cultivate lasting brand attachment and excitement. The hospitality industry's openness to innovative collaboration ensures that social media remains a fertile ground for creative, inclusive practices and adaptable strategies (Sims, 2019).

Using Metrics and Analytics to Optimise Digital Investment

Today's brands invest significantly in measuring the return on their digital efforts, employing tools such as sentiment mapping, conversion analytics, and interaction metrics. By leveraging real-time data platforms, influencer dashboards, and adaptive feedback loops, teams can maximize their impact, nurture customer loyalty, and refine campaign costs effectively. (Alicia Orea-Giner, 2026).

CASE STUDIES IN SOCIAL MEDIA - DRIVEN CUISINE BRANDING

India's Himachal Pradesh: Social Media Campaign

India's Himachal Pradesh has launched the social media campaigns, spearheaded by local tourist officials and hospitality business owners. This initiative has united local chefs, food bloggers, and regional influencers to showcase traditional dishes such as dham, siddu, and chha gosht on platforms like Facebook and Instagram. By utilizing real-time geotags and hashtags, seasonal festivals have transformed into rich content sources featuring family gatherings, artisan music, and culinary stories. Notable highlights included live-streamed "cook-along" sessions that attracted thousands of participants, generating user-created content and significantly raising awareness of Himachali cuisine among urban audiences in India (Kashyap V., 2024) (Kumar, 2021).

Spain: Valencia's "slowfoodmovement"

In Spain, Valencia's slowfoodmovement exemplifies effective international collaboration. The area's tourism board, local chefs, and Instagram influencers have created a social media campaign that leverages short-form cooking videos and region-focused hashtags. This effort has emphasized culinary authenticity and sustainability by promoting the origins of local dishes like paella. The results are evident in increased engagement and visitor interest, as reflected in booking data and analytics demonstrating the impact digital branding strategies can have on perceptions of a destination and its economic outcomes (MD, 2025).

Japanese Cuisine: YouTube and TikTok's

In Japan, the Ministry of Agriculture and various private entities have come together to promote traditional Japanese cuisine through platforms like YouTube and TikTok. Their campaigns feature creative and informative short films and vlogs that highlight sushi, soba, and festival foods. These content efforts foster both national pride and international interest, providing insights into Japan's culinary traditions, production methods, and dining etiquette. The outcome is a compelling digital brand identity for Japanese cuisine that resonates globally (Dordai, 2026).

Visual Storytelling: Food Imagery, Video, and Narrative

Food, which inherently appeals to multiple senses, gains new depth and meaning when showcased through compelling digital imagery. Today, Instagram and TikTok stand out as the primary platforms for sharing food cultures. They leverage artistic photography and inventive short-form videos like "Reels" and "Stories" along with dynamic editing to create narratives that resonate with viewers, capturing not just the food's appearance but also its mood, suspense, and emotional undertones.

Recent studies emphasize that emotionally engaged and realistic content tends to perform better in marketing. Authentic visuals are often more memorable and persuasive than conventional staged advertisements because they evoke feelings of curiosity, nostalgia, and belonging. The emotional impact of content can often be more significant than technical accuracy; the anticipation on a chef's face, laughter around a festive table, or the steam rising from a dish can all invite deeper viewer engagement and sharing (Maria Giovanna Confetto, 2023).

Successful marketing campaigns, such as Switzerland's "Taste the Alps," have effectively utilized unscripted photos and brief videos featuring farmers, craftspeople, and chefs sharing their stories. These approaches led to a considerable rise in digital mentions and tourism inquiries, focusing on unique culinary experiences, like the glimmer of olive oil on freshly cut bread or the subtle hint of smoke in mountain cheese (Giacomo Pettenati, 2025) .

UGC-DRIVEN CAMPAIGNS: REGIONAL AND GLOBAL CASE STUDIES

Himachal Pradesh- "Dham Wave" Initiative

A notable example of effective community interaction is Himachal Pradesh's "Dham Wave". The tourism authority built a self-sustaining library of authentic #HimachaliFood content by inviting visitors and residents to submit quick videos and unposed photos of traditional communal meals. The initiative, which included local music and real-time challenges like "Create Your Own Dham Platter," fostered broader participation, enhanced regional culinary pride, and significantly boosted campaign awareness within India and beyond.

The "Feast on the Capital" Food Trails in Ottawa

In Canada's capital, a collaborative branding campaign involving food trucks, upscale restaurants, and artisanal bakers promoted the hashtag #FeastOnTheCapital for tagging culinary experiences. The campaign, emphasizing seasonal events and neighborhood diversity, fostered influencer and user-generated content (UGC), resulting in measurable increases in media coverage, meal bookings, and online interactions.

Nigeria: Making Use of User-generated Content at the "Taste of Lagos" Festival

The Taste of Lagos festival exemplifies effective UGC integration, motivating attendees to document their food experiences in real-time through interactive geofencing and hashtag contests. The campaign, featuring influencer-hosted live streams, QR-coded recipe kiosks, and onsite digital photo booths, aimed to create a year-round digital archive and a positive online reputation for the city and festival partners (GTCO, 2025).

Influencer Partnerships: ROI and Best Practices

The collaboration between digital influencers and hospitality entities is most effective when it transcends mere endorsement to engage deeply with storytelling. Influencers are increasingly invited to participate in culinary creations, attend exclusive seminars, or cover entire festivals and culinary journeys. These multi-step engagements yield richer, more varied media outputs aligned with the platform algorithms and audience preferences. To enhance the measurement of return on investment for influencer initiatives, unique promo codes, reservation tracking, and referral-based analytics are being employed. Collaborating with high-engagement influencers can boost UGC creation rates significantly, leading to marked, lasting increases in bookings, brand recommendations, and positive social sentiment, as evidenced by case studies from Swedish midsummer festivals and Mediterranean food tours (Alicia Orea-Giner, 2026)

STRATEGIC CONTENT ELEMENTS: ADVANCED TACTICS

Hashtag Engineering

A distinctive digital identity and dispersion into broader topic networks are made possible by the strategic merging of community tags with brand-owned hashtags (Ishani Sharma, 2024). Keeping an eye out for "trend spikes" and incorporating socially relevant keywords, as during public holidays or harvest festivals, optimises organic reach without sacrificing brand uniqueness.

Examine the feedback loops and integration

It has been demonstrated that post-visit review prompts significantly boost customer review rates and positive sentiment, particularly when sent out via social media or SMS soon after an encounter (Chen, 2023). Accordingly, displaying the best reviews, whether on Instagram highlights, website homepages, or QR-linked displays at physical venues, acts as continuous content, encourages additional guest participation, and fortifies reputation cycles.

Thematic Partnerships and Campaigns

Whether they are based on culinary mythology, local customs, or seasonal ingredients, narrative arcs are key to maintaining follower interest and prompting deeper exploration. Collaborations with local farmers, artists, or historians create opportunities for shared storytelling that highlights local uniqueness and connects with various audience segments.

A combination of educational content with mixed media

A significant trend is the integration of entertainment and education within content. This includes live cooking demonstrations, chef Q&As, and informative films that debunk culinary myths. Such offerings not only boost the destination's image as a vibrant cultural hub but also provide value through education and entertainment for visitors.

Analytics and Ongoing Content Improvement

As content creation becomes central to hotel branding, analytics and rapid adaptation become paramount. Beyond simple metrics like likes and shares, important performance indicators include conversion rates linking posts to bookings or inquiries, engagement duration, the quality of community comments, video completion rates, and how well trends are being adopted. Continuous learning and enhancements are supported through A/B testing, which examines various image formats, caption styles, video lengths, and timing for calls to action. Hotels and restaurants are increasingly utilizing social listening platforms to monitor audience sentiment and real-time trends, allowing them to react swiftly to viral topics, emerging critiques, or seasonal shifts in content effectiveness.

Content Creation's Future in Regional Cuisine Branding

As digital platforms, AI-driven personalisation, and cross-device storytelling develop, the significance of content production principles and strategies will only grow. The next generation of destination brands will be defined by regional cuisines that can adapt to new content forms, centre authentic and interactive storytelling, and mobilise digital communities.

Most significantly, this change guarantees that the reputation of the food is created collaboratively, not just by marketers but also by chefs, residents, tourists, and ardent supporters, all of whom contribute memories, photos, and comments in an ongoing dialogue (Buhalis, 2019).

Digital First Impressions for Branding in Hospitality

In the modern hospitality and tourism industry, a destination's online reputation, or Online Destination Image (ODI), is now just as important as its traditional media or physical infrastructure. The management of ODI has changed from being a side project to a primary strategic concern for regional culinary branding as visitors increasingly interact, evaluate, and share locations via smartphones and laptops. To successfully bridge the gap between local authenticity and worldwide appeal, ODI curation combines data-driven decision-making, creative storytelling, and real-time feedback management (Rudolf, 2022).

Co-Creation in the Digital Ecosystem: The Dynamics of ODI

Online destination pictures are continually shaped by a diverse group of participants, including locals, influencers, destination marketers, food suppliers, and, most importantly, travelers. Platforms like digital maps, Instagram, TikTok, Google

Reviews, and other social media sites facilitate the sharing of both institution-driven content and user-generated content (UGC). This creates a dynamic and participative destination image (ODI) that reflects organizational strategies and collective sentiments rather than a static representation.

Food festivals, local customs, and everyday dining experiences significantly contribute to this co-creation process. For example, reviews from culinary tourists, videos showcasing local harvests, and posts from Himachali home cooks collaborate to shape how outsiders view and desire a location, often surpassing traditional branding efforts.

MEASURING AND MANAGING DESTINATION IMAGE VIA SOCIAL CHANNELS

1. Analysis of Sentiment

Recent research highlights the importance of emotional resonance in digital destination branding. Hospitality management can gauge prevalent sentiments from posts, comments, and reviews ranging from happiness and nostalgia to annoyance or skepticism through automated sentiment analysis that utilizes natural language processing and artificial intelligence. Positive sentiment spikes correlate with increased inquiries, bookings, and favorable word-of-mouth, whereas negative trends often foreshadow declines in brand reputation and intention to visit. A study on Scottish culinary regions, for instance, revealed that while infrastructure complaints or staged images led to ambivalence, reviews emphasizing local customs and sensory experiences like tastes and scents were strong predictors of sustained positive ODI. (Tussyadiah, 2017)

2. Analytics of Engagement

Beyond traditional engagement metrics likes, shares, and comments deeper behavioral data such as watch time, click-through rates to booking systems, geolocation interactions, and hashtag or UGC cascade analytics offer richer insights. Advanced engagement dashboards can transform signals from a single Himachali food post that sparks increased local search inquiries or a collection of relevant guest reviews into actionable intelligence, helping determine which menu items to emphasize or which festival themes to promote. (Ishani Sharma, 2024)

3. Textual and Visual Inspections

Content audits that analyze recurring, resonant, or fading textual or visual themes help organizations stay attuned to customer preferences. Research comparing Italian towns found that emotionally evocative images such as those depicting cooking, sharing meals, or family traditions, garnered more engagement than sterile facility images. Moreover, a textual analysis of TripAdvisor reviews for French bistros indicated that narratives capturing the "journey from plate to place" from sourcing ingredients to home-cooked nostalgia were key factors in driving patronage and referrals (Garcês, 2024).

REPUTATION MANAGEMENT IN REAL TIME

The most powerful hospitality brands view online reputation as a living asset, keeping eye on reviews, reacting promptly, and incorporating audience data into daily operations.

1. Prompt, Tailored Answers

According to research, brand sentiment can be considerably enhanced by quick, one-on-one interactions with reviewers and commentators (Borghi, 2021). In reaction to critical comments, personalized thank-you notes, return invites, or offers of resolution not only re-establish confidence but also show sincere concern. Such responsiveness works particularly well in regional cuisine branding when the response includes food-related stories or offers, such as an apology combined with a delicacy that was found locally.

2. Strengthening Voices from the Community

Authentic user voices are elevated through community management, which includes showcasing participant images, sharing guest evaluations, and incorporating influencer narratives that complement brand value. For instance, public reposting of guest paella-making films was given priority in campaigns in the Basque Country, which produced greater organic reach and destination prestige than well-produced ads (Tafesse W, 2023).

3. Openness and Education

Higher trust scores have been linked to open communication regarding changes and public recognition of flaws, particularly in industries where emotional decision-making is prevalent. For example, the organisers of a significant food festival in South Africa used Facebook posts and live Twitter threads to collect constructive criticism and explain the situation when overbooking and service delays occurred. This approach generated constructive engagement and fresh concepts for event management in the future rather than escalating hostility (Ferran Sabate, 2014).

4. Incorporating Operational Feedback

Operational innovation is increasingly leveraging online reviews and continuous user-generated content. Viral cycles of improvement are produced by analytics-driven menu modifications (such as adding gluten-free siddu in response to repeated requests), event scheduling adjustments, or training materials developed in response to service criticism. In Finland, hospitality operators have even created new regional culinary trails and festival themes based on the collective feedback (Lorgeoux, 2023).

DESIGN OF A CULINARY DESTINATION BRANDING CAMPAIGN

An enhanced understanding of audience diversity, engagement mechanisms, and digital behaviors illustrates the transition in hotel marketing from static branding to dynamic campaign design (Nuria Recuero-Virto C. V., 2024)

1. Natural Community Development

The organic tactics create lasting brand effects and promote visitor participation, such as open recipe swaps, behind-the-scenes kitchen videos, or cultural quiz challenges. Interactive initiatives produce rich involvement and strengthen local attachment, but they also demand patience and a dedication to community moderation and storytelling. For instance, guest picture competitions connected to local hashtags have been effectively employed by festivals in Thailand and Peru to produce long-lasting digital narratives and cultural memory (Benxiang Zeng, 2014).

2. Paid Advertising: Amplification and Targeting

With careful planning and analysis, paid social media efforts can increase reach and accuracy, giving even tiny regional food firms a chance to compete on a global scale. According to (Ghorbanzadeh D, 2023), targeted advertisements convert interaction into conversion, regardless of whether they are geo-mapped to festival venues, categorised by trip intent, or customised for community groups. With the use of algorithm-based distribution, creative paid content frequently blends personalised offers with urgency (e.g., "only this weekend!").

3. Geo-targeting and hyperlocal marketing

Reaching time- and location-sensitive customers is being transformed in the hospitality industry by location-based marketing, which makes use of GPS data and real-time app integration. Geo-targeted alerts doubled event participation and increased local visitor satisfaction, according to research conducted in Australian cities (Borghi, 2021). Hyperlocal marketing are frequently used by hospitality managers in rural Japan to fill restaurant seats at off-peak or festival times (Narayan, 2020). Additional value is added by cooperative local activities, such as planned "food trail" programs between nearby companies, which promote discovery and enable natural cross-promotion.

STAKEHOLDER COLLABORATION: THE STORY OF PLACE IN CULINARY BRANDING

Together, Weaving the Cultural Fabric

The establishment of intricate networks for stakeholder collaboration comprising chefs, restaurateurs, producers, marketing agencies, and local communities is essential for creating and maintaining a regional brand identity. Such collaborative ecosystems are vital for the enduring appeal and competitive success of culinary destinations. These partnerships are purposefully developed around shared objectives of growth, sustainability, and authenticity. Continuous collaboration, adaptive flexibility, and shared storytelling play integral roles in shaping a place's culinary identity (Šmid Hribar, 2021).

Chefs: Craftspeople, Pioneers, and Cultural Ambassadors

Chefs hold a unique position in the transmission of culinary traditions and the development of brand identities. Today's chefs transcend the role of mere food producers; they serve as advocates of regional culture and innovators in contemporary culinary trends. By acting as bridges between agricultural practices and culinary events, chefs connect local produce to a global audience. For example, in Himachal Pradesh, indigenous ingredients such as buckwheat and wild apples contribute to both traditional dishes and modern culinary innovations (Kashyap V. &., 2023).

Globally, Chef Yoshihiro Narisawa of Japan exemplifies this trend by showcasing local wild foods and fermentation techniques on Michelin-starred platforms through collaborations with local farmers and tourism agencies. Through initiatives such as cooking classes, social media takeovers, and television features, he has broadened awareness of his regional culinary heritage. Such chef-driven partnerships with Destination Marketing Organizations (DMOs) enhance the authenticity and appeal of culinary experiences for international visitors, while also enriching the destination's brand narrative. These collaborations often extend to joint festivals, farm tours, and live digital seminars, fostering a shared audience. (Khatami F, 2024)

Restaurants: Anchors of the Community and Curators of Experience

As key providers of hospitality, restaurateurs play a critical role in shaping public perceptions and experiences of food. Their establishments frequently serve as cultural hubs that bring together community discussions, music, art, and cuisine (Hudson, 2013). By organizing seasonal culinary events, hosting guest chefs for pop-up experiences, and spotlighting local artists and producers, effective restaurateurs assume the responsibilities of curators. These initiatives not only encourage repeat patronage but also reinforce the local brand and enhance the significance of food beyond the menu. For instance, Vancouver's Fable Kitchen collaborates with nearby wineries and farmers to host monthly "Farm Dinner" events, which are further enriched by multi-channel digital storytelling. These gatherings promote ongoing engagement through opportunities for influencer feedback, personal narratives from guests, and collective menu development (C. Michael Hall, 2005).

Orchestrators and Amplifiers of Destination Marketing Organisations (DMOs)

DMOs play a critical role in coordinating stakeholder resources into cohesive and compelling brand campaigns. Their responsibilities encompass the formulation of regional food guides, facilitating collaboration between public and private sectors, and ensuring a consistent amplification of digital messaging. In contrast to traditional top-down branding approaches, contemporary DMOs embrace participatory co-creation, allowing travelers, farmers, chefs, and restaurateurs to contribute to the storytelling process. This participatory framework can be observed in the Norwegian Tourist Board's "Innovasjon Norge" campaign, which brings together chefs, food councils, and online ambassadors to collaboratively develop festival programs, seasonal content, and digital contests, empowering both locals and visitors to shape brand perceptions under the "Taste of Norway" initiative (McPharlin, 2022).

Local Communities: Preserving Customs, Sparking Innovation

The foundation of long-term culinary branding is community engagement. Where producers, home cooks, co-ops, and festival organisers work to preserve and revitalise food heritage, the food destinations are the richest. In order to boost local pride and external appeal, women's collectives, youth organisations, and cultural associations host interactive classes, tasting events, and market partnerships.

Digital projects that document multigenerational culinary customs and cooperative food stalls at local fairs are examples of grassroots involvement in Himachal

Pradesh. In other countries, programs such as Korea's "Hansik Globalisation Project" enable local producers, traditional chefs, and recipe archivists to participate in online discussions, oppose commercialisation, and promote significant change (Ri, 2024).

PARTNERSHIP MODELS AND MECHANISMS

Collaborations Driven by Events

Cross-sector collaborations are a natural fit for food festivals. For optimum effect, regional festivals frequently bring together DMOs, regional chefs, restaurateurs, performers, and product sponsors. One example is the Guelaguetza festival in Oaxaca, which features hundreds of community stalls, chef demonstrations, artisan workshops, and international media in a celebration enhanced by in-the-moment social interaction (Hernández-Mogollón, 2019)

Service-Oriented Partnerships

The collaboration enhances brand awareness and customer service year-round. European initiatives like Italy's "Strada del Vino" create permanent networks of vineyards, restaurants, accommodation providers, and digital storytellers that bolster local economies and brand stability (C. Michael Hall, 2005).

Engagement Driven by the Community

Community-based tourism strategies prioritise interactions between tourists and residents, such as sharing stories, cooking, and harvesting. According to Kerala hosts "village cookery day" programs that link tourists with home cooks for market trips, communal meal preparation, and recipe documentation streams that are aired worldwide.

In every situation, formalising collaboration and broadening reach across platforms is accomplished through co-branded materials, uniform event calendars, and digital content creation (such as hashtag-powered picture contests) (Baby, 2024).

Obstacles to Stakeholder Cooperation

Although there is a lot of potential, there are significant obstacles to collaboration. Partnerships can be hampered by disparate commercial interests, unequal resource distribution, and gaps in digital literacy. Transparent communication, shared digital platforms, and frequent in-person interactions are necessary for coordination.

Building capacity is crucial, especially for community organisations and small producers. More inclusive and resilient branding is enabled by training in digital storytelling, brand principles, and crisis response. Local farmers and restaurateurs in Yorkshire have collaborated to establish guidelines for "local" sourcing, striking a balance between the community's demand for authenticity and provenance and business realities (Dordai, 2026).

Long-Term Effects and Success Factors

Empirical surveys and cluster analysis reveal the importance of adaptable, values-based structures in developing partnerships. Destinations that promote adaptable leadership, experiment with campaign structures, and establish feedback forums tend to see greater success in maintaining relevance and brand equity. Common values such as authenticity, sustainability, and community pride unite efforts toward a single goal. Ongoing interaction ensures that partners remain creative and committed, focusing on recognizing shared achievements and adapting to changing travel motivations (Suparak Suriyankietkaew, 2025).

Maintaining Stakeholder Cooperation as a Critical Strategic Need

Culinary destination branding transforms local cuisine from a personal indulgence into an international invitation through dynamic stakeholder collaboration. A brand that is known for authenticity, resilience, and reach emerges from the collective efforts of chefs' creativity, restaurateurs' hospitality, DMOs' vision, and community ownership. Success is measured by various factors, including long-term community attachment, repeat business, and reputation across digital platforms, alongside traditional metrics like visitor numbers and social media shares. New frameworks, interdisciplinary teams, cross-sector investments, participatory campaign design, and continuous feedback will be essential for the future of the hotel industry. Travel destinations that promote reciprocal leadership, genuine collaboration, and shared storytelling will continue to shape global culinary preferences for years to come.

MEASURING ROI AND IMPACT: FROM ENGAGEMENT TO EQUITY IN SOCIAL MEDIA HOSPITALITY BRANDING

Beyond Traffic What Constitutes Digital Success?

Traditional notions of marketing success, such as full restaurants or high hotel occupancy rates, have evolved into a complex framework that prioritizes online engagement, conversion statistics, and long-term brand equity in today's digitally focused hospitality sector. As restaurants, hotels, and destination management organizations (DMOs) strive to turn digital buzz into loyal customers and a strong reputation, the rise of social media necessitates a skillful integration of data-driven evaluation and narrative measurement.

Digital Metrics: Mapping Engagement, Reach, Conversion, and Equity

User interactions now include sentiment analysis of comments, hashtag mentions, likes, shares, and saves. Platforms like Later and Sprinklr enable influencer amplification and the filtering of emotive language. The conversion rate measures the percentage of landing page visitors who complete a transaction. Hospitality brands often utilize booking engine integrations and analytics dashboards to track these metrics. The Net Promoter Score (NPS) calculated from post-stay emails, surveys, and social polls indicates how likely customers are to recommend a service.

Participation: Both Quantitative and Qualitative

The "heartbeat" of social media performance is increasingly seen as digital engagement. Hospitality brands are now focusing on the significance of emotional resonance, comment depth, and shareability, rather than merely counting likes or views (Hudson, The Impact of Social Media on the Consumer Decision Process: Implications for Tourism Marketing, 2013).

Key performance indicators include:

- Private Engagement: Real-time feedback, booking inquiries, and direct messages signify genuine intent. Brands assign greater importance to these key performance indicators (KPIs) in conversion modeling.
- Amplification Effects: A campaign's reach and relevance can be gauged by engagement that snowballs, which happens when local reels or stories are shared by media outlets, community organizations, or influencers.

- Reach: Geographic and Scope Diffusion – The extent of individuals exposed to branded messages is referred to as social reach. This is often assessed using:
- Impressions and Unique Views: Analytics tools on platforms like Facebook, Instagram, and TikTok can track not only repeated exposures but also the number of unique users reached. Tools such as Brandwatch or Talkwalker can provide geo-targeted reach maps and identify engagement hotspots, highlighting which locations are most impacted by campaign materials.
- Temporal Analysis: Evaluating reach over time, including the time of day, campaign duration, and seasonal peaks, can optimize future campaign launches.
- Conversion and Bookings: such as bookings, RSVPs for events, and menu purchases, remain essential for return on investment (ROI) analysis. Modern strategies center around the click-through rate (CTR), which measures the percentage of visitors who proceed from an ad or post to a reservation or purchase page.
- Redemption Codes/UTMs: Special tracking mechanisms allow for accurate attribution of reservations or orders to specific campaign components.

CHALLENGES AND FUTURE DIRECTION IN SOCIAL MEDIA -DRIVEN REGIONAL CUISINE BRANDING

The Conundrum of Contemporary Marketing and Authenticity

Hospitality professionals are currently at a crossroads as digital content has become the primary means of branding regional cuisines. The challenge is to determine how companies can leverage influencer networks and commercial platforms to reach global audiences without sacrificing authenticity. The core issue in today's hospitality industry lies in this paradox: how to balance the demands of marketing scale and monetization with the need for a "real" experience (Richards, 2021).

While local stories and culinary traditions are amplified through digital media, there is a risk that prioritizing virality over genuine connections can lead to commodification, dilution, or loss of credibility. To ensure that regional cuisine branding enhances rather than weakens destination identity, strategic actions driven by values and transparency are essential.

Navigating Authenticity vs Commercialization

The Role of Narrative and Open Practice

Authentic content is grounded in honest narratives and visible engagement. The collective brand narrative is shaped by travelers sharing personal stories, restaurateurs discussing their cooking routines, and chefs revealing their sourcing practices. Research indicates that open communication about customs, provenance, and even mistakes can enhance digital trust. Self-representation on social media, such as sharing pictures of morning market visits and discussing seasonal options, generates more engagement, repeat business, and positive sentiment than generic imagery from professional campaigns, as evidenced by case studies from Vietnamese street food collectives (Thu, 2023).

Commercial Influences and Inauthenticity Risks

However, the temptation to use social media for commercialization, scaling, and monetization can have drawbacks. If not managed carefully, excessive hashtags, staged posts, and paid influencer collaborations can undermine credibility. An audience may become skeptical and criticize "inauthentic" portrayals, particularly when content is overly polished or when experiences feel productized. Smaller venues and restaurants often face operational challenges, as they may lack the technical expertise or resources of larger chains. As a result, local establishments may struggle to gain visibility or feel pressured to conform to trends, potentially sacrificing tradition. This creates a risk for rural or legacy players, who may be marginalized in powerful online ecosystems, especially in areas with existing digital literacy gaps (Sims, 2019).

Increasing the Ability to Participate Digitally

Continued education and capacity building are vital for preserving authenticity. Providing training in storytelling, social media fundamentals, and digital branding to producers, local chefs, and community leaders can help expand the media landscape and maintain a diversity of voices. Shared learning and funding can bridge competency gaps and stimulate grassroots innovation, as illustrated by policy initiatives and cooperative partnerships like India's Smart Village projects and Italy's Slow Food Movement (Bizjak, 2025).

Coping With Negative Review, Crises and Digital Fatigue

Crises to Digital Reputation and Reaction

Reputation issues, such as negative reviews, viral complaints, or service failures, can have significant repercussions due to the rapid visibility and network effects of digital media. Hospitality businesses must establish robust procedures for monitoring reviews, investigating underlying issues, and engaging in open and constructive conversations.

According to recent research, visitors are more impressed by sympathetic and practical solutions to issues, both online and offline, than by a flawless stay. Real-time updates, make-good offers, and apologies are all examples of proactive reputation recovery (Kingston, 2024).

Emotional Burnout and Digital Fatigue

Burnout in the public and professional spheres has increased due to the unrelenting pace and complexity of digital interactions. Emotional exhaustion strain from fast reaction expectations, content cycles, and campaign pivots is reported by brand managers, chefs, and hospitality marketers. Content creation, guest messaging, and crisis management increased during the COVID-19 epidemic, sometimes at the price of people's personal and professional wellbeing.

Organisations should invest in training, wellness, and community management skills in addition to rotating employees, encouraging positive storylines, and utilising automation where necessary to reduce digital weariness.

Harnessing Emerging Technologies: AI, AR/VR, and Interactive Content

Applications of Artificial Intelligence (AI) in Content, Analysis and Service

Important developments in the hospitality industry, such as managing reservations, automating feedback loops, and personalizing visitor experiences, are now enhanced by artificial intelligence (AI) and machine learning (Kyung-Hyan Yoo, 2016). Conversational AI frameworks optimize scheduling, address dietary requirements, provide round-the-clock support, and highlight relevant culinary events (Kyung-Hyan Yoo, 2016).

According to (Dordai, 2026), natural language processing systems enable proactive crisis management and rapid marketing adaptations by analyzing thousands of social media posts and generating real-time sentiment reports. Revenue optimization technologies predict event attendance, dynamic pricing, and menu needs by processing data from bookings, reviews, and competitor analysis.

AR/VR: Enhancing Training and Experience

Virtual reality (VR) and augmented reality (AR) technologies are broadening the possibilities for staff training and visitor experiences. AR overlays enhance discovery and upselling by allowing customers to explore ingredient origins, preview menu items, and access narratives about dishes. By blurring the lines between the physical and virtual worlds, VR applications from immersive venue tours to kitchen simulations address training needs, venue previews, and remote engagement. Hospitality establishments-maintained brand engagement during the pandemic by reimagining their event concepts and hosting virtual festivals and chef meet-ups.

Immersion and Interactive Content

Brand engagement increasingly relies on interactive elements. The shift from inspiration to action is facilitated by gamified cook-offs, shoppable videos, and quick booking via Instagram stories. According to (Mariani, 2016), gamification encourages viral engagement and repeated interaction through digital scavenger hunts, festival passports, and social quests.

Future Trends and Strategic Directions

Micro-Segmentation and Data-Driven Personalisation

Unprecedented personalisation is now possible because to the development of analytics and predictive modelling. In addition to geography and demographics, brands are progressively customising offers, menu items, and narrative journeys based on detailed preference, behavioural, and social network data. Personalised loyalty benefits, unique festival participation, and dynamic menus all promote lifelong value and emotional connections.

"Phygital" Experiences and Hybrid Campaigns

It is anticipated that through the late 2020s, best practices will be defined by the fusion of digital and physical (phygital) marketing components. For a smooth experience, hospitality managers combine influencer-led virtual seminars, online voting, and live events. Interactive food festivals combine location-based social questing, livestreamed chef tables, and instant digital offer redemption.

"Super Apps" and Integrated Business Management

Super apps, which combine social, reservation, payment, and service management in cohesive digital environments, are expected to take over Western hospitality marketing. They are modelled after Asian platforms like WeChat. Convenience, loyalty, and cross-selling potential are fuelled by this simplified ordering, booking, reviewing, and recommending process.

Transparency, Ethics, and Trust

The rise of influencer marketing, artificial intelligence (AI), and digital experiences has led to increased scrutiny of company practices. Customers now demand transparent partnerships, a clear distinction between sponsored and organic content, and visible local benefits. Brands that focus on ethical engagement, local outcomes, and authentic storytelling tend to have higher conversion rates and stronger trust among consumers.

Crisis-Ready Operations and Resilience

Companies need to engage in agile and continuous reputation management. Hospitality leaders should not only prioritize team training in technology and empathetic communication but also implement rapid-response protocols and build flexibility into their operational systems for event and menu planning.

Developing the Future of Hospitality Branding Together

To advance regional cuisine branding, hotel executives must balance history with economic ambition, technological innovation with community outreach, and data-driven strategies with personal connections. The future strategic landscape will be shaped by the tensions between commercialization and authenticity, the threats of crises and fatigue, and the potential of emerging technologies. Best practices will include capacity building, ethical storytelling, cross-disciplinary strategic partnerships, and diverse content creation that respects local identity and consumer preferences. Hospitality companies must leverage the full creative and analytical capabilities of digital tools while staying true to their core values in an evolving market. Brands rooted in the shared tables and memories of local communities, yet actively engaged in the conversations, platforms, and connections of the global digital world, will likely thrive in the future.

RECOMMENDATIONS

The study highlights the strategic importance of regional cuisine in shaping destination image through social media mediation. To ensure that culinary heritage is leveraged sustainably and effectively, several recommendations are proposed for different stakeholders.

For Researchers

- **Expand Cross-Cultural Studies**: Future research should examine diverse geographic contexts, particularly underexplored regions in Africa, South Asia, and Latin America, to broaden theoretical applicability.
- **Investigate Digital Authenticity**: Scholars should explore how authenticity is negotiated in online spaces, focusing on the tension between user-generated narratives and institutional branding.
- **Develop Longitudinal Models**: Long-term studies are needed to assess whether culinary branding through social media leads to sustained tourist loyalty and destination competitiveness.
- **Integrate Interdisciplinary Approaches**: Combining insights from sociology, marketing, anthropology, and digital communication can enrich theoretical frameworks and empirical findings.

For Policymakers

- **Preserve Culinary Heritage**: Governments should support initiatives that document traditional recipes, protect indigenous food practices, and promote culinary festivals as cultural assets.
- **Invest in Digital Infrastructure**: Equal access to digital platforms must be ensured so that rural and developing regions can participate in global culinary branding.
- **Regulate Commercialization**: Policies should balance commercialization with authenticity, preventing cultural homogenization while enabling economic growth.
- **Support Local Producers**: Incentives and subsidies should be provided to farmers, artisans, and small businesses to ensure equitable participation in culinary tourism.

For Practitioners and Destination Managers

- **Design Authentic Culinary Experiences**: Hospitality businesses should create immersive food encounters such as cooking workshops, farm visits, and street food tours that highlight local traditions.
- **Engage with social media Strategically**: Destinations should actively curate and amplify user-generated content, using hashtags, influencer collaborations, and interactive campaigns to strengthen online destination image.
- **Adopt Sustainable Practices**: Managers should integrate eco-friendly approaches, such as farm-to-table models, organic sourcing, and food waste reduction, into culinary tourism initiatives.
- **Measure Impact with Analytics**: Regular monitoring of engagement metrics, visitor satisfaction, and repeat visitation rates can provide actionable insights for refining culinary branding strategies.

FUTURE DIRECTIONS

The evolving relationship between *regional cuisine, destination image, and social media* presents fertile ground for future inquiry. While this study has provided a conceptual framework and empirical insights, several avenues remain open for exploration to deepen theoretical understanding and enhance practical application.

Research Directions

- **Longitudinal Studies**: Future research should adopt longitudinal designs to assess the sustained impact of culinary branding on tourist loyalty and destination competitiveness over time.
- **Cross-Cultural Comparisons**: Comparative studies across diverse cultural and geographic contexts can reveal how regional cuisine functions differently in Western, Asian, African, and Latin American settings.
- **Digital Authenticity**: Scholars should investigate how authenticity is negotiated in online spaces, particularly the tension between curated institutional narratives and spontaneous user-generated content.
- **Emerging Technologies**: The role of artificial intelligence, augmented reality, and virtual reality in enhancing culinary storytelling warrants exploration, as these technologies may redefine how tourists experience and share food.
- **Consumer Psychology**: Future studies could examine how digital culinary narratives influence consumer decision-making, identity formation, and emotional engagement with destinations.

Policy Directions

- **Inclusive Culinary Tourism Policies**: Governments should design policies that ensure equitable participation of local producers, artisans, and small businesses in culinary tourism initiatives.
- **Digital Infrastructure Development**: Investment in digital infrastructure is critical to enable rural and underrepresented regions to participate in global culinary branding.
- **Sustainability Frameworks**: Policies must integrate food security, waste reduction, and eco-friendly practices into culinary tourism strategies to align with global sustainability agendas.
- **Cultural Heritage Protection**: Future policy should prioritize safeguarding indigenous food traditions, ensuring they are not lost to commodification or homogenization.

Practical Directions

- **Innovative Culinary Experiences**: Hospitality managers should experiment with immersive experiences such as interactive cooking workshops, farm-to-table dining, and hybrid digital-physical food festivals.
- **Strategic Social Media Engagement**: Destinations must continue to refine strategies for engaging with user-generated content, leveraging influencers, and curating authentic narratives.
- **Data-Driven Decision Making**: Future practice should rely more heavily on analytics to measure the effectiveness of culinary branding initiatives, tracking engagement, satisfaction, and repeat visitation.
- **Collaborative Ecosystems**: Building partnerships among tourism boards, local communities, and digital platforms will be essential for sustaining culinary branding initiatives.

CONCLUSION

Social media has become central to how regional cuisine and destination identities are balanced, challenged, and celebrated, marking a significant transformation in hospitality marketing over the past decade. This chapter explored the journey "from plate to post," illustrating how competitive hospitality brands are now shaped in a global, digital-first travel industry through the intersection of authentic local flavors, innovative digital storytelling, collaboration with stakeholders, strict performance metrics, and flexible campaign design. Regional food does more than satisfy hunger;

it anchors the identity of places through multisensory experiences, collective memory, and narrative depth. The impact of chefs' skills and restaurateurs' aspirations is amplified by collaboration with destination marketing agencies and local customs, transforming food into cultural capital. To maintain authenticity, expand reach, and promote long-term engagement, various groups have collaborated on festivals, food trails, influencer events, and user-generated content. The surge of social media has made destination branding more approachable, enabling visitors, residents, and content creators to quickly create and share meaning. Cuisine branding has evolved from static advertisements into dynamic dialogues through powerful visuals, interactive campaigns, and omni-channel strategies, fostering emotional connections and brand loyalty that extend well beyond the dining experience. Enhanced analytical tools now provide hospitality companies with actionable data on engagement, reach, conversion rates, and brand equity. This data translates digital buzz into actual reservations and repeat business, bolstering competitive reputation. However, this landscape also presents challenges. Strategic foresight, ongoing capacity building, and ethical commitment are crucial to navigating the tension between authenticity and commercialization, adapting to ever-changing technological needs, and mitigating the risks of digital fatigue and crisis. In response to evolving consumer expectations and the emergence of new technologies like AI, augmented reality (AR/VR), and integrated "super apps," brands must remain committed to their core values, invest in inclusive and transparent storytelling, and maintain adaptability. Ultimately, hospitality marketing will reward those who strike a balance between innovation and tradition, actively seek out feedback, and foster meaningful stakeholder relationships at every stage. When the "plate-to-post" journey is grounded in community, enhanced by creativity, and guided by careful measurement, it reshapes not only how travel destinations are promoted but also how people experience, remember, and share them. In a world where every meal can become a digital memory, the stories we create together will be the true currency of destination branding, inspiring visitors to enjoy, connect, and share their experiences.

REFERENCES

Akehurst, G. (2009). User generated content: The use of blogs for tourism organisations and tourism consumers. *Service Business*. Advance online publication. DOI: 10.1007/s11628-008-0054-2

Orea-Giner, A., Fusté-Forné, F., Todd, L., & Park, E. (2026). The nexus between local food tourism events and social sustainability: Future prospects and priorities. *Tourism Management Perspectives, Volume 60, 101430, ISSN 2211-9736*. DOI: 10.1016/j.tmp.2025.101430

Ana María Munar, J. K. (2014). Motivations for sharing tourism experiences through social media. *Tourism Management*, •••, 46–54. DOI: 10.1016/j.tourman.2014.01.012

Andersson, T. D. (2017). Food and tourism synergies: Perspectives on consumption, production and destination development. *Scandinavian Journal of Hospitality and Tourism*, *17*(1), 1–8. DOI: 10.1080/15022250.2016.1275290

Ashiq, R. & Carnie, B. (2025). Maintaining Brand Authenticity Through Rebranding: A Case Study of Ponda.bio. *The Journal of Design, Creative Process & the Fashion Industry*, 1–27. DOI: 10.1080/17569370.2025.2508819

Baby, J. B. (2024). Creative Tourism: An Umbrella for Agrifood Travel Experiences? *Tourism and Hospitality*, *5*(4), 1363–1380. DOI: 10.3390/tourhosp5040076

Bansal, M. S. (2025). Synthesizing Insights: A Literature Review on Social Media Influencers. *Effulgence*. doi:https://effulgence.rdias.ac.in/user/article_pdf/Artical_vol23_1_134_148.pdf

Bizjak, M. (2025). *With Slow Food Festival, Sacramento Hopes to Enter New Era as a Food Destination City*. Retrieved from https://www.comstocksmag.com/web-only/slow-food-festival-sacramento-hopes-enter-new-era-food-destination-city

Borghi, M. (2021). Service Robots in Online Reviews: An Empirical Study of Online Robotic Discourse. *Annals of Tourism Research*, *87*, 103036. Advance online publication. DOI: 10.1016/j.annals.2020.103036

Buhalis, D. (2019). Real-time co-creation and nowness service: Lessons from tourism and hospitality. *Journal of Travel & Tourism Marketing*, *36*(5), 563–582. DOI: 10.1080/10548408.2019.1592059

Chen, Q. X. (2023). Exploring the Discrepancy between Projected and Perceived Destination Images: A Cross-Cultural and Sustainable Analysis Using LDA Modeling. *Sustainability*, *15*(12), 9296. DOI: 10.3390/su15129296

Crespi Vallbona, M. (2021). Satisfying experiences: guided tours at cultural heritage sites. *Taylor and Francis*. https://hdl.handle.net/2445/178387

Vrontis, D., Makrides, A., Christofi, M., & Thrassou, A. (2021). Social media influencer marketing: A systematic review, integrative framework and future research agenda. *International Journal of Consumer Studies*. DOI: 10.1111/ijcs.12647

Dordai, L. B. (2026). *Gastronomic Tourism: Global Trends, Sustainability Challenges, and Research Directions (2010–2025)—A Comprehensive Review*. Gastronomy. DOI: 10.3390/gastronomy4010004

Ellis, A. P. (2018). What Is Food Tourism? *Tourism Management*, *68*, 250–263. DOI: 10.1016/j.tourman.2018.03.025

Feldman, Z. (2021). Good Food' in an Instagram Age: Rethinking hierarchies of culture, criticism and taste. *European Journal of Cultural Studies*, *24*(6). Advance online publication. DOI: 10.1177/13675494211055733

Ferran Sabate, J. B.-M. (2014). Factors influencing popularity of branded content in Facebook fan pages. *European Management Journal*. Advance online publication. DOI: 10.1016/j.emj.2014.05.001

Fusté-Forné, F. & Filimon, N. (2025). From post to table: The social media marketing of food tourism. *International Journal of Gastronomy and Food Science, Volume 39, ISSN 1878-450X*. DOI: 10.1016/j.ijgfs.2025.101107

Garcês, S. (2024). Gastronomy Experiences, Authenticity, and Storytelling in Tourism Destinations: A Conceptual Paper. In Castanho, R., & Franco, M. (Eds.), *Cultural, Gastronomy, and Adventure Tourism Development*. IGI Global Scientific Publishing. DOI: 10.4018/979-8-3693-3158-3.ch009

Ghorbanzadeh, D. Z. R. (2023). Generating destination brand awareness and image through the firm's social media. *Kybernetes*, *52*(9), 3292–3314. DOI: 10.1108/K-09-2021-0931

Giacomo Pettenati, E. A. (2025). Assembling mountains through food. Typical cheese and politics of mountainness in the Italian Alps. *Geoforum*. Advance online publication. DOI: 10.1016/j.geoforum.2025.104210

Gretzel, U. F. (2006). Searching for the Future: Challenges Faced by Destination Marketing Organizations. *Journal of Travel Research, 45*(2), 116–126. DOI: 10.1177/0047287506291598

GTCO. (2025). GTCO food and drink: holiday edition. Retrieved from https://foodanddrink.gtcoplc.com/#:~:text=Venue%3A%20GTCentre%2C%20Plot%201%20Water,Attendance%20is%20FREE!

Hashimoto, A. (2006). Selling Canadian Culinary Tourism: Branding the Global and the Regional Product. *Tourism Geographies, 8*(1), 31–55. DOI: 10.1080/14616680500392465

Hernández-Mogollón, J. A.-F.-C. (2019). Food Festivals and the Development of Sustainable Destinations. The Case of the Cheese Fair in Trujillo (Spain). [*May.*]. *Sustainability, MDPI, 11*(10), 1–14.

Hudson, S. (2013). The Impact of Social Media on the Consumer Decision Process: Implications for Tourism Marketing. *Journal of Travel & Tourism Marketing, 30*(1–2), 156–160. DOI: 10.1080/10548408.2013.751276

Hudson, S. & Thal, K. (2013). The Impact of Social Media on the Consumer Decision Process: Implications for Tourism Marketing. *ournal of Travel & Tourism Marketing*, 30(1–2), 156–160. DOI: 10.1080/10548408.2013.751276

Ibrahim, M.A., Wan Mohd Zain, W.M.A., Mior Shariffuddin, N.S., Azinuddin M., Mohd Salim, M.N.H., & Zainul, N.H. (2025). Crafting food destination image in the social media age: dynamics of consumption, experience and culture differences. *Journal of Hospitality and Tourism Insights, 8*(5), 1907-1926. DOI: 10.1108/jhti-12-2023-0885

Sharma, I., Sharma, N. & Patwa, N. (2024). Mapping Social Media Research Trends in Hospitality and Tourism: A Bibliometric Perspective. *Journal of Technology Management for Growing Economies, 15*(2). DOI: 10.15415/jtmge/2024.152002

Kashyap, V. (2023). *The Comprehension of the Nichar Community for the Development and Growth of the Destination as a Creative Tourism Destination?* Asean Journal on Hospitality and Tourism.

Kashyap, V. (2024). The Creative Tourism - A New Approach of Sustainable Practices a Case Study of Kinnaur, Himachal Pradesh. *IRTTHI* (pp. 208-218 (11 pages)). Mohali: IRTTHI.

Khatami, F. S. F. (2024). Breaking barriers: The role of digital platforms in enhancing the resilience of food entrepreneurs. *British Food Journal, 126*(11), 3822–3841. DOI: 10.1108/BFJ-02-2024-0142

Kingston, P. (2024). Crisis Response Strategies in Online Reputation Management. *International Journal of Public Relation and Communication*. Retrieved from https://forthworthjournals.org/journals/index.php/IJPRC/article/view/59

Kivela, J. (2006). Tourism and gastronomy: Gastronomy's influence on how tourists experience a destination. *Journal of Hospitality & Tourism Research (Washington, D.C.)*, *30*(3), 354–377. DOI: 10.1177/1096348006286797

Ksenia Kirillova, X. F. (2014). What makes a destination beautiful? Dimensions of tourist aesthetic judgment. *Tourism Management*. Advance online publication. DOI: 10.1016/j.tourman.2013.12.006

Kumar, P. K. (2021). Retrieved from https://hospitality.economictimes.indiatimes.com/news/travel/himachal-pradesh-to-harness-the-powers-of-digital-media/87056703

Kyung-Hyan Yoo, U. G. (2016). The Role of Information and Communication Technologies (ICTs. In Experiences, M. T. (Ed.), *The Handbook of Managing and Marketing Tourism Experiences*. Marios Sotiriadis, Dogan Gursoy. DOI: 10.1108/978-1-78635-290-320161017

Law, R. B. D. (2014). Progress on information and communication technologies in hospitality and tourism. *International Journal of Contemporary Hospitality Management*, *26*(5), 727–750. DOI: 10.1108/IJCHM-08-2013-0367

Lee, H. Y. (2017). Differences in tourist ethical judgment and responsible tourism intention: An ethical scenario approach. *Tourism Management*, 298 - 307. DOI: 10.1016/j.tourman.2016.12.003

Leung, D. Law, R., van Hoof, H., & Buhalis. (2013). Social Media in Tourism and Hospitality: A Literature Review. *Journal of Travel & Tourism Marketing*, *30*(1–2), 3–22. DOI: 10.1080/10548408.2013.750919

Lorgeoux, C. P. (2023). How Foreign Social Media Influencers Help Shape Destination Country's Tourism Image: The Case of South Korea's Tourism Image in France. *Tourism Analysis*, *28*(2). Advance online publication. DOI: 10.3727/108354223x16773677647966

Maria Giovanna Confetto, F. C. (2023). Digital destination branding: A framework to define and assess European DMOs practices. *Journal of Destination Marketing & Management*, *30*. Advance online publication. DOI: 10.1016/j.jdmm.2023.100804

Mariani, M. M. (2016). Facebook as a destination marketing tool: Evidence from Italian regional Destination Management Organizations. *Tourism Management, Elsevier*, *54*(C), 321–343. DOI: 10.1016/j.tourman.2015.12.008

McPharlin, M. (2022). Retrieved from https://scanmagazine.co.uk/stolte-anton-an-old-fashioned-and-sustainable-taste-of-norway/

Bruno MD. (2025). Facebook post. Retrieved from https://www.facebook.com/BrunoMDofficial/posts/eating-paella-in-valencia-is-like-tasting-the-citys-history-born-in-the-rice-fie/1155150523263359/

Michael Hall, C. & Mitchell, R. (2005). Chapter 6 - Gastronomic tourism: Comparing food and wine tourism experiences. In M. Novelli, *Niche Tourism* (pp. 73-88). DOI: 10.1016/B978-0-7506-6133-1.50014-7

Robinson, R.N.S. & Getz D. (2014). Profiling potential food tourists: an Australian study". British Food Journal. *British Food Journal, Vol. 116 No. 4 pp. 690–706.* DOI: 10.1108/BFJ-02-2012-0030

Nuria Recuero-Virto, C. V. (2024). Culinary destination enchantment: The strategic interplay of local gastronomy in regional tourism development. *International Journal of Gastronomy and Food Science*. Advance online publication. DOI: 10.1016/j.ijgfs.2024.100931

Nuria Recuero-Virto, C. V. (2024). Culinary destination enchantment: The strategic interplay of local gastronomy in regional tourism development. *International Journal of Gastronomy and Food Science*, *36*. Advance online publication. DOI: 10.1016/j.ijgfs.2024.100931

Pahor Zvanut, A. (2025). Social Media Marketing Strategy in the Tourism Industry: A Systematic Literature Review. *Tourism Planning & Development*, 1–34. DOI: 10.1080/21568316.2025.2549069

Park, E. K. (2022). Hunger for learning or tasting? An exploratory study of food tourist motivations visiting food museum restaurants. *Tourism Recreation Research*, *47*(2), 130–144. DOI: 10.1080/02508281.2020.1841374

Phung, T. B., Nguyen, D. V. P., & Tran, V. P. T. (2025). Storytelling on social media: forging the path to tourism destination branding. *Cogent Business and Management*, *12*(1). DOI: 10.1080/23311975.2025.2482016

Phuong Minh Binh Nguyen, X. L. (2023). A bibliometric analysis of research on tourism content marketing: Background knowledge and thematic evolution. *Heliyon*, *9*(2). Advance online publication. DOI: 10.1016/j.heliyon.2023.e13487 PMID: 36816254

Piotr, G. P. (2023). The Use of Social Media in City Marketing Communication with Residents and Tourists – User Segmentation. *Polish Journal of Sport and Tourism*. Advance online publication. DOI: 10.2478/pjst-2023-0005

Ri, P. H. (2024). *Strategy to raise food industry's value to KRW 300B by 2027*. Retrieved from https://www.korea.net/NewsFocus/policies/view?articleId=246532

Richards, G. (2021). Evolving research perspectives on food and gastronomic experiences in tourism. *International Journal of Contemporary Hospitality Management*, *33*, 1037–1058. DOI: 10.1108/IJCHM-10-2020-1217

Rudolf, N. L. (2022). Social Media and Destination Branding in Tourism: A Systematic Review of the Literature. *Sustainability, MDPI*, *14*(20), 1–18.

Sims, R. (2019). Food, place and authenticity: Local food and the sustainable tourism experience. *Journal of Sustainable Tourism*, *17*(3), 321–336. DOI: 10.1080/09669580802359293

Šmid Hribar, M. R. (2021). Models of stakeholder collaboration in food tourism experiences. *Acta Geographica Slovenica*, *61*(1), 127–140. DOI: 10.3986/AGS.8756

Sofía Blanco-Moreno, A. M.-F.-G. (2024). Understanding engagement with Instagram posts about tourism destinations. *Journal of Destination Marketing & Management*. Advance online publication. DOI: 10.1016/j.jdmm.2024.100948

Suparak Suriyankietkaew, K. K. (2025). Creative tourism as a driver for sustainable development: A model for advancing SDGs through community-based tourism and environmental stewardship. *Environmental and Sustainability Indicators*. Advance online publication. DOI: 10.1016/j.indic.2025.100828

Tafesse, W. W. B. (2023). Social media influencers' community and content strategy and follower engagement behavior in the presence of competition: An Instagram-based investigation. *Journal of Product and Brand Management*, *32*(3), 406–419. DOI: 10.1108/JPBM-02-2022-3851

Tham, A. (2023). A pentadic analysis of TikTok marketing in tourism: The case of Penang, Malaysia. *Tourist Studies*, *24*(1), 75–103. DOI: 10.1177/14687976231218483

Thu, N. &. (2023). Visual marketing on promoting Vietnamese cuisine image through instagram. DOI: 10.13140/RG.2.2.25495.14240

Tussyadiah, I. P. (2017). Identifying salient attributes of peer-to-peer accommodation experience. *Journal of Travel & Tourism Marketing*, *34*(5), 636–652. DOI: 10.1080/10548408.2016.1209153

Zeng, B. R. G. (2014). What do we know about social media in tourism? A review. *Tourism Management Perspectives*. Advance online publication. DOI: 10.1016/j.tmp.2014.01.001

Chapter 16
Role of Robotics in Hotel Operations and Future Trends and Sustainability in Hospitality Robotics

Sanjeev Kumar
http://orcid.org/0000-0002-7375-7341
Lovely Professional University, India

ABSTRACT

The robotics and artificial intelligence (AI) has redefined the landscape of modern hotel operations, transforming both front-of-house and back-of-house activities. Robotics in hospitality is no longer a futuristic concept but an emerging reality that addresses the growing demand for efficiency, personalization, and safety in guest experiences. In operational domains such as housekeeping, robots support cleaning, sanitation, and linen management, ensuring consistent quality standards while minimizing human error. The self-service kiosks and humanoid robots streamline the check-in and check-out processes, reducing waiting times and enhancing customer satisfaction. Furthermore, AI-powered concierge robots and service bots have expanded the scope of guest assistance, offering multilingual support, real-time information, and contactless interactions an especially valuable feature in a post-pandemic hospitality environment. Beyond operational convenience, the integration of robotics into hotel management systems enables seamless coordination of services, predictive maintenance.

DOI: 10.4018/979-8-3373-6741-5.ch016

INTRODUCTION

Customer satisfaction is the most important role in the hospitality industry that has always been considered as one of the most dynamic and service-oriented industries. The last couple of decades have seen technological innovations constantly redefine the way the hotel industry runs, and robotics is one of the technological innovations that have become a game changer. Robotics in hotel works is not a far-fetched fantasy anymore, but it can be a reality. Auto check-in counters, robotic cleaners and concierge services are just a few examples of how robots are gradually transforming hotel services making them quicker, efficient and more dependable. The efficiency, safety, and customized guest experience are the main factors that lead to the implementation of robotics in the hospitality industry. Robots have the benefit of providing uniform services, eliminating exhaustion, minimizing human error and 24/7 availability. The adoption of robotics in hotels can not only enhance the productivity of their operations but also help them to stand out in a highly competitive market (Nam et al., 2021).

There is a broad spectrum of hotel functions that robotics is applicable to. The service robots will help with guest check-in, informing them, and even transporting luggage at the front office. Robotic vacuuming cleaners and robots that clean dishes are useful in housekeeping to ensure the hygiene level is upheld. Meal preparation, serving, and quick, contactless delivery of food and beverage services are being prepared with the help of robots. Hotels have security robots patrol their locations and maintenance robots perform regular technical inspections. This broadness also indicates the ability of robotics to assist nearly all operations within a hotel. Besides efficiency in operations, robotics also helps improve the experiences of guests (Yang et al., 2020). Consider a robot welcoming the visitors in their language of choice, offering them room service within minutes, or even having interactive entertainment in the lobby. These types of innovations make them seem new and unique, which are a favorite among tech-savvy travelers. Meanwhile, robotics can assist hotels in managing staffing issues, excessive labor expenses, and the necessity to adhere to international standards of service. But the introduction of robotics is not free of obstacles. The high cost of installation, the necessity of in-service technical maintenance, and the question of the human touch in hospitality are all serious problems (Gaur et al., 2021). Hospitality is a business that thrives on warmth, customization and emotional attachment and excessive dependence on machines may sometimes provoke a feeling of coldness. It is, therefore, crucial to find the proper balance between human service and robotic help. Going forward, hospitality robotics trends are likely to be more closely connected with the artificial intelligence (AI), the Internet of Things (IoT), and the cloud-based management system. Instead of just doing tedious jobs, robots will also be able to learn the preferences of their guests, provide them with personal recommendations and help to design smart sustainable hotels. It is especially crucial that the idea of sustainability is considered in the context where a growing pressure on the hospitality industry is imposed to decrease its impact on the environment (Talukder & Afchar, 2025). Hotels will keep in line with global sustainability requirements through energy efficient robots, intelligent resource management, and waste reduction through robotics. Robotics will be at the heart of hospitality in the future, as hotels keep adapting to evolving guest expectations and other challenges in the world. The future of robotics is the ability to develop a synergistic balance wherein technology complements, rather than disrupts the human nature of hospitality. The future of robotics in hospitality is closely tied to sustainability and innovation. Robotic technologies are expected to play a critical role in energy management, waste reduction, and eco-friendly operations (G. G. Liu et al., 2025). For example, smart robots can monitor energy consumption in real time, ensure water-efficient cleaning, and reduce reliance on disposable materials. Collaborative robots (cobots) are also likely to emerge, working alongside human staff to enhance service quality while preserving human-centric interactions. Additionally, advancements in machine learning and the Internet of Things (IoT) will allow robots to predict guest preferences, personalize services, and contribute to a more resilient hospitality ecosystem. Robotics in hotel operations represents a transformative force that combines efficiency, sustainability, and innovation. The future lies in striking a balance between robotic capabilities and human empathy, ensuring that technology enhances, rather than replaces, the core values of hospitality (Wang et al., 2022).

OBJECTIVES OF THE STUDY

I. To analyze the application of robotics in hotel operations.
II. To examine the advantages and issues of robotics in hospitality
III. To understand what is coming next in the field of hospitality robotics
IV. To evaluate the contribution of robotics to sustainability

OVERVIEW OF ROBOTICS IN HOSPITALITY INDUSTRY AND EVOLUTION OF ROBOTICS IN HOTELS

Hospitality industry is among service industries that are most rapidly developing, and technology has never been left out in influencing the development of the industry. Robotics is one of the most influential and innovative technologies in this sphere in recent years. Robotics in hospitality means that automated machines and systems based on artificial intelligence are used to carry out the work that used to be performed by human employees. All of these are focused on the main objective to provide efficiency, less cost of operation, and a unique and superior guest experience (Wang et al., 2022). Robots are now seen in different operations in the hospitality industry. Service robots can help at the front desk with the check-in and check-out procedures, direct guests to their rooms, and speak several languages. In food and beverage services, robots cook meals in robotic kitchens, service meals to rooms and also serve as waiters in restaurants. Housekeeping robots can clean, sanitize, and maintain the floor and do it with accuracy and predictability. Security robots have cameras and sensors to patrol the hotel area, whereas concierge robots provide travel tips, event news, and information to visitors. The future of robotics usage is not just concerning the convenience, but also fulfilling the expectations of modern guests (McCartney & McCartney, 2020). Modern customers, and the younger generation in particular, are very technologically advanced and demand innovative, contactless and efficient services. Robotics is also useful in handling issues such as the labour shortages, increasing wage requirements, and quality consistency that hotels require. The use of robotics in conjunction with other technological solutions such as Artificial Intelligence (AI), the Internet of Things (IoT), and data analytics only enhances robotics in building intelligent hotels (Mingotto et al., 2021).

Hotel Evolution of Robotics

The process of robotics in hotels has been slow to evolve and change with the technologies as well as with the changing consumer needs. At the beginning of the hospitality industry, robots were not viewed so much as service aids as much as as a novelty item. To illustrate this point, during the early 2000s, some luxury hotels started testing robotic bellboys or entertainment robots to impress their guests. These were very rudimentary robots and more of a symbol of innovation than usefulness. The biggest breakthrough was the opening of the first robot-staffed hotel in the world, the Henn-na Hotel in Nagasaki, Japan, in 2015 (Mingotto et al., 2021). This hotel used humanoid robots at the hotel entrance, robotic arms to store luggage and AI-based assistants in the rooms. It was the start of serious testing of robotics in hospitality, even though not all systems performed perfectly. Since that time, robotics has ceased to be a novelty, having become a part of the hotel activities. Hotels such as the Marriott, Hilton and FlyZoo Hotel run by Alibaba in China have launched robots to carry out chores such as room delivery, information delivery and cleaning. COVID-19 also contributed to this development by generating a powerful need in contactless services. The further development of robotics in the hotel industry today is implemented by the use of artificial intelligence-based robots, which can learn the preferences of their guests, understand those who visit the hotel regularly, and provide services to them individually. Robots are not a simple machine, but they are becoming intelligent helpers who can collaborate with human beings (Reis et al., 2020).

Role of Robotics in Hotel Operations

The hospitality business is founded upon providing comfort, efficiency and experience to customers. Robotics has emerged as one of the most revolutionary things in this pursuit. Robotization of hotel functioning is no longer a futuristic vision, but is already a reality in most regions of the world. Robots have been implemented in various hotel departments assisting the employees, enhancing efficiency and creating unique experiences to the travelers (Choi et al., 2020).

I. **Front Office and Guest Services:** Robotics is also most visible in the front office. Robots are used as receptionists to guide guests on the check-in and check-out procedure. They are able to check reservations, give out room keys, and even speak various languages. There are also robotic concierge usages in some hotels, answering guest questions, directions and information regarding local attractions (Xu et al., 2020).

II. **Housekeeping and Cleaning:** The other field where robotics has proved to be very useful is housekeeping. Floor scrubbers, disinfection robots, and robot vacuum cleaners ensure that the guest rooms, the lobbies, and common rooms are kept clean. These are machines that are highly precise and therefore are reliable in their hygiene standards. The disinfection robots were especially useful during the COVID-19 pandemic, which required them to sanitize rooms and other places to reduce the risk of infection (Ivanov et al., 2025). Robotics in housekeeping is increasing as hygiene and safety are given more importance.

III. **Food and Beverage Services:** Food and beverage (F&B) operations have gotten involved in robotics as well. It is now possible to have robots that cook in the kitchen, make coffee or even mix cocktails precisely (Talukder, Kumar, Singh, et al., 2025). Some hotels and restaurants use robotic waiters that can transfer the food to a specific table or a room without physical contact (Ivanov et al., 2020). Besides contributing to the safety of the visitors, it also creates a new element in the dining process. Being served by a robot is a distinctive aspect of hospitality in modern times and a memorable experience that guests (K. Singh et al., 2024).

Benefits of Using Robotics in Hotels and Cost Reduction and Productivity

The hospitality business is very competitive and efficiency, customer satisfaction and cost containment are all equally crucial in the hotel industry. Robotics has become an effective instrument in this setting that introduces various benefits to hotels. Whether it be enhancing the quality of services being offered or lowering the operational costs, the deployment of robots is changing the manner in which hotels operate (Garg et al., 2025).

I. **Enhanced Guest Experience:** Faster, smoother and personalized services are one of the biggest advantages of robotics in hotels. The reception desk will have robots to help guests check-in, respond to questions in various languages and 24/7. Room service robots bring food, beverages or other services to guest rooms in real time. The speed and efficiency will improve the satisfaction of the guests as they will enjoy their stay and remember it better (J. Liu et al., 2024).
II. **Consistency and Accuracy:** Robots are also not exhausted, distracted, or stressed the way human staff members are. They are able to do repetitive tasks with a certain degree of accuracy. Examples would include cleaning robots cleaning each room or hallway to the last item, and kitchen robots that make food with consistent taste and quality (Alma Çallı et al., 2023).
III. **Improved Hygiene and Safety:** Contactless services were emphasized during the COVID-19 pandemic. The robot reduces face-to-face interaction and health dangers to the guests and employees. Distribution of items to guest rooms does not require any physical contact as disinfection robots can better clean rooms and common areas and the delivery robots can deliver items to guests (Rosete et al., 2020). Not only does this develop trust in the minds of guests, but it also enhances the safety reputation of a hotel.
IV. **Exceptional and novel Appeal:** Robots are novel and innovative and can be exciting to many guests. It makes a great impression when you are welcomed by a humanoid receptionist or are waiting to be served by a robot waiter. These features may distinguish a hotel among its competitors and appeal to tech-savvy travelers seeking modern and innovative hospitality offerings (Kiliçhan & Yilmaz, 2020).
V. **Lower Labor Costs:** One of the biggest costs of hotels is to hire, train, and keep employees. Repetitive and routine duties like cleaning, delivery and check-in can be handled by robots. Although the initial cost of investing in robotics is high, it helps to save costs of labor in the long run (Ivanov & Webster, 2020). The ability to work around the clock without pay, breaks or overtime allows robots to assist hotels in labor shortages and lower payroll. Robots have been

created to do things more quickly than humans. E.g. a robot is able to clean a room faster or provide room service without waiting. This contributes to the productivity of hotel operations (S. (Sam) Kim et al., 2021).

VI. **Resource Efficiency:** Most present-day robots are aimed at optimization of resource consumption. In such a way, cleaning robots consume only the necessary volume of water or disinfectant without any waste. This is cost saving and also helps in ensuring sustainability. The advantages of deploying robotics in hotels are much deeper than a gimmick (Li et al., 2019). They add value to the guest experience, accuracy, hygiene and introduce innovation to hospitality services. Most importantly, they assist hotels to cut down on operations and increase productivity which is vital in a competitive industry. Incorporating robots into several departments will enable hotels to become efficient and stay financially viable in the long-term, as well as provide guests with an exclusive and high-tech experience explain the table 01.

Table 1. Comparison Table: Before vs After Robotics in Hotels:

Aspect	Before Robotics (Traditional Hotels)	After Robotics (With Automation)	Benefit
Front Office	Manual check-in, long queues, limited language support	Self check-in kiosks, robotic receptionists, multi-language support	Faster service & guest convenience
Housekeeping	Staff-dependent cleaning, inconsistent quality, time consuming	Robotic vacuums & disinfection robots with consistent cleaning	Better hygiene, less time
Food & Beverage	Human waiters, chances of delay or mistakes in orders	Robots delivering food, automated kitchens, error-free preparation	Accuracy & contactless delivery
Room Service	Manual delivery by staff, slower response	Robots deliver items directly to rooms within minutes	Quick, 24/7 reliable service
Security	Manual monitoring, staff patrols	AI-powered security robots with sensors & cameras	Safer & efficient surveillance
Labor Costs	High salaries, training, overtime costs	One-time investment, low maintenance compared to staff salaries	Cost savings
Productivity	Limited by staff availability & human fatigue	Robots work 24/7 without breaks, faster task completion	Higher efficiency
Error Rate	Human errors in billing, cleaning, and service delivery	Robots programmed for accuracy and consistency	Reduced mistakes
Guest Experience	Standard, sometimes delayed services	Personalized, innovative, and tech-driven experiences	Memorable stay
Sustainability	Higher use of water, energy, and waste	Smart robots optimize resources and reduce wastage	Cost + eco benefits

Challenges and Limitations of Robotics in Hotels

Although robotics is revolutionizing the hospitality sector in terms of efficiency, innovation, and cost-savings, its implementation is not uneventful. There are various challenges and restrictions that hotels encounter during the application of robotics in their daily businesses.

I. **High Initial Investment:** High cost of installation and setup is one of the greatest challenges of introducing robotics in hotels. Robots and, in particular, Artificial Intelligence (AI) with high-quality sensors are expensive. In the case of small and medium-sized hotels, this expense is prohibitive (Putri et al., 2023).
II. **Technical Problems and Troubles:** Like any technological device, robots can fail in their technical operation. Delays and inconvenience can be caused to a guest when a robot fails at the busiest time. Hotels should also hire qualified technicians to do repairs and maintenance which increases the cost of running the hotel. Some areas may also be difficult to locate spare parts or skilled repairmen (Ivanov & Webster, 2019).
III. **Lack of Human Touch:** Hospitality has always been associated with kindness, compassion, and human touch. Even the most sophisticated versions of robots cannot completely mimic emotions, cultural sensitivity, and a sense of being able to respond to special guest requests. This is especially important in luxury hotels, where attention to the individual is considered very important (Sapelnikova, 2025).
IV. **Guest Acceptance:** Not everybody is comfortable when communicating with robots. Others might view robots as frightening, disorienting or unreliable. Access to robotic services such as robots to check-in or deliver room supplies may be a barrier to elderly guests or those who are not familiar with technology (Naeem Abass et al., 2022). The impact of negative guest perceptions may be detrimental to the overall hotel experience, and so hotels must find the right balance between robotics and human assistance.

Concerns Around Data Privacy and Security

A lot of hotel robots are tied to the AI systems and hold information about guests like booking, preferences, and payment history. Hackers can reveal sensitive guest information when systems are compromised, which is not only harmful to the reputation of the hotel, but it also creates legal issues. Securing high quality cybersecurity is a continuous challenge (Bertino, 2016).

Job Displacement and Staff Concerns

Robotics is introducing the issue of job security among hotel workers. Automation can threaten staff and result in resistance or dissatisfaction. Even though robots can do repetitive work, hotels still need human worker to serve individuals in a personalized way (Sharma & Kumar, 2025). The hotel management finds it difficult to balance this without developing the fear of being sacked (Talukder, Kumar, & Das Tonny, 2025). Overall, although robotics offers efficiency, safety, and novelty, there are drawbacks to the hotel industry, including high prices, technical problems, loss of human touch, difficulties in getting guests to accept them, and threats to data privacy (Brand, 2006). To achieve success in the long term, hotels need to embrace a hybrid approach that involves collaboration between the robots and humans, with the latter contributing to efficiency and a sense of emotional attachment to the guests (B. Singh & Kumar, 2025).

FUTURE TRENDS IN HOSPITALITY ROBOTICS: ARTIFICIAL INTELLIGENCE INTEGRATION AND CONTACTLESS TECHNOLOGIES

Robotics is at the core of rapid technological transformation in the hospitality industry. Although the initial application of robots in hotels was limited to cleaning, carrying luggage, and reception services, much more sophisticated applications are expected in the future. As Artificial Intelligence (AI) evolves and companies increasingly rely on contactless and touchless services, robotics will have a revolutionary impact on the future of hotels (Shukla & Kulshreshtha, 2023). These trends will not only make it more efficient but also change the definition of the guest experience.

I. **Integration of Artificial Intelligence:** The next stage of robotics in hospitality is powered by Artificial Intelligence. The AI-enabled robots are capable of learning, adapting, and offering customized services to the guests, unlike the traditional robots, which were programmed to perform repetitive tasks.
II. **Individualized Guest Experience**: Robots with AI will analyze the data regarding guests, including their previous registration, preferences, and wishes to provide individual suggestions. A robot concierge can recommend restaurants, entertainment choices, or activities, based on the interests of a guest, as an example. Equally, in-room robots would be able to change the lighting, temperature and entertainment systems to suit the preferences of the guest (Chung & Tan, 2025).

III. **Natural Communication:** Robots that are integrated with AI will possess greater natural language processing (NLP) capabilities. This implies that they will be able to interact better with guests who speak different languages, respond to difficult questions, and even have meaningful conversations. This lessens the language barrier and makes the guest experience a much easier one, particularly in foreign hotels (Fernandes et al., 2024).

IV. **Anticipatory Service Provision**: AI robots will not only answer the calls but also anticipate the needs of the guests. An example would be when a guest orders coffee every morning, the robot will automatically bring coffee at the usual time without being requested. Equally, AI-powered solutions can predict room service requests or propose upgrades and promotions to generate a proactive hospitality experience.

V. **Smart Data Management:** Hotels are producing large volumes of information every day. This information can be processed by AI robots to discover patterns, control stock levels, use energy efficiently, and simplify work. This not only increases productivity but also assists the management in making better decisions as shown in the table 02.

Table 2. Challenges and Limitations of Robotics in Hotels

Area	Challenges and Limitations
High Initial Cost	High purchase, installation, and maintenance costs of robots
Technical Issues	Breakdowns, software errors, and need for regular updates
Limited Human Interaction	Robots lack emotional intelligence and personal touch
Training Requirement	Staff need training to operate and manage robots
Security & Privacy Concerns	Risk of data breaches and guest privacy issues
Limited Flexibility	Robots cannot handle complex or unexpected situations
Dependence on Technology	System failures can disrupt hotel operations

Contactless and Touchless Technologies

Contactless and touchless technologies became increasingly demanded during the COVID-19 pandemic, and this tendency will remain the same in the future. Visitors have come to demand safety, sanitation, and comfort, and robotics can provide all of them successfully.

I. **Touchless Check-in and Check-out:** The rooms have facial recognition and mobile-based robots and self-service kiosks that enable a guest to check-in and out without having to touch anyone. This shortens waiting time at reception and makes it safer due to a decrease in human contact.
II. **Touchless Room Service and Delivery:** These robots are also being used to deliver room service in a safe and efficient way. Visitors will be able to make orders via a mobile app and the robot will bring them to the room, which in many cases uses elevators independently. Not only does this ensure hygiene, but also offers 24/7 service (Rahman et al., 2023).
III. **In-Room voice-controlled technologies:** Guest rooms also have touchless. Sensors may also use voice-assisted devices to adjust the room temperature, lighting, television set, and even the curtains, without touching any of the available switches or remotes. Combined with robotics, it makes the environment in the future futuristic, comfortable, and hygienic (Dewangan & Kumar, 2024).
IV. **Sanitation Robots:** Cleanliness has taken over as a hotel priority. Robots with UV lights or high-end disinfectant sprays can clean rooms, lobbies, gyms, and other areas where people gather effectively. Their contactless nature keeps them clean all the time because they make sure that their staff is not exposed to any possible hazard.
V. **Contactless Technologies and AI Synergy:** The future of hospitality robotics is in using AI in combination with contactless systems. As an example, facial recognition-enabled AI-based check-in robots can authenticate identity and assign a room in real-time, with delivery robots under the control of AI able to locate the shortest path to a guest. Voice-controlled in-room robots would be able to blend personalization (AI) with safety (touchless control) to provide guests with the convenience and innovation in one package. Hospitality robotics of the future is shifting towards smart, touchless and guest-focused experiences (Chen & Ahmed, 2024). The use of Artificial Intelligence will help to make the robots smarter so that they can learn and predict the needs of the guest, and the use of contactless technologies will make it safer, more hygienic, and convenient. These trends will collectively not only enhance efficiency in operation, but also transform the manner in which the Hotels relate to their customers. Hotels will struggle to find a balance between automation and the warmth of human hospitality using these technologies (Buhalis & Moldavska, 2022). In the end, the combination of AI and contactless robotics will help to introduce a new world of intelligent, environmentally-friendly and guest-oriented hotels.

Sustainability in Hospitality Robotics

Sustainability is one of the most relevant aspects of the global hospitality industry. Hotels are constantly pressured to minimize their environmental footprint, use fewer resources, and cater to the needs of environmentally conscious tourists. Hospitality robotics, in this respect, is not only becoming an efficiency and innovation driver but a worthy addition to sustainability objectives. Robotics is making hotels green and more responsible by integrating the latest technology with intelligent use of resources (Ivanov et al., 2023).

I. **Energy Efficiency:** Hotel robots are increasingly being developed to work with low energy. Smart robots may be programmed to clean when no one is around, reducing electricity needs and saving all energy wastage. Other high-end robots can also be connected to the building management systems of the hotel so that lighting, air conditioning and heating are used more efficiently (Ivanov et al., 2023).
II. **Waste Reduction:** Waste management and reduction is another sustainability activity that robotics facilitates. Food waste is also reduced as automated kitchen robots are able to cook meals with high accuracy. Delivery robots deliver orders precisely, which eliminates the possibility of incorrect deliveries or excessive consumption. Also, inventory management robots are able to monitor supplies and stock better to reduce over-buying and spoilage (Talukder, Mia, et al., 2025). This is in addition to cost reduction and more sustainable utilization of resources.
III. **Cleaning and Water Saving:** Housekeeping robots usually consume less water and cleaners than the manual ones. As an example, floor cleaning robots have been programmed on how much water or disinfectant is needed, then do not waste it. This not only conserves the amount of resources used, but also decreases the quantity of harmful chemicals that are emitted into the environment (Kumar et al., 2025). The long term water and chemical savings in large hotels with extensive cleaning operations can be a significant contribution to sustainability.
IV. **Reducing Carbon Footprint:** Hotels are also able to minimize their carbon footprint with the help of robotics. The use of automated delivery robots can eliminate the use of fuel-powered vehicles in resorts or massive hotel complexes. Robot systems that consume less energy use less electricity, which in turn lowers greenhouse gas emissions indirectly. Other hotels are also trying renewable-energy-powered robots, which also conform to eco-friendly actions.
V. **Sponsoring Green Certifications:** Most hotels now seek to achieve such certifications like LEED (Leadership in Energy and Environmental Design) or the Green Globe Certification. Hotels can utilize sustainable robotics, in-

cluding energy-efficient housekeeping bots, AI-based intelligent systems, and waste-cutting technologies, to help them get these certifications (Filimonau et al., 2025). This not only enhances their image, but also attracts eco-conscious tourists who like spending their time in properties that are environmentally friendly.

VI. **Long-Term Economic Sustainability:** Sustainability does not solely refer to the environment but also to long term financial sustainability. Although the initial cost of investing in robotics may be expensive, the end-result savings in labor, energy expenses and waste-elimination benefits make hotels economically sustainable in the long-term. Robotics provides a model of sustainability that can be beneficial to both hotels and society by combining financial efficiency with environmental responsibility (M. J. Kim et al., 2025). Robotics is also making hotels friendlier to the environment and more economically sustainable through energy efficiency, waste reduction, water conservation, minimized carbon footprint, and facilitating green certifications. Due to the growing popularity of eco-conscious decisions among travelers, sustainability in hospitality robotics will become even more important.

CASE STUDIES OF HOTELS USING ROBOTICS

I. Henn-na Hotel, Japan

- **Overview:** Known as the world's first robot-staffed hotel, opened in 2015 in Nagasaki.
- **Robotics Use:**
  - Humanoid robots at the reception for check-in and check-out.
  - Robotic arms for luggage storage.
  - In-room robot assistants for guest communication.
- **Impact:** Reduced labor costs, created a futuristic guest experience.
- **Challenge:** Some robots faced technical issues and could not handle complex guest needs, highlighting the limitation of over-reliance on automation

II. Marriott International (Various Locations)

- **Overview:** Marriott has experimented with robotics in several of its global properties.
- **Robotics Use:**
  - "Relay" robots used for room delivery (toiletries, food, beverages).

- Robots operate elevators autonomously to deliver items directly to guest rooms.
- **Impact:** Improved efficiency in room service and provided a contactless delivery option, especially useful during COVID-19.
- **Guest Feedback:** Guests found the novelty of being served by robots exciting and memorable.

III. Hilton Hotels – "Connie the Robot Concierge" (USA)

- **Overview:** Hilton partnered with IBM Watson to introduce "Connie," the world's first AI-powered concierge robot.
- **Robotics Use:**
  - Connie answers guest queries about local attractions, dining options, and hotel services.
  - Uses natural language processing and AI to interact in real-time.
- **Impact:** Enhanced guest engagement and provided personalized recommendations.
- **Significance:** Showed how AI integration can make robotic services more interactive and helpful.

FUTURE OUTLOOK AND RECOMMENDATIONS

Robotics in the hospitality sector is a relatively new phenomenon that is yet to be fully developed, but the effect of its integration is indisputable. Robotics will be at the heart of defining the future of hospitality as hotels strive to achieve the three components of the hospitality business: innovation, efficiency and guest satisfaction. The future of robotics is expected to become more rooted in artificial intelligence (AI), contactless services, and robotics oriented towards sustainability. Hotels, however, should also come up with strategic recommendations to be implemented.

I. **Greater Role of Artificial Intelligence:** AI will characterize the next stage of robotics in the hospitality industry. Robots will not be engaged in mechanical duties but they will be smart helpers with ability to forecast their guests needs, make suggestions and recommendations, and communicate in a natural manner in several languages. Robots that are powered by AI will help improve the overall guest experience by developing individual experiences.

II. **Expansion of Contactless and Touchless Technologies:** The need of hygiene and safety is high after the pandemic. Contactless systems like facial recognition check-ins, mobile apps-controlled services, and voice-controlled room technologies will become standard in combination with robotics. The technologies will make the hotel ambiance seamless, safe and modern.

III. **Hybrid Human–Robot Collaboration:** Robots are effective but they fail to provide the emotional warmth and empathy of human employees. A hybrid version in which robots are used to perform the more repetitive, routine tasks (cleaning, delivery, check-in) and human staff is left to work on the more personalized services and emotional attachment is likely to happen in the future. This balance will increase efficiency as well as guest satisfaction.

IV. **Sustainability and Green Robotics:** Hotels will use robotics more and more to support sustainability as eco-friendly practices become increasingly important. Smart cleaning systems that use less water, energy-efficient robots, and waste management based on AI will allow hotels to decrease their environmental footprint. Green robotics will also help hotels to obtain sustainability certifications and attract environmentally friendly travelers.

V. **Global Standardization and Scalability:** As technology improves, robotic solutions will also be cheaper and easier to scale, making them available to not only luxury but also mid-range and low-end hotels. This will make robotics in hospitality be widely accepted worldwide as shown in table 03.

Recommendations of the Study

Table 3. Comparison Table of Challenges, Recommendation and Expected benefits

Challenge	Recommendation	Expected Benefit
High cost of robotics implementation	Adopt robotics gradually in key areas (cleaning, delivery, check-in)	Reduced financial risk, smooth integration
Fear of job loss among staff	Provide training and upskilling programs; highlight robots as assistants	Improved employee morale, better human–robot collaboration
Lack of human touch in hospitality	Use a hybrid model: robots for routine tasks, humans for personalized services	Balanced guest experience with efficiency and empathy
Data privacy and cybersecurity risks	Invest in strong data protection systems and comply with regulations	Enhanced guest trust and protection of sensitive information
Guest hesitation in using robotics	Ensure user-friendly designs, clear instructions, and option for human assistance	Increased guest acceptance and satisfaction
Sustainability concerns in operations	Deploy energy-efficient, water-saving, and AI-enabled smart robots	Lower environmental impact and improved eco-friendly reputation

I. **Make Strategic Investments in Robotics:** Hotels are advised to implement robotics slowly, first in those sectors that bring immediate benefits like room service delivery or room cleaning.
II. **Balance Human and Robotic Services:** The management must not depend too much on machines. Rather, robots are to be used as the supplement to human employees. One on one guest relations, empathy, and emotional support should always be human based, with robots taking care of the repetitive jobs.
III. **Focus on Training and Employee Engagement:** The implementation of robotics may cause employees to develop the fear of unemployment. They are also supposed to be trained in the operation and supervision of robots through training programs conducted by hotels to upskill the employees. The workers must be convinced that robots are not a substitute; they are a helper.
IV. **Ensure Data Security and Privacy:** Cybersecurity has to be a priority as AI-driven robotics gathers guest data. Those hotels that are investing in effective data protection systems must abide by regulations regarding privacy to ensure that guests do not develop distrust towards them.
V. **Promote Guest Awareness and Acceptance:** Hotels should make sure that their guests are comfortable with robotic services. Gesture instructions, ease of use, and human assistance options should always exist to improve guest satisfaction. The next phase of hospitality robotics is the development of smart, touchless and environmentally friendly hotels that balance technology and human warmth. Through proper planning, investing, and guest-focused techniques, robotics can make hotels systems highly efficient and green, as well as innovative.

CONCLUSION

The current state of robots is no longer a futuristic dream; robots are already engaged in activities like automated check-in and check-out, luggage delivery, housekeeping, service, food, and beverage delivery, and even concierge. Robotics can do more than just increase guest satisfaction, reducing repetitive work and improving efficiency, the hotel can focus on personalized services, which are the core of hospitality. Moving forward, it is anticipated that robotics in hospitality will develop as artificial intelligence, machine learning, and the Internet of Things (IoT) continue to improve. Robots will tend to be more intelligent, adaptable, and able to carry out difficult tasks more effectively. Robots will be able to engage with guests more meaningfully and personalized using features such as natural language processing, facial recognition, and predictive analytics. Additionally, robots will keep gaining popularity as guest expectations of contactless, fast and seamless services increase, particularly in luxury and high-tech hotels aiming to stand out in the market with innovation. Another area where hospitality robotics has a massive potential is in sustainability. Robots are also programmable to maximize energy efficiency, minimize waste, and ensure environmental sustainability, which may include cleaning more efficiently, or tracking food intake to limit leftovers. Through automation, green initiatives can also be assisted through precision in monitoring and controlling the use of resources. Strategically incorporating robotics in hotels will not only provide them with an advantage over the competition, but will also lead the way in terms of innovation and environmental friendliness

REFERENCES

Alma Çallı, B., Çallı, L., Sarı Çallı, D., & Çallı, F. (2023). The impact of different types of service robots usage in hotels on guests' intention to stay. *Journal of Hospitality and Tourism Technology*, *14*(1), 53–68. DOI: 10.1108/JHTT-09-2021-0266

Bertino, E. (2016). Data Security and Privacy: Concepts, Approaches, and Research Directions. *2016 IEEE 40th Annual Computer Software and Applications Conference (COMPSAC)*, 400–407. https://doi.org/DOI: 10.1109/COMPSAC.2016.89

Brand, J. E. (2006). The effects of job displacement on job quality: Findings from the Wisconsin Longitudinal Study. *Research in Social Stratification and Mobility*, *24*(3), 275–298. DOI: 10.1016/j.rssm.2006.03.001

Buhalis, D., & Moldavska, I. (2022). Voice assistants in hospitality: Using artificial intelligence for customer service. *Journal of Hospitality and Tourism Technology*, *13*(3), 386–403. DOI: 10.1108/JHTT-03-2021-0104

Chen, S.-H., & Ahmed, F. (2024). The Transformative Power of AI and AR in Customer-Centric Services in the Tourism and Hospitality Sector: Looking Back to Predict the Future Outlook. In Ho, R. C., Song, B. L., & Tee, P. K. (Eds.), (pp. 105–138). Advances in Marketing, Customer Relationship Management, and E-Services. IGI Global., DOI: 10.4018/979-8-3693-5668-5.ch005

Choi, Y., Choi, M., & Oh, M. (Moon), & Kim, S. (Sam). (2020). Service robots in hotels: Understanding the service quality perceptions of human-robot interaction. *Journal of Hospitality Marketing & Management*, *29*(6), 613–635. DOI: 10.1080/19368623.2020.1703871

Chung, K. C., & Tan, P. J. B. (2025). Artificial intelligence and internet of things to improve smart hospitality services. *Internet of Things : Engineering Cyber Physical Human Systems*, *31*, 101544. DOI: 10.1016/j.iot.2025.101544

Dewangan, S., & Kumar, S. (2024). AI and Big Data Analytics Revolutionizing Industry 5.0: Unlocking the Power of Smart Manufacturing and Beyond. In Darwish, D. (Ed.), (pp. 398–410). Advances in Business Information Systems and Analytics. IGI Global., DOI: 10.4018/979-8-3693-0413-6.ch016

Fernandes, M. D., Wani, P. S., & Shah, G. D. (2024). The Integration of Artificial Intelligence in the Hospitality Industry. In Talukder, M. B., Kumar, S., & Tyagi, P. K. (Eds.), *Advances in Hospitality, Tourism, and the Services Industry* (pp. 525–550). IGI Global., DOI: 10.4018/979-8-3693-7898-4.ch025

Filimonau, V., Ashton, M., Derqui, B., & Hernandez-Maskivker, G. (2025). Exploring How Artificial Intelligence (AI) Can Enable Sustainability in the Hospitality Industry. *Sustainable Development*, sd.70146. https://doi.org/DOI: 10.1002/sd.70146

Garg, S., Srivastava, S. P., Malhotra, R. K., & Sharma, R. (2025). Sustainable Integration of Robotic Services in the Hospitality Industry: Enhancing Operational Efficiency and Employee Satisfaction. *2025 International Conference on Intelligent Control, Computing and Communications (IC3)*, 1377–1381. https://doi.org/DOI: 10.1109/IC363308.2025.10956363

Gaur, L., Afaq, A., Singh, G., & Dwivedi, Y. K. (2021). Role of artificial intelligence and robotics to foster the touchless travel during a pandemic: A review and research agenda. *International Journal of Contemporary Hospitality Management*, *33*(11), 4079–4098. DOI: 10.1108/IJCHM-11-2020-1246

Ivanov, S., Duglio, S., & Beltramo, R. (2023). Robots in tourism and Sustainable Development Goals: Tourism Agenda 2030 perspective article. *Tourism Review*, *78*(2), 352–360. DOI: 10.1108/TR-08-2022-0404

Ivanov, S., Seyitoğlu, F., & Markova, M. (2020). Hotel managers' perceptions towards the use of robots: A mixed-methods approach. *Information Technology & Tourism*, *22*(4), 505–535. DOI: 10.1007/s40558-020-00187-x

Ivanov, S., Seyitoğlu, F., & Webster, C. (2025). The economics of service robots in hospitality companies. *Tourism Economics*, *13548166251362622*. Advance online publication. DOI: 10.1177/13548166251362622

Ivanov, S., & Webster, C. (2019). Conceptual Framework of the Use of Robots, Artificial Intelligence and Service Automation in Travel, Tourism, and Hospitality Companies. In S. Ivanov & C. Webster (Eds.), *Robots, Artificial Intelligence, and Service Automation in Travel, Tourism and Hospitality* (pp. 7–37). Emerald Publishing Limited. https://doi.org/DOI: 10.1108/978-1-78756-687-320191001

Ivanov, S., & Webster, C. (2020). Robots in tourism: A research agenda for tourism economics. *Tourism Economics*, *26*(7), 1065–1085. DOI: 10.1177/1354816619879583

Kiliçhan, R., & Yilmaz, M. (2020). Artificial intelligence and robotic technologies in tourism and hospitality industry. *Erciyes Üniversitesi Sosyal Bilimler Enstitüsü Dergisi*, *50*, 353–380. DOI: 10.48070/erusosbilder.838193

Kim, M. J., Barnes, S. J., & Kang, S.-E. (2025). Embracing sustainable diversity climates in hospitality and tourism: Insights from prospective employees on human–robot collaboration. *Journal of Sustainable Tourism*, *33*(5), 801–821. DOI: 10.1080/09669582.2025.2459628

Kumar, S., Talukder, M. B., & Singh, K. (2025). Impact of Tourist Behavior Towards the Digital Technologies in Hospitality Sectors. In Birdir, K., & Birdir, S. (Eds.), (pp. 243–262). Advances in Computational Intelligence and Robotics. IGI Global., DOI: 10.4018/979-8-3693-8769-6.ch009

Li, J., Bonn, M. A., & Ye, B. H. (2019). Hotel employee's artificial intelligence and robotics awareness and its impact on turnover intention: The moderating roles of perceived organizational support and competitive psychological climate. *Tourism Management*, *73*, 172–181. DOI: 10.1016/j.tourman.2019.02.006

Liu, G. G., Benckendorff, P., & Walters, G. (2025). Human–Robot interaction research in hospitality and tourism: Trends and future directions. *Tourism Review*, *80*(4), 847–870. DOI: 10.1108/TR-04-2024-0266

Liu, J., Gu, T., & Liao, Z. (2024). Operation design of a robot logistics system considering demand fluctuations in the hotel industry. *International Journal of Contemporary Hospitality Management*, *36*(1), 113–135. DOI: 10.1108/IJCHM-08-2022-0968

McCartney, G., & McCartney, A. (2020). Rise of the machines: Towards a conceptual service-robot research framework for the hospitality and tourism industry. *International Journal of Contemporary Hospitality Management*, *32*(12), 3835–3851. DOI: 10.1108/IJCHM-05-2020-0450

Mingotto, E., Montaguti, F., & Tamma, M. (2021). Challenges in re-designing operations and jobs to embody AI and robotics in services. Findings from a case in the hospitality industry. *Electronic Markets*, *31*(3), 493–510. DOI: 10.1007/s12525-020-00439-y

Naeem Abass, M., Abd El-Fattah Zohry, M., & Gamal Saad Soliman, S. (2022). The Possibility of using Robot as one of the Artificial Intelligence Techniques in the Food and Beverage Department in Five-star Hotels: Managers' Perspective. *مجلة كلية السياحة والفنادق. جامعة المنصورة*, *11*(2), 857–907. https://doi.org/DOI: 10.21608/mkaf.2022.254018

Nam, K., Dutt, C. S., Chathoth, P., Daghfous, A., & Khan, M. S. (2021). The adoption of artificial intelligence and robotics in the hotel industry: Prospects and challenges. *Electronic Markets*, *31*(3), 553–574. DOI: 10.1007/s12525-020-00442-3

Putri, R. N. P., Situmorang, R., & Mehrotra, A. (2023). HUMAN vs. ROBOT: THE APPLICATION OF SMART TECHNOLOGY IN THE HOTEL INDUSTRY. *Jurnal Manajemen Dan Kewirausahaan*, *25*(2), 142–151. DOI: 10.9744/jmk.25.2.142-151

Rahman, N. A. A., Hassan, A., Ahmad, M. F., & Singh, R. K. S. (2023). Contactless Hospitality Technology in Post-COVID-19 Era: Future Research Clusters. In Hassan, A., & Rahman, N. A. A. (Eds.), *Technology Application in Aviation, Tourism and Hospitality* (pp. 179–188). Springer Nature Singapore., DOI: 10.1007/978-981-19-6619-4_13

Reis, J., Melão, N., Salvadorinho, J., Soares, B., & Rosete, A. (2020). Service robots in the hospitality industry: The case of Henn-na hotel, Japan. *Technology in Society*, *63*, 101423. DOI: 10.1016/j.techsoc.2020.101423

Rosete, A., Soares, B., Salvadorinho, J., Reis, J., & Amorim, M. (2020). Service Robots in the Hospitality Industry: An Exploratory Literature Review. In Nóvoa, H., Drăgoicea, M., & Kühl, N. (Eds.), *Exploring Service Science* (Vol. 377, pp. 174–186). Springer International Publishing., DOI: 10.1007/978-3-030-38724-2_13

Sapelnikova, N. (2025). Implementation of Robotisation and Application of Artificial Intelligence in the Hotel and Restaurant Business. *Restaurant and Hotel Consulting. Innovations*, *7*(2), 220–229. DOI: 10.31866/2616-7468.7.2.2024.335180

Sharma, R., & Kumar, S. (2025). Impact of Ethical Implications of Using AI and IoT in Hotels. In Mehra, P., Abioye, O., & Kumar, P. (Eds.), (pp. 375–392). Advances in Computational Intelligence and Robotics. IGI Global Scientific Publishing., DOI: 10.4018/979-8-3693-9611-7.ch014

Shukla, U. N., & Kulshreshtha, S. K. (2023). *Post-COVID Tourism and Hospitality Dynamics: Recovery, Revival, and Re-Start* (1st ed.). Apple Academic Press., DOI: 10.1201/9781003429722

Singh, B., & Kumar, S. (2025). Eco-Friendly Practices of Ghost Kitchens Through Smart Technology: Technological Innovations in the Food-Beverage Industry. In Singh, K., Kumar, S., & Talukder, M. B. (Eds.), (pp. 359–378). Advances in Computational Intelligence and Robotics. IGI Global., DOI: 10.4018/979-8-3373-0432-8.ch017

Singh, K., Kumar, S., & Talukder, M. B. (2024). Digital Transformation and Its Impact on Tourism Business in India. In Albattat, A., Azman, N., Valeri, M., & Singh, A. (Eds.), *Advances in Hospitality, Tourism, and the Services Industry* (pp. 215–230). IGI Global., DOI: 10.4018/979-8-3693-9636-0.ch010

Talukder, M. B., & Afchar, M. N. (2025). Vision Hotels: Shaping the Future of Hospitality Through Innovation, Sustainability, and Technology. In Parashar, A., Chandel, P. S., Seetaram, N., & Agarwal, P. (Eds.), *Global Practices and Innovations in Sustainable Homestay Tourism* (pp. 269–294). IGI Global., DOI: 10.4018/979-8-3373-0427-4.ch012

Talukder, M. B., Kumar, S., & Das Tonny, O. (2025). Innovative Solutions for Employee Well-Being in the Digital Hospitality Era. In Ahmad, B., Abrar, M., & Saeed, M. (Eds.), *Advances in Hospitality, Tourism, and the Services Industry* (pp. 231–258). IGI Global., DOI: 10.4018/979-8-3693-7127-5.ch009

Talukder, M. B., Kumar, S., Singh, K., & Bhardwaj, V. (2025). Sustainable Food and Beverage Practices With AI. In Singh, K., Kumar, S., & Talukder, M. B. (Eds.), (pp. 1–14). Advances in Computational Intelligence and Robotics. IGI Global., DOI: 10.4018/979-8-3373-0432-8.ch001

Talukder, M. B., & Mia, Md. N., Masum, Md. Y., Kabir, F., & Kumar, S. (2025). Encouraging Innovative and Responsible Tourism Through Digital Advancement. In P. Thaichon, P. K. Dutta, A. K. Haghi, & S. Dutta (Eds.), *Digital Disruption in Hospitality, Sustainable Hospitality* (pp. 145–165). Emerald Publishing Limited. https://doi.org/DOI: 10.1108/978-1-83662-360-120251007

Wang, L.-H., Ho, J.-L., Yeh, S.-S., & Huan, T.-C. (Tc). (2022). Is robot hotel a future trend? Exploring the incentives, barriers and customers' purchase intention for robot hotel stays. *Tourism Management Perspectives*, *43*, 100984. DOI: 10.1016/j.tmp.2022.100984

Xu, S., Stienmetz, J., & Ashton, M. (2020). How will service robots redefine leadership in hotel management? A Delphi approach. *International Journal of Contemporary Hospitality Management*, *32*(6), 2217–2237. DOI: 10.1108/IJCHM-05-2019-0505

Yang, L., Henthorne, T. L., & George, B. (2020). Artificial Intelligence and Robotics Technology in the Hospitality Industry: Current Applications and Future Trends. In B. George & J. Paul (Eds.), *Digital Transformation in Business and Society* (pp. 211–228). Springer International Publishing. https://doi.org/DOI: 10.1007/978-3-030-08277-2_13

Chapter 17
The Impact of Robotics in Modern Hotel Industry Operations:
A Critical Review of Five Star Hotels in India

Earnest Anand
http://orcid.org/0009-0006-4298-2323
Lovely Professional University, India

Sanjeev Kumar
http://orcid.org/0000-0002-7375-7341
Lovely Professional University, India

ABSTRACT

The research examines the long-term anti-differentiation of robotic services in the hotel sector, emphasizing their dual effects on employee happiness and operational excellence. Using concepts like the service-profit chain, the study looks at how robotic services could improve workflow, reduce labor costs, and promote sustainable management practices. This study aims to investigate and assess the current and potential effects of machine learning and artificial intelligence (AI) on the world economy. It involves looking at how AI is being used in various fields, how it affects industries, the patterns of leading businesses that are leveraging AI, and the concept of crystallizing exponential growth while striking a balance between human understanding and the potential of AI in the future. Additionally, they think that service businesses should strike a balance between the labor of humans and robots, with

DOI: 10.4018/979-8-3373-6741-5.ch017

workers providing warm, individualized services and technologies doing repetitive duties. To humanize services, they favor humanoid robots in human-touch service industries.

BACKGROUND OF THE STUDY

In recent years, robotics science and artificial intelligence (AI) have been influencing several industries and business types. The experimental and theoretical study of perceptual and intellectual processes using computers, as well as the ability to make a computer see, comprehend, and act in ways that are currently only conceivable for humans, is known as artificial intelligence (AI). Decades ago, manufacturing firms began using robots, a type of artificial intelligence that resembles humans, to process products in place of tedious human labor. The fast penetration of robotics into the service industry is transforming the establishment, distribution, and assessment of customer experience in the luxurious hotels. In India, the five-star market, where cost control, brand differentiation and customer service excellence must be balanced, robots and automation are currently seen in front-of-front reception and concierge activities, back-of-house housekeeping logistics, food-and-beverage production and delivery, security monitoring and back-of-office administration(Mukherjee et al., 2023).

Instead of robots seen as experimental, ranging through autonomous delivery units that navigate guest corridors to AI-enabled concierges, to robotic process automation (RPA) in reservations and revenue management, to cobots in support of kitchens and laundries, they have become a proven part of the toolkit. Rather, it more and more has become synonymous with strategic objectives: to take personalization to new levels, reduce service lead times, and achieve consistency of quality in an environment of varying demand. There are several drivers to quicken this change. The business case in favor of automation is further on the rise due to post-pandemic hygiene expectations, chronic shortages of skilled labor, and increasing costs of wages and administrative compliance. Meanwhile, India has its upscale travelers, used to on-demand digital service, and likely to want efficacious, contact-light dealings, without loss of warmth. The future of Robotics is high tech and high touch service delivery Robotics can enable staff to concentrate on emotive, imaginative, people-rich interactions whereas machines can continues to perform routine, time-critical, or risky interactions (Talukder et al., 2023). However, these advantages have cautions: The excessive front-end capital requirements, the difficulty to integrate with legacy systems of property-management, the cyber security and data-privacy concerns, and the need to redraw workflows, as well as the cultural acceptability concerns among the guests who value human hospitality. The environmental impact of robotics such as energy consumption, e-waste and lifecycle management as well, must be scrutinized as part of the sustainability commitments within the hotels (Samala et al., 2022). This critical review analyzes the empirical and conceptual evidence on robotics within the India five star hotels in assessing the performance reported results-service quality, customer satisfaction, operational efficiency, accuracy, safety and ROI versus organizational and human factors e.g. employee attitude, job redesign, training, and union considerations. It also compiles the results of multiple deployment settings front-of-house/back-of-house; mobile service robots, cobots, RPA, chatbots, computer vision and operating models in-house, vendor-managed, and hybrid (Lukanova & Ilieva, 2019). It is anticipated that the review, through the mapping of benefits bad risks and identification of gaps in methods and measures will illuminate what works, where, and why. Finally, the paper presents a research and managerial agenda: effective cost benefit models beyond headline ROI; service design of human robot interactions with luxury aspirations; interoperable technology stacks; governance of ethics, security, and data; and paths to workforce capability-building that changes how employees appear to higher-value work. Through this, it provides evidence-based recommendations to decision-makers to align robotics to five components, including brand promise, guest intimacy and sustainable competitive advantage (Bharwani & Mathews, 2021).

OBJECTIVES OF THE STUDY

1. To investigate the level and types of adoption of robotics in the Indian five-star hotels
2. To determine how robotic recycling affects the quality of services, efficiency of work, customer satisfaction and budget-friendliness
3. To evaluate the hurdles, constraints, and business aspects of assimilating robotics
4. To critically analyze and make strategic suggestions on successful and long-term implementation of robotics

GLOBAL APPLICATIONS OF ROBOTICS IN THE HOTEL INDUSTRY:

The hospitality sector has never been identified as other than its endeavor to service excellence, innovation and efficiency. The use of robotics was gaining pace in the last few years on the global front and the use of robotics has changed the way hotels perform their services, communicate, and operate the backend folds. Robotics has been adopted by detailing luxury brands to cost-effective hotels as a measure of reaching equilibrium between increased customer's demands, employee scarcity in the hospitality sector, and safe and contactless experiences, which particularly apply to the post-COVID period (Ivanov et al., 2020). This is used mostly in front-office and guest services. The introduction of humanoid robots in the hotels operating in Asia, Europe, and North America has facilitated the execution of functions of the concierge, checking in or checking out. To give an example of such an online hotel, the Henn-na hotel in Japan was the first hotel to have all staff completely robotized, including multilingual reception robots greeting and serving the guests (Kumar et al., 2024). Likewise, Hilton Hotels partnered with IBM and developed its own robot-style concierge, named "Connie"; the device, which relies on the input of artificial intelligence, can suggest recommendations as to which restaurants to visit in a given city, what attractions to visit, and what hotel services can be availed. These inventions are not the only efficiency enhancing factor since they also provide a memorable futuristic experience to the people traveling through them. One more major sphere is the housekeeping and room service. In the United States, hotels chains like Aloft Hotels have installed the services of robots working on delivery, like Bottler which drops toiletries, towels, or snacks at the guest door. Such robots are able to move through hallways and/or elevators at their own pace, reducing time spent waiting and the burden on the housekeeping staff. In China, service delivery robots have gained popularity especially in urban business hotels where they are doing repetitive tasks and ensuring a hygienic and contact-free contact (Talukder et al., 2024).

Robotics are also being applied on food and beverage operations. Automated bartenders and robotic cooks have now been adopted in hotels and resorts. As a means of example, the Yotel brand uses robotic arms to make cocktails, and a number of high-end resorts in Dubai and Singapore have experimented with robotic kitchen assistants to standardize cooking processes and enhance consistency, as well as ensure faster food delivery (Bowen & Morosan, 2018). Buffet style restaurant is also being reinvented with robots doing the serving, which makes sure it is hygienic and reduces food wastages. In addition to its uses in guests-facing operations, robotics is also becoming involved in back of house. Hotel management systems also apply the concept of robot process automation (RPA) to simplify processes associated with and related to reservation management, inventory management, and data-related tasks (Manoharan et al., 2024). There are also robots in the laundry and logistics that have been used up to wash and fold large-scale clothing and make it easier to distribute linens. The applications bring cost-cutting opportunities to hotels and enhance accuracy levels and also enable employees to spend their time on high-value activities where they have to be creative and have emotional quotient. There are also initiatives being made concerning the use of robotics by hotels around the world in terms of health, safety, and sustainability (Tuomi et al., 2021). This is the reason why, there are numerous hotels in Europe and Asia, which have used UV-light sanitizing robots during the pandemic as they clean rooms and sanitize public areas and cut-down the use of chemical cleaning products. Likewise, sensors on robots utilize energy optimization wherein they keep track of temperature, lighting and water. In spite of these breakthroughs, there are challenges associated with the global implementation of robotics in a hotel. Costs of installations are high, there is maintenance overhead, difficulty with integrating it with legacy systems, and the cultural appeal to guests (Das et al., 2024). As prices continue to be lowered and improved with artificial intelligence, robotics will grow to become more common and will work in conjunction with human personnel as opposed to replacing them.

ROBOTICS IN HOTEL OPERATIONS AND GUEST RELATIONS AND CONCIERGE SERVICE

Hotel industry has never lagged when it comes to innovations that improve the way the industries handled their guests as well as improved operations. Robotic technology has become an influential technology, especially in hotel management, guest relation, and concierge services in the recent years. As competition has become more and more international and the expectations of the guests more challenging, robots are becoming more predominant as a device to enhance the workflow, minimize cost and provide associated reminiscent and technology-assisted hospitality (Chen et al., 2023). Robotics is essential in front-of-house and back-of-house operations in a hotel. Front-office operational roles involve the use of robots in the check-in and check-out procedures where they either take the guest throughout the digital kiosk or independently registering the guest. As an example, there are a number of hotels in Japan and Singapore that have humanoid robots, and these can scan identification documents, provide directions and key cards to rooms. This is not only waiver of time but also, it increases accuracy and efficiency in processing big load of arrivals and departures. Robotics is also very useful in back-of-house functions (Shin & Jeong, 2020). The tasks that services robots perform are waste-fulfilling as well as labor-intensive, which include deliveries on behalf of the rooms, laundry services and luggage handling. Chains have adopted robots like the Savioke (Relay) to deliver amenities and food directly to the guest rooms. Robotic vacuum cleaners and floor scrubbers are incorporated into housekeeping to ensure lobbies, corridors and common places are clean and relieve the physical stress on workers. Likewise, robotic processes are used in laundry units to automate the separation, washing, folding, and transporting of linens and guarantee quality and cost reductions in the operations (Sharma et al., 2024). Hospitality industry is powered by guest relations, and use of robotics is increasingly emerging in treating relations to boost relations with guests. Robots in the form of humanoids with natural language use abilities will be able to greet guests in the lobby, give details of the hotel and even check guests in or out. The multiple-language capability of the robots makes them extra handy in international hotels since such settings are characterized by diversity in terms of culture and language. Robots could be used to scan their passport, provide them with room keycard, accept payments, etc., which will decrease the line time and make the check-in process effortless as shown in the table 01 (Etemad-Sajadi & Sturman, 2022).

Table 1. Robotics in Hotel Operations, Guest Relations, and Concierge Services:

Area	Role of Robotics	Benefits
Hotel Operations	Automated cleaning, room delivery, and maintenance tasks	Faster operations, reduced labor cost, higher efficiency
Guest Relations	Robot assistants for greetings, check-in, and information	Improved guest experience, 24/7 support
Concierge Services	Providing directions, bookings, and local recommendations	Quick responses, personalized service, time-saving

Furthermore, robots will be able to offer simple information about the facilities, policies, or events of the hotel; accordingly, human personnel will be able to address more complicated or customized requests of the customers. Hotels can equally combine robotics and data analytics to ensure that the robots deliver customized guidance to the guests, depending on their preferences to also improve satisfaction and loyalty. One of the areas of hospitality that is as highly personalized as possible is concierge, which typically requires human capabilities, empathy, and skillful attention to detail. Nevertheless, robotics has widened the concierge-service possibilities through direct, immediate 24/7 access to information and support. Robot concierges that usually include hotel reception or that can be used via mobile applications help the guests to navigate between different places and venues, make restaurant/ transportation reservations, or recommend local sights. These robots are provided with big databases and can update information in ACT, promising their accuracy and actuality (Carroll & Murphy, 2024). Others have robotic kiosk ins or anthropomorphic robots that do not speak but only robotically talk to the guest to provide weather information, entertainment and or event list at a given time. The combination of robotics with artificial intelligence leads to the development of a more interactive, efficient, and customizable concierge that reacts to different types of customer needs, especially when it comes to the needs of travelers who need immediate support as soon as it becomes available, rather than wait for the availability of human personnel (Choi et al., 2020).

CURRENT ADOPTION LEVELS OF ROBOTICS IN FIVE STAR HOTELS IN INDIA

Unlike other hospitality technology trends in India, guest-facing robots be it concierge carts and autonomous foot-solders that ride elevators to deliver essentials are still at infancy, pilot-heavy phase in country's upper-end hotels. The clearest recent example from a large Indian hospitality company is IHCL's trial of a "robot concierge" able to do room deliveries and basic information at its Ginger Mumbai Airport hotel. Ginger, IHCL's lean-luxury brand and not a five-star upper-tier brand, is reviewed in this trial, however reflects curiosity, group-wise in service robotics that could be upscale elsewhere if respective ROI and guest feedback warrants (Mukherjee et al., 2021).

1. **Cleaning/maintenance of public space**: Present-day examples are encompassed in autonomous scrubbers and pool robots that complete routine activities done late-night or before the opening period; hoteliers demur to increased deadlines and manual contact. ITC Kohenur (Hyderabad) openly cited the practice of adopting robots on the floor cleaning; the management in Taj Hyderabad area has also mentioned about the use of robotic machines on pools and marble polishing.
2. **Pilots of limited service delivery:** Some Indian hotels tested delivery robots that interface with elevators (things common in the world). In India, the most well-known named pilot to a large group is IHCL at Ginger; on the luxury side, these robots are being used patchily, often only during high occupancy or labour-force shortages, and they are slowly rolled out under the physical barrier of elevators, security considerations and brand suitability questions
3. **Risk averse guest-oriented jobs (concierge/info):** In the academic and industry literature, there is increased acceptance of hotel robots after the pandemic, yet the question of whether a hotel should adopt in India at the luxury end of the spectrum pits the perceived demands of a guest of personalized service against novelty and affordability. One study on service-robot acceptance and customer experience highlights that usability, perceived value, and context (front desk vs. room service) are strongly linked to satisfaction- inducing factors that five-star brands are particularly careful about in their action plans (Gupta et al., 2022).

So why has adoption not galloped forward. Firstly, positioning the brand- Indian luxury hotels have positioned themselves on the end of human hospitality, crafted service; robots are introduced to complement, not substitute, that value claim. Second, integration friction: connecting robots to lifts, door locks, PMS stacks, is not trivial, and is particularly onerous in older/heritage buildings (Singh et al., 2023).

Third, economics & reliability-rate of capital expenditure, ongoing maintenance and uptime have to outperform well trained staff in a high-touch environment.

IMPACT ON SERVICE QUALITY AND GUEST EXPERIENCE ROBOTICS IN MODERN HOTEL INDUSTRY OPERATIONS

As an industry, hospitality has always led in the field of embracing the new technology to promote service delivery and customer satisfaction. Over the past years, robotics has become a revolutionary tool, changing the ways in which hotels conduct their services and communicate with guests. The introduction of robotics into the contemporary operations of hotels and restaurants has presented a dual context of opportunities and challenges to service excellence and customer satisfaction through, amongst others, front desk robots that perform hotel check-ins and robotic concierges that make personalized recommendations (Naumov, 2019). Efficiency and consistency are among the most important effects of robotics on the quality of the service that they provide. Motion: Robots are capable of doing tedious jobs like the delivery of room services, transportation of luggage and provision of housekeeping services without commuting to exhaustion. Robots, unlike the human employee, have no emotional or physical restrictions and, therefore, a standard and consistent service is guaranteed (Chiang & Trimi, 2020). As an illustration, a robotic room service assistant will bring the food or amenity at a faster-than-average rate, posing less chance of a guest waiting and therefore streamlining the customer experience. Such consistency brings about enhanced reliability in service, which is a determinant of the perception of service quality in hospitality as mentioned in the table 02.

Table 2. Impact of Robotics on Service Quality and Guest Experience in Modern Hotel Industry Operation

Aspect	Impact on Service Quality	Impact on Guest Experience
Speed of Service	Faster service delivery and response time	Reduced waiting time, greater convenience
Accuracy	Fewer human errors in tasks and orders	More reliable and consistent service
Availability	24/7 operational support	Guests receive help anytime
Personalization	Data-based service customization	More personalized and comfortable stay
Hygiene & Safety	Improved cleanliness and contactless service	Increased feeling of safety and trust
Consistency	Uniform service standards	Predictable and high-quality experience

The other important role that robotics plays is enhancing the convenience and personalization of the guests. Other hotels use AI-enabled robots concierge that can speak various languages, make recommendations about dining or entertainment activities, and help make reservations. These robotic concierges also improve the experience of the guest, which is made possible due to the 24-hour availability and instant answers when needed. In addition, robotic systems can also be combined with guest data analytics: accordingly, individual preferences can be offered to the guest in terms of the hotel recommendations and the services they can use, thereby enhancing the personalization of guest stays (Yörük et al., 2024). Robots also improve hygiene and safety, which also became a priority in the post-pandemic time. Self-service robots or kiosk check in, robotic disinfection of common rooms, and contactless delivery services reduce physical contact and helps to inspire confidence in the guest about safety and health. That would add to a safer, less-stressful environment and increases overall guest satisfaction and brand trust.

CHALLENGES AND BARRIERS IN THE ADOPTION OF ROBOTICS

Robotics in the hotel industry has been touted as an avenue into better staff efficiency, better service and out-of-the-box customer experience. Nevertheless, even with the benefits mentioned, there are numerous challenges and obstacles to overcome in the case of most hotels implementing robotic technology. These burdens arise out of financial, technical, operating and cultural elements that render implementation to be complex and in certain instances unsustainable. Becoming knowledgeable on these barriers is of importance to hospitality companies so that they make informed decisions when it comes to considering investments on technology. Among the most urgent problems is high investment cost. Robots are also high capital costs in terms of purchase, installation and connection with the current systems in the hotels. Other than the initial cost, maintenance cost, software upgrades and repair costs are also extra costs incurred, thus increasing the financial burden (Oke et al., 2024). These investments might not be so daunting in case of luxury five star hotels but in a case of mid-range or budget hotels, the costs can run into prohibitions.

The investment will not pay off instantly, which will make hoteliers reluctant to implement the use of robotics on a large scale. Complexity of technology and integration is another obstruction. Robotics systems should also be smooth in their interface with property management systems (PMS), customer relationship management (CRM) systems, among other digital platforms. Failure to merge productively has the potential to cause havoc in the operation as well as invest friendliness (Ilesanmi et al., 2025). In addition, technical issues, system crashing, or coding bugs may displease the guests. Constant inspection, a high level of technical knowledge and established IT functioning is necessary to guarantee trouble-free operation, something not all hotels can afford. The impossibility to implement the human touch is another significant problem of the introduction of robotics in the hospitality sphere. The core of the sector is the personal, caring communication, industry, and sensitivity based on culture comprehension. Although robots are highly efficient and consistent, they do not have emotional intelligence and the flexibility to address the needs of the guests. The robots are likely to replace traditional staff which will make guests, who expect to have truly human interaction, dissatisfied or alienated, posing the obstacle to acceptance. Finding the right proportion between the automation and the use of human services is always precarious. The adoption is also prevented by employee reluctance and job insecurity (Doarn & Moses, 2011). Most hotel employees see robotics as a threat to their existing job opportunities and hence, they either oppose or fail to cooperate with efforts to integrate new systems. Social and ethical implications would be of great concern in labor-intensive nations where hospitality sector is a core actor of employment, in case of large-scale automation things may not be the same (Kumar, 2024a). Hotel management should very cautiously handle this transition by retraining, up skilling and positioning the robotics as something that will complement rather than replace the human staff. Along with this is the factor of guest acceptance which is also a barrier presenting a barrier is the factor of guest acceptance Guest acceptance is a barrier However, although younger and more tech-savvy guests might share a very positive image of robotics and can fall in love with this technology, older or more traditional customers might feel confused or even intimidated by the innovation and could find it impersonal. Other aspects that come into play are cultural differences; there tends to be resistance to adopt robotics in societies that have high regard on interpersonal hospitality. Hotels put their reputation and customer loyalty at risk of not seeing robotic service as an addition to the quality of the service but as a drop in it (Kumar, 2024b).

EMERGING TRENDS IN SERVICE ROBOTICS OPPORTUNITIES FOR PERSONALIZED GUEST EXPERIENCES

Hospitality industry is at the stages of technological transformation and service robots are also increasingly used to transform the way hospitality industry treats its guests. Because passengers seek more convenience, customization, and innovation, hotels are venturing into robotics, not just as a lever toward efficiency but also as an enabler of the ability to provide customized services to individual guests (Gangwar & Reddy, 2023). The new developments of service robotics have shown promising signs of how to provide exclusive and customer-made experiences that a combination of automation and personalization allow. Among the trends, increased usage of concierge robots powered by artificial intelligence is one of them. Such robots, in many cases natural language processing and machine learning enabled, are able to communicate with guests in different languages, suggest services according to their preferences, and help to solve issues with contracts. Using the history of the guest and behavioral data, it is possible that they can make personal suggestions on dining, sight sight or entertainment. This makes the guest experience more self explanatory and there is increased fit between the recommendations and individual preferences, this improves satisfaction. The other trend is the use of robotic room service and delivery systems (Yang et al., 2020). More hotels are introducing service robots that can bring the meals, beverages, toiletries or other services within rooms. The innovativeness of this trend lies in its prospect of personalization: robots are able to know who comes to visit, what was ordered last time, and even provide them with custom choices, according to diet types or preferences they had in the past. It does not only make the operations more efficient, but it also assures a personal experience that addresses unique desires. The other emerging opportunity is represented through smart housekeeping robots. The robots that have sensors, artificial intelligence, and automation will be capable of cleaning rooms, restocking supplies, and tracking maintenance problems. Housekeeping robots, when connected to profile accounts of the guests, can modify room regulation, lighting, temperature, or the fragrant atmosphere of the room based on the individual preferences registered in the previous stays. This lends its own comfort and gives a sense of familiarity/exclusivity to repeat customers (Talukder, Swarna, et al., 2025).

IMPLICATIONS FOR HOTEL MANAGERS AND STAKEHOLDERS

Introduction of robotics in the new hotel operations changes everything in how hospitality services are conducted and operated. Although there exist prospects of efficiency, individualization, and innovativeness when adopting robotics, there are considerable ramifications to be borne by the hotel managers and stakeholders in dealing with operational, financial, and human resource issues. Knowing such implications would be critical once the decision-maker understands how to maximize the benefit of robotics and minimize risks. Strategic investment and financial planning would be one of the immediate implications that can be described as a requirement among the hotel managers. There is huge capital spending when procuring, installing, and integrating robotics technologies with the current hotel technologies. Managers should balance the cost and the supposed advantage like efficient work, lesser labor expenditure and customer satisfaction. To the stakeholders, the return on investment (ROI) is the key since robotics can bring in the long term benefits but sometimes carry a high initial cost. This requires close budgeting, staged implementing, and seeking joint venture with a technology provider to reduce the risks (Talukder, Das, et al., 2025). The other implication is the change in the management and human resource policies of the workforce. Robotics has the ability of automating routine work; however, this might cause some anxiety among employees in terms of their loss of employment. Managers should overcome this obstacle by communicating with the staff openly and proposing re-skilling programs and redeployment to jobs that focus on human interaction, creative thinking, and empathy where a machine such as a robot cannot replace the human. In the case of stakeholders, this transition amounts to emphasizing the balancing of social responsibility and technology innovation, where the implementation of robotics does not impose any reputational risks of job displacement. Another challenge of the hotel managers is to adjust the operation strategy and processes. To implement robotics, one will majorly have to redesign the conventional operations, including check-in, room services, and housekeeping.

Managers should strive to coordinate the robotic systems and human employees flawlessly to prevent the gaps in service. In its turn, stakeholders should take long-term impacts of hotel competencies into account: those hotels that manage to introduce robotics can gain advantage in terms of differentiation on the market, and the inability to manage rapid changes can be a threat to stay behind those technologically progressive companies. Robotics both offer new possibilities and establish potential problems that managers will have to negotiate with a keen eye. Though the use of robots entails increasing convenience, personalization, and safety of hotels, they are highly likely to be perceived by some guests as impersonal and intimidating. Managers of hotels will be forced to have a hybrid service model wherein efficiency-oriented tasks are done by robots, and empathy-oriented relations are left to human workers. Stakeholders should make sure that their guest satisfaction rates remain high since negative attitudes towards the idea of robotic service may affect the brand loyalty. Another deadly implication is on data management and cyber-security. Robotics usually use artificial intelligence, machine learning, and cloud-based systems to collect and analyze the data on people and offer them customized services. To safeguard the trust of the guests, managers are obliged to have severe data protection and adherence to the privacy regulations. The investors and the owners of the brands must understand that even the smallest moment of a violation of the security of the guest information may cause a loss of their financial assets and the establishment of a bad reputation in the long-term. Last, implementing robotics is associated with long-term sustainability and innovation strategy. Hotel managers should consistently review cutting-edge technologies and determine how they can apply them to operations to maintain robotics investments on par with the changes in guest needs and hospitality trends. The stakeholders will have to create a culture of innovation, which should promote experimentation without jeopardizing the financial aspect and ethics.

CONCLUSION

The use of robotics in the operations of the modern hotel industry has become an important paradigm towards the service delivery system employed by five star hotels in India, its management, and subsequent heightening of the contentment of the guests. Such a critical review points out that robotics is not exactly a far future reality anymore but social reality as it currently enacts the very essence of luxury hospitality. Whether its service robots in front office operations; robotic concierges and housekeeping aids, robotic check-in kiosk and more, the latest use of technology has transformed convenience and efficiency in the guest experience. The value of robotics is the way it ensures seamless, contactless, and standardized services, especially against the background of new hygienic requirements after the pandemic of the COVID-19 phenomenon. In the case of five-star hotels located within India, robotics has not only enhanced the quality of their services but also increased efficiency in their operations by eliminating the chance of manual error which was repetitive in nature. This has enabled hotel employees to no longer need to concentrate on transactional interaction but more on the personal level when interacting with the guest hence creating balance between the technological efficiency and the human touch. Further, robotics has played a vital role in transforming the competitive advantage by providing exclusive experiences to tech-savvy travelers and foreign tourists who are open to modernity and innovation concerning hospitality experience. Conclusively, robotics in Indian five star hotels is a hurdle and opportunity simultaneously. It is not a technological update alone but also a strategic shift that will necessitate vision as well as investment and much needed cultural adjustment. Provided that we tap its potential, robotics will enable luxury hospitality to become more progressive, robust, and customer-centric with the fusion of contemporary technologies and ancient traditions.

REFERENCES

Bharwani, S., & Mathews, D. (2021). Techno-business strategies for enhancing guest experience in luxury hotels: A managerial perspective. *Worldwide Hospitality and Tourism Themes, 13*(2), 168–185. DOI: 10.1108/WHATT-09-2020-0121

Bowen, J., & Morosan, C. (2018). Beware hospitality industry: The robots are coming. *Worldwide Hospitality and Tourism Themes, 10*(6), 726–733. DOI: 10.1108/WHATT-07-2018-0045

Carroll, E., & Murphy, C. (2024). Enhancing Event Reputations: Insights and Recommendations for Secure and Engaging Experiences. *ICHRIE Research Reports, 9*(5). Advance online publication. DOI: 10.61701/311750.093

Chen, M., Wang, X., Law, R., & Zhang, M. (2023). Research on the Frontier and Prospect of Service Robots in the Tourism and Hospitality Industry Based on International Core Journals: A Review. *Behavioral Sciences (Basel, Switzerland), 13*(7), 560. DOI: 10.3390/bs13070560 PMID: 37504007

Chiang, A.-H., & Trimi, S. (2020). Impacts of service robots on service quality. *Service Business, 14*(3), 439–459. DOI: 10.1007/s11628-020-00423-8

Choi, Y., Choi, M., & Oh, M. (Moon), & Kim, S. (Sam). (2020). Service robots in hotels: Understanding the service quality perceptions of human-robot interaction. *Journal of Hospitality Marketing & Management, 29*(6), 613–635. DOI: 10.1080/19368623.2020.1703871

Das, I. R., Talukder, M. B., & Kumar, S. (2024). Implication of Artificial Intelligence in Hospitality Marketing. In Kumar, S., Talukder, M. B., & Pego, A. (Eds.), *Advances in Hospitality, Tourism, and the Services Industry* (pp. 291–310). IGI Global., DOI: 10.4018/979-8-3693-1978-9.ch014

Doarn, C. R., & Moses, G. R. (2011). Overcoming Barriers to Wider Adoption of Mobile Telerobotic Surgery: Engineering, Clinical and Business Challenges. In Rosen, J., Hannaford, B., & Satava, R. M. (Eds.), *Surgical Robotics* (pp. 69–102). Springer US., DOI: 10.1007/978-1-4419-1126-1_4

Etemad-Sajadi, R., & Sturman, M. C. (2022). How to Increase the Customer Experience by the Usage of Remote Control Robot Concierge Solutions. *International Journal of Social Robotics, 14*(2), 429–440. DOI: 10.1007/s12369-021-00800-x

Gangwar, V. P., & Reddy, D. (2023). Hospitality Industry 5.0: Emerging Trends in Guest Perception and Experiences. In Dadwal, S., Kumar, P., Verma, R., & Singh, G. (Eds.), (pp. 185–211). Advances in Business Strategy and Competitive Advantage. IGI Global., DOI: 10.4018/978-1-6684-6403-8.ch010

Gupta, S., Modgil, S., Lee, C.-K., Cho, M., & Park, Y. (2022). Artificial intelligence enabled robots for stay experience in the hospitality industry in a smart city. *Industrial Management & Data Systems, 122*(10), 2331–2350. DOI: 10.1108/IMDS-10-2021-0621

Ilesanmi, O. O., Oke, A. E., Moyanga, D. T., Aliu, J., & Aigbavboa, C. (2025). Key Barriers to the Extensive Adoption of Robotics in the Nigerian Built Environment. In Azrour, M., Hossain, I., & Haque, A. K. M. M. (Eds.), (pp. 197–224). Advances in Computational Intelligence and Robotics. IGI Global., DOI: 10.4018/979-8-3373-1892-9.ch008

Ivanov, S., Webster, C., & Berezina, K. (2020). Robotics in Tourism and Hospitality. In Z. Xiang, M. Fuchs, U. Gretzel, & W. Höpken (Eds.), *Handbook of e-Tourism* (pp. 1–27). Springer International Publishing. https://doi.org/DOI: 10.1007/978-3-030-05324-6_112-1

Kumar, S. (2024a). The Role of Digital Marketing on Customer Engagement in the Hospitality Industry. In *Leveraging ChatGPT and Artificial Intelligence for Effective Customer Engagement* (pp. 177–191). IGI Global Scientific Publishing.

Kumar, S. (2024b). Uncertainties in the Hospitality Sector. In *VUCA and Other Analytics in Business Resilience, Part B* (pp. 183–197). Emerald Publishing Limited.

Kumar, S., Talukder, M. B., & Kaiser, F. (2024). Artificial Intelligence in Business: Negative Social Impacts. In Dadwal, S., Goyal, S., Kumar, P., & Verma, R. (Eds.), (pp. 81–97). Advances in Human Resources Management and Organizational Development. IGI Global., DOI: 10.4018/979-8-3693-0724-3.ch005

Lukanova, G., & Ilieva, G. (2019). Robots, Artificial Intelligence, and Service Automation in Hotels. In S. Ivanov & C. Webster (Eds.), *Robots, Artificial Intelligence, and Service Automation in Travel, Tourism and Hospitality* (pp. 157–183). Emerald Publishing Limited. https://doi.org/DOI: 10.1108/978-1-78756-687-320191009

Manoharan, G., Rao, C. V. G., Ashtikar, S. P., Kumar, S., & Nivedha, M. (2024). Voyage Virtuoso: Artificial Intelligence in Transforming Tourism. In Kumar, S., Talukder, M. B., & Pego, A. (Eds.), *Advances in Hospitality, Tourism, and the Services Industry* (pp. 79–97). IGI Global., DOI: 10.4018/979-8-3693-1978-9.ch004

Mukherjee, S., Baral, M. M., Nagariya, R., Venkataiah, C., Rao, U. V. A., & Rao, K. S. (2023). Systematic literature review and future research directions for service robots in hospitality and tourism industries. *Service Industries Journal, 43*(15–16), 1083–1116. DOI: 10.1080/02642069.2023.2243592

Mukherjee, S., Baral, M. M., Venkataiah, C., Pal, S. K., & Nagariya, R. (2021). Service robots are an option for contactless services due to the COVID-19 pandemic in the hotels. *Decision (Washington, D.C.), 48*(4), 445–460. DOI: 10.1007/s40622-021-00300-x

Naumov, N. (2019). The Impact of Robots, Artificial Intelligence, and Service Automation on Service Quality and Service Experience in Hospitality. In S. Ivanov & C. Webster (Eds.), *Robots, Artificial Intelligence, and Service Automation in Travel, Tourism and Hospitality* (pp. 123–133). Emerald Publishing Limited. https://doi.org/DOI: 10.1108/978-1-78756-687-320191007

Oke, A. E., Aliu, J., Fadamiro, P., Jamir Singh, P. S., Samsurijan, M. S., & Yahaya, M. (2024). Robotics and automation for sustainable construction: Microscoping the barriers to implementation. *Smart and Sustainable Built Environment, 13*(3), 625–643. DOI: 10.1108/SASBE-12-2022-0275

Samala, N., Katkam, B. S., Bellamkonda, R. S., & Rodriguez, R. V. (2022). Impact of AI and robotics in the tourism sector: A critical insight. *Journal of Tourism Futures, 8*(1), 73–87. DOI: 10.1108/JTF-07-2019-0065

Sharma, M., Tyagi, P. K., Semwal, R., Tyagi, P., Singh, V. J., & Kumari, N. (2024). Robotic Concierges and Smart Spaces: A Vision for the Future of Hospitality Services. In M. Sharma, A. K. Singh, & P. Tyagi (Eds.), *Proceedings of the International Conference on Innovation and Regenerative Trends in Tourism and Hospitality Industry (IRTTHI 2024)* (Vol. 285, pp. 511–525). Atlantis Press International BV. https://doi.org/DOI: 10.2991/978-94-6463-437-2_34

Shin, H. H., & Jeong, M. (2020). Guests' perceptions of robot concierge and their adoption intentions. *International Journal of Contemporary Hospitality Management, 32*(8), 2613–2633. DOI: 10.1108/IJCHM-09-2019-0798

Singh, G., Raheja, S., & Sharma, R. (2023). Elevating Hospitality with Smart Hotel Technologies: A Guest – Centric Perspective. *2023 IEEE Engineering Informatics*, 1–9. https://doi.org/DOI: 10.1109/IEEECONF58110.2023.10520539

Talukder, M. B., Das, I. R., & Kumar, S. (2025). From Digital Production to Digital Society in Hospitality: Industry 5.0 Perspectives. In Grima, S., Kaleli, S. S., Baygin, M., & Boztepe, E. (Eds.), *Business Challenges and Opportunities in the Era of Industry 5.0* (pp. 173–193). Emerald Publishing Limited., DOI: 10.1108/978-1-83549-676-320251010

Talukder, M. B., Kumar, S., Kaiser, F., & Mia, Md. N. (2024). Pilgrimage Creative Tourism: A Gateway to Sustainable Development Goals in Bangladesh. In M. Hamdan, M. Anshari, N. Ahmad, & E. Ali (Eds.), *Advances in Public Policy and Administration* (pp. 285–300). IGI Global. https://doi.org/DOI: 10.4018/979-8-3693-1742-6.ch016

Talukder, M. B., Kumar, S., Sood, K., & Grima, S. (2023). Information Technology, Food Service Quality and Restaurant Revisit Intention. *International Journal of Sustainable Development and Planning*, *18*(1), 295–303. DOI: 10.18280/ijsdp.180131

Talukder, M. B., Swarna, D. A., Kumar, S., & Kabir, F. (2025). Leveraging Technology for Employee Wellness in Hospitality: Smart Solutions for a Vibrant Service Culture. In Baez, M. D. (Ed.), (pp. 221–246). Advances in Logistics, Operations, and Management Science. IGI Global., DOI: 10.4018/979-8-3373-1687-1.ch008

Tuomi, A., Tussyadiah, I. P., & Stienmetz, J. (2021). Applications and Implications of Service Robots in Hospitality. *Cornell Hospitality Quarterly*, *62*(2), 232–247. DOI: 10.1177/1938965520923961

Yang, L., Henthorne, T. L., & George, B. (2020). Artificial Intelligence and Robotics Technology in the Hospitality Industry: Current Applications and Future Trends. In B. George & J. Paul (Eds.), *Digital Transformation in Business and Society* (pp. 211–228). Springer International Publishing. https://doi.org/DOI: 10.1007/978-3-030-08277-2_13

Yörük, T., Akar, N., & Özmen, N. V. (2024). Research trends on guest experience with service robots in the hospitality industry: A bibliometric analysis. *European Journal of Innovation Management*, *27*(6), 2015–2041. DOI: 10.1108/EJIM-09-2022-0530

Compilation of References

A, P., Arunprakash, A., Kulothungan, V., & Radha, P. (2025). The Role of Artificial Intelligence in Revolutionizing Customer-Centric Marketing Strategies: A Data-Driven Approach. *NPRC Journal of Multidisciplinary Research, 2*(1), 163–175. https://doi.org/DOI: 10.3126/nprcjmr.v2i1.74691

Aaker, D. A. (1996). *Building strong brands*. Free Press.

Abakouy, R., En-naimi, E. M., Haddadi, A. E., & Lotfi, E. (2019). Data-driven marketing: How machine learning will improve decision-making for marketers. *Proceedings of the 4th International Conference on Smart City Applications*, 1–5. https://doi.org/DOI: 10.1145/3368756.3369024

Abraham, S., & Krishnan, T. A. (2021). The Role of Technology In Reshaping Guest Experiences At Indian Hotels Post-Covid 19. [JTSM]. *Journal of Tourism & Sports Management, 4*(1), 692–702.

Abrol, D. (2017). Evaluating the Influence of Dynamic Capabilities on Firms' Performance: Role of Innovative Sustainability and Adaptation to Change. *Amity Journal of Management Research, 2*(2), 1–12. https://amity.edu/UserFiles/admaa/492fcPaper 1.pdf

Adeyinka-Ojo, S., Lee, S., Abdullah, S. K., & Teo, J. (2020). Hospitality and tourism education in an emerging digital economy. *Worldwide Hospitality and Tourism Themes, 12*(2), 113–125.

Afif, F., & Susanto, P. (2025). Blockchain for Marketing Transparency and Trust: Applications in Supply Chain and Customer Loyalty Programs. *Journal of Indonesian Management, 5*(2), 10. DOI: 10.53697/jim.v5i2.2422

Aggarwal, A., Baker, H. K., & Joshi, N. A. (2024). Organizational Innovation as Business Strategy: A Review and Bibliometric Analysis. *Journal of the Knowledge Economy, 16*(2), 6550–6576. DOI: 10.1007/s13132-024-01830-2

Aghaei, R., Kiaei, A. A., Boush, M., Vahidi, J., Zavvar, M., Barzegar, Z., & Rofoosheh, M. (n.d.). *Harnessing the Potential of Large Language Models in Modern Marketing Management: Applications*. Future Directions, and Strategic Recommendations.

Ahmad, N., & Rasheed, H. M. W. (2025). Tourism and hospitality SMEs and digital marketing: What factors influence their attitude and intention to use from the perspective of BRT, TAM and IRT. *Journal of Hospitality and Tourism Insights*, *8*(4), 1546–1563. DOI: 10.1108/JHTI-05-2024-0508

Ahmed, F., Kabir, M. A., & Ahmed, M. D. (2025). The Impact of Short Video Content and Social Media Influencers on Digital Marketing Success: A Systematic Literature Review of Smartphone Usage. *Innovatech Engineering Journal*, *1*(02), 1070937.

Ajzen, I. (1991). The theory of planned behavior. *Organizational Behavior and Human Decision Processes*, *50*(2), 179–211. DOI: 10.1016/0749-5978(91)90020-T

Akbar, Y. H., & Tracogna, A. (2018). The sharing economy and the future of the hotel industry: Transaction cost theory and platform economics. *International Journal of Hospitality Management*, *71*, 91–101.

Akehurst, G. (2009). User generated content: The use of blogs for tourism organisations and tourism consumers. *Service Business*. Advance online publication. DOI: 10.1007/s11628-008-0054-2

Aktan, M., Aydogan, S., & Aysuna, C. (2016). Web Advertising Value and Students' Attitude Towards Web Advertising. *European Journal of Business and Management*, *8*(9), 86–97.

al. Rasch, F., Roxana Mosteanu, N., & Teplyakova, I. (2021, December). The impact of introducing robotics and artificially based intelligence systems, on employment in hospitality sector of Uzbekistan. In *Proceedings of the 2021 4th Artificial Intelligence and Cloud Computing Conference* (pp. 194-200).

Alalwan, A. A. (2018). Investigating the Impact of Social Media Advertising Features on Customer Purchase Intention. *International Journal of Information Management*, *42*, 65–77. DOI: 10.1016/j.ijinfomgt.2018.06.001

Al-Hyari, H. S. A., Al-Smadi, H. M., & Weshah, S. R. (2023). The impact of artificial intelligence (AI) on guest satisfaction in hotel management: An empirical study of luxury hotels. *Geo Journal of Tourism and Geosites*, *48*, 810–819.

Al-Issa, N., & Thanasi, M. (2024). Mapping the Future of Tech-Infused Luxury: A Roadmap and Research Directions. *International Journal of Consumer Studies*, *48*(6), e13103.

Alma Çallı, B., Çallı, L., Sarı Çallı, D., & Çallı, F. (2023). The impact of different types of service robots usage in hotels on guests' intention to stay. *Journal of Hospitality and Tourism Technology*, *14*(1), 53–68. DOI: 10.1108/JHTT-09-2021-0266

Al-Maslam, S., Al-Msallam, S., & Alhaddad, A. (2016a). The Effects of Social Media Marketing in the Hotel Industry: Conceptual Model for Development of an Effective Online Community Building customer loyalty model in airline industry View project The Effects of Social Media Marketing In the Hotel Industry: Co. *International Journal of Business and Management Invention ISSN*, *5*(July), 1–12. www.ijbmi.org

Alnofeli, K. K., Akter, S., & Yanamandram, V. (2025). Unlocking the power of AI in CRM: A comprehensive multidimensional exploration. *Journal of Innovation & Knowledge*, *10*(3), 100731. DOI: 10.1016/j.jik.2025.100731

Alsamydai, M. J., & Hamdi Al Khasawneh, M. (2013). Antecedents and consequences of e- Jordanian consumer behaviour regarding Facebook advertising. *International Journal of Business*, *3*(4), 41–60.

Alsayat, A. (2023). Customer decision-making analysis based on big social data using machine learning: A case study of hotels in Mecca. *Neural Computing & Applications*, *35*(6), 4701–4722. DOI: 10.1007/s00521-022-07992-x

Alsetoohy, O., Ayoun, B., Arous, S., Megahed, F., & Nabil, G. (2019). Intelligent agent technology: What affects its adoption in hotel food supply chain management? *Journal of Hospitality and Tourism Technology*, *10*(3), 286–310.

Al-Shehri, M. (2021). Choosing the Best Social Media Influencer: The role of gender, age, and product type in influencer marketing. *International Journal of Marketing Strategies*, *4*(1), 1–26.

Altinay Ozdemir, M. (2021). Virtual Reality (VR) and Augmented Reality (AR) Technologies for Accessibility and Marketing in the Tourism Industry: In C. Eusébio, L. Teixeira, & M. J. Carneiro (Eds.), *Advances in Hospitality, Tourism, and the Services Industry* (pp. 277–301). IGI Global. https://doi.org/DOI: 10.4018/978-1-7998-6428-8.ch013

Aluri, A., Slevitch, L., & Larzelere, R. (2015). The effectiveness of embedded social media on hotel websites and the importance of social interactions and return on engagement. *International Journal of Contemporary Hospitality Management*, *27*(4), 670–689. https://www.emerald.com/ijchm/article-abstract/27/4/670/120497/The-effectiveness-of-embedded-social-media-on?redirectedFrom=fulltext

Ameen, N., Sharma, G. D., Tarba, S., Rao, A., & Chopra, R. (2022). Toward advancing theory on creativity in marketing and artificial intelligence. *Psychology and Marketing*, *39*(9), 1802–1825.

Aminu, M. I., & Mahmood, R. (2015). Mediating Role of Dynamic Capabilities on the Relationship between Intellectual Capital and Performance: A Hierarchical Component Model Perspective in PLS-SEM Path Modeling. *Research Journal of Business Management*, *9*(3), 443–456. DOI: 10.3923/rjbm.2015.443.456

Amitay, E., Carmel, D., Har'El, N., Ofek-Koifman, S., Soffer, A., Yogev, S., & Golbandi, N. (2009, June). Social search and discovery using a unified approach. In *Proceedings of the 20th ACM Conference on Hypertext and Hypermedia* (pp. 199-208).

Ana María Munar, J. K. (2014). Motivations for sharing tourism experiences through social media. *Tourism Management*, •••, 46–54. DOI: 10.1016/j.tourman.2014.01.012

Andersson, T. D. (2017). Food and tourism synergies: Perspectives on consumption, production and destination development. *Scandinavian Journal of Hospitality and Tourism*, *17*(1), 1–8. DOI: 10.1080/15022250.2016.1275290

Anisa, N., & Hadiprawoto, T. R. (2025). Micro vs. mega influencers: Whose endorsements and promoted brands truly spark purchase intention in Indonesia? *JMBI UNSRAT*, *12*(2), 537–565.

Anubala, R. (2023). The future of hospitality: Predictive analytics in hotel management. [IJMRP]. *International Journal for Multidimensional Research Perspectives*, *1*(3), 38–47.

Anubha, & Jain, A. (2024). In-game advertising and brand purchase intentions: An SOR perspective. *Global Knowledge, Memory and Communication, 73*(1/2), 24-44. https://doi.org/DOI: 10.1108/gkmc-02-2022-0050

Anwar, F. A., Deliana, D., & Suyamto, S. (2024). Digital Transformation in the Hospitality Industry: Improving Efficiency and Guest Experience. *International Journal of Management Science and Information Technology*, *4*(2), 428–437. DOI: 10.35870/ijmsit.v4i2.3201

Arapou, D. and Kapiki, S., 2023. Enhancing the Guest Experience in Hospitality through Technology: An Outlook of the Future.

Arma & Elma. (2025). *Best Instagram Ads Statistics 2025 (Editor's Choice)*. Retrieved August 27, 2025, from https://www.amraandelma.com/best-instagram-ads-statistics/?utm_source=chatgpt.com

Arora, R., & Arora, Y. (2019). Role and Impact of Social Media in Hospitality Industry. *Ijirmps, 7*(1), 1–6. www.ijirmps.org

Arora, J. (2024). A Study On Impact Of E-Marketing And Social Media On Small Scale Businesses And Hotel Industry Growth. *Migration Letters : An International Journal of Migration Studies*, *21*(S3), 658–663. https://pdfs.semanticscholar.org/249b/526c7b73e6779b3e3f7d177e758e9a1aacf8.pdf

Arora, T., & Agarwal, B. (2019). Empirical Study on Perceived Value and Attitude of Millennials Towards Social Media Advertising: A Structural Equation Modelling Approach. *Vision (Basel)*, *23*(1), 56–69. DOI: 10.1177/0972262918821248

Arthurs, J. D., & Busenitz, L. W. (2006). Dynamic capabilities and venture performance: The effects of venture capitalists. *Journal of Business Venturing*, *21*(2), 195–215. DOI: 10.1016/j.jbusvent.2005.04.004

Arusho Lucy. (2023). *Effect of Social Media Platforms' Use on Hotel Performance*. 11–13.

Ashiq, R. & Carnie, B. (2025). Maintaining Brand Authenticity Through Rebranding: A Case Study of Ponda.bio. *The Journal of Design, Creative Process & the Fashion Industry*, 1–27. DOI: 10.1080/17569370.2025.2508819

Ashley, C., & Tuten, T. (2015). Creative Strategies in Social Media Marketing: An Exploratory Study of Branded Social Content and Consumer Engagement. *Psychology and Marketing*, *32*(1), 15–27. DOI: 10.1002/mar

Augier, M., & Teece, D. J. (2009). Dynamic Capabilities and the Role of Managers in Business Strategy and Economic Performance. *Organization Science*, *20*(2), 410–421. DOI: 10.1287/orsc.1090.0424

Ausejo Sánchez, J. L., Soto, F. G. C., La Rosa, P. E. R., Palma, D. F. M., Campos, G. A. C., & Cadillo, A. J. R. (2024). Big data research in the business, management and accounting field: Revealing the thematic structure based on co-word analysis. *Iberoamerican Journal of Science Measurement and Communication*, *4*(1), 1–8. DOI: 10.47909/ijsmc.116

Ayeh, J. K. (2015). Travellers' acceptance of consumer-generated media: An integrated model of technology acceptance and source credibility theories. *Computers in Human Behavior*, *48*, 173–180. DOI: 10.1016/j.chb.2014.12.049

Aziz, K., Dua, S., & Gupta, P. (2024). Revolutionizing Influencer Marketing: Harnessing the Power of Data Analytics and Artificial Intelligence (AI). In Dutta, S., Rocha, Á., Dutta, P. K., Bhattacharya, P., & Singh, R. (Eds.), *Advances in Data Analytics for Influencer Marketing: An Interdisciplinary Approach* (Vol. 9, pp. 41–66). Springer Nature Switzerland., DOI: 10.1007/978-3-031-65727-6_4

Azman, N., Albattat, A., & Valeri, M. (2023). The Importance of Big Data Analysis: Developing Neuromarketing in Tourism Industry. In Valeri, M. (Ed.), *Tourism Innovation in the Digital Era* (pp. 1–24). Emerald Publishing Limited., DOI: 10.1108/978-1-83797-166-420231001

Baburao, C., Gangadhara, R. R. S., Talukder, M. B., Sheela, P., & Ouariach, F. Z. (2026). AI-Powered Smart Revenue Management in Hospitality: Integrating Innovation, Ethics, and Practical Strategies. In *Smart Operations and Enhancing Guest Experience in the Hospitality Industry* (pp. 219-240). IGI Global Scientific Publishing.https://doi.org/DOI: 10.4018/979-8-3373-2145-5.ch008

Baby, J. B. (2024). Creative Tourism: An Umbrella for Agrifood Travel Experiences? *Tourism and Hospitality*, *5*(4), 1363–1380. DOI: 10.3390/tourhosp5040076

Bacha, J., & Meghrajani, I. (2025). The strategic rise of social media influencers: Disruption and opportunities in modern marketing in hotel operations channels. *International Journal of Business and Management Practices*, *3*(4), 255–262.

Badraoui, B., & Smith, S. J. (2025). Innovative interiors: An evaluation of guest perceptions and booking responses to robotic furniture in hotel rooms. *Journal of Hospitality and Tourism Insights*, *8*(4), 1355–1373. DOI: 10.1108/JHTI-05-2024-0479

Bagozzi, R. P., & Yi, Y. (1988). On the evaluation of structural equation models. *Journal of the Academy of Marketing Science*, *16*(1), 74–94.

Baía, E. P., & Ferreira, J. J. M. (2024). Dynamic capabilities and performance: How has the relationship been assessed? *Journal of Management & Organization*, *30*(1), 188–217. DOI: 10.1017/jmo.2019.88

Bakar, N. P. S. A. (2023). Efektivitas Penggunaan Media Sosial dalam Pemasaran Restoran: A Literature Review [Review of Efektivitas Penggunaan Media Sosial dalam Pemasaran Restoran: A Literature Review]. *JURNAL LENSA MUTIARA KOMUNIKASI*, *7*(2), 181. DOI: 10.51544/jlmk.v7i2.4009

Baka, V. (2016). The becoming of user-generated reviews: Looking at the past to understand the future of managing reputation in the travel sector. *Tourism Management*, *53*, 148–162.

Balte , L. P. (2015). *Content marketing - the fundamental tool of digital marketing.* Bulletin of the Transilvania University of Brasov. Series V : Economic Sciences. http://webbut2.unitbv.ro/BU2015/series v/BILETIN I/15_Patrutiu.pdf

Bano, R., Azim, F., Mahmood, Z., Sanaullah, A., & Ali, O. (2025). The Role of Artificial Intelligence in Personalized Marketing: Enhancing Customer Experience, Predictive Targeting, and Brand Engagement. *The Critical Review of Social Sciences Studies*, *3*(2), 50–65. DOI: 10.59075/d94kvf44

Bansal, M. S. (2025). Synthesizing Insights: A Literature Review on Social Media Influencers. *Effulgence.* doi:https://effulgence.rdias.ac.in/user/article_pdf/Artical_vol23_1_134_148.pdf

Bardukova, L. (2023). Navigating the hospitality horizon: Current trends and strategies for customer attraction and retention in the hotel industry. *Economics and computer science, 2*, 88-103.

Barreto, I. (2010). Dynamic Capabilities: A Review of Past Research and an Agenda for the Future. *Journal of Management*, *36*(1), 256–280. DOI: 10.1177/0149206309350776

Belanche, D., Casaló, L. V., & Flavián, C. (2021). Frontline robots in tourism and hospitality: Service enhancement or cost reduction? *Electronic Markets*, *31*(3), 477–492.

Ben Oumlil, A., & Balloun, J. L. (2020). Millennials' attitude toward advertising: An international exploratory study. *Young Consumers*, *21*(1), 17–34. DOI: 10.1108/YC-10-2018-0865

Bennaciri, M. (2012).. . *The Effect of Social Media on Hotel Industry Customer.*, (August), 1–41.

Bennear, L. S., & Wiener, J. B. 2019. Adaptive regulation: instrument choice for policy learning over time. *Obtenido de Universidad de Harvard:* https://www. hks. harvard. edu

Bertino, E. (2016). Data Security and Privacy: Concepts, Approaches, and Research Directions. *2016 IEEE 40th Annual Computer Software and Applications Conference (COMPSAC)*, 400–407. https://doi.org/DOI: 10.1109/COMPSAC.2016.89

Bhagyalakshmi, Ms. G. S. B. Dr. R. (2023). Exploring The Effects of Conversational Marketing and Artificial Intelligence on Customer Engagement - A Comprehensive Literature Review.". Tuijin Jishu/Journal of Propulsion Technology, 44(4), 4509. DOI: 10.52783/tjjpt.v44.i4.1735

Bhagyashree, M., Dashmukhe, P., & Nath, P. P. (2024).. . *Social Media Marketing And It's Role In Hotel Brand Image Building.*, *12*(10), 451–458.

Bhardwaj, R., & Srivastava, S. (2024). Dynamic Capabilities of Social Enterprises: A Qualitative Meta-Synthesis and Future Agenda. *Journal of Social Entrepreneurship*, *15*(2), 400–428. DOI: 10.1080/19420676.2021.1972030

Bharwani, S., & Mathews, D. (2021). Techno-business strategies for enhancing guest experience in luxury hotels: A managerial perspective. *Worldwide Hospitality and Tourism Themes*, *13*(2), 168–185. DOI: 10.1108/WHATT-09-2020-0121

Bhatia, R., Bhat, A. K., & Tikoria, J. (2021). Life insurance purchase behaviour: A systematic review and directions for future research. *International Journal of Consumer Studies*, *45*(6), 1149–1175.

Bhatt, S., & Dani, R. (2022). *Social Media: Marketing Strategies in Hospitality Industry*. Research in Tourism and Hospitality Management., DOI: 10.21467/books.134.8

Bilgihan, A., & Ricci, P. (2024). The new era of hotel marketing: Integrating cutting-edge technologies with core marketing principles. *Journal of Hospitality and Tourism Technology*, *15*(1), 123–137. DOI: 10.1108/JHTT-04-2023-0095

Bizjak, M. (2025). *With Slow Food Festival, Sacramento Hopes to Enter New Era as a Food Destination City*. Retrieved from https://www.comstocksmag.com/web-only/slow-food-festival-sacramento-hopes-enter-new-era-food-destination-city

Borges-Tiago, M. T., & Avelar, S. (2025). Co-creation dynamics in tourism and hospitality: A horizon 2050 paper. *Tourism Review*, *80*(1), 194–208. DOI: 10.1108/TR-06-2024-0500

Borghi, M. (2021). Service Robots in Online Reviews: An Empirical Study of Online Robotic Discourse. *Annals of Tourism Research*, *87*, 103036. Advance online publication. DOI: 10.1016/j.annals.2020.103036

Bowen, J., & Morosan, C. (2018). Beware hospitality industry: The robots are coming. *Worldwide Hospitality and Tourism Themes*, *10*(6), 726–733.

Brackett, L. K., & Carr, B. N. (2001). Cyberspace Advertising vs. Other Media: Consumer vs. Mature Student Attitudes. *Journal of Advertising Research*, *41*(5), 23–32.

Brand, J. E. (2006). The effects of job displacement on job quality: Findings from the Wisconsin Longitudinal Study. *Research in Social Stratification and Mobility*, *24*(3), 275–298. DOI: 10.1016/j.rssm.2006.03.001

Brinson, N. H., & Lemon, L. L. (2023). Investigating the effects of host trust, credibility, and authenticity in podcast advertising. *Journal of Marketing Communications*, •••, 1–19. DOI: 10.1080/13527266.2022.2054017

Brown, S. A., & Venkatesh, V. (2005). Model of adoption of technology in households: A baseline model test and extension incorporating household life cycle. *Management Information Systems Quarterly*, *29*(3), 399–426. DOI: 10.2307/25148690

Bruno MD. (2025). Facebook post. Retrieved from https://www.facebook.com/BrunoMDofficial/posts/eating-paella-in-valencia-is-like-tasting-the-citys-history-born-in-the-rice-fie/1155150523263359/

Buhalis, D. (2019). Real-time co-creation and nowness service: Lessons from tourism and hospitality. *Journal of Travel & Tourism Marketing*, *36*(5), 563–582. DOI: 10.1080/10548408.2019.1592059

Buhalis, D., Harwood, T., Bogicevic, V., Viglia, G., Beldona, S., & Hofacker, C. (2019). Technological disruptions in services: Lessons from tourism and hospitality. *Journal of Service Management*, *30*(4), 484–506.

Buhalis, D., & Moldavska, I. (2022). Voice assistants in hospitality: Using artificial intelligence for customer service. *Journal of Hospitality and Tourism Technology*, *13*(3), 386–403.

Buhalis, D., O'Connor, P., & Leung, R. (2023). Smart hospitality: From smart cities and smart tourism towards agile business ecosystems in networked destinations. *International Journal of Contemporary Hospitality Management*, *35*(1), 369–393. DOI: 10.1108/IJCHM-04-2022-0497

Buhalis, D., & Park, S. (2021). Brand management and cocreation lessons from tourism and hospitality: Introduction to the special issue. *Journal of Product and Brand Management*, *30*(1), 1–11.

Bulchand-Gidumal, J., William Secin, E., O'Connor, P., & Buhalis, D. (2024). Artificial intelligence's impact on hospitality and tourism marketing: Exploring key themes and addressing challenges. *Current Issues in Tourism*, *27*(14), 2345–2362. DOI: 10.1080/13683500.2023.2229480

Cabanillas, F. L., Leiva, F. M., Castillo, J. F. P., & Higueras-Castillo, E. (Eds.). (2025). *Biometrics: Challenges, Trends and Opportunities*. CRC Press.

Çakar, K., & Aykol, Ş. (2021). Understanding travellers' reactions to robotic services: A multiple case study approach of robotic hotels. *Journal of Hospitality and Tourism Technology*, *12*(1), 155–174.

Carlson, J., Rahman, M., Voola, R., & De Vries, N. (2018). Customer engagement behaviours in social media: Capturing innovation opportunities. *Journal of Services Marketing*, *32*(1), 83–94.

Carroll, E., & Murphy, C. (2024). Enhancing Event Reputations: Insights and Recommendations for Secure and Engaging Experiences. *ICHRIE Research Reports*, *9*(5). Advance online publication. DOI: 10.61701/311750.093

Carvalho, I., & Ivanov, S. (2023). ChatGPT for tourism: Applications, benefits and risks. *Tourism Review*, *79*(2), 290–303. DOI: 10.1108/TR-02-2023-0088

Castillo-Picón, J., Nagadeepa, C., Rani, I., Angulo-Cabanillas, L., Vílchez-Vásquez, R., Manrique-Cáceres, J., & Allauca-Castillo, W. J. 2023, May. Guest Perception of Technology vs. Human Interaction in Hotel Check-in Process Implication for Service Quality. In *International Conference on Business and Technology* (pp. 81-95). Cham: Springer Nature Switzerland.

Cavana, R., Delahaye, B., & Sekeran, U. (2001). *Applied business research: Qualitative and quantitative methods*. John Wiley & Sons.

Centobelli, P., Cerchione, R., Vecchio, P. D., Oropallo, E., & Secundo, G. (2022). Blockchain technology for bridging trust, traceability and transparency in circular supply chain. *Information & Management*, *59*(7), 103508. DOI: 10.1016/j.im.2021.103508

Chaffey, D., & Ellis-Chadwick, F. (2019). *Digital marketing*. Pearson uk. https://thuvienso.hoasen.edu.vn/bitstream/handle/123456789/13083/Contents.pdf?sequence=1

Chakrabarti, S., Chakrabarti, S., Bhandari, A. K., Saha, D., & Mazumder, R. (2024). *Perspectives in Finance and Digital Transformations in Business* (1st ed.). Routledge India., DOI: 10.4324/9781003470229

Chakraborty, U., & Biswal, S. K. (2024). Is ChatGPT a Responsible Communication: A Study on the Credibility and Adoption of Conversational Artificial Intelligence. *Journal of Promotion Management*, *30*(6), 929–958. DOI: 10.1080/10496491.2024.2332987

Chan-Olmsted, S., & Kim, H. J. 2022. 6 Influencer marketing dynamics. *The Dynamics of Influencer Marketing*, p.99.

Chan, T. H., Hung, K., & Tse, D. K. (2023). Comparing E-Commerce Micro-and Macroinfluencers in TikTok Videos: Effects of Strategies on Audience Likes, Audience Shares, and Brand Sales. *Journal of Interactive Advertising*, *23*(4), 289–322.

Chappell, H., & Creissels, D. (2019). Topicality and the typology of predicative possession. *Linguistic Typology*, *23*(3), 467–532.

Chatterjee, S., Nguyen, B., Ghosh, S. K., Bhattacharjee, K. K., & Chaudhuri, S. (2020). Adoption of artificial intelligence integrated CRM system: An empirical study of Indian organizations. *The Bottom Line (New York, N.Y.)*, *33*(4), 359–375.

Cheah, I., & Phua, P. (2025). Generational advertising: Literature review and practitioner insights on key pitfalls and implications. *International Journal of Advertising*, *44*(2), 286–312.

Chen, J., Zhang, Y., Cai, H., Liu, L., Liao, M., & Fang, J. (2024). A comprehensive overview of micro-influencer marketing in hotel operations: Decoding the current landscape, impacts, and trends. *Behavioral Sciences (Basel, Switzerland)*, *14*(3), 226. PMID: 38540529

Chen, L., & Kozak, M. (2024). *Algorithmic Personalization and Ethics in Tourism Marketing*. Tourism Management Review.

Chen, M., Wang, X., Law, R., & Zhang, M. (2023). Research on the Frontier and Prospect of Service Robots in the Tourism and Hospitality Industry Based on International Core Journals: A Review. *Behavioral Sciences (Basel, Switzerland)*, *13*(7), 560. DOI: 10.3390/bs13070560 PMID: 37504007

Chen, P. T., & Kuo, S. C. (2017). Innovation resistance and strategic implications of enterprise social media websites in Taiwan through knowledge sharing perspective. *Technological Forecasting and Social Change*, *118*, 55–69.

Chen, Q. X. (2023). Exploring the Discrepancy between Projected and Perceived Destination Images: A Cross-Cultural and Sustainable Analysis Using LDA Modeling. *Sustainability*, *15*(12), 9296. DOI: 10.3390/su15129296

Chen, S.-H., & Ahmed, F. (2024). The Transformative Power of AI and AR in Customer-Centric Services in the Tourism and Hospitality Sector: Looking Back to Predict the Future Outlook. In Ho, R. C., Song, B. L., & Tee, P. K. (Eds.), (pp. 105–138). Advances in Marketing, Customer Relationship Management, and E-Services. IGI Global., DOI: 10.4018/979-8-3693-5668-5.ch005

Chen, S., Han, X., Bilgihan, A., & Okumus, F. (2021). Customer engagement research in hospitality and tourism: A systematic review. *Journal of Hospitality Marketing & Management*, *30*(7), 871–904. DOI: 10.1080/19368623.2021.1903644

Chen, Y., Hu, Y., Zhou, S., & Yang, S. (2023). Investigating the determinants of performance of artificial intelligence adoption in hospitality industry during COVID-19. *International Journal of Contemporary Hospitality Management*, *35*(8), 2868–2889.

Cheung, C. M. K., & Thadani, D. R. (2012). The impact of electronic word-of-mouth communication: A literature analysis and integrative model. *Decision Support Systems*, *54*(1), 461–470. DOI: 10.1016/j.dss.2012.06.008

Chiang, A.-H., & Trimi, S. (2020). Impacts of service robots on service quality. *Service Business*, *14*(3), 439–459. DOI: 10.1007/s11628-020-00423-8

Chin, W. W., & Newsted, P. R. (2020). Structural equation modeling analysis with small samples using partial least squares. In Hoyle, R. H. (Ed.), *Statistical strategies for small sample research* (pp. 307–341). Sage.

Choi, S. M., & Rifon, N. J. (2002). Antecedents and Consequences of Web Advertising Credibility. *Journal of Interactive Advertising*, *3*(1), 12–24. DOI: 10.1080/15252019.2002.10722064

Choi, Y., Choi, M., Oh, M., & Kim, S. (2020). Service robots in hotels: Understanding the service quality perceptions of human-robot interaction. *Journal of Hospitality Marketing & Management*, *29*(6), 613–635.

Chua, B. L., Al-Ansi, A., Kim, S., Wong, A. K. F., & Han, H. (2022). Examining airline employees' work-related stress and coping strategies during the global tourism crisis. *International Journal of Contemporary Hospitality Management*, *34*(10), 3715–3742. DOI: 10.1108/IJCHM-09-2021-1085

Chung, K. C., & Tan, P. J. B. (2025). Artificial intelligence and internet of things to improve smart hospitality services. *Internet of Things : Engineering Cyber Physical Human Systems*, *31*, 101544. DOI: 10.1016/j.iot.2025.101544

Chung, K.-C. (2025). The evolution of creativity: How generative AI is reshaping the hospitality landscape. *Enterprise Information Systems*, *19*(3–4). Advance online publication. DOI: 10.1080/17517575.2024.2427024

Citak, J., Owoc, M. L., & Weichbroth, P. (2021). A note on the applications of artificial intelligence in the hospitality industry: Preliminary results of a survey. *Procedia Computer Science*, *192*, 4552–4559.

Cohen, J. (1992). A power primer. *Psychological Bulletin*, *112*(1), 155–159. PMID: 19565683

Cozzio, C., Santos Arteaga, F. J., & Maurer, O. (2025). Artificial intelligence adoption in hospitality: Challenges and opportunities across hierarchical levels. *Tourism Review*.

Crespi Vallbona, M. (2021). Satisfying experiences: guided tours at cultural heritage sites. *Taylor and Francis*. https://hdl.handle.net/2445/178387

Dabas, S., Sharma, S., & Manaktola, K. (2021). Adoption of digital marketing tools in independent businesses: Experiences of restaurant entrepreneurs in India and United Kingdom. *Worldwide Hospitality and Tourism Themes*, *13*(2), 214–235. https://www.emerald.com/whatt/article-abstract/13/2/214/383568/Adoption-of-digital-marketing-tools-in-independent?redirectedFrom=fulltext

Dahl, S. (2021). *Social Media Marketing: Theories and Applications*. Sage Publications Ltd.

Daiya, D., Yadav, M., & Rao, H. S. 2024, April. Diffstock: Probabilistic relational stock market predictions using diffusion models. In *ICASSP 2024-2024 IEEE International Conference on Acoustics, Speech and Signal Processing (ICASSP)* (pp. 7335-7339). IEEE.

Dang, T. D., & Nguyen, M. T. (2023). Systematic review and research agenda for the tourism and hospitality sector: Co-creation of customer value in the digital age. *Future Business Journal*, *9*(1), 94. DOI: 10.1186/s43093-023-00274-5

Dao, W. V. T., Le, A. N. H., Cheng, J. M. S., & Chen, D. C. (2014). Social media advertising value: The case of transitional economies in Southeast Asia. *International Journal of Advertising*, *33*(2), 271–294. DOI: 10.2501/IJA-33-2-271-294

Datiko, D. B. (2024). The customer-centric-marketing (CCM) perspectives in the tourism and hospitality sector: Insight from a developing country. *International Journal of Tourism Policy*, *14*(1), 37–53.

de Moura, A. C., de Sevilha Gosling, M., Christino, J. M. M., & Macedo, S. B. (2017). Acceptance and use of technology for the choice of touristic destina-tions by persons of the third age: A study using UTAUT2. *Revista Brasileira de Pesquisa em Turismo*, *11*(2), 239. DOI: 10.7784/rbtur.v11i2.1277

de Oliveira, P. S. G., da Silva, L. F., de Oliveira, S. I., da Silva, R. C., & de Mesquita Spinola, M. (2024). Chefs' Communities of Practice for Managing Innovations in the Tourism and Hospitality Sectors. *Journal of the Knowledge Economy*, *16*(2), 8660–8686. DOI: 10.1007/s13132-023-01616-y

Dehghani, M., Niaki, M. K., Ramezani, I., & Sali, R. (2016). Evaluating the influence of YouTube advertising for attraction of young customers. *Computers in Human Behavior*, *59*, 165–172. DOI: 10.1016/j.chb.2016.01.037

Delbaere, M., Michael, B., & Phillips, B. J. (2021). Social media influencers: A route to brand engagement for their followers. *Psychology and Marketing*, *38*(1), 101–112.

Demirović Bajrami, D., Cimbaljević, M., Petrović, M. D., Radovanović, M. M., & Gajić, T. (2025). Internal marketing and employees' personality traits toward green innovative hospitality. *Tourism Review*, *80*(3), 710–724. DOI: 10.1108/TR-05-2023-0307

Dev, C. S., Buschman, J. D., & Bowen, J. T. (2010). Hospitality marketing: A retrospective analysis (19602010) and predictions (20102020). *Cornell Hospitality Quarterly*, *51*(4), 459469.

DeVellis, R. (2016). *Scale Development: Theory and Applications* (Second edi). Sage publications. https://books.google.co.in/books?id=BYGxL6xLokUC&printsec=frontcover&redir_esc=y#v=onepage&q&f=false

Devi, S. (2015). Social Media as a Tool of Marketing: A Study of Indian Automobile Industry. SSRN *Electronic Journal, 5*(12), 166–172. https://doi.org/DOI: 10.2139/ssrn.2698527

Devkota, J., Shrestha, J., Pandit, S., & Sharma, A. (2025). Marketing on consumer buying behaviors in the hospitality industry. *NPRC Journal of Multidisciplinary Research*, *2*(3), 189–203. DOI: 10.3126/nprcjmr.v2i3.76993

Dewangan, S., & Kumar, S. (2024). AI and Big Data Analytics Revolutionizing Industry 5.0: Unlocking the Power of Smart Manufacturing and Beyond. In Darwish, D. (Ed.), (pp. 398–410). Advances in Business Information Systems and Analytics. IGI Global., DOI: 10.4018/979-8-3693-0413-6.ch016

Dewangan, S., & Kumar, S. (2024). Enhancing Fraud Detection in Finance Through AI and Machine Learning. In Darwish, D., & Kumar, S. (Eds.), (pp. 267–282). Advances in Finance, Accounting, and Economics. IGI Global., DOI: 10.4018/979-8-3693-8507-4.ch014

Dewnarain, S., Ramkissoon, H., & Mavondo, F. (2019). Social customer relationship management: An integrated conceptual framework. *Journal of Hospitality Marketing & Management*, *28*(2), 172–188. https://www.tandfonline.com/doi/abs/10.1080/19368623.2018.1516588

Dhiman, N., & Jamwal, M. (2023). Tourists' post-adoption continuance intentions of chatbots: integrating task–technology fit model and expectation–confirmation theory. *foresight, 25*(2), 209-224.

Di Pietro, L., & Pantano, E. (2012). An empirical investigation of social network influence on consumer purchasing decision: The case of Facebook. *Journal of Direct, Data and Digital Marketing Practice*, *14*(1), 18–29. DOI: 10.1057/dddmp.2012.10

Dilek, S. E., & Harman, S. (2017). Hospitality marketing: A historical perspective. In *Routledge Handbook of Hospitality Marketing* (p. 920). Routledge.

Dinga, E., Oprean-Stan, C., Tănăsescu, C. R., Brătian, V., & Ionescu, G. M. (2022). *Financial market analysis and behaviour: the adaptive preference hypothesis*. Routledge.

Djafarova, E., & Rushworth, C. (2017). Exploring the credibility of online celebrities' Instagram profiles in influencing the purchase decisions of young female users. *Computers in Human Behavior*, *68*, 1–7. DOI: 10.1016/j.chb.2016.11.009

Doarn, C. R., & Moses, G. R. (2011). Overcoming Barriers to Wider Adoption of Mobile Telerobotic Surgery: Engineering, Clinical and Business Challenges. In Rosen, J., Hannaford, B., & Satava, R. M. (Eds.), *Surgical Robotics* (pp. 69–102). Springer US., DOI: 10.1007/978-1-4419-1126-1_4

Dobber, T., Kruikemeier, S., Votta, F., Helberger, N., & Goodman, E. P. (2025). The effect of traffic light veracity labels on perceptions of political advertising source and message credibility on social media. *Journal of Information Technology & Politics*, *22*(1), 82–97.

Doborjeh, Z., Hemmington, N., Doborjeh, M., & Kasabov, N. (2021). Artificial intelligence: A systematic review of methods and applications in hospitality and tourism. *International Journal of Contemporary Hospitality Management*, *34*(3), 1154–1176.

Donald, M., & Donald, A. 2024. How Marketing and Design can Enhance Customer Experience in Hospitality by Meeting Their Evolving Needs. In *Marketing and Design in the Service Sector: Enhancing Customer Experience* (pp. 175-186). Emerald Publishing Limited.

Dordai, L. B. (2026). *Gastronomic Tourism: Global Trends, Sustainability Challenges, and Research Directions (2010–2025)—A Comprehensive Review*. Gastronomy. DOI: 10.3390/gastronomy4010004

Dossa, Z., & Kaeufer, K. (2014). Understanding Sustainability Innovations Through Positive Ethical Networks. *Journal of Business Ethics*, *119*(4), 543–559. DOI: 10.1007/s10551-013-1834-8

Dou, W., Lim, K. H., Su, C., Zhou, N., & Cui, N. (2010). Brand positioning strategy using search engine marketing. *Management Information Systems Quarterly*, ●●●, 261–279.

Duarte Alonso, A., Vu, O. T. K., Tran, T. D., Nguyen, T. T., Dang, Q. T., & Maheshwari, G. (2024). Perceived advantages and disadvantages of information communication technology adoption among restaurants in an emerging economy: A diffusion of innovations view. *International Journal of Hospitality Management*, *122*, 103837. DOI: 10.1016/j.ijhm.2024.103837

Ducoffe, R. H. (1995). How consumers assess the value of advertising. *Journal of Current Issues and Research in Advertising*, *17*(1), 1–18. DOI: 10.1080/10641734.1995.10505022

Ducoffe, R. H. (1996). Advertising value and advertising on the web. *Journal of Advertising Research*, *36*(5), 21–35.

Dwinanda, B., & Syaripuddin, F. A., Hudaifi, & Hendriana, E. (2022). Examining the Extended Advertising Value Model: A Case of TikTok Short Video Ads. *Mediterranean Journal of Social & Behavioural Research*, *6*(2), 35–44. DOI: 10.30935/mjosbr/11820

Dwivedi, Y. K., Ismagilova, E., Hughes, D. L., & Carlson, J. (2021). Setting the future of digital and social media marketing research: Perspectives and research propositions. *International Journal of Information Management*, *59*(1), 1–37. DOI: 10.1016/j.ijinfomgt.2020.102168

Dwivedi, Y. K., Pandey, N., Currie, W. L., & Micu, A. (2023). Leveraging ChatGPT and other generative artificial intelligence (AI)-based applications in the hospitality and tourism industry: Practices, challenges and research agenda. *International Journal of Contemporary Hospitality Management*, *36*(1), 1. DOI: 10.1108/ijchm-05-2023-0686

Dwivedi, Y. K., Rana, N. P., Jeyaraj, A., Clement, M., & Williams, M. D. (2019). Re-examining the Unified Theory of Acceptance and Use of Technology (UTAUT): Towards a revised theoretical model. *Information Systems Frontiers*, *21*(3), 719–734. DOI: 10.1007/s10796-017-9774-y

Dzreke, S. S., & Dzreke, M. S. E. (2025). The influencer equity equation: Analyzing influencer marketing in hotel operations's effect on brand equity via the perspectives of authenticity, credibility, and engagement. 7(3):1-23; DOI: 10.36948/ijfmr.2025.v07i03.48683

Easterby-Smith, M. T., & Lowe, R. A. (2002). *Management Research: An Introduction*. SAGE Publications Ltd.

Easterby-Smith, M., & Prieto, I. M. (2008). Dynamic Capabilities and Knowledge Management: An Integrative Role for Learning? *. *British Journal of Management, 19*(3), 235–249. DOI: 10.1111/j.1467-8551.2007.00543.x

Edelman, D. C. (2010). (2010). Branding in the Digital Age: You're Spending Your Money in All the Wrong Places. *Harvard Business Review Digital Articles, 88*, 63–69. https://www.scirp.org/reference/referencespapers?referenceid=1714074

Eisenhardt, K. M., & Martin, J. A. (2000). Dynamic Capabilities: What are They? *Strategic Management Journal, 21*(10/11), 1105–1121. https://www.jstor.org/stable/3094429

Ellis, A. P. (2018). What Is Food Tourism? *Tourism Management, 68*, 250–263. DOI: 10.1016/j.tourman.2018.03.025

Elshaer, I. A., Azazz, A. M. S., Fayyad, S., Mohamed, S. A. K., Fouad, A. M., & Fathy, E. A. (2024). From Data to Delight: Leveraging Social Customer Relationship Management to Elevate Customer Satisfaction and Market Effectiveness. *Information (Basel), 16*(1), 9. DOI: 10.3390/info16010009

Ertaş, Ç., & Karakan, H. I. (2024). The future of events in the tourism industry: The case of the "Best of the Best Things to Do 2023" on TripAdvisor. *Worldwide Hospitality and Tourism Themes, 16*(4), 474–484.

Etemad-Sajadi, R., & Sturman, M. C. (2022). How to Increase the Customer Experience by the Usage of Remote Control Robot Concierge Solutions. *International Journal of Social Robotics, 14*(2), 429–440. DOI: 10.1007/s12369-021-00800-x

Evans, D. (2010). *Social media marketing: the next generation of business engagement*. Jhon Willy & Sons.

Faizal, S., Sankar, J. P., Menon, N., Abdalla, R., & Pattali, S. (2024). Factors influencing hotel decision-making through digital platforms in South Asia. *Cogent Social Sciences, 10*(1). Advance online publication. DOI: 10.1080/23311886.2024.2407933

Farwell, T. M. (2008). Book review: *Always on: Advertising, marketing, and media in an era of consumer control. Journal of Advertising Education, 12*(2), 47. DOI: 10.1177/109804820801200212

Fatima, T., & Abbas, M. T. (2016). Impact of Advertising Beliefs and Personalization on Attitude towards Advertising; Mediating Role of Advertising Value. In *International Journal of Business Management and Commerce* (Vol. 1, Issue 2).

Feldman, Z. (2021). Good Food' in an Instagram Age: Rethinking hierarchies of culture, criticism and taste. *European Journal of Cultural Studies*, *24*(6). Advance online publication. DOI: 10.1177/13675494211055733

Felix, R., Rauschnabel, P. A., & Hinsch, C. (2017). Elements of strategic social media marketing: A holistic framework. *Journal of Business Research*, *70*, 118–126. DOI: 10.1016/j.jbusres.2016.05.001

Fennell, D. A. (2009). The nature of pleasure in pleasure travel. *Tourism Recreation Research*, *34*(2), 123134.

Ferhataj, A., & Memaj, F. (2025). AI-DRIVEN PERSONALIZATION IN TOURISM: EXPLORING TOURIST BEHAVIOR, ETHICAL CONCERNS, WORKFORCE TRANSFORMATION, AND SKILL INTEGRATION. tr.iksadkongre.com/bingol

Ferran Sabate, J. B.-M. (2014). Factors influencing popularity of branded content in Facebook fan pages. *European Management Journal*. Advance online publication. DOI: 10.1016/j.emj.2014.05.001

Ferreira, J. R., Ferreira, L. V. F., & Paiva Neto, A. (2016). Analysis of the official websites of tourism destinations classified socioculturally by the report the economist inteligence unit limited. *Turismo: Visão e Ação*, *18*(3), 557–583.

Field, A. (2009). *Discovering statistics using spss*. sage.

Filieri, R., Alguezaui, S., & McLeay, F. (2015). What makes online reviews helpful? A diagnosticity-adoption framework to explain informational and normative influences in e-WOM. *Journal of Business Research*, *68*(6), 1261–1268. DOI: 10.1016/j.jbusres.2014.11.006

Filimonau, V., Ashton, M., Derqui, B., & Hernandez-Maskivker, G. (2025). Exploring How Artificial Intelligence (AI) Can Enable Sustainability in the Hospitality Industry. *Sustainable Development*, sd.70146. https://doi.org/DOI: 10.1002/sd.70146

Filimonau, V., & Naumova, E. (2020). The blockchain technology and the scope of its application in hospitality operations. *International Journal of Hospitality Management*, *87*. Advance online publication. DOI: 10.1016/j.ijhm.2019.102383

Fraga, C., Cardoso, L., de Stefano, E., Lima Santos, L., & Motta, N. (2025). Mapping Gamification for Sustainable Urban Development: Generating New Insights for Tourism Education. *Tourism and Hospitality*, *6*(1), 17. DOI: 10.3390/tourhosp6010017

Fransen, M. L., Verlegh, P. W. J., Kirmani, A., & Smit, E. G. (2015). A typology of consumer strategies for resisting advertising, and a review of mechanisms for countering them. *International Journal of Advertising, 34*(1), 6–16. DOI: 10.1080/02650487.2014.995284

Fraser, J., & Fahlman, D. (Willy), Arscott, J., & Guillot, I. (2018). Pilot Testing for Feasibility in a Study of Student Retention and Attrition in Online Undergraduate Programs. *International Review of Research in Open and Distance Learning, 19*(1), 1–14. DOI: 10.19173/irrodl.v19i1.3326

Freed, J. Q. (2021). *Hospitality CRM: Past, Present and Future*. Stayhapi. Retrieved from https://www.stayhapi.com/resources/hospitality-crm-past-present-and-future

Fusté-Forné, F. & Filimon, N. (2025). From post to table: The social media marketing of food tourism. *International Journal of Gastronomy and Food Science, Volume 39, ISSN 1878-450X*. DOI: 10.1016/j.ijgfs.2025.101107

Gabarron, E., Larbi, D., Dorronzoro, E., Hasvold, P. E., Wynn, R., & Årsand, E. (2020). Factors engaging users of diabetes social media channels on Facebook, Twitter, and Instagram: Observational study. *Journal of Medical Internet Research, 22*(9), e21204.

Gangwar, V. P., & Reddy, D. (2023). Hospitality Industry 5.0: Emerging Trends in Guest Perception and Experiences. In Dadwal, S., Kumar, P., Verma, R., & Singh, G. (Eds.), (pp. 185–211). Advances in Business Strategy and Competitive Advantage. IGI Global., DOI: 10.4018/978-1-6684-6403-8.ch010

Garcês, S. (2024). Gastronomy Experiences, Authenticity, and Storytelling in Tourism Destinations: A Conceptual Paper. In Castanho, R., & Franco, M. (Eds.), *Cultural, Gastronomy, and Adventure Tourism Development*. IGI Global Scientific Publishing. DOI: 10.4018/979-8-3693-3158-3.ch009

Gardiner, S., King, C., & Grace, D. (2013). Travel decision making: An empirical examination of generational values, attitudes, and intentions. *Journal of Travel Research, 52*(3), 310324.

Garg, A., & Kumar, J. (2021). Social media marketing influence on Boutique Hotel customers' purchase intention in Malaysia. *Tourism & Management Studies, 17*(3), 51–62. DOI: 10.18089/tms.2021.170304

Garg, S., Srivastava, S. P., Malhotra, R. K., & Sharma, R. (2025). Sustainable Integration of Robotic Services in the Hospitality Industry: Enhancing Operational Efficiency and Employee Satisfaction. *2025 International Conference on Intelligent Control, Computing and Communications (IC3)*, 1377–1381. https://doi.org/DOI: 10.1109/IC363308.2025.10956363

Garrido-Moreno, A., García-Morales, V. J., Lockett, N., & King, S. (2018). The missing link: Creating value with social media use in hotels. *International Journal of Hospitality Management*, *75*, 94–104. https://www.sciencedirect.com/science/article/abs/pii/S0278431916301670

Gaur, L., Afaq, A., Singh, G., & Dwivedi, Y. K. (2021). Role of artificial intelligence and robotics to foster the touchless travel during a pandemic: A review and research agenda. *International Journal of Contemporary Hospitality Management*, *33*(11), 4079–4098.

Gefen, D. (2000). E-commerce: The role of familiarity and trust. *Omega*, *28*(6), 725–737. DOI: 10.1016/S0305-0483(00)00021-9

Gerlich, M. (2023). The power of personal connections in micro-influencer marketing in hotel operations: A study on consumer behaviour and the impact of micro-influencers. *Transnational Marketing in hotel operations Journal, 22*(1), 131–152.

Ghorbanzadeh, D. Z. R. (2023). Generating destination brand awareness and image through the firm's social media. *Kybernetes*, *52*(9), 3292–3314. DOI: 10.1108/K-09-2021-0931

Ghosh, D., & Chatterjee, S. 2025. Embracing Digital Transformation in Hospitality: Innovations, Challenges, and Opportunities With Case Studies. In *Digital Disruption in Hospitality, AI, and Emerging Technologies: A Roadmap to Personalized Experiences, Enhanced Operations, and Revenue Growth* (pp. 189-200). Emerald Publishing Limited.

Giacomo Pettenati, E. A. (2025). Assembling mountains through food. Typical cheese and politics of mountainness in the Italian Alps. *Geoforum*. Advance online publication. DOI: 10.1016/j.geoforum.2025.104210

Giannoukou, I. (2024). Revolutionizing hospitality: Strategic integration of innovation management embracing technological innovation for enhanced customer experiences. *Technium Business and Management*, *7*, 24–39.

Gil-Saura, I., & Ruiz-Molina, M. E., Gloria Berenguer-Contrí, & Antonio Marín-García. (2024). Sustainability-oriented innovation in retailing. *Psychology and Marketing*, *41*(2), 240–253. DOI: 10.1002/mar.21922

Giordano, J., Benedikter, R., & Shook, J. R. (2024). *Neuroscience*. Neuroculture, and Neuroethics.

Giraldo, L. F. G., Pineda, V. G., Arias, J. V., Palacios-Moya, L., & López Goycochea, J. (2024). Exploring the evolution of marketing strategies in hospitality and tourism: A bibliometric study. *Progress in Industrial Ecology*, *17*(3), 240–251. DOI: 10.1504/PIE.2024.143784

Gitau, S. K. (2020). *Impact of social media marketing on the brand awareness in the hotel industry. 21*(1), 1–9. https://www.golder.com/insights/block-caving-a-viable-alternative/

Giuffredi-Kähr, A., Petrova, A., & Malär, L. (2022). Sponsorship disclosure of influencers–a curse or a blessing? *Journal of Interactive Marketing in hotel operations, 57*(1), 18–34.

Goel, P., Kaushik, N., Sivathanu, B., Pillai, R., & Vikas, J. (2022). Consumers' adoption of artificial intelligence and robotics in hospitality and tourism sector: Literature review and future research agenda. *Tourism Review*, *77*(4), 1081–1096.

Go, H., Kang, M., & Suh, S. C. (2020). Machine learning of robots in tourism and hospitality: Interactive technology acceptance model (iTAM)–cutting edge. *Tourism Review*, *75*(4), 625–636.

Gouda, R. M., & Halim, Y. T. (2025). The role of sustainable social media content in enhancing customer loyalty in the hospitality industry. *Future Business Journal*, *11*(1). Advance online publication. DOI: 10.1186/s43093-025-00516-8

Gregory, R. W., Henfridsson, O., Kaganer, E., & Kyriakou, H. (2021). The role of artificial intelligence and data network effects for creating user value. *Academy of Management Review*, *46*(3), 534–551.

Gretzel, U. (2011). Intelligent systems in tourism: A social science perspective. *Annals of Tourism Research*, *38*(3), 757–779.

Gretzel, U. (2022). The Smart DMO: A new step in the digital transformation of destination management organizations. *European Journal of Tourism Research*, *30*, 3002. DOI: 10.54055/ejtr.v30i.2589

Gretzel, U. F. (2006). Searching for the Future: Challenges Faced by Destination Marketing Organizations. *Journal of Travel Research*, *45*(2), 116–126. DOI: 10.1177/0047287506291598

Greyser, S. A. (1973). Irritation in advertising. *Journal of Advertising Research*, *13*(1), 3–10.

GTCO. (2025). GTCO food and drink: holiday edition. Retrieved from https://foodanddrink.gtcoplc.com/#:~:text=Venue%3A%20GTCentre%2C%20Plot%201%20Water,Attendance%20is%20FREE!

Guan, C., Hung, Y. C., & Liu, W. (2022). Cultural differences in hospitality service evaluations: Mining insights of user generated content. *Electronic Markets*, *32*(3), 1061–1081.

Gudmand-Höyer, K., & Johansson, W. (2025). Who holds the influence? Consumer experiences of micro- and macro-influencers on TikTok. https://hdl.handle.net/2077/89352

Guijarroa, A. J. M. (2013). Textual and compositional choices in hotel brochures. *Choice in Language*, 301.

Gulati, S. (2022). Social and sustainable: exploring social media use for promoting sustainable behaviour and demand amongst Indian tourists. *International Hospitality Review, 36*(2), 373-393. https://www.emerald.com/ihr/article/36/2/373/107042

Gupta, A., Prabhat, P., & Gulzar, B. (2022). Personal-Internet-of-Things (PIoT): A vision for hyper-personalization delivered securely. *2022 IEEE Delhi Section Conference (DELCON)*, 1–6. https://doi.org/DOI: 10.1109/DELCON54057.2022.9753314

Gupta, S., Modgil, S., Lee, C. K., & Sivarajah, U. (2023). The future is yesterday: Use of AI-driven facial recognition to enhance value in the travel and tourism industry. *Information Systems Frontiers*, *25*(3), 1179–1195.

Gupta, S., Modgil, S., Lee, C.-K., Cho, M., & Park, Y. (2022). Artificial intelligence enabled robots for stay experience in the hospitality industry in a smart city. *Industrial Management & Data Systems*, *122*(10), 2331–2350. DOI: 10.1108/IMDS-10-2021-0621

Gupta, S., Paul, J., Stoner, J. L., & Aggarwal, A. (2024). Digital transformation, online advertising, and consumer behaviour. *International Journal of Advertising*, *43*(8), 1439–1462. DOI: 10.1080/02650487.2024.2317632

Gupta, V. (2019). The influencing role of social media in the consumer's hotel decision-making process. *Worldwide Hospitality and Tourism Themes*, *11*(4), 378–391. https://www.emerald.com/whatt/article-abstract/11/4/378/383362/The-influencing-role-of-social-media-in-the?redirectedFrom=fulltext

Gursoy, D. (2018). Future of hospitality marketing and management research. *Tourism Management Perspectives*, *25*, 185–188. DOI: 10.1016/j.tmp.2017.11.008

Gursoy, D., Chi, O. H., Lu, L., & Nunkoo, R. (2019). Consumers acceptance of artificially intelligent (AI) device use in service delivery. *International Journal of Information Management*, *49*, 157–169.

Gursoy, D., Li, Y., & Song, H. (2023). ChatGPT and the hospitality and tourism industry: An overview of current trends and future research directions. *Journal of Hospitality Marketing & Management*, *32*(5), 579–592. DOI: 10.1080/19368623.2023.2211993

Gursoy, D., Malodia, S., & Dhir, A. (2022). The metaverse in the hospitality and tourism industry: An overview of current trends and future research directions. *Journal of Hospitality Marketing & Management*, *31*(5), 527–534.

Haenlein, M., Anadol, E., Farnsworth, T., Hugo, H., Hunichen, J., & Welte, D. (2020). Navigating the new era of influencer marketing: How to be successful on Instagram, TikTok, & Co. *California Management Review*, *63*(1), 5–25.

Hair, F. J., Black, C. W., Babin, J. B., & Amderson, E. R. (2010). Multivariate Data Analysis (7th ed.). Pearson prentice Hall.

Hair, J. F., & Lukas, B. (2014). *Marketing Research.* McGraw-Hill Education Australia. https://cat2.lib.unimelb.edu.au/record=b5609216~S13

Hair, J. F., Hult, G. T. M., Ringle, C. M., & Sarstedt, M. (2019). *A primer on partial least squares structural equation modeling (PLS-SEM)* (2nd ed.). Sage Publications.

Hajli, M. N. (2014). A study of the impact of social media on consumers. *International Journal of Market Research*, *56*(3), 387–404. DOI: 10.2501/IJMR-2014-025

Halkiopoulos, C., & Papadopoulos, D. (2022, April). Computational methods for evaluating web technologies and digital marketing techniques in the hospitality industry. In *Transcending Borders in Tourism Through Innovation and Cultural Heritage: 8th International Conference, IACuDiT, Hydra, Greece, 2021* (pp. 387–406). Springer International Publishing., https://link.springer.com/chapter/10.1007/978-3-030-92491-1_24

Hanaysha, J. R., & Alhyasat, K. M. (2025). Examining the Effect of Social Media Advertising Features on Customer Perceived Value and Brand Love in the Retail Industry. *Telematics and Informatics Reports*, 100208.

Han, H., Ayalew, Z. A., & Kim, S. (Sam), Quan, W., Lho, L. H., Jung, I., & Al-Ansi, A. (2024). Drivers of digital currency adoption and their configurational impact assessment in tourism and hospitality: Loss aversion under prospect theory. *Current Issues in Tourism*, •••, 1–18. DOI: 10.1080/13683500.2024.2413665

Harrigan, P., Evers, U., Miles, M., & Daly, T. (2017). Customer engagement with tourism social media brands. *Tourism Management*, *59*, 597–609. DOI: 10.1016/j.tourman.2016.09.015

Hashimoto, A. (2006). Selling Canadian Culinary Tourism: Branding the Global and the Regional Product. *Tourism Geographies*, *8*(1), 31–55. DOI: 10.1080/14616680500392465

Hassan, A. (Ed.). (2023). *Digital transformation in aviation, tourism and hospitality in Southeast Asia*. Routledge.

Hayes, J. L., & King, K. W. (2014). The Social Exchange of Viral Ads: Referral and Coreferral of Ads Among College Students. *Journal of Interactive Advertising*, *14*(2), 98–109. DOI: 10.1080/15252019.2014.942473

Hays, S., Page, S. J., & Buhalis, D. (2013). Social media as a destination marketing tool: Its use by national tourism organisations. *Current Issues in Tourism*, *16*(3), 211–239. https://www.tandfonline.com/doi/abs/10.1080/13683500.2012.662215

Healy, T. G., & Wilson, A. (2015). *Social Media Marketing in the Hospitality Industry: Is It Worth the Effort?* 10.

Helfat, C. E., & Martin, J. A. (2015). Dynamic Managerial Capabilities: Review and Assessment of Managerial Impact on Strategic Change. *Journal of Management*, *41*(5), 1281–1312. DOI: 10.1177/0149206314561301

Hennig-Thurau, T., Gwinner, K. P., Walsh, G., & Gremler, D. D. (2004). Electronic word-of-mouth via consumer-opinion platforms: What motivates consumers to articulate themselves on the Internet? *Journal of Interactive Marketing*, *18*(1), 38–52. DOI: 10.1002/dir.10073

Hernández-Mogollón, J. A.-F.-C. (2019). Food Festivals and the Development of Sustainable Destinations. The Case of the Cheese Fair in Trujillo (Spain). [*May.*]. *Sustainability, MDPI*, *11*(10), 1–14.

Hisrich, R. D., Peters, M. P., & Shepherd, D. A. (2016). *Entrepreneurship* (10th ed.). McGraw Hill.

Holliman, G., & Rowley, J. (2014). Business to business digital content marketing: Marketers' perceptions of best practice. *Journal of Research in Interactive Marketing*, *8*(4), 269–293. DOI: 10.1108/JRIM-02-2014-0013

Homans, G. C. (1958). Social behavior as exchange. *American Journal of Sociology*, *63*(6), 597–606.

Homer, P. M. (1990). The Mediating Role of Attitude toward the Ad: Some Additional Evidence. *JMR, Journal of Marketing Research*, *27*(1), 78. DOI: 10.2307/3172553

Hong, I. B., & Cho, H. (2011). The impact of consumer trust on attitudinal loyalty and purchase intentions in B2C e-marketplaces: Intermediary trust vs. seller trust. *International Journal of Information Management*, *31*(5), 469–479. DOI: 10.1016/j.ijinfomgt.2011.02.001

Hornik, J., Ofir, C., & Rachamim, M. (2024). *Out of the fog: fog computing-enabled AI to support smart marketing management.* Management Review Quarterly.

Hosmani, S.M. and Lalitha, M.D., 2025. Data Driven Insights: Machine Learning For Terrorist Attacks Region Predication. *Journal of Scientific Research and Technology*, pp.217-228.

Hossain, M. S., Sheikh, P., & Islam, P. (2025). The Role of Social Media Marketing in the Tourism and Hospitality Industry: A study on Bangladesh. *American Journal of Tourism and Hospitality*, *3*(1), 14–23. DOI: 10.54536/ajth.v3i1.4082

Ho, V. (2020). Do hotels enhance and challenge rapport with customers with the same degree of commitment? *Journal of Pragmatics*, *166*, 70–83.

Hsu, M. H., Chuang, L. W., & Hsu, C. S. (2014). Understanding online shopping intention: The roles of four types of trust and their antecedents. *Internet Research*, *24*(3), 332–352. DOI: 10.1108/IntR-01-2013-0007

HTL. H. (2024). *India Hotel Market Review 2024 The Global Leader in Hospitality Consulting*. https://horwathhtl.com/wp-content/uploads/2025/02/India-Hotel-Market-Report-2024.pdf

Huang, A., Chao, Y., de la Mora Velasco, E., Bilgihan, A., & Wei, W. (2022). When artificial intelligence meets the hospitality and tourism industry: An assessment framework to inform theory and management. *Journal of Hospitality and Tourism Insights*, *5*(5), 1080–1100.

Huang, N., Burtch, G., Gu, B., Hong, Y., Liang, C., Wang, K., & Yang, B. (2019). Motivating user-generated content with performance feedback: Evidence from randomized field experiments. *Management Science*, *65*(1), 327–345.

Hudson, S. (2013). The Impact of Social Media on the Consumer Decision Process: Implications for Tourism Marketing. *Journal of Travel & Tourism Marketing*, *30*(1–2), 156–160. DOI: 10.1080/10548408.2013.751276

Hulland, J., & Houston, M. B. (2020). Why systematic review papers and meta-analyses matter: An introduction to the special issue on generalizations in marketing. *Journal of the Academy of Marketing Science, 48*(3), 351–359. DOI: 10.1007/s11747-020-00721-7

Husain, R., Ratna, V. V., & Saxena, A. (2023). Past, present, and future of anthropomorphism in hospitality & tourism: Conceptualization and systematic review. *Journal of Hospitality Marketing & Management, 32*(8), 1077–1125.

Hussain, Z., Safeer, A. A., & Ahmed, M. J. (2025). The Role of Social Media Marketing for the Hospitality Business. In *Marketing Technology-Infused Hospitality: Upskilling Frontline Employees for Competitiveness* (pp. 181-204). IGI Global Scientific Publishing. https://www.igi-global.com/chapter/the-role-of-social-media-marketing-for-the-hospitality-business/367414

Hussain, A., Hooi Ting, D., Zaib Abbasi, A., & Rehman, U. (2023). Integrating the S-O-R Model to Examine Purchase Intention Based on Instagram Sponsored Advertising. *Journal of Promotion Management, 29*(1), 77–105. DOI: 10.1080/10496491.2022.2108185

Ibrahim, M.A., Wan Mohd Zain, W.M.A., Mior Shariffuddin, N.S., Azinuddin M., Mohd Salim, M.N.H., & Zainul, N.H. (2025). Crafting food destination image in the social media age: dynamics of consumption, experience and culture differences. *Journal of Hospitality and Tourism Insights, 8*(5), 1907-1926. DOI: 10.1108/jhti-12-2023-0885

Ilesanmi, O. O., Oke, A. E., Moyanga, D. T., Aliu, J., & Aigbavboa, C. (2025). Key Barriers to the Extensive Adoption of Robotics in the Nigerian Built Environment. In Azrour, M., Hossain, I., & Haque, A. K. M. M. (Eds.), (pp. 197–224). Advances in Computational Intelligence and Robotics. IGI Global., DOI: 10.4018/979-8-3373-1892-9.ch008

Inversini, A., De Carlo, M., & Masiero, L. (2020). The effects of customer-centricity in hospitality. *International Journal of Hospitality Management, 86*, 102436.

Islam, N., & Singh, A. (2025). Role of Digitalization into Hospitality Businesses: Innovations and Trends. In *Transforming the Service Sector With New Technology* (pp. 447–458). IGI Global Scientific Publishing.

Ivanov, S., & Webster, C. (2019). Conceptual Framework of the Use of Robots, Artificial Intelligence and Service Automation in Travel, Tourism, and Hospitality Companies. In S. Ivanov & C. Webster (Eds.), *Robots, Artificial Intelligence, and Service Automation in Travel, Tourism and Hospitality* (pp. 7–37). Emerald Publishing Limited. https://doi.org/DOI: 10.1108/978-1-78756-687-320191001

Ivanov, S., & Webster, C. (2019). Conceptual Framework of the Use of Robots, Artificial Intelligence and Service Automation in Travel, Tourism, and Hospitality Companies. Robots, Artificial Intelligence, and Service Automation in Travel, Tourism and Hospitality, 7-37. https://doi.org/DOI: 10.1108/978-1-78756-687 320191001

Ivanov, S., Webster, C., & Berezina, K. (2020). Robotics in Tourism and Hospitality. In Z. Xiang, M. Fuchs, U. Gretzel, & W. Höpken (Eds.), *Handbook of e-Tourism* (pp. 1–27). Springer International Publishing. https://doi.org/DOI: 10.1007/978-3-030-05324-6_112-1

Ivanov, S., Duglio, S., & Beltramo, R. (2023). Robots in tourism and Sustainable Development Goals: Tourism Agenda 2030 perspective article. *Tourism Review*, *78*(2), 352–360. DOI: 10.1108/TR-08-2022-0404

Ivanov, S., Seyitoğlu, F., & Markova, M. (2020). Hotel managers' perceptions towards the use of robots: A mixed-methods approach. *Information Technology & Tourism*, *22*(4), 505–535. DOI: 10.1007/s40558-020-00187-x

Ivanov, S., Seyitoğlu, F., & Webster, C. (2025). The economics of service robots in hospitality companies. *Tourism Economics*, *13548166251362622*. Advance online publication. DOI: 10.1177/13548166251362622

Ivanov, S., & Webster, C. (2020). Robots in tourism: A research agenda for tourism economics. *Tourism Economics*, *26*(7), 1065–1085.

Ivanov, S., & Webster, C. (2021). Willingness-to-pay for robot-delivered tourism and hospitality services–an exploratory study. *International Journal of Contemporary Hospitality Management*, *33*(11), 3926–3955.

Ivanov, S., & Webster, C. (2023). Restaurants and robots: Public preferences for robot food and beverage services. *Journal of Tourism Futures*, *9*(2), 229–239.

Ivanov, S., Webster, C., & Garenko, A. (2018). Young Russian adults' attitudes towards the potential use of robots in hotels. *Technology in Society*, *55*, 24–32.

Ivanov, S., Webster, C., & Seyitoğlu, F. (2023). Humans and/or robots? Tourists' preferences towards the humans–robots mix in the service delivery system. *Service Business*, *17*(1), 195–231.

Iyengar, M. S., & Venkatesh, R. 2024. A brief communication on the Top Ten Trends in the Hospitality Industry for 2024: World Scenario. *SCT Proceedings in Interdisciplinary Insights and Innovations, 2*, p.45.

Jabareen, Y. (2009). Building a Conceptual Framework: Philosophy, Definitions, and Procedure. *International Journal of Qualitative Methods*, *8*(4), 49–62. DOI: 10.1177/160940690900800406

Jae, Y. I., & Hwa, P. I. (2025). Personalized Digital Marketing Strategies: A Data-Driven Approach Using Marketing Analytics. *Journal of Management and Informatics*, *4*(1), 668–686. DOI: 10.51903/jmi.v4i1.149

Jain, P. (2024). Exploring the Impact of Digital Marketing Strategies on Customer Engagement and Loyalty in the Hospitality Industry. *International Journal Of Novel Research And Development, 9*(8). www.ijnrd.org

Jain, G., Rakesh, S., & Chaturvedi, K. R. (2018). Online video advertisements' effect on purchase intention: An exploratory study on youth. *International Journal of E-Business Research, 14*(2), 87–101. DOI: 10.4018/IJEBR.2018040106

Jalilvand, M. R., & Samiei, N. (2012). The impact of electronic word of mouth on a tourism destination choice: Testing the theory of planned behavior (TPB). *Internet Research*, *22*(5), 591–612. DOI: 10.1108/10662241211271563

Jamir, W., Jasrotia, A., & Kumar, S. (2025). The Power of Social Media: Unveiling its Impact on Millennial Travel Choices. In Talukder, M. B., & Chowdhury, H. H. K. (Eds.), *Smart Operations and Enhancing Guest Experience in the Hospitality Industry* (pp. 297–314). IGI Global., DOI: 10.4018/979-8-3373-2145-5.ch011

Jamshed, K., Qureshi, M. A., Kishwer, R., & Jamshaid, S. (2024). The benefits and challenges of artificial intelligence applications in tourism industry: How the hospitality industry in Japan is transforming. In *The role of artificial intelligence in regenerative tourism and green destinations* (pp. 129–147). Emerald Publishing Limited.

Janssen, L., Schouten, A. P., & Croes, E. A. (2021). Influencer advertising on Instagram: Product-influencer fit and number of followers affect advertising outcomes and influencer evaluations via credibility and identification. *International Journal of Advertising*, *41*(1), 101–127. DOI: 10.1080/02650487.2021.1994205

Jantunen, A., Tarkiainen, A., Chari, S., & Oghazi, P. (2018). Dynamic capabilities, operational changes, and performance outcomes in the media industry. *Journal of Business Research*, *89*, 251–257. DOI: 10.1016/j.jbusres.2018.01.037

Jaremen, D. E. (2016). Advantages from ICT usage in Hotel Industry. *Czech Journal of Social Sciences Business and Economics*, *5*(3), 6–18.

Jayawardena, C., Ahmad, A., Valeri, M., & Jaharadak, A. A. (2023). Technology acceptance antecedents in digital transformation in the hospitality industry. *International Journal of Hospitality Management, 108*, 103350. DOI: 10.1016/j.ijhm.2022.103350

Jebarajakirthy, C., Maseeh, H. I., Morshed, Z., Shankar, A., Arli, D., & Pentecost, R. (2021). Mobile advertising: A systematic literature review and future research agenda. In *International Journal of Consumer Studies* (Vol. 45, Issue 6, pp. 1258–1291). John Wiley and Sons Inc. https://doi.org/DOI: 10.1111/ijcs.12728

Jesus Jerez-Jerez, M., Sevilla-Sevilla, C., & Aguiar-Castillo, L. (Eds.). (2025). *The Role of Artificial Intelligence in the Tourism and Hospitality Sector* (1st ed.). Routledge., DOI: 10.4324/9781003545125

Jeyakumar, T. (2025). *The Evolution of CRM in the Hospitality Industry: From Bookings to Brand Loyalty*. LinkedIn. Retrieved from https://www.linkedin.com/pulse/evolution-crm-hospitality-industry-from-bookings-brand-jeyakumar-ls7ac

Jiang, Y., & Wen, J. (2020). Effects of COVID-19 on hotel marketing and management: A perspective article. *International Journal of Contemporary Hospitality Management, 32*(8), 2563–2573.

Jiménez-Barreto, J., Rubio, N., & Molinillo, S. (2021). "Find a flight for me, Oscar!" Motivational customer experiences with chatbots. *International Journal of Contemporary Hospitality Management, 33*(11), 3860–3882.

Johnson, R. (2022). *Influencer Marketing in Hospitality: Risks and Regulations*. International Journal of Hospitality Marketing.

Johnson, A. (2025). Engagement, informativeness, and intrusiveness: Unpacking social media's impact on mobile ads. *International Journal of Management and Economics Fundamental, 5*(01), 1–4.

Johnson, T. J., & Kaye, B. K. (2015). Site Effects: How Reliance on Social Media Influences Confidence in the Government and News Media. *Social Science Computer Review, 33*(2), 127–144. DOI: 10.1177/0894439314537029

Jonathan, J. (2025). THE TRANSFORMATION OF THE HOSPITALITY INDUSTRY IN FACING THE DIGITAL TECHNOLOGY ERA: OPPORTUNITIES, CHALLENGES, AND INNOVATIONS. [Artificial Intelligence Research and Applied Learning]. *AIRA, 4*(2), 79–95. DOI: 10.1234/aira.v4i2.96

Jothy, K. P. (2025). A Study on the Role of AI and Chatbots in Social Media Marketing: Enhancing Customer Engagement and Experience. *International Journal of Latest Technology in Engineering Management & Applied Science*, *14*(6), 884. DOI: 10.51583/ijltemas.2025.140600097

Jung, A. R. (2017). The influence of perceived ad relevance on social media advertising: An empirical examination of a mediating role of privacy concern. *Computers in Human Behavior*, *70*, 303–309. DOI: 10.1016/j.chb.2017.01.008

Jung, T. H., Lee, H., Chung, N., & tom Dieck, M. C. (2018). Cross-cultural differences in adopting mobile augmented reality at cultural heritage tourism sites. *International Journal of Contemporary Hospitality Management*, *30*(3), 1621–1645. DOI: 10.1108/IJCHM-02-2017-0084

Kaba, B., & Touré, B. (2014). Understanding information and communication technology behavioral intention to use: Applying the UTAUT model to social networking site adoption by young people in a least developed country. *Journal of the Association for Information Science and Technology*, *65*(8), 1662–1674. DOI: 10.1002/asi.23069

Kaban, L. M., & Augustinus, D. C. (2025). Understanding brand recommendation and loyalty strategy across local and international chain hotels. *Corporate and Business Strategy Review*, *6*(2), 52. DOI: 10.22495/cbsrv6i2art5

Kalgi, D., Desai, R., & Fatangare, S. (2022). Impact of Social Media Marketing on Accommodation Sector in the Hospitality Industry. In *Current and Futuristic Trends in Accommodation Sector*.

Kalgi, D., Dhole, V., & Naik, S. (2022). *To Study the Role of Social Media Marketing on the Hospitality and Tourism industry of India. Recent Advances in Humanities.* Management, Engineering, Science & Technology.

Kamal, S. A., Z., & Kamarulzaman, Y. (2025). Digital transformation in hotels: A meta-analysis of UTAUT-based empirical evidence. *Jurnal Pengurusan, 74*, Article 2.

Kamalul Ariffin, S., Ihsannuddin, N. Q., & Abdul Mohsin, A. M. (2021). The influence of attitude functions on Muslim consumer attitude towards social media advertising: A case of bubble tea. *Journal of Islamic Marketing*, *6315458*. Advance online publication. DOI: 10.1108/JIMA-01-2021-0015

Kandampully, J. and Solnet, D., 2024. Service Management Principles for Hospitality & Tourism in the Age of Digital Technology.

Kant, S., Niguse, T., Olubiyi, T. O., Adula, M., & Kebede, K. (2025). Sustainable Fashion-Based Innovations and Consumer Behavior in Ethiopia. In Global Impacts and Sustainable Practices in Fast Fashion (pp. 167-196). IGI Global Scientific Publishing.

Kant, S., Niguse, T., & Adula, M. (2025). Role of Social Media on Corporate Branding by Mediation of Customer Relationship Management in the Horn of Africa. In *Corporate Management in the Digital Age* (pp. 337–364). IGI Global Scientific Publishing.

Kaplan, A. M., & Haenlein, M. (2010). Users of the world, unite! The challenges and opportunities of social media. *Business Horizons*, *53*(1), 59–68. DOI: 10.1016/j.bushor.2009.09.003

Kashyap, V. (2024). The Creative Tourism - A New Approach of Sustainable Practices a Case Study of Kinnaur, Himachal Pradesh. *IRTTHI* (pp. 208-218 (11 pages)). Mohali: IRTTHI.

Kashyap, V. (2023). *The Comprehension of the Nichar Community for the Development and Growth of the Destination as a Creative Tourism Destination?* Asean Journal on Hospitality and Tourism.

Kasim, M. (2023). Beyond the Basics: Advanced Strategies for Hotels Using Social Media. *International Journal of Research Publication and Reviews*, *4*(5), 584–588. www.ijrpr.com

Keller, K. L. (1993). Conceptualizing, Measuring, and Managing Customer-Based Brand Equity. *Journal of Marketing*, *57*(1), 1–22. DOI: 10.1177/002224299305700101

Khan, R. & Shalini. (2024). Influencer Marketing Evolution: Unveiling the Power of Data Analytics and AI for Strategic Campaign Excellence. In S. Dutta, Á. Rocha, P. K. Dutta, P. Bhattacharya, & R. Singh (Eds.), *Advances in Data Analytics for Influencer Marketing: An Interdisciplinary Approach* (Vol. 9, pp. 125–147). Springer Nature Switzerland. https://doi.org/DOI: 10.1007/978-3-031-65727-6_8

Khan, A., Rezaei, S., & Valaei, N. (2022). Social commerce advertising avoidance and shopping cart abandonment: A fs/QCA analysis of German consumers. *Journal of Retailing and Consumer Services*, *67*. Advance online publication. DOI: 10.1016/j.jretconser.2022.102976

Khanna, A., & Gopinath, S. (2024). *2 0 2 4 I N D I A N Trends & Opportunities Managing Partner, Strategic Advisory Senior Associate, Strategic Advisory.* https://hotelivate.com/wp-content/uploads/2024/10/Indian-Hospitality-Trends-Opportunities-2024.pdf

Khan, S., & Rehman, A. (2024). Social media influences consumer choices in the travel industry: Examining the decision-making process of travelers. *International Journal of Applied Research, 10*(6), 303–314. DOI: 10.22271/allresearch.2024.v10.i6d.11858

Khatami, F. S. F. (2024). Breaking barriers: The role of digital platforms in enhancing the resilience of food entrepreneurs. *British Food Journal, 126*(11), 3822–3841. DOI: 10.1108/BFJ-02-2024-0142

Khatwani, D., & Bhut, G. (2020). A study on effectiveness of social media marketing in hospitality industry. *International Journal of Management and Commerce Innovations, 7*(2), 1283–1288. www.researchpublish.com

Khlusevich, A., Inversini, A., & Schegg, R. (2024). Artificial Intelligence and Hospitality: A Challenging Relationship. In Springer proceedings in business and economics (p. 247). Springer International Publishing. DOI: 10.1007/978-3-031-58839-6_27

Kiliçhan, R., & Yilmaz, M. (2020). Artificial intelligence and robotic technologies in tourism and hospitality industry. *Erciyes Üniversitesi Sosyal Bilimler Enstitüsü Dergisi, 50*, 353–380. DOI: 10.48070/erusosbilder.838193

Kim, H., So, K. K. F., Shin, S., & Li, J. (2024). Artificial Intelligence in Hospitality and Tourism: Insights From Industry Practices, Research Literature, and Expert Opinions. *Journal of Hospitality & Tourism Research (Washington, D.C.), 49*(2), 366–385. DOI: 10.1177/10963480241229235

Kim, H., So, K. K. F., & Wirtz, J. (2022). Service robots: Applying social exchange theory to better understand human–robot interactions. *Tourism Management, 92*, 104537.

Kim, M. J., Barnes, S. J., & Kang, S.-E. (2025). Embracing sustainable diversity climates in hospitality and tourism: Insights from prospective employees on human–robot collaboration. *Journal of Sustainable Tourism, 33*(5), 801–821. DOI: 10.1080/09669582.2025.2459628

Kim, M., & Qu, H. (2014). Travelers' behavioral intention toward hotel self-service kiosks usage. *International Journal of Contemporary Hospitality Management, 26*(2), 225–245.

Kim, T., Jo, H., Yhee, Y., & Koo, C. (2022). Robots, artificial intelligence, and service automation (RAISA) in hospitality: Sentiment analysis of YouTube streaming data. *Electronic Markets, 32*(1), 259–275.

Kim, Y. J., & Han, J. (2014). Why smartphone advertising attracts customers: A model of Web advertising, flow, and personalization. *Computers in Human Behavior, 33*, 256–269. DOI: 10.1016/j.chb.2014.01.015

Kingston, P. (2024). Crisis Response Strategies in Online Reputation Management. *International Journal of Public Relation and Communication*. Retrieved from https://forthworthjournals.org/journals/index.php/IJPRC/article/view/59

Kivela, J. (2006). Tourism and gastronomy: Gastronomy's influence on how tourists experience a destination. *Journal of Hospitality & Tourism Research (Washington, D.C.), 30*(3), 354–377. DOI: 10.1177/1096348006286797

Kline, R. B. (2015). *Principles and practice of structural equation modeling* (4th ed.). Guilford Press.

Knani, M., Echchakoui, S., & Ladhari, R. (2022). Artificial intelligence in tourism and hospitality: Bibliometric analysis and research agenda. *International Journal of Hospitality Management, 107*, 103317.

Korkee, N. (2024). How brands can utilize micro influencers to grow their sales among generation Z in Finland. https://urn.fi/URN:NBN:fi-fe202502038734

Kornias, G., & Hălălău, R. (2012). Factors influencing users' attitude toward display advertising on Facebook. In *Jönköping University*.

Kotler, P., Bowen, J., Makens, J., & Baloglu, S. (2017). *Marketing for Hospitality and Tourism*. Pearson. https://www.slithm.edu.lk/wp content/uploads/2022/02/marketing_for_hospitalitytourism.pdf

Kotler, P., & Keller, K. L. (2016). *Marketing management* (International Ed.). Pearson.

Krishnan, C., & Mariappan, J. (2024). The AI Revolution in E-Commerce: Personalization and Predictive Analytics. In Gaur, L., & Abraham, A. (Eds.), *Role of Explainable Artificial Intelligence in E-Commerce* (Vol. 1094, pp. 53–64). Springer Nature Switzerland., DOI: 10.1007/978-3-031-55615-9_4

Kruesi, M.A. and Remy, D., 2024. How can Hotels of Every Size Create the Right Technology Roadmap.

Ksenia Kirillova, X. F. (2014). What makes a destination beautiful? Dimensions of tourist aesthetic judgment. *Tourism Management*. Advance online publication. DOI: 10.1016/j.tourman.2013.12.006

Kumar, S. (2024b). Uncertainties in the Hospitality Sector. In *VUCA and Other Analytics in Business Resilience, Part B* (pp. 183–197). Emerald Publishing Limited.

Kumar, A., & Ayedee, N. (2018). Social media tools for business growth of SMEs. *Journal of Management*, *5*(3), 137–142.

Kumari, S., & Rekha. (2019). A study of social media marketing with reference to Hospitality sector. *International Journal of Creative Research Thoughts, Vol.6*(Issue 5), 229–239. https://www.jetir.org/papers/JETIR1905B36.pdf

Kumar, P. (2015). Green marketing innovations in small Indian firms. *World Journal of Entrepreneurship, Management and Sustainable Development*, *11*(3), 176–190. DOI: 10.1108/WJEMSD-01-2015-0003

Kumar, P. K. (2021). Retrieved from https://hospitality.economictimes.indiatimes .com/news/travel/himachal-pradesh-to-harness-the-powers-of-digital-media/ 87056703

Kumar, S. (2024a). The Role of Digital Marketing on Customer Engagement in the Hospitality Industry. In *Leveraging ChatGPT and Artificial Intelligence for Effective Customer Engagement* (pp. 177–191). IGI Global Scientific Publishing.

Kumar, S., Talukder, M. B., & Kaiser, F. (2024). Artificial Intelligence in Business: Negative Social Impacts. In Dadwal, S., Goyal, S., Kumar, P., & Verma, R. (Eds.), (pp. 81–97). Advances in Human Resources Management and Organizational Development. IGI Global., DOI: 10.4018/979-8-3693-0724-3.ch005

Kumar, S., Talukder, M. B., & Singh, K. (2025). Impact of Tourist Behavior Towards the Digital Technologies in Hospitality Sectors. In Birdir, K., & Birdir, S. (Eds.), (pp. 243–262). Advances in Computational Intelligence and Robotics. IGI Global., DOI: 10.4018/979-8-3693-8769-6.ch009

Kumar, S., Talukder, M. B., & Tyagi, P. K. (2025). The Impact of Virtual Reality and Augmented Reality in TNE Learning. In Crawford, C. M., & Gee, T. T. (Eds.), *Motivating Engagement, Belonging, and Success in Higher Education Student Experience* (pp. 359–382). IGI Global., DOI: 10.4018/979-8-3693-8089-5.ch013

Kuo, C. M., Chen, L. C., & Tseng, C. Y. (2017). Investigating an innovative service with hospitality robots. *International Journal of Contemporary Hospitality Management*, *29*(5), 1305–1321. DOI: 10.1108/IJCHM-08-2015-0414

Kushwaha, B. P., Singh, R. K., Varghese, N., & Singh, V. N. (2020). Integrating social media and digital media as new elements of integrated marketing communication for creating brand equity. *Journal of Content, Community & Communication, 11*(6), 52-64. https://www.researchgate.net/profile/Zinggara-Hidayat-2/publication/ 350639866

Kyung-Hyan Yoo, U. G. (2016). The Role of Information and Communication Technologies (ICTs. In Experiences, M. T. (Ed.), *The Handbook of Managing and Marketing Tourism Experiences*. Marios Sotiriadis, Dogan Gursoy. DOI: 10.1108/978-1-78635-290-320161017

Labib, E. (2024). Artificial intelligence in marketing: Exploring current and future trends. *Cogent Business & Management, 11*(1). Advance online publication. DOI: 10.1080/23311975.2024.2348728

Lacoste, S. M., & Dekker, J. (2016). Driving change: The role of "emotional connectedness"–A case study. *The Learning Organization, 23*(5), 357369.

Lafferty, B. A., & Goldsmith, R. E. (1999). Corporate Credibility's Role in Consumers' Attitudes and Purchase Intentions When a High versus a Low Credibility Endorser Is Used in the Ad. *Journal of Business Research, 44*, 109–116.

Lakha, R., & Bahra, R. (2020). Influence of social media marketing on the performance of hotel industry: A study in Chandigarh Tri-city. *International Journal for Research in Engineering Application & Management, 01*, 401–408. DOI: 10.35291/2454-9150.2020.0322

Lasek, M., & Jessa, S. (2013). Chatbots for customer service on hotels' websites. *Information Systems Management, 2*(2), 146–158.

Law, R., Buhalis, D., & Cobanoglu, C. (2014). Progress on information and communication technologies in hospitality and tourism. *International Journal of Contemporary Hospitality Management, 26*(5), 727–750. DOI: 10.1108/IJCHM-08-2013-0367

Law, R., Lin, K. J., Ye, H., & Fong, D. K. C. (2023). Artificial intelligence research in hospitality: A state-of-the-art review and future directions. *International Journal of Contemporary Hospitality Management.*

Lee, H. Y. (2017). Differences in tourist ethical judgment and responsible tourism intention: An ethical scenario approach. *Tourism Management*, 298 - 307. DOI: 10.1016/j.tourman.2016.12.003

Lee, C., Abdullah, T., Hallak, R., & Kallmuenzer, A. (2025). Hospitality on the streets: A mixed-method study of Indonesian street food micro-enterprises. *International Journal of Hospitality Management, 130*, 104236. DOI: 10.1016/j.ijhm.2025.104236

Lee, J., & Hong, I. B. (2016). Predicting positive user responses to social media advertising: The roles of emotional appeal, informativeness, and creativity. *International Journal of Information Management, 36*(3), 360–373. DOI: 10.1016/j.ijinfomgt.2016.01.001

Lee, J., Walter, N., Hayes, J. L., & Golan, G. J. (2024). Do influencers influence? A meta-analytic comparison of celebrities and social media influencers effects. *Social Media + Society, 10*(3), 20562660241269269.

Lee, M., Ahn, J., Shin, M., Kwon, W., & Back, K.-J. (2021). Integrating technology to service innovation: Key issues and future research directions in hospitality and tourism. *Journal of Hospitality and Tourism Technology, 12*(1), 19–38. DOI: 10.1108/JHTT-01-2019-0013

Lee, S., Shulga, L. V., Busser, J. A., & Hwang, J. (2024). Self-Service Hotel Check-In: Is There Still a Role for the In-Person Experience? *International Journal of Hospitality & Tourism Administration*, •••, 1–28.

Lei, C., Hossain, M. S., & Wong, E. (2023). Determinants of repurchase intentions of hospitality services delivered by artificially intelligent (AI) service robots. *Sustainability, 15*(6), 4914.

Lestari, N. S., Rosman, D., Chan, S., Nawangsari, L. C., Natalina, H. D., & Triono, F. (2022, October). Impact of robots, artificial intelligence, service automation (RAISA) acceptance, self-efficacy, and relationship quality on job performance. In *2022 4th International Conference on Cybernetics and Intelligent System (ICORIS)* (pp. 1-6). IEEE.

Leung, D. Law, R., van Hoof, H., & Buhalis. (2013). Social Media in Tourism and Hospitality: A Literature Review. *Journal of Travel & Tourism Marketing, 30*(1–2), 3–22. DOI: 10.1080/10548408.2013.750919

Leung, D., Law, R., Van Hoof, H., & Buhalis, D. (2013). Social media in tourism and hospitality: A literature review. *Journal of Travel & Tourism Marketing, 30*(1-2), 3–22.

Leung, F. F., Gu, F. F., & Palmatier, R. W. (2022). Online influencer marketing. *Journal of the Academy of Marketing Science, 50*(2), 226–251.

Leung, X. Y., Billy Bai, & Kurt A. Stahura. (2015). The Marketing Effectiveness of Social Media in the Hotel Industry. *Journal of Hospitality & Tourism Research (Washington, D.C.)*.

Leung, X. Y., Bai, B., & Erdem, M. (2017). Hotel social media marketing: A study on message strategy and its effectiveness. *Journal of Hospitality and Tourism Technology, 8*(2), 239–255. DOI: 10.1108/JHTT-02-2017-0012

Leung, X. Y., Bai, B., & Stahura, K. A. (2015). The Marketing Effectiveness of Social Media in the Hotel Industry: A Comparison of Facebook and Twitter. *Journal of Hospitality & Tourism Research (Washington, D.C.), 39*(2), 147–169. DOI: 10.1177/1096348012471381

Leung, X. Y., Jie, S., & Bai, B. (2021). SOCIAL MEDIA RESEARCH IN HOSPITALITY AND TOURISM: A CAUSAL CHAIN FRAMEWORK OF LITERATURE REVIEW. *Tourism and Hospitality Management, 27*(3), 455. DOI: 10.20867/thm.27.3.1

Leung, X. Y., Sun, J., & Bai, B. (2019). Thematic framework of social media research: State of the art. *Tourism Review, 74*(3), 517–531.

Liasidou, S., & Pipyros, K. (2025). Conclusion: What is the transformative relationship between tourism and technology? *Worldwide Hospitality and Tourism Themes, 17*(1), 144–148. DOI: 10.1108/WHATT-12-2024-0314

Li, H., Edwards, S. M., & Lee, J. H. (2002). Measuring the intrusiveness of advertisements: Scale development and validation. *Journal of Advertising, 31*(2), 37–47. DOI: 10.1080/00913367.2002.10673665

Li, J. J., Bonn, M. A., & Ye, B. H. (2019). Hotel employee's artificial intelligence and robotics awareness and its impact on turnover intention: The moderating roles of perceived organizational support and competitive psychological climate. *Tourism Management, 73*, 172–181.

Li, L., Lee, K. Y., Emokpae, E., & Yang, S. B. (2021). What makes you continuously use chatbot services? Evidence from chinese online travel agencies. *Electronic Markets*, •••, 1–25.

Lim, W. (2010). *The Effects of social media networks in the hospitality industry*. 44. http://digitalcommons.library.unlv.edu/thesesdissertations/693/

Li, M., & Suh, A. (2022). Anthropomorphism in AI-enabled technology: A literature review. *Electronic Markets, 32*(4), 2245–2275.

Limna, P., Siripipatthanakul, S., & Phayaphrom, B. (2021). The role of big data analytics in influencing artificial intelligence (AI) adoption for coffee shops in Krabi, Thailand. *International Journal of Behavioral Analytics, 1*(2), 1–17.

Lim, S. (Edward), Ok, C. M., & Yang, Y. (2024). A meta-analytic investigation of innovation predictors in tourism and hospitality organizations. *Tourism Management, 105*, 104965. DOI: 10.1016/j.tourman.2024.104965

Lim, W. M., Yap, S. F., & Makkar, M. (2021). Home sharing in marketing and tourism at a tipping point: What do we know, how do we know, and where should we be heading? *Journal of Business Research, 122*, 534–566.

Lina, L., Lorenzo, V., Iwai, S., & Wahyuningtias, D. (2023). The influence of e-WOM and brand image on hotel booking intention in Jakarta: A study of Generation Z. *E3S Web of Conferences, 426*, 02088. https://doi.org/DOI: 10.1051/e3sconf/202342602088

Lin, H., Chi, O. H., & Gursoy, D. (2020). Antecedents of customers' acceptance of artificially intelligent robotic device use in hospitality services. *Journal of Hospitality Marketing & Management, 29*(5), 530–549.

Lin, J. S. C., & Bhattacherjee, A. (2010). Extending technology usage models to interactive hedonic technologies: A theoretical model and empirical test. *Information Systems Journal, 20*(2), 163–181. DOI: 10.1111/j.1365-2575.2007.00265.x

Lin, T. T. C., & Bautista, J. R. (2020). Content-related factors influence perceived value of location-based mobile advertising. *Journal of Computer Information Systems, 60*(2), 184–193. DOI: 10.1080/08874417.2018.1432995

Litvin, S. W., Goldsmith, R. E., & Pan, B. (2008). Electronic word-of-mouth in hospitality and tourism management. *Tourism Management, 29*(3), 458–468. DOI: 10.1016/j.tourman.2007.05.011

Liu, G. G., Benckendorff, P., & Walters, G. (2025). Human–Robot interaction research in hospitality and tourism: Trends and future directions. *Tourism Review, 80*(4), 847–870. DOI: 10.1108/TR-04-2024-0266

Liu, H., Huang, M., & Zhang, P. (2025). The influence of social media marketing on the quality of hotel services and the behavioral intentions of tourists. *Acta Psychologica, 255*, 104881. DOI: 10.1016/j.actpsy.2025.104881 PMID: 40086229

Liu, J., Gu, T., & Liao, Z. (2024). Operation design of a robot logistics system considering demand fluctuations in the hotel industry. *International Journal of Contemporary Hospitality Management, 36*(1), 113–135. DOI: 10.1108/IJCHM-08-2022-0968

Liu, X. (2020). Analyzing the impact of user-generated content on B2B Firms' stock performance: Big data analysis with machine learning methods. *Industrial Marketing Management, 86*, 30–39.

Liu, Y. (2022). Effect of Digital Marketing Capabilities and Blockchain Technology on Organizational Performance and Psychology. *Frontiers in Psychology, 12*. Advance online publication. DOI: 10.3389/fpsyg.2021.805393 PMID: 35211056

Lorgeoux, C. P. (2023). How Foreign Social Media Influencers Help Shape Destination Country's Tourism Image: The Case of South Korea's Tourism Image in France. *Tourism Analysis*, *28*(2). Advance online publication. DOI: 10.3727/108354223x16773677647966

Louis, G. Tornatzky, Fleischer, M., & Chakrabarti, A. K. (1990). *The processes of technological innovation.* Lexington Books.

Lukanova, G., & Ilieva, G. (2019). In Ivanov, S., & Webster, C. (Eds.), *Robots, artificial intelligence, and service automation in hotels* (pp. 157–183). Robots, Artificial Intelligence, and Service Automation in Travel, Tourism and Hospitality., DOI: 10.1108/978-1-78756-687-320191009

Lu, L., Cai, R., & Gursoy, D. (2019). Developing and validating a service robot integration willingness scale. *International Journal of Hospitality Management*, *80*, 36–51.

Lu, Y., Zhou, T., & Wang, B. (2009). Exploring Chinese users' acceptance of instant messaging using the theory of planned behavior, the technology acceptance model, and the flow theory. *Computers in Human Behavior*, *25*(1), 29–39. DOI: 10.1016/j.chb.2008.06.002

Lv, L., Huang, M., Guan, D., & Yang, K. (2022). Apology or gratitude? The effect of communication recovery strategies for service failures of AI devices. *Journal of Travel & Tourism Marketing*, *39*(6), 570–587.

MacKenzie, S. B., & Lutz, R. J. (1989). An Empirical Examination of the Structural Antecedents of Attitude toward the Ad in an Advertising Pretesting Context. *Journal of Marketing*, *53*, 48–65. DOI: 10.2307/1251413

Magoutas, A. I., Manolopoulos, D., Manouka, M., & Dimitropoulou, M. (2024). Digitalization of the Alternative Tourism Marketspace: Evidence from an EU Peripheral Economy. *Tourism and Hospitality*, *5*(4), 1151–1166. DOI: 10.3390/tourhosp5040064

Mahalakshmi, S., & Bharath, H. 2025. From Check-In to Check-Out: AI Innovations in the Hospitality Sector. In Digital Disruption in Hospitality, AI, and Emerging Technologies (pp. 79-99). Emerald Publishing Limited.

Mahatmavidya, P. A., & Yasa, N. N. K. (2020). Advertising value of Instagram stories and the effect on millennial's attitude. *Russian Journal of Agricultural and Socio-Economic Sciences*, *3*(99), 29–39. DOI: 10.18551/rjoas.2020-03.04

Maiyaki, A. A., & Mokhtar, S. S. M. (2010). Determinants of customer behavioural responses: A pilot study. *International Business Research*, *4*(1), 193. https://doi.org/http://dx.doi.org/10.5539/ibr.v4n1p193

Manaman, H. S., & Jamali, S., & AleAhmad, A. (2016). Online reputation measurement of companies based on user-generated content in online social networks. *Computers in Human Behavior*, *54*, 94–100.

Mangold, W. G., & Faulds, D. J. (2009). Social media: The new hybrid element of the promotion mix. *Business Horizons*, *52*(4), 357–365. DOI: 10.1016/j.bushor.2009.03.002

Manoharan, G., & Ashtikar, S. P. 2025. AI Era in Hospitality: The New Frontier in Guest Satisfaction and Operations. In *Digital Disruption in Hospitality, AI, and Emerging Technologies: A Roadmap to Personalized Experiences, Enhanced Operations, and Revenue Growth* (pp. 59-77). Emerald Publishing Limited.

Manoharan, G., Kumar, S., & Talukder, M. B. (2024). Artificial Intelligence Enhancing Customer Relations in Financial Sectors. In Darwish, D., & Kumar, S. (Eds.), (pp. 283–300). Advances in Finance, Accounting, and Economics. IGI Global., DOI: 10.4018/979-8-3693-8507-4.ch015

Maria Giovanna Confetto, F. C. (2023). Digital destination branding: A framework to define and assess European DMOs practices. *Journal of Destination Marketing & Management*, *30*. Advance online publication. DOI: 10.1016/j.jdmm.2023.100804

Mariani, M. M. (2016). Facebook as a destination marketing tool: Evidence from Italian regional Destination Management Organizations. *Tourism Management, Elsevier*, *54*(C), 321–343. DOI: 10.1016/j.tourman.2015.12.008

Mariani, M., & Borghi, M. (2021). Customers' evaluation of mechanical artificial intelligence in hospitality services: A study using online reviews analytics. *International Journal of Contemporary Hospitality Management*, *33*(11), 3956–3976.

Martin-Fuentes, E., & Mellinas, J. P. (2018). Hotels that most rely on Booking.com–online travel agencies (OTAs) and hotel distribution channels. *Tourism Review*, *73*(4), 465–479.

Martin-Rios, C., & Ciobanu, T. (2019). Hospitality innovation strategies: An analysis of success factors and challenges. *Tourism Management*, *70*, 218–229. DOI: 10.1016/j.tourman.2018.08.018

Martins, J., Costa, C., Oliveira, T., Gonçalves, R., & Branco, F. (2019). How smartphone advertising influences consumers' purchase intention. *Journal of Business Research*, *94*, 378–387. DOI: 10.1016/j.jbusres.2017.12.047

Mastilak, L., Suchy, R., Kostal, K., & Kotuliak, I. (2023). Blockchain-Based Sustainable Retail Loyalty Program. *IEEE Access: Practical Innovations, Open Solutions*, *11*, 75063–75075. DOI: 10.1109/ACCESS.2023.3296914

Mavitha, K., & Kushe Shekhar, S. (2025). *Mapping the landscape of digital transformation and digital technologies in the hotel industry: a comprehensive bibliometric analysis*. Digital Transformation and Society.

McCarthy, L., Stock, D., & Verma, R. (2010). How travelers use online and social media channels to make hotel-choice decisions. https://ecommons.cornell.edu/server/api/core/bitstreams/29b13443-43b9-41ce-a084-d1c884ddfc82/content

McCartney, G., & McCartney, A. (2020). Rise of the machines: Towards a conceptual service-robot research framework for the hospitality and tourism industry. *International Journal of Contemporary Hospitality Management*, *32*(12), 3835–3851. DOI: 10.1108/IJCHM-05-2020-0450

McDonald, E. (2025, January 21). *Influencer Marketing in Hospitality: Grow Brand Reach & Bookings | dblspc*. Dblspc. https://dblspc.com/insights/influencer-marketing-hospitality-industry/

McKelvey, F., & Hunt, R. (2019). Discoverability: Toward a definition of content discovery through platforms. *Social Media + Society*, *5*(1), 2056305118819188.

McPharlin, M. (2022). Retrieved from https://scanmagazine.co.uk/stolte-anton-an-old-fashioned-and-sustainable-taste-of-norway/

Mehta, A. (2000). Advertising Attitudes and Ads Effectiveness. *Journal of Advertising Research*, *40*(3), 67–72.

Mengalli, N. M., de Carvalho, A. A., & Galvão, S. M. (2024). Metaverse ecosystem and consumer society 5.0: consumer experience and influencer marketing in phygital transformation. In *Influencer marketing applications within the metaverse* (pp. 33–56). IGI Global.

Meng, J., Begum, M., Na, M., & Shah Alam, S. (2025). The Impact of Innovative Culture on Adaptive Marketing and Service Innovation in Hospitality: A Strategic Perspective. *Journal of Quality Assurance in Hospitality & Tourism*, •••, 1–38. DOI: 10.1080/1528008X.2025.2509230

Michael Hall, C. & Mitchell, R. (2005). Chapter 6 - Gastronomic tourism: Comparing food and wine tourism experiences. In M. Novelli, *Niche Tourism* (pp. 73-88). DOI: 10.1016/B978-0-7506-6133-1.50014-7

Michopoulou, E., & Moisa, D. G. (2019). Hotel social media metrics: The ROI dilemma. *International Journal of Hospitality Management*, *76*, 308–315. https://www.sciencedirect.com/science/article/abs/pii/S0278431917308423

Milfeld, T., & Haley, E. (2024). Purpose advertising and the credibility gap. *Journal of Advertising Research*, *64*(1), 59–79. DOI: 10.2501/jar-2023-021

Minazzi, R. (2015). *Social media marketing in tourism and hospitality*. Springer International Publishing Switzerland. https://link.springer.com/book/10.1007/978-3-319-05182-6

Minazzi, R., & Panno, A. (2019, July). Social media marketing in the hospitality industry: the evolution of European hotels' approaches from 2012 to 2018. In *9th Advances in Hopitality and Tourism Marketing and Management Conference* (p. 345).

Mingotto, E., Montaguti, F., & Tamma, M. (2021). Challenges in re-designing operations and jobs to embody AI and robotics in services. Findings from a case in the hospitality industry. *Electronic Markets*, *31*(3), 493–510. DOI: 10.1007/s12525-020-00439-y

Mitchell, A. A., & Olson, J. C. (1981). Are Product Attribute Beliefs the Only Mediator of Advertising Effects on Brand Attitude? *JMR, Journal of Marketing Research*, *18*(3), 318–332. DOI: 10.2307/3150973

Mittal, B. (1994). Public assessment of advertising: Faint praise and harsh criticism. *Journal of Advertising Research*, *34*(1), 35–53.

Mogaji, E., Viglia, G., Srivastava, P., & Dwivedi, Y. K. (2024). Is it the end of the technology acceptance model in the era of generative artificial intelligence? *International Journal of Contemporary Hospitality Management*, *36*(10), 3324–3339.

Mohammad, A. A. A., Elshaer, I. A., Azazz, A. M. S., Kooli, C., Algezawy, M., & Fayyad, S. (2024). The Influence of Social Commerce Dynamics on Sustainable Hotel Brand Image, Customer Engagement, and Booking Intentions. *Sustainability*, *16*(14), 6050. DOI: 10.3390/su16146050

Mohammadian, N., & Valilai, O. F. (2024). Influencer-Driven Paradigm Shifts: Analyzing Sustainability and Customer Behavior in Cell Phone and E-Auto Industries via Social Media Analytics. *IEEE Access: Practical Innovations, Open Solutions*, *12*, 119133–119145. DOI: 10.1109/ACCESS.2024.3449113

Mohd Noor, M. N., Sreenivasan, J., & Ismail, H. (2013). Malaysian consumers attitude towards mobile advertising, the role of permission and its impact on purchase intention: A structural equation modeling approach. *Asian Social Science*, *9*(5), 135–153. DOI: 10.5539/ass.v9n5p135

Moisescu, O.-I., Gică, O.-A., & Herle, F.-A. (2022). Boosting eWOM through Social Media Brand Page Engagement: The Mediating Role of Self-Brand Connection. *Behavioral Sciences (Basel, Switzerland)*, *12*(11), 411. DOI: 10.3390/bs12110411 PMID: 36354388

Molina-Castillo, F. J., Meroño-Cerdán, A. L., Lopez-Nicolas, C., & Fernandez-Espinar, L. (2023). Innovation and technology in hospitality sector: Outcome and performance. *Businesses*, *3*(1), 198–219. DOI: 10.3390/businesses3010014

Molinillo, S., Rejón-Guardia, F., & Anaya-Sánchez, R. (2022). Exploring the antecedents of customers' willingness to use service robots in restaurants. *Service Business*, *17*(1), 167–193.

Mondal, S., Das, S., & Vrana, V. G. (2023). How to bell the cat? A theoretical review of generative artificial intelligence towards digital disruption in all walks of life. *Technologies*, *11*(2), 44. DOI: 10.3390/technologies11020044

Montazeri, A., Mohammadi, S. M., Hesari, P., Ghaemi, M., Riazi, H., & Sheikhi-Mobarakeh, Z. (2023). Preliminary guideline for reporting bibliometric reviews of the biomedical literature (BIBLIO): A minimum requirements. *Systematic Reviews*, *12*(1), 239. PMID: 38102710

Moran, G., Muzellec, L., & Johnson, D. (2020). Message content features and social media engagement: Evidence from the media industry. *Journal of Product and Brand Management*, *29*(5), 533–545.

Morgan, N., & Pritchard, A. (2012). *Advertising in tourism and leisure*. Routledge.

Moro, S., & Rita, P. (2018). Brand strategies in social media in hospitality and tourism. *International Journal of Contemporary Hospitality Management*, *30*(1), 343–364. https://www.emerald.com/ijchm/article-abstract/30/1/343/115837/Brand-strategies-in-social-media-in-hospitality?redirectedFrom=fulltext

Morosan, C. T., Bowen, J., & Atwood, M. (2014). The evolution of marketing research. *International Journal of Contemporary Hospitality Management*, *26*(5), 706726.

Morrison, A. M. (2022). *Hospitality and travel marketing*. Routledge.

Mukherjee, S., Baral, M. M., Nagariya, R., Venkataiah, C., Rao, U. A., & Rao, K. S. (2023). Systematic literature review and future research directions for service robots in hospitality and tourism industries. *Service Industries Journal*, *43*(15-16), 1083–1116.

Mukherjee, S., Baral, M. M., Venkataiah, C., Pal, S. K., & Nagariya, R. (2021). Service robots are an option for contactless services due to the COVID-19 pandemic in the hotels. *Decision (Washington, D.C.)*, *48*(4), 445–460. DOI: 10.1007/s40622-021-00300-x

Mu, L., Guo, Q., & Yang, L. (2025). Revolutionizing Hospitality: Unraveling the Transformative Potential of Big Data in Tourism and Hotel Management. *HighTech and Innovation Journal*, *6*(1), 201–215. DOI: 10.28991/HIJ-2025-06-01-014

Muller, C. (2010). Hospitality technology: A review and reflection. *Worldwide Hospitality and Tourism Themes*, *2*(1), 9–19. DOI: 10.1108/17554211011012568

Müller, R., Coffie, I. S., de Klerk, N., & Schalkwyk, J. H. (2025). Enhancing Consumer Social Media Brand Engagement: An Examination of the Interactive Influence of Perceived Utilitarian and Hedonic Benefit. *Business Perspectives and Research*. Advance online publication. DOI: 10.1177/22785337251342838

Murillo, E., Merino, M., & Núñez, A. (2016). The advertising value of Twitter Ads: A study among Mexican Millennials Enrique. *Review of Business Management*, *18*(61), 436–456. DOI: 10.7819/rbgn.v18i61.2471

Murniati, M., & Bawono, S. (2020). *Hotel Marketing Strategies in the Digital Age*. Hotel Marketing Strategies in the Digital Age., DOI: 10.54204/329258

Naab, T. K., & Sehl, A. (2017). Studies of user-generated content: A systematic review. *Journalism*, *18*(10), 1256–1273.

Naeem Abass, M., Abd El-Fattah Zohry, M., & Gamal Saad Soliman, S. (2022). The Possibility of using Robot as one of the Artificial Intelligence Techniques in the Food and Beverage Department in Five-star Hotels: Managers' Perspective. . , *11*(2), 857–907. https://doi.org/DOI: 10.21608/mkaf.2022.254018

Nam, K., Dutt, C. S., Chathoth, P., Daghfous, A., & Khan, M. S. (2021). The adoption of artificial intelligence and robotics in the hotel industry: Prospects and challenges. *Electronic Markets*, *31*, 553–574.

Narangajavana Kaosiri, Y., Callarisa Fiol, L. J., Moliner Tena, M. Á., Rodríguez Artola, R. M., & Sánchez García, J. (2019). User-generated content sources in social media: A new approach to explore tourist satisfaction. *Journal of Travel Research*, *58*(2), 253–265.

Narangajavana, Y., Fiol, L. J. C., Tena, M. Á. M., Artola, R. M. R., & García, J. S. (2017). The influence of social media in creating expectations. An empirical study for a tourist destination. *Annals of Tourism Research*, *65*, 60–70.

Naseem, M. J., Bardhan, M. R., & Singh, M. P. (2025). *The Digital Paradox of Childhood: Balancing Freedom & Protection in the Age of AI and Cybersecurity*. BlueRose Publishers Pvt Ltd.

Naumov, N. (2019). The Impact of Robots, Artificial Intelligence, and Service Automation on Service Quality and Service Experience in Hospitality. In S. Ivanov & C. Webster (Eds.), *Robots, Artificial Intelligence, and Service Automation in Travel, Tourism and Hospitality* (pp. 123–133). Emerald Publishing Limited. https://doi .org/DOI: 10.1108/978-1-78756-687-320191007

Nayyar, A., Mahapatra, B., Le, D. and Suseendran, G., 2018. Virtual Reality (VR) & Augmented Reality (AR) technologies for tourism and hospitality industry. *International journal of engineering & technology, 7*(2.21), pp.156-160.

Neuhofer, B., Buhalis, D., & Ladkin, A. (2014). A typology of technology-enhanced tourism experiences. *International Journal of Tourism Research, 16*(4), 340–350. DOI: 10.1002/jtr.1958

Nguyen, T. M., Le, D., Quach, S., Thaichon, P., & Ratten, V. 2021. The current trends and future direction of digital and relationship marketing: A business perspective. In *Developing Digital Marketing: Relationship Perspectives* (pp. 191-200). Emerald Publishing Limited.

Nguyen, D. H., Tan, K. L., Vi, N. L. N., Phu, N. A., & Ting, H. (2024). The Influence of Customer Relationship Management in Enhancing Hospitality Business Performance: The Conditional Mediation of Digital Marketing Capabilities. *International Journal of Hospitality & Tourism Administration*. Advance online publication. DOI: 10.1080/15256480.2024.2346142

Nguyen, T. M., Quach, S., & Thaichon, P. (2022). The effect of AI quality on customer experience and brand relationship. *Journal of Consumer Behaviour, 21*(3), 481–493.

Nielsen. (2016). Nielsen Social Media Report. In *The Nielsen Company*.

Noone, B. M., McGuire, K. A., & Rohlfs, K. V. (2011). Social media meets hotel revenue management: Opportunities, issues and unanswered questions. *Journal of Revenue and Pricing Management, 10*(4), 293–305. https://link.springer.com/article/10.1057/rpm.2011.12

Noor, U., Mansoor, M., & Shamim, A. (2024). Customers create customers! – Assessing the role of perceived personalization, online advertising engagement and online users' modes in generating positive e-WOM. *Asia-Pacific Journal of Business Administration, 16*(2), 392–409.

Nozdreva, R., & Churakova, A. (2021). Digital tools in empirical marketing strategies of global hotel companies. *Digital strategies in a global market: Navigating the Fourth Industrial Revolution*, 213-227. https://link.springer.com/chapter/10.1007/978-3-030-58267-8_16

Nunnally, J. C., & Bernstein, I. H. (1994). *Psychometric theory* (3rd ed.). McGraw-Hill.

Nurhidayah, S., & Dirgantara, I. M. B. (2025). The effect of personalized advertising on attitude towards advertising and click-through rate. *Economic and Business Horizon*, *4*(3), 469–478.

Nuria Recuero-Virto, C. V. (2024). Culinary destination enchantment: The strategic interplay of local gastronomy in regional tourism development. *International Journal of Gastronomy and Food Science*. Advance online publication. DOI: 10.1016/j.ijgfs.2024.100931

OECD. (2022). *Regulatory Approaches to Digital Advertising*. Organisation for Economic Co-operation and Development.

Oh, H., Kim, B.-Y., & Shin, J.-H. (2004). Hospitality and tourism marketing: Recent developments in research and future directions. *International Journal of Hospitality Management, 23*(5), 425–447. DOI: 10.1016/j.ijhm.2004.10.004

Oke, A. E., Aliu, J., Fadamiro, P., Jamir Singh, P. S., Samsurijan, M. S., & Yahaya, M. (2024). Robotics and automation for sustainable construction: Microscoping the barriers to implementation. *Smart and Sustainable Built Environment, 13*(3), 625–643. DOI: 10.1108/SASBE-12-2022-0275

Ononiwu, M., Azonuche, T. I., & Enyejo, J. O. (2023). Exploring Influencer Marketing Among Women Entrepreneurs using Encrypted CRM Analytics and Adaptive Progressive Web App Development. *International Journal of Scientific Research and Modern Technology*, *2*(6), 1–13.

Orea-Giner, A., Fusté-Forné, F., Todd, L., & Park, E. (2026). The nexus between local food tourism events and social sustainability: Future prospects and priorities. *Tourism Management Perspectives, Volume 60, 101430, ISSN 2211-9736*. DOI: 10.1016/j.tmp.2025.101430

Ottenbacher, M. C. (2007). Innovation Management in the Hospitality Industry: Different Strategies for Achieving Success. *Journal of Hospitality & Tourism Research (Washington, D.C.), 31*(4), 431–454. DOI: 10.1177/1096348007302352

Ottenbacher, M., & Gnoth, J. (2005). How to develop successful hospitality innovation. *The Cornell Hotel and Restaurant Administration Quarterly*, *46*(2), 205–222. DOI: 10.1177/0010880404271097

Ozdemir, O., Dogru, T., Kizildag, M., & Erkmen, E. (2023). A critical reflection on digitalization for the hospitality and tourism industry: Value implications for stakeholders. *International Journal of Contemporary Hospitality Management, 35*(9), 3305–3321.

Öztürk, O., Kocaman, R., & Kanbach, D. K. (2024). How to design bibliometric research: An overview and a framework proposal. *Review of Managerial Science, 18*(11), 3333–3361.

Page, M. J., McKenzie, J. E., Bossuyt, P. M., Boutron, I., Hoffmann, T. C., Mulrow, C. D., Shamseer, L., Tetzlaff, J. M., Akl, E. A., Brennan, S. E., Chou, R., Glanville, J., Grimshaw, J. M., Hróbjartsson, A., Lalu, M. M., Li, T., Loder, E. W., Mayo-Wilson, E., McDonald, S., . . . Moher, D. (2021). The PRISMA 2020 statement: An updated guideline for reporting systematic reviews. In *The BMJ* (Vol. 372). BMJ Publishing Group. https://doi.org/DOI: 10.1136/bmj.n71

Pahor Zvanut, A. (2025). Social Media Marketing Strategy in the Tourism Industry: A Systematic Literature Review. *Tourism Planning & Development*, 1–34. DOI: 10.1080/21568316.2025.2549069

Palenčarová, M., Hohoš, T., Correia, R., & Cunha, C. R. (2022). Social Media Marketing Research at the Hotel Industry in Slovakia. *Iberian Conference on Information Systems and Technologies, CISTI, 2022-June*, 1–2. https://doi.org/DOI: 10.23919/CISTI54924.2022.9820127

Panda, G. C., Rout, P. K., Nayak, M., Mohanty, B. R., & Sana, S. S. (2024). Social media as a catalyst for hotel business growth: a pls-Sem approach in Odisha's smart cities. *OPSEARCH*, 1-29. https://link.springer.com/article/10.1007/s12597-024-00859-w

Panda, G. C., Rout, P. K., Nayak, M., Mohanty, B. R., & Sana, S. S. (2024). *Social media as a catalyst for hotel business growth: a pls-sem approach in odisha's smart cities*. OPSEARCH., DOI: 10.1007/s12597-024-00859-w

Pandya, B., & Al Janahi, M. M. (2021). The intervention of artificial intelligence in the recruitment function in UAE's hospitality industry. *Transnational Marketing Journal, 9*(1), 89–105.

Park, E. K. (2022). Hunger for learning or tasting? An exploratory study of food tourist motivations visiting food museum restaurants. *Tourism Recreation Research, 47*(2), 130–144. DOI: 10.1080/02508281.2020.1841374

Parvez, M. O., Arasli, H., Ozturen, A., Lodhi, R. N., & Ongsakul, V. (2022). Antecedents of human-robot collaboration: Theoretical extension of the technology acceptance model. *Journal of Hospitality and Tourism Technology*, *13*(2), 240–263.

Paul, J., & Benito, G. R. (2018). A review of research on outward foreign direct investment from emerging countries, including China: What do we know, how do we know and where should we be heading? *Asia Pacific Business Review*, *24*(1), 90–115.

Paul, J., & Criado, A. R. (2020). The art of writing literature review: What do we know and what do we need to know? *International Business Review*, *29*(4), 101717. DOI: 10.1016/j.ibusrev.2020.101717

Paul, J., Lim, W. M., O'Cass, A., Hao, A. W., & Bresciani, S. (2021). Scientific procedures and rationales for systematic literature reviews (SPAR-4-SLR). *International Journal of Consumer Studies*, *45*(4), O1–O16.

Paul, J., Parthasarathy, S., & Gupta, P. (2017). Exporting challenges of SMEs: A review and future research agenda. *Journal of World Business*, *52*(3), 327–342.

Pavlou, P. A., & El Sawy, O. A. (2011). Understanding the Elusive Black Box of Dynamic Capabilities. *Decision Sciences*, *42*(1), 239–273. DOI: 10.1111/j.1540-5915.2010.00287.x

Pelau, C., Dabija, D. C., & Ene, I. (2021). What makes an AI device human-like? The role of interaction quality, empathy and perceived psychological anthropomorphic characteristics in the acceptance of artificial intelligence in the service industry. *Computers in Human Behavior*, *122*, 106855.

Pentina, I., Guilloux, V., & Micu, A. C. (2018). Exploring social media engagement behaviors in the context of luxury brands. *Journal of Advertising*, *47*(1), 55–69.

Periasamy, P., & Dinesh, N. (2024). Leveraging digital transformation technologies in the hospitality industry. In *Revolutionizing the AI-Digital landscape* (pp. 151–165). Productivity Press.

Peter, A. T. (2023). The Role of Social Media in Hotel Marketing: A Study of Customer Engagement and Brand Loyalty. [IJSR]. *International Journal of Scientific Research*, *12*(7), 1830. DOI: 10.21275/sr23721185208

Petrovici, D., & Marinov, M. (2007). Determinants and antecedents of general attitudes towards advertising: A study of two EU accession countries. *European Journal of Marketing*, *41*(3–4), 307–326. DOI: 10.1108/03090560710728354

Phung, T. B., Nguyen, D. V. P., & Tran, V. P. T. (2025). Storytelling on social media: forging the path to tourism destination branding. *Cogent Business and Management, 12*(1). DOI: 10.1080/23311975.2025.2482016

Phuong Minh Binh Nguyen, X. L. (2023). A bibliometric analysis of research on tourism content marketing: Background knowledge and thematic evolution. *Heliyon, 9*(2). Advance online publication. DOI: 10.1016/j.heliyon.2023.e13487 PMID: 36816254

Pillai, R., & Sivathanu, B. (2020). Adoption of AI-based chatbots for hospitality and tourism. *International Journal of Contemporary Hospitality Management, 32*(10), 3199–3226.

Pine, B. J., & Gilmore, J. H. (2011). *The experience economy*. Harvard Business Press.

Pine, B. J., & Gilmore, J. H. (2013). The experience economy: Past, present and future. In Sundbo, J., & Sørensen, F. (Eds.), *Handbook on the Experience Economy*. Edward Elgar Publishing., DOI: 10.4337/9781781004227.00007

Piotr, G. P. (2023). The Use of Social Media in City Marketing Communication with Residents and Tourists – User Segmentation. *Polish Journal of Sport and Tourism*. Advance online publication. DOI: 10.2478/pjst-2023-0005

Polimerou, R., & Spais, G. S. (2025). Establishing relationships between brands and customers via strategic social media chatbots for telecom goods and services. Journal of Marketing Analytics. DOI: 10.1057/s41270-025-00396-5

Pollay, R. W., & Mittal, B. (1993). Here's the Beef: Factors, Determinants, and Segments in Consumer Criticism of Advertising. *Journal of Marketing, 57*(3), 99. DOI: 10.2307/1251857

Pontes, A., & Ramos, C. (2023). How does Social Media influence the Behaviour of Hotel Consumers? *Journal of Tourism Sustainability and Well-Being, 11*(2). Advance online publication. DOI: 10.34623/784k-qg19

Prdić, N., Gajić, T., & Stepanov, S. (2025). WHOLESALE MARKETS AS SUPPLY CHANNELS FOR GREEN MARKETS AND THEIR IMPACT ON RURAL DEVELOPMENT IN SERBIA. *Ekonomika Poljoprivrede, 72*(1), 63–87. DOI: 10.59267/ekoPolj250163P

Prendergast, G., & Liu, P. yan, & Poon, D. T. Y. (2009). A Hong Kong study of advertising credibility. *Journal of Consumer Marketing, 26*(5), 320–329. DOI: 10.1108/07363760910976574

Prentice, C., Dominique Lopes, S., & Wang, X. (2020). The impact of artificial intelligence and employee service quality on customer satisfaction and loyalty. *Journal of Hospitality Marketing & Management*, *29*(7), 739–756.

Prevolšek, D., Kukurin, Ž., & Golja, T. (2024). Collaborative Synergies for Elevated Destination Experiences: A Model of Cooperation between Hotel Companies, DMOs, and Local Stakeholders. *Organizacija*, *57*(1), 20–38. DOI: 10.2478/orga-2024-0002

Pulizzi, J. (2012). The Rise of Storytelling as the New Marketing. *Publishing Research Quarterly*, *28*(2), 116–123. DOI: 10.1007/s12109-012-9264-5

Putra, A. H. P. K., Mariam, S., Tafsir, M., & Rosanti, N. (2024). Deciphering the green marketing puzzle: Understanding the interplay of green marketing strategic orientation, attitude towards green marketing, brand integrity, and purchase intention. *International Review of Management and Marketing*, *14*(4), 210.

Putri, R. N. P., Situmorang, R., & Mehrotra, A. (2023). HUMAN vs. ROBOT: THE APPLICATION OF SMART TECHNOLOGY IN THE HOTEL INDUSTRY. *Jurnal Manajemen Dan Kewirausahaan*, *25*(2), 142–151. DOI: 10.9744/jmk.25.2.142-151

Qenaj, M., & Beqiri, G. (2022). Social Media Marketing in Hospitality Industry and Its Effect on Consumer Behavior in Kosovo. *IFAC-PapersOnLine*, *55*(39), 66–69. DOI: 10.1016/j.ifacol.2022.12.012

Ra, S., Shrestha, U., Khatiwada, S., Yoon, S. W., & Kwon, K. (2019). The rise of technology and impact on skills. International Journal of Training Research, 17(sup1), 26–40. https://doi.org/DOI: 10.1080/14480220.2019.1629727

Rafiki, A., Hidayat, S. E., & Al Abdul Razzaq, D. (2019). CRM and organizational performance. *The International Journal of Organizational Analysis*, *27*(1), 187–205.

Rafiq, F., Dogra, N., Adil, M., & Wu, J. Z. (2022). Examining consumer's intention to adopt AI-chatbots in tourism using partial least squares structural equation modeling method. *Mathematics*, *10*(13), 2190.

Rahman, N. A. A., Hassan, A., Ahmad, M. F., & Singh, R. K. S. (2023). Contactless Hospitality Technology in Post-COVID-19 Era: Future Research Clusters. In Hassan, A., & Rahman, N. A. A. (Eds.), *Technology Application in Aviation, Tourism and Hospitality* (pp. 179–188). Springer Nature Singapore., DOI: 10.1007/978-981-19-6619-4_13

Raktham, W., Chaipoopirutana, S., & Combs, H. (2017). Factors Influencing Consumer Attitudes toward Social Media Advertising. *International Conference on Humanities, Social Sciences and Education*, 32–36.

Ramachandran, S., Ugokwe, C. K., Latiff, K., & Ibrahim, M. R. (2024). Continued innovation beyond COVID-19 crisis: toward mitigating the challenges in the tourism and hospitality industry. *Journal of Tourism Futures*. https://doi.org/DOI: 10.1108/JTF-10-2023-0221

Ramaprasad, J. (2001). South Asian students' beliefs about and attitude toward advertising. *Journal of Current Issues and Research in Advertising*, *23*(1), 55–70. DOI: 10.1080/10641734.2001.10505114

Ramírez, J., Baez, M., Casati, F., Cernuzzi, L., Benatallah, B., Taran, E. A., & Malanina, V. A. 2021, March. On the impact of predicate complexity in crowdsourced classification tasks. In *Proceedings of the 14th ACM International Conference on Web Search and Data Mining* (pp. 67-75).

Rasheed, H. M. W., He, Y., Khizar, H. M. U., & Abbas, H. S. M. (2023). Exploring Consumer-Robot interaction in the hospitality sector: Unpacking the reasons for adoption (or resistance) to artificial intelligence. *Technological Forecasting and Social Change*, *192*, 122555.

Rasheed, H. M. W., Yuanqiong, H., Khizar, H. M. U., & Khalid, J. (2024). What drives the adoption of artificial intelligence among consumers in the hospitality sector: A systematic literature review and future agenda. *Journal of Hospitality and Tourism Technology*, *15*(2), 211–231.

Rathore, A. K., Ilavarasan, P. V., & Dwivedi, Y. K. (2016). Social media content and product cocreation: An emerging paradigm. *Journal of Enterprise Information Management*, *29*(1), 718.

Rathore, A. K., Kar, A. K., & Ilavarasan, P. V. (2017). Social media analytics: Literature review and directions for future research. *Decision Analysis*, *14*(4), 229–249. https://pubsonline.informs.org/doi/abs/10.1287/deca.2017.0355

Raza, S. H., Bakar, H. A., & Mohamad, B. (2018). Relationships between the advertising appeal and behavioural intention: The mediating role of the attitude towards advertising appeal and moderating role of cultural norm. *The Journal of Business and Retail Management Research*, *12*(2), 185–193. DOI: 10.24052/jbrmr/v12is02/rbtaaabitmrotataaamrocn

Reis, J., Melão, N., Salvadorinho, J., Soares, B., & Rosete, A. (2020). Service robots in the hospitality industry: The case of Henn-na hotel, Japan. *Technology in Society*, *63*, 101423. DOI: 10.1016/j.techsoc.2020.101423

Ri, P. H. (2024). *Strategy to raise food industry's value to KRW 300B by 2027*. Retrieved from https://www.korea.net/NewsFocus/policies/view?articleId=246532

Rialti, R., Kvítková, Z., Pompurová, K., Kushcheva, N., & Marrucci, A. (2025). *Online Reputation Management in the Context of Tourism and Hospitality*. https://strategie.vse.cz/wp-content/uploads/7.0.-ORM-book-final-1.pdf

Richard, P. J., Devinney, T. M., Yip, G. S., & Johnson, G. (2009). Measuring Organizational Performance: Towards Methodological Best Practice. *Journal of Management, 35*(3), 718–804. DOI: 10.1177/0149206308330560

Richards, G. (2021). Evolving research perspectives on food and gastronomic experiences in tourism. *International Journal of Contemporary Hospitality Management, 33*, 1037–1058. DOI: 10.1108/IJCHM-10-2020-1217

Ridley, D. (2012). *The literature review: A step-by-step guide for students.*

Robinson, R.N.S. & Getz D. (2014). Profiling potential food tourists: an Australian study". British Food Journal. *British Food Journal, Vol. 116 No. 4 pp. 690–706.* DOI: 10.1108/BFJ-02-2012-0030

Rosário, A. T., & Cruz, R. N. (2023). Data-Driven Decision-Making in Marketing. 10.20944/preprints202501.0354.v1

Rosete, A., Soares, B., Salvadorinho, J., Reis, J., & Amorim, M. (2020). Service Robots in the Hospitality Industry: An Exploratory Literature Review. In Nóvoa, H., Drăgoicea, M., & Kühl, N. (Eds.), *Exploring Service Science* (Vol. 377, pp. 174–186). Springer International Publishing., DOI: 10.1007/978-3-030-38724-2_13

Roshandel, A., Miöen Dahlström, F., & Ekström, K. (2023). Unveiling the art of illusion: Exploring the fabrication of authenticity and trustworthiness by social media micro-influencers.

Roth-Cohen, O., Rosenberg, H., & Lissitsa, S. (2022). Are you talking to me? Generation X, Y, Z responses to mobile advertising. *Convergence, 28*(3), 761–780. DOI: 10.1177/13548565211047342

Roy, P., Ramaprasad, B. S., Chakraborty, M., Prabhu, N., & Rao, S. (2020). Customer acceptance of use of artificial intelligence in hospitality services: An Indian hospitality sector perspective. *Global Business Review*, 0972150920939753.

Rózsa, Z., Ferenčáková, L., Zámek, D., & Firstová, J. (2025). Generation Z's perception of privacy on social media: Examining the impact of personalized advertising, interpersonal relationships, reference group dynamics, social isolation, and anxiety on self-disclosure willingness. *Oeconomia Copernicana, 15*(1), 229–266.

Rudolf, N. L. (2022). Social Media and Destination Branding in Tourism: A Systematic Review of the Literature. *Sustainability, MDPI, 14*(20), 1–18.

Ruel, H., & Njoku, E. (2021). AI redefining the hospitality industry. *Journal of Tourism Futures*, *7*(1), 53–66.

Ryan, R. M., & Deci, E. L. (2024). Self-determination theory. In *Encyclopedia of quality of life and well-being research* (pp. 6229–6235). Springer International Publishing.

Saadeghvaziri, F., & Hosseini, H. K. (2011). Mobile advertising: An investigation of factors creating positive attitude in Iranian customers. *African Journal of Business Management*, *5*(2), 394–404. DOI: 10.5897/AJBM10.431

Sackey, B. B., Yang, J., Quansah, P. E., Ekumah, C. A., Arboh, F., & Boadu, B. (2025). Internal marketing orientation and employee innovative behaviour: The mediating role of workforce agility and moderating role of psychological empowerment. *Journal of Hospitality and Tourism Insights*, *8*(2), 674–693. DOI: 10.1108/JHTI-01-2024-0063

Sağtaş, S. (2022). The effect of social media marketing on brand equity and consumer purchasing intention. *Journal of Life Economics*, *9*(1), 21–31. DOI: 10.15637/jlecon.9.1.02

Saini, H., Kumar, P., & Verma, R. (2025). Social media and its influence on travel decision making. In *Decoding tourist behavior in the digital era: Insights for effective marketing* (pp. 261–282). IGI Global.

Salazar, A. (2018). Hospitality trends: Opportunities and challenges. *Worldwide Hospitality and Tourism Themes*, *10*(6), 674–679. DOI: 10.1108/WHATT-07-2018-0047

Samala, N., Katkam, B. S., Bellamkonda, R. S., & Rodriguez, R. V. (2020). Impact of AI and robotics in the tourism sector: a critical insight. *Journal of tourism futures, 8*(1), 73-87.

Samala, N., Katkam, B. S., Bellamkonda, R. S., & Rodriguez, R. V. (2022). Impact of AI and Robotics in the Tourism Sector: A Critical Insight. *Journal of Tourism Futures*, *8*, 73–87. DOI: 10.1108/JTF-07-2019-0065

Sam, S. J. I., & Jasim, K. M. (2025). Diving into the technology: A systematic literature review on strategic use of chatbots in hospitality service encounters. *Management Review Quarterly*, *75*(1), 527–555.

Sánchez Jiménez, M. Á., Gómez Carmona, D., & Moral Moral, M. (2024). Evolution of the impact of social media in hospitality: A bibliometric analysis. *Journal of Destination Marketing & Management*, *31*, 100868. DOI: 10.1016/j.jdmm.2024.100868

Sánchez-González, G., & González-Fernández, A. M. (2021). The Influence of Quality on eWOM: A Digital Transformation in Hotel Management. *Frontiers in Psychology, 11*. Advance online publication. DOI: 10.3389/fpsyg.2020.612324 PMID: 33519629

Sanjeev, G. M., & Birdie, A. K. (2019). The tourism and hospitality industry in India: Emerging issues for the next decade. *Worldwide Hospitality and Tourism Themes*, *11*(4), 355–361.

Sapelnikova, N. (2025). Implementation of Robotisation and Application of Artificial Intelligence in the Hotel and Restaurant Business. *Restaurant and Hotel Consulting. Innovations*, *7*(2), 220–229. DOI: 10.31866/2616-7468.7.2.2024.335180

Saraiva, M. F., & Lues, H. T. (2024). Generation Y's view on print media advertisements: Variances in its perceived informativeness, entertainment, irritation, credibility, and value. *Journal of Contemporary Management*, *20*(si1), 1–21.

Saravanakumar, S., & Narayanan, M. B. (2018). The service automation and robotics in hospitality industry: A study on business implications. *International Journal of Mechanical and Production Engineering Research and Development*, *8*(6), 91–100.

Sârbu, R., Alecu, F., & Dina, R. (2018). Social media advertising trends in tourism. *Amfiteatru Economic*, *20*(12), 1016–1028.

Sarin, T. (2023). Significance of social media on the hospitality industry. *International Journal of Technical Research and Applications*, *8*(8), 22–28.

Sarkar, D., Suhag, N., & Kumar, S. (2025). Sustainable Practices in India's Hotel Industry: Navigating Challenges and Opportunities. In Nadda, V., Sharma, A., Mediratta, H., & Dadwal, S. S. (Eds.), *Addressing Contemporary Challenges in the B2B Hospitality Sector* (pp. 337–352). IGI Global., DOI: 10.4018/979-8-3693-9760-2.ch012

Saura, J. R., Škare, V., & Došen, Đ. O. (2024). Is AI-based digital marketing ethical? Assessing a new data privacy paradox. *Journal of Innovation & Knowledge*, *9*(4), 100597. DOI: 10.1016/j.jik.2024.100597

Saxena, A., & Khanna, U. (2013). Advertising on Social Network Sites: A Structural Equation Modelling Approach. *Vision: The Journal of Business Perspective*, *17*(1), 17–25. DOI: 10.1177/0972262912469560

Schultz, V. A. B. J. P. D. (2016). Social media and consumer engagement: A review and research agenda. *Journal of Research in Interactive Marketing*, *10*(4). Advance online publication. DOI: 10.1016/0031-9201(92)90209-e

Scott, I. J., De Castro Neto, M., & Pinheiro, F. L. (2023). Bringing trust and transparency to the opaque world of waste management with blockchain: A Polkadot parathread application. *Computers & Industrial Engineering*, *182*, 109347. DOI: 10.1016/j.cie.2023.109347

Sekaran, U., & Bougie, R. (2016). *Research Methods for Business: A Skill Building Approach*. John Wiley and Sons. https://www.wiley.com/en-in/Research+Methods+For+Business:+A+Skill+Building+Approach,+7th+Edition-p-9781119266846

Şener, G., & Çobanoğlu, C. (2022). Analysis of International Hotels' Social Media Strategies. *Journal of Mediterranean Tourism Research*, *1*(2), 123. DOI: 10.5038/2770-7555.1.2.1010

Seo, Y. (2023). David and Goliath: Micro-influencers versus mega-influencers. *University of Auckland Business School Research Paper Series*. https://dx.doi.org/ DOI: 10.2139/ssrn.4905436

Seo, K. H., & Lee, J. H. (2021). The emergence of service robots at restaurants: Integrating trust, perceived risk, and satisfaction. *Sustainability*, *13*(8), 4431.

Sesar, V., Martinčević, I., & Boguszewicz-Kreft, M. (2022). Relationship between Advertising Disclosure, Influencer Credibility and Purchase Intention. *Journal of Risk and Financial Management*, *15*(7), 276. DOI: 10.3390/jrfm15070276

Setiyanto, A., & Syakir, A. (2019). The influence of perceived ease of use, perceived usefulness, and consumer satisfaction on online purchasing behaviour. *Journal of Applied Accounting and Taxation*, *4*(2), 214–222. DOI: 10.30871/jaat.v4i2.1081

Shareef, M. A., Mukerji, B., Dwivedi, Y. K., Rana, N. P., & Islam, R. (2019). Social media marketing: Comparative effect of advertisement sources. *Journal of Retailing and Consumer Services*, *46*, 58–69. DOI: 10.1016/j.jretconser.2017.11.001

Sharma, A. B. (2024). Content Creation in Transition: Analyzing YouTube, YouTube Shorts, and Facebook's Influence on Content Creators Amidst and Beyond COVID19.

Sharma, C., 2024. The Influence of Technological Innovations on Customer Satisfaction in the Hospitality Industry. *ATITHYA: A Journal of Hospitality, 10*(1).

Sharma, I., Sharma, N. & Patwa, N. (2024). Mapping Social Media Research Trends in Hospitality and Tourism: A Bibliometric Perspective. *Journal of Technology Management for Growing Economies, 15*(2). DOI: 10.15415/jtmge/2024.152002

Sharma, K. K., Tomar, M., & Tadimarri, A. (2023). AI-driven Marketing: Transforming Sales Processes for Success in the Digital Age. *Journal of Knowledge Learning and Science Technology ISSN: 2959-6386 (Online), 2*(2), 250–260. https://doi.org/ DOI: 10.60087/jklst.vol2.n2.p260

Sharma, M. and Singh, A., 2024. Embracing Technological Innovation: A Review of Hi-Tech Services in Hospitality Industry.

Sharma, M., Tyagi, P. K., Semwal, R., Tyagi, P., Singh, V. J., & Kumari, N. (2024). Robotic Concierges and Smart Spaces: A Vision for the Future of Hospitality Services. In M. Sharma, A. K. Singh, & P. Tyagi (Eds.), *Proceedings of the International Conference on Innovation and Regenerative Trends in Tourism and Hospitality Industry (IRTTHI 2024)* (Vol. 285, pp. 511–525). Atlantis Press International BV. https://doi.org/DOI: 10.2991/978-94-6463-437-2_34

Sharma, K., Dhir, S., & Ongsakul, V. (2022). Artificial intelligence and hospitality industry: Systematic review using TCCM and bibliometric analysis. *Journal for International Business and Entrepreneurship Development, 14*(1), 48–71.

Sharma, N., Khatri, B., Khan, S. A., & Shamsi, M. S. (2023). Extending the UTAUT model to examine the influence of social media on tourists' destination selection. *Indian Journal of Marketing, 53*(4), 47–64. DOI: 10.17010/ijom/2023/v53/i4/172689

Sharma, R., & Kumar, S. (2025). Impact of Ethical Implications of Using AI and IoT in Hotels. In Mehra, P., Abioye, O., & Kumar, P. (Eds.), (pp. 375–392). Advances in Computational Intelligence and Robotics. IGI Global Scientific Publishing., DOI: 10.4018/979-8-3693-9611-7.ch014

Shavitt, S., Lowrey, P., & Haefner, J. (1998). Public attitudes toward advertising: More favourable than you might think. *Journal of Advertising Research, 38*(4), 7–22.

Shimp, T. A. (1981). Attitude toward the AD as a mediator of consumer brand choice. *Journal of Advertising, 10*(2), 9–48. DOI: 10.1080/00913367.1981.10672756

Shin, H. H., & Jeong, M. (2020). Guests' perceptions of robot concierge and their adoption intentions. *International Journal of Contemporary Hospitality Management, 32*(8), 2613–2633. DOI: 10.1108/IJCHM-09-2019-0798

Shin, H. H., Shin, S., & Gim, J. (2023). Looking back three decades of hospitality and tourism technology research: A bibliometric approach. *International Journal of Contemporary Hospitality Management, 35*(2), 563–588. DOI: 10.1108/IJCHM-03-2022-0376

Shoib, G., & Nandhakumar, J. (2003). Cross-cultural IS adoption in multinational corporations: A study of rationality. *Information Technology for Development*, *10*(4), 249–260. DOI: 10.1002/itdj.1590100404

Shokohyar, S., Tavalaee, R., & Karamatnia, K. (2017). Identifying effective indicators in the assessment of organizational readiness for accepting social CRM. *International Journal of Information, Business and Management*, *9*(4), 209–226.

Shukla, U. N., & Kulshreshtha, S. K. (2023). *Post-COVID Tourism and Hospitality Dynamics: Recovery, Revival, and Re-Start* (1st ed.). Apple Academic Press., DOI: 10.1201/9781003429722

Sigala, M., Goh, E., Leung, X., Rasoolimanesh, S. M., Su, C.-H. (Joan), & Tham, A. (2025). 30 Years of contribution and future directions in tourism, hospitality, and events research: A Quo Vadis perspective from the Journal of Hospitality and Tourism Management. *Journal of Hospitality and Tourism Management, 62*, 258–265. https://doi.org/DOI: 10.1016/j.jhtm.2025.02.001

Simola, J., Kivikangas, M., Kuisma, J., & Krause, C. M. (2013). Attention and memory for newspaper advertisements: Effects of ad-editorial congruency and location. *Applied Cognitive Psychology*, *27*(4), 429–442. DOI: 10.1002/acp.2918

Sims, R. (2019). Food, place and authenticity: Local food and the sustainable tourism experience. *Journal of Sustainable Tourism*, *17*(3), 321–336. DOI: 10.1080/09669580802359293

Singh, G., Raheja, S., & Sharma, R. (2023). Elevating Hospitality with Smart Hotel Technologies: A Guest – Centric Perspective. *2023 IEEE Engineering Informatics*, 1–9. https://doi.org/DOI: 10.1109/IEEECONF58110.2023.10520539

Singh, B., & Kumar, S. (2025). Eco-Friendly Practices of Ghost Kitchens Through Smart Technology: Technological Innovations in the Food-Beverage Industry. In Singh, K., Kumar, S., & Talukder, M. B. (Eds.), (pp. 359–378). Advances in Computational Intelligence and Robotics. IGI Global., DOI: 10.4018/979-8-3373-0432-8.ch017

Singh, K., Kumar, S., & Talukder, M. B. (2024). Digital Transformation and Its Impact on Tourism Business in India. In Albattat, A., Azman, N., Valeri, M., & Singh, A. (Eds.), *Advances in Hospitality, Tourism, and the Services Industry* (pp. 215–230). IGI Global., DOI: 10.4018/979-8-3693-9636-0.ch010

Singh, S., & Dhir, S. (2019). Structured review using TCCM and bibliometric analysis of international cause-related marketing, social marketing, and innovation of the firm. *International Review on Public and Nonprofit Marketing*, *16*(2), 335–347.

Sinha, M., & Srivastava, M. (2023). Augmented reality: New future of social media influencer marketing. *Vision (Basel)*, 09722629221147124.

Sivakami, R., & Thapa, P. (2025). Influencer scale in marketing in hotel operations: Examining the impact of mega, macro, micro, and nano influencers on brand loyalty and engagement in the Indian merchandise market. *Asian Journal of Management, 16*(2), 94–100.

Šmid Hribar, M. R. (2021). Models of stakeholder collaboration in food tourism experiences. *Acta Geographica Slovenica, 61*(1), 127–140. DOI: 10.3986/AGS.8756

Smith, J. (2023). *Data Privacy in Hospitality Apps*. Journal of Hospitality Technology.

Smith, M. J., Buckton, C., Patterson, C., & Hilton, S. (2023). User-generated content and influencer marketing involving e-cigarettes on social media: A scoping review and content analysis of YouTube and Instagram. *BMC Public Health, 23*(1), 530. DOI: 10.1186/s12889-023-15389-1 PMID: 36941553

Smith, M. J., & Hilton, S. (2022). Adolescents' views on user-generated content and influencer marketing of e-cigarettes on social media: A focus group study. *Lancet, 400*, S77. DOI: 10.1016/S0140-6736(22)02287-5

Sofía Blanco-Moreno, A. M.-F.-G. (2024). Understanding engagement with Instagram posts about tourism destinations. *Journal of Destination Marketing & Management*. Advance online publication. DOI: 10.1016/j.jdmm.2024.100948

Soliman, M., Gulvady, S., Elbaz, A. M., Mosbah, M., & Wahba, M. S. (2024). Robot-delivered tourism and hospitality services: How to evaluate the impact of health and safety considerations on visitors' satisfaction and loyalty? *Tourism and Hospitality Research, 24*(3), 393–409.

Sota, S., Chaudhry, H., & Srivastava, M. K. (2019). Customer relationship management research in hospitality industry: A review and classification. *Journal of Hospitality Marketing & Management, 29*(1), 39–64.

Sousa, N., Alén, E., Losada, N., & Melo, M. (2024). Virtual reality in tourism promotion: A research agenda based on a bibliometric approach. *Journal of Quality Assurance in Hospitality & Tourism, 25*(2), 313–342. DOI: 10.1080/1528008X.2022.2112807

Spais, G. S., & Chryssochoidis, G. (2025). Trends and future of artificial intelligence (AI), machine learning (ML) algorithms, and data analytics and their applications and implications for digital marketing and digital promotions. Journal of Marketing Analytics. DOI: 10.1057/s41270-025-00406-6

Stone, M., Aravopoulou, E., Ekinci, Y., Evans, G., Hobbs, M., Labib, A., Laughlin, P., Machtynger, J., & Machtynger, L. (2020). Artificial intelligence (AI) in strategic marketing decision-making: A research agenda. *The Bottom Line (New York, N.Y.)*, *33*(2), 183–200. DOI: 10.1108/BL-03-2020-0022

Subramanian, H., Mitra, S., & Ransbotham, S. (2021). Capturing value in platform business models that rely on user-generated content. *Organization Science*, *32*(3), 804–823.

Suharto, S., & Hoti, A. (2023). Relationship Marketing, Customer Experience and Customer Satisfaction: Testing Their Theoretical and Empirical Underpinning. *Jurnal Manajemen Bisnis*, *14*(1), 21–35. DOI: 10.18196/mb.v14i1.17805

Sukach, O., Kozlovska, S., & Sushko, N. (2021). Modern management technologies in the hospitality industry. *Baltic Journal of Economic Studies*, *7*(3), 168–176.

Suparak Suriyankietkaew, K. K. (2025). Creative tourism as a driver for sustainable development: A model for advancing SDGs through community-based tourism and environmental stewardship. *Environmental and Sustainability Indicators*. Advance online publication. DOI: 10.1016/j.indic.2025.100828

Susilo, D., & Santos, M. C. K. (2023). Digital marketing communication sustainable hotel practice of accor group in social media. *International Journal of Economic, Business, Accounting, Agriculture Management and Sharia Administration (IJEBAS)*, *3*(3), 730-743. https://pdfs.semanticscholar.org/5fca/79ab11b745e4d3ebbcaa5e2b63fada1d8b11.pdf

Tafesse, W. W. B. (2023). Social media influencers' community and content strategy and follower engagement behavior in the presence of competition: An Instagram-based investigation. *Journal of Product and Brand Management*, *32*(3), 406–419. DOI: 10.1108/JPBM-02-2022-3851

Taher, A., El Kolaly, H., & Tarek, N. (2025). Examining crisis communication in geopolitical conflicts: The micro-influencer impact model. *Journalism and Media*, *6*(3), 226.

Tahereh, N., & Zahra, G. T. (2012). Investigating effective factors on the perceived values and attitudes of Internet advertisements users. *Journal of Basic and Applied Scientific Research*, *2*(5), 4392–4399.

Talukder, M. B., & Mia, Md. N., Masum, Md. Y., Kabir, F., & Kumar, S. (2025). Encouraging Innovative and Responsible Tourism Through Digital Advancement. In P. Thaichon, P. K. Dutta, A. K. Haghi, & S. Dutta (Eds.), *Digital Disruption in Hospitality, Sustainable Hospitality* (pp. 145–165). Emerald Publishing Limited. https://doi.org/DOI: 10.1108/978-1-83662-360-120251007

Talukder, M. B., Kumar, S., Kaiser, F., & Mia, Md. N. (2024). Pilgrimage Creative Tourism: A Gateway to Sustainable Development Goals in Bangladesh. In M. Hamdan, M. Anshari, N. Ahmad, & E. Ali (Eds.), *Advances in Public Policy and Administration* (pp. 285–300). IGI Global. https://doi.org/DOI: 10.4018/979-8-3693-1742-6.ch016

Talukder, M. B., & Afchar, M. N. (2025). Vision Hotels: Shaping the Future of Hospitality Through Innovation, Sustainability, and Technology. In Parashar, A., Chandel, P. S., Seetaram, N., & Agarwal, P. (Eds.), *Global Practices and Innovations in Sustainable Homestay Tourism* (pp. 269–294). IGI Global., DOI: 10.4018/979-8-3373-0427-4.ch012

Talukder, M. B., Das, I. R., & Kumar, S. (2025). From Digital Production to Digital Society in Hospitality: Industry 5.0 Perspectives. In Grima, S., Kaleli, S. S., Baygin, M., & Boztepe, E. (Eds.), *Business Challenges and Opportunities in the Era of Industry 5.0* (pp. 173–193). Emerald Publishing Limited., DOI: 10.1108/978-1-83549-676-320251010

Talukder, M. B., Khan, M. R., & Kumar, S. (2025). The Impact of Gig Economy Trends on Traditional Employment Models: Evidence From Hotel Industry. In Nozari, H. (Ed.), *Dynamic and Safe Economy in the Age of Smart Technologies* (pp. 253–276). IGI Global., DOI: 10.4018/979-8-3693-4369-2.ch016

Talukder, M. B., Kumar, S., & Kabir, F. (2025). Marketing Strategies for Promoting Heritage Tourism in Bangladesh. In Sousa, B. B., & Santos, V. R. (Eds.), *Intersections of Niche Tourism and Marketing* (pp. 113–134). IGI Global., DOI: 10.4018/979-8-3693-8417-6.ch005

Talukder, M. B., Kumar, S., & Khan, M. R. (2024). The Integration of Sustainable Practices in Cultural and Gastronomic Tourism. In Munuhwa, S. (Ed.), (pp. 467–484). Advances in Civil and Industrial Engineering. IGI Global., DOI: 10.4018/979-8-3693-3755-4.ch017

Talukder, M. B., Kumar, S., Singh, K., & Bhardwaj, V. (2025). Sustainable Food and Beverage Practices With AI. In Singh, K., Kumar, S., & Talukder, M. B. (Eds.), (pp. 1–14). Advances in Computational Intelligence and Robotics. IGI Global., DOI: 10.4018/979-8-3373-0432-8.ch001

Talukder, M. B., Kumar, S., Sood, K., & Grima, S. (2023). Information Technology, Food Service Quality and Restaurant Revisit Intention. *International Journal of Sustainable Development and Planning, 18*(1), 295–303. DOI: 10.18280/ijsdp.180131

Talukder, M. B., Swarna, D. A., Kumar, S., & Kabir, F. (2025). Leveraging Technology for Employee Wellness in Hospitality: Smart Solutions for a Vibrant Service Culture. In Baez, M. D. (Ed.), (pp. 221–246). Advances in Logistics, Operations, and Management Science. IGI Global., DOI: 10.4018/979-8-3373-1687-1.ch008

Tarvainen, S. (2023). *Social Media Marketing Plan for Original Sokos Hotel Tapiola Garden.*

Teece, D. J. (2007). Explicating dynamic capabilities: The nature and microfoundations of (sustainable) enterprise performance. *Strategic Management Journal, 28*(13), 1319–1350. DOI: 10.1002/smj.640

Teece, D. J. (2014). A dynamic capabilities-based entrepreneurial theory of the multinational enterprise. *Journal of International Business Studies, 45*(1), 8–37. DOI: 10.1057/jibs.2013.54

Teece, D. J., Pisano, G., Shuen, A., & Jose, S. (1997). Dynamic capabilities and strategic management. *Strategic Management Journal, 18*(7), 509–533. DOI: 10.1002/(SICI)1097-0266(199708)18:7<509:AID-SMJ882>3.0.CO;2-Z

Thakur, A. (2022). Technological innovations in the hospitality and tourism industry. In *Mobile computing and technology applications in tourism and hospitality* (pp. 72–97). IGI Global.

Thakur, A. S., Kumar, N., Chamoli, V., & Goyal, N. (2024). Social media marketing in the Himalayas: An examination of its influence on tourist decision-making in Himachal Pradesh. *International Journal of Business Competition and Growth, 9*(1), 43–60. https://www.inderscienceonline.com/doi/abs/10.1504/IJBCG.2024.142220

Thakur, R., & Srivastava, M. (2014). Adoption readiness, personal innovativeness, perceived risk and usage intention across customer groups for mobile payment services in India. *Internet Research, 24*(3), 369–392. DOI: 10.1108/IntR-12-2012-0244

Tham, A. (2023). A pentadic analysis of TikTok marketing in tourism: The case of Penang, Malaysia. *Tourist Studies, 24*(1), 75–103. DOI: 10.1177/14687976231218483

Thu, N. &. (2023). Visual marketing on promoting Vietnamese cuisine image through instagram. DOI: 10.13140/RG.2.2.25495.14240

Tlili, A., Altinay, F., Altinay, Z., & Zhang, Y. (2021). Envisioning the future of technology integration for accessible hospitality and tourism. *International Journal of Contemporary Hospitality Management, 33*(12), 4460–4482. DOI: 10.1108/IJCHM-03-2021-0321

Trainor, K. J., & Andzulis, J. (Mick), Rapp, A., & Agnihotri, R. (2014). Social media technology usage and customer relationship performance: A capabilities-based examination of social CRM. *Journal of Business Research, 67*(6), 1201–1208. DOI: 10.1016/j.jbusres.2013.05.002

Trivedi, S., Grover, V., & Balusamy, B. (2025). Exploring AI in Data-driven Marketing: Understanding the Intersection of Data Engineering and Marketing. In Balusamy, B., Grover, V., Nallakaruppan, M. K., Rajasekaran, V. A., & Milanova, M. (Eds.), *Data Engineering for Data-driven Marketing* (pp. 1–16). Emerald Publishing Limited., DOI: 10.1108/978-1-83662-326-720251002

Tsang, M. M., Ho, S. C., & Liang, T. P. (2004). Consumer attitudes toward mobile advertising: An empirical study. *International Journal of Electronic Commerce, 8*(3), 65–78. DOI: 10.1080/10864415.2004.11044301

Tsou, H.-T., Chen, J.-S., Mai, T. O., & Jade, N. B. N. (2025). Soft HRM Practices Fostering Service Innovations and Performance in Hospitality Firms. *Sustainability, 17*(3), 895. DOI: 10.3390/su17030895

Tsymbal, O., Mercorelli, P., & Sergiyenko, O. (2021). Predicate-based model of problem-solving for robotic actions planning. *Mathematics, 9*(23), 3044.

Tuomi, A., Tussyadiah, I. P., & Hanna, P. (2021). Spicing up hospitality service encounters: The case of Pepper™. *International Journal of Contemporary Hospitality Management, 33*(11), 3906–3925.

Tuomi, A., Tussyadiah, I. P., & Stienmetz, J. (2021). Applications and Implications of Service Robots in Hospitality. *Cornell Hospitality Quarterly, 62*(2), 232–247. DOI: 10.1177/1938965520923961

Turban, E., Outland, J., King, D., Lee, J. K., Liang, T. P., & Turban, D. C. (2017). *Electronic commerce 2018: a managerial and social networks perspective*. Springer. https://econpapers.repec.org/scripts/redir.pf?u=https%3A%2F%2Fdoi.org%2F10.1007%252F978-3-319-58715-8;h=repec:spr:sptbec:978-3-319-58715-8

Tussyadiah, I., & Miller, G. (2019). Perceived impacts of artificial intelligence and responses to positive behaviour change intervention. In *Information and Communication Technologies in Tourism 2019: Proceedings of the International Conference in Nicosia, Cyprus, January 30–February 1, 2019* (pp. 359-370). Springer International Publishing.

Tussyadiah, I. P. (2017). Identifying salient attributes of peer-to-peer accommodation experience. *Journal of Travel & Tourism Marketing*, *34*(5), 636–652. DOI: 10.1080/10548408.2016.1209153

Tussyadiah, I. P., Jung, T. H., & Tom Dieck, M. C. (2018). Embodiment of wearable augmented reality technology in tourism experiences. *Journal of Travel Research*, *57*(5), 597–611.

Tu, Y., Liu, W., & Yang, Z. (2023). Exploring the influence of service employees' characteristics on their willingness to work with service robots. *Journal of Service Management*, *34*(5), 1038–1063.

Unnava, V., & Aravindakshan, A. (2021). How does consumer engagement evolve when brands post across multiple social media? *Journal of the Academy of Marketing Science*, *49*(5), 864–881.

Valença, M. N., Sobral, M. F. F., Andrade Lima, T. L. D., & Farias, D. D. M. P. (2020). Innovation radar in hospitality: A new procedure to evaluate the innovation in hotels. *Journal of Hospitality and Tourism Technology*, *11*(2), 313–326. DOI: 10.1108/JHTT-10-2017-0119

Valos, M. J., Haji Habibi, F., Casidy, R., Driesener, C. B., & Maplestone, V. L. (2016). Exploring the integration of social media within integrated marketing communication frameworks: Perspectives of services marketers. *Marketing Intelligence & Planning*, *34*(1), 19–40. https://www.emerald.com/mip/article-abstract/34/1/19/295719/Exploring-the-integration-of-social-media-within?redirectedFrom=fulltext

Varkaris, E., & Neuhofer, B. (2017). The influence of social media on the consumers' hotel decision journey. *Journal of Hospitality and Tourism Technology*, *8*(1), 101–118. https://www.emerald.com/jhtt/article-abstract/8/1/101/225562/The-influence-of-social-media-on-the-consumers?redirectedFrom=fulltext

Vasumathi, A., & Ambrose, J. (2024). A study on the factors that impact consumer decision making process in the context of using social media for choosing a hotel in India among students. *International Journal of Business Process Integration and Management*, *11*(3), 221–236. https://www.inderscienceonline.com/doi/abs/10.1504/IJBPIM.2024.140157

Venkatesh, V., Morris, M. G., Davis, G. B., & Davis, F. D. (2003). User acceptance of information technology: Toward a unified view. *Management Information Systems Quarterly*, •••, 425–478.

Venkatesh, V., Thong, J. Y., & Xu, X. (2012). Consumer acceptance and use of information technology: Extending the unified theory of acceptance and use of technology. *Management Information Systems Quarterly*, •••, 157–178. DOI: 10.2307/41410412

Venkatraman, N., & Ramanujam, V. (1986). Measurement of Business Performance in Strategy Research: A Comparison of Approaches. *Academy of Management Review*, *11*(4), 801. DOI: 10.2307/258398

Verhoef, P. C., Broekhuizen, T., Bart, Y., Bhattacharya, A., Qi Dong, J., Fabian, N., & Haenlein, M. (2021). Digital transformation: A multidisciplinary reflection and research agenda. *Journal of Business Research*, *122*, 889–901. DOI: 10.1016/j.jbusres.2019.09.022

Verhoef, P. C., Reinartz, W. J., & Krafft, M. (2010). Customer Engagement as a New Perspective in Customer Management. *Journal of Service Research*, *13*(3), 247–252. DOI: 10.1177/1094670510375461

Verissimo, M., & Menezes, N. (2015). Social media as a tool to enhance customer experience in hospitality industry. *Portuguese Journal of Marketing/Revista Portuguesa de Marketing*, (34).https://openurl.ebsco.com/openurl?sid=ebsco:plink:scholar&id=ebsco:gcd:114258387&crl=c

Verma, S., & Diwan, H. (2025). Marketing innovation for sustainability: Review, trends, and way forward. *Business Ethics, the Environment & Responsibility*, *34*(3), 912–935. DOI: 10.1111/beer.12686

Vermeulen, I. E., & Seegers, D. (2009). Tried and tested: The impact of online hotel reviews on consumer consideration. *Tourism Management*, *30*(1), 123–127. DOI: 10.1016/j.tourman.2008.04.008

Vishwakarma, V. K., Kapur, S., ... (2021a). Analysing the impact of social media marketing on guests hotel selection. ... *Journal of Hospitality and ..., September*, 37–49. https://acspublisher.com/journals/index.php/pjhas/article/view/3371

Vishwakarma, V. K., Kapur, S., ... (2021b). Analysing the impact of social media marketing on guests hotel selection. ... *Journal of Hospitality and ..., September*, 9–14. https://acspublisher.com/journals/index.php/pjhas/article/view/3371

Vivek, S. D., Beatty, S., & Morgan, R. M. (2012). *(PDF) Customer Engagement: Exploring Customer Relationships Beyond Purchase*. ResearchGate., DOI: 10.2307/23243811

Vrontis, D., Makrides, A., Christofi, M., & Thrassou, A. (2021). Social media influencer marketing: A systematic review, integrative framework and future research agenda. *International Journal of Consumer Studies*. DOI: 10.1111/ijcs.12647

Wang, C. L., Senaratne, C., & Rafiq, M. (2015). Success traps, dynamic capabilities and firm performance. *British Journal of Management, 26*(1), 26–44. DOI: 10.1111/1467-8551.12066

Wang, F. (2020). Digital marketing capabilities in international firms: A relational perspective. *International Marketing Review, 37*(3), 559–577. DOI: 10.1108/IMR-04-2018-0128

Wang, L.-H., Ho, J.-L., Yeh, S.-S., & Huan, T.-C. (Tc). (2022). Is robot hotel a future trend? Exploring the incentives, barriers and customers' purchase intention for robot hotel stays. *Tourism Management Perspectives, 43*, 100984. DOI: 10.1016/j.tmp.2022.100984

Wang, P., & Wen, M.-J. (2017). Personalization, privacy, and attitudes towards online advertising. *Decision Science Letters, 22*(9), 1–12.

Wang, T. Y., & Park, J. (2023). Destination information search in social media and travel intention of generation Z university students. *Journal of China Tourism Research, 19*(3), 570–588.

Wang, W.-L., Malthouse, E. C., Calder, B., & Uzunoglu, E. (2019). B2B content marketing for professional services: In-person versus digital contacts. *Industrial Marketing Management, 81*, 160–168. DOI: 10.1016/j.indmarman.2017.11.006

Wang, Y., & Genç, E. (2019). Path to effective mobile advertising in Asian markets: Credibility, entertainment, and peer influence. *Asia Pacific Journal of Marketing and Logistics, 31*(1), 55–80. DOI: 10.1108/APJML-06-2017-0112

Wang, Y., & Sun, S. (2010). Examining the role of beliefs and attitudes in online advertising: A comparison between the USA and Romania. *International Marketing Review, 27*(1), 87–107. DOI: 10.1108/02651331011020410

Webster, C., & Ivanov, S. (2020). Future tourism in a robot-based economy: A perspective article. *Tourism Review, 75*(1), 329–332.

Webster, C., & Ivanov, S. (2020). *Robotics, artificial intelligence, and the evolving nature of work*. Springer International Publishing.

Webster, C., & Ivanov, S. (2020). *Robots in travel, tourism and hospitality: Key findings from a global study*. Zangador.

Wedel, M., & Kannan, P. K. (2016). Marketing Analytics for Data-Rich Environments. *Journal of Marketing*, *80*(6), 97–121. DOI: 10.1509/jm.15.0413

Weiss, A., Bernhaupt, R., & Tscheligi, M. (2011). The USUS evaluation framework for user-centered HRI. *New Frontiers in Human–Robot Interaction*, *2*, 89–110.

Whitehead, A. L., Julious, S. A., Cooper, C. L., & Campbell, M. J. (2016). Estimating the sample size for a pilot randomised trial to minimise the overall trial sample size for the external pilot and main trial for a continuous outcome variable. *Statistical Methods in Medical Research*, *25*(3), 1057–1073. DOI: 10.1177/0962280215588241 PMID: 26092476

Wibowo, S. E., Almasari Aksenta, Hartanto, S., & Politeknik Negeri Samarinda. (2024). The Strategic Role Of Brand Storytelling In Enhancing Marketing Management And Brand Awareness On Social Media Platforms-Sarwo Eddy Wibowo et.al The Strategic Role Of Brand Storytelling In Enhancing Marketing Management And Brand Awareness On Social Media Platforms. *Jurnal Multidisiplin Sahombu*, *4*(2), 343–348. https://doi.org/DOI: 10.58471/jms.v4i02

Wilkesmann, M., & Bassyiouny, M. (2025). From leisure to labor: How workations are reshaping hospitality and destination marketing in the era of New Work. *Journal of Destination Marketing & Management*, *36*, 100991. DOI: 10.1016/j.jdmm.2025.100991

Williams, A. (2006). Tourism and hospitality marketing: Fantasy, feeling and fun. *International Journal of Contemporary Hospitality Management*, *18*(6), 482–495. DOI: 10.1108/09596110610681520

Willie, P. (2019). Can all sectors of the hospitality and tourism industry be influenced by the innovation of Blockchain technology? *Worldwide Hospitality and Tourism Themes*, *11*(2), 112–120. DOI: 10.1108/WHATT-11-2018-0077

Wilson, A., Murphy, H., & Fierro, J. C. (2012). Hospitality and travel: The nature and implications of user-generated content. *Cornell Hospitality Quarterly*, *53*(3), 220–228.

Wright, L. T., Gaber, H., Robin, R., & Cai, H. (2018). Content Strategies for Facebook Marketing: A Case Study of a Leading Fast-Food Brand Page. *Academy of Marketing Science*, 779–791. https://doi.org/DOI: 10.1007/978-3-319-66023-3_246

Wu, I.-L., Hsiao, W.-H., Wu, I.-L., & Hsiao, W.-H. (2017). Involvement, content, and interactivity drivers for consumer loyalty in mobile advertising: The mediating role of advertising value. *International Journal of Human-Computer Studies, 15*(6), •••.

Wu, P. C. S., Yeh, G. Y. Y., & Hsiao, C. R. (2011). The effect of store image and service quality on brand image and purchase intention for private label brands. *Australasian Marketing Journal, 19*(1), 30–39. DOI: 10.1016/j.ausmj.2010.11.001

Wu, Q., Yan, D., & Umair, M. (2023). Assessing the role of competitive intelligence and practices of dynamic capabilities in business accommodation of SMEs. *Economic Analysis and Policy, 77*, 1103–1114. DOI: 10.1016/j.eap.2022.11.024

Xiang, Z., Du, Q., Ma, Y., & Fan, W. (2017). A comparative analysis of major online review platforms: Implications for social media analytics in hospitality and tourism. *Tourism Management, 58*, 51–65.

Xu, D. J. (2006). The influence of personalization in affecting consumer attitudes toward mobile advertising in China. *Journal of Computer Information Systems, 47*(2), 9–19. DOI: 10.1080/08874417.2007.11645949

Xu, H., Teo, H.-H., Tan, B. C. Y., & Agarwal, R. (2010). The role of push-pull technology in privacy calculus: The case of location-based services. *Journal of Management Information Systems, 26*(3), 135–174. DOI: 10.2753/MIS0742-1222260305

Xu, S., Stienmetz, J., & Ashton, M. (2020). How will service robots redefine leadership in hotel management? A Delphi approach. *International Journal of Contemporary Hospitality Management, 32*(6), 2217–2237. DOI: 10.1108/IJCHM-05-2019-0505

Yang, L., Henthorne, T. L., & George, B. (2020). Artificial Intelligence and Robotics Technology in the Hospitality Industry: Current Applications and Future Trends. In B. George & J. Paul (Eds.), *Digital Transformation in Business and Society* (pp. 211–228). Springer International Publishing. https://doi.org/DOI: 10.1007/978-3-030-08277-2_13

Yang, K. C., Huang, C. H., Yang, C., & Yang, S. Y. (2017). Consumer attitudes toward online video advertisement: YouTube as a platform. *Kybernetes, 46*(5), 840–853. DOI: 10.1108/K-03-2016-0038

Yang, M., Ren, Y., & Adomavicius, G. (2019). Understanding user-generated content and customer engagement on Facebook business pages. *Information Systems Research, 30*(3), 839–855.

Yang, Y., Liu, Y., Lv, X., Ai, J., & Li, Y. (2022). Anthropomorphism and customers' willingness to use artificial intelligence service agents. *Journal of Hospitality Marketing & Management, 31*(1), 1–23.

Ye, G., Guan, X., Hudders, L., Xiao, Y., & Li, J. (2024). A Meta-Analysis of the Antecedents and Consequences of Advertising Value. *Journal of Advertising*, *54*(1), 117–138. DOI: 10.1080/00913367.2024.2309923

Ye, Q., Law, R., Gu, B., & Chen, W. (2011). The influence of user-generated content on traveler behavior: An empirical investigation on the effects of e-word-of-mouth to hotel online bookings. *Computers in Human Behavior*, *27*(2), 634–639.

Yoganathan, V., Osburg, V. S., Kunz, W. H., & Toporowski, W. (2021). Check-in at the Robo-desk: Effects of automated social presence on social cognition and service implications. *Tourism Management*, *85*, 104309.

Yörük, T., Akar, N., & Özmen, N. V. (2024). Research trends on guest experience with service robots in the hospitality industry: A bibliometric analysis. *European Journal of Innovation Management*, *27*(6), 2015–2041. DOI: 10.1108/EJIM-09-2022-0530

Youn, S., & Kim, S. (2019). Understanding ad avoidance on Facebook: Antecedents and outcomes of psychological reactance. *Computers in Human Behavior*, *98*, 232–244. DOI: 10.1016/j.chb.2019.04.025

Zachurzok-Srebrny, E. (2024). USING ARTIFICIAL INTELLIGENCE FOR CUSTOMER ENGAGEMENT IN SOCIAL MEDIA. *Scientific Papers of Silesian University of Technology Organization and Management Series*, *2024*(209), 5.

Zade, A. A. R. O. H. I., & Sethi, S. U. R. I. N. D. E. R. (2024). Transforming hospitality: The digital revolution in post-pandemic hotel management. *International Journal of Cultural Studies and Social Sciences*, *20*(2), 42–51.

Zakić, N., Ćurčić, N., & Leković, K. (2022). Hospitality digital marketing and technology transformation challenges. *International Journal of Qualitative Research*, *16*(4), 1133–1148. DOI: 10.24874/IJQR16.04-12

Zeng, B. R. G. (2014). What do we know about social media in tourism? A review. *Tourism Management Perspectives*. Advance online publication. DOI: 10.1016/j.tmp.2014.01.001

Zeng, Z., Shen, C., Wang, H., & Lin, I. Y. (2024). Luckin Coffee in China: An Innovative Coffee Brand Dominating the Chinese Market amid the Covid-19 Pandemic. *Journal of Hospitality & Tourism Cases*, *12*(1), 3–10. DOI: 10.1177/21649987241241913

Zeqiri, A. (2024). From Traditional to Digital: The Evolution of Business Models in Hospitality Through Platforms. *Platforms*, *2*(4), 221233.

Zhang, M., & Li, J. (Justin), & Li, X. (2025). Can esports help with hospitality marketing for Generation Z? The interaction of esports, novelty seeking, and subjective knowledge. *International Journal of Hospitality Management, 124*, 103963. DOI: 10.1016/j.ijhm.2024.103963

Zhang, X., & Jin, H. (2023). How does smart technology, artificial intelligence, automation, robotics, and algorithms (STAARA) awareness affect hotel employees' career perceptions? A disruptive innovation theory perspective. *Journal of Hospitality Marketing & Management, 32*(2), 264–283.

Zhao, X., Yang, J., Xie, T., & Wang, Z. (2017). Examining advertising intrusiveness on Instagram: Hedonic and utilitarian attributes of brand and sponsored content. *In American Academy of Advertising*, 243.

Zhao, H., Lan, J., Lyu, T., & Zeng, G. (2023). Working with artificial intelligence surveillance during the COVID-19 pandemic: A mixed investigation of the influence mechanism on job engagement in hospitality industry. *Current Issues in Tourism, 26*(20), 3318–3335.

Zheng, Y., Li, Y., Own, C. M., Meng, Z., & Gao, M. (2018). Real-time predication and navigation on traffic congestion model with equilibrium Markov chain. *International Journal of Distributed Sensor Networks, 14*(4), 1550147718769784.

Zhou, T. (2011). Understanding mobile Internet continuance usage from the perspectives of UTAUT and flow. *Information Development, 27*(3), 207–218. DOI: 10.1177/0266666911414596

Zikmund, W., Babin, B., Carr, J., & Griffin, M. (2013). *Business Research Methods*. Cengage Learning. https://books.google.co.in/books/about/Business_Research_Methods.html?id=veM4gQPnWHgC&redir_esc=y

Zobnina, M., & Rozhkov, A. (2018). Listening to the voice of the customer in the hospitality industry: Kano model application. *Worldwide Hospitality and Tourism Themes, 10*(4), 436448.

Zollo, M., & Winter, S. G. (2002). Deliberate Learning and the Evolution of Dynamic Capabilities. *Organization Science, 13*(3), 339–351. DOI: 10.1287/orsc.13.3.339.2780

About the Contributors

Ankit Shukla is an accomplished educator and researcher with a robust background in the hospitality and tourism industry. His career spans various roles, from frontline food and beverage service to academic leadership and extensive research contributions. Ankit's journey exemplifies a blend of practical experience, academic acumen, and a passion for advancing knowledge in his field. Early Career and Industry Experience Ankit's career in the hospitality industry began at the Hyatt Regency Chandigarh in September 2015, where he worked in the Food & Beverage Service department. His responsibilities included taking room service orders, managing point-of-sale systems, and setting up banquets for events. This role provided Ankit with hands-on experience in the operational aspects of the hospitality industry. Following his time at the Hyatt Regency, Ankit transitioned into academia, joining Kumaun University Nainital as a teaching personnel in September 2016. He took on multiple responsibilities, including lecturing MBA Tourism students, overseeing practical training, and designing course curricula. This marked the beginning of his journey in education, where he contributed to shaping the next generation of hospitality professionals. Academic Leadership and Teaching Ankit's academic career continued to flourish as he assumed the role of Assistant Professor at SIHMCT & AN Tehri Garhwal in July 2017. He became the head of the Food & Beverage Service department, where he coordinated events, designed course curricula, and managed the department's overall functioning. From February 2018 to April 2022, Ankit served as an Assistant Professor at Shoolini University Solan. Here, he expanded his responsibilities to include training and placement coordination, NAAC coordination for the Hospitality Management department, and handling operations of a hotel with eight rooms. His leadership skills and ability to manage complex tasks were instrumental in the smooth functioning of the university's hospitality department. Contributions to Research and Academia Ankit's passion for research is evident through his significant contributions to academic literature. He has presented research papers at various international conferences, focusing on topics such as ecology, local and regional food in destination marketing, and the influence of technological amenities on hotel guest satisfaction. His research has been published in reputable journals, with manuscripts addressing safety and security measures in hotels, tobacco consumption in India, and the role of Indian spices in Indian history. In addition to his research publications, Ankit has filed 40 patents, copyrights, and utility applications, with several already granted. His commitment to innovation and intellectual property rights underscores his dedication to advancing knowledge in his field. Current Role and Future Endeavors As of July 2023, Ankit is a lecturer at Raja Mangala University of Technology Thanyaburi in Thailand. In this role, he continues to inspire and educate students in the field of hospitality while pursuing his research interests. Ankit's extensive experience in both industry and academia, coupled with his passion for teaching and research, positions him as a key figure in the ongoing development of the hospitality and tourism sector. Ankit Shukla's journey from industry practitioner to esteemed academic is a testament to his dedication, expertise, and unwavering commitment to excellence in hospitality and education.

Nagendra Yadav is a highly regarded expert in hospitality, bringing over 12 years of extensive experience in both academia and the hotel industry. He holds a Ph.D. in Hospitality and a Master's degree in Hotel Management from Kurukshetra University. Currently, he serves as a distinguished faculty member at the Welcomgroup Graduate School of Hotel Administration (WGSHA) at Manipal Academy of Higher Education (MAHE) in Manipal, India. With a robust professional background, Dr. Yadav has successfully collaborated with prestigious hotel brands, including Taj Hotels, The Leela Group, Lemon Tree Hotels, and Piccadilly Hotel, in addition to his academic tenure at Shoolini University. His significant contributions to research and academia include over 45 patents and copyrights, alongside more than 15 Scopus-indexed papers and books published in leading journals. Dr. Yadav's research interests are pivotal in the field, focusing on gastronomic tourism, culinary heritage, hospitality innovation, and experiential learning. His ability to merge industry insights with academic rigor positions him as an influential leader in shaping the future of hospitality professionals.

Karan Berry, an alumnus of prestigious IHM Pusa, New Delhi, is a passionate tourism and hospitality professional with a rich blend of industry and academic experience of over 19 years. He holds a Ph.D. in Hotel Management, along with being UGC-NET qualified in Tourism Administration and Management. He also bears a Masters in Tourism Management, and Masters in Hospitality and Catering Management. Possessing a thorough knowledge of the challenges and prospects of gastronomy tourism, Dr. Berry has authored several Scopus indexed research publications, book chapters, and a textbook titled “The Chef: A Guide to Becoming a Culinary Master” (ISBN: 9788184578676). He also runs a YouTube channel by the name "Research Bay" focusing upon Research methodology & Data analysis techniques, especially for all the beginners.

Siddharatha Sharma is an M.Sc. Ph.D. of Panjab University, Chandigarh (India). He did his Bachelor’s degree in Bioinformatics and that of the Master’s in Anthropology (Honours) from the same University. He, then, qualified the National Eligibility Test (N.E.T.) of his Country i.e. India. He did his Ph.D. in Forensic Anthropology under the Deptt. of Anthropology of Panjab University, Chandigarh (India). Dr. Siddharatha had been a University Grants Commission’s (U.G.C.) Senior Research Fellow under the aforementioned University of that Country. He is a Member of ‘The Chartered Society of Forensic Sciences’, U.K.(United Kingdom). Dr. Siddharatha Sharma has associated himself with the Wildlife Conservation Activities for the last fourteen years. He is a Member of the Zoological Society. He has been a part of many Wildlife Conservation Programmes. Besides, he has also associated himself with the Fossil Collection Work for the last about Eleven years. Presently, he has been working as a Mission Facilitator in the Directorate of Environment & Climate Change under the Government of Punjab at Chandigarh.

Ghamaliel M. Villalobos is an English Foreign Teacher at Rajamangala University of Technology Thanyaburi (RMUTT), Thailand. She is pursuing a Master of Arts in English for Career Development and has experience in higher education, secondary education, and customer service. Her work focuses on language teaching methodologies, educational technology, and career-focused English instruction.

***

Earnest Anand is a Professor in Lovely Professional University Punjab India. He received Undergraduate in Hotel Management from Manipal University, Postgraduate in Tourism Management from Madurai Kamaraj University. He completed Doctor of Philosophy in Hospitality Management in 2023 from G D Goenka University Gurugram India. His research areas lies in food Service Industry, his research focuses on Alcoholic beverages, Event management and Sustainable Management Practices, Front Office operation, Event Management, Tourism Ethics, Destination Marketing. Dr Earnest is an active researcher and has published numerous research articles in prestigious national and international journals and books. He has participated in various National and International Conferences as a Session Chair and Resource person and he also reviewed the various papers and book chapters in renowned publication houses.

Samuel Ayertey is currently a business lecturer at Arden University, UK and a visiting lecturer at the University of Cumbria, UK. He has a PhD in marketing from the University of Plymouth, UK, and MBA from the University of Wales, UK. His teaching covers key areas such as organisational behaviour, leadership, strategic management and postgraduate research supervision. Samuel has worked as a digital marketing executive for a number of marketing companies in the UK and Africa. He has presented several conference papers in the field of digital marketing, particularly on the impact of emerging technologies on service failure and recovery strategies. He has published extensively in academic books and journals, including Interdisciplinary Journal of Economics & Business Law. Samuel is a fellow of the Higher Education Academy (FHEA). He is currently undertaking the UK's Higher Education Academy programme which confers senior fellow (SFHEA) recognition for leadership in teaching and learning.

Mukunda B. G., M.T.A. (5-year Integrated), IATA, UGC-NET & K-SET, Ph.D., (M.B.A. in Aviation Management), currently serves as an Assistant Professor in the School of Humanities and Social Sciences within the Department of Travel and Tourism at Mount Carmel College, Autonomous, Bangalore, Karnataka. With more than 11 years of teaching experience across esteemed institutions, he possesses a profound expertise in travel, tourism, hospitality, and aviation. His academic pursuits are complemented by a robust research portfolio, characterized by the publication of 20 research papers in the UGC care, and Scopus-indexed journals from globally renowned publishing houses such as Longdon, IGI, Taylor, and Francis. Additionally, he has actively participated in academic discourse, having delivered over 15 research papers at national and international seminars and conferences, authored two textbooks, and three design patents have been published. His areas of specialization encompass a diverse spectrum, spanning Travel Agency and Tour Operations, Air Ticketing, Airline Management, Hospitality Management, and Air Cabin Crew Management. His research interests include Community-Based Tourism, Heritage Tourism, Sustainable Tourism, Rural Tourism, and Tourist Satisfaction. Received many national awards and published textbooks in tourism, hospitality and aviation fields. He has served on the Board of Studies (BOS) and Board of Examiners (BOE) in various universities and colleges in Bangalore.

Gaurav Bathla is having over fifteen years of experience in Academia & Industry and presently working as Professor in School of Hotel Management, Airlines and Tourism at CT University Punjab. He has received his Doctorate (PhD) in Hotel Management and Tourism from GNA University, Punjab. Dr. Bathla has authored more than 35 research papers in Scopus Indexed, UGC Approved and Peer Review Journals. He has been associated with many universities and hotel management institutions for their curriculum development and examination system. Dr. Bathla is editorial / reviewer board member of more than 8 National & International Journals. He has also organized various conferences and Faculty Development Programs in the field of Hospitality and Tourism.

Bharat Bhushan is a seasoned academic and researcher at ICFAI University, Himachal Pradesh. He specializes in Finance and Business Management, focusing on contemporary management practices, financial strategies, and emerging trends in business.

Gigi G.S. is an Associate Professor at Saveetha School of Management, SIMATS, Chennai, with over 15 years of experience in academia. She holds a B.Sc., an MBA with University 3rd rank, and a Ph.D. in Management, specializing in employee engagement in the IT industry. She is also UGC NET qualified. Her teaching philosophy focuses on fostering a dynamic, inclusive learning environment that promotes critical thinking and practical skills. Dr. Gigi has guided three Ph.D. scholars and served as a Research Advisory Committee (RAC) member for eight others across various universities. She actively contributes to student mentoring and institutional service through her involvement in committees and organizations like the Rotaract Club and UBA. She has received several awards and has presented and published widely at national and international conferences.

John Garrick is a distinguished academic and strategic consultant with expertise in inclusive education, curriculum innovation, and creative branding. Holding degrees from the University of Huddersfield and the University of Salford including a PhD in Business Management, he lectures across UK institutions such as Arden University and the London School of Commerce. With extensive experience in higher education, he specialises in student supervision, blended learning design, and evidence-informed teaching that empowers diverse learners. Beyond academia, Dr. Garrick supports startups and SMEs in developing impactful brand identities and business strategies, seamlessly integrating theory with practice. His dual role enhances classroom relevance and fosters strategic insight. Committed to continuous professional development, he actively engages in CPD focused on inclusive pedagogy, curriculum co-creation, and digital innovation. Whether mentoring students or collaborating with peers, Dr. Garrick champions equitable, engaging, and transformative learning experiences that reflect his dedication to educational excellence and strategic impact.

Vikesh Kashyap is an accomplished academic and professional in the field of Hospitality and Tourism. With a robust career spanning over a decade, he has held key positions, including Associate Professor and Head of Department at prestigious institutions like Bahra University and Chandigarh Group of Colleges. He holds a Ph.D. in Tourism Studies from Himachal Pradesh University and an MBA in International Hotel and Tourism Management from Vatel International School, France. A prolific researcher, he has substantial contributions to research, with publications in esteemed journals and with multiple book authorships. His work spans areas like creative tourism, community-based tourism, and sustainable practices in the Hospitality industry. He is an active member of "The Indian Society for Technical Education" and has chaired sessions and co-convened International Conferences on Sustainable Development and Innovation in Hospitality and Tourism. In addition to his academic achievements, He has industry expertise, having worked with prestigious organizations, including Boscolo Plaza Hotel, France. His dedication to advancing the field is reflected in his patents, conference contributions, and initiatives in promoting tourism's economic and cultural dimensions.

Koroye Ebimoboere is a dedicated scholar and educator specialising in Financial Accounting and management. She holds a PhD and MSc from the university of Bradford, UK. and a BSc in Accounting from the University of Benin, Nigeria. With a strong foundation in both academic and theory and practical application, Dr. Ebimoboere has lectured across institutions in the UK and Ghana respectively, delivering courses in Economics, accounting and finance, business and management at both undergraduate and post graduate levels. Her teaching philosophy emphasizes critical thinking, ethical decision making and inclusive learning. She is proficient in data analytics and educational technologies and actively contributes to curriculum development and student mentoring. Beyond academia, she serves as a volunteer accounting officer, demonstrating her commitment to community service and financial integration. Dr Ebimoboere's research interest span from financial reporting, corporate governance, and contemporary business practices, and she continues to inspire future professionals through her innovative and student-centered approach to education.

Dilip Kumar is a seasoned academician with a Ph. D. (Marketing) with more than 20 years of experience with various reputable organisations. Presently, he is working with Great Lakes Institute of Management, Gurgaon, India. He has published one book titled "Hotel and Resort Management" under the Paradise Press. He has also published various articles in Scopus and the Web of Science-indexed journals. His area of research revolves around tourism, hospitality, food, sustainable development goals, sustainability, and artificial intelligence. He has organised two international conferences as a convenor and published the conference proceedings as edited books.

Niraj Kumar is a Lecturer at the Dr. Ambedkar Institute of Hotel Management (AIHM), Chandigarh, and a Research Scholar at Chandigarh University. With over 15 years of teaching experience in the field of tourism and hospitality, he has contributed significantly to academic development and student mentorship. His research interests lie in tourism and hospitality management, with a focus on emerging trends and innovations shaping the industry. In addition to his teaching and research work, Mr. Kumar has also demonstrated strong editorial and leadership skills, serving as the Editor-in-Chief of his institute's magazine for more than six years. Through this role, he actively promoted academic writing, creative expression, and professional development among students and faculty members. Committed to advancing knowledge and practice in hospitality education, he continues to explore the integration of modern approaches in tourism and hospitality studies, contributing to both academia and the professional community.

Pankaj Kumar is currently working as an Assistant Professor in School of BFSI, Symbiosis University of Applied Sciences, Indore, Madhya Pradesh. He has completed his Ph.D. in Finance from Faculty of Commerce, Banaras Hindu University and published number of research papers in SCOPUS, ABDC and Care listed journals.

Sanjeev Kumar Is a Professor in Lovely Professional University Punjab India. He received Undergraduate in Hotel Management from Osmania University, Postgraduate in Tourism Management from Madurai Kamaraj University. He completed Doctor of Philosophy in Hospitality Management in 2019 from Amity University Jaipur India. His research areas lies in food Service Industry, his research focuses on Alcoholic beverages, Event management and Sustainable Management Practices, Metaverse, AI Machine Learning and Artificial Intelligence. He published more than 80 research papers, articles and chapters in Scopus Indexed, UGC Approved and peer reviewed Journals and books. Dr. Sanjeev Kumar participated and acted as resource person in various National and International conferences, seminars, session chair, research workshops and industry talks and his work has been widely cited. Dr. Sanjeev also edited more than 20 books with various International Publishers such as IGI Global, Cambridge Scholars, Emerald, CABI, Bentham Science, Taylor & Francis. Dr Sanjeev is an active researcher and has published numerous research articles in prestigious National and International journals and books.

Vinoth Kumar S. is a dedicated research scholar who has completed his undergraduate and postgraduate studies from institutions affiliated with the University of Madras and is currently pursuing his Doctorate (Ph.D.) at the same university. His research expertise centers on Sustainability, Environmental, Social, and Governance (ESG) frameworks, Green Human Resource Management (Green HRM), and the integration of the United Nations Sustainable Development Goals (SDGs) within organizational practices. He has contributed to the body of scholarly literature through the publication of three Scopus-indexed book chapters and has disseminated his research at reputed national and international conferences, where he has also been honored with Best Paper Awards. Vinoth has further advanced his academic proficiency by actively participating in a wide range of research-oriented workshops, seminars, faculty development programs, and capacity-building initiatives hosted by leading institutions. In addition, he has served as a research assistant in several government-funded projects, supporting critical activities such as data collection, field engagement, and analytical processes. Through sustained scholarly involvement and a focused commitment to sustainability-driven research, he continues to contribute meaningfully to the disciplines of commerce and interdisciplinary studies.

Farhana Yeasmin Lina is a Lecturer (Senior Scale) in the Department of Tourism & Hospitality Management at Daffodil International University, where she specializes in research areas such as digital detox, artificial intelligence in tourism, and community-based tourism development (CBT). Currently pursuing an MPhil in Tourism and Hospitality Management, she holds both a BBA and an MBA from the University of Dhaka. Lina's work focuses on understanding the potential impacts of tourism development in Bangladesh, promoting sustainable tourism, and empowering local communities. Her research also explores how emerging technologies can revolutionize the tourism industry, enhancing both academic and practical insights in the field.

Abdullah Malik is currently serving as an Associate Professor in the Department of Commerce and also holds the position of Research Head for JAIN Online.

Michael Nii Laryeafio is an accomplished Information systems and business lecturer with a passion for inspiring and equipping the next generation of students and professionals for over 10 years. Known for his dynamic teaching style and ability to simplify complex concepts, Michael has received accolades for his ability to connect with students and foster a stimulating learning environment. Michael is currently a business lecturer, Module leader and dissertation supervisor at Arden University, UK. With a bachelor's degree in economics from the Kwame Nkrumah University of Science and Technology, Michael holds a PhD and an MSc in Information systems from the University of Salford, UK – with the focus on educational technology. Michael is also a member of UKAIS and has a fellowship

(FHEA). Dr. Michael Nii Laryeafio mentors' students by fostering idea generation mindset and encouraging innovative thinking. He integrates real-world case studies into his teaching, guiding students to identify opportunities and develop creative solutions. His hands-on approach empowers aspiring entrepreneurs to refine their ideas and succeed in dynamic business environments.

Varinder Singh Rana Passionate, resourceful, and innovative professional, with 22 years Academic and Industry career demonstrating consistent success as an Administrator and Educator at higher education levels. Outstanding track record in assuring student success. Recognized for teaching excellence based on technical, research, and design fundamentals. Strong follow-through, administrative and time management capabilities. Highly articulate, demonstrating refined interpersonal skills across all levels and backgrounds. Effective communicator with excellent planning, organizational, and negotiation strengths as well as the ability to lead, reach consensus, establish goals, and attain results. Received Doctorate (PhD) in Hospitality from Amity University, Noida and postgraduate in Hotel Management and Catering Technology from St Peters University, Chennai and obtained his Bachelors in Hotel Management from Bangalore University in 2001. 21 years of experience in Academia and Industry. Provided services to Lovely Professional University, GNA University, Punjab Tourism Development Corporation and various reputed hotels. Have 11 Limca Records in account. General Secretary of Chefs Association of Five Rivers which is the nodal body of Indian Federation of Culinary Associations (IFCA). Member of Board of Management and Academic Council of GNA University and Board of Studies member of various Universities. Authored 12 books and 30 Research papers. Served as head chef to honourable President of India and President of Republic of Afghanistan during their visit to Punjab. Certified Master trainer of Food Safety and Standards Authority of India. Awarded by Phagwara Administration for outstanding professional work in 2017. Star Achiever Award for regional culinary development from Indian Federation of Culinary Associations. Honoured by Tourism Minister of Punjab for initiating a Bakery Unit at Central Jail, Ludhiana. Presence as Jury of Master Chef Punjabi- A Cookery Reality Show of DD National Punjabi. Cooking shows on National Television. Represented State of Punjab in Republic day Celebration at Red Fort, New Delhi. Jury in ICF and IFCA events at National and International Level. He has been awarded with Best Culinary Educator award by Indian Federation of Culinary Association (A Nodal Body of Ministry of Tourism, Government of India). Won Two silver Medals and one bronze medal for Republic of India (Our Nation) at International Culinary Challenge, Uzbekistan where 22 countries participated. Associated with many projects of Punjab Heritage and Tourism Promotion Board.

Harini S is an accomplished academic with dual postgraduate degrees-MBA and M.Com-as well as a Post Graduate Diploma in Business Management (PGDBM) and worked as an Assistant Professor with four years of teaching experience, Harini is recognized for her research-oriented mindset and dedication to academic innovation. Currently doing her research in human resource management in Saveetha School of Management During her MBA, Harini was honored as the Best Outgoing Student and received a coveted gold medal, reflecting her commitment to excellence and leadership. Her passion for research is evident in her extensive work with various scholarly articles, particularly those employing quantitative approaches. Harini's innovative spirit and analytical skills have earned her the prestigious Young Researcher Award. In addition to her research contributions, Harini has reviewed several research chapters, further establishing her reputation as a meticulous and insightful scholar. She is driven by a passion for advancing knowledge, fostering academic innovation, and inspiring the next generation of researchers.

Vinay Seth is currently pursuing his Ph.D. from the Department of Commerce, Mahatma Gandhi Kashi Vidyapith, Varanasi, Uttar Pradesh. He has completed his graduation and post graduation from the Faculty of Commerce, Banaras Hindu University and published a number of research papers in Scopus, ABDC, UGC Care listed journals and in peer reviewed journals.

Abhinav Shandilya is an educationist with a Ph.D. (Management), Master in Business Administration (HRM), Master in Tourism Management, Post Graduate Diploma in Retail Management, and B.Sc. in Hospitality and Hotel Administration having more than 20 years of teaching and industry experience. He is presently working as an Associate Professor, Department of Management, Birla Institute of Technology, Mesra, Patna Campus, India. His core competence is in Marketing and hospitality Management. He has conference/seminar presentations, edited books, and journal articles to his credit. He was resource person for Orientation programs and capacity-building programs sponsored by different State Govt. agencies of Jharkhand. He was empanelled as National Level Monitor for National Level Monitoring, 2012-13, Phase-I and Phase-II, under the Ministry of Rural Development, Government of India.

Dharna Shukla is a hotel management educationist and an experienced hotelier with over two decades of experience in academia hospitality operations. Dr. Shukla has worked in India and abroad in the hospitality sector with chains of The Park, The Taj and Coral Hotels. She has also taught hospitality and tourism management at IHM Lucknow, Christ University Bangalore and was the founding faculty and program leader, hospitality and tourism, at Amity University Dubai. Dr.Shukla has reviewed hospitality and tourism content of Aptech and is a consultant inspector for NEBOSH certifications in India for a UK-based organization. She is also a Lifetime Member of the Professional Housekeepers Association (PHA). Dr. Shukla has authored and co-authored three books, research papers and book chapters on contemporary topics of significance in the hospitality and tourism industry. She holds a PhD in Management from Banasthali University, Rajasthan and currently is the Program Leader of BBA (Tourism Management) and an Assistant Professor at Amity School of Hospitality, Amity University Uttar Pradesh, Lucknow Campus.

Amrik Singh is working as Professor and HOD in the School of Hotel Management and Tourism at Lovely Professional University, Punjab, India. He has obtained his Ph.D. degree in Hotel Management from Kurukshetra University, Haryana, India. He has published 130 Scopus-indexed publications. He has published 12 patents, and 01 patent has been granted in the inter-disciplinary domain. Dr. Amrik Singh participated and acted as a resource person in various national and international conferences, seminars, research workshops, and industry talks. He has published 20 books with IGI Global Publication, Emerald Publication, Bentham Publication, Nova Publication etc., on trending areas such as Food waste, Artificial Intelligence, Mountain Tourism, Virtual tourism, Healthcare Tourism, Guest behavior in tourism and hospitality. His area of research interest are Accommodation management, sustainability, Green practices, Human Resource Management in Hospitality, Artificial Intelligence, AR VR in hospitality, Hotel pricing, Employee Disability, Work life balance, women empowerment etc.

Balgopal Singh is an Associate Professor of the Department of Commerce and Management at Banasthali Vidyapith, Jaipur, Rajasthan. With over 23 years of academic and research experience. He specializes in the Business Management domain. His research focuses areas are Consumer Behaviour, Branding, and Aviation Management. He has published 60+ research papers in national and international academic journals indexed in Scopus and peer-reviewed journals.

Princy Singh is currently pursuing his Ph.D from the Department of Commerce, Mahatma Gandhi Kashi Vidyapith, Varanasi, Uttar Pradesh. She has completed her graduation from the Faculty of Commerce, Banaras Hindu University and post graduation from Department of Commerce, Mahatma Gandhi Kashi Vidyapith Varanasi and published a number of research papers in ABDC and peer reviewed journals.

Vishal Kumar Singh is an Assistant Professor at the School of Management Science (SMS), Varanasi. He holds a Ph.D. with Senior Research Fellowship (SRF) from the Institute of Management Studies, Banaras Hindu University (BHU),

Varanasi, India. He completed his MBA from the Faculty of Management Studies, BHU. He has qualified UGC-NET (2017, 2018) and UGC-NET with JRF (2019). With a strong commitment to quality research, he has published papers in SCOPUS Q1 & Q2, ABDC B & C category, Web of Science, and UGC-CARE listed journals. Vishal has actively participated in national and international conferences, including those organized by IIMs, where he has presented research papers. Additionally, he serves as a reviewer for reputed international publishers, such as Sage, Emerald, Taylor & Francis and Inderscience.

Pravin Chandra Singh is an assistant professor at MSMSR, MATS University, Raipur. He holds a Ph.D. from the Institute of Management Studies, Banaras Hindu University (BHU), Varanasi, India. He has completed his MBA from I.C.C.M.R.T. and also qualified UGC-NET. With a strong commitment to quality research, he has published papers in SCOPUS Q1, Web of Science, and UGC-CARE-listed journals. Dr. Pravin has actively participated in national and international conferences, where he has presented research papers. Additionally, he serves as a reviewer for reputed international publishers, such as Sage, Emerald, and Inderscience.

Mohammad Badruddoza Talukder is an Associate Professor at the College of Tourism and Hospitality Management at the International University of Business Agriculture and Technology (IUBAT) in Dhaka, Bangladesh. Holding a PhD from Lovely Professional University, India, he is renowned for his innovative integration of cutting-edge technologies such as Artificial Intelligence (AI), the Internet of Things (IoT), and Blockchain into tourism and hospitality management. His research explores the transformative impact of these technologies on smart tourism, cloud kitchens, and the broader industry landscape. As a prolific author, Dr. Talukder has published numerous scholarly articles and books, with forthcoming titles that address AI innovations in hospitality, the evolution of cloud kitchens, and the enhancement of digital literacy within hospitality education. His work shapes contemporary tourism and hospitality practices, skillfully marrying technological advancements with practical industry applications. Since 2008, Dr. Talukder has imparted his knowledge through a diverse array of courses in tourism and hospitality across various universities in Bangladesh.

Megha Tamang is currently pursuing her Ph.D. from Christ (Deemed to be University), Bengaluru, with her research focusing on the intersections of tourism, community development, and social entrepreneurship. She serves as an Assistant Professor in the Department of Travel and Tourism, Mount Carmel College Autonomous, Bengaluru, affiliated with Bengaluru City University. Hailing from the picturesque hill town of Darjeeling, Ms. Tamang brings with her a deep appreciation for culture, sustainability and the transformative power of tourism in local communities. She holds an MBA in Tourism from the Indian Institute of Tourism and Travel Management (IITTM), Bhubaneswar, which has laid a strong foundation for her academic and professional journey in the field of tourism education and research. A passionate educator and lifelong learner, Ms. Tamang believes in the philosophy of learning, unlearning and relearning as a continuous process that enriches both personal and professional growth. Her academic interests include sustainable tourism development, destination branding, aviation and community-based tourism initiatives. A small-town girl with big dreams, she aspires not only to keep her own ambitions alive but also to inspire and empower others to pursue theirs. Through her teaching, research and mentorship, she strives to contribute meaningfully to the evolving landscape of tourism studies and to nurture future leaders in the industry.

Pankaj Kumar Tyagi is an accomplished academician, researcher, and consultant. He is presently working as Professor at Chandigarh University, Mohali, India. Dr. Tyagi is an alumnus of Hemwati Nandan Bahuguna Garhwal University (Central University) and Kurukshetra University. He has over 2 decades of experience in the industry, teaching, training, consultancy, and expertise in destination management, travel process and disruptive technologies. He has published over 40 research papers in international journals indexed in the quality database and authored/edited 15 books with premium publications Like IGI-GLOBAL, Emerald Publications, CRC, Apple Academic Press and many more. He is a reviewer for many international tourism, management, and technology journals. His area of expertise is Travel Technologies, Sustainable Development Goals, Disruptive Technologies, Community Based Tourism, Meaningful Tourism, Hospitality Operations, Events and Festivals, Digital Innovation in Service Sector etc.

Richa Verma is currently serving as Head of the Department of Hotel Management at Swami Vivekanand Faculty of Technology and Management, Banur. She specializes in hospitality management and focuses on academic leadership, curriculum development, and industry-oriented training.

Index

A

B

C

D

M

O

P

R

S

www.ingramcontent.com/pod-product-compliance
Lightning Source LLC
LaVergne TN
LVHW061531290926
849162LV00004B/760